THE PEOPLE'S REPUBLIC OF CHINA

To the memory of Paul Selden

THE PEOPLE'S REPUBLIC OF CHINA

A DOCUMENTARY HISTORY OF REVOLUTIONARY CHANGE

Edited and with an Introduction by
MARK SELDEN
With Patti Eggleston

Monthly Review Press
New York and London

Grateful acknowledgment is made to the following for permission to reprint previously published material.

Loren Fessler, "Delayed Marriage and Planned Birth. Translation of a Chinese Birth Control Manual," LF-1-'73, Field Staff Reports, East Asia Series, Vol. 20, no. 1 (1973):2-5. Copyright © 1973 by American Universities Field Staff, Inc. Mao Tsetung, "The Sixty Articles," translated by Stuart Schram, The China Quarterly 46 (April-June 1971): 226-29. Copyright © 1971 by The China Quarterly. C. S. Chen, ed., Rural People's Communes in Lien-chiang, pp. 81ff, 90ff. Copyright © 1969 by The Hoover Institution on War, Revolution and Peace. "CCP Central Committee Directive Concerning the Question of Distribution in Rural People's Communes," Issues and Studies 9, no. 2 (November 1972). Copyright © 1972 by Issues and Studies. Alan Winnington, The Slaves of the Cool Mountains, pp. 88-92. Copyright © 1959 by Lawrence and Wishart Ltd., London. Reprinted by permission. Mao Tsetung, A Critique of Soviet Economics, translated by Moss Roberts. Copyright © 1977 by Moss Roberts. Reprinted by permission of Monthly Review Press. "Premier Chou En-lai Talks to William Hinton About Classes and Customs in Chinese Society," New China, Spring 1975. Copyright © 1975 by New China. William Hinton, Interview with Ch'en Yung-kuei, New China, Fall 1977. Copyright © 1977 by New China. Delia Davin, Woman-Work. Women and the Party in Revolutionary China. Copyright © 1976 by Oxford University Press. Reprinted by permission. Stuart Schram, ed., Chairman Mao Talks to the People, pp. 92ff. Copyright © 1974 by Stuart Schram. The same material is reprinted with permission of Penguin Books Ltd., who holds the international copyright. "The Placement Is Good, the Education Is Good, the Utilization Is Good," Chinese Education 8, nos. 2,3 (1977). Copyright © 1977 by M. E. Sharpe Inc. Mao Tsetung, "Speech at the Second Chengchow Conference," translated by Pierre Perrolle, Chinese Law and Government (Winter 1976-77). Copyright © 1977 by M. E. Sharpe Inc. CCP Documents of the Great Proletarian Cultural Revolution 1966-1977, pp. 116-19, 331-33, 630-33; and Tibet: 1950-1967, pp. 78-92; and "Let the Brilliance of Mao Tse-tung Thought Forever Shine on the Road to Agricultural Mechanization," Union Research Service, 48, pp. 296-300. All Copyright © Union Research Institute. Richard Baum and Frederick Tiewes, eds., Ssu-Ch'ing: The Socialist Education Movement of 1962-1966. Copyright © 1968 by The Regents of the University of California.

Library of Congress Cataloging in Publication Data
Main entry under title: The People's Republic of China.
Bibliography: p. 716
1. China—History—1949-1976—Sources. I. Selden, Mark.
DS777.55.P423   951.05   78-13916

Monthly Review Press
62 West 14th Street, New York, N.Y. 10011
47 Red Lion Street, London WC1R 4PF

Manufactured in the United States of America
10 9 8 7 6 5 4 3 2

CONTENTS

* Documents preceded by an asterisk are of major importance in defining
China's socialist development path.

III. The Great Leap Forward, 1958–1959

IV. The Two-Line Struggle
in City and Countryside, 1959–1965

PREFACE AND ACKNOWLEDGMENTS

This book is at once an interpretation of China's socialist development and a documentary record presented in the words and deeds of its participants.

The basic documentation for an understanding of Chinese socialist development has not been widely available previously. A number of documents are translated here for the first time; the majority are gathered from diverse translated sources. In sum, they present an extraordinarily rich record of highlights of three decades of revolutionary change.

Collected here are the major laws and directives which defined the land revolution; the four constitutions of the People's Republic; documents of the first five-year plan, illustrating its theory and practice in city and countryside; guidelines for the Great Leap Forward and the Cultural Revolution; major theoretical statements of Mao Tsetung, including many items recently published for the first time; and documents defining the working-class struggle, the women's movement, and the revolution in education, which reveal in detail central problems, goals, and clashing approaches of successive stages of the uninterrupted revolution.

A balance has been sought between documents of the center represented by Mao and the party leadership, and the record of the revolution in action, particularly the words and deeds of participants at the grassroots level in farms and factories. An attempt has been made to capture the views of major protagonists in successive debates that shaped the formation of an independent road to socialism. The documents have been selected to clarify the dynamic linking the masses of Chinese people with the Communist Party and its leader, Mao Tsetung, a

xi

relationship which at its best can be understood in terms of a mass line political process of interaction and mutual learning, repeatedly redefining the frontiers of socialist development.

A number of documents are presented here in English for the first time; many others have previously been translated but are generally inaccessible. Taken as a composite, it is my hope that they bring to life a measure of the richness and vitality, the trauma, the contradictions, the unquenchable striving and creative achievement of the Chinese people, and that in their particularity, their concrete exploration of problems, they help to clarify universal themes of revolutionary change, socialist transition, and development.

The juxtaposition of protagonists in major debates clarifies distinctive features of Mao's thought and practice, and the continuity and development of each over time. It also sheds light on the interaction among Mao, the party, and the people in charting a course which repeatedly burst the constraints of plans and inherited models.

The selections from Mao's writings include major items from the *Selected Works* as well as a variety of writings, speeches, and informal remarks collected and published by red guards during the Cultural Revolution. Many of the former were revised by Mao for inclusion in the *Selected Works* in the 1950s; I have used the original text where available to capture the thought and language of the time of presentation. In none of the documents included here, however, are the differences between the original and revised version substantial. The later, often informal, speeches and writings provide fascinating insight into the man in the leader at various stages of the revolution. They also include some of Mao's most important and carefully crafted works.

In light of the wealth of documentation spanning three decades of revolutionary change, it has been necessary to excerpt. The tone and substance of the original have been preserved wherever possible while highlighting new theoretical or practical contributions. In all cases references are provided to facilitate access to the complete document. In a number of cases where it has been possible to compare the original, minor revisions have been made in available translations.

The preparation of this volume would not have been possible without the cooperation of many people. Edward Friedman, Carl Riskin, Peter Seybolt, and Benedict Stavis made valuable suggestions of texts for inclusion in the documents.

Ch'iu Cheng-chang, Linda Grove, John Gittings, John Gurley, Victor Lippit, Donald Long, Muto Ichiyo, Nakagane Katsuji, Carl Riskin, James Scott, David Wilson, Yabuki Susumu, and especially Joseph Esherick, Kojima Reiitsu, and Mitch Meisner provided invaluable commentary and criticism of the manuscript during successive stages of its preparation.

Lauress Ackman, Patti Eggleston, Don Long, Pierre Perrolle, and Robert Salasin made available original translations. In addition, I have relied on the work of numerous anonymous translators in China, Hong Kong, the United States, and elsewhere for much of the work included here.

Patti Eggleston made the preliminary selection of the documents on rural transformation during the first five-year plan and the Great Leap Forward, drafted introductions to those documents, and helped to shape the conception and analysis during the early stages of preparation. Lauress Ackman selected a number of documents and provided introductory material on industry during the cultural revolution.

I would like to express my appreciation to all those mentioned above, to the numerous writers and scholars whose works and insights I have drawn on in preparing this volume, and to the Chinese people whose struggle is recorded here.

The completion of this book was facilitated by research grants from Washington University and the National Endowment for the Humanities.

Tokyo
June 30, 1978

CHINA

USSR

MONGOLIA

SINKIANG

KANSU

NINGHSIA

Lanchow

CHINGHAI

TIBET

SZECHUAN

Chungking

YUNNAN

Kunming

INDIA

BURMA

VIETNAM

LAOS

Abbreviations

CB   *Current Background*

CC Documents *Documents of the Chinese Communist Party Central Committee, 1950–1969*

CD   *China Digest*

FBIS   *Foreign Broadcast Information Service*

HC   *Hung-ch'i* (Red Flag)

JMJP   *Jen-min jih-pao* (People's Daily)

JPRS   *Joint Publications Research Service*

NCNA   *New China News Agency*

SCPRM   *Selections from People's Republic of China Magazines* (Prior to 1960 *Extracts from China Mainland Magazine*)

SCPRP   *Selections from People's Republic of China Press*

SR   *Selected Readings from the Works of Mao Tsetung*

SW   *Selected Works of Mao Tsetung*

URS   Union Research Service

Statistical Units

Chin (catty) = .5 kilograms = 1.1 pounds
Mou = 1/6 acre = 0.07 hectares = 667 square meters
Tan = 50 kilograms = 110 pounds = 100 catties
Tael = 1.1023 ounces
Li = 1/3 mile

Administrative Units

Hsien = county
Ch'u = district (sub-unit of county)
Hsiang = township

A Note on Pronunciation

The romanization used here is the modified Wade-Giles system. An apostrophe following a letter or combination of letters as in k', p', t', ch' and ts' changes the original sound by aspirating.

Wade-Giles romanization	Approximate English pronunciations as in
a	father
ai	eye
ang	ahng
ao	ouch
ch	jar
ch'	chart
e	uh
ei	pay
erh	girl
f	far
h	ham
hs	between seat and sheet
i	machine
ia	reality
iao	meow
ieh	eeyeh
ih	turn
in	in
ing	ring
iu	you
j	between red and jet

k	*g*o
k'	*c*ola
l	*c*ola
m	*m*ore
n	*n*ow
ou	*n*o
p	*b*all
p'	*p*all
s	*s*op
sh	*sh*oe
ssu or szu	ssuh
t	*d*o
t'	*t*o
ts or tz	su*ds*
ts' or tz'	ba*ts*
u	fo*o*l or y*u*le
ueh	ueh
ui	q*ua*ver
w	*w*ater
y	*y*ear

INTRODUCTION

For more than half a century Chinese revolutionaries have grappled with the central problems of our era: war, revolution and peace, national liberation, independence and unity, development of productive resources and human capacities, self-reliance, and the elimination of oppression and inequality. Some of the landmarks on the Chinese road to socialism are here explored through the words and deeds of the participants who traveled it.

This book examines the theoretical and practical issues of Marxism and development during successive stages of revolutionary transformation. It gauges the roles of working people, more than 85 percent of them peasants, in remaking their society in dynamic interaction with the Chinese Communist Party and its leader, Mao Tsetung. In particular, it highlights the interaction between national and class struggles directed toward the creation of a new political and social environment free from the exploitation and poverty of the old order and advancing toward prosperity and socialism.

The Chinese revolutionary record challenges reigning assumptions in Western and some Third World and socialist societies about the problems and prospects for human development. To be sure, certain of its distinctive features represent a creative response to specific Chinese conditions, but surely others equally address universal problems of our era. Recognizing that neither Western nor Chinese views are uniform or static (and their practice still less so), the following capsule summary of conflicting approaches highlights six critical issues in the contemporary global development debate which the Chinese experience illuminates and which will be explored below.

Perspectives on Development*

Western Orthodox View	*Chinese Revolutionary View*
1. The future of the underdeveloped nations lies in extensive utilization of foreign capital, expertise, and technology provided through international aid and investment.	1. The essential precondition for effective development is breaking the grip of foreign domination. Revolutionary change opens the way to self-reliant (though not autarkic) utilization of untapped human and material resources.
2. The most effective means for internal capital accumulation and high speed growth in the developing nations lies in export-oriented industrialization strategies.	2. Coordinated development of agriculture, domestic industry, and commerce are primary; exports are secondary. Export-first strategies ensure the continued subordination of the nations of Asia, Africa, and Latin America to those of the metropolitan centers and to international capital and impede overall coordination of the national economy.
3. Rapid development proceeds through concentration of resources and application of advanced technology in high growth sectors of urban industry. The countryside serves urban industry primarily through provision of food, resources, and, above all, cheap labor. (There is also a vigorous orthodox school which emphasizes the primacy of agricultural development but typically here, too, by concentrating inputs	3. Development of a comprehensive industrial base including heavy industry is important, but agriculture is critical to overall (including industrial) development and welfare in predominantly agrarian countries. The task is to coordinate multi-level industrial development using modern and indigenous technology to serve agriculture and the countryside. Regions and local communities must retain initiative through control over re-

* The Western views expressed here are drawn from the development literature of the 1970s. While they constitute a coherent package, individual points have been subject to criticism by particular authors. The Chinese view is my synthesis of core principles of the political economy of Mao Tsetung as developed during and after the Great Leap Forward of 1958.

into high growth, commercially oriented sectors.)

4. The central roles in the development process are played by the entrepreneurial bourgeoisie, professional managers, and a technological elite closely integrated with foreign capital and technology and operating in a private enterprise system which richly rewards these groups.

5. Principal obstacles to development are overpopulation, lack of entrepreneurial drive, and primitive technology; remedies include population control, foreign inputs of capital and technology, reliance on rich peasant initiative, and, in some cases, urban migration.

6. Development is above all technological progress which is best fostered by an entrepreneurial elite and measured by high GNP or per capita GNP; some economists also emphasize "human capital."

sources for self-reliant development including the combination of industry and agriculture, rural mechanization, and electrification.

4. The organized workers and peasants with state support play a leading role. Incentive systems emphasize the collective well-being of all and progressive reduction of income differentials.

5. The landlord order, in squandering the rural surplus and repressing the peasantry, is the main internal obstacle to development. Redistribution of land and income, that is, agrarian revolution, is the first step; socialization of the means of production and cooperative transformation the second step in solving the apparent population problem and embarking on self-reliant rural development.

6. Development is the fuller realization of human and natural potential in all its dimensions. Technology is important, but most critical is the human consciousness that by working together and adapting technology to community needs, people can improve the livelihood of all.

The origins and development of these principles shall be sought in China's revolutionary experience.

I. People's War and the Origins of the
Chinese Road to Socialism

A generation ago China was "the sick man of Asia," a nation ravaged by a century of successive wars waged by imperial powers and native warlords, and by the plunder of corruption-ridden governments and a parasitic landlord-commercial class. The economy of this agrarian nation of four hundred million people was so fragile that waves of famine sent millions to death by starvation, and tremors in the world economy reverberated with disastrous consequences for currency, finance, and trade. China's humiliation was the product of foreign domination feeding on internal weakness and corruption.

In the early nineteenth century, opium and gunboats spearheaded the initial phase of Western invasion. Nowhere do we find a more telling example of the thirst for profit, hypocritically rationalized by the call for "free trade," than in British piracy and then war to force opium upon the Chinese nation and eventually to submit the entire economy to foreign penetration. United States merchants quickly followed the British lead to become the second major opium traders at the expense of a prostrate China. In 1841, explaining that the Anglo-Chinese War was not about opium, John Quincy Adams leaped to support the moral imperative of British policy:

> The moral obligation of commercial intercourse between nations is founded entirely, exclusively upon the Christian precept to love your neighbor as yourself. . . . But China, not being a Christian nation, its inhabitants do not consider themselves bound by the Christian precept to love their neighbor as themselves. . . . The fundamental principle of the Chinese nation is anti-commercial. . . . It admits no obligation to hold commercial intercourse with others. . . . It is time that this enormous outrage upon the rights of human nature, and upon the first principles of the rights of nations should cease.[1]

For the next half century opium was China's leading import while successive wars and occupying forces progressively facilitated the Western advance in China. Already in the nineteenth century the Chinese people rose in resistance to foreign conquest and waves of rebellion challenged a moribund state and society, only to be repressed with immense bloodshed.

Following China's defeat in the Sino-Japanese War of 1894-1895, territorial dismemberment by the West and Japan took the form of exacting concessions, colonial territories, and leased areas, and foreign capital began to flow into modern industry. Foreign economic, financial, and administrative power centered in the treaty ports but radiated outward to the entire nation. By stages the powers deprived the Chinese government of much of its sovereign authority. Extraterritoriality, for example, gave foreigners immunity to Chinese law. Unequal treaties, beginning in about 1840 and continuing over the next century, placed control of tariffs on imported goods in foreign hands. China became locked in the grip of foreign debt and indemnity payments which by the 1930s claimed up to one-third of the national budget. And Japanese researchers have estimated the cost of the destruction wrought by Japanese invasion in the years 1937-1945 in the range of $50 to $55 billion. Sun Yat-sen, the leader of the 1911 republican revolution, described the foreign impact as "triple oppression, political, economic, and ethnic," reducing China to a "sub-colony." It was a view shared by Chinese of diverse political persuasions.

The scattered fragments of a modern industrial base, key elements of which were foreign owned or controlled, rather than contributing toward comprehensive industrialization and rural prosperity, largely serviced the interests of foreign capital. A critical instance of industrial subjugation is the iron and steel industry, which became a fully integrated component of the Japanese economy. Centered in Manchuria at Anshan, the leading steel center ever since its founding in 1915, Chinese iron and steel provided a major boost to Japanese industrialization. The iron, coal, and other raw materials of the region not only feuled resource-poor Japan's industrialization (and war machine) but provided impetus to invade and annex the region.

While Chinese-owned modern industry also continued to grow, in 1920, in addition to controlling 99 percent of pig iron and iron ore, foreign firms held 75 percent of the coal mined by modern methods, over 90 percent of the railroads (via loans), and they dominated shipping to and from China and on inland waterways.

The influx of foreign manufactures devastated important sectors (though by no means all) of traditional industry. By 1920, as a result of the import of yarn, cotton spinning, the most important Chinese handicraft, suffered a 50 percent reduction; foreign iron and steel and Standard Oil's kerosene virtually destroyed native iron and vegetable oil (for lighting). And beginning with Western penetration in the early nineteenth century and accelerating in the twentieth century, China suffered a serious decline in the terms of international trade as the price of its raw material exports fell relative to imported manufactures.

With the state paralyzed by a century of successive wars and loss of such sovereign rights as tariff autonomy and control over investment, foreign enterprises succeeded in appropriating and exporting substantial revenues. At the same time landlords, warlords, officials, and moneylenders squeezed the peasantry and channeled the income into speculation, luxury consumption, weapons, and other nonproductive purposes. For example, in the nineteenth century, the landlords, who comprised approximately 2 percent of the population, appropriated 22 percent of national income and made no significant productive contribution. What productive investment occurred centered on the export sector, had few linkages to agriculture or to other domestic industries, and was concentrated overwhelmingly in Shanghai and Manchuria. The result was severe imbalance between growing but parasitic treaty port enclaves and the stagnating countryside and inland areas. China was a prototype of those underdeveloped nations with large agrarian populations, limited arable land, primitive technology, and low per capita income whose options were circumscribed by foreign power. It should nevertheless be noted that even in this state China enjoyed certain opportunities for independent action which fully colonized areas did not.

International and domestic forces combined to thwart Chinese aspirations for national independence, wealth, and power. But in the final analysis it was the moribund quality of a landlord- and bureaucrat-ridden society which opened the way to foreign conquest and which continued to block aspirations for revolutionary change.

By 1920 China's industrial working class, its origins and

character intimately bound up with imperialist investment, had emerged as a small but significant social force. The 1.5 million industrial workers, although less than 1 percent of the population, were heavily concentrated in six urban areas, of which Shanghai was by far the largest and most important. The majority worked in large plants with 500 or more workers in a few critical industries, notably textiles, transport, and mining, and over 650,000, nearly half, found employment in foreign firms.

This first-generation proletariat had deep roots in the countryside. Most of its members, recently smallholders, tenants, or agricultural laborers, had been forced by famine or the loss of land to migrate to the cities. Female and child labor accounted for a significant portion, in many industries the majority of the workforce, as shown in a 1924 survey of the Shanghai textile industry (see Table 1).

Table 1
Composition of the Workforce in Shanghai Textile Factories, 1923-1924

Industry	Men		Women		Boys under 12		Girls under 12	
Silk		%		%		%		%
39 Chinese factories	2,274	9.6	17,895	74.5	105	0.4	3,461	15.5
27 Foreign factories	797	3.5	12,458	55.5	1,364	6.1	8,566	34.9
7 American factories	140	3.1	3,050	68.6	—	—	1,250	28.1
Cotton								
18 Chinese mills	8,682	26.9	19,822	62.8	1,005	2.9	2,610	6.4
24 Japanese and British mills	15,048	26.1	38,157	65.9	1,615	2.8	2,690	5.2

Source: A. Kotenev, *Shanghai, Its Municipality and the Chinese.* (Shanghai, 1927), pp. 306-10; cited in Jean Chesneaux, *The Chinese Labor Movement, 1919-1927* (Stanford: Stanford University Press, 1968), p. 74.

Extensive reliance on child labor brought the average age of the workforce in the textile industry, China's largest, to below twenty years of age. Like men, women and children worked the standard twelve-hour shift seven days a week, but for a fraction of the wages. Many, due to such various pretexts as "apprenticeship training," received no wages at all, and labor gang bosses siphoned off a large share of the wages of most others. A visitor to several Shanghai silk factories in 1926 concluded that many of its child employees were no more than seven years old and some probably younger. In the late 1930s another described the work of a nine-year-old girl who was "privileged" to accompany her mother to a Shanghai silk-reeling factory where she, like many others, worked as an apprentice in return for her food: "for eleven hours each day this tot stood upon a raised platform wielding a small brush in a steaming brazier full of boiling cocoons." The working conditions which prevailed in Chinese factories gave rise to horrendous rates of accidents, death, and diseases with virtually no compensation.

Paul Henry, the International Labor Organization delegate to China, in 1925 compared conditions in the traditional factories such as match, carpet, and silk factories to Dante's descriptions of the infernal regions:

> Pale, sickly creatures move around there in almost total darkness, amidst indescribable filth, and breathing an atmosphere that is insupportable to anyone coming in from outside. At ten o'clock at night, or sometimes even later, they are still at work, and the feeble light of a few oil lamps lends the factories a still more sinister aspect. . . . When the time to stop work finally comes, these miserable creatures doss down in any place they can find—the lucky ones on bales of waste material or in the attics if there are any, and the rest on the workshop floor, like chained dogs.[2]

Summing up the evidence on workers' income and livelihood in the 1920s, Jean Chesneaux concluded that "workers and their families simply didn't have enough to live on." The wages of average workers in most industries barely covered the most minimal requirements for survival for a single person, not to mention their families. Most working-class families spent 60 to 75 percent of their meager income on food and many were in permanent debt. As for housing, families crowded into a single room, when they could afford that, while thousands slept on factory floors, in company dormitories, or in squatter huts fashioned of flotsam and jetsam.

The extreme misery of the proletariat, its geographical and industrial concentration, and the high visibility of foreign capital provided fertile ground for organization. In the 1920s, under the leadership of the newly formed Communist Party, this strategically placed and well-organized proletariat played a critical role in the revolutionary and anti-imperialist movement. The legacy of the struggles of that era would leave a deep imprint on the subsequent course of revolution. However, in 1927, having unified much of China with the help of the Communist-led mass movement, Chiang Kai-shek and his Kuomintang Party broke with their Communist allies and launched a bloody repression of the working-class movement. With subsequent state control of the cities by Kuomintang, warlord, and imperialist forces, the locus of revolution shifted to the countryside.

Ninety percent of the Chinese people were peasants, truly the wretched of the earth. But it was also the peasantry which was the bearer of a rebel tradition spanning two millennia. The vast majority were tenant farmers or small cultivators living off tiny, fragmented plots of land, or hired laborers. They eked out a living—or attempted to do so—from the overworked soil while a small and parasitic landlord class reaped a large share of the harvest. The American writer Edgar Snow captured the desperation of the situation in the countryside in drought-stricken North China in 1929 at the height of a famine which sent three to five million to their death and forced countless others to abandon their land. "Have you ever seen a man," Snow asked,

—a good honest man who has worked hard, a "law-abiding citizen," doing no serious harm to anyone—when he has had no food for more than a month? It is a most agonizing sight. His dying flesh hangs from him in wrinkled folds; you can clearly see every bone in his body; his eyes stare out unseeing and even if he is a youth of twenty he moves like an ancient crone, dragging himself from spot to spot. If he has been lucky he has long ago sold his wife and daughters. He has also sold everything he owns—the timber of his house itself, and most of his clothes. Sometimes he has, indeed, even sold the last rags of decency, and he sways there in the scorching sun, his testicles dangling from him like withered olive seeds—the last grim jest to remind you that this was once a man!

Children are even more pitiable, with their little skeletons bent over and misshapen, their crooked bones, their little arms like twigs, and their purpling bellies filled with bark and sawdust, protruding like tumors.[3]

Yet as Snow wrote his classic *Red Star Over China,* world war was about to transform the international order and a new stage began in the Chinese Revolution. In 1937, anticipating rapid conquest of a prostrate Chinese nation, Japan launched an all-out invasion, only to find itself mired in the quicksand of a people's war from which neither victory nor extrication was possible. While the national government, comprised of the Kuomintang and allied warlords, retreated to the Southwest in order to preserve its armies intact, throughout North China the Communist Party led guerrilla forces which engulfed and eventually whittled away Japanese occupied territory. By 1945 approximately 100 million people lived in Communist-led liberated areas in the countryside. The Pacific War, waged by the United States and its allies after Pearl Harbor, contributed to Japan's defeat. It is worth emphasizing, however, that the Chinese people had already resisted Japan singlehandedly for the entire decade following Japan's 1931 seizure of Manchuria, and throughout the Pacific War Communist-led forces directly aided the U.S. military by tying down hundreds of thousands of Japanese troops.

How could a nation with a century-long unbroken record of defeat at the hands of foreign powers repulse a technologically powerful country? What conditions permitted the Chinese Communists, driven from the cities in 1927 and virtually destroyed in 1934–1935, to emerge at the head of a peasant-based national revolutionary movement? These questions and the lessons of people's war are important for the subsequent reconstruction of the Chinese nation and its efforts to build a socialist society.

Geographically isolated in base areas behind Japanese lines, Communist forces could not but rely on their own resources, above all on a mobilized population, to fight Japan. Under these circumstances, self-reliance and the creation of firm bonds between guerrilla army and people were virtues born of necessity. Consistent with but not derived directly from Marxist revolutionary principles, their origins lay in the concrete experience of guerrilla warfare in the countryside after 1927, plus some inspiration from elements of China's heritage of peasant rebellion. China's liberation was the fruit of two decades of sacrifice, during which the Communist Party forged powerful bonds of unity with the people, above all the peasantry, bonds which would shape the future possibilities of revolutionary change.

Confronted with full-scale Japanese invasion in 1937 the Communists entered a united front with the Kuomintang. While preserving the autonomy of their armed forces and independent territorial base, they sought to unite with all classes prepared to resist Japanese conquest. As the Kuomintang would soon discover, the appeal to nationalism divorced from an effective social program was inadequate to the task of fully mobilizing the Chinese people. In the end, successful mobilization was rooted in the ability of the Communists to concretely identify with and serve the interests of the peasant majority and elicit their active support for a program responsive to their economic and social needs. The heart of that program was the reduction of rent and interest implemented directly by tenants and poor peasants. In the process, the peasantry gained both organization and consciousness of collective power. In this way, as well as through peasant participation in Communist-led village governments, militia units, and cooperatives, a generation of peasant activists broke the economic and political monopoly of landlords and rich peasants. Peasant participation on every front—military, political, economic, social, and cultural—produced the popular and dynamic quality of the era. Were these the same men and women who had endured exploitation at the hands of landlords, warlords, and foreign powers?

Popular mobilization was the hallmark of success of both the new political economy of the liberated areas and the Communist guerrilla warfare strategy for defeating Japan. The Chinese people rose to resist an enemy which enjoyed overwhelming superiority in technology, weapons, and wealth. The ability of the Communist Eighth Route and New Fourth Armies to forge a common identity with local people made it possible to encircle and wear down Japanese forces. People's war meant unity between the cooperative principles of the emerging political and economic order and military innovations in the guerrilla struggle.

The Chinese resistance provided the first successful challenge to the outward sweep of Western (and Japanese) power, placing it at the forefront of the world-wide movement for decolonization and national independence which emerged from World War II. Looking at it closely, one can discern five interrelated principles of people's war at the heart of the wartime linkage of party and peasantry which subsequently infused the practice and conceptualization of Chinese socialist development.

Equality

> One day Wang Kou-ho took me with him when he went out to the sheep. That was in the summer and it was hot. We went eight li from the village. At dinner time I was sent back to fetch his food. First he took off my cloth shoes and pissed in them, then he said: 'You must be back with my food before my piss has dried.' It was a hot summer day and I had to run barefoot across sand and I could not stop and rest on the way. I ran as fast as I could, but when I got back the landowner's piss had already dried because the sun was strong and Wang Kou-ho beat me after he had eaten. [Weeps.] I was only twelve.
>
> [Recollection of a North China peasant, 1962.[4]]

Such incidents, characteristic of the absolute power—and degradation—of the landlords, and the tyranny many exercised over their tenants and servitors, etched deeply into peasant consciousness. They help to explain the passion and power of the peasant struggle to wrest their land and their lives from landlord control.

In the liberated areas, as the balance shifted to the revolutionary forces, the rigid hierarchical structure of traditional Chinese society embodied in the dominance of landlords over tenants, rich over poor, officials over the common people, the old over the young, and men over women, gave way in often striking ways to egalitarian practice in political, economic, and social life. Within the framework of a new alignment of military and political power, the attack on landlord prerogatives was central. Not only in popular movements to reduce rent and interest, but in participation in elected local governments, the poorest strata of the rural population took important steps toward equality. To be sure, equality could not be achieved at a single stroke. Rather, one observes in China's uninterrupted revolution continuing efforts to transform relationships between exploiters and exploited and between officials and the people, striking at barriers of status, income, and opportunity.

Not only did officials in the liberated areas receive subsistence incomes comparable to local consumption standards, they engaged in productive labor themselves. Thus, many army units and government offices reduced the burden of taxation on the peasantry by achieving substantial self-sufficiency in their supply needs. Here was one basis for firm unity between army and people, and between state and society, breaking the cycle of exploitation in favor of common income levels and mutual efforts to produce and to fight in the service of the resistance. The Communists further challenged the special position of officialdom through the practice of criticism and self-criticism which helped to undermine privilege and provided a basis for dialogue and cooperation between officials and people.

The egalitarian spirit in the base areas contrasted sharply with the rigid divisions which pervaded landlord society elsewhere in China. Journalist Jack Belden commented:

> I was ashamed to go from one Kuomintang general to another, eating special delicacies from their well-laid tables, while peasants were scraping the fields outside the yamens for roots and wild grass to stuff into their griping stomachs. But I was more than ashamed—I was overcome with a feeling of loathing—when I learned that these same generals and the Kuomintang officials were buying up land from starving farmers for arrears in taxes and were holding it to wait tenants and rainy days.[5]

As Belden observed, wartime conditions heightened class polarization in the Kuomintang- and Japanese-occupied regions while class oppression was under attack in the liberated areas.

Life was harsh under the pressure of attack and blockade. Yet the shared hardship and a clear sense of purpose united leaders and led and produced a spirit of optimism which distinguished the liberated areas.

Participation

In the course of the resistance the Communists encouraged peasants to form local peasant associations, militia units, and, in the case of activists, to join the party. Through participation in the new organizations, and on the basis of initial successes against the local landlords and the Japanese, peasants experienced political organization first hand and learned how to use it to change the circumstances of their lives. As peasant horizons expanded with participation in political and military activities and in shaping decisions which would determine the survival of their villages, rural life took on new dimensions. Women as well as men joined in acts of redistributive justice and economic restructuring in the rent reduction, cooperative, and production movements, and all found roles in supporting the guerrillas.

People's war with its emphasis on the total human contribution gave rise to a distinctive conception of the human ideal, the all-round individual. Such a person might till the fields or spin yarn by day, join the local militia and teach or study in a part-time school at night, all the while playing unaccustomed political roles in the community. Closing the gap between those who worked with their hands and those who worked with their minds enabled all to contribute their creativity and their labor to the common goal which linked national liberation with individual and community welfare.

Cooperative Organization

A century of recurring war compounding rural immiseration had disrupted village life and intensified class antagonisms in the countryside. During the War of Resistance, however, there began the process of reconstituting rural communities on the basis of new egalitarian and cooperative principles. An essential step in revitalizing rural society was the formation of production cooperatives in the aftermath of rent and interest reduction struggles. Building on bonds of class solidarity, rent reduction led increasing numbers of poor and middle peasants to the realization that their well-being and political rights rested on the ability to sustain collective action and prevent the resurgence of Japanese, warlord, and landlord power. New forms of mutual aid modified and extended traditional cooperative practices to pool labor, draft animals, and tools. Rural women, many entering social productive labor for the first time, made important contributions to newly established mutual aid and cooperative units of five, ten, or more families. Cooperatives frequently provided leadership for the village militia or school. They became the nuclei for the full range of village activities. Although private ownership of land and other means of production were continued under the party's wartime program known as the new democracy, organizational forms emerging in the liberated areas bore within them the seeds of a society resting on the predominance of cooperative and community goals. Features of the cooperatives and of government-run industrial enterprises would re-emerge a decade later in the course of socialist transition in the countryside.

Self-Reliance

One imperative of survival in people's war was self-reliance in the basic necessities of life, in weapons, and in policy implementation, not only for each of the more than twenty geographically discrete liberated areas, but often for each county and village in the war zone. The party and military center provided overall strategic unity and articulated a clear conception of national liberation. It coordinated military and political activity, repeatedly summing up and clarifying advanced experiences to serve as models which people could learn from and adapt to their own experiences in the base areas. However, local communities had to assume basic responsibility for their own actions in the face of Japanese onslaught. Not infallible organizational techniques, still less the use of manipulation or terror, can explain the popular achievements of the base areas. The strength of the resistance rested on popular support; in China's liberation war, as in Vietnam's two decades later, it was foreign invaders who relied on naked terror in the futile attempt to quell a population in arms. The articulation of popular goals and broad-based commitment to their implementation at the grassroots level was the *sine qua non* of the resistance. People's war tested the vision that the people, given appropriate leadership and relying on their own collective energy and insight, can ultimately conquer foreign armies, domestic oppressors, and a harsh natural environment. When contrasted with the fatalism and passivity characteristic of pre-revolutionary peasant consciousness, self-reliance provides a dynamic antithesis to reigning values.

The Mass Line

At the heart of the party's wartime conception, and of Mao Tsetung's lifelong revolutionary strategy, is the mass line approach to leadership rooted in the conviction that the people are the motive force of history. "Weapons are an important factor in war," Mao observed in 1938, "but not the decisive factor; it is people, not things, that are decisive. The contest of strength is not only a contest of military and economic power, but also a contest of human power and morale."

The role of leaders begins with investigating and understanding existing patterns of oppression and crystallizing and articulating popular desires for change. This requires an intimate grasp of concrete conditions as well as clarity of ultimate goals tested and refined in a continuous two-way learning process between leaders and the people. Leaders must be pupils as well as teachers of the masses. Legitimation must reside not in status conferred by office, position, or theoretical versatility but in repeated testing of the ability of leaders to forge and sustain effective relationships with the people. Mao put it this way in 1943 in his classic formulation of the mass line:

> all correct leadership is necessarily "from the masses, to the masses." This means: take the ideas of the masses (scattered and unsystematic ideas) and concentrate them (through study turn them into concentrated and systematic ideas), then go to the masses and propagate and explain these ideas until the masses embrace them as their own, hold fast to them and translate them into action, and test the correctness of these ideas in action. Then once again concentrate ideas from the masses and once again go to the masses, so that the ideas are persevered in and carried through. And so on, over and over again in an endless spiral, with the ideas becoming more correct, more vital and richer each time.[6]

We can trace the origins of the mass line from Marx and Engels, notably in *The Communist Manifesto*, through elements of the Bolshevik experience.* At the same time, the mass line

---

* At various times in his revolutionary career, Lenin offered suggestive approaches to leadership and participation strikingly different from his well-known vanguard formulations and much of the practice of the

developed in the milieu of people's war as a response to elitist and authoritarian tendencies in traditional Chinese practice which were reinforced by top-down, centralized conceptions of the vanguard party inherited from the Soviet Union.

Ideas of liberation when firmly grounded in popular understanding, Mao held, can become a powerful material force. Once correct ideas "are grasped by the masses, these ideas turn into a material force which changes society and changes the world." The same peasants who stand mute beneath the landlords' lash or cower before advancing Japanese armies today, Mao held, may rise as one tomorrow. The masses of people, above all the most oppressed elements of the peasantry, provide the motor of revolutionary change in achieving national independence and waging class struggle; the same is true of the drive to build a prosperous developing nation. The entire history of the Chinese Revolution may be considered a search for conditions which foster new levels of consciousness and more effective interaction between leaders and led, between party and a mobilized people.

"Men make their history," Karl Marx observed, "but they do not make it exactly as they please." Periods of war, economic and political crisis, and social disintegration as well as the experimental stages of a new political and economic order—that is, the entire period of the Chinese Revolution—provide abundant opportunity for conscious political action. But effective action must be grounded both in clarity of ultimate goals and in detailed knowledge of concrete social conditions, popular con-

---

Bolshevik Party. In *"Leftwing" Communism: An Infantile Disorder,* he called on the party "to link itself, to keep in close touch with, and to a certain extent, if you like, to merge itself with the broadest masses of the toilers—primarily with the proletarian, but also with the nonproletarian toiling masses."[7] However, in sharp contrast with Chinese Communist practice during the Anti-Japanese Resistance and land revolution, the Bolshevik Party never succeeded during Lenin's lifetime in establishing firm organic links between the vast peasant majority and the party. Hence one sees the adoption in Russia of Jacobin strategies of minority revolution to seize power and effect revolutionary change from above. The Chinese Communist attempt to formulate and achieve a mass line style of leadership under conditions of people's war and subsequently, has centered on the necessity to redefine politics and party, and the relationship between leaders and led, in ways which expand the active and creative role of the people.

sciousness, and human capabilities. The critical importance of both popular and leadership consciousness in the formulations of Mao Tsetung and in Chinese revolutionary practice underline the necessity to correctly gauge the contradictions inherent in each stage of development. Throughout this study we will explore changing perceptions of the potential for revolutionary change and the complex dialectic involving the people, the Communist Party, and Mao in initiating or impeding it.

China has broken important new ground in theory as well as in practice of the mass line. In the early 1940s, nearly a decade prior to liberation, Mao and the Communist leadership turned their attention to a problem which haunted Lenin in his final years following the October Revolution: the potential dangers of corruption, privilege, and bureaucratism by any leadership which becomes divorced from the people. A Communist Party was no exception. The Chinese party approached the problem by repeatedly launching campaigns for study, criticism, and internal reform to sensitize and rededicate the leadership at every level to the task of forging effective bonds with the people in order to learn from them as well as lead them and to break down manifestations of elitism.

The corollary of the mass line, and a theme which runs through party theory and practice since the War of Resistance, is "serve the people." This has meant above all ensuring the welfare of the peasantry. To be sure, under enemy attack the party and army entered into intensified competition with the people for resources to finance the war effort. Yet in 1942, at the very height of the Japanese counteroffensive, in his first extended analysis of political economy, Mao defined the priority task of serving the people as contributing directly to their prosperity. In a theme he would reiterate throughout the subsequent transition to socialism, Mao insisted that:

> All empty words are useless, we must give the people visible material wealth. . . . The primary aspect of our work is not to ask things of the people; it is to give things to the people. . . . we can organize, lead and help the people develop production, increase their material wealth, and, on this basis, step by step we can raise their political consciousness and cultural level.[8]

We will observe both in Mao's leadership conception and in

China's revolutionary practice the enduring emphasis on popular welfare and rapid economic development as means of improving the livelihood of all (and particularly of the poorest classes) and deepening of consciousness en route to higher stages of social development. The point is central to understanding the strength of the loyalty which linked the great majority of the peasantry to the party through successive phases of revolutionary change, although, as we will observe, these ties were not without strains in periods when this principle was violated. It is also essential for understanding the impressive economic development which has continued on the basis of deepening cooperative foundations throughout a protracted period of class and institutional upheavals.

Wartime experience suggested that the critical question was how to link revolution with higher productivity to mobilize broad-based support for eliminating privilege and raising consciousness in ways which strengthened the war economy.

The ideals and social practice drawn from the party's concrete experience in people's war may be called the Yenan Way, named after the movement's wartime capital. Synthesized and given their clearest expression in the writings of Mao, they constitute both the essence of the collective experience of an era and a reference point in the subsequent history of the revolution.

In Russia in 1917 the Bolsheviks, with firm roots in the proletariat but lacking a significant rural base, carried out a minority revolution centered in the leading cities in predominantly peasant Russia. Having seized political power they initiated radical social change. But the Bolsheviks clashed with the most powerful and radical peasant movement in the early 1920s and then in the New Economic Policy deferred the socialist transformation of the rural areas. After 1928 the state and army imposed collectivization on the countryside under conditions of virtual civil war, mass executions, and the arrest of hundreds of thousands of kulaks.

It is difficult to overestimate the significance of the bonds formed between the Chinese Communist Party and the peasantry during the War of Resistance and subsequent land revolution. The war provided an environment in which prefigurative elements of the future socialist society, particularly equality, participation, cooperation, and self-reliance, were tested and adapted to Chinese conditions on the basis of mass line principles. This experience, in contrast with that of the pre-1917 Bolshevik Party which concentrated its activity in the cities, would provide firm foundations and legitimation for the subsequent social revolution.

II. Social Transformation and Economic Development

From the standpoint of world history, the bourgeois revolutions and the establishment of the bourgeois nations came before not after the Industrial Revolution. The bourgeoisie first changed the superstructure and took possession of the machinery of state. . . . Only then did they push forward great changes in the production relations. . . . To be sure, the revolution in the production relations is brought on by a certain degree of development of the productive forces, but the major development of the productive forces always comes after changes in the production relations.

Mao Tsetung, 1960

In the immediate aftermath of the Japanese surrender, as China plunged into civil war, the Communists, pitted against U.S.-backed Kuomintang forces, embarked on a program of intense revolutionary change centered in the countryside. Beginning with land revolution in the years 1947–1952, it proceeded by discrete stages to the formation of socialist institutions and implementation of national development programs designed to achieve comprehensive industrialization, agricultural modernization, and abundance. The land revolution was a social revolution, one of the most far-reaching of this century. But it was not a socialist revolution. Nevertheless, in destroying the privilege of the landlord class it created crucial political preconditions for socialism in agrarian China.

In the 1950s Paul Baran, drawing both on Marxist theory and the practice of the Soviet Union, hypothesized that "the degree of maturity of society's productive resources . . . determines the general character of social, political and intellectual life . . .

[therefore] socialism in backward and underdeveloped countries has a powerful tendency to become a backward and underdeveloped socialism."[9] The magnitude of the challenge facing Chinese revolutionaries in 1949 is underscored by the fact that China's fragile, imperialist-dominated industrial base was less than half that inherited by the Bolsheviks in 1917, and less than one-eighth in per capita terms. Drawing both positive and negative lessons from Soviet experience, China would seek to apply the strength of a mobilized people and the rationality of socialist institutions to stimulate the development of productive forces so as to eliminate poverty and accelerate national development in the service of socialism.

The basic precondition for achieving higher stages of development, whether en route to feudalism, capitalism, or socialism, is not the level of economic development but the seizure of political power by a class or classes committed to and capable of generating fundamental change. The seizure of political power preceded both the Industrial Revolution in the West and the first socialist revolution carried out in the Soviet Union. Therefore, the Chinese Communist leadership concluded, a national liberation struggle focusing on driving out the foreign invaders, followed by a full-scale social revolution in the countryside, could create preconditions for China's socialist development. The sequence was critical, for as long as imperialism and moribund Chinese social classes held sway, China could neither initiate significant internal development nor contemplate socialism. Having paved the way for national liberation with the defeat of Japan, the next challenge was to sweep aside those anachronistic social forces, above all the landlord class, which held back the Chinese nation. Already during people's war, as we have seen, in North China liberated areas peasants organized under party leadership broke the landlords' monopoly on rural power. But it was only with the defeat of Japan that the Communists launched a full-scale attack on the landlord system in its entirety.

In China, agrarian revolution would precede and set the stage for industrial revolution and socialist transition. In this respect

Classes are large groups of people distinguished by their position in an historically determined economic system, by their relation to ownership and control of the means of production, by their position in the social organization of the work process, and, consequently, by their access to the wealth and opportunities available in society. Class status determines the ability to appropriate—or to have appropriated—the fruits of human labor, that is, to exploit or to be exploited. Yet class consciousness, values, and behavior, while decisively shaped by all the preceding factors (some of which are determined at birth) are also the product of education, experience, and class struggle. In particular, human beings can transcend their class origins and present class status in the revolutionary process. Likewise, revolutionary classes and individuals may degenerate to become guardians of special privilege. Hence, continued advance toward socialism and the eradication of inequality require that the issue of class be repeatedly addressed in the realm of social production, ideas, and individual and collective action.

China's trajectory toward industrialization, like that of European capitalist nations, would begin with the agrarian revolution (radically different in content to be sure, but both comprising profound changes in relations of production and paving the way for subsequent efforts to transform technology). By contrast, export-oriented industrialization stressing the primacy of foreign over domestic markets is being carried out in many Third World nations today while stagnation prevails in landlord-dominated rural areas, or the "green revolution" accelerates concentration of land and wealth while foreign capital dominates the modern sector. In the late 1950s Mao provided a theoretical basis for the primacy of the land revolution and its integral relationship to the subsequent technological revolution.

It was possible to destroy the old productive relations only after we had overthrown a backward superstructure in the course of revolution. After the old productive relations had been destroyed new ones were created, and these cleared the way for the development of new social productive forces. With that behind us we were able to set in

motion the technological revolution to develop social productive forces on a large scale.[10]

The critical challenge, beginning in the land revolution and
continuing through the entire period of socialism, lay in linking
social revolution and economic development. Revolutionary
change, Mao suggested, could set the stage for rapid advances in
productivity in the first instance by eliminating those classes, particularly landlords, which blocked development, and by stimulating productive enthusiasm and organization among the peasants. But further economic progress required planning and the
continued transformation of ideas, institutions, and technology.

Forces of production are the land, resources, tools, and
machinery, together with the labor power, knowledge,
skill, and technology of the people applied to the productive process. Among the forces of production, human
labor, technology, and creativity are decisive; and people
define themselves as human beings through labor.

Relations of production comprise ownership and work
relations. The ownership and control of the means of
production (including land, resources, factories, and labor
power) is the principal determinant of wealth, power, and
social stratification. The relations of production are class
relations manifested in the work process and in the allocation of society's goods. Together forces of production
and relations of production comprise the economic base or
foundation of society.

The superstructure is the realm of ideas and institutions,
including culture, customs, and political, military, educational, religious, and judicial systems of society. The superstructure invariably reflects significant features of the economic base, and above all the values and interests of the
ruling class, but in class societies it also incorporates
competing value systems which reflect the interests of
other classes. Changes in the superstructure may precipitate changes in the base and vice versa. The dynamic
relationship between forces of production, relations of
production, and superstructure gives rise to revolutionary
change.

The Chinese road to socialism entailed progression by means of class struggle and development of the productive forces through discrete stages beginning with the new democracy. The new democratic economy gradually introduced cooperation and planning features into a predominantly small-scale peasant economy beginning in the phase of people's war and culminating by 1952 with the land revolution and state control of critical industries. In the early 1950s the new democratic economy was an amalgam of reformed capitalist relations of production—private ownership of land and light industry—with a critical and growing state sector (public ownership of major industries), and incipient socialist relations of production, reflected, for example, in small-scale mutual aid. The new democracy was a milestone on the road to socialism.

In 1956 at a decisive moment in the evolution of an independent Chinese development path, Mao briefly summarized national goals: "We promote socialism because we want to develop our country, develop a national economy and culture that is better than the system of private ownership and to ensure our national independence." Here we find the promise of socialism wedded to the strivings of China's century-long revolutionary struggle. The necessity to direct revolutionary change in the service of accelerated development of the productive forces in ways which reinforce socialist values is particularly urgent in a poor nation such as China. Socialism is, in short, projected as the touchstone of economic growth and prosperity, of humane social values and cultural norms, and finally as the basis for ending a century of humiliation through self-reliance.

This study will consider three yardsticks for measuring socialist society: (1) cooperative and state (all people) ownership and control of the means of production and distribution, and planned allocation of society's resources; (2) elimination of inequities and privileges that retard economic development and the full realization of human potential; and (3) mastery by the immediate producers of the workplace and of working people in all spheres of society, including the allocation of national resources and control over the realm of politics and ideas.

It is worth emphasizing in light of the revolutionary record of this century that if only the first of these is achieved, the liberating potential of socialism may still be denied. Concentrated economic and political power in the hands of a state and a party is subject to such abuses as the formation of a new class, an elite which behind the mask of socialist rhetoric uses its power to repress the people and monopolize wealth and status. Only progress toward the attainment of all three mutually related goals is sufficient to earn designation as a socialist society. Yet socialism is a process, and the achievement of the first yardstick may be a milestone in the passage to socialism.

The continuing search for socialist institutions, human relations, and ideas appropriate to constantly changing Chinese conditions is reflected in these documents. In his major philosophical essay "On Contradiction," Mao pointed out:

> Changes in society are due chiefly to the development of the internal contradictions in society, that is, the contradiction between the productive forces and the relations of production, the contradiction between classes and the contradiction between the old and the new; it is the development of these contradictions that pushes society forward and gives the impetus for the supersession of the old society by the new. [11]

At each stage of development the specific character and interrelationship among contradictions change. For example, the principal contradiction between imperialism and the Chinese people is transformed by the victory of people's war; the contradiction between landlord and peasant is resolved by land revolution. In each case, however, new contradictions arise and old ones assume new forms whose resolution is the task of politics and economics. We may note a series of contradictions whose persistence in various forms would challenge revolutionary forces throughout the entire duration of the People's Republic; the study which follows will explore the roles of class struggle and the party's use of mass line and other methods in addressing these persistent problems for clues to the distinctive qualities of China's development. They include:

(1) the contradiction between centralism and democracy, reflected, for example, in the relationship between central planning and resource allocation on the one hand and local initiative and self-reliance on the other, and between the concentration of power in the hands of a state and party on the one hand and popular initiative and control on the other;

(2) the contradiction between promise of national unity and

shared community (the basis for flourishing democracy among the people) and the imperative to continue the revolution to eliminate class oppression, vestiges of privilege, and the ideas associated with former ruling classes.

(3) the contradiction among state, collective, and individual, for example in determining the proportion of the surplus produced by society to be allocated to consumption, investment, or defense; and

(4) the contradictions inherent in the "three great differences" between city and countryside, worker and peasant, and mental and manual labor, as well as those between men and women and between Han and minority peoples.

China's progress and the prospects of continued advance toward communism may be evaluated in light of its success in confronting and resolving these and other contradictions while overcoming the legacy of poverty during successive phases of the revolution.

Throughout the long period of socialist transition toward communism classes exist and momentum toward higher stages rests on the dialectic of class struggle and expansion of the productive forces. What are the conditions which permit the transition from socialism to communism? In one of his rare discussions of communist society, Marx observed:

> In a higher phase of communist society, when the enslaving subordination of the individual to the division of labor, and therewith also the antithesis between mental and physical labor, has vanished; after labor has become not only a means of life but life's prime want; after the productive forces have also increased with the all-round development of the individual, and all the springs of co-operative wealth flow more abundantly—only then can the narrow horizon of bourgeois right be crossed in its entirety and society inscribe on its banner: From each according to his ability, to each according to his needs![12]

A protracted process is required to prepare the social, material, and ideological preconditions for the transition from socialism to the higher stage of communist society.

Marx offered few guidelines to chart the course for the achievement of communism which would have to emerge from the social practice of societies in revolution. Yet the diverse experiences of the Soviet Union and China amply confirm, in the words of Charles Bettelheim, that

> what is hardest is not the overthrow of the former dominant classes: the hardest task is, first, to destroy the former social relations—upon which a system of exploitation similar to the one supposed to have been overthrown for good can be reconstituted—and then to prevent those relations from being constituted on the basis of those elements of the old that still remain present for a long time in the new social relations.[13]

And, we may add, to do so while progressively overcoming the legacy of poverty and backwardness which China inherited at liberation.

III. Land Revolution and the New Democracy, 1946–1952

> In a very short time, in China's central, southern and northern provinces, several hundred million peasants will rise like a mighty storm, like a hurricane—a force so swift and violent that no power, however great, will be able to hold it back. . . . Every revolutionary party and every revolutionary comrade will be put to the test. . . . There are three alternatives. To march at their head and lead them? To trail behind them gesticulating and criticizing? Or to stand in their way and oppose them?
>
> Mao Tsetung, 1927

What contribution did the land revolution make to socialist transition and economic development? To what extent did it fulfill its dual promise of eliminating oppression and stimulating production? To answer these questions we must consider briefly the nature of socioeconomic relations in the Chinese countryside.

Rural poverty was the product of a complex social order rooted in myriad forms of oppression. Based in the first instance on highly unequal land ownership, religion and values reinforced peasant powerlessness in the face of nature and class superiors while the family perpetuated the domination of men over women and the old over the young. Prior to the land revolution, landlords who comprised 3 percent of the population owned approximately 26 percent of the land while 69 percent of the farming families, the poor peasants (including small landowners, tenants, and landless laborers) owned only 22 percent. More than half of all Chinese farmers were tenants, one-third being full tenants and nearly one-fourth part tenants. Tenancy rates were highest, and land concentration and absentee landlordism most pronounced, in Central and South China. In some areas tenants comprised 60 to 80 percent of the farming population and rents often exceeded 60 percent of the harvest. But tenancy was only one form of rural exploitation. Millions more, perhaps 10 percent of the rural workforce, were hired laborers. In 1930 John Buck found that two-fifths of all peasant households were in debt, paying an average of 32 percent of annual interest on an average debt of 76 yuan, and just three years later a Nationalist government survey placed the debtor population at 56 percent. With the war-accelerated disintegration of rural society in the twentieth century, peasants found themselves increasingly pressed by a variety of irregular exactions from official and unofficial predators—landlords, bandits, and tax collectors. Thus while the rural crisis was most acute for the poor, middle peasants also suffered as a result of the ravages and exactions of the landlord-warlord order in the countryside. All of these problems were compounded by the devastation of the land accompanying the century-long breakdown of the social order: denuded forests inviting flash floods, neglected irrigation works and river dykes, and overworked soil.

In early 1945, Mao had emphasized that "the social productive forces of China can be liberated only by destroying the Japanese aggressors, carrying out land revolution, emancipating the peasants, developing modern industry and establishing an independent, free, democratic, united, prosperous and powerful new China." The land revolution was the first step toward emancipating the vast majority of the Chinese people, paving the way for a comprehensive national development program. We can identify four major periods in the unfolding of land revolution.

1. *The eruption of land revolution from below,* *August 1945 to October 1947*

Building on peasant activity to control their own villages and curb landlord power during the War of Resistance, the first spontaneous wave of land revolution was the radical peasant response triggered by Japan's surrender. This initially took the form of revenge against wartime collaborators. Since collaborator and landlord were frequently one and the same, in many areas the peasantry quickly exceeded the bounds of the wartime rent reduction guidelines and initiated full-scale land redistribution. Whether to march at their head . . . or trail behind? As the nation plunged toward civil war in the spring of 1946, the Communists issued their first postwar land directive. The secret May Fourth Directive hailed the seizure and distribution of land that had already occurred and sanctioned confiscation of land belonging to traitors who had supported Japan, but its central thrust lay in guidelines designed to replace confiscation with a program of "voluntary" sale of landlords' surplus land and to protect rich peasants. The goal was to fulfill peasant demands for land while isolating the hardcore landlords and giving others the choice of cooperation or resistance. The priority right of tenants to purchase land would realize the promise of "land to the tiller," first put forward decades earlier by Sun Yat-sen. The May Fourth Directive curbed seizure of the land by an aroused peasantry in favor of legalized transfer. The goal of full equality was downplayed in this initial restraining directive, with its emphasis on the achievement of broad unity. December 1946 legislation in the Shensi–Kansu–Ninghsia border region, for example, permitted landlords in this old liberated area to retain up to 50 percent more land than the average middle peasant. The balance was to be sold to the state at prices twice the value of the annual yield (well below the market price, but far from outright confiscation). In theory peasants could then purchase the land from the government at half the state purchase price with installments paid over ten years. The concept—which the party subsequently repudiated—seemed to be one of administered land reform with initiative centered in the state and bypassing a mobilized peasantry.

As Kuomintang-Communist negotiations to avert civil war

dragged on, the Communists adhered to a moderate land program predicated on broad united front principles. We will observe time and again the explosion of class forces bursting through careful administrative guidelines established by planners and officials. The actual effect of the May Fourth legislation was to intensify the rural class struggle—had it not given sanction to already completed land seizures? In practice its main provisions were honored in the breach. Peasant activists and lower level cadres swung into action throughout North China. By 1947 land revolution was in full swing.

2. The high tide of land revolution, October 1947 to February 1948

With all-out civil war under way, in October 1947 the Communists issued the major postwar guidelines, "The Basic Agrarian Law." Here the ambiguities of earlier directives yielded to unequivocal commitment to revolution. The premise: "China's agrarian system is unjust in the extreme." The conclusion: "The agrarian system of feudal and semifeudal exploitation is abolished. The agrarian system of 'land to the tiller' is to be realized." In lucid jolting statements, the voice of a peasantry in revolt, the basic law sounded the deathknell of a landlord order rooted in exploitation.

In the following months, as the civil war entered its most bitterly contested phase, the Communists prepared to shift from the defensive to nation-wide offensive. Military offensive coincided with the high tide of peasant radicalism in North China as poor and landless peasants advanced to expropriate the landlords, wipe clean the slate of debt and oppression, and share in the division of land and other resources. The party now threw its full weight behind a process which, with varying degrees of intensity and myriad local variations, eventually penetrated to every village across the land. As a result of the struggle against the landlords, redistribution of land and property and testing and retesting of new village leadership, the peasantry and the party transformed the parameters of power and wealth throughout the countryside.

3. Toward the moderation of the land revolution, January 1948 to June 1950

The ink was scarcely dry on the Basic Agrarian Law when party leadership began to warn of excesses in the struggle for the land. More than any other twentieth-century leader, Mao has been associated with the notion that a mobilized peasantry, above all its most oppressed elements, can provide a powerful motor for revolutionary change. Yet the fact is that he combined empathy for the poor peasants with a keen sensitivity to the legitimate desires and importance of the middle sectors, which also in various ways suffered under the landlord order. The challenge of land revolution centered on uniting the vast majority of poor and middle peasants to isolate and strike a blow at landlord power. To ensure broad popular unity in the land revolution, Mao held that mobilization of the poor peasants must be coupled with absolute guarantees that the middle peasants would retain their land intact. Given the scarcity of distributable land (particularly in North China liberated areas where landlord holdings were relatively small initially and had already been reduced prior to land revolution) this meant that absolute equality of land ownership could not be achieved. Land revolution eliminated the most glaring inequities within the villages, yet middle peasants frequently retained advantages over poor peasants in land and tools. The party, whose first task lay in mobilizing the peasants to confront the landlords, had a second major task, to curb peasant demands for absolute leveling down to hoes and rakes and pots and pans.

Success in civil war required uniting the vast majority to isolate the Kuomintang and its landlord defenders. It also posed the difficult challenge of expanding the production and distribution of grain and supplies in the service of revolutionary forces and the people. A policy of complete equalization, by threatening to reduce the livelihood of middle peasants, would have undermined these national priorities. The principle of achieving the broadest unity and striking a concentrated blow against the main enemy was reaffirmed in land revolution.

Mao's inner-party directive of January 1948 initiated the moderating phase which continued for the duration of the land revolution. The party sought to tread a fine line between mobilizing peasant activists to seize power and preventing indiscriminate beating and killing—however justified by humiliations and crimes long borne in silence. Here as in every campaign we will observe the dual role of the party as a mobilizing and a restraining force. Thus, even landlords, if they had committed no serious crimes, were guaranteed an equal share of the land after expropriation. The landlords would be eliminated root and branch—as a class, not as individuals. To be sure, peasant anger sometimes exploded in summary justice and as many as 500,000 to 1,000,000 landlords may have been killed in the course of the land revolution and civil war. Yet the great majority of landlords emerged from the revolution stripped of political rights but as small owner-cultivators. The party helped mobilize the peasantry to rise, seize the land, and liberate itself from the strictures of overwhelming poverty and subordination to the landlord class. It then sought to channel the momentum of the revolution into increased productivity to eliminate poverty and support the war effort. By liberation in 1949, 20 percent of the peasants, centered in North and Northeast China, had completed land revolution.

4. Land revolution in the service of production, June 1950 to spring 1953

The Agrarian Reform Law of June 1950 summed up the critical shift in emphasis in the land revolution that had begun in the final years of the civil war and been extended after its conclusion. Whereas the 1947 law stressed the injustice of the landlord order, in the early 1950s land revolution would above all rectify its *irrationality*. Its central goal was to "set free the rural productive forces, develop agricultural production and thus pave the way for new China's industrialization." And indeed, agricultural production, rebounding from a century of war, increased at a rate of 15 percent per year from 1949 to the virtual completion of the movement in 1952.

The most important changes which had evolved in practice since 1947 concerned the treatment of the rich peasants. Emphasizing that the land revolution was antifeudal, not anticapitalist, the party placed a premium on rapid economic recovery based in part on preserving and even fostering the "rich peasant economy." Rich peasants hiring agricultural laborers and regularly participating in and directing farming were perceived as advanced elements of rural capitalism who could lead the way to higher productivity; landlords who rented out their land and typically made no productive contribution were feudal elements who impeded development. The 1950 law had stipulated that only those portions of rich peasant land rented out to tenants were to be redistributed. This policy, strongly emphasized in the early 1950s, encouraged rich peasants to raise productivity and also reassured middle peasants that their livelihood was not threatened. In South and Central China, land revolution nevertheless significantly reduced rich peasant landholdings (by confiscation of tenant lands and sometimes by exceeding the provisions of the law). Yet rich peasants retained economic advantages. In 1952, in the immediate aftermath of land revolution, the average rich peasant family's holdings of land, draft animals, and tools, as well as income, exceeded those of poor peasants by margins of better than 2:1. (The gap was slightly less in per capita terms since rich peasant families were larger.) Average poor peasant holdings of 12 mou (a 100 percent increase) compared with 26 mou for rich peasant families, and the advantages were more pronounced with respect to draft animals and equipment. During the new democratic phase, when development hinged significantly on private ownership, the rich peasants who emerged from the revolution with advantages in land and productive resources, and sometimes with commercial and industrial holdings as well, would make important economic contributions.

By further isolating the landlords, the rich peasant policy permitted smoother consolidation of the land revolution and reduced the economic dislocation which accompanied earlier more radical phases. Under the 1950 law, land revolution began with rent reduction and unfolded systematically by stages. In many southern and central provinces it extended over two to three years. The slower pace of land revolution (although accelerated in some areas by the Korean War) reinforced the leadership consensus that socialization of the countryside was a distant prospect requiring prior industrialization. The postliberation leadership appeared unified in the view that while experiments with mutual aid linking individual landowners would proceed, the rich peasant economy based on private ownership would be preserved as a relatively long-term policy. Socialist transformation of the countryside would *follow* industrialization.

In *The German Ideology* Karl Marx observed that revolution is necessary "not only because the ruling class cannot be over-thrown in any other way, but also because the class over-throwing it can only in a revolution succeed in ridding itself of all the muck of ages and become fitted to found society anew." The intense personal and collective experience of land revo-lution produced the *fanshen* of millions of peasants. *Fanshen* literally means "turn the body." Here it suggests beginning a new life in the material sense that the destitute obtain land, tools, and grain. At the same time, transcending deeply rooted fears and tasting power for the first time, many began to transform their world view of passivity, fatalism, and depen-dence. The revolution gave birth to a new generation of peasant activists, many of whom became party members and leaders in reconstructing their villages. Poor peasants particularly ex-perienced the revolutionary truth that in their unity lay the strength to turn the heavens upside down and defeat the land-lords. Peasant women played vital roles and women won property rights and a measure of equality in family relations in conjunction with the land revolution.

Direct participation was an essential element of *fanshen.* For the army, party, or state to administratively redistribute the land would reinforce peasant passivity before authority. Direct participation led a mobilized peasantry to discover its own power and ability by seizing and redistributing the land. As one cadre put it, "land revolution is a whole series of political, economic, and cultural revolutions, with dividing up the land as the core, in order to destroy the old and build the new. Land revolution involves the peasants using revolutionary means to struggle and seize the land. It is definitely not a case of land-lords giving up the land as a favor." Work teams comprised of peasant activists, party cadres, students, and intellectuals dispatched to the villages were to stimulate and provide sup-port, guidance, and coordination. While supporting peasant activism they sought to prevent excessive violence and to focus the attack on the worst enemies during the long and complex struggle enacted within each village.

There could be no substitute, however, for direct peasant participation. In the revolutionary struggles a century earlier, Marx had told the European proletariat: "You have to undergo fifteen, twenty, fifty years of civil wars and popular struggles not only to change the relations but to change yourselves for political mastery." In the 1940s, when this process occurred in China, it centered not in the ranks of the proletariat but in the peasantry. Intense revolutionary praxis gave rise to revolutionary classes with new consciousness.

Fanshen gave birth to hopes and aspirations based on a new lease on life (land) and the glimmerings of the possibility of a society created by the peasants themselves, responsive to their needs, and ultimately capable of ensuring prosperity for all. For most of rural China, the Communist Party entered the villages in the land revolution and successfully forged bonds with the new peasant leadership. This was the critical step in integrating the villages with the party and with national goals in ways that would facilitate subsequent waves of revolutionary change throughout the countryside.

To assess the achievement of land revolution we must consider conditions in the countryside prior to and following it. Two conflicting schools of thought rooted in two political perspectives have dominated the debate over the nature of China's agrarian crisis since the 1930s. Moreover, the issues are directly relevant to the choices that confront many nations presently experiencing acute agrarian problems. One perspective, stressing the inherent *oppression* of the landlord-dominated order, compounded by the ravages of bandits, warlords, and imperialist armies and the toll exacted by usurers and tax collectors, saw revolution as the necessary first step in resolving the rural crisis en route to raising productivity. The other, viewing the rural economy as consisting of roughly equal smallholders, emphasized *technological* obstacles, including lack of mechanization, irrigation, and fertilizer, and the increasingly noneconomic size of farms as a result of population growth. It concluded that by the early twentieth century Chinese agriculture had become incapable of generating any substantial surplus that could fund development. The only solution, therefore, lay with the injection of capital and technology from the cities or from abroad to modernize agriculture and raise productivity while curbing population growth. In this view social revolution was at best irrelevant and at worst counterproductive.

Recent research by Victor Lippit and Carl Riskin has demolished the pillar of the technological argument that the Chinese rural economy was incapable of producing a substantial surplus. John Buck's exhaustive survey data of the 1930s—Buck was the leading Western exponent of the technological view— showed that 34 percent of cultivable land was rented to tenants at an average rent of 40 percent of the gross output and that in 1933 land rent accounted for a minimum of 10 percent of national income. Adding the surplus above wages paid to hired laborers and the interest on rural debt, the figure rises to 17 percent, and if rural taxes are included, a total of 19 percent of income was taken from the peasants.

Moreover, if we consider underutilized land and labor, in 1933 the potential surplus of the rural economy at prevailing levels of technology was approximately 25 percent of national income and this figure excludes the heavy exactions in the form of bandit and warlord stealing and protection rackets. In short, China's rural economy, despite a century of the ravages of war, payment of large-scale indemnities to the imperialist powers, paucity of investment, high population growth, and the depletion of the soil, produced a substantial surplus above consumption and was capable of producing more without further modern inputs.

The fact that the existing surplus was used largely for nonproductive purposes, principally for war and luxury consumption by a parasitic elite composed of Chinese and foreign landlords, warlords, bandits, and usurers, led to the conclusion that revolutionary change was the precondition to development. Land revolution in this densely populated agrarian nation would have to precede modernization. Land revolution could not itself break the grip of poverty, but without it there was little prospect of effectively attacking the problems of development.

The logic of land revolution thus rested on foundations of peasants striving to eliminate exploitation and poverty at the same time that it paved the way for economic development. Its overriding achievement lay in eliminating the landlord class, improving the economic and political position of the great majority of landless, poor, and some middle peasants—*fanshen* in material and spiritual terms—and generating new peasant leadership rooted in local communities, firmly committed to the Communist Party, and eager to work to build rural prosperity on foundations of basic equality in privately owned land. In national terms, 300 million peasants, nearly two-thirds of the rural population, won control of 700 million mou (117 million acres), 44 percent of all arable land, as well as draft animals, tools, and grain (see Table 2).

Table 2
Land Transfer in the Land Revolution

	Percent of households	Percentage of crop land owned		Average size of landholding (in mou)*	
		Before reform	After reform	Before reform	After reform
Landlords	2.6	28.7	2.1	116.1	12.0
Rich peasants	3.6	17.7	6.4	35.7	26.3
Middle peasants	35.8	30.3	44.8	15.8	18.5
Poor peasants & farm laborers	57.1	23.5	46.8	6.2	12.1

Sources: John Buck, *Land Utilization in China* (Nanking: University of Nanking, 1937), pp. 271, 368; and *T'ung-chi kung-tso* (Statistical Work) 10 (1957):31-32, cited in Peter Schran, *The Development of Chinese Agriculture 1950-1959* (Urbana: University of Illinois Press, 1969), pp. 21-22.

*1 mou is equal to 0.166 acres or 0.07 hectares.

Land revolution dramatically increased equality in the countryside by eliminating the power of the landlord class, weakening the rich peasants, eradicating the most extreme manifestations of rural poverty, substantially expanding the ranks of the middle peasantry, and enabling the poorest strata living at the brink of subsistence to increase landholdings and consumption. Given the paucity of land and wealth, land revolution could neither create full equality nor eliminate poverty. Despite the impetus of land revolution in elevating many to middle peasant status, in 1950 China had only one acre of arable land per person and in many densely populated southern regions barely one-third of an acre.

The land revolution created a nation of roughly equal small landowners. Hundreds of millions of peasants became landowners for the first time or expanded their holdings. This stimulated productive enthusiasm and raised expectations of impending prosperity. In responding to the basic peasant demand for land, however, the revolution reinforced the system of private land ownership. It left for the future not only the promise of socialism but the problems of land fragmentation, primitive technology, and the acute shortage of tools and draft animals in a premechanized rural economy.

From a developmental perspective, comparison of data for 1933 (a representative prewar year for which unusually detailed data is available) and 1952 (the concluding year of land revolution) reveals striking economic changes directly attributable to the outcome of the struggle for the land. In 1933 China's net investment, the critical indicator of potential development, amounted to just 1.8 percent of net domestic expenditure. Neither the government nor the private sector engaged in significant productive investment. By 1952 net investment had risen to 15.4 percent. The following year it reached the extraordinarily high level of 20.2 percent, which it sustained and even raised slightly during the first five-year plan. Land revolution played an essential role in freeing resources for productive purposes.

By 1952 not only had peasant food consumption improved considerably, but the state was able to obtain 5 billion yuan from the agrarian sector in the form of taxes and income on purchases of industrial goods, accounting for a full 45 percent of its 11.3 billion yuan net investment. Even at the height of the Korean War, 43 percent of the government budget was allocated to economic construction, with the countryside providing a substantial portion. In breaking the grip of landlord power and in contributing to the formation of a government committed to comprehensive development, land revolution facilitated the dramatic increase in investment which fueled rapid economic recovery and set the stage for subsequent economic growth. Land revolution was a *precondition* for significant primary accumulation to finance China's drive for development.

The land revolution liberated not only men and women, it also liberated, in Mao's phrase, "the broad world of nature." As we will observe below, the transformation of ownership relationships which began with land revolution and culminated in the formation of the communes was the precondition for revitalization of China's forests, turning back her expanding wasteland and deserts, taming uncontrolled rivers, and restoring the fertility of the depleted soil. Increasingly, agrarian communities would mobilize resources for the long-range task of improving the environment in the interests of the whole people and of future generations.

In the land revolution China opened an important new page in the history of modern revolution. Neither Marx nor Lenin had fully anticipated the explosive power and revolutionary potential of an aroused peasantry. That power had now been demonstrated twice, first in a people's war and subsequently in the struggle for the land. But in satisfying its most basic desire rooted in the deepest memories of peasant society—the desire for land—it remained to be seen whether the peasantry would stand as a bulwark of conservatism against socialist development.

IV. Socialist Transformation, the First Five-Year Plan and the Soviet Model, 1953-1957

If we see to it that the working class retains its leadership over the peasantry, we shall be able to develop our large-scale machine industry, to develop electrification. . . .

In this, and in this alone, lies our hope. Only when we have done this shall we, speaking figuratively, be able to change horses, to change from the peasant *muzhik* horse of poverty, from the horse of an economy designed for a ruined peasant country, to the horse which the proletariat is seeking and must seek—the horse of largescale machine industry, of electrification.

V. I. Lenin, 1923

An upsurge in the new, socialist mass movement is imminent throughout the countryside. But some of our comrades, tottering along like a woman with bound feet, are complaining all the time, "You're going too fast, much too fast." . . . The high tide of social transformation in the countryside, the high tide of cooperation, has already swept a number of places and will soon sweep the whole country.

Mao Tsetung, 1955

In March 1949 Mao observed that after two decades in the countryside the period "of the city leading the village has now begun. The center of gravity of the party's work has shifted from the village to the city."[14] With the approach of liberation, for the first time the party confronted the challenge of governing China's major cities and directing large-scale industry. The view that the center of gravity had shifted reflected a leadership consensus that national development and the formation of socialist institutions hinged on the acceleration of industrialization and the leading role of the cities.

Industry and the Cities

When Chinese Communist forces took control of the cities in the years 1947-1949 they encountered a staggering array of problems, ranging from the destruction of the small industrial base to massive unemployment, uncontrollable inflation, starvation, rampant gangsterism, prostitution, opium addiction and disease, endemic corruption, and a near total breakdown of administration and social services. The new government's rapid solution to these problems—with the exception of urban unemployment to which we will return below—stands in dramatic contrast to the failure of the Kuomintang during the decades of its administration.

The eradication of opium addiction, which had plagued China throughout the preceding century, illustrates successful application of the mass line in the urban context and one of the bases of popular support for the new government. At the outset the party mobilized the people to identify and arrest opium dealers and to locate addicts. In every major city family members rose at mass meetings to denounce opium dealers and describe the ravages of opium. Popular tribunals condemned to death a small number of the biggest dealers. Addicts, however, were treated not as criminals but as victims. They received rapid and effective medical treatment and education about the relationship between opium, imperialism, and gangster-ridden Chinese governments. But solution to the problem required eradicating the social roots of addiction, embedded in poverty, degradation, and joblessness. Addicts who had recently come from the countryside were sent home to obtain land and work, and wherever possible, the state provided urban jobs for other former addicts. In just two years a scrupulously honest government working with the people solved once and for all the problem of opium addiction as well as the prostitution and gangsterism that beset the cities. It also moved vigorously to throw off the foreign yoke, eliminating alien control of the treaty ports and other foreign enclaves of privilege, and expelling all foreign troops, missionaries, and adventurers and, eventually, foreign businessmen. These acts, among the most popular carried out by the new government, provided visible evidence that the Chinese people had stood up, as Mao proclaimed at the founding of the People's Republic. But they were only a beginning.

The new government inherited an industrial structure shaped in every way by the role of foreign power in China. The outstanding feature of China's industry was substantial foreign control of its leading sectors, variously estimated at from one-third to nearly half of total modern industry. Industry remained confined to the coastal regions, oriented toward export markets with few links to the domestic economy and centered preponderantly in light industry. The result was that in 1949 coastal areas with 10 percent of the land area produced 77 percent of factory output value. The core of an industrial economy—producer goods such as steel, electric power, and machine tools—amounted to a small fraction of industrial output. Consumer industry accounted for 92 percent of the total industrial output in China south of the Great Wall. Moreover, the War of Resistance and above all the subsequent civil war left China's cities a shambles, with much of their modern industry destroyed or dismantled.

Following liberation China could nevertheless build on the rudimentary foundations of an industrial complex begun in the colonial era. The most important assets were Manchuria, which Japan had designed as the heavy industrial heartland of its Asian empire, and Shanghai, the leading center of foreign and domestic light industry. Between 1931 and 1945 Japan invested $2.7 billion in Manchuria, expanded industrial output more than 5.5 times, and created a substantial iron and steel complex at Anshan. This provided the main base for the subsequent development of China's heavy industry.

Japan monopolized not only the output of the mines but also the technology, using Chinese almost exclusively as coolie labor. At Anshan, for example, in 1943 all 310 of the leading technical personnel were Japanese. Anshan was decimated by Japanese sabotage in 1945, again in the civil war (in 1948 alone the city changed hands seven times), but above all by Soviet plundering of an estimated $2 billion worth of industrial equipment, carried across the border during the brief occupation following Japan's surrender.

Reminiscent of the fate of the Soviet Union's working class in the civil war and invasion which followed the Bolshevik Revolution, by 1949, just 10,000 of the 120,000 industrial workers of Anshan remained, of whom 100 were skilled workers. Not until 1954 did Anshan surpass prewar production peaks, and then only as a result of concentrated Sino-Soviet technical cooperation in the area. Nevertheless, as we will observe, Manchuria in general and Anshan in particular provided foundations for the creation of a heavy industrial base and, despite subsequent industrial decentralization, it is the most important—though no longer the only—center of heavy industry today.

After World War II the Kuomintang took over large-scale Japanese investment. More than 2,000 industrial and mining enterprises and other major industries were placed under state control within a framework of bureaucratic capitalism which preserved significant elements of private profit. Those industries could be readily nationalized by the new government of the People's Republic. This enabled the state quickly and smoothly to secure control of leading sectors of the economy—accounting for one-third of the value of industrial output but 80 percent of fixed assets, including the lion's share of heavy industry—while allowing private capital to function in other sectors. By the end of 1949 the state sector employed 700,000 workers, nearly two-thirds in large enterprises with more than 1,000 skilled workers.

Moving rapidly yet with sensitivity to the complex and unfamiliar problems of urban and industrial areas, the Communists secured control of the lifelines of the modern sector of the economy, the leading banks, mines, railroads, steel mills, and virtually all Japanese and Kuomintang enterprises. By the end of 1950, for example, government banks held 98 percent of all deposits. The state permitted and in many cases encouraged private (including some foreign) enterprises to operate while restricting private capital to light industry, commerce, and handicrafts.

In contrast to the annihilation of the landlord class, the party attempted with a high degree of success to win over China's small but strategically placed capitalists, managers, and technicians and to secure their services for national development. Capitalist enterprises were guaranteed supplies, markets and fixed profits while the scope, products, and management of their operations were subject to progressively tightened controls. As early as June 1952, in an internal document, Mao signaled that a new stage had been reached in the party's relations with the national bourgeoisie, that is, those Chinese capitalists not subordinate to foreign capital: "With the overthrow of the landlord class and the bureaucrat-capitalist class, the contradiction between the working class and the national bourgeoisie has become the principal contradiction, therefore the national bourgeoisie should no longer be defined as an intermediate class." [15] There nevertheless remained a role for the national capitalists, and by 1953 the number of privately owned industrial firms had increased from 23,000 to 150,000, employing 2.2 million workers, the bulk of the Chinese proletariat.

Mao described the mixed economy of the new democracy as "a particular kind of capitalist economy, namely, a state-capitalist economy of a new type. It exists not chiefly to make profits for the capitalists but to meet the needs of the people and the state." Proceeding by stages, significant portions of capitalist industry passed into state hands. Beginning in 1953, as China proclaimed the transition from the new democracy to socialism, this took the form of creating joint state-private enterprises. By the end of 1954 more than 1,700 factories employing over .5 million workers became joint state-private enterprises enabling the state to capture control of raw material inputs, production and management decisions, and marketing operations. Chinese capitalists would continue to reap profit without power. In Mao's words, the basic policy toward the urban bourgeoisie was one of "utilization, restriction, and transformation."

Two years later, in 1956, China completed well ahead of schedule the socialist transition and reorganization of capitalist industry as well as commerce and handicrafts (see Table 3). In striking contrast to the mass mobilization and expropriation of landlord property, the state compensated capitalists by paying 5 percent interest on their shares for a full decade from 1956 to 1966. Many former capitalists subsequently served as managers or advisers. The result was a smooth transition in which factories not only continued to produce but expanded through the years of transfer from capitalist to socialist ownership, and a portion of the national bourgeoisie put its services at the disposal of socialist industry even as it entered its death throes as a class.

What role did the proletariat play in the changes which led

Table 3
Socialist Transformation of Industry
Percentage Distribution of Gross Output of Industry
(excluding handicrafts)

	I Socialist industry	State capitalist industry	II Composition of state capitalist industry		III Capitalist industry (produced and mar- keted independently)
			Joint state- private enterprise	Privately owned en- terprises executing state orders	
1949	34.7	9.5	2.0	7.5	55.8
1950	45.3	17.8	2.9	14.9	36.7
1951	45.9	25.4	4.0	21.4	28.7
1952	56.0	26.9	5.0	21.9	17.1
1953	57.5	28.5	5.7	22.8	14.0
1954	62.8	31.9	12.3	19.6	5.3
1955	67.7	29.3	16.1	13.2	3.0
1956*	67.5	32.5	32.5	—	—

Source: State Statistical Bureau, *Ten Great Years* (Peking: Foreign Languages Press, 1960), p. 38.

*In 1956, capitalist enterprises became joint state-private enterprises by entire trades, that is, they came under direct state management. Subsequently, the only significant distinction between state-capitalist and socialist industry was that the state continued to pay capitalists fixed interest on their holdings for the next decade.

Chinese industry from capitalism to the new democracy toward socialism? In its initial encounters with the cities in Manchuria in 1947, as in the two preceding decades, the Communists sharply differentiated the historical roles of the peasantry and proletariat. In 1947, at the height of rural class struggle, the party leadership ruled out revolution from below in urban and rural industry and commerce. Although Mao called for enlargement of worker participation in running the factories, in his authoritative December pronouncement "On the Current Situation and Our Tasks," he emphasized stabilizing production and minimizing disruption in taking control of the cities and industry. The Communist Party and army, not the working class, seized power in the factories and cities at the time of liberation.

As the Communists entered the cities they encountered the expectations—but also the uncertainty—of the proletariat, whose revolutionary role in recent decades was marginal at best. Pressure arose for substantial wage increases and concrete steps toward making the workers the masters of the factories and the cities. In striking contrast with its Kuomintang and warlord predecessors, the new government rapidly provided relief, training, and jobs for many of the 4 million urban unemployed and in less than a year, using price and currency levers, controlled the rampant inflation which had wrecked economy and people in the preceding decade.

Between 1948 and 1950, however, the party criticized as "guerrillaism" and "agrarian socialism" worker and cadre attempts to seize power from the capitalists and independently run the factories. Where workers actually seized power bankruptcy frequently occurred, leading to production decline and a rise in unemployment. Workers were to concentrate on raising productivity and strengthening labor discipline. The party also rejected demands for immediate pay hikes, insisting that wages be directly tied to overall productivity. At this time progressive wage systems, including piece work, rewarded outstanding workers with higher incomes in an effort to stimulate productivity. In the years 1947–1956 the class conflict pitting proletariat against bourgeoisie was carefully channeled to ensure continuity in industrial production while the state administratively took direct control of leading sectors of industry and restricted the independence of remaining capitalist enterprise. The proletariat mobilized on occasion, as in the three-anti and five-anti movements of 1951 and 1953, to criticize and curb capitalist and corrupt bureaucratic practices; yet it was the state which employed administrative measures to effect the change from capitalist to socialist ownership of industry. The party was only just creating with the proletariat those deep organic ties which it had forged with the peasantry in the course of people's war and land revolution. For this and other reasons, the proletariat, which by 1953 still accounted for less than 10 percent of party membership, had yet to become a significant factor in the revolutionary changes which were sweeping Chinese society.

In 1918, shortly after the Bolshevik Revolution, Lenin observed that "Until workers' control has become a fact . . . it will be impossible to pass . . . to the second step toward socialism, i.e. to pass on to workers' regulation of production."[16] That second step, whose difficulty is borne out by six decades of Soviet experience, would likewise provide a major challenge to the Chinese Revolution.

In China, from the earliest entry of the Communists into the cities in 1947, we may observe two approaches to industrial management. One of these, the Shanghai system of committee decision-making, developed in both state and capitalist factories in areas where there was effective worker organization prior to liberation. Workers and party members with administrative or technical experience, along with the manager, participated in a factory management committee. Building on the wartime tradition of collective responsibility and mass participation, the Shanghai system fostered experiments in formation of worker and staff congresses with elected representatives and prompted active union work in the factories.

The alternative approach, modeled directly on "advanced Soviet practice," was the system of "one-man management," which vested ultimate authority and responsibility for the work of the factory in its manager. A 1953 article in the newspaper *Ta Kung Pao* invoked the authority of Lenin to explain the necessity for implementing one-man management in industry:

> Unless there is one unified command to direct all operations, there is no way of getting economic efficiency. Lenin once said: "Any large-scale industry—which is the material source and foundation of production in socialism —unconditionally must have a rigorous unified will to direct the collective work of hundreds of thousands, and even millions of men. But how can the rigorous unity of will be assured? Only by the wills of the thousands and millions submitting to the will of a single individual."[17]

While the author hastened to add the caveat that managers must closely rely on the masses, the essence of one-man management lay in the vast powers entrusted at each level of the chain of command to a single individual, particularly to the factory manager. "One-man management" symbolized the triumph of technical over political factors and the authority of the managers over the party and the workers.

"One-man management" was widely implemented first in Manchuria, where Soviet economic influence permeated earliest and was concentrated throughout the first five-year plan. In 1953, with the advent of the first five-year plan, it was officially designated the model of industrial management. The system rested on three principles: (1) clearly defined hierarchical division of labor distinguishing managerial, technical, and worker roles with authority vested in the former; (2) a rigid chain of command penetrating from powerful central ministries to the factory, with basic targets and decisions handed down from above and detailed regulations defining all aspects of factory work; and (3) heavy reliance on material incentives, particularly in the form of piece-work rates (for most workers) and bonuses (particularly for managers).

By the early 1950s most of the democratic and participatory features of the Shanghai system had yielded to the powerful authority of the factory manager and the planning system. While not implemented in every factory, "one-man management" was ascendant. Worker participation as a check on bureaucratic and elitist tendencies and as the prerequisite for worker control, failed to develop extensively in contrast with the role of peasant activism at each stage in the decade-long rural transformation. In 1955 and 1956 the state administratively carried out large-scale nationalization of industry and commerce in the absence of significant class struggle in the factories. These trends, running directly counter to the party's mass line heritage and to the socialist vision of worker control, but consistent with the drive to be "modern and Soviet," would be reinforced by the priorities of the first five-year plan.

The First Five-Year Plan, 1953–1957

In the fall of 1953 with the completion of the land revolution, basic recovery from the ravages of foreign invasion, armistice in the Korean War, and conclusion of the Sino-Soviet agreement providing Soviet industrial aid and credits, China announced the general line for the transition to socialism centered on the socialist transformation of industry and agriculture and the first five-year plan for national development. The leading role of the state would make possible accelerated industrialization, above all the formation of heavy industry to overcome China's economic backwardness. The essence of the plan and of China's socialist development strategy in the early 1950s may be summarized as follows:

(1) Primacy is given to capital-intensive socialist heavy industry, particularly large-scale, integrated complexes centered in large industrial inland cities.

(2) The private agrarian sector supplies food, resources, and much of the capital required for industrialization, exports, and growing cities.

(3) A high-growth command economy centralizes power and resources in national ministries and within enterprises in the factory manager. Central planning, strict hierarchy, and elaborate regulations guide the economy.

(4) The Soviet Union provides foreign capital, machinery, and technical assistance.

Drawn up with the close collaboration of Soviet planners, predicated on substantial Soviet financial and technical aid, the plan was modeled on the early Soviet five-year plans to achieve rapid industrialization. Yet the difficulty of meeting its major targets of investment and industrial growth was vastly greater in a China which began with much lower per capita agricultural and industrial production levels, rates of investment, and margins of subsistence, and much higher population density and growth rates.

In the early 1950s the Chinese leadership, which had carved out an independent road in national liberation war and in land revolution, consciously patterned its strategy of socialist development on Soviet experience. As a *People's Daily* editorial put it shortly before embarking on the plan, "the Soviet path to industrialization is the very road that China should and must follow." The reasons for this decision were complex. Persistent efforts, beginning in 1944 by Mao, Chou En-lai, and other party leaders to preserve China's options by opening economic and political channels to the United States and other capitalist countries, had failed. China in 1949 was isolated. United States policy, crystallizing in the Korean War and sustained in two decades of blockade, thus ensured "the loss of China" in the sense that it left the Chinese leadership with few options other than, in Mao's words, to "lean to the side of the Soviet Union." While China rapidly eliminated the most humiliating internal symbols and sinews of foreign domination—gunboats, extraterritoriality, missionaries, and alien control of leading industries and schools—China lived in a hostile world system defined in large part by the capitalist nations under United States leadership.

There were also important positive reasons for becoming a member of the Soviet-led socialist bloc. The Soviet Union was not only the first socialist state, but it had succeeded in transforming a backward agrarian nation into a leading industrial power in just one generation. Soviet aid promised to greatly facilitate China's industrialization, indeed, at the time it was difficult to conceive of rapid progress toward heavy industry without such aid. While the Chinese Communists had extensive experience to draw on in the countryside, they were novices in administering the cities and in designing and administrating large-scale industry. Finally, the Sino-Soviet alliance provided the best available guarantee against foreign invasion in a hostile world.

The central assumption of the first five-year plan was that mobilization of all available financial and technical resources for the construction of heavy industry would provide the most rapid route to all-round development and create the preconditions for socialist transformation. The corollary: agriculture would both finance industrialization and continue to develop in the absence of inputs of capital, technology, or consumer goods prior to the formation of heavy, and then light industry. Or, failing that, it was hoped that, as in the Soviet Union, industry could continue its rapid growth despite agricultural stagnation.

In practice, China succeeded by dint of great effort in channeling over 20 percent of total output to investment. Approximately 40 percent of this investment capital came from agriculture and the lion's share of it was allocated to heavy industry. Of the ambitious 76 billion yuan projected for the state's capital construction, 77 percent was slated for industry and transport while agriculture, water conservancy, and forestry

would receive just 8 percent. Eighty-eight percent of investment in industry was allocated to heavy industry. The imbalance in the Chinese plan, focusing on heavy industry and
slighting agriculture, was even more extreme than in the Soviet
first and second plans. It should be noted, however, that the
planners assumed that landowning peasants would continue
private agricultural investment while the state concentrated
scarce resources on industry.

The core of the plan was 156 projects to be built with Soviet
aid, blueprints, and the contributions of 14,000 Soviet technical
personnel sent to China. Moreover, the Soviet Union trained
more than 6,000 Chinese scientists and technicians at the university level and 7,000 workers received on-the-job training in
Soviet factories. As in the early Soviet plans, the highest
priority was given to the iron and steel industries, including to
the furnaces, the coal and iron ore, iron and steel processing,
rail transport, and specialists which this required. As the world
leader in steel technology in the mid-1950s, the Soviets could
provide invaluable assistance. Forty-eight Soviet projects, fully
one-third of the total, were constructed in the Anshan steel
complex alone, exclusive of railroads and mines to serve it.
Thirty-five thousand Chinese technicians, engineers, and skilled
workers were transferred to Anshan from other areas, and in
1951 a Soviet-supported five-year program began to train 5,000
technical personnel and 30,000 skilled steel workers. As a
result, by 1957 China possessed some of the world's most
advanced steel technology and Anshan produced 60 to 70
percent of the nation's iron and steel—the backbone of the
industrialization drive. The Soviet Union also designed,
financed, and built two new integrated iron and steel complexes
at Wuhan in Central China and Pao-t'ou in Inner Mongolia. The
first five-year plan, in addition, emphasized the development of
machine building, metal working, power, fuel, nonferrous
metals, and chemicals as the core of a heavy industrial structure
constructed with Soviet aid.

Soviet aid made immense contributions to China's rapid
industrialization. A 1975 U.S. government study correctly concluded that China benefited from

> undoubtedly the most comprehensive technology transfer
> in modern industrial history. . . . The Soviet contribution

encompassed much more than production technology. It ran the gamut from scientific and technical education to project design, and from production engineering to creating a modern industrial organization, complete with planning, budgeting, and management systems.[18]

The limits of aid, provided at a time when the Soviet Union was itself recovering from a devastating war, should nevertheless be noted. The $430 million provided in the years 1950–1956 took the form of short-term, low-interest loans. Mao later compared economic relations with Stalin with getting "a piece of meat from the mouth of a tiger." Total aid was 3.1 percent of state investment during the first five-year plan. By contrast, countries like India and Indonesia received foreign aid in the postwar years in the range of one-third to one-fourth of their state investment budgets. China, moreover, not only fought in the Korean War but provided $2.2 billion in Soviet weapons free to its Korean ally, repaying this sum to the Soviet Union for its military "aid" over the next decade. And between 1953 and 1957 China actually registered a net outflow of economic aid. It was the Chinese people who provided the basic financing for industrialization.

At first glance the countryside appears peripheral to the plan's conception. But its success rested unequivocally on the rapid expansion of the marketable agricultural surplus to feed the growing cities, provide raw materials and markets for industry, sustain an investment rate of 20 percent of national income, generate sufficient exports to meet China's heavy loan payments to the Soviet Union, and provide additional foreign exchange. While the five-year output of producer goods was slated to grow by 126 percent, and agriculture by only 23 percent, we will observe that the plan's 1955 target of a 4.3 percent annual growth figure for agriculture and comparable expansion of marketable agricultural commodities created the critical bottleneck (1953 and 1954 projections were higher—5.3 and 4.6 percent per year respectively). It is not an exaggeration to say that the countryside, starved of resources by the planners, held the key to the success of the plan.

Chinese planners recognized that the question of industrialization was ultimately inseparable from the institutional transformation of agriculture. Teng Tzu-hui, head of the Rural Work

Department, in 1953 expressed the leadership consensus that China must "wait until state industrial development is able to supply agriculture with the machinery it needs and at that time Soviet-type collective farms, using machines, can gradually grow in China and greatly spread. That is, we can complete the socialist reform of agriculture." But popular pressures for institutional change had begun to build in the Chinese countryside. As early as the late 1940s, beginning with the formation of mutual aid teams, peasants had begun to pool land and labor on a small scale. From 1951 elementary agricultural producers' cooperatives gradually extended the scope of cooperation within the framework of private ownership of land. A process had begun of phased advance in rural cooperation based on voluntary participation and mutual benefit. Where mutual aid teams typically involved five to ten families in seasonal cooperation, elementary cooperatives pooled the efforts of an average of twenty-seven families (in 1955), draft animals and labor for more efficient resource utilization, and capital accumulation on a year-round basis. Cooperative members divided income on the dual bases of input of land and other means of production, and labor contribution. Through cooperation peasants sought to overcome the shortage of capital, draft animals and tools, and land fragmentation. Cooperation reduced the individual risk of natural disaster and facilitated small-scale capital construction which improved yields.

In 1954 the rural class struggle centered on the stepped-up campaign to form cooperatives. While poor peasants short of land and other means of production tended to favor cooperatives, rich peasants, fearing expropriation, often preferred to go it alone, in some cases relying on hired labor or engaging in speculation and usury. In other instances rich peasants dominated the cooperatives, ensuring high return on property and low remuneration for labor to the detriment of poorer members. It was also frequently the case, however, that cadres, eager to stimulate rural cooperation, violated principles of voluntary participation and mutual interest by pressuring prosperous peasants to join cooperatives and underassessing their land and draft animals or turning private fishponds and orchards into cooperative property without compensation. Such practices could gravely undermine productive efforts and cooperative morale.

Between 1954 and 1956 several factors restricted production and local investment in the countryside. First, uncertainty about future prospects led many, particularly rich peasants, to cut back on agricultural investment. One critical indicator of this uncertainty was the decline in the number of pigs in 1955 and 1956 as many peasants rushed to sell or slaughter to preclude the possibility of confiscation by the cooperatives. The number of pigs, which had risen from 57 million to 102 million between 1949 and 1954, dropped to 88 million in 1955, reaching a low point of 84 million in 1956 before resuming its upward curve in 1957. Second, in 1954, despite extensive floods, the state increased tax levies and compulsory grain sales, the latter by 7 billion catties over 1953. The result was severe hardship and discontent in many areas, forcing party and state leaders to publicly criticize their error and cut procurement by 7 billion catties in 1955, despite a grain shortage in the cities. Finally, as the state purchased larger quantities of cotton and other commercial crops for efficient processing and export by state-run factories, rural handicrafts suffered a blow.

We can observe two divergent patterns with respect to rural handicraft and industry during the first five-year plan. Industries which did not conflict with the state's centralizing and marketing plans, such as local cement, indigenous coal and iron, toolmaking, and so on, grew steadily, though without significant state support, to meet the growing demands of the rural sector and to provide supplemental income. But the state, by centralization and industrialization, virtually eliminated such important handicrafts and sources of supplemental income as cotton spinning and weaving and food processing. What imperialism had accomplished imperfectly in a matter of decades in the early twentieth century, the Chinese state achieved with brutal efficiency in the years 1954–1956. The number of handicraft workers, including cooperative members, declined from 8.9 million in 1954 to 6.5 million in 1956 before a policy reversal initiated by Mao led to an increase in the total number of handicraft workers and eventually to rural industrialization. The Soviet comparison is again illuminating. Soviet handicrafts suffered a far more devastating and permanent blow during the first plan. The number of workers fell by two-thirds, from 2.4 million in 1927 to 861,000 in 1933.

The reduction of Chinese handicraft employment dealt the peasantry a double blow. Not only did many peasant and family members depend on handicrafts for a significant part of their income, but resource centralization reduced the supply of goods in the countryside. As in many other respects, emphasis on urban industry and exports placed intense pressures on the rural sector.

One notable effect of these policies was the rush of peasants to the cities in search of jobs, higher incomes, and the promise of urban life so prominently featured during the first plan period. Despite government restrictions, the urban population swelled from 57 million in 1949 to 89 million in 1957. Rural migrants accounted for two-thirds of the increase, more than 20 million people. The capital-intensive strategy of the first five-year plan, however, produced only one million new non-agricultural jobs a year, while agricultural employment increased only slightly in the early years of the plan (see Table 9). At this time the total labor force grew at a rate of 8 million per year. Official estimates placed urban unemployment at 3 million in 1952 prior to the plan, but by 1957 unemployment was approaching crisis proportions. And it was compounded by the increasing difficulty of obtaining sufficient marketable grain to feed the cities. The problem of the flight to the cities and massive urban unemployment is one that has plagued every developing country; here we note that in China the first five-year plan priorities exacerbated the problem.

In the late 1920s, the Soviet strategy of industrial centralization at the expense of the countryside produced rapid industrialization, while agriculture embarked on a cycle of stagnation which it has never fully broken. Comparable, but much less severe, state procurement policies in China during the early 1950s strained but did not produce the collapse of agriculture. There was nevertheless cause for grave concern, particularly since the challenge confronting China was far greater. Given its relatively favorable position in resource endowment, technology, land to population ratio, and per capita income, stagnating agriculture in the Soviet Union did not preclude milking the countryside of a substantial surplus to finance rapid industrial expansion. China, operating much closer to the margin of subsistence, had to simultaneously increase agricultural productiv-

ity and rates of investment if rapid industrialization was not to
be bought at the price of mass starvation.

By the spring of 1955, lagging agricultural productivity, and
particularly, marketed grain, cotton, and commercial crops,
clearly threatened attainment of the ambitious targets of the
plan. As shown in Table 4, grain had increased by less than
one-third of plan projections, while cotton, the basis for the
textile industry, China's leading light industry and a major
source of foreign exchange, *fell* by nearly 10 percent in 1953
and again in 1954.

Table 4
Targets and Production of Grain and Cotton, 1952–1955

	1952 output	Planned rise for 1953 (%)	1953 output	1953 change over 1952 (%)	Planned rise for 1954 (%)	1954 output	1954 change over 1953 (%)	Planned rise for 1955 (%)
Grain	3,275	9	3,359	+2.5	9.4	3,390	+0.9	6.0
Cotton	2,584	16	2,352	–9.1	17.8	2,130	–9.4	21.0

Source: Kenneth Walker, "Collectivisation in Retrospect," *The China
Quarterly* (April–June 1966):23. Compare slightly different official grain
statistics given in the State Planning Commission's *Ten Great Years*, which
show a slightly lower increase in grain output for the years 1952–1954.

Industrial growth could not be sustained if urban population
could not be fed and clothed and if agriculture failed to produce the export commodities required to obtain foreign exchange. The central issue debated by the party leadership at
that time was whether to halt temporarily the advance of rural
cooperation and stress the productive contributions of the rich
peasants, or to encourage the poorer strata of the peasantry
who continued to press for higher levels of cooperation. Fearing
possible disruption of production in the event of rapid cooperativization, and mindful of the disastrous human and economic
consequences of forced collectivization in the Soviet Union, the
Central Committee called a halt to cooperative formation and in
the spring of 1955 even ordered the disbandment of 20,000 of

the nation's 670,000 cooperatives on the ground that their economic foundations were weak.

Socialist Upsurge in the Countryside

Mao's dramatic speech on agricultural cooperation of July 31, 1955, the day after the publication of the first five-year plan, sent shock waves through the party leadership. Reverberations were soon felt throughout the society. Bypassing the Central Committee to take his message directly to a specially convened meeting of provincial and regional party secretaries, Mao initiated the process of charting an independent Chinese road to socialism. In his first major public statement since liberation, Mao proclaimed that "an upsurge in the socialist mass movement is imminent throughout the countryside" and chided those comrades who "are tottering along like a woman with bound feet and constantly complaining 'You're going too fast.'" In language reminiscent of the 1927 "Report on the Peasant Movement in Hunan," in which Mao made his initial call for a peasant-based strategy, he insisted that "we must guide the movement boldly and must not always 'fear the dragons ahead and the tigers behind.'"[19] Once again, as in 1927, Mao held that the peasantry was showing the way forward to the party. In the countryside the critical agent of change would not be the slowly maturing productive forces or future support from urban industry as envisaged in the first five-year plan, but a mobilized peasantry with its poorest strata in the lead.

Mao repeatedly invoked the authority of the Soviet Union and reiterated certain premises of the first five-year plan, but he did so to justify drawing on China's heritage of peasant mobilization to accelerate cooperative formation. He pointed out that although heavy industry "produces tractors, farm machinery, chemical fertilizers, modern means of transport, oil, electric power, etc., for agricultural use . . . all these things can only be used or used extensively, on the basis of large-scale cooperative agriculture." Therefore, "In agriculture, with conditions as they are in our country, cooperation must precede the use of big machinery (in capitalist countries agriculture develops in a capitalist way)."[20] For Mao, the success of pacesetting units in advancing to cooperatives demonstrated the possibility that the entire countryside could follow suit with proper leadership.

If Chinese agriculture were to develop, if it were to develop along *socialist* lines, and if it were to develop in support of industrialization, immediate accelerated progress toward rural cooperation was imperative. Advanced elements of the peasantry had once again shown the way, but successful implementation required the active leadership of the party to insure not only the formation of cooperatives but to help iron out the myriad problems they encountered and ensure their economic viability.

In the summer of 1955, having re-examined the premises of China's socialist transition, Mao analyzed four contradictions inherent in the first five-year plan.

1. *The contradiction between the low production of marketable grain and raw materials and the state's high and growing demand.* The plan projected an essentially one-way flow of resources out of the countryside to urban heavy industry, downgraded production of consumer goods which could be sold in the countryside, and restricted rural handicrafts through compulsory sales of raw materials to the state for centralized processing, all of which retarded agricultural production, above all, the production of marketable commodities.

In 1955 the first large Soviet loans fell due, and during the next decade China would repay a total of $2 billion until the loans were cleared. Higher forms of cooperation, Mao held, would both contribute to increased productivity and facilitate state access to marketable crops and tax revenues. Failure to complete the transformation to cooperatives and large-scale mechanized farming within three five-year plans would result in a shortage of marketable grain and industrial raw materials and could jeopardize hopes for industrialization.

2. *The contradiction between projected production of tractors, chemical fertilizer, and electric power by heavy industry and the small scale of agricultural production.* Without cooperation and economies of scale, peasants, with the exception of a small number of rich peasants, could neither afford to purchase nor effectively employ the means of mechanization. Therefore, the development of socialist agriculture must occur in step with socialist industry. The alternatives were rural stagnation or

further class polarization, with the rich growing richer and the poor lagging behind.

3. *The contradiction between the need for large amounts of capital for industrialization and agricultural mechanization and the fact that agriculture is itself the source of a major part of these funds.* If the state drained the countryside of resources, industrialization too would be left short of capital. Draining the pond to catch the fish would not suffice. This perception focused attention on light industry and pointed toward reconsidering the overwhelming priority placed on heavy industry. Precision on this point is essential. Mao rejected neither the primacy of heavy industry nor the necessity to import equipment, using deficit financing with Soviet loans. At issue were questions of degree. Light industry, in providing goods for peasant consumption, Mao reasoned, would rapidly stimulate the production of marketable commodities. With few consumer goods available in the countryside, what incentive did peasants have to increase marketable output? Agriculture would provide both the indispensable source of raw materials for light industry and a market to stimulate its growth. With profit margins set high and given the rapid return on investment, light industry provided a potential source of capital even as it raised the quality of life in town and country. But in the absence of expanded rural purchasing power via agricultural cooperation and development, light industry's expansion would be restricted.

An important related issue not specifically addressed by Mao until the following year is the question of scissors pricing, that is, the low and declining price of agricultural goods relative to industrial goods. Throughout a century of imperialist inroads, agricultural prices had declined drastically vis-à-vis foreign goods, such as textile imports and machinery. Between 1949 and 1952 China narrowed the gap between agricultural and industrial prices by raising the relative price of agricultural commodities 20 percent over those of industrial goods. However, despite these promising beginnings, during the first plan, with consumer goods priced high, the gap was not significantly narrowed. At this time the state relied on three methods for extracting the agricultural surplus: taxation, compulsory sales, and scissors pricing.

4. *The contradiction between the desire to build socialism and the continued polarization between rich and poor in the countryside.* "The spontaneous forces of capitalism have been steadily growing in the countryside in recent years," Mao observed, "with new rich peasants springing up everywhere and many well-to-do middle peasants striving to become rich peasants. On the other hand, many poor peasants are still living in poverty for lack of sufficient means of production, with some in debt and others selling or renting out their land."[21] The legacy of incomplete equalization of land, draft animals, and tools in the land revolution, far from being overcome in the following years, had increased. A number of village surveys in North China liberated areas showed that within three years of the completion of land redistribution, 20 to 25 percent of peasant households, lacking draft animals and tools, were forced to sell portions of their land, and many others had fallen into debt. A 1954 national survey found significant inequality in ownership of the means of production between poor peasants and rich. The rich enjoyed advantages of three or four to one.

Table 5
Ownership of Means of Production per Household

	Poor peasants	Rich peasants
Land (mou)	11.7	34.6
Draft animals	0.5	2.0
Ploughs	0.3	1.0
Water wheels	0.1	0.3

Source: Tung Ta-lin, *Agricultural Cooperation in China* (Peking: Foreign Languages Press, 1959), pp. 30, 38.

There is ample evidence that the more prosperous continued to increase their advantage over poorer families even after the formation of elementary cooperatives. Observing the growing class polarization in the countryside and the income and opportunity gap between city and countryside, Mao concluded that continuation of the trends of the first plan jeopardized the worker-peasant alliance, the foundation of China's advance to socialism. If the gap continued to widen, rural collectivization might require a second and more violent land revolution rather than smooth, step-by-step transition based on principles of voluntary participation and mutual benefit.

The poorer strata of the peasantry whose poverty rested on the inability to purchase draft animals, tools and equipment, stood to gain most from cooperation. For 60 to 70 percent of the rural population by Mao's reckoning, "socialism is the only way out. . . . The only way for the majority of the peasants to shake off poverty, improve their livelihood and fight natural calamities is to unite and go forward along the high road of socialism." [22] Rather than wait passively for sufficient maturation of the productive forces to provide the peasants with tractors and other modern inputs, cooperatives would accelerate development by mobilizing surplus labor and promoting capital construction. "We are now carrying out a revolution not only in the social system, the change from private to public ownership, but also in technology, the change from handicraft to large-scale modern machine production, and the two revolutions are interconnected." [23] The dual imperatives of social revolution and economic advance converge in Mao's analysis.

Mao's bombshell unified the party and the peasantry. The result was acceleration of the upsurge in cooperative formation which was already beginning in advanced areas at the grassroots level. The chain reaction detonated in the fall of 1955 and climaxing in the spring of 1956 overran the bounds of all previous projections, including Mao's, and led eventually to scrapping the basic framework of the first five-year plan. In the year following his speech, the party and the peasantry closed ranks and China basically completed the socialization of industry and agriculture as well as of handicrafts and commerce a full decade ahead of schedule. In startling contrast to Soviet collectivization, the process of transition was accomplished in the virtual absence of violence and with continued, modest production increases.

The socialist upsurge centered on the formation of rural cooperatives illustrates the mass line at work. The initial phases of the popular upsurge in advanced units directly challenged the timetable and strategic priorities of the national plan. Activity at the grassroots level led first Mao and subsequently a majority of the party leadership to overturn the premise of the first plan that mechanization must precede collectivization. Once the party, from the highest levels to the village, swung behind the new program, the movement could expand from pacesetting units to the entire countryside and, on the basis of synthesis of broad experience, could correct errors and improve the new institutions.

The initiation of advanced cooperatives (collectives) which expanded rapidly in 1956 inaugurated a new stage in the transformation of the Chinese countryside. By appropriating all agricultural land as cooperative property without compensation, they fulfilled the egalitarian promise implicit in the land revolution and essentially abolished the relationship between private ownership of land and income. In one stroke advanced cooperatives eliminated the principal remaining source of intravillage inequity, ending the period of rich peasant economy. Henceforth, labor would provide the single yardstick for income. Or nearly so: draft animals and tools still remained private property. They could be purchased, theoretically at market prices, but during the upsurge, they frequently passed to the cooperatives at a fraction of their value. The cooperatives also allocated private plots of land to individual households.

Advanced cooperatives facilitated scientific land management, making possible economies of scale and overcoming the parochialism and inefficiency associated with tiny scattered individual plots of land. With the 1956 expansion of the average cooperative size to 344 families (reduced in 1957 to 164 and frequently coinciding with natural villages), the peasants themselves initiated more ambitious irrigation and reforestation projects.

The cooperatives' appropriation of the land for common use eliminated rental payments to individual owners. In 1955, elementary cooperatives paid 22 percent of agricultural produce in rent, with a disproportionate share going to rich and prosperous middle peasants. The advanced cooperatives now controlled the entire product and their members could dispose of it as they saw fit. This opened the way to significant increases in cooperative accumulation and purchase of intermediate technology, particularly improved ploughs and tools. Cooperative accumulation increased dramatically in the critical year of the transition to advanced cooperatives, rising from 300 million yuan to 2.8 billion yuan or two to three times per cooperative member between 1955 and 1956 as the membership also grew. The formation of advanced cooperatives made possible income distribution exclusively on the socialist principle "to each according to one's work."

In the transition from elementary to advanced cooperatives progress occurred unevenly by fits and starts and with rapid bursts, repeatedly rendering obsolete official guidelines concerning the speed and nature of collectivization. Such profound changes as those which swept the countryside during collectivization invariably produced a wide range of problems, the most serious of which in this case was "commandism." In their zeal to advance to higher forms of cooperation and to curb the prerogatives of individual rich peasants, cadres sometimes attempted to move too quickly or resorted to force. Under the best of circumstances new cooperatives would experience extreme difficulties in organizing production on a scale more than ten times that of previous cooperatives. Some communities, caught up in the enthusiasm of the cooperative movement, initiated a wide variety of new activities ranging from construction of irrigation works to small factories for part-time schools, only to find their central task of agricultural production jeopardized by a shortage of labor. Moreover, this same enthusiasm affected the party leadership, including Mao, who promoted certain technical innovations prematurely. The most notable failures were the double-wheel, double-blade plough and new corn and rice seed varieties widely introduced without adequate testing. For all this, the net results of rapid cooperation were impressive. The process of transition was peacefully effected by the peasants and the vast majority of cooperatives moved toward consolidation and higher levels of investment, production, and income.

Part of the credit in sustaining the transition undoubtedly belongs to the state's careful preparatory work in preceding years. Although events moved with a rush in 1955–1956, the state had previously closed most channels for independent rich peasant activity such as free trade and speculation. The Unified Purchase and Supply Order of November 1953, which required the sale of all surplus grain to the state at fixed prices, essentially ended speculation and the free market in the single most important commodity. Once leadership consensus was achieved on the upsurge in the countryside, the state smoothed the path for revolutionary change with infusions of loan capital. In 1956 agricultural loans from the People's Bank more than tripled, to 3.4 billion yuan. Both peasants and cadres successfully applied lessons of earlier mobilization and the experience of a decade of mutual aid and elementary cooperative forms to new tasks. Above all, the smoothness of the transition can be attributed in large measure to the fact that cooperation rested on a foundation of perceived economic well-being of the majority of the peasants and enjoyed the firm support of the party and the state. While mobilization took place to the accompaniment of drums and gongs, the fact is that at each stage rising personal income for peasants and the prospect of future gains smoothed the path of cooperative formation.

Whereas the Soviet Union's forced collectivization and procurement policies drove a deep wedge between the peasantry and the state, the Chinese approach reinforced the peasant-party and worker-peasant alliances and paved the way for the continued advance of socialism in the countryside. That achievement rested on the ability of successively higher levels of cooperation to produce higher incomes for the great majority and particularly for the poor and lower middle peasants.

In the socialist upsurge of 1955-1956 advanced forms of cooperation replaced the predominantly individual cultivation that had prevailed in the countryside for thousands of years. The link between ownership of land and personal wealth was severed. The mobilized poor and middle peasants, striving for equality and cooperation, frequently telescoped stages of cooperation and in some instances coercion (though rarely physical violence) occurred. In a single year 88 percent of the peasants joined *advanced* cooperatives. In South and Central China, where land revolution had only recently been concluded, hundreds of millions of peasants made the direct transition from individual farming or mutual aid to advanced cooperatives in a matter of weeks or months. A root principle of the first five-year plan with respect to agriculture was overturned. Full-scale collectivization thus *preceded* mechanization in China and created the basis for effective use of modern technology in agriculture. Under peasant initiative, but with the party playing an important leadership and coordinating role, individual ownership of land and other means of production yielded to socialist ownership and planning through the medium of advanced collectives.

In 1956 city and countryside, industry and agriculture, handicrafts and commerce, completed the basic transition from private (capitalist) ownership of the means of production to socialist ownership. Socialist ownership took two basic forms: ownership by the whole people (through the state) and ownership by a collective. The state owned and operated industry, commerce, and a small number of state farms. Income that accrued to these enterprises returned to the state budget; their workers were salaried state employees and national planning guided their operations. Agriculture as well as handicraft and some small-scale rural industries were owned and operated collectively by their members. Cooperative units pooled their own capital, made most decisions about production and labor allocation (though with reference to local and national planning), and divided income among their members. These two forms of ownership provided the basic framework within which Chinese socialism has developed since the mid-1950s.

The National Program for
Agricultural Development, 1956–1967

The "high tide" not only exploded the notion that the countryside must wait for salvation (and socialism) dispensed by urban industry and the state, but initiated a surge of peasant economic and social activity. The National Program for Agricultural Development, 1956–1967, drafted by Mao in coordination with rural leaders in January 1956, encapsulated a new vision of rural possibilities informed by the events and achievements of the preceding year. Prior to this time, the future presented to the Chinese people was cast in the mold of the city and dominated by large-scale, state-owned heavy industry; it essentially bypassed more than 85 percent of the people who lived in the countryside. The National Program, by contrast, outlined in detail the possibilities offered by advanced cooperatives to raise productivity of land through rational use of abundant labor power and, on this foundation, to improve the quality of rural life. The future of a rejuvenated countryside, it implied, would rest principally on the expanded activity of 500 million pairs of hands and the creative achievement of rural people. The following points are good examples.

Mobilization of underutilized labor. The program called for expanded rural activity, to ensure 250 working days a year for every able-bodied male and 120 days for every female. Women formed the major untapped pool of surplus social labor, and were thus drawn into production on a large scale, although it is worth noting that the program assumed the restriction on women's social labor based on their family responsibilities.

Economic diversification. New sources of cooperative labor and the end of private ownership of scattered plots of land would make possible not only multiple cropping and use of improved seed strains, but also the expansion of tree planting and water conservancy and the proliferation of rural industry.

Expansion and transformation of education. The emphasis in education in the first five-year plan was on training high-level technicians and engineers appropriate to the requirements of advanced and imported technology. By contrast, the National Program stressed eliminating illiteracy and training five to six million primary- and intermediate-grade technicians to spur technical transformation of the countryside. The educational explosion of 1956 was in part a response to the new cooperatives' demand for bookkeepers, technicians, and innovators to improve seed strains and production techniques and keep production and income records.

Technological innovation. Rather than wait passively for tractors, electrification, and so on, the plan initiated a drive to introduce and disseminate new and improved farm tools. The emphasis was on adaptation to suit local conditions and the major innovators frequently cited were peasants with abundant practical experience and little formal schooling.

Expansion of health, social and cultural services. On the basis of projected income expansion over the coming decade, the program outlined steps to enrich rural life, including expansion of housing, elimination of major diseases, diffusion of radio and telephone services. In short, the program called for peasant initiative to improve the quality of rural life in ways consistent with socialist transformation and sustained development. Collective self-reliance, not salvation at the hands of the urban sector or the state, would show the way forward for the countryside.

On the Ten Major Relationships

In his April 1956 speech, "On the Ten Major Relationships," Mao drew on insights from the socialist upsurge to explicitly challenge premises of the first five-year plan and, for the first time, important features of the Soviet development path. This controversial and highly sensitive speech—it was not officially published until after Mao's death in 1977—is a landmark in the formulation of an independent Chinese socialist development strategy and a classic formulation of the dialectics of development.

Mao affirmed the primacy of heavy industry, but he did so as the basis for suggesting substantial readjustment of the overall balance in favor of light industry and agriculture. "If your desire [to develop heavy industry] is genuine or strong," Mao suggested, "then you will attach importance to agriculture and light industry so that there will be more grain and more raw materials for light industry and a greater accumulation of capital." [24] In this way heavy industry could develop more rapidly, but the immediate call was to step up the pace in light industry and agriculture.

Examining the relationship among state, collective, and individual, Mao suggested strengthening self-reliant cooperatives and protecting them against excessive centralizing tendencies of the state. Criticizing tendencies to concentrate "everything in the hands of the central authorities, shackling the local authorities and denying them the right of independent action," Mao insisted that regions and localities "should all enjoy their own proper independence and rights." And, he added, "they should fight for them." [25]

Lashing out at blind imitation and adulation of the Soviet Union, Mao implied that the most vital models derived from China's own continuing revolutionary experience. The speech illustrates two pivotal roles that Mao played throughout his revolutionary career. One, as the conscience of the revolution, rested on his empathy for and appreciation of the revolutionary potential of the peasantry. Mao repeatedly intervened against powerful forces within the state and party bureaucracies to advocate policies favorable to the peasantry and to the extension of socialism in the countryside. He repeatedly bypassed state and party channels to communicate directly with peasants, grassroots leaders, and (on rare occasions) with workers, thus defining one of the unique characteristics of his personal mass line leadership. His method was not that of the mass rally as favored, for example, by Cuba's Fidel Castro, nor did it emphasize on-the-spot visits to communes and factories, as in the case of Korea's Kim Il Sung. It involved a combination of direct addresses to party cadres and, above all, written letters, directives, editorials, and instructions to cadres and the people, circulated through party channels and in the press. Second, we see Mao intervening as early as 1927 and at subsequent critical junctures to oppose blindly copying Soviet practice in favor of an independent road to socialism rooted in Chinese conditions and needs and, after 1945, drawing on the heritage of the Yenan Way.

The Hundred Flowers, Chinese Intellectuals, and Socialist Transition

With the socialist upsurge of 1955–1956 China was well on the way to creating an independent road to socialism. Yet in 1956 significant countercurrents emerged as the party held its Eighth Congress to sum up the achievement of socialist transition in industry and agriculture, assess the results of the first five-year plan, and ratify outlines of a second plan. Declaring that "the contradictions between the proletariat and the bourgeoisie in our country has been basically resolved," the congress embraced the Soviet position that socialist ownership of the means of production essentially resolves questions of oppression and class struggle, leaving only the development of the productive forces:

> The major contradiction in our country is already that between the people's demand for the building of an advanced industrial country and the realities of a backward agricultural country. . . . This contradiction, in essence, is between the advanced socialist system and the backward productive forces of society.[26]

The logic led to a second five-year plan which paralleled the first in its emphasis on urban-based heavy industry. At the same time, under pressure from economic planners who viewed with alarm the economic dislocation and overheating of early 1956, the party quietly shelved the National Program for Agricultural Development. The initiative within the party rested with planners who viewed the central problem as one of economic development to be achieved through centralization of resources, emphasis on the urban-industrial sphere, and an end to the mobilization approaches of the transition period. Mao, who played a conspicuously minor role and later criticized major theses of the Eighth Congress, had earlier made plain his commitment to rapid development in framing the National Program and in his April speech, "On the Ten Major Relationships," but his approach was clearly at odds with that formulated by the planners.

Critical to the success of the development drive—and here Mao joined hands with Chou En-lai and planners in the State Council—was the role of intellectuals, particularly those with scientific and industrial skills. In 1956, in a bid to gain an increase in their support, Chou En-lai had called for greater professional autonomy for intellectuals, and to reinforce the point the 1956 wage reform increased material incentives, particularly at higher levels. The wage reform also enlarged the income gap between city and countryside to a ratio officially estimated at two to one in 1957.

Immediately following the Eighth Congress, Mao restated his view that "the contradiction between the proletariat and the bourgeoisie, between the socialist road and the capitalist road, is undoubtedly the principal contradiction in China's present day society." The socialist transition which had begun with the transfer of ownership of the means of production could only be consolidated through continued class struggle including conflict between competing ideas and ideologies. And in 1956 and early 1957 Mao sought to direct that struggle against two targets: bureaucratic and elitist tendencies he perceived eroding the revolutionary vigor of the party and state and producing contradictions between leaders and led; and uncritical copying of Soviet policies. His method: a rectification campaign modeled in significant respects on the party rectification and education movement initiated in 1942 at a critical juncture in the War of Resistance. This was the Hundred Flowers Movement, based on Mao's call to "let a hundred flowers bloom, let a hundred schools of thought contend." In calling on the intellectuals for criticism, Mao sought simultaneously to reform the party and the state and to strengthen the active contribution of intellectuals on behalf of economic development.

In 1956 Mao's speeches revealed his preoccupation with problems of legitimation and dissent that then wracked the entire international communist movement in the wake of Khrushchev's denunciation of Stalin and protest and rioting in Poland and Hungary. Noting China's success in depriving the landlords and bourgeoisie of their power through land revolution, nationalization, and cooperativization, Mao observed that the antisocialist ideas of these classes remained alive. He noted, moreover, that fewer than 20 percent of college students were drawn from the ranks of the proletariat and the poorer peasants. This meant that not only the old intellectuals but many of the new came from exploiting or elite classes. Mao nevertheless argued that the great majority of the 5 million intellectuals were, in varying degrees, loyal to the nation and to socialism and willing to learn. One way to deal with the problem of conflicting values and ideas which inevitably persist throughout the period of socialist transition was to eliminate antagonistic classes and silence all heterodox thinking. Such methods had recently been applied, for example, to the landlord class. Mao, however, proposed another approach. Noting that "in Hungary, great democracy toppled the party, the government and the army once it was set in motion," Mao expressed optimism that China had no cause to "be afraid of great democracy. If there is a disturbance, it will help get the festering sore cured, and that's a good thing." [27] The way to deal with contradictions was to bring them into the open. "Truth stands in contrast to falsehood and develops in struggle with it."

The campaign, on again and off again in 1956, reflecting strong resistance to it among the party leadership, received powerful impetus from Mao's speech of February 1957 "On the Correct Handling of Contradictions Among the People." Mao urged intellectuals to freely criticize the party in the interest of exposing contradictions among the people and advancing socialism. When speeches and wall posters swelled from a trickle to a flood, culminating in "the storm in the universities" in May and June, the Communists faced the harshest criticism leveled by the people since the founding of the People's Republic. The most telling, but by no means the only criticisms, were those which held up to the party the mirror of its own ideals and found that a process of degeneration had set in leading to the formation of a new class of privileged officials increasingly divorced from the people. As one critic put it, "instead of standing among the masses," the party increasingly "stood on the back of the masses and ruled the masses." Others criticized the party's failure to reduce the gap between city and countryside, some even claiming that the revolution had brought no improvement to the peasantry. Many intellectuals and students bitterly attacked the party's monopoly on power and demanded the full implementation of democratic rights, particularly calling for expanded intellectual and political freedoms for themselves.

On June 8 the party initiated a vigorous counteroffensive against its critics, whom the *People's Daily* proceeded to denounce as rightist and antisocialist. The brunt of the criticism which had been directed against the party was now turned against the intellectuals. Mao together with Chou En-lai and Teng Hsiao-p'ing had been the most outspoken advocates of the movement within the party; they now found themselves on the defensive.

From the outset, much of the party bureaucracy had opposed the campaign that made it a target of criticism. Mao had personally launched the movement and supported significant elements of the criticism it produced. For example, in March he, too, decried increasing tendencies of cadres to "contend for fame and position . . . comparing salaries, food, clothing, and comforts."[28] In June Mao nevertheless joined the party leadership to suppress the Hundred Flowers and initiate the antirightist movement. The heart of the matter lay in conflicting interpretations between Mao and many of the intellectual critics over the meaning of freedom and democracy. "Poisonous weeds have been growing side by side with fragrant flowers and ghosts and monsters appearing together with the unicorn and phoenix," Mao observed. The urgency with which he led the counterattack in the summer suggests that Mao had underestimated the nature and extent of rightist criticism which the campaign produced. For many of the critics democracy principally meant the expansion of individual freedom, power, and prerogatives for the intellectuals, the very tendencies Mao had sought to curb in the party. Mao and his supporters insisted that democracy was not an end in itself. It must be judged by class criteria, particularly whether it contributed to the advance to socialism or the restoration of capitalism, whether it was directed toward overcoming bureaucratic and elitist tendencies or whether it led to new forms of privilege or the reassertion of old privileges, whether it served to revitalize or weaken the revolutionary party and, above all, whether it served the interests of the workers and peasants. The great debate touched off by the Hundred Flowers Movement, extended in the subsequent antirightist campaign and the transfer of large numbers of intellectuals and cadres to work in the countryside, culminated ultimately in a new strategy for socialist development departing sharply from many of the guidelines of the first five-year plan in favor of a Great Leap Forward. The pressing issues of freedom and democracy, the individual and the party, revolution and bureaucracy, which the movement had raised but left unresolved, would erupt throughout the society during the Great Leap, in the Great Proletarian Cultural Revolution, and in the debate over modernization during the late seventies. In July 1957, as the reaction to the Hundred Flowers took shape within the party, Mao gave perhaps his fullest definition of the problem:

> Our aim is to create a political situation in which we have both centralism and democracy, both discipline and freedom, both unity of will and personal ease of mind and liveliness, and thus to promote our socialist revolution and socialist construction, make it easier to overcome difficulties, build a modern industry and modern agriculture more rapidly and make our Party and state more secure and better able to weather storm and stress. . . . The method is to seek truth from facts and follow the mass line. The derivative methods are those of holding meetings attended by both Party and non-Party people to discuss major policies, conducting the rectification movement publicly, and criticizing many of the Party's and government's shortcomings and mistakes in the press.[29]

The First Five-Year Plan:
Accomplishments and Problems

We have examined the Soviet-inspired first five-year plan with its emphasis on bureaucratic rationality, centralized planning, and urban focus, and the dialectic involving the Chinese peasantry, the proletariat, the party, and Mao Tsetung for clues to the emergence of a distinct Chinese road to socialist development. It remains to assess its accomplishments and contradictions. By 1957, China had achieved economic growth rates which had few parallels in world history. It did so in a period of war, isolation, and profound social change, and with little net injection of foreign capital despite Soviet aid. The accomplishments were most visible in the priority sectors, that is, heavy industry and selected cities. Between 1952 and 1957 China's gross national product increased by 40 percent. Industry achieved the most rapid gains, doubling output. Agricultural production also increased by a respectable 20 percent. Industry, the growth rate of which exceeded that of the Soviet Union during its first plan period, increased its share of gross national product from 18 percent in 1952 to 26 percent in 1957. In key sectors the record was still more impressive. Between 1952 and 1957 the output of steel quadrupled, as did chemical fertilizers; oil and pig iron tripled, and coal, electric power, and cement doubled. (See Table 13.) In the course of a very brief period of time, China had laid the groundwork for comprehensive industrialization and basically completed the transition from private enterprise to socialist ownership of the means of production in city and countryside, in industry, agriculture, handicrafts, and commerce. Moreover, this was accomplished simultaneously with rising personal incomes for nearly everyone and a substantial expansion of educational, health, cultural, and social services. China's overall growth rate throughout the first decade of the People's Republic was extremely rapid, probably outstripping Japan, the Soviet Union, and Germany in comparable periods of their development.

Yet by 1957, despite new possibilities opened up by rural cooperation, viewed from two perspectives China was rapidly approaching the limits of the road taken in the first plan.

First, the plan's priorities ran counter to ideals which the party had fought for and which continued to guide the vision of its future for many of its leaders and people. The reliance on Soviet technology, the predominance of urban-based capital-intensive heavy industry, the long-term extraction of rural resources to serve the cities, the emphasis on a specialized technical elite and a planning network concentrating power at the center at the expense of the localities, stood in direct conflict with the egalitarian, participatory, cooperative, self-reliant, and mass line principles of the Yenan Way. In practice, class struggle centered in the countryside had significantly modified the original plan, most strikingly in the completion of rural collectivization a decade ahead of schedule. Nevertheless, the plan set in motion the growing predominance of the city over the countryside and fostered a managerial structure narrowly attuned to technical priorities and negating the role both of party and working class in running industry and the cities; its educational priorities were training small numbers of high-level technicians, and it favored health and welfare systems oriented toward the urban areas, particularly its more privileged sectors. To be sure, many of these tendencies common to the modernizing process were much more weakly developed than in most other countries as a result of continued eruption of class struggle. Yet the tendencies were clear, and the Hundred Flowers Movement of 1957 brought them into the arena of public debate.

There was a second range of problems which lent urgency to these matters. Stated simply, the first five-year plan strategy of rapid industrialization had been pressed to its limits. Unless the problem of lagging agricultural growth rates and its corollary, the blind rush of peasants to the cities, could be resolved, the overall pace of growth would have to be slowed. Agriculture held the key to development of all other sectors: it provided 80 percent of the raw materials for light industry and, as late as 1957, 72 percent of the value of exports. It fed the cities and provided the largest potential market for both light and heavy industry. With 15 million additional mouths to feed each year and the cities expanding more rapidly than the countryside, the agrarian sector had to register significant productivity gains if the plan were to succeed. Yet the state not only extracted a significant part of the rural surplus but deferred to the distant future any significant return either in terms of consumer goods or such inputs as tractors, fertilizer, steel, and cement. The countryside, for three decades the storm center of the revolution, continued to pose the central challenge to China's socialist development. By 1957 the growing contradictions between industry and agriculture, between city and countryside, between mass line and Soviet practice, and between party and peasantry had reached acute proportions.

V. The Great Leap Forward and the Formation of the People's Communes, 1958–1959

> We work at such white heat,
> If we bump the sky it will break,
> If we kick the earth it will crack,
> If the sky falls, our commune'll mend it,
> If the earth splits, our commune'll patch it.
>
> Peasant Song, Great Leap Forward

> Now our enthusiasm has been aroused. Ours is an ardent nation, now swept by a burning tide. There is a good metaphor for this: our nation is like an atom.... When this atom's nucleus is smashed the thermal energy released will have tremendous power. We shall be able to do things which we could not do before.
>
> Mao Tsetung, 1958

In the fall and winter of 1957, unprecedented numbers of peasants engaged in water conservancy, forestry, and other projects. Finding their activities restricted by the limited size of even advanced cooperatives, in some areas units merged to facilitate coordination. Large-scale participation in slack season capital construction and cooperative mergers opened the way to the Great Leap Forward, the formation of people's communes, and many of the most distinctive and enduring features of China's socialist development path. Once again much of the initiative sprang from the countryside; as in 1955 Mao was quick to grasp the potential of the new upsurge. Building on the momentum of the antirightist offensive of the summer of 1957, Mao led the party and the people on a new phase of rapid advance.

The Rise of the Rural People's Communes

In the spring of 1958 a sense of exhilaration and limitless possibility swept much of the countryside. The slogan of the hour was "let the mountain lower its head; let the river course be moved." The American writer Anna Louise Strong, observing the communes at their birth, described the experience of one small island off the Chekiang coast. In 1954 its 2700 residents had merged four fishing cooperatives, creating, in effect, a commune.

> When the movement for communes began, this little island not only took the new name at once but was ready for a big drive. It set up a fish-processing industry, established trade with the mainland, and sent a number of young men to Shanghai to learn to operate motor junks. By December they had built eighteen motor junks and ordered two trawlers: some of the young men already commanded motor vessels at sea. They had a dozen small factories for motor repair, iron smelting, making fish nets. They had a broadcasting station, a library, a "palace of culture," a school for fishery, a maternity home, electric lights and telephones.[30]

The rural people's communes constitute the central institutional contribution not only of the Great Leap but of the entire period of China's socialist transformation. Beginning spontaneously and experimentally in the spring, under party leadership they spread throughout the entire countryside in the summer. Here is how the August 1958 Pei-tai-ho Resolution, which formally sanctioned and provided guidelines for the nation-wide formation of rural people's communes, described their multiple activities and mission:

> The establishment of people's communes with all-round management of agriculture, forestry, animal husbandry, side occupations and fishery, where industry (the worker), agriculture (the peasant), exchange (the trader), culture and education (the student) and military affairs (the militiaman) merge into one, is the fundamental policy to guide the peasants to accelerate socialist construction, complete the building of socialism ahead of time and carry out the gradual transition of communism.[31]

The name *commune*, introduced in the summer of 1958, linked the experiment under way with Marx's perception that the Paris Commune of 1871 provided the historical model for the dictatorship of the proletariat in which a mobilized people smashed existing bureaucratic rule, destroyed the state and army apparatus, and concentrated power in its own hands to guide the advance to communism. Characteristically, however, the commune, in its most highly developed Chinese form, was a rural institution.

Previous institutional change in the countryside had centered on larger and more advanced cooperative *economic* units. The commune conception likewise gave priority to accelerated economic and technological development, but it went further in creating an all-embracing unit to reconstruct the social, political, cultural and even the familial foundations of rural life. The commune at its formation, with approximately 20,000-25,000 members, coincided with the township, thus merging the basic cooperative unit, owned and operated by its members, with the lowest echelon of government administration. By 1963, when their size was reduced to more manageable proportions and their number increased from 26,000 to 74,000, communes averaged approximately 8,000 members and their boundaries normally coincided with the standard marketing community, which had long been the local inter-village center of rural trade and intercourse. In the late 1970s, membership in the approximately 50,000 communes averages approximately 13-16,000.

The communes from their inception have been organized with three levels of ownership and management, to facilitate both solidarity based on face-to-face working relationships (in daily agricultural tasks at the team level) and economies of scale that make possible crop diversification, mechanization, technological innovation, and rural industrialization (brigade and commune levels). The basic unit of ownership and production in most of the countryside since 1962 is the team, comprised typically of twenty to thirty-five families (though sometimes including more than a hundred families) that since the early 1960s own, operate, and divide the income from their land and sideline activities. The production brigade, comprised of five to fifteen teams, together with the commune, coordinates use of tractors and irrigation equipment, some capital construction and local industry as well as most health, cultural, and educational activities. The commune, made up of ten to thirty brigades, initiates and coordinates such large-scale economic activities as water conservancy, electrification, and rural industry. It also provides overall planning and logistics, and establishes crop quotas and targets for its constituent units. In their initial phase in 1958 and 1959 the communes also attempted to directly manage agricultural and sideline production and coordinate income distribution on a commune-wide scale.

The rural people's communes, which originated as a grassroots response to economic and organizational problems, in the course of 1958 became the centerpiece of a full-blown vision and incorporated a set of strategic principles that directly challenged premises of the first five-year plan. They set China on a course that combined technological with social and cultural revolution, that sought to transform the productive forces and nature itself on the basis of new relations of production. This was the Great Leap Forward.

The Strategy of the Great Leap Forward

The economic ambitions of the leap are suggested by Chou En-lai's statement "that an annual increase of 20 percent or more in industrial output is a leap forward, an increase above 25 percent is a Great Leap Forward, and an increase of 30 percent or more, an exceptionally Great Leap Forward."[32] In 1958 the Chinese leadership announced the drive to "Catch Up with Great Britain in Fifteen Years." The critical question was how an already strained economy could accelerate development. The basic answer lay in bringing into play two factors that had been relatively neglected during the earlier plan: China's abundant labor reserves and the consciousness and creativity of working people. Both would be applied to liberate the forces of nature and increase productivity. This required overcoming premises, widely held in the twentieth century, that development could be equated with urban industrialization and centralization of resources.

The Great Leap strategy in essence was simultaneous acceleration of modern industry and traditional agriculture and handicrafts. The countryside would continue to provide resources for

Table 6
Socialist Transformation of the Countryside
Percentage of Participating Peasant Households

	Mutual aid teams	Elementary agricultural producers' cooperatives	% age change, June to December 1955	Advanced agricultural producers' cooperatives	% age change December 1955 to June 1956	Communes	% age change August to September 1958
1950	11						
1952	40						
1954	60	11					
June 1955	65	14					
Dec. 1955		59	+45	4			
Jan. 1956		50		11			
Feb. 1956				51			
June 1956		28		63	+59		
Dec. 1956		8		88			
Spring 1958				100			
August 1958				70		30	
Sept. 1958						98	+68

Sources: Kenneth Walker, *Planning in Chinese Agriculture* (London: Frank Cass, 1965), p. 14; Peter Schran, *The Development of Chinese Agriculture* (Urbana: University of Illinois Press, 1969), p. 28; and *Ten Great Years*, p. 35.

heavy and light industry and exports. At the same time, self-sustaining rural development would rest on mobilization of abundant labor reserves, diversification of rural labor into industry, handicrafts, and capital construction, organized through large-scale cooperation and relying heavily on peasant initiative. Light industry, growing rapidly in both the modern and traditional sectors, would stimulate agriculture by providing consumer goods and simultaneously generating rapid accumulation. This was, in short, a strategy of "walking on two legs," simultaneously emphasizing development of countryside and city, farm and factory, and indigenous and advanced technology. It provided the greatest stimulus, however, to the rural sector.

During the Great Leap, rural people, peasants, expanded their horizons and their economic prospects by initiating a broad range of local industries as well as extending agriculture and diverse sideline activities. President Liu Shao-ch'i observed in his May 1958 report on the leap:

> The growth of social productive forces calls for a socialist revolution and the spiritual emancipation of the people; the victory of this revolution and emancipation in turn spurs a forward leap in the productive forces and this in turn impels progressive change in the social relations of production and an advance in man's ideology. In their ceaseless struggle to transform nature, the people are continuously transforming society and themselves.[33]

New levels of consciousness and the social reorganization which they prompted, Liu suggested, opened new possibilities for economic development.

The communes played a central role in expanding economic activity by bringing into play abundant underutilized resources of labor and reversing the centralizing tendencies of the earlier plan which had tended to restrict the countryside to agricultural production to service the cities. The accelerated capital construction which led to the formation of the communes set off a chain reaction. When the demand for more tools exceeded the supply capacity of urban industry, localities began to produce their own, but this in turn generated demand for iron and steel and other resources.

During the first nine months of 1958, according to official statistics, China established no less than 7.5 million new industrial and handicraft plants and workshops, including 6 million commune enterprises utilizing local capital, technology, labor, and raw materials. This approach, relying on local resources and initiative, addressed the pressing problem of rural unemployment and underemployment. Unfortunately, in the phase of rapid expansion in the summer and fall of 1958, however, it also placed a heavy burden on agriculture by siphoning off labor during the peak harvest season.

Many of the new factories, including iron and steel foundries, machine shops, and chemical fertilizer plants, expanded into new areas or had few rural precedents; others such as oil pressing, food processing, and tool making built on foundations of traditional rural handicrafts and industry which recent state policy had weakened or eliminated. The new decentralized, small-scale industry, its proponents claimed, had a capital-output ratio one-fourteenth that of the giant complexes favored in the earlier plan, that is, it required much less capital to initiate production. And instead of requiring three to five years' lead time, factories began producing goods in a matter of months. Local industry also solved the problem of primitive transport which retarded the urban-rural flow of goods.

Table 7 suggests the scope and sequence of the changes as the leap generated new demands, capabilities, and confidence, and the rural areas began the process of change from agricultural to agricultural-industrial economies.

Rural industrialization during the Great Leap relied principally on the self-reliant efforts of peasants pooling resources and skills through the communes. But beginning in 1957 the process was reinforced by the transfer to the countryside of technical and managerial personnel. Here was an example of an important state subsidy of the countryside reversing the one-way flow of resources to the cities.

As communes expanded the range of productive activities from capital construction to small-scale industry, the acute

Table 7
Internal Logic of Rural Small-Scale Industrial Development
During the Great Leap Forward

Stage	Events	Date
One	Shortage of agricultural and industrial tools, fertilizer, and agricultural chemicals perceived.	December 1957
Two	Rural production of agricultural and industrial tools, chemical fertilizer factories, and cement factories inaugurated.	February-April 1958
Three	Factories producing machinery, transport equipment, iron and steel, aluminum, copper, and chemicals inaugurated.	June-November 1958

Source: Kojima Reiitsu, *Chūgoku no keizai to gijutsu* (China's Economy and Technology) (Tokyo: Keiso Shobo, 1975), p. 124.

shortage of field workers gave married women, many of whom worked primarily in the home and on private family plots, an opportunity to contribute to collective labor. In the land revolution and 1950 marriage law women achieved full legal equality. However, in the Great Leap millions of women in both city and countryside advanced out of the home as full (though not yet fully equal) participants in the economy. As women expanded their economic activities, the communes initiated a wide range of community services that further expanded economic and social opportunities (see Table 8).

The expansion of day care, dining halls, and other services in turn released women from family duties traditionally defined as women's work and facilitated their further advance into social labor, politics, and other activities. In the cities, where women

Table 8
Rural Women's Participation in Social Labor
and the Expansion of Social Services

	Participation of rural women in social labor	Public dining halls	Nurseries
1957 (Fall)	60-80 percent of women participate in social labor (including the peak agricultural season); women account for 166 days labor per year, 30 percent of the total labor days.	Scattered experiments	6 million children
1958	Nearly all participate; 55 million more women in city and countryside participate in social labor; women constitute 1/3 of agricultural labor days.	90 percent of villages	67 million children
1959	Women average 250 days labor, and 40-45 percent of total labor days; 20 million more rural women participate in social labor.	3,600,000 public dining halls; 70 percent of rural families participate.	70 percent of rural children

Source: Kojima, *China's Economy and Technology*, p. 157. The data, derived from numerous local sources, reflect broad orders of magnitude.

organized and staffed small-scale neighborhood industries, the expansion of social services was more comprehensive and the gains more durable. In 1958 in both the city and countryside the provision of social services reduced the burden of women's work in the home. The convention of women's exclusive responsibility for the remaining family duties, including housework and children, remained intact.

The Great Leap emphasized technological development, both advanced modern technology and grassroots innovation serving local industry and agriculture. It particularly fostered scientific and technological inquiry among working people. Peasant innovations received wide recognition and for the first time peasants and workers gained membership in the prestigious and exclusive National Academy of Sciences. This brought worker and peasant innovators together with one another and with their university-educated colleagues to share techniques, bolster theoretical understanding, and adapt technology to local production needs. The approach to technology reflected the dual concern for accelerating economic development and bridging the gap between city and countryside. Simultaneous technological and social revolution required the transformation of values and priorities of elite science and encouragement of grassroots innovators. The conception of technology and, above all, the composition of the technical and scientific community had changed. In 1956 the attention of the party had centered on the cultivation of a technical intelligentsia. During the leap it fostered and recognized the achievements of outstanding workers and peasants among the bearers of technology and sought to integrate modern and indigenous technology in the service of development.

The proliferation of productive activity in the countryside is shown in Tables 9 and 10. The expanded utilization of labor began with the mini-leap of 1956 and then accelerated during 1958 and 1959 at the height of the Great Leap.

Between 1955 and 1959 China doubled the number of rural labor days. Agricultural employment expanded rapidly, but the most striking increases centered on communal industry, capital construction, and community services. Between 1950 and 1955, in part because of the decline of handicrafts, the number of labor days did not increase significantly. It was not until 1956

Table 9
Rural Population, Employment, and Labor Days, 1952–1959

	Peasant population (millions)	Total employed peasants (millions)	Average annual labor days	Total annual labor days (billions)	Index of total annual labor days (1952=100)
1950	479.7	222.6	119.0	26.5	97.5
1952	491.9	228.3	119.0	27.2	100.0
1955	523.8	243.3	121.0	29.4	108.4
1956	532.2	255.6	149.0	38.1	140.2
1957	541.3	260.3	159.5	41.5	152.8
1958	550.5	271.3	174.6	47.5	174.7
1959	539.6	309.1	189.0	58.4	215.0
Collectivization					
1955–57	+17.5	+17.0	+38.5	+12.1	+44.4
Communization					
1957–59	−1.7	+48.5	+29.5	+16.9	+62.2

Sources: Schran, *The Development of Chinese Agriculture*, pp. 47, 75; John Gurley, *China's Economy and the Maoist Strategy* (New York: Monthly Review Press, 1976), p. 244.

Table 10
The Structure of Rural Employment by Labor Days, 1950–1959

	Farm work	Subsidiary work*	Corvee basic construction	Communal industry	Collective affairs and communal services
1950	75.2	19.2	3.1		0.0
1952	77.1	19.7	3.2		0.0
1955	83.0	21.0	3.9		0.4
1956	104.3	23.7	8.7		3.5
1957	113.4	25.8	9.7		3.8
1958	120.3	28.8	10.9	3.9	10.9
1959	151.7	29.5	12.3	7.5	13.9

Source: Schran, *The Development of Chinese Agriculture*, p. 75.

*Subsidiary work includes gathering activities, domestic handicrafts, professional services, care of private plots, and animal husbandry.

that advanced cooperatives, followed shortly by communes, encouraged rural diversification and other policies conducive to expanding employment.

The vast labor reserves tapped during the leap consisted principally of women and of labor previously idle during the winter slack season. These additional labor inputs raised total output while per capita productivity of agricultural labor declined since newly mobilized labor tended to be less efficient and because of diminishing returns on a basically constant cultivated area. The problem of raising total output and income, not productivity per unit of labor, is the most pressing problem for the Chinese economy, as it is in other developing nations. The promise of the Great Leap, however, rested not only on drawing on new sources of labor but also on raising labor efficiency through cooperation and a technological revolution bringing about rural mechanization, electrification, and industrialization. The technological revolution that is again being vigorously pursued in the late 1970s began during the Great Leap.

The leap thus expanded the conception of accumulation applied to rural development. In initiating a technological revolution, it looked both to improvement of indigenous tools, technology, and processes (accumulation as the extension of the hand), and to such modern industrial inputs as electricity and tractors. In stressing irrigation systems and other large-scale capital construction it sought to transform nature (the extension of the land) to increase productivity and eliminate the ravages of natural disaster. But perhaps the most important new source of capital was China's abundant labor power. In tapping large labor reserves and encouraging the initiative of those already in the workforce, the leap emphasized the extension of the mind, that is, the acquisition of knowledge and skills applied to the work process.[34]

The emphasis on technological innovation and grassroots initiative was reflected in education. The communes, for example, initiated a variety of schools. Part-time and popularly run rural schools exemplify the relationship between education and the economic and social transformation of the countryside, as education was closely geared to the economic demands of the communes (see Table 11).

Simultaneously with the productive and organizational drive, tens of millions of people, predominantly peasants and workers,

Table 11
Students in Part-Time Schools and Newly Literate
(thousands)

	Newly literate	Part-time primary schools	Part-time middle schools	Part-time technical middle schools
1949	657	—	—	—
1952	656	1,375	249	1
1955	3,678	4,538	1,167	195
1956	7,434	5,195	2,236	563
1957	7,208	6,267	2,714	588
1958	40,000	26,000	5,000	—

Source: *Ten Great Years*, p. 198.

entered the classroom, many for the first time in their lives. Large numbers of the new schools were organized, run, and financed by working people with the curriculum tailored to local priorities during the leap.

The Central Committee's December (Wuhan) Resolution pointed out that the rural people's communes opened

> the way to the gradual industrialization of the rural areas, the way to the gradual transition from collective owner-ship to ownership by the whole people in agriculture, the way to the gradual transition from the socialist principle "to each according to his work" to the communist princi-ple "to each according to his need," the way to gradually lessen and finally eliminate the differences between town and country, between worker and peasant and between mental and manual labor, and the way gradually to lessen and finally to eliminate the internal function of the state.[35]

The Wuhan Resolution, which raised the issue of the immi-nent advance to communism, and which introduced for the first time the socialist goal of eliminating the three great differences, was the most radical statement issued by the center during the Great Leap. The earlier Pei-tai-ho Resolution, which defined the communes as the institutional form for the *future* transition to ownership by the whole people and eventually to communism, had emphasized the continued adherence to socialist principles of distribution according to labor throughout the extended period of economic scarcity. At Wuhan Mao tentatively raised the issue of the transition to communism.

> In regard to the socialist system, two types of ownership exist simultaneously in the socialist stage. They are opposites and also united. They are a unity of opposites. Collective ownership contains the nucleus of socialist ownership by the whole people. Its basic essence is collective ownership but it also contains elements of communist ownership by all the people . . . in nations under the leadership of the Communist Party, one can and should allow the elements of communism to grow.[36]

Mao was suggesting that prefigurative elements of the future communist society should gradually grow during the transition process. In the promethean atmosphere of the Great Leap, however, many communes immediately implemented policies embodying significant communist elements, particularly partial free supply systems which provided members grain at no charge through public dining halls (that is, the commune, not the individual, bore the costs) and diverse services including nurseries, day care, and homes for the aged. Anna Louise Strong described the system implemented in the small Paimao Commune, a two-hour drive from Shanghai. With its slogan, "Equal Shanghai in conveniences and the West Lake of Hangchow in beauty," the commune was "going 'high, wide, and handsome' " in making available free services.

> Besides the normal free food, education and nurseries, their free list included: "free clothing, up to the limit of the cotton ration, all tailored to individual taste," free medical services, for which already they had 52 medical personnel, and a hospital of 32 beds. . . . Free education was contemplated "up through the university"; free theater and cinema right in their midst; free haircuts and baths and barbers; free weddings, including needed photographs and wedding feast for up to twenty guests; free funerals up to a cost of fifty yuan; free tooth-brushes, tooth-paste and cosmetics for "women between 16 and 45 years of age"; free laundry and mending.[37]

A bit "dizzy with success," Strong commented. To be sure, few communes went as far even at the height of Great Leap expectations. Nevertheless, despite warnings by the leadership that communism could not be achieved overnight, the mood of anticipation of the imminent advent of communist society and of abundance for all prevailed in many quarters, fanning enthusiasm for yet bolder experimentation ... and sowing seeds of disaster.

The Proletariat, Industry, and the Cities in the Great Leap Forward

China's development prior to the leap suggests the paradox that while the Communist Party led the nation toward socialism in the name of the proletariat, and industry provided the cutting edge of technological and economic advance, the driving force of social revolution and of class struggle remained centered in the poor and lower middle peasants. Working-class struggles to restrict and then eliminate entirely the power of the capitalist class did occur at the time of liberation of the cities, in subsequent anticorruption movements and in the 1956 nationalization of industry. But class struggle in factories and the cities did not approach the intensity achieved in the countryside.

In 1958 the Chinese proletariat re-emerged as a powerful revolutionary force for the first time since 1927. The changing role of workers is best illustrated in the realm of industrial management. During the first five-year plan industrial management featured concentration of power in central ministries which controlled production down to the factory level; "one-man management," that is, individual responsibility at each administrative level within a rigid chain of command, and sharply differentiated division of labor; and emphasis on individual material incentives, including piece-rate wages and bonuses. These principles, consistent with Soviet practice, preserved the basic structure of authority within the factories in a period of transition from capitalist to state ownership. Changes were already under way, however, in 1956 and 1957, when the party responded to worker demands, officially rejected "one-man management," and began to experiment with new approaches to planning, management, and incentives.

Despite the productive achievements of industry during the

first plan period, serious contradictions lurked beneath the surface. The technical rationalizations of the industrial management system clashed fundamentally with the party's revolutionary heritage and with the liberating and antibureaucratic premises of Chinese socialism. The decision to vest power in central ministries at the top and factory managers at the base negated both the mobilizing role of the party and the activism of the workers. Rigid rules and the elaborately graded wages that replaced the wartime supply system in 1955 widened the gap between managerial/technical personnel and the workers. Clear status lines were emerging between workers and managers and between skilled and unskilled workers. Finally, piece rates, widely implemented in modern plants by 1956, fostered divisions rather than a sense of collective enterprise. In short, the division of labor, hierarchical organizational tendencies, emphasis on technical rationality over human solidarity, and reliance on material incentives concentrated power in the hands of managers and technicians (the majority of bourgeois backgrounds) and sharply restricted the role of the proletariat. The sacrifice of mass line principles of participation, collective decision-making, and decentralized management at the altar of efficiency reinforced the subordinate position of workers in industry.

We have seen that in the course of the 1950s it became increasingly clear that the Soviet model could not comfortably be imposed on Chinese reality. The centralized planning system, for example, produced a situation in which major industries attained such extensive autonomy that their activities could not be effectively coordinated and adapted to meet changing provincial and local needs. Excessive concentration of economic and financial power at the center crippled the initiative of the locales and held back the integration and overall advance of the economy.

Moreover, the elaborate Soviet system of regulations narrowly defining each task confined the scope of activity of the workers, hampered understanding of the larger industrial process, and blocked worker initiative and technical innovation. In any event, the system could not be efficiently applied under conditions in which variations from factory to factory made unification of quotas impossible. In short, managerial principles implanted during the first five-year plan not only conflicted sharply with revolutionary values and goals of cadres and workers but posed increasingly serious technical and economic problems. Early in the leap, Mao approvingly quoted the Hunanese saying that "straw sandals have no pattern—they shape themselves in the making." The imported shoe clearly pinched here as in so many other areas.

From the fall of 1957 class struggle erupted within the factories and the party began to support transformation of Chinese industrial practice. The first step was ending the absolute authority of the ministries over planning and resources exercised by means of vertical integration. The system of dual rule replaced the centralized, hierarchical structure with one which emphasized decentralized administration, coordinated planning among industries, and flexibility at intermediate and lower levels. The concept redefining the relationship between center and locality was one of centralized planning and leadership coupled with decentralized administration and implementation.

Vertical rule had emphasized the inviolability of the chain of command running for example from the railroad, machine building, or commerce ministry at the center direct to local bureaus and individual factories. Dual rule broke the exclusive power of the ministries by emphasizing coordinating functions at the central, regional, and local levels, thus expanding local initiative. Coordination at each level (provincial, county, and enterprise) ensured the compatibility of plans formulated by each ministry with overall priorities and resources and facilitated adjustments. Dual rule placed a premium on collective, coordinated decision-making and on flexibility under varying and rapidly changing local conditions, in contrast with the rule bound, centralized and technically oriented vertical model. This change paralleled the elimination within the factory of "one-man management" in favor of collective leadership with the party committee rather than the factory manager assuming primary responsibility.

The changes did not stop here. During 1958-1959, experimentation in thousands of factories gave rise to a managerial system of "two participations, one reform and triple combination." Where the system took root it began the process of transforming relationships among manager, technicians, cadres, and production workers. Indeed, it called into question the meanings of those very categories. A May 1957 directive, striking both at bureaucratic tendencies within the party and at elitist tendencies among intellectuals and technical personnel, had stipulated that all cadres must regularly participate in labor. The two participations went further in stipulating both worker participation in management and participation by managers, technicians, and cadres in labor.

While practice varied from factory to factory, cadre participation in labor directly challenged the hierarchical division of labor and brought technical and supervisory personnel into direct contact with the workers in ways designed to overcome disdain for labor, break down elitism, and familiarize managers with problems and possibilities of equipment and personnel. One reform referred to the workers' reform and elimination of outmoded or irrational rules and regulations. Triple combination technical innovation teams of workers, cadres, and technicians helped to narrow the gap between mental and manual labor, made use of the practical experience of veteran workers, and stimulated the entire workforce to upgrade technical skills. At this time, triple combination teams typically functioned only at the team and small workshop levels, and often with workers subordinate to technical personnel. The groundwork was nevertheless being laid for the emergence of the workers as the masters of the factories.

Under modern industrial conditions, was it possible for workers and cadres to master sufficient advanced technology to genuinely challenge the power of the technocrats? The Great Leap addressed the problem from several directions. First, mass line principles stressing "politics in command" resulted both in worker participation in management committees and direct interaction between cadres and workers at the point of production. Moreover, during the leap virtually the entire middle level of technical and managerial personnel transferred to the production line, making possible greater initiative and planning at the workshop level. But how to overcome the divisions among workers fostered by the piece-rate system? How to challenge the passivity and lack of confidence which "one-man management" had reinforced? And how to upgrade a technically limited workforce so that decisions would conform not only with political but with production imperatives?

The abolition of the piece-rate system was an important step in reversing the tendencies on the part of workers to establish low quotas (to increase their bonuses), to privately covet rather than share technological advances, and to emphasize individual profit over the collective needs of the factory and the nation. In contrast with the countryside, where bold and sometimes utopian experiments occurred with free supply, the factories did not significantly modify the 1955 graded wage system. The 1955 reform had established rational income distribution guidelines which applied uniformly in each industry based on skill levels and seniority, thus eliminating gross intra-industry inequities in income between different plants and regions. During the leap, industry restricted and transformed piece-rate and bonus systems, eliminating them entirely in many plants and awarding bonuses to work teams rather than to individuals in others to reinforce collective spirit.

Table 12 indicates the wage pattern in effect in 1959 and, except for minor wage hikes, unchanged until the wage change and reform of 1977. Differentials between the highest and lowest wages in most industries ran in the neighborhood of three to one, but it is important to note that seniority accounted for a large share of the differences and most workers would advance from the lower to the upper end of the scale in the course of their working lives. As of 1955, when the system was introduced, more than half the workers clustered in grades three to five of the eight grades with monthly wages of 47 to 61 yuan. The 1955 wage reform had also established an eight grade scale for highly skilled technicians and engineers, ranging from 88 to 210 yuan per month. The twenty-six grade scale for cadres in state organs ranged from 30 to approximately 100 yuan for most workers and cadres up to the level of county department heads, with the highest salaries up to 560 yuan reserved for ranking cadres, including a few thousand in the top six grades earning over 300 yuan at the highest levels of provincial and national organs.

These differentials, small in comparison with those in preliberation China or with prevailing norms in the United States as well as in the developing countries, geared wages to differences in skill levels on the basis of the socialist principle "to each according to one's work." In abolishing piece rates and large bonuses and in expanding worker participation in management and planning, the reforms of the Great Leap opened the way to active cooperation among workers to stimulate production and sharply reduced personal material incentives. The leap did not seriously question income inequities based on skill levels and rank.

Table 12
Wages in Industry by Wage Grades, 1959
(in yuan per month)

Industry and enterprise	1	2	3	4	5	6	7	8
Coal, Fu-shun mine	34.50	40.74	48.13	56.82	67.10	79.25	93.60	110.40
Steel, Anshan I&S Co.	34.50	40.74	48.11	56.82	67.10	79.25	93.59	110.40
Machinery, Mukden works	33.00	38.90	45.80	54.00	63.60	74.90	88.20	104.00
Electric power Hu-shun station	34.00	40.05	47.19	55.59	65.48	77.15	90.88	107.10
Petroleum Northeast Petroleum	34.00	39.88	46.78	54.88	64.36	75.48	88.54	103.70
Lumber Forest industries	33.00	38.61	45.17	52.85	61.83	72.34	84.64	99.00
Chemicals Mukden plant	33.00	38.61	45.18	52.87	61.84	72.37	84.68	99.00
Cereal Mukden flour mill	29.00	34.00	39.90	46.80	54.90	64.60	75.40	—
Construction Fu-shun	33.66	39.95	47.43	56.28	66.82	79.44	92.40	—

Source: Chūgoku Kenkyūjo, *Chūgoku Nenkan 1959* (China Yearbook 1959) (Tokyo: Iwazaki Shoten, 1960); cited in Charles Hoffmann, *The Chinese Worker* (Albany: State University of New York, 1974), p. 101.

Education was central to the elimination of barriers between workers and management. The Great Leap in the cities as in the rural areas pioneered in educational innovation directly related to elevating technical levels. Virtually every major factory initiated technical training programs. Shanghai factories alone established more than 1,200 middle schools and 197 colleges, and many plants reported that 60 to 70 percent of their workers enrolled in part-time courses. In 1958 the emphasis shifted from receiving and mastering Soviet technology and managerial practices to Chinese innovation and the adaptation of industrial management to rapid socialist development.

The leap thus challenged root principles of Soviet industrial practice: under the slogans "politics in command" and "walking on two legs," centralization gave way to radical decentralization, hierarchy and elitism to mass participation. In leadership, planning, and technical innovation, workers contested exclusive and irrational prerogatives of managers and cadres.* The model of the specialized worker or technician, master of a single technique or process, yielded to the ideal of the all-round hand and to the combination of "red and expert" traits, that is, unification of political consciousness and technical skills in both workers and cadres. In the spring of 1958 Mao contrasted Lenin and Stalin to illustrate his concept of a dialectical link between politics and technology:

> Stalin's two slogans are insufficiently dialectical. If "Technology decides everything," what about politics? If "Cadres decide everything," what about the masses? Lenin put it well: "Communism equals the Soviets plus electrification." The Soviets mean politics, and electrification means technology. The union of politics and professional work leads to communism.[38]

---

* 1957 was also the year when the Soviet Union initiated sweeping decentralization measures (the Liberman plan). However, the two approaches were diametrically opposed. Soviet reforms emphasized piece rates, bonuses, individual material incentives, the hierarchy of managers, technicians, and workers. They provided factories wider latitude on condition that they increase profits. China's decentralization stressed the coordinating roles of the region, political mobilization, elimination of hierarchy, and reduction of individual material incentives.

Red and Expert

The "red and expert" ideal requires that revolutionary cadres and working people master higher levels of technology, and managerial and technical personnel practice mass line ideals in the work process. The concept was Mao's response to the demands of the intellectuals in 1956 and 1957 for greater autonomy and privilege and to the tendencies of party leadership to become both divorced from the people and insensitive to the need to master technology. With industrial decentralization and proliferation of economic activity, the Great Leap fostered the combination of red and expert as one approach to overcoming the gap between mental and manual labor. A decade later, during the Great Proletarian Cultural Revolution, the theme would receive increased emphasis. In the course of the modernization drive in 1978 the concept would be redefined for scientists in ways which deprived it of political content by automatically classifying devotion to scientific work as "red."

In the course of the Great Leap workers began to play expanded roles in factory and workshop decision-making, in plan formulation, and in technical innovation. Here as in so many other respects, it revised and extended themes consonant with the mass line approaches of the War of Resistance.

The Great Leap Forward: An Assessment

In 1958 China achieved rapid production gains in virtually every field, followed by a mixed picture in 1959 comprised of sharp decline in agriculture and continued rapid industrial advance.* The years 1960 and 1961 marked the nadir of post-leap economic reverses. In industry, even at the lowest point, critical

---

* The statistical data presented throughout this study are the generally conservative conclusions derived by U.S. government economists from official Chinese data. See Tables 12, 13, 14.

sectors such as steel, oil, coal, electricity, and chemical fertilizer continued to produce at levels substantially above those prior to the leap. The situation was more critical in agriculture. Beginning in 1960, food shortages resulted in serious malnutrition and starvation in some areas. The three-year food shortage was extremely severe. Yet in contrast with comparable natural disasters which in the first half of the twentieth century sent millions of Chinese to their graves and wreaked havoc on the economy, communal institutions and the supporting role of the state made it possible to minimize the damage and restore the economy. Recovery began in 1962 with the first of what the Chinese government has subsequently described as an unbroken succession of good-to-excellent harvests, and the pattern of rapid though uneven growth has continued throughout the last fifteen years.

The leap has been widely regarded in the West as Mao's folly, an example of the heavy price that revolutionary nations invariably pay for "ideologically motivated" policies. Ignoring both the difficult options which China faced in 1958, diverse factors in the subsequent setbacks, and the economic performance since the early 1960s, some have concluded that the experiment cost China a decade of development. How then are we to assess the long-range economic consequences of the pattern which began with rapid growth, followed by sharp decline, then by resumption of significant long-term growth? The preceding analysis has suggested some of the bases for the productive gains of 1958. Most important were the effort to turn labor into capital through the substantial expansion of the workforce; the role of rural people's communes in coordinating large-scale, self-reliant economic activity and facilitating capital construction, industrialization, and technical advance; local initiative at the levels of province, county, factory, and worker; and fine weather. Moreover, with the exception of the last, these gains could be expected to be cumulative as new workers mastered skills, communes and localities learned to coordinate large-scale diverse industrial and agricultural enterprises, and education bore fruit in higher levels of skill.

Nevertheless, the Great Leap gave way to the "three hard years" and bequeathed a controversial legacy. Three factors are essential to understanding the costly economic reverses which began with agriculture in 1959 and in the following three years produced the most severe economic and political crisis China had experienced since 1949.

First, in 1959-1961 China suffered a series of natural disasters brought on by some of the worst weather of the century. Typhoons struck South China and the Northeast, drought crippled substantial parts of the Yellow River basin. Overall, more than 60 percent of the cultivated areas suffered from drought or flood. Natural disaster of this magnitude just a decade earlier would have sent millions to their death. Yet despite severe food shortages, partially alleviated by foreign grain purchases, few died and China neither sought nor received international aid. The large-scale water conservancy carried out between 1957 and 1959 and the ability of the communes to mobilize labor and share income cushioned nature's blow and turned around the depression in a short time.

Second, the deepening rift between China and the Soviet Union, exacerbated by China's choice of an independent, self-reliant development strategy, resulted in the abrupt withdrawal of all Soviet technicians in 1960. The withdrawal halted major projects, many for a decade or more, and delayed others which relied on Soviet technology, blueprints, and advisers. Since virtually the entire modern sector depended on Soviet spare parts and equipment, the withdrawal delivered a severe blow at a moment of economic crisis.

The consequences for the two new major steel centers under Soviet-sponsored construction, at Wuhan and Pao-t'ou, highlight its impact. From 1961 until at least 1965 Chinese reports indicate that the Wuhan mills operated at less then 25 percent of planned capacity. At Pao-t'ou, which blew in its first blast furnace a year ahead of schedule in 1959, construction ground to a complete halt. The first rolling mill was not completed until 1969 and throughout the decade Pao-t'ou's production remained at approximately one-third projected capacity. The withdrawal revealed that, despite impressive progress, China lacked the capacity to independently design and construct large-scale efficient steel facilities. The sharp two-year decline in China's overall industrial production from 1961, after virtually doubling output between 1957 and 1960, testifies to the severe consequences of the Soviet withdrawal.

Against this background of both urban and rural reverses, it is worth recalling the intensity and duration of the Great Depression of the 1930s in the United States and Europe. In the United States, the world's most dynamic industry, trade and finance collapsed for an entire decade. The Roosevelt administration's policies patently failed to break the depression; it took World War II to generate a new economic upsurge. Likewise we note the pervasive, though less dramatic, impact on production and income in every industrial country of the post-1973 world recession before drawing sweeping conclusions about the post-leap reverses.

Nevertheless, while the overall strategy of the leap opened new possibilities for China's socialist development, the leadership must bear responsibility for excesses and errors in implementation. The most important of these were associated with the "communist wind," that is, the belief that the advance to communism was imminent, and that the people, if challenged to assume full initiative, could immediately accomplish any task. Riding the communist wind, some Communists dispensed entirely with the institutions and incentives associated with the period of socialist transition. For example, the short-lived free supply system undermined the structure of incentives developed in earlier cooperatives. Mao himself, architect of the Great Leap and its most articulate spokesperson, in March 1959 analyzed three such excesses:

> The first was the levelling of the poor and the rich brigades, the second was that capital accumulation by the commune was too great, and the commune's demand for labor without compensation was too great, and the third was the "communization" of all kinds of property. . . . As things went on in this way, the communist wind blew up. In certain areas, it actually produced situations in which there was a taking over of other people's labor without compensation.[39]

As in previous peak periods of mobilization—in 1943 at the height of people's war, in 1947 as radicalism reached its peak in the struggle for land, and in the mini-leap in the countryside in 1955-1956—the leadership challenge lay in encouraging activism while at the same time directing it into channels which served the goals both of advanced social relations and higher productivity. The communist wind (encouragement for which Mao bore personal responsibility with the party leadership at central and grassroots levels) carried the leap to extremes which seriously undercut productive advances. In leveling poor and rich units by setting the large commune rather than the team as the unit for income distribution and expanding the free supply system, the more prosperous frequently felt that they were subsidizing by their labor the less diligent. The goal was, of course, to reduce inequality and stimulate collective consciousness. But the practical result of free supply was to eliminate the direct relationship between labor and income. This frequently reduced work motivation. Above all, the transfer of jurisdiction over work and income from the team to larger units eliminated the reinforcement provided by face-to-face relationships of trust and mutuality rooted both in traditional village loyalties and patterns of cooperation that had evolved in the course of the revolution. The enthusiasm of the leap at its peak overrode the problem of labor incentives; but as it faded, the lack of a direct and immediate connection between work and income and the weakening of the fabric of personal relations posed increasing difficulties. The problem of sustaining the drive of a mobilized peasantry remained central.

Capital accumulation of the commune and its demand for unpaid labor proved excessive. As commune capital construction, industry, and services rapidly increased, communes sought both to centralize funds and allocate labor to long-range projects such as irrigation and tree planting. These projects, vitally important for future economic growth, often brought little immediate and visible benefit and in some cases siphoned labor away from agriculture. Carried to extremes, this resulted both in falling individual income and in further erosion of the relationship between work and income; as economic hardships developed this would call into question the viability of the communes and the Great Leap itself. Communization of all kinds of property meant the appropriation not only of pigs and private plots of land but in some instances even pots, pans, and bowls in support of new collective functions such as dining halls and day care centers. In all of these areas communes failed to provide equal value, that is, they essentially appropriated people's labor without compensation.

As the boom year of 1958 gave way to increasing dislocation and economic difficulties in 1959, some of the problems inherent in the practice of the leap produced sharpened conflict, both within the party and among the people. Voices such as Mao's, noting the danger of excesses but affirming the basic soundness of the new institutional order and the all-round gains of the leap, were challenged by party leaders and economic planners distraught at the dangers of disequilibrium and economic collapse. Elements of the debate which erupted in the party in early 1959 recapitulated the two lines of 1955 and 1956. The debate pitted important features of the Soviet model, particularly the emphasis on control, material incentives, and the expanded role of foreign technology, against the leap's emphasis on mobilization, decentralization, self-reliance, and "walking on two legs."

The iron and steel industry was as central to the leap as it had been to the first five-year plan. During the first plan period more than 60 percent of the entire metallurgical budget was allocated to Anshan and the new Wuhan and Pao-t'ou complexes. In 1958 the Chinese sought to break out of the straitjacket imposed by shortages of capital, expertise, machine-building capacity, high-grade iron ore, coal, and rail transportation to greatly accelerate and decentralize iron and steel production. At Mao's initiative a mass mobilization began to expand production by native methods, within an overall strategy of simultaneously accelerating production in large, medium, and small plants, using both native and modern methods.

The small native ("backyard") furnaces which mushroomed throughout the nation in the summer of 1958 formed an essential component of the conception of accelerated industrialization and overcoming the distinction between city and countryside, between worker and peasant, and between industry and agriculture. After just two months' trial experience and with virtually no advance warning or planning, the press reported construction of 30,000 to 50,000 small-scale iron furnaces in July 1958; in September 700,000; in October 1 million.

In 1958 China's steel output topped 11 million tons, more than doubling the previous year's figure. The total included 3 million tons of steel produced by 60 to 100 million peasants in newly built small native furnaces. Yet in November-December 1958, the Central Committee called a halt to the native steel movement, ending the most massive industrialization in human history. By October 1960 just over 3,000 of the 1 million furnaces remained in operation, presumably those operating long before the leap. Perhaps the simplest explanation was provided by the candid *People's Daily* editorial of August 1, 1959: "We must face the problem frankly: Last year's small furnaces could not produce iron." And Mao himself, taking personal responsibility for the operation, acknowledged that "it was a great catastrophe." Central to the failure of the hastily launched indigenous iron movement, though not necessarily to the concept of decentralized iron and steel production, were the following factors:

Quality. Using local ore and primitive furnaces, the quality of the product was frequently so poor as to be useless even for producing cheap consumer goods and tools for local use.

Labor shortage. The deflection of a substantial part of the male workforce from agriculture to steel making at the height of the summer harvest produced a severe agricultural labor shortage. In some areas crops were left rotting unharvested in the fields.

Resource depletion. In the drive to increase the *quantity* of iron and steel, wanton waste of resources occurred, including the destruction of forests for fuel in cases where coal was lacking, with subsequent adverse effects on agriculture, such as flooding. In addition, local mines were often ravaged without regard to preparing them for optimum future utilization.

Exorbitant costs. Per-unit cost of local iron and steel, even ignoring quality differentials, proved many times higher than production costs in modern mills, the effectiveness of which was undercut by the backyard steel movement.

The indigenous steel campaign was quietly abandoned in the fall of 1958, but the leap in iron and steel nevertheless continued in new form. The dual emphasis was on simultaneous rapid expansion of large and medium-size modern enterprises favored during the first plan period together with hundreds of small, modern blast furnaces tapping local resources and dispersed throughout the nation. M. Gardner Clark, who has provided a close study of the industry, concludes:

October 1958 marks the high point of economic irrationality [as] the Chinese acted as though all of the resources needed to produce iron and steel were practically free goods, as though they were living in a world where economic and technical choices no longer had to be made, as though they could do everything at once.[40]

For example, of sixty new medium and large plants, ranging in size from 100,000 to 3 million tons, constructed without Soviet aid during the leap (capacity 34 million tons of pig iron, 30 million tons of steel—more than was then being produced by any country in the world except the United States and the Soviet Union), none ever approached designed capacity. By 1961 nearly all had ceased to function, along with hundreds of small, modern blast furnaces.

China dramatically expanded iron and steel production in the years 1958-1960, and even at the lowest point in subsequent years output figures remained well above earlier peaks. But the costs included a sharp deterioration in quality, an immense waste of resources, a sharp rise in unit cost, the disruption of agriculture, and large-scale transportation bottlenecks. In the end, rather than contributing to the viability of the communes, the overall effect of the vast experiment in decentralized steel production must have demoralized many peasants, weakened the rural collective base, and undermined the overall premises of the leap itself among the leadership and the people. The indigenous steel movement addressed genuine needs of China's 500 million peasants and provided millions with their first experience with industrial technique. The campaign nevertheless represents perhaps the most vivid example of how a movement, borne aloft by the communist wind and ignoring technical factors, can go awry.

However, while recognizing the costly failure of the indigenous steel and other programs there is a more important point, and that is the long-range possibilities revealed by numerous reforms during the leap and consolidated on a firm basis during subsequent decades. Rural industrialization, where it took effective root—and in 1958 it often did in the production of cement, bricks, fertilizer, tools, and food processing—marked a quantum step toward realizing the vision of eliminating the urban-rural gap and bringing prosperity and technological advance to the countryside. Here, as in so many aspects of the leap, the soundness of the essential strategy would be borne out by subsequent developments, particularly those of the Cultural Revolution.

The Great Leap, beginning with the upsurge of 1955-1956, was the third great period of revolutionary transformation in China's advance toward an independent strategy of socialist development, following and building on people's war and land revolution. This time mobilization included both peasantry and proletariat, city and countryside.

The Great Leap produced important and lasting gains in the realms of production relations and consciousness. It gave rise to a major institution, the rural people's commune, which remains China's most important institutional contribution to socialist development. But it also gave rise to excesses and errors—Mao compared them to one finger out of ten—and it led to sharp conflict in the party and among the people, with consequences to be considered below.

Viewed from the perspective of the emergence of a distinctive Chinese road to socialist development, the leap broke with the logic of urban-industrial–dominated growth. It revealed the potential of organized rural communities to effectively utilize the rural surplus through expansion of industry as well as agriculture. No longer would it be possible to justify a development strategy at the expense of the countryside, or one which failed to utilize China's abundant labor power to overcome deficiencies in capital and technology. The Great Leap initiated a national experiment in community-based mobilization of human and material resources in the service not only of economic advance but of social, cultural, and political progress. It also incorporated an educational and intellectual revolution to overcome technological and psychological barriers to challenging the "three great differences" between city and countryside, worker and peasant, and mental and manual labor as entire communities sought to discover within themselves the initiative and resources for advance. Finally, it posed challenges to the structure of existing inequalities of farm and factory, of power, rank, access to education, and income. The overriding significance of the leap lies in opening new possibilities in the search for equality, participation, self-reliance, and socialist development which would define tasks for the coming decades.

VI. The Aftermath of the Great Leap Forward
and the Struggle Between the Socialist and Capitalist Roads, 1960–1965

In the historical period of socialism, there are still classes, class contradictions and class struggle, there is the struggle between the socialist and the capitalist road, and there is the danger of capitalist restoration. . . . We must conduct socialist education. We must correctly understand and handle class contradictions between ourselves and the enemy from those among the people and handle them correctly. Otherwise a socialist country like ours will turn into its opposite and degenerate, and a capitalist restoration will take place.

Tenth Plenum, Eighth Central Committee, 1962

Going forward to communism means moving towards the abolition of all classes and class differences. A communist society which preserves any classes at all, let alone exploiting classes, is inconceivable. Yet Khrushchev is fostering a new bourgeoisie, restoring and extending the system of exploitation and accelerating the class polarization in the Soviet Union. A privileged bourgeois stratum opposed to the Soviet people now occupies the ruling position in the party and government and in the economic, cultural, and other departments. Can one find an iota of communism in all this?

"On Khrushchev's Phony Communism,"
People's Daily and *Red Flag*, 1964

The Great Leap Forward opened the way to a distinctive Chinese path to socialist development. It also reaped a harvest of division within society in general and the party leadership in particular. In the summer of 1959 Mao, on the defensive, withdrew from day-to-day involvement in national affairs and the reconstituted party and state hierarchy sought to restore order and prosperity as China plunged into the gravest crisis period since liberation. Beginning with economic reverses, the crisis rapidly extended to leadership conflict, bitter antagonism between China and the Soviet Union, and widespread demoralization among the people, particularly the peasantry.

The countryside provided the clearest warning signals. By the early 1960s, with the contraction of the rural economy and nation-wide grain shortage, many innovations of the leap had been eliminated, including most part-time schools, communal dining halls and nurseries, and the majority of the new factories and mines. Peasant participation in water control, afforestation, and land improvement projects fell to a fraction of pre-leap levels. Most ominous was the reduction by many peasants of labor commitment to the collective economy to concentrate more of their energies on private production. The commune continued to provide the basic institutional framework for rural development, but most of its authority passed to the brigade and team levels and some communes retained little power and controlled few resources. At this time many communes expanded private plots for family cultivation and even established individual household production quotas to replace cooperative farming. And urban communes, propagated briefly in 1960, disappeared entirely in most cities within a year.

In the face of economic and political crisis, many among both leadership and people sought protection in familiar prerevolutionary defense mechanisms, ranging from bureaucratic administrative methods to renewed emphasis on the individual economy. And with the "three hard years" came the revival of the black market and speculation, superstitious practices, and such customs as bridal purchase, which had been curbed during the preceding period of rapid social change.

Three developments during the years 1962–1965 are central to understanding the subsequent course of the Chinese revolution. First, in 1962 the party initiated a socialist education movement to heighten peasant appreciation of socialism, reverse the trend toward individual economy, and, above all, rectify bureaucratic tendencies in the leadership and corruption among local cadres.

Second, from the late 1950s, and particularly during the early 1960s, Mao was preoccupied with the analysis and critique of the domestic and international policy of the Soviet Union, that is, with the reversal of the advance to higher stages of socialism and the problem of capitalist restoration. In contrast with and in reaction to the Soviet leadership, which had declared a state of the whole people and the end of class struggle, in November 1962 the Tenth Plenum of the Chinese Communist Party affirmed that class struggle continues throughout the protracted period of socialist transition. It also formally reversed the economic priorities of the first five-year plan, placing agriculture first, followed by light industry and heavy industry. Henceforth China would emphasize the contribution of industry to the countryside as in accelerated tractor and fertilizer production, rural electrification, and supply of consumer goods.

Third, in 1964 Mao personally issued the calls, "In agriculture learn from Tachai" and "In industry learn from Tach'ing," emphasizing independent, self-reliant socialist development. The Tachai brigade and the Tach'ing oil fields extended the vision of the leap, providing symbols of coordinated human activity triumphing over natural adversity and achieving productivity gains independent of state support or foreign technology.

We now know that the highest levels of the party leadership were sharply divided over all three of these policies, and particularly over the socialist education movement in the countryside. Mao advocated peasant mobilization to overcome bureaucratic and individualistic tendencies in the party and society that were undermining the communes. The vast majority of the peasants, especially the poor and lower-middle peasants, as well as the overwhelming number of cadres, Mao held, remained committed to cooperation. Their future depended on it. Given proper leadership, they would resume the advance temporarily reversed during the three hard years and in the process contribute to the revitalization of the party.

Liu Shao-ch'i, who directed the party organization at this time, gave priority to social stability and technological change as prerequisites for economic recovery. Fresh from the post-leap reverses, he opposed a large-scale political mobilization which threatened to undermine the authority of the party and which might set back economic recovery. Moreover, perceiving both the peasant masses and a substantial part of the local leadership as basically unreliable allies in furthering socialism, Liu, with the support of much of the party leadership, proposed to rely heavily on outside work teams to propagate socialist ideas and, where necessary, replace local leadership. Where Mao saw a central task as rectification of the party *at all levels*, Liu sought to rectify the peasants and grassroots leadership. Work teams of urban intellectuals and party activists had played important roles in supporting and coordinating peasant activism during the land revolution, and again during the Great Leap. In the socialist education movement, however, charged with rooting out corrupt leadership, their primary functions proved to be discipline and control, in effect reinforcing higher authority rather than mobilizing the peasantry. In essence, mass line leadership clashed with a bureaucratic top-down approach to social change, and Mao's basically optimistic perspective on the revolutionary role of the peasantry came up against the pessimistic assessment of Liu and the party bureaucracy. The socialist education movement, sharply restricted by the party leadership, never developed into a major mobilization.

Polarization within the leadership was intensified by other critical issues of the period. In the early 1960s, Mao and his closest allies, preoccupied with the question of revisionism in China and abroad, moved toward rupture in relations with the Soviet Union on the basis of the conclusion that capitalist restoration had led the Soviets to abandon socialist domestic and international policies. Liu and other military leaders, however, continued efforts to resolve conflicts with the Soviet Union. The issues were far from simple. Mao's opponents not only hoped to restore economic and political ties with the Soviet Union; in 1965 they also sought unity in the socialist camp to block United States aggression in Vietnam, a war which threatened to engulf China as had the Korean War a decade earlier. Thus, questions of an independent domestic development strategy were intertwined with issues of unity with the socialist countries, particularly with respect to the Vietnam War.

By January 1965, having analyzed capitalist restoration in the Soviet Union and the bitter post-leap struggle within the Chinese party, Mao concluded that the Chinese Revolution was in jeopardy and the enemy were those in authority in the party leadership taking the capitalist road. The Great Proletarian Cultural Revolution was about to begin.

VII. The Great Proletarian
Cultural Revolution, 1966–1976

Where do correct ideas come from? Do they drop from the skies? No. Are they innate in the mind? No. They come from social practice, and from it alone; they come from three kinds of social practice, the struggle for production, the class struggle and scientific experiment. It is man's social being that determines his thinking. Once the correct ideas characteristic of the advanced class are grasped by the masses, these ideas turn into a material force which changes society and changes the world.

The Central Committee of the
Chinese Communist Party, 1963

Although the bourgeoisie has been overthrown, it is still trying to use the old ideas, culture, customs, and habits of the exploiting classes to corrupt the masses, capture their minds and endeavor to stage a comeback. . . . The aim of the Great Proletarian Cultural Revolution is to revolutionize people's ideology and as a consequence to achieve greater, faster, better, and more economical results in all fields of work. . . . The Great Proletarian Cultural Revolution is a powerful motive force for the development of the social productive forces in our country.

The Central Committee of the
Chinese Communist Party, 1966

You are making the socialist revolution, and yet don't know where the bourgeoisie is. It is right in the Communist Party—those in power taking the capitalist road.

Mao Tsetung, early 1970s

In the summer of 1966, in a series of whirlwind moves, Mao Tsetung returned to the center of the Chinese political stage to inaugurate a new phase of the uninterrupted revolution. Having demonstrated fitness and determination with his much publicized swim in the Yangtse River in July, the next month Mao confronted the Central Committee's Eleventh Plenum with his big character poster, "Bombard the Headquarters," and then (barely) won party support for launching the Great Proletarian Cultural Revolution. In the coming weeks Mao threw his support behind newly formed red guard organizations of revolutionary youth. At T'ien An Men Square he reviewed as many as 11 million red guards, the shock troops of the movement, many of whom came to Peking from across the land. The mass movement for the creation of a proletarian culture, society, and politics was in full swing.

To understand its origins and import we must recall the intense conflict within the party in the post-leap period and the questions it posed. Was only the Soviet Union subject to capitalist restoration? What was to prevent China from succumbing to the logic of revolutionary degeneration leading to bureaucratic retrenchment, the formation of a new elite class, and the abandonment in mid-passage of socialist institutions and ideals? The retreat from cooperation toward individual cultivation in many areas during the early sixties called into question the viability of the communes. Mao gave the problem its most startling formulation in a 1963 comment, publicly quoted after the outbreak of the Cultural Revolution, in which he warned of the danger of the Communist Party becoming "a revisionist party or a fascist party," with the result that "the whole of China would change its color." The conclusion that significant elements within the party had already degenerated, including some at its highest levels of leadership, led Mao to initiate the full-scale attack to purify and reform the party on the basis of the mass line, and to train a generation of revolutionary successors in the only way possible, by making revolution. The intensity and duration of the movement suggests the depths of conflict in Chinese society between revolutionary ideals and political practice, and the immense difficulty for any society to resist tendencies toward routinization and consolidation of elite privilege.

If the danger lurked in capitalist restoration, where was the bourgeois enemy and what was the appropriate solution consistent with the attainment of higher levels of socialist development? Although the movement began with an attack on the "four olds"—ideas, culture, customs, and habits—and particularly remnants of the hierarchical and repressive ideas prevalent in the old society, as it unfolded it became clear that the real problem centered on a *new* bourgeoisie, a privileged managerial and cadre elite with its power base in the party and the state. Its commitment to consolidating the gains of previous revolutions (and its own position) blocked those who sought to continue the revolution to eliminate remaining inequalities and

overcome the three great differences in order to achieve higher
levels of socialism and development.

The problem of bureaucratic and elitist leadership in varying
forms confronts every modern society. In China, however, with
the weight of several thousand years of bureaucratic and manda-
rin rule, reinforced in part by centralist and vanguard tendencies
of the Soviet heritage, and with the concentration of economic
and political power in the hands of the party and the state, the
problem assumes formidable proportions. The revolutionary
experience of nearly half a century suggested that social progress resided in the continuing movement of working people to
expand their collective power over the workplace and outward
to every nook and cranny of society. In Mao's view, by 1966
the principal obstacle to this course lay in elements within the
party itself. It would have to be attacked and reformed by the
people. The mass line provided a method for testing and renew-
ing the revolutionary commitment of leadership, for injecting
new energies into the political process, and for training revolutionary successors from among the generation of youth that had
personally experienced neither the oppression of foreign invasion and landlord rule in the old society nor the revolution
which had given birth to the new society.

Throughout his revolutionary career Mao had frequently
looked for allies outside the party, particularly to the peasant
masses, as in the socialist upsurge of 1955, but also to the
intellectuals, as in the Hundred Flowers Movement of 1957. In
1965 he sought allies among revolutionary intellectuals, youth,
and the army, under the command of Lin Piao. And, in new and
striking ways, he drew on his enormous personal prestige to
mobilize the people when the party dragged its feet. Since the
early 1960s Lin Piao had led the army on a course which
emphasized the mass line and the mobilization politics associated with Mao's thought at a time when very different tendencies held sway within the party. It was Lin who compiled
the Little Red Book of quotations from Mao's works which
circulated in the hundreds of millions of copies and made
possible the dissemination of Mao's thought on a vast scale. Yet
in the hands of book-waving youth it also became a symbol of
the Mao cult, which flourished during the Cultural Revolution

and represents the antithesis of the best in Mao's revolutionary thought and practice.

In 1965 and 1966 Yao Wen-yuan and other intellectual protégés of Mao fired the opening shots in the Cultural Revolution in the form of exposés of thinly veiled satires of Mao and the Great Leap published in the early sixties. On June 1, 1965, the newly installed editors of the *People's Daily*, who would play a leading role in the movement, hailed Mao's call for "sweeping away a horde of monsters that have entrenched themselves in ideological and cultural positions. With the tremendous impetuous force of a raging storm, they have smashed the shackles imposed on their minds by the exploiting classes for so long in the past, routing the bourgeois 'specialists,' 'authorities,' and 'venerable masters' and sweeping every bit of their prestige into the dust."[41] In the course of three tumultuous years, the cultural movement penetrated every institution, every factory, commune, school, and party and mass organization. It demanded the re-examination of every mode of operation, measured the conduct and values of individuals against the standards of the mass line and socialism, and produced challenges and new institutional responses to leadership and bureaucracy. Yet as the power struggle in the party and throughout the society intensified, it also carried to unprecedented levels a personal cult of Mao, gave rise to a politics of demagoguery and hero worship, created an environment in which debate and political struggle repeatedly deteriorated into violence, and left a legacy of suspicion and conflict which a decade failed to heal.

"The Sixteen Points," the Central Committee's August 8, 1966 directive, provided the principal guidelines for the movement, although it rapidly became apparent that no directive and no leader could contain the forces which erupted in Chinese society at this time. The directive called on revolutionary youth to become "courageous and daring pathbreakers" in criticizing and overturning bourgeois remnants in society. The methods involved relying on the revolutionary principles embodied in Mao's thought and the mass line, with the people themselves directly participating in re-examining and reshaping leadership, values, and socialist institutions. The goal of criticism was transformation, the goal of struggle, new higher forms of unity based on the ability to successfully resolve contradictions, all (or nearly all) of which were among the people.

Article 14 of the directive linked the cultural and economic revolutions, stating that "the Great Proletarian Cultural Revolution is a powerful motive force for the development of the social productive forces in our country." As in the Great Leap Forward, it held, the key lay in mobilizing working people at all levels to achieve rapid economic and technical advance.

In the initial phases of the movement, the primary target was "capitalist roaders" in the party; the goal was the transformation of consciousness and popular "seizure of power" to continue the revolution. Yet this goal proved extraordinarily elusive. In earlier struggles against Japanese invaders, landlords, and capitalists, the target was relatively clear. Moreover, the party had always played an important coordinating and leadership role. Virtually its entire leading core, which crystallized around Mao following the Long March in 1935, had traversed the course from people's war through the new democracy and early stages of socialist transition culminating in the Great Leap. This leadership unity, based on successful mediation of sometimes intense differences at the highest levels, fractured in the postleap reverses. But the depths of the divisions became clear only during the Cultural Revolution, with the disgrace and dismissal in the course of a decade of most of the top and second echelon levels of party, state, and military leadership—with the exceptions of Mao and Chou En-lai. The party's paralysis, its inability to provide coherent national leadership during three years of frontal attack and internal division, and Mao's strategy of encouraging grassroots activism, meant that the frequently sectarian movements of the period would take shape with little direction except occasional communiques from Chairman Mao and the newly formed ad hoc Cultural Revolution Group, whose authority essentially replaced that of the Central Committee and the state from the summer of 1966 to early 1968.

Thus the party, which had earlier developed a rigorous empirical class analysis of rural society as the basis for the land revolution, and of the bourgeoisie for the socialist transformation of industry, failed to produce an effective analysis of the classes in society during and after the Cultural Revolution. And, from the summer of 1966, much of the initiative and driving force of the movement would spring from outside the party and in opposition to it.

Four sequential but overlapping stages brought new participants and leading forces to the fore. First, in 1965 and early 1966 revolutionary intellectuals initiated the movement in cultural and university circles. Reacting against the persistence of traditional and bourgeois values and forms in the arts and education, they prepared public opinion for the subsequent mass movement. Then, in the summer of 1966, university and middle school students, organized as red guards and sensitive to the gap between revolutionary ideals and an educational system that trained specialists divorced from production and political engagement and oriented toward urban industry, launched the attack on the "four olds" and against capitalist roaders within the party, the state, and the schools. Having rebelled in the name of the party's revolutionary ideals and against bureaucratic and elitist tendencies in society, the red guard youth movement in many instances gave rise to extreme forms of factionalism, Mao worship, and physical violence. Third, in late 1966 and 1967, workers seized control of factories and major cities and proceeded to transform the political institutions at every level on the basis of the characteristic new institution of the Cultural Revolution, the revolutionary committees. Finally, the army, which played an important role throughout the entire movement, in 1967 intervened directly to avert civil war and restore order on the basis of the new revolutionary committees. In the process, it extended its own authority throughout the political system on a scale not witnessed since the early 1950s.

The discussion of the Cultural Revolution which follows focuses on two major issues: (1) the politics of socialist transition reflected in issues of mass line and bureaucracy and culminating in the formation of revolutionary committees; and (2) the political economy of socialist transition, particularly the changing relationships between revolution and production, city and countryside, workers and peasants, and mental and manual labor. Shanghai, Tachai, and Tach'ing illustrate three critical dimensions of the movement with wide ramifications for socialist development in the city and countryside.

The Shanghai Working Class, the Commune,
and the Formation of Revolutionary Committees

In late 1966 and early 1967 in a number of cities the working class emerged onto the national political stage as a powerful, disciplined revolutionary force in the attack on bureaucratism and the reshaping of factory and municipal politics. Shanghai, China's largest, most industrialized, and most cosmopolitan city, initiated the Cultural Revolution in the ranks of the intellectuals and then led the political struggles of the working class. Throughout the preceding decade, working-class struggles centered on the control of the factories had given rise to a militant and experienced core of activists. In 1966 the workers extended their political sphere from the factories to the struggle against the Shanghai party leadership.

By the fall of 1966 political lines had hardened as Shanghai worker militants demanded the overthrow of the city's two top officials, Ch'en Pei-hsien, secretary of the party's East China Bureau, and Mayor Ts'ao Ti-ch'iu. In November hundreds of militant worker groups coalesced and established a city-wide Headquarters of the Revolutionary Revolt of Shanghai Workers. Reduced to essentials, the issue was direct power exercised by the working class versus continued party and bureaucratic control of the factories and the city.

The militants' unity resided in commitment to a vision of equality, participation, and worker power. Yet important cleavages divided the workers, particularly more conservative older workers and young militants, and regular state employees and contract or day laborers (the most privileged and the most disadvantaged sections of the proletariat). Building on reserves of support and patronage, particularly among older workers grateful for its role in improving their livelihood, and taking advantage of divisions in the rebel camp, in November the party refused official recognition and spurned the Headquarters' demand to organize freely in factories.

Up to this point the dynamics of the struggle derived from the initiative of conflicting Shanghai forces. When Shanghai authorities rejected their demands, workers seized a train bound for Peking to carry their case to the highest levels, only to have it halted by the authorities at Anting. Negotiations as well as directives from Peking failed to break a three-day seige. At that point the Anting Incident brought the struggle for Shanghai to the center of national politics. The Cultural Revolution Group dispatched one of its members, Chang Ch'un-ch'iao, the former deputy secretary and propaganda head of the Shanghai party committee, to resolve the issues. When Chang endorsed the worker demands legitimizing the Headquarters, it was the beginning of the end for the Shanghai party leadership. Yet by the end of the year, while the Headquarters had grown in strength, it was outnumbered by a new coalition, the scarlet guards, claiming 800,000 workers and later alleged to have been covertly organized by the party authorities to stem the revolt. With Shanghai in turmoil, worker demands proliferated and large-scale confrontation between the two coalitions repeatedly ended in violence. At this critical juncture the Shanghai party committee, fighting for its life, employed two tactics to win support: one was buying off the worker opposition with higher wages and illegal cash payments; the other was to launch a strike which closed major plants and immobilized the railroads and the docks.

On January 5, 1967, the Workers' Headquarters issued a call to the people of Shanghai for unity and the restoration of the city's paralyzed production and services. The next day a televised rally of more than 1 million people brought down the party committee and government. Secretary Ch'en, Mayor Ts'ao, and the entire party standing committee made public confessions and were stripped of their positions. Shanghai was now in rebel hands, and the new government they formed reflected in the purest form the aspirations of the militant worker movement. The city's new provisional leading body, the Fighting Line Command, consisted of fifty representatives nominated by the Workers' Headquarters from factories, government offices, and universities. Attempting to break with the bureaucratic practice of its predecessor, leadership emphasized on-the-spot investigation and solution to problems, that is, the antithesis of bureaucratic practice. With rebel workers frequently joined by students working around the clock, the new government quickly broke the strike, restored municipal services, and extended worker control in the factories.

The historical model of the Shanghai workers was the Paris Commune. And indeed, in the fiercely antibureaucratic and democratic ideals which inspired the January storm we find echoes of the earlier commune. Workers in one factory described their new executive committee as "a political committee, production committee, and workers' committee self-consciously organized by the masses. . . . It is a committee born of the full election system of the Paris Commune."[42]

Yet it was one thing to overthrow the Shanghai party committee, another to unify hundreds of rebel groups, and quite another to devise and implement nonbureaucratic means to effectively govern a city of 12 million which was the nerve center of the complex Chinese economy. Following the fall of the party committee and the end of the strike, rebel unity disintegrated and sharp factional struggles re-emerged. On February 5, after a month of intense efforts to forge unity, the Shanghai people's commune was inaugurated. With Chang Ch'un-ch'iao as its first secretary the organization rested on a "three-in-one alliance" of rebel organizations, the People's Liberation Army, and leading cadres. The commune provisionally replaced the Shanghai people's council and the party as the city's leading body, pending city-wide elections. Yet organizations representing nearly half the city's rebels refused to participate and continued to challenge the new leadership.

Like its predecessors in Paris in the 1870s and the city of Canton in the 1920s, the commune proved short-lived. In the end Mao himself, who had first championed the Paris Commune model, drew back from its radical implications. Having pondered the violence and the factional strife generated in the Cultural Revolution and the difficulty in attaining broad unity, Mao posed the dilemma: "If everything were changed into the commune, then what about the party? . . . There must be a nucleus, no matter what we call it. . . . The commune must have a party."[43]

In early 1967, as Mao moved vigorously to end the violence and factionalism and restore unity based on seizures of power at every level throughout the country, the national model proposed was not Shanghai's commune but the much more moderate revolutionary committee form adopted in Heilungkiang province. There the highest leadership, vested in a five-member committee, included not only the former first secretary of the party but the commander and vice commander of the PLA garrison and two red guard leaders. The message was clear: the process had begun of rebuilding the party, a revitalized party, as the nucleus of the new revolutionary committees. Revolutionary committees rather than the commune eventually provided the institution for leadership at every level of administration and in every commune, factory, school, and office, not by replacing the party but as a popular vehicle through which a reconstituted party leadership could exercise power. At this time Chou En-lai employed all his powers of persuasion (and the authority of Mao's decision) to bring together warring red guard factions with elements of the leadership they had been attacking to forge unity in revolutionary committees based on the Heilungkiang model. As he explained to conflicting red guard activists:

> Revolutionary committees are newborn organs of power. The power, seized from the hands of bourgeois power-holders, is placed in the hands of proletarian revolutionaries. . . . Combat selfishness includes the closing of ranks between two organizations. Contradictions between revolutionary mass organizations are contradictions among the people and should be solved by means of unity-criticism–unity. . . . The majority faction should welcome the minority faction back into the fold . . . don't pay off old scores any more.[44]

Revolutionary committees in the course of the next year of factionalism and near civil war eventually established leadership at every level throughout the country. Party and administrative cadres served beside the activists of the Cultural Revolution, although not always, to be sure, in harmony. In most areas the PLA played the role of midwife to the new organizations that sought to bring together and assure unity—or at least peaceful coexistence—among rivals who had fought unremittingly throughout the preceding year. The revolutionary committees typically included three-in-one combinations uniting former cadres, rebels, and the PLA. Revolutionary committees contributed to the democratization of the political process and an expansion of the political power and supervisory role of working people at all levels in factories, government offices, offices, and schools.

Revolutionary committees throughout China varied greatly in

their composition, function, and mode of operation. Their salient features, however, typically include the following:

Selection of three-in-one leadership combinations. Selection by direct election or, more frequently, by extensive consultative processes to insure representativeness. Factory three-in-one combinations, for example, frequently included revolutionary worker activists, former cadres, and technicians, with an effort made as well to include representatives of old, middle-aged, and young men and women workers. Where deeply entrenched factions defied unity, PLA representatives often played a leading role in the new leadership as part of the three-in-one combination.

Leadership by a rejuvenated party subject to popular participation and control. As the revolutionary committees developed, the reconstructed party played an increasingly powerful leadership role, and eventually the dominant role. At the same time, through expanded participation, including "open door rectification," that is, mass criticism of government and party, emphasis was placed on the supervisory role of the people and the need for responsive government.

Integration of leadership and production. Worker or commune members of revolutionary committees continued in most cases to hold their factory jobs and received no additional pay for their leadership responsibilities. Activists were to remain workers with firm roots in the problems of working life and in close contact with fellow workers. The sharp (but temporary) reduction of bureaucracy which accompanied the Cultural Revolution reinforced this trend.

At the start of the Cultural Revolution, Mao and the Sixteen Articles had affirmed that 95 percent of the cadres were basically good, that is, they continued to stand on the side of the revolution. Yet in the urban areas in 1966 and 1967, leadership at virtually every level of state and party was criticized and overthrown. With the restoration of the party in 1968 the vast majority of leaders, including those savagely criticized as "capitalist roaders" shortly before, returned to political activity. From 1968, when the movement entered a period of consolidation, the pendulum swung sharply against the most militant leadership of the Cultural Revolution. As they sought to extend the struggle they found themselves denounced as "ultra-left." In

1968 much of the leadership of the Cultural Revolution Group was disgraced, and the group itself shortly disbanded, although the purge of its most powerful figures—Lin Piao, Ch'en Po-ta, Chiang Ch'ing, and Chang Ch'un-ch'iao—remained in the future.

Nevertheless, in important but less dramatic ways, central goals and priorities of the Cultural Revolution continued to penetrate and reshape life in city and countryside. One approach to understanding these changes at the grassroots level is to consider the two national models widely propagated for emulation during and since the Cultural Revolution: Tachai in agriculture and Tach'ing in industry. These are not, of course, "typical" of the experience of commune members and factory workers. As national pacesetters each had highly distinctive traits. Yet thousands of units throughout China have sought to apply the spirit and adapt elements of the practice of these and comparable models to the concrete conditions of their own commune, factory, workshop, or school in order to "grasp revolution, promote production." Analysis of these two models clarifies important aspects of the effort to build industry, agriculture, city, and countryside along socialist lines appropriate to Chinese conditions.

The Tachai Model and the Great Proletarian Cultural Revolution in the Countryside

The Tachai Brigade is a small village with only eighty-eight households and in 1974, 440 people, farming 56.7 hectares of land in the T'aihang Mountains of North China's Shansi province. Spanning seven gullies and the intermediate ridges, it is the symbol par excellence of a mobilized community, starting with little more than bare hands and the collective spirit of moving mountains, striving to conquer nature, eliminate famine, ensure basic security, and open broad new vistas for its citizens. Since 1964 Tachai has been the standard bearer of Chinese agriculture as the embodiment of Mao's proposition that "the masses have boundless creative power. They can organize themselves and concentrate on places and branches of work where they can give full play to their energy; they can concentrate on production in breadth and depth and create more and more undertakings for their own well-being."

Our concern here is with the forms of human solidarity which Tachai devised during a quarter of a century of painstaking labor to carve homes and fields out of the mountains, to rebuild virtually from scratch following destruction by raging floods, and to become a pacesetter in achieving high yields and creating advanced socialist forms of cooperative labor and income distribution.

Tachai's experience is unique, but it also mirrors aspects of the protracted struggle over rural policy. Beginning in the early 1950s when its leader Ch'en Yung-kuei organized an advanced cooperative over the objection of higher leadership which criticized his plan as "adventurist" and sought to reverse it, through the dark period of the socialist education movement, when the brigade fought attempts by outside work teams to overturn its leadership, to the present, it has been in the throes of the struggle to define appropriate collective modes for socialist development and technological change.

In the initial phases of its development, by full mobilization of labor, above all by turning the desolate idle winter months into periods of productive capital construction, Tachai solved two basic problems of the natural environment: land (too little, too scattered, too steep, too barren) and water (too little most of the year, but with periods of flash floods and severe erosion). The people of Tachai *created* the land out of the crags and gullies, opening new areas and leveling and merging old plots to form plains sufficiently large and level to ensure high and stable yields and to permit mechanization. Tachai solved its water problem through construction of a four-mile canal to the village, by building water storage facilities against prolonged drought and dams which solved the problem of flash floods. Tachai's refusal to accept state aid in 1963 when flood swept away land, crops, houses, everything, symbolized the possibilities for self-reliant cooperative development. In a series of innovations, the most important being devising new principles for construction of terraces, the community applied native skills, ingenuity, and local materials to technical innovation. And in the diversification of local industry, transport, animal husbandry, and forestry, Tachai suggested the rich possibilities of overall development of the rural economy. For example, the

Tachai commune, of which the brigade is a part, manages seven enterprises, including an agricultural implements workshop, an aluminite plant, a coal pit, and a motorized transport team. By 1973 Tachai Brigade's total grain production reportedly surpassed 385 tons, with yields exceeding 7 tons per hectare in four consecutive years. While Tachai's production record is unusual for communities operating under such adverse conditions (it is worth recalling that fully one-third of China's arable land and rural population is in mountainous areas), others, particularly suburban communes and those in the fertile southern and central rice belts, have much higher income and grain yields two to three times that of Tachai. Tachai's accomplishment is the steady expansion of productivity and income for individual, collective, and state, in ways which reinforce communal bonds and values of cooperation.

Tachai's remuneration system, perfected during the Cultural Revolution, exemplifies unusually advanced forms of socialist relations. Thus, while it has been held up as a model for the future, the leadership has warned other communes of the danger of mechanical copying. Four principles are central to income distribution in Tachai: (1) ensuring the welfare of the state, the collective, and the individual; (2) simplicity of implementation; (3) mass participation in decisions; and (4) implementation of the socialist principle, "to each according to one's work," coupled with progressive restriction of income inequalities.

The annual brigade meeting of the entire membership assesses the contribution and need of each individual, each family, the collective, and the nation, using the method of "self-report and public appraisal." Each member is evaluated on the basis of attitude (politics), skill, and work output, and a work point figure is then set on a scale of one to eleven points. Income is calculated by multiplying the work point figure by the number of days worked. For example, a worker with a 10-point rating who worked 320 days would earn 3,200 work points. Dividing total brigade work points into overall income, after subtracting tax, accumulation, and welfare fund deductions, gives the value of 1 work point and the basis for calculating income. In the Tachai Brigade per capita income rose from 23 yuan in 1953 to

123 yuan in 1965 and 180 yuan in 1973. The brigade simultaneously allocates progressively larger sums (24 percent in 1973) for capital construction and mechanization. In 1967 the value of the labor day in the entire commune was 1.15 yuan (having more than doubled from .52 yuan in 1966), with the range between poorer and more prosperous brigades extending from .9 to 1.5 yuan. The principle of self-reliance, taking the team (in most cases) or, as in Tachai, the brigade, as the accounting unit, perpetuates such income inequalities between neighboring units. But as the collective economy of the brigade and commune grow, the basis is laid for raising the accounting unit to the brigade and eventually the commune and reducing intracommunal inequities without significantly reducing the income and production incentives of the more advanced teams or brigades, that is, without impairing the productive enthusiasm of the pacesetters.*

Distribution on the basis of work points is only one aspect of the system. The brigade also guarantees the grain needs of each household. Every family draws grain from brigade reserves as required throughout the year with the value subtracted from disposable income at year end. The brigade welfare fund subsidizes any labor-short or otherwise handicapped family which earns less than the value of its grain allotment. The Tachai community—not the state—thus provides the most important subsistence guarantees, eliminating the fear of starvation on the basis of community self-reliance. What Tachai (and many others) are doing to ensure the livelihood of all at the level of brigade or team anticipates eventual implementation of communist principles of distribution according to need. "Perhaps," Mao hypothesized, "when the principal material goods can be adequately supplied we can begin to carry out such distribution

---

* This goal of raising the unit of work and distribution to the brigade, commune, and eventually the whole people, implicit in the original commune concept and since repeatedly reaffirmed by the leadership, is seen as central to the transition to communism, and it is without question essential both to overcoming inequality between units and ending commodity production. Yet in the last two decades, powerful pressures have preserved the lowest level, the team, as the main unit of account, in part (at least under present conditions) because it best reinforces bonds of human solidarity and effective face-to-face working and community relations.

with those goods, extending the practice to other goods on the basis of further development of the productive forces."*

The Tachai system reduces, though does not eliminate, differences in income, while ensuring the primacy of collective over individual work incentives. Unlike most other units, which tally not only days but hours worked, specific jobs performed, and in some cases performance at each task, Tachai's simplified system requires recording only the number of days worked. This system, which reduces the need for supervision and bookkeeping, rests on high levels of consciousness of the people. In one important area, however, Tachai lags behind many other units. Despite the impressive economic contribution of Tachai women, and the fact that Ch'en Yung-kuei's successor as brigade leader is a woman, the average work point differential between men and women reported in 1973 was a comparatively high 2.5 points, 7 to 9 for women, 10 to 11 for most men.

Throughout China during the Cultural Revolution experiments were encouraged to curb income differentials while expanding collective consciousness and work incentive. Among the most important were those in which the team or brigade distributes equally to its members a fixed portion of income, often 40 to 60 percent, with the remainder allocated on the basis of work points. This method emphasizes the progressively expanded contribution of the collective in determining one's income while preserving the relationship between income and work through the work point system.

The Tachai system reduces supervision and encourages everyone to pitch in wherever assistance is needed. The role of leadership is critical here and throughout the commune system.

---

* Just how far China has to go toward attaining the conditions for communist distribution is suggested by a Kwangtung peasant refugee's account of the persistence of individual income drives among the peasantry and the still unresolved conflict between individual and collective income, conflicts which reach critical proportions in times of economic pinch or breakdown of collective leadership:

> On the mountainsides there's grass that can be sold to the village brickworks for 1.4 yuan per 100 catties; in a good year you'd only earn one yuan for a whole day's collective work, while some folks can cut up to 200 catties of grass in the same day. As soon as collective work stopped for lunch, folks would immediately clamber up the mountainsides, running along cutting grass fit to kill and stuffing rice-cakes in their mouths at the same time. . . . When collective labor resumes they're pooped and so relax in the fields a

Leaders act as pacesetters who play an integral part in the work process. As leadership supervision is reduced, it becomes everyone's responsibility and everyone's interest to ensure quality work. This counters impulses to maximize one's personal income by fast but shoddy work, and to rely on leadership initiative.

Tachai's success lies in harmonizing the interests of individual, collective, and state. The brigade's economic performance has generated rising personal income and made possible provision of subsistence guarantees against natural disaster as well as an increasingly rich cultural and political life. Collective accumulation has taken the form not only of expanded capital but also the dramatic improvement of the quality of the land, the level of mechanization, and the collective skills of its members. And the state has received steadily increasing supplies of marketable grain from a self-reliant unit. As Tachai's people see it, its gains have been primarily the result of class struggle centered on successive changes in the relations of production in step with changing productive forces and popular consciousness, development of a style of leadership and mobilization emphasizing participation in the work process, preserving brigade unity rooted in mass line practice in the face of bureaucratic tendencies to outside leadership, and the continuing struggle to place public interest above self.

But Tachai's success has also hinged on a grassroots scientific revolution requiring fundamental changes in the relationship between humanity and nature. Ch'en Yung-kuei understands the significance of mechanization and of technical innovation in ways which highlight its political significance: it "consolidates the worker-peasant alliance, promotes socialist industrialization and reduces the differences between the workers and the peasants." In short, the Tachai model exemplifies the unity of

---

bit by working at a leisurely pace. Then, through this, they recoup and go off to work at their private stuff, such as more grasscutting when the workday ends.[45]

This contradiction between individual and collective interests can be reduced, and progress has been made, for example, through mechanization and industrialization of collectives which can raise the value of collective labor above that which can be earned by individuals. But the contradiction cannot be entirely eliminated so long as individual, collective, and state ownership forms continue to exist side by side.

the three great revolutionary movements: the struggle for production, the class struggle, and the scientific revolution.

During the Cultural Revolution the highest levels of the party divided sharply over issues of rural policy. Two aspects of the debate had a strong impact on the transformation of the countryside and on rural-urban relations.

Rural mechanization. Liu Shao-ch'i, the head of state denounced as "China's Khrushchev" and deposed during the Cultural Revolution, is said to have argued in the early 1950s that collectivization could not proceed until productivity increased to the point at which 80 percent of peasant families had three horses, an ox, and a cart in at least 70 percent of the villages. Such views, consistent with the first five-year plan, were repudiated in the socialist upsurge and Great Leap. However, in the 1960s China's few tractors became state property, garaged in county towns and driven by state employees whose lives, income, and future were tied to the cities. Communes, particularly those located near county seats, received the "gift" of tractor time (at a price, of course), but did not control the technology. Driving, repairing, and ownership remained in the hands of the state. Criticism during the Cultural Revolution resulted in commune and brigade purchase of tractors and other equipment and training in their use, maintenance, and repair. The result was that the poorer and more remote units gained control over and access to tractors and equipment.

This illustrates the downward transfer of technology and the means of mechanization from the state and the cities directly into the hands of the peasants' communal organization. The transfer of tractors broke the "gift" relationship; tractors came to be driven and repaired by peasants whose income and future rested on the effective functioning of the communes. This change in the relations of production occurred as China's tractor production expanded rapidly from just 1,100 standard units (15 horsepower) in 1958 to 79,000 in 1970 and 190,000 in 1976.

Rural industrialization. In the early 1960s the Great Leap experiments in rural industrialization aborted when the state channeled scarce resources into centralized industry and directed the communes to concentrate on food production. From 1966 industrialization and electrification along with mechanization again expanded rapidly, and this time on a firmer technical foundation. With the Cultural Revolution, taking advantage of abundant widely scattered resources, slack season surplus labor, and local skills, rural industry provided an important complement to agriculture. Ranging from upgraded village crafts to small modern plants, and including state and industry at the county level, and collectively owned and operated industry at the commune and brigade levels, by 1974 China had an estimated 500,000 industrial units, including 100,000 mines, 50,000 small hydropower plants, and numerous iron and steel plants, cement factories, fertilizer and other chemical plants, and machinery and repair plants. The estimated 10 to 17 million workers at county level and below constitute less than 5 percent of the rural workforce, yet already they number approximately half of all mining and manufacturing employees. China is approaching a situation in which a majority of the industrial workforce lives and works in rural people's communes. Rural industrialization and mechanization coupled with restriction on urban growth and the transfer of intellectual youth to the countryside constitute the heart of a strategy for achieving common prosperity in the rural areas while bridging the gap between agriculture and industry and countryside and city.

The Tach'ing Model and Industrial Revolution.

Construction of Tach'ing, China's largest oil field, began in 1960 at the time of withdrawal of Soviet technicians and China's decision to independently accelerate the search for oil. Tach'ing has contributed significantly to China's transformation from an oil-dependent country to an oil exporter. It also exemplifies a new type of industry uniting city and countryside, industry and agriculture, and worker, technician, and cadre.

We will focus on Tach'ing's experience in transforming worker-management relationships; in building a new type of industrial complex; and in expanding the concept of the factory from the realm of production to political, social, educational, and cultural realms—the totality of human life.

By 1966, Tach'ing had developed a managerial system embodying mass line principles designed to transform the relations among workers, technicians, and managers. It guaranteed the workers' right to criticize and struggle against all industrial practices and acts contrary to party policy, to elect basic-level cadres, and to refuse to work in the absence of appropriate safety or quality standards.

Tach'ing's two-line system stressed leadership at the point of production. The second line, comprised of the leading cadres of the oil field, freed from distinct responsibility for routine administration, provided overall direction by going to selected points of production for detailed investigation and on-the-spot leadership of work in progress. On this basis of direct experience, it summed up the overall situation and conveyed guidelines to the first line which was responsible for implementation in day-to-day operations. The method was designed to maximize contact between leadership and production workers, and to ensure that policy grew out of continuous observation of and participation in the work process.

Tach'ing was also a leader in implementation of triple-combination technical innovation teams involving workers, cadres, and technicians, and in the participation in labor of technicians and cadres, the great majority of whom rose from the ranks of workers in the field. In 1977 11,000 Tach'ing workers reportedly participated in its scientific research network and 59 percent of its 5,000 professional and scientific researchers, and the majority of its cadres, were drawn from the ranks of the workers.

Located in the desolate Sung-liao basin of Heilungkiang province in the Northeast, Tach'ing pioneered a new approach to industrial and urban life, redefining the relationship between work and the full range of human activities. This is mirrored in the design of the oil fields. Tach'ing broke first with the concept of building a single large urban center which would inevitably stand as a monument to the gulf dividing peasants from industrial workers and management, entail high construction costs, and separate workers from their families as well as presenting a vulnerable military target. Its decentralized design was conceived as the basis for "a new socialist mining district where town and countryside, industry and agriculture, and government and enterprise are integrated."[46]

The Tach'ing model and others implemented during the Cultural Revolution sought to integrate city and countryside by bringing agriculture to industry and the cities. In Tach'ing this primarily took the form of seeking food self-sufficiency by dependents opening virgin land and creating sideline production. In 1977 Tach'ing dependents reportedly sowed more than 30,000 acres of wheat, ran numerous subsidiary enterprises, and earned an average of 400 yuan per year (in work points in the manner of communes), a sum equivalent to a second-class worker in the oil fields. This experience is integrally linked to the decentralized design of the fields, which are divided into regions each of which contains a central village of approximately 500 households and three to five smaller villages of 100 families each.

The Tach'ing influence is reflected in a major 1974 article on urban-rural planning and the environment in *Red Flag:*

> [I]ndustries are dispersed and widely distributed in the various provinces, while in a small locality the industries are concentrated and close to each other, and we have built many small towns. This is a strategic measure that helps reduce the difference between countryside and city and also an effective way of solving the contradiction between developing industry and protecting the environment.[47]

While the spatial dimensions of Tach'ing distinguish it from large industrial cities, since the Cultural Revolution integration of industry and agriculture in the latter has taken the form of farming within and on the periphery of the city, integration of suburban communes within the municipality, and emphasis on the contributions of urban industry, education, and health services to the surrounding countryside.

The Tach'ing concept emphasizes the workplace as the center of community life: economic, political, military, cultural, social, and educational. Features of Tach'ing, above all its decentralized design, cannot be readily applied to existing large industrial cities. For this reason, and because Tach'ing never produced a working-class leader of the caliber of Tachai's Ch'en Yung-kuei, it has not received national attention on a scale comparable to that accorded Tachai. Yet its stress on self-reliance and thrift, its concrete efforts to expand worker participation and control and to transform leadership, and the attempt to integrate industry, agriculture, education, and military training with the enterprise as the center of human activity—in short, to replicate for industry certain organic features unifying labor and social life in the manner of the rural commune—these are components which have been studied and applied selectively throughout China in the context of the movement to learn from Tach'ing.

The Great Proletarian Cultural Revolution: Toward an Assessment

China is the first nation to seriously confront the problems of bureaucratism, elitism, and routinization which challenge every revolutionary society (indeed, every modern society) and which, if unresolved, may halt or even reverse socialist development. In this light the most important areas of progress during the Cultural Revolution, many building on and extending the Great Leap vision, include the following:

(1) Extension of the power of working people over the workplace and, through mechanisms of criticism of authority, seizure of power and formation of revolutionary committees, to the political realm.

(2) Transformation of the relationship between city and countryside through the integration of industry and agriculture, the strengthening and diversification of activities of the rural people's commune, transfer of resources to the countryside, and a new stress on integrating agriculture with the cities.

(3) Further development of a Chinese path to socialist development rooted in mass line practice applied in the realm of ideas, institutions, culture, relations of production, and national priorities.

In the course of the Cultural Revolution the people subjected the party and its leaders to severe criticism; the party at the national level and in many localities was temporarily paralyzed and thrust aside by new grassroots organizations of working people, then reconstituted and rejuvenated with the inclusion of activists who emerged from the movement.

These are accomplishments worthy of the designation revolution. There is, however, a dark side to the Cultural Revolution which must be understood to assess the overall record and to understand the reaction of the Chinese leadership and many of the people since the deaths of Mao and Chou En-lai in 1976.

The sometimes probing criticism of the Cultural Revolution exhibited powerful tendencies to degenerate into factionalism, physical and mental torture, and even armed confrontation. These proclivities of the red guard youth in particular were by no means confined to them. At every level, as conflicting groups formed and put forward demands, factions, each convinced of its own revolutionary purity, resorted to physical force. The result was that battle lines hardened and, for a full decade, the promise of the early Cultural Revolution that great disorder across the land would give rise to great order, proved unattainable.

The Cultural Revolution gave rise to a cult of Mao, sloganeering, and hero worship which in many ways represent the antithesis of the striving of working people to mastery in the society. It is true that Mao's image bolstered the determination of many to rebel against reactionary or corrupt authority in the name of higher revolutionary legitimacy. Yet the ritualistic praise for the "Great Leader, Great Teacher, Great Supreme Commander and Great Helmsman," the Red Book waving and chanting of millions of red guards, and Lin Piao's proclamation that "one of his sentences is worth 10,000 of ours," infused the movement with the quality of a religious revival which detracted from critical thought and mass line politics. In retrospect this must diminish the stature of the leader who fostered such adulation. Lin Piao and others bear responsibility for carrying the cult to grotesque extremes. But it is clear that Mao, who earlier had resisted such temptations, during the early Cultural Revolution himself exploited them for political purposes.* In

---

* Lenin, by contrast, is an example of a leader who implacably rejected attempts by his colleagues and the people to erect a cult of personality around him during his lifetime. A prime example occurred shortly after he was shot, an event which elicited an outpouring of public praise for Lenin's leadership. "What is this? How could you permit it?" he admonished his aide on discovering it. "Look what they are saying in the papers. Makes one ashamed to read it. They write that I'm such-and-such, exaggerate everything, call me a genius, a special kind of man. . . . Next they'll be holding public prayers for my health. . . . All our lives we have carried on an ideological struggle against the glorification of personality."[48] When this message was carried to *Pravda* and *Izvestia*, the accolades reportedly ceased immediately.

these and other ways the persistence of traditional Chinese political norms converged with corrupt elements of Stalinist political practice. I have in mind particularly the pattern of denunciation of purged leaders, which, of course, neither began nor ended with the Cultural Revolution but was perhaps perfected at the time. For example, Lin Piao, a highly successful general since 1927 and Mao's "closest comrade-in-arms" and designated successor during the Cultural Revolution, was described following his fall from power (he died in a plane crash while reportedly attempting to flee to the Soviet Union) as seeking to build a "revisionist, fascist party . . . subvert the dictatorship of the proletariat and restore capitalism . . . institute a feudal-compradore-fascist dictatorship . . . and capitulate to Soviet revisionism and social imperialism." He had, moreover, committed "bourgeois idealist errors" at every stage of his career. The wholesale writing off of revolutionary careers, invariably including the belated discovery of Trotskyite, Kuomintang, and fascist ties prior to liberation, was not limited to Lin. It befell every disgraced leader of note (and there were many, including most of the surviving group of leaders of the Long March generation) from Liu Shao-ch'i and Teng Hsiao-p'ing in 1966–1968 to Chiang Ch'ing and Chang Ch'un-ch'iao a decade later. The results of such "historical interpretation" surely include demeaning the revolutionary record of the party and undermining its credibility by calling into question the judgment of Mao and others who had long fought alongside such "fascists" and "Kuomintang agents."

The movement which began in the realm of culture and ideas in the course of a decade leveled some of its fiercest attacks on intellectuals and called for the re-evaluation of every aspect of cultural and intellectual life. To achieve these ends, the Cultural Revolution essentially sought to wipe the slate clean. The universities closed entirely for nearly five years and other schools more briefly, not only to permit students to devote themselves to the revolution but also to permit radical restructuring of the schools. A decade later, despite the influx of workers and peasants, the number of university students did not yet approach pre-1966 levels and many universities functioned at a fraction of earlier levels. The bookshelves were swept clear, not only in the areas of social science and the arts, but even in the natural sciences, for several years leaving the field to the works of Mao. Preparation began to produce appropriate new books in tune with the times, yet in the course of a decade few appeared. Likewise in the theater, film, and music, performance virtually ceased save for eight model revolutionary operas and ballets prepared under the personal direction of Chiang Ch'ing.

Among the achievements of the Chinese Revolution from the War of Resistance through the land revolution and the Great Leap, was the ability, despite often severe conflicts, to win the active support of large numbers of intellectuals. Today, many scientists, teachers, engineers, technicians, writers, and artists perceive the Cultural Revolution as essentially a lost decade. Criticized sharply and often justly during 1966 and 1967, rather than being reintegrated to put their knowledge and skills to work in the service of socialist development, many remained in limbo politically and intellectually.

While special enclaves such as China's nuclear program apparently continued to function relatively undisturbed, and while significant technical and scientific work increased at the grassroots level (for example in the field of earthquake prediction), the attack on intellectuals paralyzed most scientific research institutes and virtually eliminated postgraduate training in all fields for a full decade.

The Cultural Revolution marked the culmination of the revolutionary career of Mao Tsetung, extending and deepening his lifelong critique of bureaucratism and the search for mass line methods to extend the mastery of working people from the workplace to the political institutions and ultimately to control of the realm of culture, values, and ideas.

The first predominantly urban mass movement since 1927, the Cultural Revolution nevertheless reaffirmed the priority of the countryside and concretized the role of the cities and industry in serving it. Both the vision and significant elements of the practice of the new relationships between city and countryside, workers and peasants, and mental and manual laborers extended the contributions of the Great Leap Forward. As in the leap, the unfolding of a vast mass movement produced a variety of excesses. In the leap these principally took the form of utopianism, that is, losing sight of the constraints imposed by the backwardness of the productive forces and the limits of consciousness. The Cultural Revolution solved certain problems which the leap had left unresolved. For example, it succeeded in establishing a firm economic base for diversification of the rural economy of the commune, specifically through effective steps to industrialize the countryside. It also extended the egalitarian and participatory features of the people's commune and urban industrial life as summed up in the Tachai and Tach'ing models.

Both its strengths and weaknesses relate to the attack on and virtual disintegration of the party. The activists of the era correctly gauged the threat of bureaucratism in party and state and the need to address the problem through mass mobilization. Yet with the virtual collapse at many levels of the party, which had provided vital leadership and coordinating roles in previous phases of the revolution, a critical element of successful mass line practice, the party-mass relationship was fractured. For all its accomplishments, the mass movement tended to move toward extremes of violence, factionalism, and utopianism and for a full decade the goal of building unity on new foundations laid by the movement proved elusive. The implications of this complex legacy for the future of China's socialist development will be taken up again below.

VII. The Proletariat, the Peasantry, and Economic Development, 1949–1976

Mao Tsetung shared with every great Third World leader a passion to achieve economic development as the foundation of national prosperity and overall advance. One distinguishing feature, however, of Mao's thought and of Chinese revolutionary practice at its best is the overriding importance attached to the *quality* of development. Mao consistently held that the key to both quality and rate of advance lay in proper leadership of mass movements centered in the peasantry and proletariat and transforming human relationships throughout the entire society.

Tables 13, 14, and 15 provide a statistical profile of China's economic performance in the years 1949 to 1976. The data presented here, summarizing the conclusions of the most authoritative U.S. government-sponsored studies, probably err on the conservative side.

From 1949 to 1976 China's GNP increased at an annual rate of 7 percent (6 percent since 1952) or close to 5 percent in per capita product. Real per capita income has doubled since 1952 and more than tripled since 1949. This is a record which few nations have attained and it is all the more impressive when we recall that throughout the Republican period, from 1911 to 1949, China's per capita output remained stagnant.

In statistical terms the largest gains have been achieved in industry (13 percent growth per year) while agricultural growth rates estimated at 2.5 to 3 percent a year exceeded population growth by narrow margins.* Since 1964 China has carried out a green revolution based on introduction of new strains of rice and wheat together with extension of irrigation, electrification, and mechanization which have continuously raised yields. These results were achieved by a combination of hard work, effective leadership, planning and cooperation, multiple cropping, irrigation, and land reconstruction to produce high and stable yields in large areas *without* widening the intra-village gap between rich and poor as green revolution strategies have done in India and other capitalist nations. Likewise, in contrast to the widening gap between urban and rural incomes common in many countries, Chinese wage, tax, and price policies over two decades have progressively reduced this gap. For example, as a result of rising state purchase prices of farm products and price reductions on industrial goods in the rural areas, the real purchasing power of the countryside rose by 64 percent between 1953 and 1974 (approximately 100 percent since 1949), while in the same two-decade period the agricultural tax declined from 12 percent of output to just 5 percent.

The problem has not, however, been eliminated. In 1978 an official of the State Planning Commission estimated that despite substantial progress the price differential continued to favor industry and the cities by 14 percent; moreover, while the issue is presently under active study, no significant change has occurred in raising the state purchase price of agricultural commodities since 1963.[49]

---

* The agrarian performance can be appreciated by comparison with that of India, the other major continental Asian power. In 1977 China grew 30 to 40 percent more food per capita on 14 percent less arable land and distributed it far more equitably to a population which is 50 percent larger.

Table 13
Major Economic Indicators, 1949–1976

Year	GNP (billions of 1975 $)	GNP per capita (1975 US $)	Agricultural (1957 = 100)	Industrial production (1957 = 100)	Grain output (million metric tons)	Steel output (million metric tons)	Foreign trade Exports f.o.b. (billions current $)	Foreign trade Imports c.i.f. (billions current $)
1949	49	91	54	20	108	0.2	0.4	0.4
1952	82	144	83	48	154	1.3	0.9	1.0
1953	87	149	83	61	157	1.8	1.0	1.3
1954	91	153	84	70	160	2.2	1.1	1.3
1955	100	164	94	73	175	2.8	1.4	1.7
1956	108	173	97	88	183	4.5	1.6	1.5
1957	115	180	100	100	185	5.3	1.6	1.4
1958	137	209	108	142	200	11.1	1.9	1.8
1959	129	193	83	173	165	13.4	2.2	2.1
1960	129	189	78	181	160	18.7	2.0	2.0
1961	99	143	77	105	160	8.0	1.5	1.5
1962	113	160	92	111	180	8.0	1.5	1.2
1963	125	174	96	134	185	9.0	1.6	1.2
1964	142	193	106	161	195	10.8	1.8	1.5
1965	163	217	114	199	210	12.5	2.0	1.8
1966	177	231	116	232	215	15.0	2.2	2.0
1967	172	219	123	202	230	12.0	1.9	2.0
1968	173	216	116	221	215	14.0	1.9	1.8
1969	192	234	118	266	220	16.0	2.0	1.8
1970	219	261	129	316	240	17.8	2.0	2.2
1971	236	273	134	349	246	21.0	2.4	2.3
1972	246	280	130	385	240	23.0	3.1	2.8
1973	272	303	138	436	250	25.5	5.0	5.1
1974	283	309	143	455	260	23.8	6.6	7.4
1975	299	320	141	502	260	26.0	6.0	7.4
1976	306	321	n.a.	523	n.a.	23.0	7.0	6.2

Sources: U.S. Central Intelligence Agency, *People's Republic of China: Handbook of Economic Indicators* (Washington, 1976), pp. 3, 5, 11, 22; U.S. Department of Commerce, *The Chinese Economy and Foreign Trade Perspective—1976* (Washington, 1977), p. 2; Joint Economic Committee of Congress, *China: A Reassessment of the Economy* (Washington: U.S. Government Printing Office, 1975), p. 23.

Table 14
Selected Production Indices, 1949 to 1976
(in million metric tons unless otherwise specified)

	Crude oil	Coal	Electric power (billion kwh)	Chemical fertilizer	Tractors (thousand 15 hp units)	Powered irrigation equipment (thousand hp units)	Cotton	Cement
1949	0.1	32.4	4.3	—	—	—	.4	.7
1952	0.4	66.5	7.3	.2	—	—	1.3	2.9
1957	1.5	130.7	19.3	.8	1.1	52	1.6	6.9
1959	3.7	300.0	42.0	1.9	9.4	1,255	1.2	12.2
1965	11.0	220.0	42.0	7.6	23.9	1,150	1.9	15.2
1970	28.2	310.0	72.0	14.0	79.0	n.a.	2.0	19.7
1973	54.8	377.0	101.0	24.8	166.0	5,948	2.5	30.5
1975	74.5	427.0	121.0	27.9	180.0	7,000	2.3	40.0
1976	84.0	448.0	133.0	n.a.	190.0	n.a.	2.3	49.3

Sources: U.S. Central Intelligence Agency, *People's Republic of China: Handbook of Economic Indicators*, pp. 3, 5, 11, 13, 15, 17, 20, 22, 23, 24; U.S. Department of Commerce, *The Chinese Economy and Foreign Trade Perspective—1976*, p. 2; *China Trade Report*, December 1977, p. 8.

Table 15
Long-term Economic Growth, 1949–1975
(average annual growth rates in percentages)

	1949-1975	1952-1975	1949-1952	1952-1957	1957-1975	1970-1975
Gross national product	7	6	19	7	5	6
Agricultural production	4	2	15	4	2	2
Industrial production	13	11	32	16	9	10

Source: U.S. Central Intelligence Agency, *People's Republic of China: Handbook of Economic Indicators*, p. 3.

This is the record of a thriving and dynamic agricultural-industrial nation with a firm grip on its key economic levers. It was achieved in the face of protracted blockade by the leading world economic powers, a major war in Korea, in the absence of long-term financial aid (Soviet loans were repaid by the mid-1960s) and in the midst of uninterrupted revolutionary transformation on a scale and intensity unmatched elsewhere. Its significance increases when we recall the grinding poverty, stagnation, hopelessness, and economic distortions characteristic of the preceding century of humiliation which ended less than three decades ago. And it attains still more impressive proportions when we grasp the fact that the prospering of city and countryside as well as laying the basic groundwork of industrialization and mechanization have been achieved without squeezing dry the vast peasant population, selling out the nation's economic birthright to foreign powers, or creating a privileged elite class. Chinese development has yielded gradually rising income for virtually everyone, led to the revitalization of local communities, and the expansion of economic, social, educational, political, and cultural opportunities for women and men of all nationalities. These gains have been achieved by a nation whose productivity and level of mechanization, despite marked advances, still remain low. China continues to confront the staggering reality that the labor of approximately four-fifths of the workforce is required to feed a population in the vicinity of 1 billion people. It is this reality that underlies the urgency of the Chinese people and leadership to accelerate the pace of mechanization and industrialization. The critical question remains whether this can be accomplished in ways consistent with the goals and values of socialism.

VIII. *Class Struggle, Modernization, and the Future of Socialist Development*

We must be soberly aware that there is still the danger for China to turn revisionist . . . because new bourgeois elements are, as Lenin put it, being engendered daily and hourly.

Chang Ch'un-ch'iao, 1975

It is by the adoption of the most advanced technologies that the industrially backward countries catch up with the industrially advanced countries in the world. We must also do the same.

Teng Hsiao-p'ing, 1975

In order to make China a modern, powerful socialist country by the end of the century . . . in the final analysis what is of decisive importance is the rapid development of our socialist economy.

Hua Kuo-feng, 1978

In 1975, with the incapacitation and imminent death of Mao and Chou En-lai, the Chinese leadership was increasingly polarized. Two antagonistic groups developed with fundamentally different assessments of the national interest and policy options. One had emerged close to Mao during the Cultural Revolution and in the 1970s sought to extend the radical thrust of that movement. The power of this Cultural Revolution Group centered in the Politburo and among young party recruits (fully half of the 35 million party members have joined since the start of the Cultural Revolution), in control of the national media, leading universities, and cultural affairs, in a reinvigorated militia, and with regional bases in Shanghai and Liaoning province. Its most prominent members included three Shanghai leaders— Chang Ch'un-ch'iao, writer Yao Wen-yuan, and labor leader Wang Hung-wen—and Mao's wife, Chiang Ch'ing.

Its antagonists, a diverse group of seasoned party and military leaders, many of them targets of struggle during the Cultural Revolution, shared the goals of national unity, party reconstruction, and modernization. The central figures in this modernization group, all veterans of the Long March, wartime military leaders, and close associates of Chou En-lai, included Teng Hsiao-p'ing (officially condemned in 1969 as the number two capitalist roader in the party), General Yeh Chien-ying, and economic planner Li Hsien-nien. Members of this group, though divided among themselves on many issues, controlled the major levers of the army, the party bureaucracy, the national economy, and major regional power bases.

While analyzing the issues which have shaped Chinese priorities since the death of Mao, a brief chronology may be helpful in locating the tumultuous changes which culminated in the leadership of Hua Kuo-feng and a new stage in Chinese development (see next page).

At the Fourth National People's Congress in February 1975, Chou En-lai called for a drive to implement the four modernizations so that by the year 2000 "our national economy will be advancing in the front ranks of the world." After a decade of the Cultural Revolution, Chou held, the time had come to realize Mao's dictum that "great disorder across the land leads to great order," that is, to consolidate unity in the service of the nation's modernization.

Mao did not attend the Fourth Congress. Within a month, however, his call for the "restriction of bourgeois right," centering on the reduction of inequalities in income and privilege, suggested a very different set of priorities. The imminent danger of capitalist restoration, in this view, required a focus on class struggle ("The capitalist roaders are still on the capitalist road").

At the center of the policy debate was this question: What are the appropriate means and priorities for advancing the interrelated goals of revolutionary change and economic development a decade after the start of the Cultural Revolution? And its corollary: How should the Cultural Revolution be evaluated and carried to its conclusion?

In April 1976, following the death of Chou En-lai, a massive demonstration at T'ien An Men honoring the premier (and including posters criticizing Mao, though not by name) exploded in violence. The Politburo's swift reaction was once again to strip Teng Hsiao-p'ing of all posts and denounce him as an "unrepentant capitalist roader." The State Council documents on modernization which he sponsored were labeled the "three poisonous weeds." The initiative had passed into the hands of the Cultural Revolution Group.

Teng Hsiao-p'ing's 1975 modernization program and its subsequent criticism provide a clear vantage point from which to assess the options debated by the Chinese leadership and people then and subsequently. The documents (included in this volume), consisting of a general program and reports on industry

Political Chronology, 1972–1978

1972. Chou En-lai first hospitalized with heart disease and cancer (permanently from 1974).

April 1973. Teng Hsiao-p'ing rehabilitated as a vice premier.

August 1973. Tenth Party Congress. Thirty-eight-year-old labor leader Wang Hung-wen appointed vice chairman of the Central Committee, the ranking party official after Mao and Chou. Mao makes his last official appearance.

January 1975. Teng Hsiao-p'ing appointed a vice chairman of the party, first vice premier (in fact he serves as acting premier) and chief of staff of the army.

February 1975. Fourth National People's Congress. Chou En-lai calls for comprehensive modernization of agriculture, industry, national defense, and science and technology (the four modernizations).

Spring 1975. Mao and the Cultural Revolution radicals initiate a mobilization campaign to restrict bourgeois right.

Summer-Fall 1975. Teng Hsiao-p'ing drafts three State Council documents to chart China's modernization.

September 1975. Vice Premier Hua Kuo-feng delivers keynote address at First National Conference on Learning from Tachai in Agriculture.

January 1976. Chou En-lai dies.

February 1976. Enlarged Politburo meeting appoints Hua Kuo-feng acting premier, bypassing the higher ranking Teng Hsiao-p'ing and Chang Ch'un-ch'iao.

April 1976. The T'ien An Men incident. Teng Hsiao-p'ing, held responsible for mass demonstrations honoring Chou En-lai which end in violence, again stripped of all

and science, constitute a blueprint for the achievement of modernization and rapid economic growth. Did they, as critics charged, ignore the question of whether China's development would be socialist or capitalist, whether it would primarily serve the interests of working people or those of a managerial and party elite?

The documents contain numerous references to the dictatorship of the proletariat, class struggle, combating revisionism, official positions but retains party membership. Hua Kuo-feng appointed first vice chairman of the party and premier.

July 1976. General Chu Teh, co-founder of the Red Army, dies. With the death of four members in one year, the standing committee of the Politburo is reduced to five members: Mao, Yeh Chien-ying, Chang Ch'un-ch'iao, Wang Hung-wen, and Hua Kuo-feng.

August 1976. T'angshan earthquake, the worst in recent centuries, takes 700,000 lives, leaves more than one million homeless, severely damages leading coal and transportation center.

September 1976. Mao dies. Hua Kuo-feng's memorial address includes praise for Mao's leadership of the Cultural Revolution which "triumphed over the revisionist lines of Liu Shao-ch'i, Lin Piao, and Teng Hsiao-p'ing."

October 1976. Hua orders the arrest and leads the denunciation of the "gang of four": Chang Ch'un-ch'iao, Chiang Ch'ing, Wang Hung-wen, and Yao Wen-yuan. Central Committee designates Hua chairman of the Central Committee and commander-in-chief of the army. He defines national priorities as achieving stability and unity, implementing the four modernizations, and rooting out the influence of the "gang of four."

July 1977. Third Plenum, Tenth Party Congress. Hua Kuo-feng confirmed as party chairman. Teng Hsiao-p'ing appointed vice chairman of the party, vice premier, and assistant chief of staff of the army. The "gang of four" officially expelled from the party.

February 1978. Fifth National People's Congress affirms the modernization program as the nation's priority task.

and the relationship between politics and economics. It is the definition given these problems which strikingly distinguishes them (along with most official statements following Mao's death in 1976) from approaches enunciated during the Cultural Revolution and advocated subsequently by its proponents. The "anti-Marxist class enemies" which the State Council documents attacked are not the capitalist roaders in the party, the bureaucrats, or new bourgeois elements. They are instead those who "practice revisionism while holding the antirevisionist banner," "some comrades" who "still use metaphysics," who "talk only about politics but not economics; only about revolution but not production." In short, the documents explicitly pinpoint the main danger rising from "ultra-left" forces whose program of class struggle undermines national goals of modernization and development. The spearhead of criticism pointed directly at the Cultural Revolution Group.

The 1975 modernization documents reaffirm a number of concrete proposals to strengthen the socialist character of development including triple-combination technical innovation teams, cadre participation in physical labor, and worker participation in management. Yet in contrast with the writings of the Cultural Revolution Group, heavy emphasis is placed on control, combating anarchy, and fulfilling production targets. The documents point in the direction of consolidating, rationalizing, and overcoming excesses stemming from the Cultural Revolution's reforms of the factory.

The modernization programs emphasize expanded introduction of foreign technology to "catch up with the industrially advanced countries." Already between 1972 and 1975 Chou En-lai had initiated (with Mao's approval) the first major purchases of technology since the start of the Cultural Revolution, with orders totaling $2.6 billion in complete plants from the West and Japan. By the 1970s the debate was no longer whether to purchase foreign technology but the extent and nature of such purchases, the relationship between foreign technology and self-reliance, and the means to pay for expensive foreign equipment. In August 1975 Teng Hsiao-p'ing used characteristically blunt language to call for import of "the latest and the best equipment from foreign countries. . . . To import, we must export a little more. The first that comes to my mind is oil. We must develop oil production as far as possible and export as much oil as we can. That is the most reliable thing to do." [50]

Teng's critics responded that such a policy—not modernization goals in and of themselves—threatened to deprive China of the opportunity to retain

> economic initiative in her own hands. Charging that massive exports would exhaust valuable resources required for development at home, in 1975 the critics initiated a debate

at the highest policy levels over the question of oil and other non-renewable resources. "What should be relied on in bringing about the four modernizations?" one critic asked. According to Teng Hsiao-p'ing's logic, only "importing foreign advanced technology" is "most reliable," only "exchanging for the best and latest equipment of foreign countries" is "most reliable." Does this mean that maintaining independence and achieving rejuvenation through self-reliance and calling into play the creative power of the masses of people are all "unreliable"?[51]

Such policies would reduce China to "an appendage of imperialism and social imperialism."

Teng's speech touched on the related and equally sensitive issues of finance and control of technology: "We may consider importing foreign technical equipment for coal mining. We may sign long-term contracts with them and pay them in coal. This does not mean external borrowing." Did this not mean, the critics responded, scrapping self-reliance as Mao had formulated it: "Rely mainly on our own efforts while making external assistance subsidiary, break down blind faith, go in for industry, agriculture and technical and cultural revolution independently . . .?"

A final critical issue posed by the modernization program is the role of intellectuals and specialists. The Cultural Revolution had sharply attacked intellectuals and placed its emphasis on the development of indigenous technology and the creative contributions of workers and peasants. Indeed, as we have seen, after a full decade, large numbers of specialists and researchers still remained idle, universities after closing for five or more years had yet to attain pre-1966 enrollments, post-graduate training had virtually ceased, and while important achievements had been made in some areas of research, others remained at low ebb. The success of the State Council's modernization and technology import programs, however, rested heavily on the contribution of highly trained specialists. The modernization group advocated new approaches to win the enthusiastic support of intellectuals and specialists; in particular, it called for an end to the incessant criticism of the Cultural Revolution and sought broad national unity as the basis for accelerated development.

Bourgeois right. Marxism holds that the socialist principle of distributive justice, "from each according to one's ability, to each according to one's work," under conditions of abundance and higher consciousness, yields to the higher stage of communism honoring the principle, "from each according to one's ability, to each according to one's need." Socialist distribution, which eliminates the capitalist's appropriation of a share of the fruits of labor and numerous irrational income discrepancies, marks a quantum advance for the worker who *should* now receive full compensation for the value of work. (Note: *should.* Another possibility exists, namely, that a proliferating state bureaucracy will monopolize an increasing share of the surplus.) But as Marx observed, since physically or mentally superior people may contribute more labor in the same time, so *"equal* right is an unequal right for unequal labor. . . . It recognizes no class differences . . . but it tacitly recognizes unequal individual endowment and thus productive capacity as natural privilege." [52] These differences in ability and situation plus the "bourgeois right" which, in the early stages of socialism, rewards individuals

Beginning in the spring of 1975 and continuing in 1976, the principal counter to this modernization program took the form of a campaign to restrict bourgeois right by the Cultural Revolution Group.

While Mao himself initiated the campaign, its archetypal statement came in Chang Ch'un-ch'iao's April 1975 article "On Exercising All-Round Dictatorship Over the Bourgeoisie." Chang cited Mao's recent observation:

In a word, China is a socialist country. Before liberation she was much the same as a capitalist country. Even now she practises an eight grade wage system, distribution according to work and exchange through money, and in all this differs very little from the old society. What is different is that the system of ownership has been changed. [53]

For the Cultural Revolution Group this perception, underlining on the basis of their contribution to production, give rise to differences in income. In short, socialist distribution according to work eliminates the largest inequality between capitalist and workers, but perpetuates other inequalities among workers of different skill and strength levels, between workers and peasants, and among different economic sectors. These differences may give rise to privilege and vested interests. Marx cautioned, "Right can never be higher than the economic structure of society and its cultural development conditioned thereby." The Cultural Revolution, like the Great Leap earlier, had restricted bourgeois right in ways which anticipated the future transition to communism, for example, in commune distribution systems that provided subsistence guarantees to all members regardless of their ability to work. Yet inequalities remained, as in the eight-grade wage system in industry and differences in income between neighboring teams and brigades. The campaign to restrict bourgeois right reopened the question of remaining inequalities and sought to introduce mass line methods to challenge or restrict some of them.

the fragility of China's socialist transition, suggested that the priority task was to mobilize the people to restrict and transform remaining inequalities, privilege, and elitist ideas in the party and among the people.

Nevertheless, despite support from Mao and the national media, the campaign failed to gain momentum through the society. In retrospect it marked the final abortive attempt to extend the Cultural Revolution into its second decade, and the prelude to the fall of the Cultural Revolution Group.

Before turning to an evaluation of the modernization program which the new Chinese leadership has made its highest priority since the fall of 1976, a word is in order about Hua Kuo-feng, who rose rapidly to national prominence in the mid-1970s to become Mao's successor. After serving in the PLA in his native Shansi province in the late years of the civil war, beginning in 1951 Hua distinguished himself as a local and provincial official in Mao's home province of Hunan. Active in promoting rural cooperation in the early 1950s (when his work may already have come to Mao's attention), he rose rapidly through the ranks, serving with notable effectiveness in a variety of capacities centering on rural work, ranging from water conservancy, finance, and mechanization to local industry. As a provincial-level official after 1958 his responsibilities broadened to include education, security, and, as the major provincial spokesperson in denouncing the U.S. intervention in Vietnam in 1965, foreign affairs. The evidence suggests that Hua actively supported the Great Leap (when significant elements of the Hunan leadership remained cool to it) without being swept away by its euphoria. And he alone among the ranking party leadership in Hunan survived the storms of the Cultural Revolution. When Hunan became the first province to establish a new party committee in December 1970, Hua was its first secretary, and in 1973, after serving under Chou En-lai in the State Council, he was elected a member of the Politburo.

In March 1958, shortly after announcing his intention to resign as chairman of the People's Republic, Mao observed that "comrades working in the center will sooner or later either die or leave the scene. Khrushchev came from a local area. At the local level the class struggle is more acute, closer to natural struggle, closer to the masses. This gives the local comrades advantages over those at the center." [54] Hua was one such cadre with ample testing at the grassroots level. In the early seventies he rose to become director of public security and a Politburo standing committee member, and in April 1976 there are indications that Mao designated him as his successor.

As Mao neared death in 1975 and 1976, of the highest party leaders Hua was least clearly identifiable with and least objectionable to either of the two conflicting camps. Three decades of local party organizational work distinguished him from the radical urban intellectuals at the center of the Cultural Revolution Group. His relative youth (born in 1920) and above all his role in the Cultural Revolution distinguished him from most of the Long March generation of party and army veterans who led the modernization group and who had been criticized severely and in many instances deprived of their positions during the Cultural Revolution. Tested as a national leader in his comprehensive address defining rural policy at the 1975 Tachai Conference, during and after the T'ien An Men incident, and in the August 1976 earthquake, Hua enhanced his stature prior to Mao's death. He also had the opportunity to assess the relative merits of the conflicting camps, and in particular to gauge the strength of the forces favoring unity and modernization in the upper ranks of the party and army.

Following Mao's death in the midst of intense jockeying for power between the two groups, Hua ordered the arrest of the "gang of four." He subsequently rehabilitated Teng Hsiao-p'ing and concluded the Cultural Revolution. The new era would stress the modernization strategy proposed by Chou En-lai, given concrete (and extreme) expression in Teng Hsiao-p'ing's State Council documents, and subsequently embodied (but with greater attention to socialist innovations and institutions of the Cultural Revolution) in the speeches and resolutions of the Eleventh Party Congress and Fourth National People's Congress.

Three aspects of the modernization strategy provide the basis for a preliminary assessment of its contribution to socialist development and its relationship to China's trajectory in the era of Mao Tsetung's leadership: industry and the cities; the countryside; and education, science, and technology. Does modernization mark a new stage in socialist development and correction of excesses of the Cultural Revolution? Or is it the first step leading China toward the reimposition of bureaucratic power, the hegemony of the cities over the countryside, class polarization, and eventually toward capitalist restoration?

Modernizing Industry and the Cities

A striking dimension of current Chinese industrialization strategy is its emphasis on advanced, including imported, technology and the exploitation of oil, coal, and other natural resources both to fuel domestic industry and provide foreign exchange. Current plans include construction by 1985 of 120 large-scale projects including ten iron and steel complexes, nine nonferrous metal complexes, ten oil and gas fields, eight coal mines, six new trunk railways, and five harbors. The plan calls for more than doubling steel output to produce 60 million tons by 1985, the first significant wage rise since 1956 for state employees, and a seven-year Sino-Japanese trade agreement committing China to purchase $10 billion in Japanese plants and equipment with payment predominantly in oil and coal.

Shanghai's $2 billion Japanese-made integrated steel complex to produce 6 million tons a year symbolizes important features of the current plan. Steel remains the highest industrial priority, although it now shares the spotlight with oil. To a far greater degree than at any time since the early sixties, industrialization is linked to the international economy. Not only does China pay for its purchases in unrefined oil and coal, but, Japanese specialists report, the high-grade ore requirements of the plant's advanced design will require China, like Japan, to import ore from such countries as Australia and Brazil that export iron of close to 70 percent purity. (China has abundant low quality ore.) In return, China receives the most advanced steel technology from the world leaders.

The modernization program projects substantial increases in purchase of foreign plants and in present levels of imports and exports. Yet, given the development of the domestic economy over the last two decades, and in light of China's potential as an oil exporter, China has the potential to substantially expand technology imports without draining the countryside of the capital required for its own development or plunging the nation into a cycle of debt and foreign control of its economic levers, the fate experienced by such high-growth, export-oriented economies as South Korea and Brazil. The question nevertheless remains open whether the new plant and equipment will provide a substantial boost to the agrarian economy or whether the drive for advanced technology will be pressed to the detriment of rural development and financial self-reliance.

The elimination of revolutionary committees in the factories —though made official in 1978, many had ceased to function effectively years earlier—represents a setback but by no means the end of worker participation in management and technological innovation. Two decades after the eruption of struggles for mastery of the factories produced during the Great Leap, workers have made important strides, yet China has produced no viable industrial institutions comparable to the rural people's communes that can provide a framework for the progressive expansion of worker control over industry and the factory. This remains a critical task for the future of Chinese socialism.

The Cultural Revolution, which emphasized the eradication of inequalities between city and countryside, froze worker salaries. Responding to strong working-class pressures, the Hua administration reversed this policy, returning to guidelines of the early fifties which emphasized that worker salaries must rise along with the increase in productivity of labor. The result is the first significant wage rise in several decades, officially estimated at 10 percent for 62 percent of the workforce. Centered overwhelmingly on the lower rungs of the pay scale, the hikes largely bypassed higher paid workers, technicians, and intellectuals, thus reducing inequalities within the industrial workforce.

Since 1977, many factories have also begun to experiment with piece rates, quota systems, and bonuses to raise productivity. As of the summer of 1978, many of these changes, as in the case of Canton and Shanghai dockworkers, provide group rather than individual production incentives and tend to be modest in scope. It remains to be seen whether this is the opening wedge leading toward reliance on individual material incentives, thus undermining the socialist content of industry.

Present policy, which emphasizes raising industrial productivity, continues to extend such socialist elements as worker participation in technical innovation and planning and the requirement that management participate in productive labor. Achievement of the socialist goal of worker mastery over the workplace, however, will require renewed initiative from below if workers are eventually to control all aspects of administration and factory life.

Modernizing the Countryside

The focus of attention in Chinese development planning has shifted to urban industry. But in contrast to the first five-year plan period, during which the countryside was neglected, the Hua administration has proposed and vigorously supported ambitious plans for agricultural mechanization, industrialization, electrification, and increased productivity. It was, after all, as a specialist in rural cooperation and development that Hua rose through the ranks, and his vigorous promotion of the

Tachai county movement first established him as a national leader. The success of current national development plans once again rests heavily on the simultaneous and interrelated advance of city and countryside, and of industry and agriculture.

Two elements of the rural program of particular importance are the drive to achieve basic mechanization of agriculture by 1980 and the effort to spur comprehensive rural development through the creation of Tachai-type counties. At the 1976 National Tachai Conference Hua summed up the goals of 70 percent mechanization in "all major operations in agriculture, forestry, animal husbandry, sideline occupations and fisheries." Specific targets for the years 1978–1980 include a 70 percent increase in the number of large and medium-sized tractors, a 110 percent increase in tractor-drawn equipment, a 36 percent increase in walking tractors, and a 32 percent increase in the number of drainage and irrigation machines. The fulfillment of these plans, a key step in the rural modernization effort, would reportedly be equivalent to a 100 percent increase in rural labor power.

In the movement to emulate Tachai the Hua administration has made plain the primacy of self-reliance in rural development, in this respect continuing and extending earlier policies. State policy is nevertheless crucial, both in terms of preserving sufficient surplus in the countryside for rural mechanization and industrialization, and in providing direct financial and technical support for industry and mechanization, particularly for poorer communes and regions.

For example, China in 1978 has more than 1,600 farm machine factories in every province except Tibet, including 26 which manufacture medium or large tractors. Despite the high degree of decentralization and local initiative, the center plays critical roles in sustaining and expanding this sector. National and provincial factories, for example, provide 30 percent or more of the equipment and material, including such items as precision steel parts and motors. And in early 1978 the state announced its commitment by 1980 to increase by 25 percent the supply of rolled steel to the countryside. In short, the prospects for rural mechanization and industrialization are integrally tied to the national industrialization drive.

The modernization strategy gives prominence to two important but potentially conflicting goals. One is the rapid increase in productivity, particularly of marketable commodities and commercial crops, centering on high growth areas with easy access to transport and the cities. The second is overcoming the income gap between poorer and richer brigades, communes and regions. The state has targeted twelve priority regions as the focus of a program for rapid increase in marketable grain and commercial crops by 1985. Will this lead to a situation of increased inequality in the countryside with target areas prospering while others stagnate, a situation familiar to many Third World countries which have carried out the green revolution?

Information obtained in discussions with Hopei provincial officials in June 1978 suggests that both aspects of the problem are being vigorously addressed at the provincial level. While accelerating development in two regions along major railway lines in Hopei, by far the largest state investment is allocated for water conservancy projects which will transform the poor and disaster-prone Heilungkang region into a stable high-yield area. Moreover, the province allocates approximately 100 million yuan per year (one-seventh of its total capital construction budget) for direct support of poorer communes and brigades, particularly those in mountain areas. The result is that provincial targets for 1975 show an actual decline in the percentage of marketable grain provided by the two high-yield areas along the railways, with poorer and more remote regions, particularly Heilungkang, expanding overall at a slightly more rapid rate.

The drive to create Tachai-type counties throughout the countryside is likewise directed both at encouraging rapid growth and reducing inequalities. China has set a goal of creating 700 Tachai-type counties in 700 of the 2,100 counties by 1980. But what is the meaning of a Tachai-type county? As of 1978 primary emphasis is being placed on the achievement of high levels of productivity, including a renewed emphasis on quota systems and material incentives to stimulate production. However, two criteria for a Tachai-type county are successful implementation of the system of cadre participation in agricultural production (300 days a year at the team level, 200 at the brigade, 100 at the commune) and narrowing the income differentials between poorer brigades and communes. A critical yardstick for assessing the current modernization program will be its impact not only on production and income but on reducing the differences between poorer and more prosperous units, between city and countryside, and between cadres and working people.

China's agricultural development since the fifties has rested on self-reliant cooperative units, the communes, brigades, and teams. After two decades of testing, this system can be expected to provide an effective socialist framework for mechanization, electrification, and industrialization. Yet it will also be subject to new strains with the diversification and expansion of the rural economy and the increasing integration of the village in national life, a process which is now rapidly occurring with the diffusion of education, of radio, and particularly of television throughout the countryside.

Ambitious agricultural production targets of 4 to 5 percent per year, substantially above national growth rates since the fifties, underline the centrality of agriculture for the overall national plan. A critical question for agriculture in the coming decade is whether the high priorities of urban industry and foreign technology will squeeze the countryside dry and undermine self-reliant growth, or whether industry will serve the countryside and continue to contribute to overcoming the three great differences. At this writing, the evidence suggests a leadership preoccupied with the modernization drive yet aware of the necessity to modernize in ways which ensure that the countryside retains the resources for self-reliant development and for industry to directly serve agriculture on a large scale.

For half a century the countryside has been the center of revolutionary change. The peasantry, which has eliminated landlord oppression and the heaviest burdens of poverty through the formation of effective communal institutions, nevertheless remains a disadvantaged sector of society. With the death of Mao it has lost a powerful voice in the highest councils of state and party. Yet there is abundant reason to anticipate that even as official emphasis swings toward modernization and productivity, the sinews of communal life that have matured over two decades will retain their efficacy. Current national policy, in any event, is no carbon copy of the agrarian and industrial strategy of the early fifties. It builds on important elements of the Great Leap and the Cultural Revolution even as it seeks to restore imbalances generated during the last decade.

Table 16 highlights the major changes and continuities in successive phases of development from the 1950s to the current modernization strategy.

The Intellectuals and the Modernization of Education, Science, and Technology

In no area does the modernization strategy break so sharply with the Cultural Revolution as in policies concerning the intellectuals, education, and science. In none was the impact of the Cultural Revolution more profound and more divisive; in none did greater unresolved antagonisms and issues remain; and none is more crucial to the overall success of the modernization strategy.

The Cultural Revolution's educational achievements included expanding peasant and worker educational opportunities both at the basic levels and up through the universities; taking concrete measures to link education to egalitarian and productive goals through work-study programs (including "open-door education" with students going out to work and study in communes and factories) and the proliferation of factory-and-commune-run part-time schools; reorienting research, particularly to serving the countryside; transferring large numbers of intellectuals, cadres, and specialists from managerial to production tasks in city and countryside; and in a variety of ways attacking elitism among intellectuals and educators. Yet the attack on elitism over the course of a decade tended to strike at and discredit all intellectuals and intellectual work and, as the Cultural Revolution wore on, important areas of education and intellectual life remained moribund. To a great extent, education failed to play its intermediary role in linking revolution and production, in stimulating the advance of the socialist economy. The unresolved and hotly controversial issues surrounding intellectuals and education came to a head in 1975.

The debate and struggle augured major changes in the field of education, particularly in higher education. The Fourth National People's Congress in January 1975 re-established the Ministry of Education, which had ceased to function in 1967, and abolished the Science and Education Group that had directed education since the early 1970s. The new minister of education, Chou Jung-hsin, was an experienced administrator

Table 16

Stages in China's Development Priorities: The First Five-Year Plan, the Great Leap Forward, the Post-Leap Retrenchment, the Great Proletarian Cultural Revolution, the Modernization Era

	First five-year plan	Socialist upsurge and Great Leap Forward	Post-leap retrenchment	Great Proletarian Cultural Revolution	Modernization era
1. Main objective	Rapid industrialization centered on heavy industry	Simultaneous accelerated growth of socialist industry and agriculture, city and countryside	Agricultural recovery, industrial recovery	Rapid growth of industry and agriculture, reduce three great differences	Accelerated growth of industry and agriculture
2. Order of economic priorities	Heavy industry, light industry, agriculture	Simultaneous development	Agriculture, light industry, heavy industry	Same as post-leap	Leading role of modern heavy industry with agriculture as the base
3. Rural versus urban priority	Primacy of cities, urban idea	Primacy of countryside, proletarianization of peasants through communes & rural industry	Recovery rural agriculture, urban industry	Rural priority. Integrate industry in countryside, agriculture in cities	Greater urban emphasis, extend rural industrialization and mechanization
4. Economic role of city and countryside	Urban industry, rural agriculture	Urban industry, rural industry and agriculture	Urban industry, rural agriculture	Urban industry and agriculture, rural agriculture and industry	Rural agriculture and industry, urban mainly industry
5. Urban-rural economic relations	Countryside provides food, foreign exchange, investment capital for cities, industry	Countryside provides food; cities provide consumer goods, personnel to country; both accumulate capital	Countryside provides food, city provides producer goods for rural modernization in delta areas	As in post-leap, but cities provide more technology, skills to countryside	As in Cultural Revolution but resource squeeze may threaten countryside
6. Self-reliance versus foreign technology priority	Heavy reliance on Soviet technology; countryside provides foreign exchange	Self-reliance in indigenous and modern technology city and countryside	Rely on foreign technology in advanced industry	As in leap	Emphasize foreign, especially Japanese, technology while developing Chinese technology; extractive industries main ... of exch...

7. Choice of technology. labor (indigenous) versus capital intensive (modern)	Capital intensive focus	Labor intensive and indigenous technology emphasis	Labor intensive in agriculture, capital intensive in industry	As in leap, but greater emphasis on advanced technology	Replace labor by technology in city and country; advanced and intermediate
8. Mobilization versus technology priority	Technology	Mobilization first, technology second	Technology	As in leap	Technology first, mobilization second
9. Emphasize change in superstructure versus economic base	Base	Superstructure and base	Base	Superstructure	Base
10. Incentive structure	Stress individual material incentives	Stress collective, nonmaterial incentives; experiment with free supply briefly	Stress individual material incentives	Stress collective, nonmaterial incentives	Greater reliance on material incentives, stress collective
11. Industrial planning and management system	Central planning, one-man management	Decentralized planning, worker participation, workers upgraded to technician, engineer	Centralized planning, nominal worker participation, re-establish technical, managerial authority	As in leap, further develop worker role	Renew stress on central planning, expert decisionmaking; continue worker participation but abolish revolutionary committees
12. Position of scientists and intellectuals	Leaders of urban industry and education	"Red and expert"; stress serving countryside	Stress urban education and role in urban industry	Heavily criticized; learn from workers and peasants	Builders of modern socialist society
13. Principal slogans	"Let's be modern and Soviet"	"Catch up with Great Britain in 15 years," "Walking on two legs," "Politics in command"	"Take the whole country as a single chessboard"	"To rebel is justified," "Grasp revolution," "promote production"	"Make China a modern powerful socialist country by the end of the century"

and educator closely associated with Chou En-lai. His background and experience contrasted sharply with that of his major antagonist, Ch'ih Ch'un. Ch'ih, who led a propaganda team to Tsinghua University during the Cultural Revolution, eventually headed the university's revolutionary committee and served as deputy head of the Science and Education Group before his arrest following the fall of the "gang of four."

A number of Chou Jung-hsin's 1975 statements on education capture the thrust of his attempt to reform what he regarded as serious excesses brought about by the Cultural Revolution:

> These days, the standard of our universities is no higher than that of the old technical middle schools, either in terms of politics or professional competence.
>
> In the universities now: no more culture, no more theory, no more scientific research.
>
> When I speak like this there are people who attack me, saying that it is right-wing opportunism; today there are deviations that interfere with the revolutionary line of Chairman Mao. . . . The danger of these years is that, in the field of education, no one actually studies.
>
> The intellectuals must be treated correctly. We must not, on the one hand, use them to teach and, on the other, treat them as stinking intellectuals. How can they continue to teach well under such conditions?
>
> [In placing university graduates] if one places thoughtless emphasis on the principle "from the commune to the commune," how will the needs of other departments be satisfied?[55]

Whatever his private thoughts, Chou Jung-hsin did not explicitly reject the basic reforms of the Cultural Revolution. But he sought to overcome the paralysis in higher education and research which resulted from carrying them to disastrous extremes: the function of universities, he asserted, was to teach students to study in order to serve the people effectively, not to become an official or to become rich.

Since the summer of 1977 the major lines of a new educational strategy have become clear. They include substantially increasing the number of university students, particularly those specializing in science, technology, and engineering; raising admission standards (to the equivalent of senior middle school graduate) and curriculum standards; rapid expansion of postgraduate and specialist training; reopening the examination system to select academically qualified students; reopening special key point and experimental schools to train outstanding students and serve as a model for educational innovation; permitting selected students to proceed directly from high school to the university without an intervening period of work; raising the status and authority of teachers, researchers, and intellectuals; strengthening discipline in the schools; increasing study time and reducing the amount of time students spend in political activity and productive labor. Hua Kuo-feng's instruction sums up the present emphasis in education: "study, study, again study. Unity, unity, again unity."

These changes are designed to strengthen the basic educational content of the schools and the contribution of intellectuals after a decade of sharp political struggle. The danger is genuine that the new key point schools, tracking systems, and college entrance examination procedures will favor urban and educationally privileged children and work to the disadvantage of the poorer and rural areas. Yet it is difficult to deny the urgency at present of setting China's educational system on a firm foundation to expand its role in support of socialist development. Schools which fail to teach, however high their egalitarian and socialist standards, cannot serve the best interests of the disadvantaged in any society. The present expansion and the seriousness of purpose surrounding education will strengthen the technical basis for confronting the problems of poverty which retard development and above all the development of the countryside.

The fundamental tone and emphasis in higher education, in particular, have shifted dramatically since 1975. If the overwhelming educational stress of the Cultural Revolution Group was on education as a "tool of the dictatorship of the proletariat" and the class struggle, in 1978 it is on raising standards of education and research to propel forward China's modernization. As the August 1977 *Red Flag* put it, schools "are places where qualified people are trained" as well, it added, as given a "firm socialist orientation." Where the emphasis during the Cultural Revolution was on training *revolutionary* students, since late 1976 it has been on training *specialists* to serve China's socialist development.

Parallel themes dominate the fields of science and technology, which since 1977 have been promoted on a scale unparalleled since the founding of the People's Republic. Kuo Mo-jo, the eighty-six-year-old revolutionary poet, writer, and president of the Academy of Sciences, in 1978 in his final address spoke of a "springtime for science" in a lyrical manner formerly reserved for praise of revolutionary martyrs or Chairman Mao. "Today, suffering humiliation no more, we can say this with our chins up: The time when the reactionaries can trample on science has indeed gone for ever! The springtime of science is here!" Those reactionaries included not only the imperialist powers and the Kuomintang, but also, in Kuo's view, the "gang of four."

> Vindicated by my lifelong experience, one unassailable truth has dawned upon me: only socialism can liberate science, and the building of socialism is possible only when it is done on the basis of science. . . .
>
> Science deals with things in a practical way. Science means honest, solid knowledge, allowing not an iota of falsehood, and it involves herculean efforts and grueling toil. At the same time, science also calls for creativeness and imagination.[56]

Kuo's words, after a decade dominated by the militant language of politics, undoubtedly touched a responsive chord among many in China, above all, of course, scientists and intellectuals, but also perhaps large numbers of young people eager to learn and serve.

The Cultural Revolution had analyzed and sought to combat problems of elitism in Chinese society. Yet in moving beyond the critique of the abuses of an intellectual and political elite to a full-scale attack on virtually the entire party and state, and in effect condemning intellectuals as a group, it sowed the seeds of reaction against the sectarianism, clique politics, and demagogy which the movement bred.

As in much of the national debate since 1975, it was Teng Hsiao-p'ing who posed the problem most bluntly and articulated the extreme position with respect to science and intellectuals. Noting soberly that several hundred million Chinese are busy producing food, he observed that the average American farmworker produces more than fifty times the 1,000 kilograms of grain of his Chinese counterpart. "If we do not modernize our country, raise our scientific and technological level, develop the social productive forces, strengthen our country and improve the material life of our people," he told the March 1978 National Science Conference, "our socialist political and economic system cannot be fully consolidated and there will be no sure guarantee for our country's security."[57] Teng stressed that intellectuals ("brain workers trained by the proletariat") are part of the proletariat: "Those who labor, whether by hand or by brain, are all working people in socialist society." But it was in his discussion of the problem of red and expert that Teng provided the sharpest challenge to a cultural revolution perspective:

> If a person loves our socialist motherland and is serving socialism and the workers, peasants and soldiers of his own free will and accord, it should be said that he has initially acquired a proletarian world outlook and, in terms of political standards, cannot be considered white but should be called red. . . . To devote oneself to our socialist science and contribute to it is an important manifestation of being red, the integration of being red with being expert.[58]

With this definition, Teng essentially equated science with socialism and nationalism, thus emasculating Mao's concept of red and expert by discarding its political core and exempting scientists from political concerns. Teng's statements reflect the current high priority on the complete rehabilitation and integration of scientists and intellectuals into the mainstream of Chinese life. In criticizing the "gang of four" for its one-sided emphasis on politics at the expense of study, the danger exists that current policies will swing to the opposite extreme, likewise failing to integrate politics and knowledge in the service of socialist development. In statements such as those of Teng's we see the basis for dissolving entirely the bonds linking red and expert, politics and profession.

In 1978 Chinese education and science continue to incorporate perceptions and experiments of the Cultural Revolution era while sharply reducing their prominence. Seventy to eighty percent (but no longer 100 percent) of incoming university students are drawn from those with two or more years of work experience; many, though probably a smaller percentage, are drawn from worker and peasant backgrounds; "open-door schooling," linking education and labor, remains an integral though reduced part of the curriculum; many students drawn from communes and factories will return to those units after graduation, although more graduates will be assigned to other posts; significant research is being directed toward the countryside while once again, after a lapse of a decade, theoretical research is being conducted. At the same time China is embarking on a major educational expansion. Education is to be universally extended to eight years in the countryside and ten years in the cities. A decade after the Cultural Revolution China urgently needs to strengthen educational and technical standards and extend its cultural horizons. Perhaps more than in any other sphere the danger exists, however, that the current reforms will swing to an extreme which divorces education from socialist and egalitarian values underlined in the philosophy of Mao and the Cultural Revolution.

In 1957, during the Hundred Flowers Movement, in a passage which has been widely cited since his death, Mao offered this definition of the goal of Chinese politics, of the people's democratic dictatorship:

> to protect all our people so that they can devote themselves to peaceful labor and build China into a socialist country with a modern industry, agriculture, science and culture. Who is to exercise this dictatorship? Naturally the working class and the entire people under its leadership. Dictatorship does not apply within the ranks of the people. The people cannot exercise dictatorship over themselves, nor must one section of the people oppress another. [59]

The policies toward intellectuals and scientists associated with the drive toward modernization rest on explicitly extending these guarantees to reintegrate within the ranks of the people a vitally important group for the future of a socialist nation which is expanding access to education and technology to large numbers of people. At the same time it remains essential to guard against the dangers of elitism and bureaucracy so brilliantly exposed during the Cultural Revolution.

In 1976 the deaths of Mao Tsetung and Chou En-lai deprived China of the two leaders who had guided not only the revolution and reconstruction of the People's Republic but the movement for national liberation which preceded its founding. Following a decade of intense political turmoil, frequently verging on civil war, it is hardly surprising that the new leadership of Hua Kuo-feng would take as its first priority the establishment of unity and order as the foundation for socialist modernization and development. A successful beginning of these tasks is the prerequisite for the continued advance of Chinese socialism. And in the institutional formation of the people's communes and the Communist Party, above all in the rich experience of the Chinese people, the basis exists for continuing the revolution in new forms appropriate to changing economic and political conditions of Chinese socialism. Yet as we know, the forces of routinization and bureaucratic privilege are extremely powerful. Revolutions atrophy and die. The swing of the policy pendulum to redress problems inherent in the Cultural Revolution cannot but raise legitimate fears that the momentum will bring to an end a century of uninterrupted revolution. To conclude that the issues have been resolved, however, denigrates the commitment of people and leadership to continued socialist development and exaggerates the important contributions of a single leader. What is certain is that devising appropriate forms for continuing the revolution under new conditions constitutes the challenge of the next generation.

Toward the beginning of this study we noted central contradictions and tensions the resolution of which would provide difficult tests to Chinese socialism: between centralism and democracy; between national unity and shared community on the one hand and the necessity to eliminate class privilege on the other; between state, collective, and individual; and between city and countryside, worker and peasant, mental and manual labor, men and women, and Han and minority peoples. In the course of three decades impressive achievements have been made in addressing these problems. Their ultimate resolution in ways which reinforce economic growth and extend the frontiers of human self-realization remains the yardstick for gauging the quality of socialist life in the People's Republic of China.

Notes

1. *Niles' National Register*, January 22, 1842, pp. 327-28; cited in Harry Magdoff, *The Age of Imperialism. The Economics of U.S. Foreign Policy* (New York: Monthly Review Press, 1969), p. 174.
2. Paul Henry Report, Archives of the International Labor Office, Geneva, Part II, Working Condition, p. 3; cited in Jean Chesneaux, *The Chinese Labor Movement, 1919-1927* (Stanford: Stanford University Press, 1968), p. 86.
3. Edgar Snow, *Red Star Over China* (London: Victor Gollancz, 1937), pp. 216-17.
4. Jan Myrdal, *Report From a Chinese Village* (New York: Pantheon, 1965), p. 126.
5. Jack Belden, *China Shakes the World* (New York: Monthly Review Press, 1970), p. 97.
6. Mao Tsetung, "Some Questions Concerning Methods of Leadership," in *Selected Readings from the Works of Mao Tsetung* (hereafter *SR*) (Peking: Foreign Languages Press, 1971), p. 290.
7. V. I. Lenin, "Left-wing Communism—An Infantile Disorder," in Robert Tucker, ed., *The Lenin Anthology* (New York: W. W. Norton, 1975), p. 553.
8. Mao Tsetung, *Ching-chi wen-t'i yu ts'ai-cheng wen-t'i* (Economic and Financial Problems) (Hong Kong: Hsin min-chu ch'u-pan-she, 1947), p. 200.
9. Paul Baran, *The Political Economy of Growth* (New York: Monthly Review Press, 1962), p. viii.
10. Mao Tsetung, *A Critique of Soviet Economics* (New York: Monthly Review Press, 1977), p. 51.
11. Mao Tsetung, "On Contradiction," *SR*, p. 89.
12. Karl Marx, "Critique of the Gotha Program," in Robert Tucker, ed., *The Marx-Engels Reader* (New York: W. W. Norton, 1972), p. 388.
13. Charles Bettelheim, *Class Struggles in the USSR. First Period: 1917-1923* (New York: Monthly Review Press, 1970), p. 18.
14. Mao Tsetung, "Report to the Second Plenary Session of the Seventh Central Committee," *Selected Works of Mao Tse-tung* (Peking: Foreign Languages Press, 1965), IV:363. Hereafter, these works will be denoted by *SW* and the volume number.
15. Mao Tsetung, "The Contradiction Between the Working Class and the Bourgeoisie is the Principal Contradiction in China," *SW*, V:77.
16. V. I. Lenin, cited in Bettelheim, *Class Struggle in the Soviet Union*, pp. 145-46.
17. Tientsin *Ta Kung Pao*, December 31, 1953; cited in Franz Schurmann, *Ideology and Organization in Communist China* (Berkeley: University of California Press, 1966), p. 255. The quote is taken from Lenin's

"The Immediate Tasks of the Soviet Government," in Tucker, ed., *The Lenin Anthology*, p. 455.

18. Hans Heymann, Jr., "Acquisition and Diffusion of Technology in China," in Joint Economic Committee of Congress, *China: A Reassessment of the Economy* (Washington: Joint Economic Committee of Congress of the United States, 1975), p. 686.

19. Mao Tsetung, "On the Question of Agricultural Cooperation," *SR*, p. 390.

20. Ibid., pp. 405-6.

21. Ibid., pp. 411-12.

22. Ibid., pp. 402-3.

23. Ibid., p. 406.

24. Mao Tsetung, "On the Ten Major Relationships," *Peking Review* January 1, 1977, p. 11.

25. Ibid., pp. 14, 17.

26. "Resolution of the Eighth National Congress of the Communist Party of China," in *Eighth National Congress of the Communist Party of China*, 3 vols. (Peking: Foreign Languages Press, 1956), I:116.

27. Mao Tsetung, "Talks at a Conference of Provincial, Municipal and Autonomous Region Party Committees," *SW*, V:358.

28. Mao Tsetung, "Persevere in Plain Living and Hard Struggle, Maintain Close Ties With the Masses," *SW*, V:437.

29. Mao Tsetung, "The Situation in the Summer of 1957," *SW* V: 473-74.

30. Anna Louise Strong, *The Rise of the Chinese People's Communes— and Six Years After* (Peking: New World Press, 1964), p. 16.

31. "Resolution of the Central Committee of the Chinese Communist Party on the Establishment of People's Communes in the Rural Areas," in Robert Bowie and John Fairbank, eds., *Communist China 1955-1959: Policy Documents with Analysis*, (Cambridge, Mass.: Harvard University Press, 1962), p. 45.

32. Chou En-lai, "Report on the Adjustment of Major Targets in the National Economic Plan for 1959 and Further Development of the Campaign for Increasing Production and Practising Economy"; cited in K. C. Yeh, "Soviet and Communist Chinese Industrialization Strategies," in Donald Treadgold, ed., *Soviet and Chinese Communism. Similarities and Differences* (Seattle: University of Washington Press, 1967), p. 350.

33. Liu Shao-ch'i, "The Present Situation, the Party's General Line for Socialist Construction and its Future Tasks," in Bowie and Fairbank, eds., *Policy Documents*, p. 491.

34. The analysis here draws on Nakamura Hisashi, *Accumulation and Interchange of Labor* (Tokyo: Institute of Developing Economies, 1976), pp. 99-105.

35. "Resolution on Some Questions Concerning the People's Communes"

adopted by the Eighth Central Committee of the Party at its Sixth Plenary Session, in Bowie and Fairbank, eds., *Policy Documents*, p. 491.

36. Mao Tsetung, in *A Critique of Soviet Economics*. (New York: Monthly Review Press, 1978).

37. Strong, *The Rise of the Chinese People's Communes*, p. 49.

38. *Miscellany of Mao Tse-tung Thought (1949-1968)* (Arlington, Virginia: Joint Publications Research Service, 1974), I:115.

39. Mao Tsetung, "Speech at the Second Chengchow Conference," *Chinese Law and Government*, 1977.

40. M. Gardner Clark, *The Development of China's Steel Industry and Soviet Technical Aid* (Ithaca, N.Y.: Cornell University Press, 1973), p. 78.

41. "Sweep Away All Monsters," included in *The Great Socialist Cultural Revolution* (Peking: Foreign Languages Press, 1966), p. 2.

42. *People's Daily*, January 23, 1967; cited in Victor Nee, "Revolution and Bureaucracy: Shanghai in the Cultural Revolution," in Victor Nee and James Peck, eds., *China's Uninterrupted Revolution, From 1840 to the Present* (New York: Pantheon, 1975), p. 340.

43. *Miscellany of Mao Tse-tung Thought*, II:451.

44. "Premier Chou En-lai's Comment on the Situation in Northeast China," September 28, 1967, in David Milton, Nancy Milton, and Franz Schurmann, eds., *People's China. Social Experimentation, Politics, Entry onto the World Scene, 1965 through 1972* (New York: Vintage, 1974), p. 358.

45. Jonathan Unger, "Collective Incentives in a Peasant Community: Lessons From Chin Village," *Social Scientist*, May/June 1977, p. 48.

46. Hsu Chin-chiang, "Hold High the Great Red Banner of the Thought of Mao Tsetung, Further Deepen the Revolutionization of Enterprises. Basic Experience in Revolutionizing the Tach'ing Oil Field," *Ching-chi yen-chiu* (Economic Research), in *Selections from People's Republic Magazine* (SCPRM) (Hong Kong U.S. Consulate-General), 538, April 20, 1965, p. 25.

47. Kuo Huan, "Chung-shih huan-ching pao-hu kung-tso" (Emphasize environmental protection work), *Red Flag*, September 1974, p. 23.

48. Quoted in introduction to Tucker, ed., *The Lenin Anthology*, p. lx.

49. Interview, Shihchiachuang, June 1978.

50. Teng Hsiao-p'ing, "On Accelerating the Development of Industry," *Selections from People's Republic of China Magazines* (SCPRM), 926, May 23, 1977. p. 22.

51. Kung Hsiao-wen (pseudonym), "Teng Hsiao-p'ing and the Twenty Articles," *Hsueh-hsi yu p'i-p'an* (Study and Criticism), SCPRM, 879, July 12, 1976, p. 6.

52. Karl Marx, "Critique of the Gotha Program," in Tucker, ed., *The Marx-Engels Reader*, p. 387.

53. Chang Ch'un-ch'iao, "On Exercising All-Round Dictatorship Over the Bourgeoisie," *Peking Review*, April 4, 1975, p. 6.
54. Mao Tsetung, "Talks at the Ch'engtu Conference," in Stuart Schram, ed., *Chairman Mao Talks to the People* (New York: Pantheon, 1974), p. 114.
55. Cited in John Gardner, "Chou Jung-hsin and Chinese Education," *Current Scene*, November-December 1977, pp. 12-13.
56. Kuo Mo-jo, "Springtime for Science," *Peking Review*, April 7, 1978.
57. Teng Hsiao-p'ing, "Speech at Opening Ceremony of National Science Conference," *Peking Review*, March 24, 1978, p. 10.
58. Ibid., pp. 13-14.
59. Mao Tsetung, "On the Correct Handling of Contradictions Among the People," *SR*, p. 436.

I

LAND REVOLUTION AND THE NEW DEMOCRACY
1946-1952

A. POLICY GUIDELINES

1. MAO TSETUNG,
THE PRESENT SITUATION AND OUR TASKS

In "The Present Situation and Our Tasks," the first compre-hensive statement following the defeat of Japan, Mao Tsetung defined the strategy for defeating the Kuomintang and for implementing new democratic policies with respect to the agrarian revolution and urban industry. Writing at the moment when the revolutionary forces shifted to the offensive from the defensive strategy characteristic of two decades of guerrilla resistance against the Kuomintang (1927–1937) and the Jap-anese (1937–1945), Mao carefully delineated a class policy designed to carry forward the agrarian revolution and the nationalization of bureaucratic capital while guarding against excessively radical policies which threatened to damage the economy. This was the heart of rural and urban policies that would mobilize the Chinese people in support of the People's Liberation Army offensive and lay the groundwork for a new political economy to destroy feudalism (the landlord-dominated rural economy) and bureaucratic capitalism (in the form of Kuomintang-linked large-scale enterprise) while fostering the controlled development of capitalism in the economic activity of rich peasants, small capitalists, and craftsmen.

The Present Situation and Our Tasks. Report to the Central Committee, December 25, 1947. In: *The Selected Works of Mao Tse-tung*, IV (SW). The text presented here modifies the 1961 official translation on the basis of the original text. The original English translation is available in *China Digest* (CD), January 13, 1948.

In the agrarian revolution, the party's policy was to "rely on the poor peasants and unite solidly with the middle peasants" in order to tap the explosive force of China's peasant majority while avoiding costly divisiveness in the ranks of the peasantry. The backbone of this effort lay in support for the poor peasants' leagues. At the same time Mao sharply delineated rich peasants from landlords. To stimulate the economy and isolate the main enemy, the party protected the bearers of rural capitalism, the rich peasants. Here was one of the central principles of Mao's revolutionary strategy: unite with all who could be united to defeat the main enemy; the corollary, attend simultaneously to revolution and to production.

The strategy of isolating the most powerful enemy while encouraging the neutrality or even support of progressive elements of a nascent capitalism was also applied to the cities where bureaucratic capitalism was nationalized and administered by the state while those small capitalists, who were themselves victimized by Kuomintang policy and the inroads of foreign capital, were encouraged to expand. Mao indicated that, in light of the backwardness of the Chinese economy, even after liberation it would be necessary to permit the existence of capitalism "for a long period of time," to build a "flourishing economy taking into account both public and private interests and benefits to both labor and capital."

Mao's report not only established the party's major guidelines for the next five years; it also represented the first full exposition of the strategy of development by clearly differentiated stages toward national liberation, new democracy, and, eventually, toward socialism.

The Chinese people's revolutionary war has now reached a turning point. That is, the Chinese People's Liberation Army has beaten back the offensive of several million reactionary troops of Chiang Kai-shek, the running dog of the United States of America, and gone over to the offensive. . . . This is a turning point in history. It is the turning point from growth to extinction for Chiang Kai-shek's twenty-year counter-revolutionary rule. It is the turning point from growth to extinction for imperialist rule in China, now over a hundred years old. . . .

After the Japanese surrender, the peasants urgently demanded land, and we made a timely decision to change our land policy from reducing rent and interest to confiscating the land of the landlord class for distribution among the peasants. The directive issued by the Central Committee of our party on May 4, 1946, marked this change. In September 1947 our party called the National Land Conference and drew up the Outline Land Law of China, which was promptly carried out in all areas. This measure not only reaffirmed the policy set forth in last year's May Fourth Directive but also explicitly corrected a certain lack of thoroughness in that directive (the landlords obtaining more land and properties than the peasants; the land and properties of rich peasants being left untouched in principle). The Outline Land Law provides for equal distribution of land per head, based on the principle of abolishing the land system of feudal and semifeudal exploitation and putting into effect the system of land to the tillers. This is a method which most thoroughly abolishes the feudal system and fully meets the demands of the broad masses of China's peasants. To carry out the land reform resolutely and thoroughly, it is necessary to organize in the villages, as lawful bodies for carrying out the reform, not only peasant associations on the broadest mass basis, including farm laborers, poor peasants, and middle peasants and their elected committees, but first of all poor peasant leagues composed of poor peasants and farm laborers and their elected committees; and these poor peasants' leagues should be the backbone of leadership in all rural struggles. Our policy is to rely on the poor peasants and unite solidly with the middle peasants to abolish the feudal and semifeudal system of exploitation by the landlord class and by the old-type rich peasants. Landlords or rich peasants must not be allotted more land and property than the peasant masses. But there should be no repetition of the wrong ultra-left policy, which was carried out in 1931-1934, of "allotting no land to the landlords and poor land to the rich peasants." Although the proportion of landlords and rich peasants in the rural population varies from place to place, it is generally only about 8 percent (in terms of households), while their holdings usually amount to 70 to 80 percent of all the land. Therefore the targets of our land reform are very few, while the people in the villages who can and should take part in the united front for land reform are many— more than 90 percent (in terms of households). Here two fundamental principles must be observed. First, the demands of the poor peasants and farm laborers must be satisfied; this is the most fundamental task in the land reform. Second, there must be firm unity with the middle peasants, and their interests must not be damaged. As long as we grasp these two basic principles, we can certainly carry out our tasks in the land reform successfully. The reason why, under the principle of equal distribution, the surplus land and part of the property of the old-type rich peasants should be handed over for distribution is that the rich peasants in China generally and to a great degree have the character of feudal and semifeudal exploiters; most of them also rent out land and practice usury and they hire labor on semifeudal terms. Furthermore, as the rich peasants have more and better land, the demands of the poor peasants and farm laborers cannot be satisfied unless this land is distributed. However, in accordance with the Outline Land Law, rich peasants should generally be treated differently from landlords. In the land reform, the middle peasants show approval of equal distribution because it does no harm to their interests. Under equal distribution, the land of one section of the middle peasants remains unchanged and that of another is increased; only the section of well-to-do middle peasants has a little surplus land, and they are willing to hand it over for equal distribution because their burden of land tax will then be lightened. Nevertheless, in carrying out equal distribution of land in different places, it is necessary to listen to the opinions of the middle peasants and make concessions to them if they object. During the confiscation and distribution of the land and property of the feudal class, the needs of certain middle peasants should receive attention. In determining class status care must be taken to avoid the mistake of classifying middle peasants as rich peasants. The active middle peasants must be drawn into the work of the peasant association committees and the government. With respect to the burdens of the land tax and of supporting the war, the principle of being fair and reasonable must be observed. These are the specific policies our party must follow in carrying out its strategic task of uniting solidly with the middle peasants. The whole party must understand that thoroughgoing reform of the land system is a basic task of the Chinese Revolution in its present stage. If we can solve the land problem universally and completely, we shall have obtained the most fundamental condition for the defeat of all our enemies. . . .

Confiscate the land of the feudal class and turn it over to the peasants. Confiscate monopoly capital, headed by Chiang Kaishek, T. V. Soong, H. H. Kung, and Ch'en Li-fu, and turn it over to the new democratic state. Protect the industry and commerce of the national bourgeoisie. These are the three major economic policies of the new democratic revolution. During their twenty-year rule, the four big families, Chiang, Soong, Kung, and Ch'en, have piled up enormous fortunes valued at ten or twenty thousand million U.S. dollars and monopolized the economic lifelines of the whole country. This monopoly capital, combined with state power, has become state monopoly capitalism. This monopoly capitalism, closely tied up with foreign imperialism, the domestic landlord class and the old-type rich peasants, has become compradore, feudal, state monopoly capitalism. Such is the economic base of Chiang Kai-shek's reactionary regime. This state monopoly capitalism oppresses not only the workers and peasants but also the petty bourgeoisie, and it injures the middle bourgeoisie. This state monopoly capitalism reached the peak of its development during the War of Resistance and after the Japanese surrender; it has prepared ample material conditions for the new democratic revolution. This capital is popularly known in China as a bureaucrat-capital. This capitalist class, known as the bureaucrat-capitalist class, is the big bourgeoisie of China. Besides doing away with the special privileges of imperialism in China, the task of the new democratic revolution at home is to abolish exploitation and oppression by the landlord class and by the bureaucrat-capitalist class (the big bourgeoisie), change the compradore, feudal relations of production and unfetter the productive forces. The petty bourgeoisie and middle bourgeoisie, oppressed and injured by the landlords and big bourgeoisie and their state power, may take part in the new democratic revolution or stay neutral, though they are themselves bourgeois. They have no ties, or comparatively few, with imperialism and are the genuine national bourgeoisie. Wherever the state power of new democracy extends, it must firmly and unhesitatingly protect them. . . . The new democratic revolution aims at wiping out only feudalism and monopoly capitalism, only the landlord class and the bureaucrat-capitalist class (the big bourgeoisie), and not at wiping out capitalism in general, the upper petty bourgeoisie or the middle bourgeoisie. In view of China's economic backwardness, even after the country-wide victory of the revolution, it will still be necessary to permit the existence for a long time of a capitalist sector of the economy represented by the extensive petty bourgeoisie and middle bourgeoisie. In accordance with the division of labor in the national economy, a certain development of all parts of this capitalist sector which are beneficial to the national economy will still be needed. This capitalist sector will still be an indispensable part of the whole national economy. The petty bourgeoisie referred to here are small industrialists and merchants employing workers or assistants. In addition, there are also great numbers of small independent craftsmen and traders who employ no workers or assistants and, needless to say, they should be firmly protected. After the victory of the revolution all over the country, the new democratic state will possess huge state enterprises taken over from the bureaucrat-capitalist class and controlling the economic lifelines of the country, and there will be an agricultural economy liberated from feudalism which, though it will remain basically scattered and individual for a fairly long time, can later be led to develop, step by step, in the direction of cooperatives. In these circumstances the existence and development of these small and middle capitalist sectors will present no danger. The same is true of the new rich peasant economy which will inevitably emerge in the rural areas after the land reform. It is absolutely impermissible to repeat such wrong ultra-left policies toward the petty bourgeois and middle bourgeois sectors in the economy as our party adopted during 1931–1934 (unduly advanced labor conditions, excessive income tax rates, encroachment on the interests of industrialists and merchants during the land reform, and the adoption as a goal of the so-called "workers' welfare," which was a shortsighted and one-sided concept, instead of the goal of developing production, promoting economic prosperity, giving consideration to both public and private interests and benefiting both labor and capital). To repeat such mistakes would certainly damage the interests both of the working masses and of the new democratic state. One of the provisions in the Outline Land

Law of China reads, "The property and lawful business of industrialists and merchants shall be protected from encroachment." "Industrialists and merchants" refers to all small independent craftsmen and traders as well as all small and middle capitalist elements. To sum up, the economic structure of new China will consist of: (1) the state-owned economy, which is the leading sector; (2) the agricultural economy, developing step by step from individual to collective; and (3) the economy of small independent craftsmen and traders and the economy of small and middle private capital. These constitute the whole of the new democratic national economy. The principles guiding the new democratic national economy must closely conform to the general objective of developing production, promoting economic prosperity, giving consideration to both public and private interests and benefiting both labor and capital. Any principle, policy, or measure that deviates from this general objective is wrong.

2. MAO TSETUNG,
THE PEOPLE'S DEMOCRATIC DICTATORSHIP

Mao's address "On the People's Democratic Dictatorship" succinctly defined principles of the domestic and international policy which would guide the People's Republic. "To sum up our experience and concentrate it into one point," he stated, "it is: the People's Democratic Dictatorship under the leadership of the working class (through the Communist Party) and based upon the alliance of workers and peasants. This dictatorship must unite as one with the international revolutionary forces." Underlining the fact that the broad united front which had carried the Communist Party to the brink of victory would continue under the People's Republic, Mao defined the People's Democratic Dictatorship as a system which would guarantee "democracy for the people and dictatorship over the reactionaries."

From 1927, when it was driven into the countryside to take

On the People's Democratic Dictatorship. CD, June 30, 1949, and July 13, 1949. In: *Selected Readings from the Works of Mao Tse-tung* (SR).

up arms, the Communist Party had experienced more than two decades of extreme isolation. The civil war period beginning in 1945 had further dramatized that isolation as the Communists found themselves attacked by Kuomintang forces armed and supported by the United States while the Soviet Union urged a settlement which would have partitioned the nation. Despite prolonged efforts to prevent isolation and to avoid a situation of all-out hostility by the capitalist nations, by 1949 the party leadership concluded, in Mao's words, that China "must lean either to the side of imperialism or to the side of socialism."

Twenty-four years have passed since Sun Yat-sen's death, and the Chinese Revolution, led by the Communist Party of China, has made tremendous advances both in theory and practice and has radically changed the face of China. Up to now the principal and fundamental experience the Chinese people have gained is twofold:

1. Internally, arouse the masses of the people. That is, unite the working class, the peasantry, the urban petty bourgeoisie and the national bourgeoisie, form a domestic united front under the leadership of the working class, and advance from this to the establishment of a state which is a people's democratic dictatorship under the leadership of the working class and based on the alliance of workers and peasants.

2. Externally, unite in a common struggle with those nations of the world which treat us as equals and with the peoples of all countries. That is, ally ourselves with the Soviet Union, with the people's democracies, and with the proletariat and the broad masses of the people in all other countries, and form an international united front.

"You are leaning to one side." Exactly. The forty years' experience of Sun Yat-sen and the twenty-eight years' experience of the Communist Party have taught us to lean to one side, and we are firmly convinced that in order to win victory and consolidate it we must lean to one side. In the light of the experiences accumulated in these forty years and these twenty-eight years, all Chinese without exception must lean either to the side of imperialism or to the side of socialism. Sitting on the fence will not do, nor is there a third road. . . .

"We want to do business." Quite right, business will be done. We are against no one except the domestic and foreign reactionaries who hinder us from doing business. Everybody should know that it is none other than the imperialists and their running dogs, the Chiang Kai-shek reactionaries, who hinder us from doing business and also from establishing diplomatic relations with foreign countries. When we have beaten the internal and external reactionaries by uniting all domestic and international forces, we shall be able to do business and establish diplomatic relations with all foreign countries on the basis of equality, mutual benefit, and mutual respect for territorial integrity and sovereignty.

"Victory is possible even without international help." This is a mistaken idea. In the epoch in which imperialism exists, it is impossible for a genuine people's revolution to win victory in any country without various forms of help from the international revolutionary forces, and even if victory were won, it could not be consolidated. This was the case with the victory and consolidation of the great October Revolution, as Stalin told us long ago. This was also the case with the overthrow of the three imperialist powers in World War II and the establishment of the people's democracies. And this is also the case with the present and the future of People's China. . . .

"You are dictatorial." My dear sirs, you are right, that is just what we are. All the experience the Chinese people have accumulated through several decades teaches us to enforce the People's Democratic Dictatorship, that is, to deprive the reactionaries of the right to speak and let the people alone have that right.

Who are the people? At the present stage in China, they are the working class, the peasantry, the urban petty bourgeoisie, and the national bourgeoisie. These classes, led by the working class and the Communist Party, unite to form their own state and elect their own government; they enforce their dictatorship over the running dogs of imperialism—the landlord class and bureaucrat-bourgeoisie, as well as the representatives of those classes, the Kuomintang reactionaries and their accomplices—suppress them, allow them only to behave themselves and not to be unruly in word or deed. If they speak or act in an unruly way, they will be promptly stopped and punished. Democracy is practiced within the ranks of the people, who enjoy the rights of freedom of speech, assembly, association and so on. The right to vote belongs only to the people, not to the reactionaries. The combination of these two aspects, democracy for the people and dictatorship over the reactionaries, is the People's Democratic Dictatorship. . . .

The serious problem is the education of the peasantry. The peasant economy is scattered, and the socialization of agriculture, judging by the Soviet Union's experience, will require a long time and painstaking work. Without socialization of agriculture, there can be no complete, consolidated socialism. The steps to socialize agriculture must be coordinated with the development of a powerful industry having state enterprise as its backbone. The state of the People's Democratic Dictatorship must systematically solve the problems of industrialization. . . .

The People's Democratic Dictatorship is based on the alliance of the working class, the peasantry and the urban petty bourgeoisie, and mainly on the alliance of the workers and the peasants, because these two classes comprise 80 to 90 percent of China's population. These two classes are the main force in overthrowing imperialism and the Kuomintang reactionaries. The transition from new democracy to socialism also depends mainly upon their alliance.

The People's Democratic Dictatorship needs the leadership of the working class. For it is only the working class that is most farsighted, most selfless and most thoroughly revolutionary. . . .

To sum up our experience and concentrate it into one point, it is: the People's Democratic Dictatorship under the leadership of the working class (through the Communist Party) and based upon the alliance of workers and peasants. This dictatorship must unite as one with the international revolutionary forces. This is our formula, our principal experience, and our main program.

3. MAO TSETUNG,
FROM THE COUNTRYSIDE TO THE CITY

Mao's "Report to the Second Plenary Session of the Seventh Central Committee" constitutes the fullest overview of the economic problems, and the basic approach to reconstructing a new democratic economy on the eve of liberation. Warning of the danger to the revolution of "sugar-coated bullets" provided by a bourgeoisie which had been defeated on the battlefield but not eliminated, Mao for the first time in more than two decades emphasized that the cities must play the leading role in the new stage of the revolution. As the party looked beyond war to reconstruction, management of industry, particularly heavy and state-owned industry, provided a formidable challenge to a movement which had fought for more than two decades in the countryside.

Mao analyzed the strength and class composition of each economic sector in charting the first steps toward the creation of a multifaceted economy en route to socialism. In industry, the core lay in a socialized sector formed by nationalization of large-scale industry and finance directly administered by the Kuomintang in its final years. In agriculture and handicrafts the first steps toward semisocialist cooperatives would begin to transform the dominant small-scale pattern of individual ownership and cultivation. State control of foreign trade would end the days when imperialism set the rules for China's economy. At the same time, Mao clearly delineated a continuing if subordinate role for private enterprise. In contrast to the class struggle played out in every village and hamlet in rural China, the transition in industry and finance would emphasize orderly transfer of power to the state (in the case of bureaucratic capital) and the necessity for sustaining output in all enterprises. And it would require mastery of technical and managerial skills if revolutionaries were to successfully reconstruct society.

Report to the Second Plenary Session of the Seventh Central Committee of the Communist Party of China, March 5, 1949. SW IV.

From 1927 to the present the center of gravity of our work has been in the villages—gathering strength in the villages, using the villages in order to surround the cities, and then taking the cities. The period for this method of work has now ended. The period of "from the city to the village" and of the city leading the village has now begun. The center of gravity of the party's work has shifted from the village to the city. In the south the People's Liberation Army will occupy first the cities and then the villages. Attention must be given to both city and village and it is necessary to link closely urban and rural work, workers and peasants, industry and agriculture. Under no circumstances should the village be ignored and only the city given attention; such thinking is entirely wrong. Nevertheless, the center of gravity of the work of the party and the army must be in the cities; we must do our utmost to learn how to administer and build the cities. In the cities we must learn how to wage political, economic, and cultural struggles against the imperialists, the Kuomintang, and the bourgeoisie and also how to wage diplomatic struggles against the imperialists. We must learn how to carry on overt struggles against them. If we do not pay attention to these problems, if we do not learn how to wage these struggles against them and win victory in the struggles, we shall be unable to maintain our political power, we shall be unable to stand on our feet, we shall fail. After the enemies with guns have been wiped out, there will still be enemies without guns; they are bound to struggle desperately against us; we must never regard these enemies lightly. . . .

On whom shall we rely in our struggles in the cities? Some muddle-headed comrades think we should rely not on the working class but on the masses of the poor. Some comrades who are even more muddle-headed think we should rely on the bourgeoisie. As for the direction of industrial development, some muddle-headed comrades maintain that we should chiefly help the development of private enterprise and not state enterprise, whereas others hold the opposite view, that it suffices to pay attention to state enterprise and that private enterprise is of little importance. We must criticize these muddled views. We must wholeheartedly rely on the working class, unite with the rest of the laboring masses, win over the intellectuals and win over to our side as many as possible of the national bourgeois elements and their representatives who can cooperate with us—or neutralize them—so that we can wage a determined struggle against the imperialists, the Kuomintang and the bureaucrat-capitalist class and defeat these enemies step by step. Meanwhile we shall set about our task of construction and learn, step by step, how to administer cities and restore and develop their production. Regarding the problem of restoring and developing production we must be clear about the following: first comes the production of state industry; second, the production of private industry; and third, handicraft production. From the very first day we take over a city, we should direct our attention to restoring and developing its production. We must not go about our work blindly and haphazardly and forget our central task, lest several months after taking over a city its production and construction should still not be on the right track and many industries should be at a standstill, with the result that the workers are unemployed, their livelihood deteriorates and they become dissatisfied with the Communist Party. Such a state of affairs is entirely impermissible. Therefore, our comrades must do their utmost to learn the techniques of production and the methods of managing production as well as other closely related work such as commerce and banking. Only when production in the cities is restored and developed, when consumer-cities are transformed into producer-cities, can the people's political power be consolidated. Other work in the cities, for example, in party organization, in organs of political power, in trade unions and other people's organizations, in culture and education, in the suppression of counter-revolutionaries, in news agencies, newspapers, and broadcasting stations—all this work revolves around and serves the central task, production and construction. If we know nothing about production and do not master it quickly, if we cannot restore and develop production as speedily as possible and achieve solid successes so that the livelihood of the workers, first of all, and that of the people in general is improved, we shall be unable to maintain our political power, we shall be unable to stand on our feet, we shall fail. . . .

Before the War of Resistance against Japan, the proportions

of industry and agriculture in the entire national economy of China were, modern industry about 10 percent, and agriculture and handicrafts about 90 percent. This was the result of imperialist and feudal oppression; this was the economic expression of the semicolonial and semifeudal character of the society of old China; and this is our basic point of departure for all questions during the period of the Chinese Revolution and for a fairly long period after victory. . . .

1. China already has a modern industry constituting about 10 percent of her economy; this is progressive, this is different from ancient times. As a result, China has new classes and new political parties—the proletariat and the bourgeoisie, proletarian and bourgeois parties. The proletariat and its party, because they have been oppressed by manifold enemies, have become steeled and are qualified to lead the Chinese people's revolution. Whoever overlooks or belittles this point will commit right opportunist mistakes.

2. China still has scattered and individual agriculture and handicrafts, constituting about 90 percent of her entire economy; this is backward, this is not very different from ancient times—about 90 percent of our economic life remains the same as in ancient times. We have abolished, or will soon abolish, the age-old feudal ownership of land. . . . In their basic form, however, our agriculture and handicrafts today are still scattered and individual, somewhat as they were in ancient times, and they will remain so for a fairly long time to come. Whoever overlooks or belittles this point will commit "left" opportunist mistakes.

3. China's modern industry, though the value of its output amounts to only about 10 percent of the total value of output of the national economy, is extremely concentrated; the largest and most important part of the capital is concentrated in the hands of the imperialists and their lackeys, the Chinese bureaucrat-capitalists. The confiscation of this capital and its transfer to the People's Republic led by the proletariat will enable the People's Republic to control the economic lifelines of the country and will enable the state-owned economy to become the leading sector of the entire national economy. This sector of the economy is socialist, not capitalist, in character. Whoever overlooks or belittles this point will commit right opportunist mistakes.

4. China's private capitalist industry, which occupies second place in her modern industry, is a force which must not be ignored. Because they have been oppressed or hemmed in by imperialism, feudalism, and bureaucrat-capitalism, the national bourgeoisie of China and its representatives have often taken part in the people's democratic revolutionary struggles or maintained a neutral stand. For this reason and because China's economy is still backward, there will be need, for a fairly long period after the victory of the revolution, to make use of the positive qualities of urban and rural private capitalism as far as possible, in the interest of developing the national economy. In this period, all capitalist elements in the cities and countryside which are not harmful but beneficial to the national economy should be allowed to exist and expand. This is not only unavoidable but also economically necessary. But the existence and expansion of capitalism in China will not be unrestricted and uncurbed as in the capitalist countries. It will be restricted from several directions—in the scope of its operation and by tax policy, market prices, and labor conditions. However, in the interest of the whole national economy and in the present and future interest of the working class and all the laboring people, we must not restrict the private capitalist economy too much or too rigidly, but must leave room for it to exist and develop within the framework of the economic policy and planning of the People's Republic. The policy of restricting private capitalism is bound to meet with resistance in varying degrees and forms from the bourgeoisie, especially from the big owners of private enterprises, that is, from the big capitalists. Restriction versus opposition to restriction will be the main form of class struggle in the new democratic state. It is entirely wrong to think that at present we need not restrict capitalism and can discard the slogan of "regulation of capital"; that is a right opportunist view. But the opposite view, which advocates too much or too rigid restriction of private capital or holds that we can simply eliminate private capital very quickly, is also entirely wrong; this is a "left" opportunist or adventurist view.

5. Scattered, individual agriculture and handicrafts, which make up 90 percent of the total value of output of the national economy, can and must be led prudently, step by step and yet actively to develop towards modernization and collectivization; the view that they may be left to take their own course is

wrong. It is necessary to organize producers', consumers', and credit cooperatives and leading organs of the cooperatives at national, provincial, municipal, county, and district levels. Such cooperatives are collective economic organizations of the laboring masses, based on private ownership and under the direction of the state power led by the proletariat. . . . If there were only a state-owned economy and no cooperative economy, it would be impossible for us to lead the individual economy of the laboring people step by step toward collectivization, impossible to develop from the new democratic society to the future socialist society, and impossible to consolidate the leadership of the proletariat in the state power. Whoever overlooks or belittles this point will also commit extremely serious mistakes. The state-owned economy is socialist in character and the cooperative economy is semisocialist; these plus private capitalism, plus the individual economy, plus the state capitalist economy in which the state and private capitalists work jointly, will be the chief sectors of the economy of the People's Republic and will constitute the new democratic economic structure.

6. The restoration and development of the national economy of the People's Republic would be impossible without a policy of controlling foreign trade. When imperialism, feudalism, bureaucrat-capitalism, and the concentrated expression of all three, the Kuomintang regime, have been eliminated in China, the problem of establishing an independent and integrated industrial system will remain unsolved and it will be finally solved only when our country has greatly developed economically and changed from a backward agricultural into an advanced industrial country. It will be impossible to achieve this aim without controlling foreign trade. After the country-wide victory of the Chinese Revolution and the solution of the land problem, two basic contradictions will still exist in China. The first is internal, that is, the contradiction between the working class and the bourgeoisie. The second is external, that is, the contradiction between China and the imperialist countries. Consequently, after the victory of the People's Democratic Revolution, the state power of the People's Republic under the leadership of the working class must not be weakened but must be strengthened. The two basic policies of the state in the economic struggle will

be regulation of capital at home and control of foreign trade. Whoever overlooks or belittles this point will commit extremely serious mistakes.

7. China has inherited a backward economy. But the Chinese people are brave and industrious. With the victory of the Chinese people's revolution and the founding of the People's Republic, and with the leadership of the Communist Party of China, plus the support of the working class of the countries of the world and chiefly the support of the Soviet Union, the speed of China's economic construction will not be very slow, but may be fairly fast. The day is not far off when China will attain prosperity. There is absolutely no ground for pessimism about China's economic resurgence.

Old China was a semicolonial country under imperialist domination. This imperialist domination manifests itself in the political, economic, and cultural fields. . . . Refuse to recognize the legal status of any foreign diplomatic establishments and personnel of the Kuomintang period, refuse to recognize all the treasonable treaties of the Kuomintang period, abolish all imperialist propaganda agencies in China, take immediate control of foreign trade and reform the customs system—these are the first steps we must take upon entering the big cities. When they have acted thus, the Chinese people will have stood up in the face of imperialism. As for the remaining imperialist economic and cultural establishments, they can be allowed to exist for the time being, subject to our supervision and control, to be dealt with by us after country-wide victory. As for ordinary foreign nationals, their legitimate interests will be protected and not encroached upon. . . . As for doing business with foreigners, there is no question; wherever there is business to do, we shall do it and we have already started; the businessmen of several capitalist countries are competing for such business. So far as possible, we must first of all trade with the socialist and people's democratic countries; at the same time we will also trade with capitalist countries. . . .

Very soon we shall be victorious throughout the country. This victory will breach the eastern front of imperialism and will have great international significance. To win this victory will not require much more time and effort, but to consolidate it will. The bourgeoisie doubts our ability to construct. The imperialists reckon that eventually we will beg alms from them in order to live. With victory, certain moods may grow within the party—arrogance, the airs of a self-styled hero, inertia and unwillingness to make progress, love of pleasure and distaste for continued hard living. With victory, the people will be grateful to us and the bourgeoisie will come forward to flatter us. It has been proved that the enemy cannot conquer us by force of arms. However, the flattery of the bourgeoisie may conquer the weak-willed in our ranks. There may be some communists, who were not conquered by enemies with guns and were worthy of the name of heroes for standing up to these enemies, but who cannot withstand sugar-coated bullets; they will be defeated by sugar-coated bullets. We must guard against such a situation. To win country-wide victory is only the first step in a long march of ten thousand *li*. Even if this step is worthy of pride, it is comparatively tiny; what will be more worthy of pride is yet to come. . . . We are not only good at destroying the old world, we are also good at building the new. Not only can the Chinese people live without begging alms from the imperialists, they will live a better life than that in the imperialist countries.

4. THE COMMON PROGRAM
FOR THE PEOPLE'S REPUBLIC OF CHINA

The Chinese People's Political Consultative Congress, composed of representatives of major political parties and organizations under the leadership of the Chinese Communist Party, was the principal embodiment of the united front policy which would continue under the People's Republic. The Common Program, which it adopted on September 30, 1949, on the eve of the official formation of the People's Republic of China, remained for five years the official policy guideline for the new government, providing national legitimization and broad policy direction during the new democratic era of transition.

The Common Program. Adopted by the First Plenary Session of the Chinese People's Political Consultative Congress on September 29, 1949. CD, October 5, 1949.

The Congress, along with the democratic and nationalist parties which participated in its work, continues to exist today (it met again in 1978) as a living symbol of the united front policy, although its functions have been vastly diminished.

Preamble

The great victories of the Chinese people's War of Liberation and people's revolution have ended the era of the rule of imperialism, feudalism, and bureaucratic capitalism in China. From the status of the oppressed, the Chinese people have become the masters of a new society, and a new state, and replaced the feudal, compradore, fascist, dictatorial KMT reactionary rule with the republic of the People's Democratic Dictatorship. The Chinese People's Democratic Dictatorship is the state power of the people's democratic united front of the Chinese working class, peasantry, petty bourgeoisie, national bourgeoisie, and patriotic democratic elements based on the alliance of workers and peasants and led by the working class. The Chinese People's Political Consultative Conference, composed of the representatives of the Communist Party of China, all democratic parties and groups, people's organizations, all-areas People's Liberation Army; all national minorities, overseas Chinese and patriotic democratic elements, is the form of organization of the Chinese people's democratic united front. The Chinese People's PCC, representing the will of the people throughout the country, proclaims the establishment of the People's Republic of China and organizes the people's own central government. The Chinese People's PCC unanimously agrees that the new democracy, namely the people's democracy, shall be the political foundation for national construction of the People's Republic of China.

General Principles

Article 1. The People's Republic of China is a state of new democracy, that is, people's democracy. This republic carries out the People's Democratic Dictatorship led by the working class, based on the alliance of workers and peasants, and rallying all democratic classes and all nationalities in China. This republic opposes imperialism, feudalism, and bureaucratic capitalism and strives for the independence, democracy, peace, unification, prosperity, and strength of China.

Article 2. The Central People's Government of the People's Republic of China must undertake to wage the people's War of Liberation to the very end, liberate all the territory of China and accomplish the cause of unifying China. . . .

Article 4. The right of the people of the People's Republic of China to elect and be elected is prescribed by law.

Article 5. The people of the People's Republic of China shall have freedom of thought, speech, publication, assembly, association, correspondence, person, domicile, moving from one place to another, religious belief and the freedom to hold processions and demonstrations.

Article 6. The People's Republic of China abolishes the feudal system which holds women in bondage. Women shall enjoy equal rights with men in the political, economic, cultural, educational, and social life. Freedom of marriage for men and women shall be enforced. . . .

Article 7. The People's Republic of China must suppress all counter-revolutionary activities, severely punish all KMT counter-revolutionary war criminals and other obdurate arch counter-revolutionary elements who collude with imperialism, commit treason to the fatherland and oppose the cause of people's democracy. Reactionary elements, feudal landlords, bureaucratic capitalists in general, must, according to law, also be deprived of their political rights within a necessary period after they have been disarmed and their special power abolished; but they shall at the same time be given a means of living and compelled to reform themselves through labor to become new men. If they continue their counter-revolutionary activities, they shall be severely punished.

Article 8. It is the duty of every national of the People's Republic of China to defend the fatherland, to observe the laws, to maintain labor discipline, to protect public property, to perform public service and military service, and pay taxes.

Article 9. All nationalities in the People's Republic of China have equal rights and duties. . . .

Article 10. The armed forces of the People's Republic of China, that is, the People's Liberation Army, the people's public security forces and people's police are armed forces belonging to the people. Their tasks are to defend the independence, integrity of territory, and sovereignty of China and the revolutionary fruits and all legitimate rights and interests of the Chinese people. The Central People's Government of the People's Republic of China shall endeavor to consolidate and strengthen the people's armed forces to enable them to accomplish their tasks effectively.

Article 11. The People's Republic of China unites with all peace and freedom loving countries and peoples throughout the world, first of all the Soviet Union, all people's democracies and all oppressed nations, and stands in the camp for international peace and democracy to oppose jointly imperialist aggression and defend lasting world peace.

Economic Policy

Article 26. The basic principle for economic construction of the People's Republic of China is to attain the goal of developing production and bringing about a prosperous economy through the policies of taking into account both public and private interests, benefits to both labor and capital, mutual aid between the city and countryside and interflow of goods at home and abroad. The state shall coordinate and regulate state-owned economy, cooperative economy, individual economy of peasants and handicraftsmen, private capitalist economy, and state capitalist economy in the spheres of operation, supply of raw materials, markets, labor conditions, technical equipment, policies of public finance, etc., so that all components of the social economy can play their part and effect division of work and cooperate under the leadership of the state-owned economy to promote the development of the entire social economy.

Article 27. The agrarian reform is the essential condition for the development of the productive power and the industrialization of the country. In all areas where the agrarian reform has been carried out, the right of ownership over the land obtained by peasants shall be protected.

In areas where the agrarian reform has not yet been carried out, the peasant masses must be set in motion to organize peasant organizations and realize "land to the tiller" through such measures as the elimination of local bandits and despots, reduction of rents and interest and distribution of land.

Article 28. State-owned economy is of a socialist nature. All enterprises vital to the economic life of the country and to the people's livelihood shall come under unified operation by the state. All state-owned resources and enterprises are the common property of all the people. They are the main material basis of the People's Republic for developing production and bringing about a prosperous economy and are the leading force of the entire social economy.

Article 29. Cooperative economy is of a semisocialist nature and is an important component of the entire people's economy. The people's government shall foster its development and accord it preferential treatment.

Article 30. The people's government shall encourage the active operation of all private economic enterprises beneficial to the national welfare and people's livelihood and foster their development.

Article 31. The economy of cooperation between state and private capital is of a state capitalist nature. Whenever necessary and possible, private capital shall be encouraged to develop along the direction of state capitalism, for example, producing for state-owned enterprises, operating jointly with the state, or operating state-owned enterprises and exploiting the state-owned resources through the form of concessions.

Article 32. The system of workers taking part in the administration of production shall, at present, be put into practice in state-owned enterprises, that is, factory administrative committees shall be set up under the leadership of the factory director. In privately operated enterprises, collective contracts should be signed by the trade union, representing the workers and employees, and the employer in order to carry out the principle of benefits to both labor and capital. At present, an eight- to ten-hour day shall in general be enforced in publicly and privately operated enterprises, but this may be dealt with at discretion under special circumstances. The people's government shall fix the minimum wage according to the conditions in various places and trades. Labor insurance shall be gradually carried out. The special interests of juvenile and women workers shall be protected. Inspection of industries and mines shall be carried out to improve safety devices and sanitary facilities of the industries and mines.

Article 33. The Central People's Government shall as early as possible draw up a general plan for rehabilitating and developing the main branches of public and private economy of the entire country, determine the division of work and cooperation between the central and local governments in economic construction and carry out unified coordination of the mutual relations between the economic departments of the central and local governments. Under the unified leadership of the Central People's Government, the various economic departments of the central and local governments should give full play to their creativeness and initiative.

Article 34. Agriculture, forestry, fishery, and stock-raising: In all areas where the agrarian reform has been thoroughly carried out, the people's government shall take as its central task the organization of peasants and all labor power that can be employed in agriculture to develop agricultural production and side occupations, and shall guide the peasants to organize step by step various forms of labor mutual aid and production cooperation according to the principle of voluntariness and mutual benefit. In newly liberated areas, every step of the agrarian reform should be linked up with reviving and developing agricultural production. . . .

Article 35. Industry: To lay down the foundation for the industrialization of the country, work shall be centered on the planned, systematic rehabilitation and development of heavy industry such as mining industry, steel and iron industries, power industry, machine-building industry, electrical industry, and the main chemical industries. At the same time, the production of the textile industry and other light industries beneficial to the national welfare and people's livelihood shall be restored and increased so as to meet with the daily consumption needs of the people.

Article 36. Communications: Railways and highways must be swiftly restored and gradually increased; rivers must be dredged and waterway transportation expanded; postal and telegraphic service must be improved and developed; air communication facilities must be built up and civil aviation inaugurated step by step according to plan.

Article 37. Commerce: All legitimate public and private trading shall be protected. Control of foreign trade shall be enforced and the policy of protecting trade shall be adopted. Domestic free trade shall be adopted under a unified economic plan of the state, but commercial speculation disturbing the market is strictly prohibited. The state-owned trading organs shall undertake to adjust supply and demand, stabilize commodity prices, and foster the people's cooperatives. . . .

Article 38. Cooperatives: The broad masses of the working people shall be encouraged and assisted to develop cooperatives according to the principle of voluntariness. Supply and marketing cooperatives, consumers' cooperatives, credit cooperatives, producers' cooperatives, and transport cooperatives shall be organized in towns and villages and consumers' cooperatives shall first be organized in factories, institutions, and schools.

Article 39. Finance: Financial enterprises shall be strictly controlled by the state. The right of issuing currency belongs to the state. The circulation of foreign currencies within the country is forbidden. . . .

Article 40. Public finance: The system of budget and final account shall be instituted. The financial spheres of the central and local governments shall be defined. Retrenchment and economy shall be enforced. The balancing of the budget shall be gradually attained and capital accumulated for the country's production. . . .

Cultural and Educational Policy

Article 41. The culture and education of the People's Republic of China are new democratic, that is, national, scientific, and popular. The main tasks of cultural and educational work of the people's government shall be the raising of the cultural level of the people, training of personnel for national construction work, liquidating of feudal, compradore, fascist ideology, and developing of the ideology of serving the people.

Article 42. Love for the fatherland and the people, love of labor, love of science, and the taking care of personal property shall be promoted as the public spirit of all nationals of the People's Republic of China.

Article 43. Efforts shall be made to develop the natural sciences to place them at the service of industrial, agricultural, and national defense construction. Scientific discoveries and inventions shall be encouraged and rewarded and scientific knowledge shall be popularized. . . .

Article 47. In order to meet the widespread needs of revolutionary work and national construction work, universal education shall be carried out, middle and higher education shall be strengthened, technical education shall be stressed, the education of workers during their spare time and education of cadres who are at their posts, shall be strengthened, and revolutionary political education shall be accorded to young intellectuals and old-style intellectuals in a planned and systematic manner. . . .

Policy Toward Nationalities

Article 50. All nationalities within the boundary of the People's Republic of China are equal. . . .

Article 51. Regional autonomy shall be carried out in areas where national minorities are concentrated. . . .

5. THE MARRIAGE LAW

"A wife married is like a pony bought; I'll ride her and whip her as I like." In such ancient sayings, in the institution of footbinding which crippled women and bound them to the home, in the exclusion of women from education, politics, and many occupations, and in the subjugation of women in the family, China's traditional marital and family patterns rested on an oppressive patriarchal base.

The Marriage Law of the People's Republic of China. Adopted by the Central People's Government Council on April 13, 1950. Promulgated on May 1, 1950. In: *The Marriage Law and Other Documents* (Peking: Foreign Languages Press, 1950).

The 1950 Marriage Law is the principal legislation defining abolition of the feudal marriage system and setting forth rights and privileges in the new democratic family. Chang Chih-jung, vice president of the Supreme People's Court, summed up its goals as:

> freedom of marriage for both men and women, monogamy, equal rights for both sexes, and the protection of the lawful rights of women and children. The chief aim of the law is to set our women free from the bondage imposed upon them by the old system, protect the lawful rights of women and children, ensure equality and cooperation between husband and wife, promote their mutual aid, love, and joint endeavor for a common cause.

The law staunchly defended the sanctity of marriage and the family, but marriage free from the bondage of the old order.

As in the land revolution, the party defined the task as elimination of the oppression inherent in the old order, not abolition of the institution of land ownership or the family. And it was in the context of land revolution that millions of women mobilized to stand up for their rights both to a share of the land and to equality within the family. At this time many women seized the opportunity to obtain divorces. The high divorce rate of the late 1940s and early 1950s soon tapered off with rectification of the worst abuses and the increased state role in mediating disputes between husband and wife.

Yet the high hopes and conviction among communist leaders that women's emancipation would be rapidly or smoothly achieved with the destruction of the feudal order and their advance into the work force were not to be realized. Like other oppressed groups, women would have to fight for equal rights in the family, the workplace, in politics and—above all—in the basic system of values. That struggle continues in China today and the 1950 law continues to define an important part of the terrain on which it is waged.

General Principles

Article 1. The feudal marriage system based on arbitrary and compulsory arrangements and the supremacy of man over woman, and in disregard of the interests of the children, is abolished.

The new democratic marriage system, which is based on the free choice of partners, on monogamy, on equal rights for both sexes, and on the protection of the lawful interests of women and children, is put into effect.

Article 2. Bigamy, concubinage, child betrothal, interference in the remarriage of widows, and the exaction of money or gifts in connection with marriages, are prohibited.

The Marriage Contract

Article 3. Marriage is based upon the complete willingness of the two parties. Neither party shall use compulsion and no third party is allowed to interfere.

Article 4. A marriage can be contracted only after the man has reached twenty years of age and the woman eighteen years of age.

Article 5. No man or woman is allowed to marry in any of the following instances:

(a) Where the man and woman are lineal relatives by blood or where the man and woman are brother and sister born of the same parents or where the man and woman are half brother and half sister. The question of prohibiting marriage between collateral relatives by blood (up to the fifth degree of relationship) is determined by custom.

(b) Where one party, because of certain physical defects, is sexually impotent.

(c) Where one party is suffering from venereal disease, mental disorder, leprosy, or any other disease which is regarded by medical science as rendering a person unfit for marriage.

Article 6. In order to contract a marriage, both the man and the woman should register in person with the people's government of the district or township in which they reside. If the proposed marriage is found to be in conformity with the provisions of the law, the local people's government should, without delay, issue marriage certificates.

If the proposed marriage is not found to be in conformity with the provisions of this law, registration should not be granted.

Rights and Duties of Husband and Wife

Article 7. Husband and wife are companions living together and enjoy equal status in the home.

Article 8. Husband and wife are in duty bound to love, respect, assist and look after each other, to live in harmony, to engage in productive work, to care for their children, and to strive jointly for the welfare of the family and for the building up of the new society.

Article 9. Both husband and wife have the right to free choice of occupation and free participation in work or in social activities.

Article 10. Husband and wife have equal rights in the possession and management of family property.

Article 11. Husband and wife have the right to use his or her own family name.

Article 12. Husband and wife have the right to inherit each other's property.

Relations Between Parents and Children

Article 13. Parents have the duty to rear and to educate their children; the children have the duty to support and to assist their parents. Neither the parents nor the children shall maltreat or desert one another.

The foregoing provision also applies to foster parents and foster children.

Infanticide by drowning and similar criminal acts are strictly prohibited.

Article 14. Parents and children have the right to inherit one another's property.

Article 15. Children born out of wedlock enjoy the same rights as children born in lawful wedlock. No person is allowed to harm them or discriminate against them.

Where the paternity of a child born out of wedlock is legally established by the mother of the child or by other witnesses or material evidence, the identified father must bear the whole or part of the cost of maintenance and education of the child until the age of eighteen.

With the consent of the mother, the natural father may have custody of the child.

With regard to the maintenance of a child born out of wedlock, if its mother marries, the provisions of Article 22 apply.

Article 16. Neither husband nor wife may maltreat or discriminate against children born of a previous marriage by either party and in that party's custody.

Divorce

Article 17. Divorce is granted when husband and wife both desire it. In the event of either the husband or the wife alone insisting upon divorce, it may be granted only when mediation by the district people's government and the judicial organ has failed to bring about a reconciliation.

In cases where divorce is desired by both husband and wife, both parties should register with the district people's government in order to obtain divorce certificates. The district people's government, after establishing that divorce is desired by both parties and that appropriate measures have been taken for the care of children and property, should issue the divorce certificates without delay.

When one party insists on divorce, the district people's government may try to effect a reconciliation. If such mediation fails, it should, without delay, refer the case to the county or municipal people's court for decision. The district people's government should not attempt to prevent or to obstruct either party from appealing to the county or municipal people's court. In dealing with a divorce case, the county or municipal people's court should, in the first instance, try to bring about a reconciliation between the parties. In case such mediation fails, the court should render a decision without delay.

After divorce, if both husband and wife desire the resumption of marriage relations, they should apply to the district people's government for a registration of remarriage. The district people's government should accept such a registration and issue certificates of remarriage.

Article 18. The husband is not allowed to apply for a divorce when his wife is pregnant, and may apply for divorce only one year after the birth of the child. In the case of a woman applying for divorce, this restriction does not apply.

Article 19. In the case of a member of the revolutionary army on active service who maintains correspondence with his or her family, that army member's consent must be obtained before his or her spouse can apply for divorce.

Divorce may be granted to the spouse of a member of the revolutionary army who does not correspond with his or her family for a period of two years subsequent to the date of the promulgation of this law. Divorce may also be granted to the spouse of a member of the revolutionary army, who had not maintained correspondence with his or her family for over two years prior to the promulgation of this law, and who fails to correspond with his or her family for a further period of one year subsequent to the promulgation of the present law.

Maintenance and Education of
Children After Divorce

Article 20. The blood ties between parents and children are not ended by the divorce of the parents. No matter whether the father or the mother has the custody of the children, they remain the children of both parties.

After divorce, both parents continue to have the duty to support and educate their children.

After divorce, the guiding principle is to allow the mother to have the custody of a breast-fed infant. After the weaning of the child, if a dispute arises between the two parties over the guardianship and an agreement cannot be reached, the people's court should render a decision in accordance with the interests of the child.

Article 21. If, after divorce, the mother is given custody of a child, the father is responsible for the whole or part of the necessary cost of the maintenance and education of the child. Both parties should reach an agreement regarding the amount and the duration of such maintenance and education. Lacking such an agreement, the people's court should render a decision.

Payment may be made in cash, in kind, or by tilling land allocated to the child.

An agreement reached between parents or a decision rendered by the people's court in connection with the maintenance and education of a child does not obstruct the child from requesting either parent to increase the amount decided upon by agreement or by judicial decision.

Article 22. In the case where a divorced woman remarries and her husband is willing to pay the whole or part of the cost of maintaining and educating the child or children by her former husband, the father of the child or children is entitled to have such cost of maintenance and education reduced or to be exempted from bearing such cost in accordance with the circumstances.

Property and Maintenance After Divorce

Article 23. In case of divorce, the wife retains such property as belonged to her prior to her marriage. The disposal of other family property is subject to agreement between the two parties. In cases where agreement cannot be reached, the people's court should render a decision after taking into consideration the actual state of the family property, the interests of the wife and the child or children, and the principle of benefiting the development of production.

In cases where the property allocated to the wife and her child or children is sufficient for the maintenance and education of the child or children, the husband may be exempted from bearing further maintenance and education costs.

Article 24. In case of divorce, debts incurred jointly by husband and wife during the period of their married life should be paid out of the property jointly acquired by them during this period. In cases where no such property has been acquired or in cases where such property is insufficient to pay off such debts, the husband is held responsible for paying them. Debts incurred separately by the husband or wife should be paid off by the party responsible.

Article 25. After divorce, if one party has not remarried and has maintenance difficulties, the other party should render assistance. Both parties should work out an agreement with regard to the method and duration of such assistance; in case an agreement cannot be reached, the people's court should render a decision.

By-Laws

Article 26. Persons violating this law will be punished in accordance with law. In cases where interference with the freedom of marriage has caused death or injury to one or both parties, persons guilty of such interference will bear responsibility for the crime before the law.

Article 27. This law comes into force from the date of its promulgation.

In regions inhabited by minority nationalities in compact communities, the people's government (or the military and administrative committee) of the greater administrative area or the Provincial People's Government may enact certain modifications or supplementary articles in conformity with the actual conditions prevailing among minority nationalities in regard to marriage. But such measures must be submitted to the government administration council for ratification before enforcement.

6. REGIONAL AUTONOMY
FOR MINORITY NATIONALITIES

The fifty-four minority nationalities, comprising 6 percent of the population and occupying over one-half of China's land area including strategic borderlands and resource-rich territories, presented special challenges to the Chinese leadership, both in forging a unified nation and in dealing with complex and varied societies and levels of economic and political development.

The General Program of 1952 is the basic document defining the policy of regional autonomy guiding relations with minority nationalities. (With the Marriage Law it is a rare example of legislation of the new democracy which was not replaced by comprehensive new guidelines during the period of socialist transition.)

General Program of the People's Republic of China for the Implementation of Regional Autonomy for Nationalities. Promulgated by Central People's Government, August 9, 1952. In: *Policy Toward Nationalities of the People's Republic of China* (Peking: Foreign Languages Press, 1953).

By June 1952 the People's Republic had already created 130 national autonomous regions with more than four million inhabitants and this experience provided the basis for framing a comprehensive policy.

Already at this time the central problem and tension in the relations among nationalities was being addressed at the highest levels. Li Wei-han, chairman of the Commission of Nationalities' Affairs, underlined in a December 1951 report the fact that the formation of autonomous regions does not solve the national question:

The real solution of our national question has to await the emergence of the national minorities from their political, economic and cultural backwardness which, for them, is a kind of historical liability. It is this backwardness which has hampered their full enjoyment of the right to national equality. According to Comrade Stalin, this situation constitutes "actual inequality." The policy of the People's Republic of China towards nationalities not only ensures equal rights for all different nationalities in their political, economic, cultural and social life, but also helps them to develop in all these fields, so that they will gradually emerge out of their backwardness into actual equality.

Such issues are not, however, broached in the General Program and the policies of the early 1950s emphasized regional autonomy, caution, and fostering unity among all nationalities.

In 1953 Mao sharply criticized Han chauvinism in a striking formulation of the problem: "We must go to the root and criticize Han chauvinist ideas which exist to a serious degree among party members and cadres, namely, the reactionary ideas of the landlord class and bourgeoisie, or the ideas characteristic of the Kuomintang, which are manifested in the relations between nationalities. Mistakes in this respect must be corrected at once." And he consistently pointed out thereafter that between Han chauvinism and minority chauvinism, the former remained the primary obstacle to effective nationality policy.

In the early to mid-1950s the focus of policy was the rehabilitation of the pastoral economy as the key to overall economic development in the minority areas with assistance provided by state subsidies and in some areas formation of rudimentary cooperative farms.

General Provisions

Article 1. This General Program is drawn up in accordance with the provisions of Articles 9, 50, 51, 52, and 53 of the Common Program of the Chinese People's Political Consultative Conference:

Article 9. All nationalities within the boundaries of the People's Republic of China shall have equal rights and duties.

Article 50. All nationalities within the boundaries of the People's Republic of China are equal. They shall establish unity and mutual aid among themselves, and shall oppose imperialism and public enemies in their midst so that the People's Republic of China will become a big fraternal and cooperative family comprising all its nationalities. Greater nationalism and local nationalism shall be opposed. Actions involving discrimination, oppression and splitting the unity of the various nationalities shall be prohibited.

Article 51. Regional autonomy shall be exercised in areas where national minorities are concentrated, and various kinds of autonomous organs for the different nationalities shall be set up according to the size of the respective populations and regions. In places where different nationalities live together and in the autonomous areas of the national minorities, the different nationalities shall each have an appropriate number of representatives in the local organs of state power.

Article 52. All national minorities within the boundaries of the People's Republic of China shall have the right to join the People's Liberation Army, and to organize local people's public security forces in accordance with the unified military system of the state.

Article 53. All national minorities shall have freedom to develop their spoken and written languages, to preserve or reform their traditions, customs and religious beliefs. The people's government shall assist the broad masses of all national minorities to develop their political, economic, cultural, and educational construction work.

Article 2. Each national autonomous region is an integral part of the territory of the People's Republic of China. The autonomous organ of each national autonomous region is a local government led by the people's government of the next higher level, under the unified leadership of the Central People's Government.

Article 3. The Common Program of the Chinese People's Political Consultative Conference is the general line along which all nationalities of the People's Republic of China unite in their common struggle at the present stage. In administering the internal affairs of their own nationality, the people in each national autonomous region shall advance along this general line.

Autonomous Regions

Article 4. In areas where national minorities are concentrated, the following types of autonomous regions may be established according to the relations obtaining between the nationalities of the locality and to the conditions of local economic development, with due consideration of the historical background:

(1) Autonomous regions established on the basis of an area inhabited by one national minority.

(2) Autonomous regions established on the basis of an area inhabited by one large national minority, including certain areas inhabited by other national minorities with very small populations who, likewise, shall enjoy regional autonomy.

(3) Autonomous regions jointly established on the basis of two or more areas, each inhabited by a different national minority. Whether a separate national autonomous region will be established in each of these areas depends on the actual conditions in the respective areas and on the wishes of the nationalities concerned.

Article 5. According to the economic, political and other requirements of the locality and with due consideration of the historical background, each national autonomous region may include some districts, towns or cities inhabited by Hans. In localities within a national autonomous region where the Hans are concentrated, no regional autonomy is necessary, but the organs of state power there shall be of the type generally adopted in the rest of the country. However, in localities within a national autonomous region where the number of Hans is exceptionally large, a democratic coalition government of nationalities shall be established. . . .

Autonomous Organs

Article 11. The autonomous organ of a national autonomous region shall be set up according to the basic principles of democratic centralism and of the system of people's congresses.

Article 12. The people's government in a national autonomous region shall be composed mainly of members from the nationality or nationalities exercising regional autonomy, with the participation of an appropriate number of members from other national minorities and the Hans inhabiting the same region. . . .

Rights to Autonomy

Article 14. The actual form which the autonomous organ of a national autonomous region is to take shall be determined in accordance with the wishes of the majority of the nationality or nationalities exercising regional autonomy and the wishes of the local leaders who are associated with the people.

Article 15. The autonomous organ of a national autonomous region may adopt the language most commonly used in the region as the chief medium of intercourse in the exercise of its authority. But when the autonomous organ exercises its authority over a nationality to whom this language is unfamiliar, the language of the latter nationality shall also be adopted.

Article 16. The autonomous organ of a national autonomous region may adopt the spoken and written language of the nationality (or nationalities) of the region for developing their culture and education.

Article 17. The autonomous organ of a national autonomous region may take necessary steps to train cadres from among the nationalities in the region who have a highly developed sense of patriotism and close contact with the local population.

Article 18. Internal reforms shall be carried out in a national autonomous region in accordance with the wishes of the majority of its people and of the local leaders who are associated with the people.

Article 19. The autonomous organ of a national autonomous region may, subject to the unified financial control of the state, administer the region's finances within a sphere prescribed by the Central People's Government and the local people's governments above its level.

Article 20. The autonomous organ of a national autonomous region may freely develop the region's economy in accordance with the unified economic system and plan for economic construction of the state.

Article 21. The autonomous organ of a national autonomous region may take necessary and appropriate steps to develop the culture, education, arts, and health services of the various nationalities inhabiting the region.

Article 22. The autonomous organ of a national autonomous region may organize its own local security forces and militia within the unified military system of the state. . . .

Relations Between the Nationalities of an Autonomous Region

Article 25. The autonomous organ of a national autonomous region shall protect the right to national equality of all nationalities in the region; educate the people of different nationalities to respect each other's languages, both spoken and written, customs, traditions, and religious beliefs; and prohibit national discrimination and oppression, and all acts liable to provoke disputes between nationalities.

Article 26. The autonomous organ of a national autonomous region shall guarantee to all people in the region, irrespective of nationality, freedom of thought, speech, publication, assembly, association, correspondence, person, domicile, change of domicile, religious belief, and the freedom to hold processions and demonstrations, as stipulated in the Common Program of the Chinese People's Political Consultative Conference, and the right to elect and to be elected according to law.

Article 27. The autonomous organ of a national autonomous region shall, in accordance with the provisions of Article 4 of this General Program, help the other national minority or minorities concentrated in the region to practice regional autonomy.

Article 28. The autonomous organ of a national autonomous region shall enter into full consultation with representatives of other nationality or nationalities living in the region on all problems relating particularly to that nationality or nationalities.

Article 29. The autonomous organ of a national autonomous region shall educate and guide the people living in the region towards unity and mutual assistance between all nationalities of the country, and towards love for the People's Republic of China in which all nationalities live together in a spirit of fraternity and cooperation like one big family.

Principles of Leadership for the People's Governments of Higher Levels

Article 30. The people's governments of higher levels shall respect the rights to autonomy of the national autonomous regions and help to put them into practice.

Article 31. The people's governments of higher levels shall make an adequate appraisal of the special characteristics and actual conditions of each national autonomous region at the present stage of development, so that their directives and orders will conform both to the general line as laid down in the Common Program of the Chinese People's Political Consultative Conference and to these special characteristics and actual conditions.

Article 32. The people's governments of higher levels shall assist the autonomous organs of the national autonomous regions in the planned training of cadres from among the nationalities in the area, and assign suitable cadres for work in the autonomous regions according to requirements.

Article 33. The people's governments of higher levels shall assist the national autonomous regions in their political, economic, cultural, and educational development, as well as in the expansion of health services.

Article 34. The people's governments of higher levels shall take appropriate measures to acquaint the people of the national autonomous regions with the advanced experiences and conditions about political, economic, and cultural development. Article 35. The people's governments of higher levels shall educate and assist the people of all nationalities in observing an attitude of equality, fraternity, unity, and mutual assistance among the nationalities, and in overcoming all tendencies to domination by the majority nationality or to narrow nationalism.

B. THE LAND REVOLUTION

1. THE MAY FOURTH DIRECTIVE ON SETTLING ACCOUNTS, RENT REDUCTION, AND LAND

The land revolution exploded throughout North China not at the behest of the Communist Party leadership but as an eruption from below, thrusting aside the moderate rent reduction program that had been the keystone of party land policy for nearly a decade. The May Fourth Directive, the first major postwar statement on land policy, marked the party's attempt to regain leadership over a peasant movement whose radicalism could not be contained within the united front program of rent and interest reduction.

Here the party addressed for the first time in the postwar period the dilemma of attempting to stimulate land reform while winning the support of the middle peasantry and preserving from confiscation commercial and industrial enterprises, even though these were owned for the most part by landlords and rich peasants.

Declaring the resolution of the land problem in the liberated areas the "most fundamental task," the Central Committee endorsed previous peasant land seizures but at the same time it attempted to restrict land confiscation to big landlords and traitors and provided property guarantees not only to rich and middle peasants but also to small and medium landlords. (Small

The Central Committee Directive Concerning the Land Problem, May 4, 1946. Translated by Lauress Ackman and Patti Eggleston.

*and medium landlords would be encouraged to voluntarily
distribute excess lands and were to be spared sharp struggle.)
The effort simultaneously to press forward with land reform
and to strengthen the broadest possible united front as armed
conflict with the Kuomintang intensified, produced an interim
policy which was fraught with contradictions and ambiguities.
The directive, subsequently criticized by Mao and other leaders,
is distinguished from subsequent policies in its emphasis on
landlords "voluntarily" providing part of their land to the
peasants rather than advocating direct seizure by the peasants, a
gift rather than the fruit of class struggle.*

According to the reports of comrades who have recently
come to Yenan, from all the liberated areas in Shansi, Hopei,
Shantung, and Central China, there is an extremely broad mass
movement. In the struggles of opposing traitors, settling accounts, and reducing rent and interest, the masses took land
directly from the hands of the landlords and enthusiasm is
running very high. In the areas where the mass movement has
penetrated, we have basically solved or are in the process of
solving the land problem. Some places, as a result of the
movement, have reached the point where they have realized
land equalization: all of the people (including the landlords)
have obtained three mou of land. On the other hand, some bad
gentry, evil tyrants, and landlords have fled to the cities where
they criticize the mass movement in the liberated areas. Some
middle-of-the-roaders have thus developed misgivings. Even
within the party there are a few people who feel that the mass
movement has been too excessive. Under these circumstances,
our party must have a consistent policy. We must firmly support the direct action of the broad masses in carrying out land
reform and provide systematic leadership so that the land reform in each liberated area may be quickly accomplished in
accordance with the scale and intensity of the development of
the mass movement. The party committee in each area at the
forefront of the mass movement need not fear universally
changing land relations in the liberated areas; it need not fear

peasants receiving large amounts of land or the landlords losing their land; it need not fear the destruction of feudal exploitation in the villages; it need not fear the curses and slander of the landlords; it need not fear the temporary dissatisfaction and wavering of the middle-of-the-roaders. On the contrary, it should resolutely support all the just ideas and righteous actions of the peasants and approve the land which peasants already received or just now are receiving. Against the slanders of the traitors, bad gentry, and landlords, you must provide refutation; against the doubts of the middle-of-the-roaders, you must supply explanation; and against incorrect viewpoints within the party, you must supply education. Every local party committee must clearly understand that the solution of the land problem in the liberated areas is now our most fundamental historical task. It is the key link in all our present activities. With the greatest determination and effort, we must wholeheartedly mobilize and lead the present mass movement to complete this historic task. Moreover, based on the following principles, we should provide the current mass movement with correct guidance:

1. Following the demands of the broad masses, our party firmly supports the peasants so that in their struggle to purge traitors, reduce rent and interest, and rescind rent and interest, they obtain land from the landlords' hands.

2. We must firmly use every method to draw in the middle peasants to participate in the movement, and cause them to benefit. Never infringe upon the land of the middle peasants. All the land of the middle peasants which has been encroached upon must either be returned or compensation paid. The entire movement must gain the genuine sympathy and satisfaction of all of the middle peasants (including the prosperous middle peasants).

3. Generally, do not change the land of the rich peasants. If, during the time of the liquidation and remission of land rents and land reform due to the demands of the broad masses, there is some unavoidable infringement, we still should not attack rich peasants too fiercely but must draw a distinction between rich peasants and landlords: toward the former we must emphasize rent reduction and preservation of that part of the land which they cultivate themselves. If we attack the rich peasants

too severely, this will cause the middle peasants to waver and impede production in the liberated areas.

4. We must give fair consideration to the livelihood of the middle and small landlords. Attitudes for treating the medium and small landlords should be differentiated from attitudes for treating big landlords, bad gentry, and evil tyrants: toward the former we should, wherever possible, adopt a style of mediation and arbitration to solve their disputes with the peasantry.

5. We must handle with care the dependents of the anti-Japanese soldiers and cadres who belong to the bad gentry or the landlord class, and the enlightened gentry and others who cooperated with us and were not anticommunist during the Anti-Japanese War, regardless of whether they lived in the liberated or Nationalist areas, and give them proper consideration during the mass movement. . . .

6. We must concentrate on carrying out resolute struggle against the traitors, bad gentry, and evil tyrants, completely isolate them and seize their land. However, we must let them retain land necessary for maintaining livelihood, that is to say, provide them with food. Toward those running dogs used by the traitors, bad gentry, and evil tyrants who come from middle peasant, poor peasant, and poor families, we should adopt a discriminating policy. We must urge them to make a candid self-examination but need not confiscate their land. After they have done so, they should be given the benefits they are entitled to.

7. Excepting the mines, factories, and shops owned by criminal and extremely wicked traitors which should be confiscated, all mines, factories, and shops established by rich peasants and landlords should not be encroached upon but should, instead, be protected so as not to affect our industrial and commercial development. We must not apply the same methods we used in solving the land problem and opposing feudal classes within the villages in opposing the industrial and commercial class; the two are fundamentally different. In some areas, the method of settling accounts with feudal landlords used in the villages was mistakenly applied to the cities, thereby destroying factories and stores. This ought to stop immediately, otherwise it will produce extremely bad effects.

8. Excepting criminal and extremely wicked traitors and

public enemies whose execution is demanded by the great popular masses in the area (we should support these demands and formally carry out capital punishment through the sentencing of the court), we should apply a lenient policy. Don't kill, beat people to death, or make too many arrests. This will keep the reactionaries from making excuses for attacking the movement as a whole, and keep the masses from becoming isolated. . . .

9. We must make the utmost effort to win over all intellectuals who can be educated and give them an opportunity to study and work. With regard to the enlightened gentry, others outside the party, or the liberal bourgeoisie in the cities, as long as they endorse our democratic program, notwithstanding their serious faults or their doubts and dissatisfaction with the present land reform, we should continue to cooperate with them (do not abandon even one) in order to consolidate an antifeudal, antidictatorial united front, striving for peace and democracy. We should allow those landlords and others who have fled to return home and give them the means to earn a living. . . .

10. The masses have already created various methods for solving the land problem. For example: (a) confiscation and redistribution of the land of arch-traitors; (b) following rent reduction, the landlords voluntarily sell land and the tenant farmers have first right to purchase this land; (c) since the peasants' tenancy rights were guaranteed after the rent reduction movement, the landlords voluntarily gave the peasants 70 to 80 percent of their land and requested to keep 20 to 30 percent of their land to cultivate themselves; (d) in settling accounts of rent and interest, of usurpation of land, of burdens and of other unjust exploitation, the landlords sell their land to compensate the peasants.

The peasants, using all the above methods, obtained land. Moreover, the vast majority have obtained land titles written by landlords. In this way they fundamentally solved the land problem in the villages, yet this is very different from the method adopted in solving the land problem during the civil war period. Using the various methods explained above to solve the land problem placed the peasants in a legal and reasonable position. Each area can adopt different policies according to different objectives.

11. All fruits which have been obtained during the movement must be fairly and rationally distributed to the poor descendents of the martyrs, the anti-Japanese soldiers, cadres and their dependents, and the landless or small land-owning peasants. After the peasants have fairly and reasonably obtained land, we ought to consolidate their ownership and develop their productive enthusiasm, encouraging them to become more industrious and frugal, to establish their own family and career, and to become wealthy and prosperous and follow in the footsteps of Wu Man-yu* so as to promote production in the liberated areas. As soon as the land problem has been solved, all those who, as a result of their own industry and thrift, skill and management, have become prosperous ought to have their property safeguarded against encroachment. Consequently we must not have endless settling of accounts and struggle which would undermine the productive enthusiasm of the peasantry. We ought to educate those who are idle, lazy loafers so that they may engage in production and improve their livelihood. . . .

13. During the movement and after the resolution of the land problem, we should pay attention to the consolidation and development of peasant associations and the people's militia, develop the party organization, train and promote cadres, reform the district and village governments, and educate the masses to struggle for defending both the land they have obtained and the democratization of the nation.

14. In those border areas where our control is not consolidated and is vulnerable, generally we do not want to mobilize the tenants to rise up and demand land. Even a movement to reduce rent and interest should be handled with caution. . . .

15. The party committee in each area should go all out to mobilize and lead the mass movement in the liberated areas. According to the principles explained above, we must resolutely solve the land problem. As long as we can grasp the principles given above, retain the support of over 90 percent of the village population which is united with the party (in the villages, farm laborers, poor peasants, middle peasants, handicraftsmen, and other poor people constitute approximately 92 percent of the population and the landlords and rich peasants constitute the

* A prominent labor hero in North Shensi in the early 1940s.

other 8 percent), and maintain a broad-based antifeudal united front, then we will not make adventurist errors. . . .

18. The Central Committee's land policy decision of 1942 in the past few years has correctly mobilized the broad mass movement and supported the War of Resistance against Japan. However, as a result of the deep penetration and development of the movement to settle accounts and reduce rent in practice, the policy needs some changes according to the demands of the broad masses. This is not yet a complete change because we still have not entirely abolished the policy of reducing rent.

2. THE BASIC AGRARIAN LAW

"China's agrarian system is unjust in the extreme."

"The agrarian system of feudal and semifeudal exploitation is abolished. The agrarian system of 'land to the tillers' is to be realized."

"All debts incurred in the countryside prior to the reform of the agrarian system are cancelled."

The 1947 land law, the basic and most radical postwar official directive on the land revolution, spelled the doom of China's landlord order. The directive sanctioned full-scale mobilization of the party and army behind a program of land confiscation and redistribution. Four principles were at the core of the new policy:

*1. Land to the tiller on the basis of equal distribution to women and men, old and young, with the administrative village (*hsiang) *as the normal unit of distribution.*

2. The peasant association of each village takes charge of confiscation and redistribution of the land.

3. All land of the landlords and surplus land of the rich peasants is subject to confiscation; these classes then enjoy the same right to equal ownership of land as do the peasants.

Basic Program on Chinese Agrarian Law. Promulgated by the Central Committee of the Communist Party, October 10, 1947. In: William Hinton, *Fanshen. A Documentary of Land Reform in a Chinese Village* (New York: Vintage Books, 1966).

4. *Land following distribution may be freely bought and sold, and (with certain restrictions) rented.*

The 1947 directive touched off the most radical phase of the land revolution in late 1947 and early 1948.

Resolution:

China's agrarian system is unjust in the extreme. Speaking of general conditions, landlords and rich peasants who make up less than 10 percent of the rural population hold approximately 70 to 80 percent of the land, cruelly exploiting the peasantry. Farm laborers, poor peasants, middle peasants, and other people, however, who make up over 90 percent of the rural population hold a total of approximately only 20 to 30 percent of the land, toiling throughout the whole year, knowing neither warmth nor full stomach. These grave conditions are the root of our country's being the victim of aggression, oppression, poverty, backwardness, and the basic obstacles to our country's democratization, industrialization, independence, unity, strength, and prosperity.

In order to change these conditions, it is necessary, on the basis of the demands of the peasantry, to wipe out the agrarian system of feudal and semifeudal exploitation, and realize the system of "land to the tillers." . . .

Basic Program:

Article 1. The agrarian system of feudal and semifeudal exploitation is abolished. The agrarian system of "land to the tillers" is to be realized.

Article 2. Land ownership rights of all landlords are abolished.

Article 3. Land ownership rights of all ancestral shrines, temples, monasteries, schools, institutions, and organizations are abolished.

Article 4. All debts incurred in the countryside prior to the reform of the agrarian system are cancelled.

Article 5. The legal executive organs for the reform of the agrarian system shall be the village peasants' meetings, and the committees elected by them; the assemblies of the poor peasants' leagues and organized and landless and land-poor peasants of villages, and the committees elected by them; *ch'u, hsien,* and provincial, and other levels of peasants' congresses, and committees elected by them.

Article 6. Except as provided in Article 9, Section B, all land of landlords in the villages, and all public land, shall be taken over by the village peasants' associations, and together with all other village land, in accordance with the total population of the village, irrespective of male or female, young or old, shall be unifiedly and equally distributed; with regard to the quantity of land, surplus shall be taken to relieve dearth, and with regard to the quality of land, fertile land shall be taken to supplement infertile, so that all the village people shall obtain land equally; and it shall be the individual property of each person.

Article 7. The unit for the distribution of the land shall be the *hsiang* or administrative village equivalent to *hsiang.* . . .

Article 8. Village peasants' associations shall take over the landlords' animals, agricultural implements, houses, grain, and other properties, shall further expropriate the surplus animals, agricultural implements, houses, grain, and other properties of rich peasants; and these shall be distributed to peasants lacking in these properties, and to other poor people, and furthermore an equal portion shall be distributed to the landlords. The property distributed to each person shall be his personal property, thus enabling all the village people to obtain proper materials for production and for life.

Article 9. Methods for dealing with certain special lands and properties, provided as follows:

Section A: Woods and hills, irrigation and waterworks, land in reeds, orchards, pools, waste land and other distributable land shall be divided in accordance with the ordinary standards for land.

Section B: Great forests, great hydraulic engineering works, large mines, large pasture land, large wastelands, and lakes shall be administered by the government. . . .

Article 10. Methods for dealing with certain special questions in the distribution of the land, provided as follows:

Section A: Poor peasants with only one or two persons in the family may be given land equivalent to that of two or

three people by the village peasants' meetings, in consideration of prevailing conditions.

Section B: Rural laborers, individual professionals, and
their families, in general, shall be given land equivalent to
that of peasants; but if their profession is sufficient for
constant maintenance of all or most of their living expenses,
they shall not be given land, or shall be given a partial portion
of land, as determined by the village peasants' meetings and
their committees in consideration of prevailing conditions.

Section C: For all personnel of the People's Liberation
Army, democratic governments, all people's organizations,
whose home is in the countryside, they and their families
shall be given land and properties equivalent to that of
peasants.

Section D: Landlords and their families shall be given land
and properties equivalent to that of peasants.

Section E: For KMT army officers and soldiers, KMT
government officials and personnel, KMT party members and
other enemy personnel, whose homes are in rural areas, their
families shall be given land and properties equivalent to that
of the peasants.

Section F: For all national traitors, collaborators, and civil
war criminals, they themselves shall not be given land or
properties. If their families live in the countryside, have not
taken part in criminal activities, and are willing to cultivate
the land themselves, they shall be given land and properties
equivalent to that of the peasants.

Article 11. The government shall issue deeds to the ownership of the land given to the people, and moreover recognize
their right to free management, buying and selling, and under
specially determined conditions to rent out the land. All land
deeds and all notes on debts from prior to the reform of the
agrarian system shall be turned in and shall be null and void.

Article 12. The property and legal operations of industrial
and commercial elements shall be protected from
encroachment.

Article 13. For the sake of making the land reform thorough
and complete, people's courts shall be established to try and
punish those who resist or violate the provisions of this law. The

people's courts shall be organized from personnel elected by peasants' meetings or peasants' congresses and from personnel appointed by the government.

3. DECISIONS ON CLASS STATUS IN THE COUNTRYSIDE

The Decisions Concerning the Differentiation of Class Status in the Countryside *were issued as guidelines for implementation of the land reform in the months following promulgation of the October 1947 land law. Comprised of two parts, "How to Analyze Class Status in the Countryside," and "Decisions Concerning Some Problems Arising From Agrarian Reform," the decisions were first issued in 1933 under Mao's signature by the Kiangsi Soviet government. In 1948 they served as reference materials for the nation-wide reform and were reissued with amendments accompanying a new land law on August 4, 1950. A number of major changes and amendments of 1950, reflecting both increasing sophistication in class analysis and shifting national priorities, are indicated in the supplementary decisions accompanying the document.*

The guidelines on class differentiation attempt to cut through the immense complexity of the rural environment to expose the roots and nature of exploitation that is siphoning off the fruits of the land from the immediate producer to the landlord and usurer. Landlords, for example, were defined as owning land and depending on exploitation rather than labor for their livelihood. But exploitation could take myriad forms such as rent, hiring laborers, and money lending. Rich peasants likewise de-

Decisions Concerning the Differentiation of Class Status in the Countryside (including "How to Analyze Class Status in the Countryside" and "Decisions Concerning Some Problems Arising from Agrarian Reform"). First passed October 10, 1933, by the Central Soviet Government, Kiangsi, revised and published by the CCP Central Committee, May 25, 1948, and updated and supplemented by the Government Administration Council, People's Republic of China, August 4, 1950. See: *The Agrarian Reform Law of the People's Republic of China and Other Documents* (Peking: Foreign Languages Press, 1950).

pended on exploitation for a part of their income, but were principally distinguished from landlords by the fact that family members participated in labor; rich peasant exploitation tended to take the form of hired labor (capitalism) rather than tenancy (the semifeudal form characteristic of the landlord class). Middle peasants owned land and basically supported themselves by their own labor, though some hired a small amount of labor and others were themselves part tenants.

Perhaps the most crucial distinction—and the most difficult to implement in practice—lay between the rich and middle peasants, between exploiters and the people. As the Communist Party moved vigorously to protect the rich peasant economy after 1948, it also modified its definition of these classes. The 1950 revision of the basic guidelines extended the ranks of the middle peasantry by raising the permissible ceiling for middle peasant income derived from exploitation from 15 to 25 percent.

Poor peasants, while typically owning part of the land they cultivated, were principally distinguished from middle peasants by the necessity to sell part of their labor for limited periods as well as by their shortage of farm implements. Finally, agricultural workers lacked both land and tools; they relied for their income principally on hiring themselves as laborers. The decisions provide concrete examples of each category and detail policies for classification and treatment of traitors, idlers, intellectuals, former landlords, soldiers of landlord origin, etc.

The issues of classification decisively shaped the land revolution, defined enemy and friend, and drew the battle lines in the countryside. For example, classification changes expanding the ranks of the middle peasants reflected their crucial role in determining the battle for the countryside. As Jen Pi-shih emphasized in a major policy statement of January 12, 1948, the ability to win over the middle peasantry was crucial to the strategy of uniting all who could be united with to effectively carry out the land revolution. Noting that as much as 30 to 40 percent of the People's Liberation Army was composed of middle peasants, and that in the old liberated areas where rent reduction had been completed the middle peasants constituted roughly half the population, Jen insisted that middle peasant property rights be guaranteed and that they be actively incorpo-

rated in peasant associations and new village governments. In this way 90 percent of the rural population could be united, providing the preconditions for successful land reform and for victory in the civil war. As the movement unfolded throughout 1948 the theme of curbing leftist excesses would be heard with mounting frequency, and among the voices heard would be that of Mao Tsetung. Together with the land law the decisions on class analysis provided reference points around which the struggle for the land unfolded.

I. How to Analyze Class Status
in the Countryside

1. Landlord—A person shall be classified as a landlord who owns land, but does not engage in labor or only engages in supplementary labor, and who depends on exploitation for his means of livelihood. Exploitation by the landlords is chiefly in the form of land rent, plus money lending, hiring of labor, or the simultaneous carrying on of industrial or commercial enterprises. But the major form of exploitation of the peasants by the landlords is the exacting of land rent from the peasants. . . .

Any person who collects rent and manages the landed property for landlords and depends on the exploitation of peasants by the landlords as his main means of livelihood and whose living conditions are better than those of an ordinary middle peasant shall be treated in the same manner as a landlord.

Supplementary Decisions Adopted by the Government Administration Council:

(A) Any person who rents large areas of land from landlords, who does not himself engage in labor but sublets the land to others for rent, and whose living conditions are better than those of an ordinary middle peasant, shall be classified as a sub-landlord. Sub-landlords should be treated in the same manner as landlords. A sub-landlord who cultivates part of his land should be treated in the same manner as a rich peasant. . . .

2. Rich Peasant—A rich peasant generally owns land. But there are also rich peasants who own only part of the land they cultivate and rent the rest from others. There are others who own no land but rent all their land from others. Generally

speaking, they own better means of production and some float-
ing capital and take part in labor themselves, but are as a rule
dependent on exploitation for a part or the major part of their
means of livelihood. Exploitation by rich peasants is chiefly in
the form of exploiting the wage-laborer (hiring long-term laborers). In addition, they may also let out part of their land for
rent, lend out money, or carry on industrial or commercial
enterprises. Most of the rich peasants also manage the landholdings owned by public bodies. Some own a considerable amount
of fertile land, engage in labor themselves and do not hire any
laborers. But they exploit the peasants in the form of land rent
and loan interest. In such cases, they should be treated in the
same manner as rich peasants. Exploitation by rich peasants is
of a constant character, and in many cases the income from
such exploitation constitutes their main means of livelihood.

*Supplementary Decisions Adopted by the Government
Administration Council:*
    (A) If the area of land rented out by a rich peasant exceeds
in size the land cultivated jointly by himself and by hired
laborers, he shall be referred to as a rich peasant of a semi-
landlord type. . . .
    3. Middle Peasant—Many middle peasants own land. Some
possess only a portion of the land which they cultivate while
the remainder is rented. Some of them are landless and rent all
their land from others. Middle peasants own a certain number
of farm implements. They depend wholly or mainly upon their
own labor for their living. In general they do not exploit others.
Many of them are themselves exploited on a small scale by
others in the form of land rent and loan interest. But generally
they do not sell their labor power. Some of them (the well-to-
do middle peasants) practice a small degree of exploitation, but
such exploitation is not of a constant character and the income
therefrom does not constitute their main means of livelihood.
    4. Poor Peasant—Some poor peasants own inadequate farm
implements and a part of the land they cultivate. Some have no
land at all and own only some inadequate farm implements. In
general, they have to rent land for cultivation and are exploited
by others in the form of land rent, loan interest, or hired labor
in a limited degree. These people shall be classified as poor
peasants.

In general, the middle peasants need not sell their labor power, but the poor peasants have to sell their labor power for limited periods. This is the basic criterion for differentiating middle peasants from poor peasants.

5. Worker—Workers (including farm laborers) generally have neither land nor farm implements. Some of them have a very small amount of land and implements. They depend wholly or mainly upon the sale of their labor power for their living.

II. Decisions Concerning Some Problems Arising from Agrarian Reform

1. Labor and Supplementary Labor—Under ordinary circumstances a family is considered as being engaged in labor if one member of the family is engaged in essential labor for one-third of a year. A family is considered as being engaged in supplementary labor if one member is engaged in essential labor for less than one-third of a year; or if he is engaged in labor, but not in essential labor, for one-third of a year.

Explanation. Attention should be paid to the following:

Rich peasants engage in labor, while landlords do not engage in labor, or only engage in supplementary labor. Thus labor is the basic criterion for differentiating rich peasants from landlords. . . .

Labor is the basic criterion for differentiating rich peasants from landlords. A person shall still be treated as a landlord, who merely hires long-term farm laborers but does not himself engage in essential labor, though he may assume responsibility for directing production and practice no exploitation in the form of land rent, loan interest, etc. . . .

2. Well-to-do Middle Peasant—Well-to-do middle peasants are part of the middle peasants. Their living conditions are better than those of the ordinary middle peasants and in general they practice a small degree of exploitation. The amount of income from such exploitation should not exceed 15 percent of the total annual income of the whole family. . . .

Under democratic rule the interests of well-to-do middle peasants shall receive the same protection as that accorded to ordinary middle peasants.

Explanation. . . . Well-to-do middle peasants constitute a considerable proportion of the population in the countryside. In the land distribution and land investigation movement it happened in many localities that well-to-do middle peasants were treated as rich peasants. This is not correct. In most cases the middle peasants whose interests have been encroached upon are well-to-do middle peasants. This should be corrected immediately.

Illustration: . . . A family has five mouths to feed, with one member engaged in full-time labor and another in half-time labor. It owns land with a potential yield of 25 piculs of grain, but an actual yield of 17 piculs. It rents from others a further amount of land with a potential yield of 75 piculs of grain, but an actual yield of 42 piculs of grain. It has been paying an annual rent of 25 piculs of grain for ten years. The family's annual income from the production of non-staple food and the rearing of hogs is 50 silver dollars. It has been hiring a herd-boy for three years. For four years it has been lending out 60 silver dollars at an annual interest rate of 30 percent or 18 silver dollars. It has five rooms, an ox and a tallow tree grove with an annual production of 30 piculs of nuts.

Conclusion: This family depends on its own labor as the main means of livelihood. It exploits others only slightly, amounting barely to 20-odd silver dollars a year (including the hiring of the herd-boy and the lending out of money), while the family is exploited by others in the form of rent up to 25 piculs of grain a year. After defraying all the family expenses, very little is left. This family should be classified as an ordinary middle peasant family, and not as a well-to-do middle peasant family.

3. Rich Peasant Exploitation—Its Duration and Degree—A person shall be classified as a rich peasant, who for three consecutive years counting backward from the time of the liberation of the locality had engaged in production himself and had depended for part or the major part of his family's means of livelihood on exploitation, the income from which exceeded 15 percent of the total annual income of his whole family. . . .

Illustration: A family has eleven mouths to feed, with two members of the family engaged in labor. The family owns land with a potential yield of 160 piculs of grain, but an actual yield of 120 piculs of grain (worth 480 silver dollars). It owns two tea groves which bring in an annual income of 30 silver dollars and a pond which brings in an annual income of 15 silver dollars. The annual income from the production of non-staple food and the rearing of hogs is about 150 silver dollars. It had hired, for seven years prior to the liberation, a long-term laborer and exploited his surplus labor to the value of 60 silver dollars a year. It had lent out, during the five years prior to the liberation, 250 silver dollars at an annual interest rate of 30 percent (or 75 silver dollars).

Conclusion: This family itself engages in labor, but it hires a long-term laborer, makes big loans, and its income from exploitation is more than 15 percent of the total income of the whole family. Although the family is a large one, there has still been a considerable surplus left after meeting all family expenses. Therefore, this family should be classified as a rich peasant family. . . .

Supplementary Decisions Adopted by the Government Administration Council:

(A) The line of demarcation between rich peasants and well-to-do middle peasants, according to the aforementioned Sections 2 and 3, lies in whether or not the income from exploitation exceeds 15 percent of the total annual income of the whole family. It is hereby changed to whether or not the income from exploitation exceeds 25 percent of the total annual income of the whole family. A person whose income from exploitation does not exceed 25 percent of the total annual income shall be classified as a middle peasant or well-to-do middle peasant as the case may be. . . .

4. Reactionary Rich Peasant—A rich peasant who engaged in serious counter-revolutionary activities before, and especially after the liberation, shall be classified as a reactionary rich peasant. The land and other property of such reactionary rich peasants and of their family members who took part in those counter-revolutionary activities shall be confiscated. . . .

8. Intellectual—The intelligentsia should not be considered as a class in itself. The class origin of intellectuals is to be determined according to the status of their families. The class status of the intellectuals themselves is to be determined in accordance

with the means they employ to earn the major part of their income. . . .

Supplementary Decisions Adopted by the Government Administration Council:

(A) Any person who is employed on the staff of institutions, enterprises, and schools of the state, or of cooperative societies or of private individuals, and who depends entirely or mainly on salary for his means of livelihood, shall be classified as a staff member. Staff members are part of the working class.

(B) Intellectuals who have technical skill and special knowledge, who are employed in brain work by the institutions, enterprises, and schools of the state, of cooperative societies or of private individuals, and who depend wholly or mainly on high salaries for their means of livelihood—such as engineers, professors, and specialists—are to be classified as senior staff members, whose class status shall be the same as that of the ordinary staff members. But in private economic institutions and enterprises, the representatives of the management shall not be classified as staff members. . . .

11. The Red Army Man of Landlord or Rich Peasant Origin and His Land—All Red Army men of landlord or rich peasant origin (be they commanders or fighters) and their dependents shall have the right to share in the distribution of land provided they fight determinedly for the interests of the workers and peasants.

4. MAO TSETUNG, PROBLEMS OF LAND REFORM

In this directive, written within months of the October 1947 land law, Mao offers his fullest and most penetrating analysis of rural classes during the civil war period as a basis for overcoming "excesses" which threatened to erode broad support during

On Some Important Problems of the Party's Present Policy. Central Committee inner party directive, January 18, 1948. Drafted by Mao Tsetung. SW IV.

1947. In one important respect, the directive extends the October land law by emphasizing the primacy of poor peasant and farm laborer interests and the decisive role of poor peasants' leagues in the land reform. In this and subsequent directives, however, Mao's emphasis lies in protecting the interests of the middle peasants. Thus the central problem—and tension—in the land reform: how to stimulate peasant activism while curbing "excesses" which may alienate many and impede productivity. The middle peasant, Mao emphasizes, must receive absolute protection against encroachment, and careful distinctions must be made between large and small landlords, rich peasants, upper middle peasants, etc. Commerce and industry must receive protection while the roots of feudal landlordism are destroyed.

This document provides Mao's definitive statement on the question of killing landlords in response to the demands of angry peasants and in the midst of civil war. The few heinous criminals among them, Mao insists, must be tried, sentenced by people's courts and executed, but indiscriminate beating and killing must be eliminated. The great majority of rich peasants and even landlords, which number around ten million, should be reformed to enable them to contribute to national development. In short, landlords must be eliminated as a class, not as individuals. Individuals can transcend class origins and status. The line would prove an extremely difficult one to tread. The striking fact, however, is not only that the party acted to shield many landlords from extreme peasant retribution but that the great majority of landlords and rich peasants did in fact survive the land reform and subsequent transitions.

Some Concrete Problems of Policy in the Land Reform and Mass Movements

The interests of the poor peasants and farm laborers and the forward role of the poor peasants' leagues must be our first concern. Our party must launch the land reform through the poor peasants and farm laborers and must enable them to play the forward role in the peasant associations and in the government organs of the rural districts. This forward role consists in forging unity with the middle peasants for common action and not in casting aside the middle peasants and monopolizing the work. The position of the middle peasants is especially important in the old liberated areas where the middle peasants are the majority and the poor peasants and farm laborers a minority. The slogan, "the poor peasants and farm laborers conquer the country and should rule the country," is wrong. In the villages, it is the farm laborers, poor peasants, middle peasants, and other working people, united together under the leadership of the Chinese Communist Party, who conquer the country and should rule the country, and it is not the poor peasants and farm laborers alone who conquer the country and should rule the country. In the country as a whole, it is the workers, peasants (including the new rich peasants), small independent craftsmen and traders, middle and small capitalists oppressed and injured by the reactionary forces, the students, teachers, professors and ordinary intellectuals, professionals, enlightened gentry, ordinary government employees, oppressed minority nationalities and overseas Chinese, all united together under the leadership of the working class (through the Communist Party), who conquer the country and should rule the country, and it is not merely some of the people who conquer the country and should rule the country.

We must avoid adopting any adventurist policies toward the middle peasants. In the cases of middle peasants and persons of other strata whose class status has been wrongly determined, correction should be made without fail, and any of their belongings that have been distributed should be returned, as far as that is possible. The tendency to exclude middle peasants from the ranks of the peasants' representatives and from the peasants' committees and the tendency to counterpose them to the poor peasants and farm laborers in the land reform struggle must be corrected. . . .

We must avoid adopting any adventurist policies toward middle and small industrialists and merchants. The policy, adopted in the past in the liberated areas, of protecting and encouraging the development of all private industry and commerce beneficial to the national economy was correct and should be continued in the future. The policy of encouraging landlords and rich peasants to switch to industry and commerce, adopted during the period of rent and interest reduction, was also correct; it is wrong to regard such switching as a "disguise" and therefore to oppose it and confiscate and distribute the property so switched. The industrial and commercial holdings of landlords and rich peasants should in general be protected; the only industrial and commercial holdings that may be confiscated are those of bureaucrat-capitalists and of real counter-revolutionary local tyrants. . . . In each public enterprise, the administration and the trade union must set up a joint management committee to strengthen the work of management in order to reduce costs, increase output, and see that both public and individual interests are benefited. Private capitalist enterprises should also try out this method in order to reduce costs, increase output, and benefit both labor and capital. The workers' livelihood must be appropriately improved, but unduly high wages and benefits must be avoided. . . .

The heart of land reform is the equal distribution of the land of the feudal classes and of their property in grain, animals, and farm implements (rich peasants hand over only their surplus property); we should not overemphasize the struggle to unearth hidden wealth and in particular should not spend too much time on this matter lest it should interfere with the main work. . . .

After the people's courts have given the handful of arch-criminals who are really guilty of the most heinous crimes a serious trial and sentenced them and the sentences have been approved by appropriate government organizations (committees organized by local governments at county or sub-regional level), it is entirely necessary for the sake of revolutionary order to shoot them and announce their execution. That is one side of the matter. The other side is that we must insist on killing less and must strictly forbid killing without discrimination. To advocate killing more or killing without discrimination is entirely wrong; this would only cause our party to forfeit sympathy, become alienated from the masses and fall into isolation. Trial and sentence by the people's courts, a form of struggle provided in the Outline of Agrarian Law, must be carried out in earnest; it is a powerful weapon of the peasant masses for striking at the worst elements among the landlords and rich peasants; it also avoids the mistake of beating and killing without discrimination. At the proper time (after the land struggle has reached its height), we should teach the masses to understand their own long-term interests—to regard those landlords and rich peasants who do not persist in wrecking the war effort or the land reform and who number tens of millions in the country as a whole (as many as 36 million out of a rural population of about 360 million) as a labor force for the country and to save and remold them. Our task is to abolish the feudal system, to wipe out the landlords as a class, not as individuals. In accordance with the land law we must give them means of production and means of livelihood, but not more than to the peasants.

5. WOMEN'S WORK
IN THE RURAL AREAS

Women's rights and the transformation of their social role were inextricably linked to the outcome of the struggle for the land. The December 20, 1948, decision on women's work provided both a penetrating critique of shortcomings and a framework for the women's movement during the land reform and early postliberation years.

The central task was defined as facilitating women's full entry into society through the economy. Women's important contributions to the war effort were seen in their growing economic role and in numerous direct support activities for the front. The expansion of women's economic role hinged on carrying through the land revolution which guaranteed full equality of property rights and challenged ideas which held women back from fully participating in economic, social, and political life. But laws alone could not guarantee equality, nor could equal property rights. Attacking the notion that equal distribution of land would automatically solve the problem of women's liberation, and at the same time rejecting approaches which isolated men as the main enemy (and thereby divided the class ranks), the directive called for actively challenging feudal

Decisions of the Central Committee of the Communist Party of China on Women's Work at Present in the Rural Districts of the Liberated Areas, December 20, 1948. In: Delia Davin, *Woman-Work: Women and the Party in Revolutionary China* (Oxford: Oxford University Press, 1976).

*ideas which held women back. It also called for special training
to prepare women to assume larger economic and leadership
roles. Women's liberation was inseparable from the ongoing
struggles for land revolution, economic growth, and wartime
victory.*

Women, who form half the population, have played a big role
and have become an indispensable force for defeating the
enemy and building a new China. Woman-work has been especially successful since February 1943, when the Central Committee issued "Decisions of the Central Committee of the
Chinese Communist Party on the Present Orientation of
Women's Work in All the Anti-Japanese Base Areas." This gave a
clear direction to women's work in the liberated areas, and
where it was put into practice there were noticeable changes in
the work. Ordinary village women of the liberated areas were
further mobilized and organized to work in handicrafts, supplementary enterprises, and agriculture, and to contribute to
the war effort with all their strength. In land reform all the
liberated areas mobilized even more women to take an active
part in the sharing out of land and the struggle to eliminate
feudalism. In the districts where land reform is already complete there has been a fundamental change in class relations in
the villages, land has been distributed to both men and women,
young and old, and quite a few women have become district or
village representatives, and have even been elected village heads,
deputy heads, or cadres above the village level. Women have
become much more aware and enthusiastic, and consequently
there has been a fundamental change in their political and
economic position and in their position in the family and in
society, opening the way to complete liberation.

But there are certain shortcomings in women's work in the
liberated areas. In a few places the party organization and the
women's association have not given enough recognition to the
Central Committee decisions of February 1943 or have not
understood them properly. The central task in women's work is
to organize women to take an active part in production. This is
also a guarantee of women's special interests and the key to
freeing them from the constraints on them which still survive.
Some areas have even completely disregarded these decisions

and so have not carried them out conscientiously or thoroughly. Moreover, in some districts conscientious care has not been given to eliminating the survivals of feudalism which hold women back or to satisfying women's special interests and demands in the course of mobilizing women for production, land reform, and work to aid the front. It has been supposed that when women are mobilized for production and land reform, everything will naturally be solved in consequence. Women's work has also been mechanically isolated from other work. Because of this, many of the special sufferings of women cannot be ended when they should be, and their full mobilization is thus obstructed. . . .

The orientation of women's work in the liberated areas should still be based on mobilizing and organizing women for an active part in production. The basic policies laid down by the Central Committee decisions of February 1943 are still completely appropriate. The whole party, all cadres engaged in women's work, and all women activists must understand that under new democratic government, all the laws of the old society which constrained or mistreated women and forced them into a humiliating position of obedience have ceased to exist. The new laws guaranteeing absolute equality of the sexes in the economy, in politics, and in society have been formulated or basically formulated in the first period of new democratic power. The question is whether these laws can truly be realized. The attitude of valuing men and despising women handed down from the old society, all kinds of constraining feudal customs, especially the economic dependence of women on men and the handicaps of not excelling at all sorts of labor and even despising it, have obstructed the rapid realization by women of the rights already granted to them in law. So if women's rights are to be properly realized, the work must be done. In the first place, women must not only be given equal economic rights and position with men, and in the countryside get and keep an equal share of land and property, above all they must be made to understand fully the importance of labor and must look on it as glorious. They must participate actively in all the productive jobs which are within their physical capabilities and become the creators of wealth in both the family and society. Only by going to work with a will, so that they gradually become economically independent, can women gain the respect of their parents-in-law, their husbands, and society at large, and increase the harmony and unity of the family; only thus can the economic, social, and political position of women be easily consolidated, and only thus can all the laws concerning sexual equality acquire a strong base on which to be implemented. . . .

There must be government orders to guarantee women's rights to land. When the family is taken as a unit for issuing land deeds, a note must be made on the deeds that the men and the women have equal rights to land. Every member of the family has democratic rights in the disposal of possessions. When necessary, land deeds for women can be issued separately. . . .

To promote the healthy development of women's production, we must carry out the policy, "get organized" correctly, and do our best to get women to take part in all sorts of cooperatives (e.g., production cooperatives such as mutual aid groups and weaving groups, etc.). In agriculture women find that inter-household cooperation and mutual aid groups in which both men and women can participate are convenient. In handicrafts and supplementary enterprises they find supply and marketing cooperatives convenient. As to methods, our principle must be that all is done voluntarily in the interests of both sides, to promote the democratic spirit and foster the creativity of the masses, and we must restrain ourselves from interfering too much and refrain from commandism and formalism, but at the same time, we should not just let things drift.

Take production as the focal point, and in the course of production improve educational work among women, raise their political consciousness and cultural level and mobilize them to participate in new democratic government. Improve health standards among women and children (e.g., by organizing training classes for infant and maternal health workers, Chinese and Western medicine cooperatives, etc.) and safeguard the special interests of women. Step by step, we must purposefully eliminate the feudal thought, constraints, and customs which prevent women's participation in political, cultural, and economic activities (of which the most important is production). It should not be thought that once women take part in production all the remnants of feudalism in society which still constrain them will just naturally disappear and there will be no need to do any more work. This way of just letting things drift ignores the special interests of women and is erroneous. In the course of production, at all mass meetings, and in the mass organizations, all peasants should be given constant ideological education on the equality of the sexes; feudal thought, constraints, and customs must be criticized, and it should be pointed out that all the feudal customs constraining women must be eliminated. . . . It must be understood that this sort of struggle is an ideological struggle among the peasants and should be radically different from the class struggle against feudal landlords. Moreover, the purpose of this type of struggle is to educate all the peasants more effectively and to help to mobilize women to engage in production and other constructive enterprises and to build a truly democratic and harmonous family. It should also strengthen and further consolidate the unity between the peasants. At the same time, it must also be recognized that this is work to change the peasants' ideas and is a long, demanding job which cannot be hurried. We should oppose both just letting things drift and impetuosity. The government must issue orders against foot-binding, infanticide, purchase marriage, taking in child brides, etc., and must also educate the masses so as to bring about the realization of these laws. . . .

As to the problem of the form of women's organizations, the elimination of independent women's organizations or their existence in name only, which occurred in some places in the past, was inappropriate. Because of the actual situation of women in China at present, independent organizations are needed to lead and inspire women's work, to unite and educate ordinary women, and to serve them constantly. Women's congresses are the best form of organization to bring women together on a larger scale and more democratically. . . .

In accordance with what is necessary to the development of the present revolutionary situation, a large group of party and nonparty women cadres must be boldly educated and fully utilized and pushed forward to take up posts of every sort and reinforce the cadres in women's organizations at every level. The same work should be allocated and the same training and educational opportunities given to men and women cadres of equal ability without discrimination. Moreover, taking into account the special position of women cadres, greater attention should be given to raising their political, theoretical, and cultural levels and their ability at work. In order to assist with their special difficulties, day care centers and nurseries should be set up and mutual aid groups of women cadres should be organized to care for children. This will not only lighten the burden of the women cadres, it will also be a start in the nursery care of children by society. . . .

From now on the whole party must recognize properly that the mobilization of ordinary women for revolutionary struggle is indispensable to the revolutionary victory in the whole country. . . .

6. AGRARIAN POLICY
OF THE PEOPLE'S REPUBLIC OF CHINA

The 1950 Agrarian Reform Law replaced the 1947 land law as the basic guide to land revolution after liberation. The new law, four times the length of its predecessor, spelled out in detail an approach to the rural problem following consolidation of the military victory: Above all, rapid restitution and expansion of the rural economy consonant with social justice in the countryside. The difference in tone and approach between the two land laws is suggested by their opening passages.

1947: "China's agrarian system is unjust in the extreme."

1950: "Feudal exploitation by the landlord class shall be abolished and the system of peasant land ownership shall be introduced in order to set free the rural productive forces, develop agricultural production and thus pave the way for new China's industrialization." [italics added] In language, in style, and in approach the documents reflect a shift from the direct expression of peasant justice in the midst of civil war to the tasks of economic reconstruction and industrialization.

Liu Shao-ch'i's report introducing the 1950 agrarian reform

Report on the Question of Agrarian Reform, June 14, 1950. In: *The Agrarian Reform Law and Other Documents* (Peking: Foreign Languages Press, 1950).

*law, delivered on behalf of the party leadership, is the principal
document defining post-liberation land policy. The core of that
policy lay in preserving the rich peasant economy while extending the land reform throughout the new liberated areas of
Central and South China, restoring the economy and paving the
way for rapid industrialization.* On June 6, 1950, Mao Tsetung called for a

change in our policy towards the rich peasants, a change
from the policy of requisitioning the surplus land and
property of the rich peasants to one of preserving a rich
peasant economy in order to further the early restoration
of production in the rural areas. This change of policy will
also serve to isolate the landlords while protecting the
middle peasants and those who rent out small plots of
land.

*Where the 1947 land law had emphasized the injustice of the
old order, the 1950 law emphasized its irrationality in shackling
China's productive forces and holding back her overall development. The rich peasant economy, Liu emphasized, was central
to a strategy "designed to set free the rural productive forces
from the shackles of the feudal land ownership system of the
landlord class in order to develop agricultural production and
thus pave the way for new China's industrialization." Moreover,
"preserving a rich peasant economy is of course not a temporary but a long-term policy" for building China's productive
forces. In his May Day 1950 speech, Liu expanded on his view
of the long-term nature of the rich peasant economy: "Only
when the conditions mature for the wide use of mechanical
farming, for the organization of collective farms and for the
socialist reform of the rural areas, can the need for a rich
peasant economy cease, and this will take a somewhat lengthy
time to achieve." The rich peasant economy, in short, would
extend until such time when, in Liu's view, large-scale agricultural mechanization would create the conditions for the collectivization of agriculture. Liu and Mao would clash on this
issue in the early 1950s and on the nature and pace of rural
collectivization subsequently.*

*From Liu's speech and from major articles published at the
time, it can be seen that the following additional considerations
underlay the rich peasant policy:*

(1) In contrast to the Soviet Union and Eastern Europe where the kulaks posed a powerful threat, China's rich peasants controlled only 10 to 15 percent of the land. Confidence reigned that they would make contributions to development as the most productive sector of the rural population without seriously challenging the party.

(2) Absolute egalitarianism constituted a threat to China's development. Protecting the rich peasants isolated the landlords while middle and rich peasants, reassured that their economic interests would be safeguarded, would be stimulated to strive for higher productivity.

(3) Because of their close association with rural industry and commerce, protection of rich peasant and other capitalist interests would stimulate these sectors essential to China's orderly development. Rich peasants also constituted an important potential market for the industrial sector, thus providing industry a growing market in the countryside.

(4) The defeat of the Kuomintang in the civil war removed the imperative for attacking the rich peasants, who could no longer pin their hopes on restoration of the old order.

A. Liu Shao-ch'i,
Agrarian Reform and the Rich Peasant Economy

At present, agrarian reform in China has been completed, or in the main completed, in an area with a rural population of about 145 million (total population of the area is about 160 million). There is still an area with a rural population of about 264 million (total population of the area about 310 million) where agrarian reform has not been carried out. Requests for permission to proceed with agrarian reform in the winter of this year have been made by various areas with a total rural population of about 100 million—3.5 million in North China, 8 million in Northwest China, 35 million to 40 million in East China and 47 million to 56 million in Central and South China—covering more than 300 counties in all. . . .

Besides, there is still an area with a rural population of about 164 million where it is not planned to carry out agrarian reform this winter. In the greater part of this area, agrarian reform may be carried out after the autumn of 1951. In a smaller part of the area, it may be carried out after the autumn of 1952. . . .

We should give the national minorities more time to consider and prepare for reform among themselves and we must not be impetuous. . . . This means that we plan to complete agrarian reform throughout China in the main, but not entirely, in two and a half to three years, beginning from this winter. . . .

To sum up, chaotic conditions must not be allowed to occur and no deviation or confusion may be allowed to remain uncorrected for long in our agrarian reform work in the future. Agrarian reform must be carried out under guidance, in a planned and orderly way, in complete accordance with the laws and decrees promulgated by the Central People's Government and the people's governments at various levels, and in accordance with the principles, policies, and steps decided by them. . . .

Why Agrarian Reform Should Be
Carried Out

The essential content of agrarian reform is the confiscation of the land of the landlord class for distribution to the landless or land-poor peasants. Thus the landlords as a class in society are abolished and the land ownership system of feudal exploitation is transformed into a system of peasant land ownership. This is indeed the greatest and most thorough reform in thousands of years of Chinese history.

Why should such a reform be made? In a nutshell, it is because the original land ownership system in China is extremely irrational. . . .

Herein lies the basic reason why our nation has become the object of aggression and oppression and has become impoverished and backward. This also constitutes the principal obstacle to our nation's democratization, industrialization, independence, unification and prosperity. Unless we change this situation, the victory of the Chinese people's revolution cannot be consolidated, the productive forces in the rural areas cannot be set free, the industrialization of new China cannot be realized and the people cannot enjoy the fundamental gains of the victory of the revolution. . . .

This basic reason for and the aim of agrarian reform are

different from the view that agrarian reform is only designed to relieve the poor people. The Communist Party has always been fighting for the interests of the laboring poor, but the viewpoints of communists have always been different from those of the philanthropists. The results of agrarian reform are beneficial to the impoverished laboring peasants, helping the peasants partly solve their problem of poverty. But the basic aim of agrarian reform is not purely one of relieving the impoverished peasants. It is designed to set free the rural productive forces from the shackles of the feudal land ownership system of the landlord class in order to develop agricultural production and thus pave the way for new China's industrialization. The problem of poverty among the peasants can be finally solved only if agricultural production can be greatly developed, if the industrialization of new China can be realized, and if China can embark upon the road to socialism. . . .

The basic reason for and the basic aim of agrarian reform are intended for production. Hence, every step in agrarian reform should in a practical way take into consideration and be closely coordinated with the development of rural production. Precisely because of this basic reason and aim, the Central Committee of the Communist Party of China has proposed that rich peasant economy be preserved and be free from infringement in future agrarian reform. This is advantageous to the development of the people's economy in our country. It is, therefore, also beneficial to the broad peasant masses. . . .

Preserve Rich Peasant Economy

The various provisions in the Draft Agrarian Reform Law regarding land and other properties of the rich peasants are aimed at preserving the rich peasant economy and, in the course of land reform, at neutralizing the rich peasants politically and rendering better protection to middle peasants and persons renting out small parcels of land in order to isolate the landlord class and unite all the people to carry out agrarian reform and eliminate the feudal system in an orderly manner. . . .

If the people's government pursues a policy of preserving the rich peasant economy, the rich peasants can be won over to a neutral attitude in general and better protection can then be given to the middle peasants, thus dispelling certain unnecessary misgivings of the peasants during the development of production. Therefore, in the present situation, the adoption of a policy to preserve the rich peasant economy in the coming agrarian reform is necessary both politically and economically. . . .

The policy adopted by us of preserving a rich peasant economy is of course not a temporary but a long-term policy. In a quite long period to come, our policy is to permit the rich peasant economy to remain while restricting the exploitation by the rich peasants. On the basis of the success in our agrarian reform we will develop the mutual aid and cooperative movement in agricultural production and gradually carry out socialist transformation in the countryside. The completion of such transformation and the final elimination of the exploitation by rich peasants will become a fact only in the rather distant future. . . .

Points for Attention During Agrarian Reform

Agrarian reform is a systematic and fierce struggle. Our general line to be followed in the forthcoming agrarian reform is that reliance should be placed on the poor peasants and farm laborers, while uniting with the middle peasants, neutralizing the rich peasants in order to eliminate the feudal exploitation system step by step and with discrimination and to develop agricultural production. . . .

Measures and plans for agrarian reform are to be worked out beforehand from the *hsiang* upwards and are to be operated after endorsement by the higher level. If any problem arises which a lower organ cannot solve, it should be submitted to an organ of a higher level for instruction. The higher organ should at once dispatch personnel to help solve the problem. . . .

The main leadership of the peasants' associations must be chosen from among the poor peasants and farm laborers. But real alliance with the middle peasants and, above all, real protection of their land and property (including that of the well-to-do middle peasants) from encroachment is indispensable. At the same time, active middle peasants must be absorbed into the leadership of the peasants' associations. It should be stipulated that one third of the leadership of the peasants' associations at all levels should be chosen from among the middle peasants. This is absolutely necessary. No poor peasants' leagues should be organized in addition to the peasants' associations. . . .

The peasants' associations must, in practice, pay attention to recruiting the women of peasant families as members and to drawing active women into participation in the leadership. It is necessary to call women's meetings or women's representative meetings within the peasants' associations so as to safeguard the interests of women during the agrarian reform, to safeguard the social rights of women, and to discuss all kinds of women's problems. . . .

To carry out these tasks and the other tasks of agrarian reform correctly, the key lies in remolding the working style of our cadres and especially in correcting "commandism." The completion of the agrarian reform will create the decisive condition for bringing about a fundamental turn for the better in our country's financial and economic situation. Moreover, it will organize the broad masses of the peasants politically. Then our country and the people's government will be stronger and more consolidated than ever before.

B. The Agrarian Reform Law of 1950

General Principles

Article 1. The land ownership system of feudal exploitation by the landlord class shall be abolished and the system of peasant land ownership shall be introduced in order to set free the rural productive forces, develop agricultural production, and thus pave the way for new China's industrialization.

The Agrarian Reform Law of the People's Republic of China. Promulgated by the Central People's Government, June 30, 1950. In: *The Agrarian Reform Law and Other Documents* (Peking: Foreign Languages Press, 1950).

Confiscation and Requisition of Land

Article 2. The land, draft animals, farm implements, and surplus grain of the landlords, and their surplus houses in the countryside shall be confiscated, but their other properties shall not be confiscated.

Article 3. The rural land belonging to ancestral shrines, temples, monasteries, churches, schools and organizations, and other land owned by public bodies shall be requisitioned.

Article 4. Industry and commerce shall be protected from infringement.

Industrial and commercial enterprises operated by landlords and the land and properties used by landlords directly for the operation of industrial and commercial enterprises shall not be confiscated. . . .

Article 5. Revolutionary army men, dependents of martyrs, workers, staff members, professional workers, peddlers and others who rent out small portions of land because they are engaged in other occupations or because they lack labor power shall not be classified as landlords. If the average per capita landholding of such families does not exceed 200 percent of the average per capita landholding in the locality, it shall remain untouched. . . .

Article 6. Land owned by rich peasants and cultivated by themselves or by hired labor and their other properties shall be protected from infringement.

Small portions of land rented out by rich peasants shall remain untouched. But in certain special areas, the land rented out by rich peasants may be requisitioned in part or in whole with the approval of the people's governments at provincial level or above.

If the portions of land rented out by rich peasants of a semi-landlord type exceed in size the land tilled by themselves and by their hired labor the land rented out should be requisitioned. . . .

Article 7. Land and other properties of the middle peasants (including well-to-do middle peasants) shall be protected from infringement.

Distribution of Land

Article 10. All land and other means of production thus confiscated and requisitioned, with the exception of those to be nationalized as stipulated in this law, shall be taken over by the *hsiang* peasants' association for unified, equitable and rational distribution to poverty-stricken peasants who have little or no land and who lack other means of production. Landlords shall be given an equal share so that they can make their living by their own labor and thus reform themselves through labor.

Article 11. Land shall be distributed by taking *hsiang* or an administrative village corresponding to a *hsiang* as a single unit. Land shall be distributed in a unified manner according to the population therein, based upon the principle of allotting the land to its present tiller and making necessary readjustment in landholdings by taking into consideration the amount, quality and location of the land. . . .

Article 12. Under the principle of allotting land to the present tiller, land owned by the tiller shall not be drawn upon for distribution during land distribution. When rented land is drawn upon for distribution, proper consideration should be given to the present tiller. The land he acquires through land distribution plus his own landholding (if he has land) shall be slightly and suitably more than the landholding, after distribution, of the peasants who had little or no land. The principle in this connection should be that the present tiller should retain the approximate average per capita landholding in the locality. . . .

Article 15. During land distribution, the people's governments at or above the county level may, in accordance with the local land conditions, set apart a certain amount of land to be nationalized and used for establishing experimental farms for one or more counties or model state farms. . . .

Organizations and Methods for Carrying Out
Agrarian Reform

Article 28. In order to strengthen the leadership of the people's governments in the work of agrarian reform, the people's governments at county level or above should, at the time of agrarian reform, organize agrarian reform committees to be composed of persons elected by people's representative conferences or persons appointed by the people's governments of a higher level. . . .

Article 29. *Hsiang* and village peasant meetings, peasant representative conferences and committees of peasants' associations elected at such conferences, the peasant congresses at *ch'u,* county, and provincial levels, and committees of peasants' associations elected at such congresses are the legal executive organizations for reforming the agrarian system.

Article 30. After agrarian reform is completed, the people's government shall issue title deeds and shall recognize the right of all landowners to manage, buy, sell, or rent out land freely.

Article 31. The determination of class status shall be carried out according to the decisions on class differentiation in the countryside issued by the Central People's Government. It shall be determined by democratic estimation and decision at the village peasant meetings and peasant representative conferences under the leadership of the village people's governments, by the method of self-assessment and public discussion. . . .

Article 32. In the course of agrarian reform a people's tribunal shall be set up in every county. . . . Indiscriminate arrest, beating or killing of people, corporal punishment, and the like are strictly forbidden.

Article 34. To ensure that all agrarian reform measures conform to the interests and wishes of the overwhelming majority of the people, the people's governments at all levels shall be responsible for effectively safeguarding the democratic rights of the people. The peasants and their representatives shall have the right to freely criticize and impeach functionaries of any sphere or level at all meetings.

7. A CADRE'S LAND REFORM DIARY

The daughter of a small landlord family, Chang Su was a graduate of the prestigious Tsinghua University, an editor, and mother. In 1951 she joined 3,000 other men and women cadres

Chang Su. A Cadre's Land Reform Diary. *People's China,* May 16, 1952, and June 1, 1952.

from Peking, and tens of thousands from other cities, as members of land reform teams dispatched to the rural areas. Hers is a rare personal account of land revolution at the village level.

Chang captures elements of the process of awakening and growth in the course of the struggle for the land which transpired with myriad variations in each of China's hundreds of thousands of villages. In contrast to the twists and turns characteristic of land reform in its early stages, in the 1950s the process of social revolution was far more orderly and closely attuned to unshackling the productive forces. As in earlier phases of land reform in the North, however, the stages of rent reduction, anti-traitor movements, and eventually the denunciation of the landlords and seizures of the land were enacted by an aroused and politicized peasantry. In the process, many peasants cast off the bonds of superstition and fatalism and became activists in the new political order.

Chang's account, which glosses over many of the twists and turns born of internal conflicts among the people in this Szechuan village is perhaps most valuable in conveying the flavor of young intellectuals participating in and learning from the land revolution.

It was mid-November. But the Szechuan winter is a mild affair. After walking for three hours, we were in fact feeling a bit too warm, although it was late in the afternoon and the sun was on the wane.

There were twelve of us, all from Peking. We had all volunteered for land reform work, had been accepted and were now on our way along a Southwest China pathway to our assignment in Hsinglung *hsiang,* Kuanghan county, some fifty kilometers north of Chengtu, Szechuan province. We were a few of the more than three thousand cadres from government institutions, people's organizations, democratic parties, college students, and teachers, who had been accepted and received special training for this work. This was only one of the groups totalling many tens of thousands of cadres who had volunteered and gone out from the cities to aid the countryside.

I myself had eagerly seized the opportunity to volunteer. Everyone in my office was eager to go. . . .

I am an assistant editor in a government publication office in Peking. Before liberation I had been studying at Tsinghua University and did not take much part in political life. My husband's work as veterinary surgeon kept us in comfortable circumstances; I myself came from a comfortable life in a small landlord's family. I studied literature, and in the old days, I really hid myself in my studies. . . .

For eight days we attended lectures given by experts on land reform, both about policy and method. Then we set off on our assignments. . . .

My own group included four other journalists besides myself, three medical and four educational workers. The oldest among us was forty-five years old, a doctor at Peking Union Medical College; the youngest was twenty-two, a girl working in the Ministry of Education.

Moving through the rich Chengtu plain, we followed the course of a clear, swift-running stream shaded by clumps of bamboo. . . . Suddenly I was assailed by doubts—could I be of real help to the land reform work, when I was so ignorant about farming and village life? How could I make friends with the peasants when I did not even know what they were planting? . . .

The Hsinglung *hsiang* Land Reform Work Team was formed of the twelve cadres from Peking and forty local cadres from Chengtu and Kuanghan, several of whom were experienced land reform workers. The team leader was Kuo Ping, a veteran fighter in the Chinese Red Army and a Communist Party member. He had directed land reform work already in two other districts in the southwest. Our group included also ten peasant cadres, with rich experience of land reform behind them. We had a strong Communist Party group among us.

Hsinglung *hsiang* embraces thirteen villages, with a population of 14,200 and 28,900 mou of land. . . .

Chengtu was freed in December 1949. In August and September 1950, peasant associations were established to replace the old landlord-dominated village authorities. The peasants formed their own militia to protect the people's rule. Then from October 1950 to April 1951 the "four-point movement" was carried through in the Southwest China villages: the liquidation of bandits, the overthrow of local tyrants, the reduction of rent, and the refund of extortionate deposits paid to the landlords. All this paved the way for land reform.

During the four-point movement, twenty-seven reactionary leaders in Hsinglung *hsiang* had been arrested and tried by the people's court. Those who had committed murders were sentenced to death. . . .

Land Reform—Part of Class Struggle

The peasants were eager for land reform. But they were not yet fully awakened politically. There were still some of them who looked on the land reform as simply a technical matter of distributing land to them, and these expected our work team of cadres sent by the government to start this right away. Because the bandits had been arrested and the landlords seemed quiescent, even humble, they overlooked the fact, which the peasant activists told us, that there were still hidden counter-revolutionary landlord elements and tyrants who were biding their time, hiding their property and otherwise preparing to sabotage the reform. One of the first tasks, therefore, was the mobilization of all the peasant masses for the coming struggle that was to wipe out the roots of feudal landlordism for good and all. . . .

The very first night after we arrived at Hsinglung, our whole team came together in a meeting with the village cadres, representatives from the peasant associations of the thirteen villages. The team was divided into fourteen groups, one for each village and one for the market center on the main road. Three local cadres and I were appointed to work in Village Number 1, and we went there the same night.

Division of Work

Different branches of work were entrusted to each of us. The leader of our small group was Chang Hua-sung, a poor peasant himself. He had taken a very active part in the land reform at his own village in the spring of 1951, and had later been elected to the *hsiang* people's representative conference. He had only just learned to read and write. Kuo Feng-ling, an eighteen-year-old graduate of the Chengtu Revolutionary College, naturally worked with the youth of the village. She sang beautifully, and could dance and act. My special field was to carry on work among the village women. . . .

The day after our arrival in Village Number 1, hundreds of peasants gathered at a mass meeting of the whole *hsiang* at the central village. This really marked the beginning of the land reform. At this meeting, the work team leader did much to explain the government policy on how the reform should be carried out. When the peasants returned to their own villages, the discussions continued on various questions related to land reform. We of the work team acted as counselors to the peasants at these discussions. . . .

On the fourth day, the peasant association called a conference of peasant delegates. Each village sent about thirty representatives. . . .

The problem discussed was how to root out the remaining influence of the reactionaries and their agents, so that the land reform should not be sabotaged. The chairman of the meeting recounted the facts that were known already, then asked the work team to explain the government's policy which combines leniency and re-education for the misguided followers of the reactionaries, with severe punishment for the handful of leading diehard reactionary criminals. . . .

I had heard before of the cruelty of the Szechuan landlords. Now I heard from the mouths of the peasants themselves about the ruinous rents they paid, of beatings and terror. It emerged that several of the bandit-landlord elements were still at large. One hidden landlord, Chou Tsung-ming, had been a close associate-in-crime of "Chung the Lazy King." . . .

The conference of the peasant delegates lasted for three days. Thirteen active counter-revolutionaries were exposed along with Chou. This awakened the masses to the fact that the reactionary elements had not been completely eliminated as many had thought. . . .

When an accusation meeting was held in our own village, two bandits were accused by the people. A picture of robbery and murder, torture and ruthless exploitation was unfolded. The peasants had had to suffer in silence. Now they could pour out their complaints and accuse the tyrants face to face. From early in the morning until dusk, one peasant after another accused these criminals. Many bitter tears were shed in memory of the past. . . .

Similar meetings were taking place in other villages. A few days later, the county people's court came on circuit to Hsing-lung *hsiang* and, after accusations and evidence produced by the peasants, sentenced several of the counter-revolutionaries.

Finding the "Roots of Poverty"

The peasants had a clear-sighted hatred for the bandits. But some of them did not yet fully realize how cruelly they had been exploited by the landlord class in general. Some even still believed that the land belonged to the landlords, and that it had been "reasonable" for them to pay rents as high as 80 percent of the land's yield. Some backward peasants still thought they were poor just because "fate" was against them.

It was at this point that we cadres could help the peasant activists find and explain to the rest all "the roots of poverty" and draw up "the account of the debt of exploitation." We were helped in this, too, by cadres of a cultural work team from Chengtu who brought the film, *The White-Haired Girl*, and gave short plays showing landlord exploitation. By now, too, the main driving forces of the movement were emerging more clearly: the farmhands and poor peasants, those who had suffered most from the old order and who therefore were most interested in fighting for the new.

With this preparation, a conference of farmhands and poor peasants' representatives was called to discuss the guilt of the landlord class as a whole. The leader of our small group, Chang Hua-sung, related how his father had died when the landlord came to their house to take away their last bag of grain, and he had been beaten up by the landlord's thugs. . . .

Case after case was brought up, the village women taking a leading part in exposing local landlord tyrants. The "debt of exploitation" added up. How much grain, how many lives, how much happiness had the landlords stolen! The peasants' bitterness turned into hatred for what they now saw was feudal landlord exploitation. They understood why they were poor and the landlords rich—they had found where the roots of poverty lay. . . .

After one month of intensive preparation through meetings with peasant representatives, with women, young people, and the militia, the time was ripe to reorganize the peasants' association—which had previously led the "turning-over" in the village—and develop within it the peasants' representative conference as the leading organ to carry out the land reform. . . .

The principle for the initial organization of the peasants' representative conference was that the leadership should firmly belong to the farm hands and poor peasants. The middle peasants should comprise one-third of the members. One-third and one-quarter of the total membership, respectively, should be women and young people. . . .

From the first day of our arrival, we had read with the peasant activists newspapers and documents on the land reform. We had given them short talks on the history of the revolution, the Communist Party, the world struggle for peace. We had told them about the Soviet Union and its great state and collective farms, and also about the mutual aid teams and agricultural cooperatives in Northeast China and other parts of the country. All this information was eagerly absorbed.

Now, after the establishment of the peasants' representative conference, the peasant representatives gathered every morning for study and discussion. . . .

For three days, the elected peasant representatives of the thirteen villages of Hsinglung *hsiang* gathered to discuss how to determine class status. First they discussed what is a class and what is the meaning of class differentiation. When it became clear to everyone that the meaning of class differentiation is to make a clear demarcation line between our enemies and ourselves as land reform is a class struggle, they proceeded to discuss concretely how to differentiate classes in the countryside, with the *Decisions Concerning the Differentiation of Class Status in the Countryside* as the standard. The decisions they agreed on in these meetings were later taken back to the villages for further discussion. In small and big meetings, peasants also learned the policy and standard and the significance of class differentiation, and applied it to concrete cases. Finally, the masses agreed on each case at a mass meeting. However, each case was submitted to the district people's government for ratification. . . .

Village Number 1 gathered in the early morning in the village temple. After the chairman of the peasants' representative conference had announced and explained the meaning of class differentiation and the standard of class differentiation, he called on Chang Hu-yu, the most obvious landlord in the village, to come forward. Chang, dressed in a long gown and with his whitish whiskers bristling, slowly walked up and faced the meeting.

"What is your class status?" the chairman asked.

"I am a rich peasant," Chang replied, somewhat guiltily.

"Rich peasant? Do you know that a rich peasant himself works a lot in the fields? Do you ever labor?"

The landlord was silent.

"Well, perhaps you'll tell us what you live on? Who feeds you?"

Landlord Chang remained silent. . . .

"Since he won't admit anything, let us tell him," said the chairman. For a few moments there was a confused competition of voices. Nearly everyone wanted to "draw up the debt of exploitation" and accuse the landlord.

Finally the floor was given to Liu Ching-hsiang, a farm hand and once one of Chang's tenants, who confronted the landlord directly. "You cheated me. You exploited me. It was you who kept my family almost starving. My family was broken up. My wife had to seek her food in Lungshan village," he charged. "And even lately, you dared to try and bribe me. You offered a fur coat to me, addressing me as Representative Liu! Can't you see, Chairman Mao has given us peasants a whole new world, and you think I care for your fur coat!" He spat contemptuously on the floor. . . .

One after another, they brought evidence against Chang, accusing him of countless cruelties. A bent old woman, whose son he had worked to death, still hardly dared accuse him even at this meeting. She spoke in a voice hardly more than a whisper. Only when she felt the great support of the masses, urging her on, she raised her voice and shook her small fist in his face. . . .

Four other landlords in the village also appeared before this meeting.

All had cruelly exploited the peasant tenants. Rents of 40 to 80 percent of the land's yield were not unusual in addition to other dues and services. . . .

The rich peasants were also classified at a mass meeting. They were advised to work hard in production and not to do anything to distract the land reform. After the land reform, individual rich peasants may be admitted into the peasants' association, on approval of a *hsiang* peasant mass meeting.

Then the peasants held small group meetings, to decide their own status among themselves: farm hands, poor and middle peasants, handicraftsmen, etc.

The name lists and class status of every inhabitant were posted up for all to see; the peasants' on a red board; the rich peasants' on a yellow board; and the landlords' on a white board. If anyone felt he had been wrongly classified, he was free to appeal within fifteen days to the county people's court for a reclassification.

Landlords' Power Broken

As soon as the class differentiation had been started, the peasants' representatives formed a group to confiscate the landlords' "five big properties," that is surplus grain (after leaving enough to last the house members till the next harvest), farm implements, draft animals, houses, and furniture, after leaving the landlord an average holding of land and the means of working it. When this was done, the political and economic power of the landlords was broken—and the peasants were enabled to start production on their new lands.

After class differentiation, the peasant representatives of the whole *hsiang* met at the West Forest Temple again. They were to investigate the land acreage and yield. . . .

Back in the village, in small group meetings, every peasant reported what land he tilled with its acreage and yield, and his neighbors discussed each report. . . .

An investigation committee, comprising several old and experienced peasants, inspected each field and its assessment. . . . The masses also went into the fields to investigate each other's land. But the investigation committee had the final say.

The work team helped in the calculations needed to distribute the land. We worked with and trained several literate peasants to check the acreage and yield. Our village, with a population of 520 but with only about 1,000 mou of land, had a shortage of land, that is, below the average holding which each should receive, on the basis of the total population and land of the *hsiang*. Those villages which had a land surplus contributed part of their surplus to the land-poor villages. . . .

Distribution of Land

A mass meeting was held to announce the average amount of land and yield each person should get. Those tenants who tilled more than the average—the "fat households"—themselves reported how much land they could give to the pool for the distribution. The rest decided if these reports were just. Then the "lean households" reported their holdings and how much extra they needed. Their neighbors confirmed these reports. . . .

The peasants knew exactly which land was suitable, considering the distance, water supply, and so on. All that I did during land distribution was to write down the acreage and yield of the land, as the peasants told about their share and as it was confirmed by their committees. : . .

Surplus grain, farm implements, draft animals, houses and furniture were all distributed according to need. . . .

Summing Up

Gathered for the homeward journey at the *hsiang* work team headquarters, Kuo Ping, the team leader, assessed the work of the twelve Peking comrades. He pointed out our particular success in two things. We had successfully helped in rousing the political consciousness of the peasants. The fact that the accusation meetings against the counter-revolutionary despots were effective had a decisive influence in mobilizing the masses and dealing successfully with the landlords. The other good point was that we had strictly performed our duty as propagandists of government policy and had encouraged the peasants to do what they could and ought to do, instead of doing things for them. We had also effectively helped the peasant representatives to set up systematic methods of work and the correct practice of criticism and self-criticism. But we had made some initial mistakes while helping the peasants decide the land acreage and yield. We had thought that the peasants were already universally progressive enough to give absolutely frank reports on the yield of their land. We had forgotten that the selfishness of some was not to be discarded at once. . . . Those of us participating in such a mass movement for the first time got a more concrete understanding of what are classes and what is the class struggle. We, no less than the peasants, had learned where the roots of poverty lay.

It was early in February. The day was clear and warm. We were ready to go. The work team headquarters was crowded with peasants from various villages in which the Peking comrades had worked. They performed a *yangko* dance to send us off. Many accompanied us for a long distance down the main road.

C. RETURN TO THE CITIES: THE ORIGINS OF URBAN AND INDUSTRIAL POLICY

1. THE ORIGINS OF URBAN AND INDUSTRIAL POLICY

As the balance of forces in the civil war shifted inexorably in their favor, the Communists inaugurated industrial and commercial policies for the towns and cities which they would soon govern for the first time in over two decades.

One critical element, as Jen Pi-shih explained in early 1948, lay in maximizing output of existing capitalist industry and commercial enterprise. Only large-scale bureaucratic capital closely tied to the Kuomintang and to foreign interests was subject to confiscation. In contrast with radical peasant-initiated land revolution, the party urged factory workers to accept the basic structure of industrial management; the new democratic revolution set out not only to destroy feudalism but to curb capitalism and place it in the service of the nation.

The analog of the policy of protecting rich peasant interests was the fostering of capitalist industry. Jen lashed out at such policies as expropriation or excessive taxation which hampered industrial growth, threw workers out of jobs, and undermined self-reliance. His speech is also among the earliest statements concerned with winning over intellectuals and technical specialists which the party would require to run the nation.

The guiding principles of urban policy received their most

Policy on Industry and Commerce. Speech to enlarged session, Northwest People's Liberation Army Front Committee, January 12, 1948. FBIS April 17, 1948.

succinct summation in an inner-party directive drafted by Mao on February 27, 1948:

> Precautions should be taken against the mistake of applying in the cities the measures used in rural areas for struggling against landlords and rich peasants and for destroying the feudal forces. A sharp distinction should be made between the feudal exploitation practiced by landlords and rich peasants, which must be abolished, and the industrial and commercial enterprises run by landlords and rich peasants, which must be protected. A sharp distinction should also be made between the correct policy of developing production, promoting economic prosperity, giving consideration to both public and private interests and benefiting both labor and capital, and the one-sided and narrow-minded policy of "relief," which purports to uphold the workers' welfare but in fact damages industry and commerce and impairs the cause of the people's revolution. Education should be conducted among comrades in the trade unions and among the masses of workers to enable them to understand that they should not see merely the immediate and partial interests of the working class while forgetting its broad, long-range interests. Under the local government's leadership, workers and capitalists should be led to organize joint committees for the management of production and to do everything possible to reduce costs, increase output and stimulate sales so as to attain the objectives of giving consideration to both public and private interests, benefiting both labor and capital and supporting the war.

By the spring of 1948 the Communists were beginning for the first time to administer large cities and modern industry. The Central Committee's telegram of April 18, drafted by Mao, while emphasizing the necessity to preserve the capitalist framework of industry, also called for cautious first steps of industrial democratization in the form of worker and technician participation in management while cautioning against the use of mobilization methods adapted to the agrarian revolution.

A. Jen Pi-shih,
Industrial and Commercial Policy

Adventuristic policies must not be adopted toward industry and commerce. Cases of damaging industry and commerce have already occurred in various places. For example, when our army recovered Kuochiapo, in north Shensi's Shenmu region, confiscation was even employed against small merchants. This is yielding to a suicidal policy. The Basic Program on Chinese Agrarian Law stipulates that "the property and legal operations of industrial and commercial businessmen shall be protected from infringement." Industry and commerce in general should be protected. Not even industry and commerce operated by landlords and rich peasants should be confiscated; it should likewise receive the protection of the democratic government.

Do not think that, because this industry and commerce is invested in by landlords and rich peasants, it should be discriminated against. This is incorrect. It should be seen that the existence of this industry and commerce is beneficial to the present-day social economy. The party's policy is only to confiscate the industry and commerce of bureaucratic capital and really big, despotic, counter-revolutionary elements, and place them under the ownership of the state of the people. . . .

Chairman Mao Tsetung says, "Owing to the backwardness of China's economy, it will still be necessary to permit the existence for a long period of the capitalist economy represented by the broad, petty bourgeoisie and the middle bourgeoisie even after the nation-wide victory of the revolution. Furthermore, in accordance with the division of labor in the national economy, the development of all sections among them . . . will still be necessary; they will still be an indispensable part of the entire national economy."

We must clearly explain this principle of Chairman Mao's to the masses of workers, peasants, and soldiers so that they understand why industry and commerce are needed, and teach all the laboring people to understand that partial temporary interests must be subordinated to the overall, long-term interests. For example, if the landlord operates coal deposits, the peasants may, from the point of view of their present partial interests, show their hands in support of confiscating and distributing them, because if everyone is distributed a portion of the tools and materials from the coal pits, it may temporarily solve his own problems.

If we permit this to be done, it would seem in form to be following the mass line of work, but in essence it would be committing the error of tailism. Under these circumstances, we must persuade the peasants to understand the advantages of having the coal pits in existence intact, and that, if dispersed, the coal pits will be ruined and they themselves will have no coal to burn. This would hinder the economic development of the liberated areas. . . .

At present, the government trading companies within the liberated areas do not yet have the strength to set up stores universally. . . . Cooperatives have not developed universally and are sometimes badly run. Therefore, the existence of private commerce is necessary. Merchants, of course, engage in exploitation; the commercial activity of merchants, in itself, does not produce any value. They either share a portion of the capitalists' profits, or directly exploit the producer and consumer. Sometimes they engage in hoarding and speculation, doing even more harm. But the answer is not to destroy commerce, but to lead commerce. We must grasp the overall development of commerce, we must use the merchants and not be utilized by them. While this sort of policy is beneficial to the people, it is also beneficial to legitimate merchants.

As for small merchants and peddlers, most of them are poor, their livelihood is only equivalent to those of poor peasants, middle peasants, or well-to-do middle peasants and we should even more not injure them. . . .

What is our view of the intelligentsia? The majority of professors, teachers, scientists, engineers, artists, and so forth, come from landlord, rich peasant, or capitalist families. But the work they themselves do is a sort of gentle labor. Toward these mental laborers, the democratic regime should adopt policies of protection, and should as much as possible win them to serve the People's Republic. . . .

We are in the process of building a new democracy. There is a population of 160 million in the liberated areas, which is continuing to grow. Within three to five years, it is possible that the revolution may be victorious throughout the country. If we want to build a new democratic country, we must have knowledge. . . . At present, we still do not have many specialists. We must unreservedly win over and use China's existing intelligentsia and specialists to work for the people. On the one hand, we may use this group of intelligentsia, and on the other hand we must educate and reform them, correcting their isolation from the masses and habits of slighting the people. Most of them have enthusiasm for construction and in the great construction work of the new democracy, most of them can certainly be made to progress. . . .

At the same time, we must pay even more attention to training an intelligentsia of worker and peasant origin, enabling the workers and peasants who have emancipated [themselves] or their sons to shoulder the tasks of construction. If we are only able to use the old intelligentsia and do not pay special attention to training a worker-peasant intelligentsia, we will commit errors.

B. Mao Tsetung,
The New Democratic Urban Policy

Loyang* is now recaptured and can probably be securely held. In our urban policy, pay attention to the following points:

1. Be very prudent in the liquidation of the organs of Kuomintang rule, arrest only the chief reactionaries and do not involve too many persons.

2. Set a clear line of demarcation in defining bureaucrat-capital; do not designate as bureaucrat-capital and do not confiscate all the industrial and commercial enterprises run by Kuomintang members. The principle should be laid down that the democratic government should take over and operate all industrial and commercial enterprises which are definitely verified as having been run by the Kuomintang's central, provincial,

---

Telegram to the Headquarters of the Loyang Front, April 18, 1948. SW IV.

* A major city and Kuomintang stronghold in Honan province.

county, or municipal governments, that is, enterprises operated wholly by official bodies. But if, for the time being, the democratic government is not yet ready to take them over or is unable to do so, the individuals previously in charge should be temporarily entrusted with the responsibility of management so that these enterprises can function as usual until the democratic government appoints people to take over. The workers and technicians in these industrial and commercial enterprises should be organized to participate in management, and their competence should be trusted. If the Kuomintang personnel have fled and the enterprise has suspended operations, a management committee of representatives elected by the workers and technicians should be set up, pending the appointment by the democratic government of managers and directors who will manage it together with the workers. Enterprises run by notorious big bureaucrats of the Kuomintang should be dealt with in conformity with the principles and measures stated above. Industrial and commercial enterprises run by small bureaucrats or by landlords, however, are not subject to confiscation. Encroachment on any enterprise run by the national bourgeoisie is strictly prohibited.

3. Forbid peasant organizations to enter the city to seize landlords and settle scores with them. Landlords whose land is in the villages but who live in the city should be dealt with by the democratic municipal government according to law. Upon the request of the village peasant organizations those who have committed the most heinous crimes may be sent back to the villages to be dealt with.

4. On entering the city, do not lightly advance slogans of raising wages and reducing working hours. In wartime it is good enough if production can continue and existing working hours and original wage levels can be maintained. Whether suitable reductions in working hours and increases in wages are to be made later will depend on economic conditions, that is, on whether the enterprises thrive.

5. Do not be in a hurry to organize the people of the city to struggle for democratic reforms and improvements in livelihood. These matters can be properly handled in the light of local conditions only when the municipal administration is in good working order, public feeling has become calm, careful surveys

have been made, a clear idea of the situation has been gained and appropriate measures have been worked out.

6. In the big cities, food and fuel are now the central problems; they must be handled in a planned way. Once a city comes under our administration, the problem of the livelihood of the city poor must be solved step by step and in a planned way. Do not raise the slogan, "open the granaries to relieve the poor." Do not foster among them the psychology of depending on the government for relief.

7. Members of the Kuomintang and its Three People's Principles Youth League must be properly screened and registered.

8. Plan everything on a long-term basis. It is strictly forbidden to destroy any means of production, whether publicly or privately owned, and to waste consumer goods. Extravagant eating and drinking are forbidden, and attention should be paid to thrift and economy.

9. Appoint as secretaries of the party's municipal committee and as mayor and deputy mayors only persons who have a grasp of policy and are capable. They should train all their personnel and explain urban policies and tactics to them. Now that the city belongs to the people, everything should proceed in the spirit that the people themselves are responsible for managing the city. It would be entirely wrong to apply our policies and tactics for cities under Kuomintang administration to a city under the people's own administration.

2. CH'EN YUN,
INDUSTRY, COMMERCE, AND TAXATION

How would the new government of the People's Republic set about the tasks of stabilizing the war-devastated economy, curbing inflation and building public confidence in its economic policies? It is worth recalling the destructive toll of inflation during the final years of the Kuomintang regime. It is estimated

Questions on the Economic Situation and Readjustment of Industry, Commerce, and Taxation. Report to the National Committee of the People's Political Consultative Conference, June 15, 1950. CB 2.

that commodity prices rose 8.5 million times between 1937 and
1949, so that in 1949 the value of Nationalist currency had
plummeted to 300 billion yuan to one U.S. dollar! The origins
of China's extraordinary success in achieving three decades of
currency and price stability, and the government's ability to win
substantial support among Chinese businessmen can be traced
to measures taken in the immediate aftermath of liberation.

Eight months after the establishment of the People's Repub-
lic, the party's leading economic specialist, Central Committee
member Ch'en Yun, analyzed the major steps in the early
transition to "an independent, free new democratic economy,"
and addressed some of the formidable economic and financial
problems to be tackled. Ch'en could report that, in a very brief
period of time, "Centralized control of economic and financial
work has been effected, revenue and expenditure in public
finance are approaching equilibrium and our currency and
prices of commodities are becoming stable." In line with the
policy of fostering a healthy capitalist sector of the economy
and winning the support of Chinese industrialists and mer-
chants, Ch'en reiterated that, "In China, which is backward in
industry, it will be progressive and beneficial to the country and
the people for the national capitalists to develop industry and
make investments in it for a long time." He proceeded to
outline the ways in which state investment, commercial, and
taxation policies would facilitate the continued growth of the
private sector.

At the present time, our country's economic and financial
situation is at a great historic turning point—of transformation
from a semicolonial, semifeudal economy into an independent,
free new democratic economy, from retrogressive and adverse
conditions to progressive and favorable conditions. . . .

Centralized control of economic and financial work has been
effected, revenue and expenditure in public finance are approaching equilibrium, and our currency and prices of commodities are becoming more stable. . . .

Certain industrial commodities and a certain kind of commerce, which developed in conformity with colonial and semicolonial economy, have entirely lost their markets because of

the elimination of imperialism, feudalism, and bureaucratic capitalism in China. Many other commodities, too, do not fit the standards required by the people. This gives rise to closing down of a certain section of industry and commerce, which in turn brings unemployment to a section of workers, who need to be given relief or to turn to other trades. . . .

Swollen organization of many private enterprises, their irrational methods of operation, their high costs and low profits or even losses, have also given rise to the phenomenon that many industrial and commercial enterprises are reducing their scale of business or even closing down. There must be readjustment in order to find a way out for them. . . .

Planlessness and blind competition among enterprises in the same trade and disharmony of supply and demand between various places also result in a falling off in production, suspension of production and closing down of enterprises. Moreover, protracted war and the great reduction in people's buying power have brought about a slackening in industry and commerce. . . .

Chairman Mao set forth the three conditions for solving these sufferings and difficult problems. They are: (1) the completion of land reform; (2) rational readjustment of existing industry and commerce; (3) drastic economy in expenditure by state organs.

We can win these conditions throughout the country in about three years. All pessimistic views on economic questions are groundless. . . .

In China, which is backward in industry, it will be progressive and beneficial to the country and the people for the national capitalists to develop industry and make investments in it for a long time.

Although Chinese commercial capital is overinflated in the big cities, at the same time we know that China is a vast country where scattered small production predominates and the existence of private merchants is, therefore, inevitable. The state allows private capital to conduct commercial activities in order to develop the circulation of commodities. This is beneficial to both the state and the people.

The people's government protects the interests of all capitalists who benefit the nation's welfare and the people's livelihood.

Of all the components of the social economy, the state's economy is the leading force.

These are our basic points of departure in carrying out the various tasks of readjusting the relations of public and private economy. . . .

We believe that the people's government should take the following steps to achieve harmony between public and private relations in order to alleviate the difficulties which have arisen during this historic turning point in the economy of our country.

In the sphere of industry:

1. Whenever possible, the government and the state-owned enterprises will entrust private factories with processing work and place orders with private factories. The Committee of Financial and Economic Affairs under the government administration council will centralize the orders for processing work and goods placed by state-owned enterprises, government organs and the army. . . .

2. The government will purchase part of the products of agriculture, and provide facilities for industrial goods which can be exported but which are having difficulties at present. In this way it is expected that both home and foreign markets for industrial goods will expand.

3. The government will combine public and private resources in organizing the turnover of industrial capital.

4. The government will call on private enterprises to improve management methods, improve relations between labor and capital and to overcome their business difficulties jointly.

5. In order to adjust the relationship between public and private enterprise, the government is prepared to unify in stages and readjust the dispersed productive enterprises of all government offices, army units, and organizations which are outside the sphere of state enterprises. It can thus bring them into harmony rather than into conflict with private enterprises, handicraft industry, and the subsidiary occupations of the peasantry.

6. The government will periodically inform the country which branches of industry have temporary overproduction or are reaching a saturation point, so that the people may take warning and minimize the harmful effects of lack of planning.

7. The government will undertake employment relief at key points, organizing as many as possible of the unemployed to take in state and public works projects, such as water conservancy, city reconstruction and so on.

In the sphere of commerce:

1. It is provided in the Common Program that: "State-owned trading organizations shall assume the responsibility of adjusting supply and demand, stabilizing commodity prices and assisting the people's cooperatives." This requires the government to fix suitable price policies from time to time in accordance with the economic conditions—that is, to maintain an appropriate difference between wholesale and retail prices, and between prices in various areas. . . .

2. Retail and department stores operated by the state trading organizations will be restricted to a number sufficient to stabilize prices in the retail market and to halt speculative merchants from deranging the market. These retail stores may only sell six kinds of daily necessities—grain, coal, cotton cloth, edible oils, table salt, kerosene. It is the responsibility of state wholesale companies to recall currency and to stabilize wholesale prices.

3. The people's livelihood is greatly influenced by the existence and rate of turnover of the market for agricultural produce. Today purchasing by the state trading organizations is still confined to only part of the main agricultural products and export goods, and part of the peasants' major subsidiary products. Cooperatives and private merchants must be encouraged to buy the remainder.

4. An appropriate price for agricultural produce must be maintained to protect the legitimate productive interests of the peasantry. But consideration must be given to the profits of marketing and transport, thus providing agricultural products a wide market which is beneficial to the peasantry.

5. In order to speed up the interflow of goods between the town and countryside, which will benefit both peasants and urban dwellers, the local people's governments must provide ample marketing and transport facilities for private merchants. . . .

Regarding industrial and commercial taxation:

1. The policy of taxing industry and daily necessities more lightly than commerce and luxuries should be continued.

2. Tax collection must not exceed the prescribed rate.

3. The innumerable tax items must be simplified. Over 200 tax items will be simplified or consolidated. (For example, various kinds of cotton piece goods will be taxed only once in the form of a uniform tax on yarn. Various kinds of woolen piece goods will be taxed only once in the form of a uniform tax on woolen yarn.) Altogether about five hundred items of tax will thus be eliminated.

4. The salt tax to be reduced for the benefit of the broad masses of consumers.

5. The method of tax assessment and calculation must be unified and uniform interpretations should be made in accordance with actual conditions. . . .

Our aim is to achieve rehabilitation and development of the people's economy, and at the same time, to reduce and wipe out the deficit in the state budget.

3. CH'EN PO-TA, LABOR AND WAGE POLICY

Policy toward the tiny proletariat in the Communist base areas had been the source of intense internal debate throughout the preceding decades. Now in 1948, as the Communists returned to the cities, the issue of labor policy was authoritatively set forth by Ch'en Po-ta, Mao's secretary and a ranking Central Committee member. Lashing out at advocates of "absolute egalitarianism" and at those who favored special privileges and higher wages for the proletariat vis-à-vis the peasantry, Ch'en defined a policy geared to maximizing productivity in line with Mao's slogan of benefits to labor and capital.

While hailing the working class as "the most advanced, most revolutionary class," Ch'en emphasized piece wages, not revolutionary mobilization, to stimulate higher productivity. Thus the essence of what Ch'en described as the "liberal capitalism" of

The Labor Policy and Tax Policy for Developing Industry. FBIS April 26-28, 1948.

the new democracy lay in establishing wage guidelines and trade union policies which maximized production incentives within the framework of capitalist management of the industrial sector. At the same time Ch'en outlined modest steps toward worker participation in issues pertaining to managerial planning and wage decisions and the role of unions.

The industrial policy of the Chinese Communist Party is the policy of "developing production, making the economy prosperous, taking into account both public and private interests, and benefiting both labor and capital," raised by Comrade Mao Tsetung. . . .

In the trade union movement, after lifting the feudal oppression and constrictions remaining on the workers, the Communist Party firmly opposes the "leftist" adventurism of excessive raising of wages and destroying production. The democratic government under the leadership of the Communist Party furthermore strives to provide convenient conditions for loans and for the circulation of goods and so forth to develop industry. . . .

On the question of wages, such mistakes as the following existed in certain old liberated areas in the past. Disregarding the general level of production and standard of living, and neglecting concrete factory conditions, excessively high wages and conditions of labor were set forth. Workers fared especially well and, at the same time, it was not easy to sell the goods produced because the cost of production was too great, nor was it possible for that factory to expand production.

Some factories could not even support themselves and some publicly operated factories—in ordinary industries—even required much financial supplement from the government to enable them to continue operating. Certain comrades who uphold this method feel that this is protecting the interests of the workers. This conception and method are wrong because their result is not only that industry cannot be developed, but also that newborn or young industries inevitably shrivel up or shut down. This is a suicide policy in the workers' movement.

At the same time this sort of forced, artificial, unprincipled, blind, unreasonable method of excessively raising wages cannot raise the political consciousness of the working class, and neither can it encourage their efforts for production and frugality. Furthermore, it may cause some workers to form a mistaken conception, cause them to take the road of vulgar economism and feel that they can have special privileges in livelihood which may cause mutual discrimination between workers and other laboring people in society, especially the peasants.

Therefore, this is not at all protecting the workers' interests but, to the contrary, is fundamentally violating the interests of the working class. Therefore, we must absolutely not adopt this sort of policy. This is one side of the question.

On the other hand, after opposing the above erroneous deviation, it is also possible that another kind of deviation may occur, or will already have occurred: That is, to neglect the fact that the correct handling of the question of wages can impel the formation and development of the forces of production with great strides, and—heedless of whether production efficiency is enhanced—to uniformly deflate wages at the first, low levels, with no appropriate rewards for the workers and employees who make special efforts to raise production and lower costs, and no appropriate punishment of workers and employees who go slow or waste materials or who commit graft or fraud, and so forth.

Very clearly this sort of policy will also injure the initiative of the workers and employees in production. There is also very mistaken advocacy of so-called "equal livelihood" for technical personnel and ordinary workers, forcing the salaries of technical personnel and employees excessively low. This, of course, would injure the initiative of technical personnel in production and would, in turn, injure the initiative of the workers in seeking progress.

Of course, the working class is the most advanced, most revolutionary class of the Chinese people, the leading class of the Chinese Revolution. It can accept correct political mobilization and thus heighten its own initiative in production. In many newly liberated places the initiative in production of workers, especially workers in publicly operated industry, is enhanced first of all by the stimulus of political liberation. But this sort of initiative cannot continuously be enhanced and cannot even be constantly maintained if it does not have the constant, rational, new democratic economic system to consolidate it, but rather relies exclusively on political stimulus. Therefore, there must be a correct policy on wages which can constantly stimulate the initiative in production of workers and employees.

A correct policy on wages is one which, in accordance with the general living conditions of the particular place and time, with the old pre-liberation wages as the basis, makes reasonable and proper adjustments of wages, and on this basis carries out a reasonable and proper progressive wage system by the piece, by grade, by share of work, and by frugality—that is, decreasing the cost of production and so forth—and carries out a progressive award system such as issuing dividends in accordance with work done.

This kind of system must be based on the concrete circumstances of the various branches of industry and the concrete conditions of various factories, with the factory superintendent responsible for consulting with the factory management committee and the wage committee consulting with the workers' representatives and the masses of workers, drawing on the past and present experiences of the factory in question and other factories, deciding to adopt this or that method or flexibly interlacing and adopting two or more methods.

Furthermore, the management and the workers should enter into a concrete agreement on the production plan, wage terms, or methods of award while the appraisal of work must give attention to quantity and quality of production alike. Wages and hours of work should be agreed upon among various factories, uniformly arriving at reasonable provisions but based on concrete circumstances. Certain discrepancies should be allowed.

Complete uniform equality is impossible. To sum up, the precondition for deciding everything should be that it must be favorable to the constant raising of production. A similar attitude likewise must be adopted with regard to the salaries of technicians and employees. . . .

Unquestionably, according to both old and new experiences, establishing this kind of wage and award system will greatly stimulate the production enthusiasm of workers and employees, make their labor discipline more serious, improve the labor organization of the factory, raise the quantity and quality of the product, eliminate waste, guard against theft, corruption, and fraud, decrease all kinds of unproductive consumption, and continuously raise the skill of workers and employees so that the technically backward catch up with the advanced and the advanced seek new progress.

This is an extremely important system for impelling the advance of productive forces. This is the material base for consolidating and giving full play to a new labor attitude on the part of workers and employees. Realizing this kind of system makes it possible for the production efficiency of the factory to increase 50 percent, 100 percent, or even more.... Some comrades feel that carrying out this kind of system will encourage the workers' "employee" concept. This is also very much mistaken....

Do not forget that we are now establishing the economic system of a new democracy still permitting the development of liberal capitalism, and are not already realizing communist society, so that wiping out the workers' "employee" concept is impossible. In reality, this is a kind of reactionary illusion which violates the laws of social development. Under the system of piece-work wages and so forth, the workers' "employee" concept of obtaining increased emoluments because of increased production—or carrying on increased production to acquire increased emoluments—is not detrimental but rather is rational and progressive.

The workers obtain increased emoluments because they have put forth increased labor and energy. On one hand, this promotes the advance of the social productive forces; on the other hand, it can supply the peasants with more, comparatively cheaper industrial products produced at lower costs. It will also be considered reasonable by the peasants and all laboring elements of society, and will strengthen the solidarity of the workers with them....

This sort of system of wages and awards must be established on the basis of what is possible and the willingness of the masses. This sort of system of wages and awards represents the interests of the development of the social productive forces and also represents the individual and mass interests of the workers. Therefore, it will readily arouse and should constantly maintain the competitive, conscious enthusiasm of the masses of workers for production and frugality.

With regard to another important question on labor policy,

the trade union question, entirely new problems have been raised in the liberated areas. The trade union movement and trade union work of the liberated areas should, under the above correct slogan, "Establish a new labor attitude," encourage the workers' production initiative, promote making production plans and wage agreements by consultation in common among the workers and managements of publicly and privately operated factories (in publicly operated factories the management comprises the superintendent, manager, and factory management committee; in privately operated factories it comprises the private capitalist, manager, and so forth) and constantly compile production experience to teach the workers, turning our trade unions into political and production schools of new democracy.

4. MANAGEMENT AND REFORM IN THE FACTORIES

The heart of China's industrialization program, the focal point for Soviet aid and technical assistance, and the first region in which the Communists managed large-scale industry was the Northeast which, as Manchuria under Japanese rule, was the most advanced industrial region prior to World War II. The leading figure in the Northeast, secretary of the party and vice chairman of the Central People's Government, Kao Kang, defined guidelines for industrial management heavily influenced by Soviet practice: (1) responsibility systems emphasizing the role of the factory manager; (2) democracy and centralization in management emphasizing the necessity for managers to actively consult management committees but to retain ultimate responsibility in their own hands; and (3) skill and productivity graded wages to provide incentives to labor. In all three areas we see efforts to rationalize the party's wartime practice as it had developed in small-scale industry in the base areas.

At the Forefront of Economic Reconstruction in the Northeast. Report to the First Conference of Representatives of the Communist Party in the Northeast, March 30, 1950. CB 6.

In the early years of the People's Republic, the new demo-
cratic industrial policy, whether in transforming bureaucratic
capital into state-owned firms or in continuing capitalist owner-
ship, provided no arena for mobilization of the working class
comparable to the fanshen *experienced by the peasantry in land*
revolution. Industrial policy emphasized a smooth transition to
ensure continued productivity.

In the spring of 1951, confident of its expanded industrial
capability and of its organizational base in the proletariat, the
party began mobilizing to make the workers masters of the
factories. One important step lay in overthrowing the old
system of labor bosses, many of them gangster remnants who
before liberation controlled hiring and took a share of workers'
salaries. At this time it became clear that some former gang
bosses continued to wield power in the factories as managers
and even party and union leaders. The campaign which ran from
May to December 1951 was the first major mobilization in
China's industrial sphere.

A. Kao Kang,
On Factory Management

I wish to stress here three aspects of industrial management:
the institution of a system of responsibility, the implementation
of democratic management, and the adoption of the system of
economic accounting. . . .

Comrades! Numerous facts have told us that negligence in
responsibility will often bring about inestimable losses, and is a
crime itself. One who neglects his duties will be held responsible
for the unhappy consequences and the crime thus engendered.
Now, our economic system is so closely linked in all its aspects
that any negligence in one aspect may produce evil influences
upon many others. For example, the work of one lathe may
affect the whole machine shop, which in turn may affect the
whole factory and even the entire enterprise. We, therefore,
must positively build up in all industrial and economic units a
system of responsibility in order to exercise effective
management. We must root out the phenomenon that "everybody is responsible and yet no one is really responsible." Respon-

sibility for anything in a factory should be definitely attributed and clearly defined. Thus we shall be able to organize all enterprises effectively. . . . The system of responsibility is the most important one in our work of reconstruction, especially economic reconstruction. We must conscientiously establish this system in all enterprises. And all members of the Communist Party should strive to be model responsible workers.

Secondly, I want to talk about the problem of democratization of management.

The democratization of management is our most important method of transforming imperialist and bureaucratic enterprises into enterprises of the people. The principal duty at the present stage is to make the factory management committees a success. In these committees the communist organizations and the labor unions functioning in the enterprises should be represented. The purpose is to oppose bureaucracy, to bring workers, technicians, and staff members together through the progressive elements among them, and to centralize the views of the masses, so as to solve problems in the factories, to raise the political consciousness of all, to change their attitude toward labor, and to fight against sabotage and wrecking activities.

This is not inconsistent with the system of responsibility, but rather, an integral part of it. Our system of responsibility must be built upon popular consciousness and a positive attitude toward production. Otherwise, no favorable result will come of it. Our system of responsibility is founded on a democratic basis, and our system of democratic management is a responsible system of democracy. Our factory management committees under the leadership of factory managers are both democratic and centralized institutions. It is a gross mistake to assume that the system of responsibility and the system of democratization are incompatible.

A factory manager, who is appointed by a superior economic department to carry out the state economic plan, is of course answerable to his superiors. But he should also listen to, and pass on to his superiors, the opinions and suggestions of his subordinates so that they may be accepted, if found to be correct. He should submit his production plan to the factory management committee for discussion. In addition, all his monthly, quarterly, or yearly production plans have to be fully discussed at the conferences of the representatives of workers and staff members. It is a big mistake for anyone to take arbitrary actions, to resist or neglect the work of democratic management, and to be unwilling to rely on the strength of the masses, the party, and the labor unions.

Some of our comrades entertain the idea that the secretary of the party committee or the party branch in the enterprise should take on the duties of the factory manager. This is an absurd idea. The party committee or the party branch is not the executive body in a factory; it is but the leader of the proletarian vanguard in it. Its duty is to call upon all party members in the factory to stand as model workers at the forefront to fulfill the production plan. It is to supervise and facilitate the execution of the plan. It may make timely suggestions when and if necessary, but it cannot act for the manager, nor can it replace the function of the system of managerial responsibility. . . .

The third is the system of economic accounting. It is a big problem in our industrial management work. . . .

It is known to all that we have lived under the government issue system for quite a long time. Even today our comrades working in many departments continue to live like that. Under that system, accounting plays a very small part. Although one's revolutionary background, qualifications, and physical condition are taken into consideration in deciding his treatment, his achievement is never a determining factor. No matter whether he works or not he gets his share. "Work or no work, one and a half catties of rice all the same," as the saying goes. On the other hand, although we did some economic work and ran some factories in the past, strictly speaking, we never had proper accounting. The majority of our factories in the previous years were to serve the purpose of the War of Liberation. We never took cost into consideration, so long as the output was needed for the war. This fact has engendered a harmful state of mind among our comrades who have been doing economic work. They have not acquired the concept of cost in the course of revolutionary work. So long as they can produce they are satisfied, and do not bother about any cost accounting.

Undoubtedly the government issue system has served its purpose in sustaining our prolonged revolutionary work. In some of our organizations, it remains a good system at present. It is still an indispensable system in the army. Indeed, to produce war supplies without regard to their cost in the past had proved to be, after all, to the best interests of the people. But now the situation has undergone a great change. We are now managing the entire national economy, and especially in managing a modern economy, if we do not have accounting of receipts and payments, production records, wages scales, or in other words, if we have no idea of the cost of production and do not implement this system of economic accounting, we shall have no industrial management at all. We shall not be able to know the present condition of an enterprise and we cannot estimate its possible development in the future. . . .

B. Liu Tzu-chiu,
Democratic Reform in Factories and Mines

For imperialism, feudalism, and bureaucratic capitalism to maintain their rule and control over the broad masses of workers and employees in factories and mines, they not only relied on reactionary political forces (such as reactionary troops, gendarmes, police, law courts, and prisons), but also fell back upon certain reactionary social forces. These reactionary social forces in factories and mines are called *t'ou-lao* (head) in Hankow, "number one" in Shanghai, and *pa-t'ou* (gang labor head) in Tsingtao. Though different in name, they were the same in character. Very often these *t'ou-lao*, "number ones," or *pa-t'ou* in factories and mines were at the same time organizers, heads, or backbones of such organizations as the KMT and Nationalist Youth Corps, secret services (party secret service and military secret service), reactionary religious societies (the *I-kuan-tao* the *Chiu-kung-tao*, the *Kan-chu-er-hua-tao*, etc.) and feudal brotherhoods (the Green Society and the Red Society). . . .
    The aim and purpose of democratic reform is to introduce a

Democratic Reform in Factories and Mines. *Kung-jen, Jih-pao*, September 12, 1951. CB 123.

thorough reform of the labor gang system which imperialism, feudalism, and bureaucratic capitalism purposely established and cultivated in factories and mines to rule the masses of workers. This will be carried out in a democratic way on the basis of systematic organization, proper leadership, and extensive mass mobilization and in accordance with the requirements of production and the demands of the masses. . . .

The development of democratic reform generally can be divided into the following three stages:

The first step is democratic struggle. Adopting the method of recall and comparison of hardships, we should carry out struggles of reasoning at mass meetings (most of these will be mass meetings of shop workers; some may be all-factory meetings or section meetings). These struggles will be directed against *pa-t'ou, t'ou-lao*, "number ones," heads of reactionary religious societies, leaders of secret brotherhoods, and backbones of reactionary parties and youth corps, who "earned their positions not by their merits, but by their backgrounds," who never or seldom took part in production, and who rode on the heads of the workers and exercised feudal oppression and exploitation. The struggles of reasoning over these people will be dealt with according to the nature of their past offenses, their abilities in production, their attitude towards labor after liberation and the degree of repentance they have shown. They may be given such treatment as demotion, reduction of salary, transfer of work, public surveillance, or suspension of trade union membership. There may be persons whose offenses were of a serious nature, who have incurred public hatred. These people may be sent to people's courts for trial or dismissed from their posts in accordance with public demand. This is the most important stage in mobilizing the masses. The laboring masses have referred to such meetings of struggle as real "delivery meetings," "liberation meetings," or "meetings to see the sun." . . . At this stage the main hesitation of the laboring masses is fear of insufficient backing from the leadership after their struggle against the gang labor heads. They are afraid of trouble and retaliation and getting "small shoes to wear."

The second step is democratic unity. This means unburdening the mind, confession, discussion, criticism and self-criticism to relieve the workers and employees of various burdens loaded on them in the past, such as joining under coercion reactionary parties, youth corps, quasi-religious societies, secret brotherhoods, the Nationalist Army and police, etc. We should also remove the misunderstandings that exist among the workers themselves, between employees and workers, between cadres and the workers (i.e., between the party, the management, the trade union officials on the one hand, and workers on the other), between workers in one department and another, and finally between workers in one locality and another. This will consolidate the unity among the working class.

As to the question of mobilizing the masses, it is a stage that demands careful handling and extensive action. To accomplish this well, experience advises us to carry out self-criticism among administrative and trade union leaders first and to encourage the masses to express their opinions. . . .

The third step in democratic reform is democratic construction. This means constructive establishment on a completely voluntary basis of various agencies and systems conducive to production and improvement of living standards after the broad masses of workers and employees have improved in political awakening and consolidated their unity. Concerning this part of democratic reform, the results obtained in successfully reformed establishments are as follows: introduction of a responsibility system, contract system and supervision for production work, re-election of trade union committees and factory control committees, and registration and re-examination of labor insurance cards. . . . The most important thing to observe is to inform the masses of the policy and procedure to be pursued and then encourage discussion and full expression of opinions from the lower ranks upwards. Do not pull strings or dominate the workers (this does not mean surrender of leadership) and do not emphasize "official safeguards of correctness." . . .

In factories, railways, and mines where the masses have been fully mobilized and democratic reform completed, a new attitude toward labor has been formed among the workers, labor discipline has been strengthened, and efficiency has increased. In some factories democratic reform took up 20 percent of the working hours for one whole month. Yet production targets which had not been fulfilled in the past were overfulfilled on time. The relationship between employees and workers and between cadres and the masses has also been improved. When party and trade union cadres arrive at the workshops, they are no longer greeted with indifference or looked askance at by the workers. . . .

In one word, after democratic reform, the factories are completely changed and rejuvenated. This bears out one truth: that before the masses are mobilized and their class consciousness deepened, everything tends to drift into mere formality.

II

THE SOCIALIST TRANSFORMATION OF CITY AND COUNTRYSIDE AND THE FIRST FIVE YEAR PLAN 1953-1957

A. POLICY GUIDELINES
FOR A DEVELOPING SOCIALIST SOCIETY

1. THE CONSTITUTION AND THE GENERAL LINE FOR THE TRANSITION TO SOCIALISM

In the fall of 1953 two major events punctuated the transition from the post-liberation period of the new democracy and postwar reconstruction. These were the initiation of the first five-year plan in September and the promulgation of the general line for the transition period on October 1. With the land revolution completed, the Korean War armistice on July 27, and the economy basically recovered from the ravages of a century of invasion and war, the leadership turned to the dual tasks of socialist transformation of city and countryside and planned national development centering on industrialization.

In August 1953 Mao summed up the tasks of the era of the transition to socialism:

> *The time between the founding of the People's Republic of China and the basic completion of socialist transformation is the period of transition. The party's general line or general task for the transition period is basically to accomplish the country's industrialization and the socialist transformation of agriculture, handicrafts and capitalist industry and commerce over a fairly long period of time. This general line should be the beacon illuminating all our work.*

This meant restricting and eventually eliminating capitalist

Report on the Draft Constitution of the People's Republic of China, September 15, 1954. In: *Selected Works of Liu Shao-ch'i* (Hong Kong: Union Research Institute, 1969).

*ownership of industry and commerce and the rich peasant rural
economy.*

*The 1954 Constitution defined the class basis and issued
guidelines for step-by-step socialist transformation of the remaining privately owned components of the urban and rural
economy. Stating that "China's advance along the road to
socialism is fixed and irrevocable," Liu Shao-ch'i addressed the
central question of the role of class struggle in the projected
peaceful transition to socialism. Explicitly rejecting the idea
that "there is no longer class struggle," he insisted that China
could restrict and then eliminate capitalist exploitation "by
peaceful struggle, through the control of the administrative
bodies of state, the leadership of the state-owned economy, and
supervision by the masses of the workers." Peaceful struggle
would be conducted both with respect to the national bourgeoisie in the industrial sector and the rich peasants in the
countryside. In each case, flexible methods involving transitional forms of state capitalism in industry and cooperatives in
agriculture and handicrafts would facilitate the smooth transition to socialism.*

*"Our policy, to solve the contradiction between socialism
and capitalism," Liu stated, "is to permit the existence of
capitalist ownership, utilize the qualities of capitalist industry
and commerce which are beneficial to the national welfare and
the people's livelihood, and restrict the qualities of capitalist
industry and commerce which are not so." The strength of the
worker-peasant alliance lay at the heart of Liu's confident
prediction that many from the ranks of national capitalists and
rich peasants could be won over to contribute to China's socialist development.*

A. Liu Shao-ch'i,
Report on the Constitution

We all know that China is now in a transition period, building
a socialist society. This period is also called in our country the
new democratic period, a period during which our economy is
characterized by both socialist and capitalist elements. Some
people hope that this condition can be permanently maintained,

and that it would be best not to make any change at all. They say that the Common Program is quite sufficient: why should we have a constitution? In the last few years, we have often heard talk about "consolidation of the new democratic order." This kind of talk reflects the idea of maintaining the status quo. But is there any real possibility of doing this? It is impossible for two conflicting relationships of production under socialism and capitalism to develop side by side in a country without interfering with each other. China will change either into a socialist state or a capitalist state; to keep China from changing means to halt all movement—and this is absolutely impossible. . . .

It can therefore be seen that China's advance along the road to socialism is fixed and irrevocable. There is no other road for China to take. . . .

Since 1953 China has already entered the period of planned economic construction with socialism as its goal. It is therefore essential for us now to take another step forward on the basis of the Common Program: to adopt a constitution like the one now submitted to you, in order to set down in legal form the central tasks of our country in the transition period.

To bring about the socialist industrialization and socialist transformation of our country is an extremely arduous and complicated task. To carry out such a task, we need to mobilize the forces of the people of the whole country, develop the initiative and enthusiasm of the masses and, under a correct and highly centralized leadership, overcome all kinds of difficulties. . . .

It is obvious that the experience of the advanced socialist states, headed by the Soviet Union, has been of great help to us. Our Draft Constitution embodies the experience of our own country and that of other countries. It is not only the product of the people's revolutionary movement in China but also a product of the international socialist movement. . . .

Content of the Draft Constitution

Continuous consolidation and strengthening of the worker-peasant alliance is the basic guarantee of successful leadership by the working class. . . . In the course of gradual transition to socialism, the peasants are bound to change, and have, in fact, begun to do so. The change takes the form of gradual transformation of individual peasants leading a precarious life into socialist cooperative farmers. Only when the working class leads the peasantry to advance along this path of cooperation can the peasants' livelihood be steadily improved and the worker-peasant alliance made closer and firmer. . . .

The fact that our state is led by the working class and based on the worker-peasant alliance shows the fundamental character of our state. . . . The true masters of the state are the overwhelming majority of the people.

The intellectuals of our country played a very important part in the revolutionary movement of the past, and they will play a still more important role in building socialism. Emerging from different social classes, intellectuals cannot by themselves form an independent social class. They can, however, when they align themselves with the working people, become working-class intellectuals, or, when they align themselves with the bourgeoisie, bourgeois intellectuals; and, to the extent that they align themselves with the overthrown feudal and the compradore class, a handful of them have become reactionary intellectuals. . . .

The Preamble to the Draft Constitution points out: "This people's democratic united front will continue to play its part in mobilizing and rallying the whole people in common struggle to fulfill the fundamental task of the state during the transition and to oppose enemies within and without." This signifies the important role to be played in the transition period by the people's democratic united front led by the working class and composed of the various democratic classes, democratic parties and groups, and people's organizations. . . .

Our country in the transition period still has its national bourgeoisie. It is recognized that in any society where exploiting and exploited classes exist, the class struggle always persists. But owing to special historical circumstances in our country—that she was formerly a nation oppressed by foreign imperialism—there was not only a conflict between the Chinese working class and the national bourgeoisie; there was also an alliance between them which still exists. The national bourgeoisie, under the leadership of the working class, joined the national and democratic revolution in the past. . . . In the transition period the national bourgeoisie still plays an important role in our national economy. . . .

In the transition period of our country there are still many different economic sectors. Ownership of the means of production in our country at present falls mainly into the following categories: state ownership, that is, ownership by the whole people; cooperative ownership, that is, collective ownership by the working masses; ownership by individual working people; and capitalist ownership. The task of the state is to strive to strengthen and extend the first two categories, that is, the socialist sector of our economy, and to bring about step by step the socialist transformation of the latter two categories, that is, the nonsocialist sector of our economy. . . .

The chief transitional form for the socialist transformation of agriculture and handicrafts is the cooperative. . . .

The transitional form for the socialist transformation of capitalist industry and commerce is state capitalism. . . .

In eliminating the system of capitalist exploitation in our country, we do not have to adopt the methods used in carrying out the land reform in 1950–1952, when we launched a broad mass movement over a short period of time and eliminated the feudal land system at one stroke. The socialist transformation of capitalist industry and commerce by the state will be gradually realized over a relatively long period of time, through various forms of state capitalism. . . . The idea that there is no longer class struggle in our country is completely wrong. Punishment will have to be meted out to those capitalists who engage in unlawful pursuits or disruptive activity. It is inconceivable that there should be no complicated struggle as we pass from the process of restricting capitalist exploitation to that of eliminating it. But the aim can be achieved by peaceful struggle, through the control of the administrative bodies of state, the leadership of the state-owned economy, and supervision by the masses of the workers. . . .

We all know that rich peasant economy is capitalist economy in the countryside; the rich peasants are the last remaining exploiting class in the countryside. In our country, rich peasant economy has never been well developed; that portion of the land rented out by the rich peasants was redistributed in the land reform. . . . Though a small number of new-type rich peasants emerged in the countryside, rich peasant economy, generally speaking, has not grown but declined. . . . In our country it is therefore possible to eliminate capitalism in the countryside step by step, through the building of cooperatives and by restrictions on the development of rich peasant economy. Struggle is of course unavoidable. Disruptive activity by the rich peasants cannot be overlooked. . . . However, in view of the general political and economic situation of our country, it will not be necessary to start a special movement, as was the case in land reform, to eliminate the rich peasants. In the future, those rich peasants who have already given up exploitation may be allowed to join cooperatives on certain conditions and continue to reform themselves, provided the agricultural producers' cooperatives have been consolidated, and the agreement of the peasants obtained. . . .

Our policy, to solve the contradiction between socialism and capitalism, is to permit the existence of capitalist ownership, utilize the qualities of capitalist industry and commerce which are beneficial to the national welfare and the people's livelihood, and restrict the qualities of capitalist industry and commerce which are not so. Transitional forms will be employed to create conditions for the gradual replacement of capitalist ownership with ownership by the whole people. . . .

Some bourgeois newspapers in foreign countries have discovered to their disappointment that the road our country will take, as laid down in our Draft Constitution, is "the road that the Soviet Union has traversed." True, the road we shall take is the road traversed by the Soviet Union. About this we have not the slightest doubt. The Soviet road is the road all humanity will eventually take, in accordance with the laws of development of history. To by-pass this road is impossible. We have always believed that Marxism-Leninism is universal truth.

B. The 1954 Constitution

Preamble

In the year 1949, after more than a century of heroic struggle, the Chinese people, led by the Communist Party of China, finally achieved their great victory in the people's revolution against imperialism, feudalism, and bureaucrat-capitalism; and so brought to an end a long history of oppression and enslavement and founded the People's Republic of China, a people's democratic dictatorship. The system of people's democracy—new democracy—of the People's Republic of China guarantees that China can in a peaceful way banish exploitation and poverty and build a prosperous and happy socialist society.

From the founding of the People's Republic of China to the attainment of a socialist society is a period of transition. During the transition the fundamental task of the state is, step by step, to bring about the socialist industrialization of the country and, step by step, to accomplish the socialist transformation of agriculture, handicrafts, and capitalist industry and commerce. . . .

General Principles

Article 1. The People's Republic of China is a people's democratic state led by the working class and based on the alliance of workers and peasants.

Article 2. All power in the People's Republic of China belongs to the people. The organs through which the people exercise power are the National People's Congress and the local people's congresses.

The National People's Congress, the local people's congresses and other organs of state practice democratic centralism.

Article 3. The People's Republic of China is a single multinational state.

Adopted September 30, 1954. In: *Documents of the First Session of the First National People's Congress* (Peking: Foreign Languages Press, 1955).

All the nationalities are equal. Discrimination against, or oppression of, any nationality, and acts which undermine the unity of the nationalities are prohibited.

All the nationalities have freedom to use and foster the growth of their spoken and written languages, and to preserve or reform their own customs or ways.

Regional autonomy applies in areas where people of national minorities live in compact communities. National autonomous areas are inalienable parts of the People's Republic of China.

Article 4. The People's Republic of China, by relying on the organs of state and the social forces, and by means of socialist industrialization and socialist transformation, ensures the gradual abolition of systems of exploitation and the building of a socialist society.

Article 5. At present, the following basic forms of ownership of means of production exist in the People's Republic of China: state ownership, that is, ownership by the whole people; cooperative ownership, that is, collective ownership by the working masses; ownership by individual working people; and capitalist ownership.

Article 6. The state sector of the economy is a socialist sector, owned by the whole people. It is the leading force in the national economy and the material basis on which the state carries out socialist transformation. The state ensures priority for the development of the state sector of the economy.

All mineral resources and waters, as well as forests, undeveloped land, and other resources which the state owns by law, are the property of the whole people.

Article 7. The cooperative sector of the economy is either socialist, when collectively owned by the working masses, or semisocialist, when in part collectively owned by the working masses. Partial collective ownership by the working masses is a transitional form by means of which individual peasants, individual handicraftsmen, and other individual working people organize themselves in their advance towards collective ownership by the working masses.

The state protects the property of the cooperatives, encourages, guides, and helps the development of the cooperative sector of the economy. It regards the promotion of producers' cooperatives as the chief means for the transformation of individual farming and individual handicrafts.

Article 8. The state protects the right of peasants to own land and other means of production according to law.

The state guides and helps individual peasants to increase production and encourages them to organize producers', supply and marketing, and credit cooperatives voluntarily.

The policy of the state toward rich peasant economy is to restrict and gradually eliminate it.

Article 9. The state protects the right of handicraftsmen and other nonagricultural individual working people to own means of production according to law.

The state guides and helps individual handicraftsmen and other nonagricultural individual working people to improve their enterprise and encourages them to organize producers', and supply and marketing cooperatives voluntarily.

Article 10. The state protects the right of capitalists to own means of production and other capital according to law.

The policy of the state towards capitalist industry and commerce is to use, restrict, and transform them. The state makes use of the positive sides of capitalist industry and commerce which are beneficial to national welfare and the people's livelihood, restricts their negative sides which are not beneficial to national welfare and the people's livelihood, encourages and guides their transformation into various forms of state capitalist economy, gradually replacing capitalist ownership with ownership by the whole people; and it does this by means of control exercised by administrative organs of state, the leadership given by the state sector of the economy, and supervision by the workers.

The state forbids capitalists to engage in unlawful activities which injure the public interest, disrupt the social-economic order, or undermine the economic plan of the state.

Article 11. The state protects the right of citizens to own lawfully earned incomes, savings, houses and other means of life.

Article 12. The state protects the right of citizens to inherit private property according to law.

Article 13. The state may, in the public interest, buy, requisition, or nationalize land and other means of production both in cities and countryside according to provisions of law.

Article 14. The state forbids any person to use his private property to the detriment of the public interest.

Article 15. By economic planning, the state directs the growth and transformation of the national economy to bring about the constant increase of productive forces, in this way enriching the material and cultural life of the people and consolidating the independence and security of the country.

2. CHINA'S INDUSTRIALIZATION AND THE MODEL OF THE SOVIET UNION

China's first major planning effort, the first five-year plan, was predicated on the belief that China, with extensive Soviet aid, would follow the basic lines of development charted by the Bolshevik Revolution and above all Stalin's focus on centralized heavy industry during the early plan periods. The present article reflects the abiding faith in the Soviet model as a blueprint for China, above all in the industrial sphere where Soviet achievement was most impressive and where Chinese revolutionaries lacked extensive experience. While revolutionary change continued to transform the countryside, the bulk of state planning and investment focused on industry, especially centralized heavy industry. The present article reflects the contemporary tendency to equate China's modernization with industrialization and the progress of the urban areas.

The five-year construction plan, to which we have long looked forward, has now commenced. Its basic objective is the gradual realization of the industrialization of our state.

Industrialization has been the goal sought by the Chinese people during the past one hundred years. From the last days of the Manchu dynasty to the early years of the republic, some

Chi Yun: How China Proceeds With the Task of Industrialization. JMJP, May 23, 1953. CB 272.

people had undertaken the establishment of a few factories in the country. But industry as a whole has never been developed in China. . . . It was just as Stalin said: "Because China did not have her own heavy industry and her own war industry, she was being trampled upon by all the reckless and unruly elements." . . .

We are now in the midst of a period of important changes, in that period of transition, as described by Lenin, of changing "from the stallion of the peasant, the farm hand and poverty, to the stallion of mechanized industry, electrification."

We must look upon this period of transition to the industrialization of the state as one equal in importance and significance to that period of transition of the revolution towards the fight for political power. . . .

It was through the implementation of the policies of the industrialization of the state and the collectivization of agriculture that the Soviet Union succeeded in building up, from an economic structure complicated with five component economies, a unified socialist economy; in turning a backward agricultural nation into a first class industrial power of the world; in defeating German fascist aggression in World War II; and in constituting itself the strong bastion of world peace today.

We are looking upon the Soviet Union as our example in the building of our own country. Soviet experiences in the realization of industrialization are of great value to us. . . .

The foundation of socialism is large industrial development. Lenin said, "There is only one real foundation for a socialist society, and it is large industry. If we do not possess factories of great size, if we do not possess a large industrial structure with the most advanced equipment, then we shall generally not be able to talk of socialism, much less in the case of an agricultural country."

Accordingly, in order to enable your state to progress victoriously toward socialism, we must construct large industries. . . . Numerous facts have proved that it is futile to attempt the enforcement of socialism on the foundations of small agriculture or small handicrafts. Industry must first be developed to provide possibilities for the collectivization and mechanization of agriculture, for the socialist reform of agriculture.

At the same time, only with the industrialization of the state may we guarantee our economic independence and nonreliance on imperialism. . . .

What, then, is industrialization? To what extent must a country's industry be developed to justify the claim to being industrialized?

Industrialization is first reflected in the comparatively greater importance of industry over agriculture in the system of national economy as a whole. . . .

Even after victory in the revolution and three years of economic recovery efforts, industry has been slowly developed to the stage of constituting barely more than 20 percent of our national economy. . . . .

The Soviet Union was also an agricultural country before the victory of its revolution. At the time, industry in Russia constituted 42.1 percent of the national economy. Lenin and Stalin referred to Russia as extremely backward. As a matter of fact, the level of industrial development there at the time was much higher than our present level. This also explains that our mission of industrialization is an even more difficult task. . . .

In the year 1929–1930 industry had already risen to 53 percent of the national economy, and agriculture constituted only 47 percent. It was then that Stalin announced that in the general system of the national economy, the importance of industry had begun to exceed that of agriculture, and he said, "We are now on the eve of the transformation from an agricultural country to an industrial country." . . .

On the completion of the first five-year plan, industry in the Soviet Union had risen in importance to constitute 70.4 percent of the national economy, while agriculture only constituted 29.6 percent. It was then that Stalin announced, "This is to say, our state has finally definitely and reliably been transformed into an industrial nation." . . .

This shows that industrialization means that industry must constitute about 70 percent of the national economy as a whole.

There must be the development of heavy industry.

The mere fact that industry occupies greater importance compared with agriculture does not constitute industrialization. Take the example of a country where industry has been well developed, but all the enterprises belong to the category of light industry, with no or very little heavy industry. The machinery and other production materials used by its factories have to be imported from countries where heavy industry is more developed. This means that the country in question is still not economically independent, still reliant on other countries. Obviously a country not economically independent cannot be considered an industrialized country. . . .

Only with the development of heavy industry, with the equipment of all production departments including heavy and light industry with self-produced capital goods, may economic independence be guaranteed and subservience to a capitalist state with great heavy industrial development be prevented. Only then will real industrialization be achieved. . . .

Industrialization must begin with the development of heavy industry.

It is clear by now that industrialization calls for the development of heavy industry. But are we to develop heavy industry immediately on our commencement of the task of industrialization? Or are we to develop light industry first and then develop heavy industry later? The distinction is of great importance. They represent two different methods in industrialization. To start with heavy industry is the socialist method for industrialization. To start with light industry is the capitalist method for industrialization. . . .

We are many years behind the economy of capitalist countries. We cannot afford to pursue the old path of the capitalist countries, but embark on a different course to catch up with the capitalist countries within a short time. The Soviet Union has opened before us a new road toward industrialization. The Soviet Union realized socialist industrialization in only thirteen years. In thirteen years the Soviet Union traveled the course which took the capitalist countries one hundred years to cover. From this we may also see the superiority of the socialist method over the capitalist method in the achievement of industrialization.

3. LI FU-CH'UN,
ON THE FIRST FIVE-YEAR PLAN

The first five-year plan was finalized at the National People's Congress in July 1955 after two years of provisional implementation. Heavy industry was the keystone of the plan which was predicated on extensive Soviet aid in the form of loans, blueprints, and technical assistance in building 156 core projects. Investment priorities were ranked in the order of heavy industry, light industry, and agriculture. Industrialization would pave the way for step-by-step socialist transformation first in industry and subsequently in agriculture.

Large-scale heavy industry, it was held, would subsequently *create the basis for the rapid expansion of light industry and agriculture. Citing the authority of Mao Tsetung, Li projected completion of the transition to socialism in city and countryside in the course of three five-year plans or fifteen years. Chinese planners anticipated that forty or fifty years would be required to build a powerful, industrialized, socialist nation. The iron and steel industry was the core of the plan with investment centered on the reconstruction and expansion of the Anshan Iron and Steel Works and establishment of two new centers at Wuhan and Pao-t'ou. China's maximum pre-liberation steel output was slightly over 900,000 tons. By 1952, when recovery was concluded, it had risen to 1,350,000. Projected steel production was 4.1 million tons at the end of the plan in 1957; in 1962 when the three integrated steel centers were scheduled for completion, China was to produce approximately 10 million tons.*

By contrast, just 7.6 percent of the plan's state investment was allocated to agriculture, water conservancy, and forestry based on the rationale that extensive mechanization was premature and larger water conservancy programs were not yet possible. This did not mean halting agricultural investment; it

Report on the First Five-Year Plan for Development of the National Economy of the People's Republic of China in 1953–1957, July 5 and 6, 1955. In: Robert Bowie and John Fairbank, eds., *Communist China 1955–1959. Policy Documents with Analysis* (Cambridge, Mass.: Harvard University Press, 1962).

did ensure that investment in agriculture took place predominantly outside the state plan as the responsibility of individual peasants and cooperatives.

Modeled in essential respects on Soviet practice, China's plan offers interesting contrasts with the first Soviet plan of 1928–1933. The respective plans were initiated at times when the share of large-scale industry and of socialized enterprise were substantially higher in the Soviet national economy. In per capita terms, at the start of their respective plans, steel output was 27.6 kilograms in the Soviet Union, more than ten times that of China (2.4 kilograms); power was more than 2.5 times greater, and grain more than 1.5 times greater.

The 58 percent of total investment China allocated to heavy industry actually exceeded the Soviet figure in its plan (49 percent), while state investment in agriculture (8 percent) was less than half that of the Soviet Union (19 percent) where collectivization of agriculture was already advanced by 1928 on the eve of the plan. In short, the Chinese plan looked to the peasantry to provide the capital and foreign exchange to construct a socialist heavy industrial base and offered little immediate return. Eventually, after an estimated three five-year plans, heavy industry would contribute to rural development in the form of tractors, fertilizer, electricity, etc., paving the way for the advance from elementary forms of cooperation to full-scale agricultural collectivization and bringing prosperity to the countryside.

1. The Fundamental Task of the State in the Period of Transition

Socialist industrialization is the keystone for building socialism in our country; the socialist transformation of agriculture and handicrafts and capitalist industry and commerce are two essential elements in this undertaking. The three are inseparable. . . .

Socialist industrialization is the central task of our country during the transition period, and the main link in socialist industrialization is to give priority to the development of heavy industry. Only by building a powerful heavy industry, that is, by establishing modern iron and steel, machine-building, power, fuel, nonferrous metals and basic chemical industries, etc., can we produce various kinds of modern industrial equipment, and make possible the technical reconstruction of heavy industry itself as well as the light industries. Only thus can we supply agriculture with tractors and other modern farm machines and sufficient quantities of fertilizers, and make possible the technical reconstruction of agriculture. . . .

To build socialism, we must solve the contradiction between small peasant economy and socialist industrialization. Socialism cannot be built on the basis of a small-peasant economy; it must have a foundation of large-scale industry and large-scale collective farming. Socialist industrialization demands that the scattered and backward mode of production in agriculture be changed to a collective and advanced mode of production, that more grain and industrial crops be produced on the basis of collectivization and mechanization, and also that individual handicrafts take the path of cooperation. . . .

The capitalist system of private ownership of the means of production hinders the further development of the productive forces of our country. The anarchy of capitalist economy runs counter to the planned development of socialist economy. With the planned development of the national economy, the contradiction between capitalist and socialist economy becomes more clear-cut and acute. That is why we must carry through the socialist transformation of capitalist industry and commerce. . . .

2. Outline of the First Five-Year Plan

The general task set by China's first five-year plan was determined in the light of the fundamental task of the state during the transition period.

It may be summarized as follows: We must center our main efforts on industrial construction; this comprises 694 above-norm* construction projects, the core of which are the 156

---

* To facilitate management and control of major capital construction projects, the state has, in the light of actual conditions in China, set an "investment norm" for every category of capital construction. Any construction project, whether it is new, rebuilt or restored, is classified as "above-norm" or "below-norm" according to whether its invested capital

projects which the Soviet Union is designing for us, and which will lay the preliminary groundwork for China's socialist industrialization; we must foster the growth of agricultural producers' cooperatives, whose system of ownership is partially collective, and handicraft producers' cooperatives, thus laying the preliminary groundwork for the socialist transformation of agriculture and handicrafts; and, in the main, we must incorporate capitalist industry and commerce into various forms of state capitalism, laying the groundwork for the socialist transformation of private industry and commerce. . . .

The total outlay for the country's economic construction and cultural and educational development during the five-year period will be 76,640 million yuan, or the equivalent in value of more than 700 million taels of gold. Such an enormous investment in national construction would have been absolutely inconceivable in the past. This is possible only for a government led by the working class and working whole-heartedly in the interests of the people.

Investments in capital construction will amount to 42,740 million yuan, or 55.8 percent of the total outlay for economic construction and cultural and educational development during the five-year period. Of the remaining 44.2 percent, or 33,900 million yuan, part will be spent on work occasioned by the needs of capital construction, such as prospecting resources, engineering surveying and designing, stockpiling of equipment and materials, etc. Part will be spent to develop industrial production, transport, and posts and telecommunications, including such items as overhaul of equipment, technical and organizational improvements in production, trial manufacture of new products, purchase of miscellaneous fixed assets, etc.; another part will serve as circulating capital for the various economic departments; and still another part will go to funds allocated to all economic, cultural and educational departments for operating expenses and for the training of specialized personnel.

---

is above or below the "normal" figure. In industry, for example, the investment norm for the iron and steel, motor vehicle, tractor, shipbuilding, and locomotive and rolling stock manufacturing industries is ten million yuan. For the nonferrous metals, chemical, and cement industries it is 6 million yuan.

The sum of 42,740 million yuan for investments in the five-year capital construction program is distributed as follows:

Industrial departments, 24,850 million yuan, or 58.2 percent of the total amount to be invested;

Agriculture, water conservancy and forestry departments, 3,260 million yuan, or 7.6 percent;

Transport, posts and telecommunications departments, 8,210 million yuan, or 19.2 percent;

Trade, banking and stockpiling departments, 1,280 million yuan, or 3 percent;

Cultural, educational and public health departments, 3,080 million yuan, or 7.2 percent;

Development of urban public utilities, 1,600 million yuan, or 3.7 percent;

Other items, 460 million yuan, or 1.1 percent. . . .

The proportion of state investments in agriculture is not large in our first five-year plan, because agriculture cannot yet be extensively mechanized and it is not yet possible to undertake bigger projects in water conservancy and forestry on a large scale in this five-year period. Furthermore, capital investments in agriculture, water conservancy and forestry departments do not include relief funds for rural areas, agricultural loans and other items, nor do they include capital invested in production by the peasants themselves. If all these items are taken into account, the total amount of capital used to develop agriculture in the five-year period comes close to the total investment in industry. . . .

There are 694 above-norm projects, including those which the Soviet Union is helping China to build, among the new projects and reconstruction projects under our five-year program of capital construction in industry. If we add to these the 252 projects in agriculture, water conservancy and forestry, the 220 projects in transport, posts and telecommunications, the 156 projects in culture, education and public health, the 118 projects in urban public utilities, and the 160 projects in other spheres, the total number of above-norm capital construction projects reaches 1,600. In addition to these, there are more than 6,000 below-norm construction projects, of which about 2,300 are in industry.

By 1957, the proportion of the output of modern industry in

the total value of industrial and agricultural output will have risen from 26.7 percent to 36 percent.

The gross value of China's industrial output will increase by 98.3 percent in 1957 compared with 1952, giving an average increase of 14.7 percent a year as compared with the year before. The increase in value of modern industrial output will be 104.1 percent, with an average annual increase of 15.3 percent. Such a rate of industrial development is obviously fairly rapid. It has never been, nor could it be achieved in capitalist countries.

Markedly increased output of various industrial products will be achieved in the five-year period. The actual output of major items in 1952 and the planned output for 1957 compare as follows:

Steel: 1,350,000 tons to 4,120,000 tons (3.1 times).

Electricity: 7,260 million kilowatt-hours to 15,900 million kilowatt-hours (2.2 times).

Coal: 63,530,000 tons to 113 million tons (1.8 times).

Generators: 30,000 kilowatts to 227,000 kilowatts (7.7 times).

Electric motors: 640,000 kilowatts to 1,050,000 kilowatts (1.6 times).

Lorries: 4,000 (not yet produced in 1952).

Cement: 2,860,000 tons to 6,000,000 tons (2.1 times).

Machine-made paper: 370,000 tons to 650,000 tons (1.8 times).

Cotton piece goods: 111,630,000 bolts to 163,720,000 bolts (1.5 times).

Machine-processed sugar: 249,000 tons to 686,000 tons (2.8 times). . . .

The industrialization that our country is striving to achieve is socialist industrialization, modeled on Soviet experience and carried out with the direct assistance of the Soviet Union and the people's democracies. It is not capitalist industrialization. Therefore, our industry, particularly those branches producing means of production, is capable of rapid development. As provided for in the first five-year plan, investments in industries producing means of production account for 88.8 percent of the total capital investment in industry, while investments in consumer goods industries make up 11.2 percent. At the same time, according to the plan, the value of output of means of production will grow by 126.5 percent within the five-year period, and that of consumer goods, 79.7 percent.

Within the five-year period, half of the capacity (measured in value of output) of private industrial enterprises will be incorporated into joint state-private industry. By 1957, therefore, the proportion of the value of output of the state, cooperative (including the processing plants of supply and marketing cooperatives and consumers' cooperatives but excluding handicraft producers' cooperatives), and joint state-private industries will rise to 87.8 percent of the total value of the country's industrial output, while the proportion of the value of output of the state, cooperative (including the processing plants of supply and marketing cooperatives and consumers' cooperatives but excluding handicraft producers' cooperatives), and joint state-private industries will rise to 87.8 percent of the total value of the country's industrial output, while the proportion of the value of output of private industry will fall to 12.2 percent. Furthermore, the major part of private industry will be engaged on government contracts for the manufacture and processing of goods and will thus be drawn into the orbit of state capitalism.

The first five-year plan sets suitable targets for increased agricultural output. In the five-year period, the total value of output of agriculture and subsidiary rural production is to increase by 23.3 percent, an average rise of 4.3 percent a year as compared to the year before. . . .

4. TRANSFORMING CAPITALIST INDUSTRY
AND COMMERCE

In November 1955, four months after his decisive call to speed the pace of agricultural cooperation, Mao Tsetung presided over a meeting of the Executive Committee of the All-China Federation of Industry and Commerce, the forum for China's embattled but still strategically placed capitalists. Stimulated by the high tide of collectivization in the countryside, the meeting established guidelines which eliminated capitalist ownership of industry and commerce far ahead of the schedule proposed in the first five-year plan. The process, as Mao described it, proceeded "with the striking of gongs and the beating of drums." Addressing those who urged caution and gradualism in transforming capitalist industry, Mao commented, "In this matter we are quite heartless: Marxism is all that is cruel and it doesn't have much mercy; it is bent on exterminating imperialism, feudalism, capitalism, and small production to boot."

By February 1956, entire trades which had but recently passed into forms of state-private joint enterprises were reorganized under exclusive state ownership, eliminating the grip of private capitalists on the Chinese economy. In the process, through trade-wide "trusts," entire industries were reorganized for greater efficiency and to ensure provision of needed services.

In June 1952 Mao had pointed out that "with the overthrow of the landlord class and the bureaucratic capitalist class, the contradiction between the working class and the national bourgeoisie has become the principal contradiction in China; therefore, the national bourgeoisie should no longer be defined as an intermediate class." Nevertheless, in contrast to practices of Soviet nationalization of industry, China's national capitalists were not expropriated. They collected dividends based on the value of their investment for the entire decade 1956–1966. This method ensured their managerial and, in some cases, technical services to industry which had passed into the hands of the state. It also gave former capitalists the opportunity to transform their outlook to serve the nation in its advance toward socialism. From early 1956 socialist ownership of industry and commerce was essentially completed, having passed through a series of stages designed to ensure smooth transition.

In 1956 handicraft cooperativization was also accelerated. Handicrafts had suffered disastrous setbacks as a result of the resource centralization policies of the five-year plan. They accounted for a full 25 percent of the value of manufactures, a substantial share of the value of exports, and were a vital source of peasants' supplementary income and supplied urban and rural services. Here Mao underlines their importance and spells out the goals to preserve unique traditions of craftsmanship, to raise productivity, and to transform the crafts from individual to cooperative endeavors.

A. Hsu Ti-hsin,
From Capitalist to Socialist Industry

The ultimate aim of China's socialist transformation of capitalist industry and commerce is to abolish the capitalist system, with its exploitation of those who work, to eliminate the bourgeoisie as a class, and replace capitalist ownership by ownership by the whole people.

How to Abolish Capitalist Ownership

How is capitalist ownership in China to be abolished?

The simplest way, it would seem, would be to take over the property without compensation. This was what was done with the bureaucrat-capitalists in 1949, when the people's revolution was victorious.

The bureaucrat-capitalists were Kuomintang officials and warlords who took advantage of their political power to become large-scale industrial and commercial monopolists. They were closely linked with imperialism. Their property was seized outright, on behalf of the people, and became the foundation of the socialist, state-owned sector of China's economy.

But we cannot deal with the national bourgeoisie in the same way. The national bourgeoisie is not quite the same as the bureaucrat-bourgeoisie which has always been the reactionary and bitter enemy of national independence and the people's revolution. The national bourgeoisie has a dual character. When China was under imperialist oppression and the yoke of feudalism, it took its place, at certain periods and to a certain extent, as a revolutionary force against imperialism without, and against the government of bureaucrats and warlords within the country. At the same time it lacked the courage to fight against imperialism and feudalism to the end. . . .

Another thing to keep in mind in this connection is the extreme economic backwardness of China. In 1949, the output of China's modern industry, in terms of value, constituted only

Transforming Capitalist Industry and Commerce: A New Stage. *People's China*, February 1, 1956.

about 17 percent of her total industrial and agricultural production. Small production, scattered and backward, was the dominating force in the national economy. Despite the negative qualities of capitalism which are detrimental to the national economy, capitalist industry and commerce still had a positive part to play in benefiting the national economy. . . .

The Method of Redemption

The line of the Chinese Communist Party on the abolition of capitalist private ownership is one of peaceful transformation. It is the socialist transformation of capitalist enterprises, and of the bourgeoisie, through the method of redemption. While the redemption is going on, the working class not only turns out products to meet the demands of the people and the state; it also produces profits for the capitalist class.

Redemption, however, does not mean that the state pays a definite sum to buy these enterprises outright. The buying out is gradual. In the process, both capitalist enterprises and the bourgeoisie itself are to be transformed. In the enterprises, capitalist ownership will eventually give way to ownership by the state, that is, the whole people. As for the capitalists, they will become people living on their own labor instead of exploiting others. . . .

A New Stage

The history of the People's Republic of China, since its founding six years ago, has shown that the principle of gradual, peaceful transformation of capitalist industry and commerce is appropriate and very effective. In the first half of 1955, about 80 percent of the output of capitalist industry throughout the country (by value) was produced by enterprises included in the intermediate form of state capitalism (processing goods for the state and executing state orders). About 2,000 industrial enterprises had also been transformed into the highest form of state capitalism (state-private joint ownership). In the first half of 1955, the value of production by state-private joint enterprises constituted 36.8 percent of the combined output of private industry and state-private joint industry. In commerce, the orbit of state capitalism included private concerns dealing in goods wholesaled through state and cooperative channels. Such private concerns had become agents or distributors for the state. . . .

In commerce, the main trades, having become agents or distributors for the state, could be included in state planning. Blindness in business management was in the main curbed. But the relation between the capitalists and the shop assistants was still that of exploiters and exploited. The socialist sector had not yet penetrated inside the shops, and therefore could not exercise leadership in a direct way. The unplanned growth of private commerce in the past, moreover, had resulted in unreasonable distribution of shops and trading concerns. . . .

In the national economy as a whole, the socialist economic sector has attained a position which was decisively superior to that of the capitalist economic sector. . . . We have passed out of the stage in which private enterprises changed over to state-private joint ownership as individual units, took orders or processed goods for the state, or acted as its agents or distributors. We have entered the new stage of socialist transformation by entire trades. All important trades in various parts of the country have become mainly or wholly state-private joint-owned. . . .

Unified Production Arrangements

Since the beginning of 1956, capitalist industry and commerce everywhere in our country have been brought, trade by trade, under unified production arrangements. In this way, the work of the transformation of capitalist industry and commerce is linked to the state plan. . . .

Since production is now arranged by entire trades, and since enterprises in each trade are to be reorganized *en bloc*, it is natural and inevitable that the changeover to state-private ownership should proceed trade by trade instead of individually as before. . . .

Two Steps

The changeover is divided into two steps. First, the government approves applications to turn private concerns into joint state-private enterprises. Secondly, economic reorganization takes place. The switch to joint ownership and the economic reorganization are closely integrated. It is now possible to break the line between one factory and another, to combine scores or hundreds of factories into a single enterprise. Profit and loss are no longer on the scale of one factory, but of the entire trade. Productive forces are increased. Very favorable conditions are provided for the ultimate transition—to ownership by the whole people.

The trade-wide organizational form that is adopted is the "trust." But it is a trust of the socialist, not the capitalist type. According to statistics for the end of 1954, China had over 134,000 private industrial enterprises and over 4,500,000 private commercial units. With a trust for each of the different trades, we can organize all the private industrial or commercial concerns within it, and bring them under one management. . . .

The trust for each trade has two tasks: one economic and one political. The economic task is finding ways to ensure that all units in a trade can fulfill state orders and contracts, to arrange production rationally, to improve technique, and to reform the enterprises that have come under joint operation. The political task is to educate the capitalists along socialist lines, to conduct united front work among them.

In this new stage in the socialist transformation of private industry and commerce, shareholders receive dividends in the form of fixed payments.

Formerly we followed the "one-fourth each" principle. That is, the profits of an enterprise were divided into four parts, one going to the state in the form of tax, one to reserve funds for expanding production, one to a fund for improving the welfare of the workers, and one to the capitalists. Thus the capitalists generally netted 25 percent of the profits of an enterprise. But this gave rise to a contradiction—the capitalists got the benefit through increased dividends, from both the improvement in management and the workers' keenness to produce more in joint enterprises. Obviously this did not help to stimulate the workers' enthusiasm. Nor did it increase the productive forces of society.

Such contradictions are solved by the new method of fixed percentage. By this method, during the period of joint state-private ownership, private shareholders will get a fixed rate of interest, say so many percent, on their investment. Whether the enterprise suffers a loss or makes more profit, dividends at a fixed amount will be paid to private shareholders just the same. Thus it solves the contradiction arising from the "one-fourth-each" principle. State accumulation for socialist construction can increase greatly.

At the same time, the shift marks a tremendous change in the production relations within the joint enterprise. The capitalists can no longer direct the enterprises, or sell them. The means of production of such enterprises are completely at the disposal of the state. . . .

Secondly, though the capitalist can take part in the management of the joint enterprise, his work is no longer that of a capitalist owner. He is now an employee of the state. His exploitation of the workers is limited to the drawing of interest.

Reforming the Capitalists

As has been said, the socialist transformation of private industry and commerce involves more than the enterprises. It includes the reform of the outlook of the individual bourgeois. . . .

In 1952 the government started the *wu fan* campaign among private industrialists and traders. Since then fewer capitalists have been found to be guilty of the malpractices against which it was directed. Labor-capital relations in private enterprises have, by and large, improved. Workers' supervision has been set up in many enterprises. . . .

We expect to win most of the bourgeoisie over to accept socialist transformation.

B. Mao Tsetung, Speed Up the Socialist Transformation of Handicrafts

1. It seems to me that the pace of the socialist transformation of independent handicrafts was a little too slow. I said so in January this year at the conference of secretaries of provincial and municipal party committees. By the end of 1955 only two

million handicraftsmen had been organized. In the first two months of this year, however, three million more have been organized, so in the main the work can be accomplished this year; that is fine. You are contemplating an average annual increase of 10.9 percent in the total value of handicraft production over a period of three five-year plans; that seems a bit too small. We set too low a target in the first five-year plan and have suffered a little in consequence; it need not be changed now, but you should use your discretion.

2. As for the size of handicraft cooperatives, generally speaking, about one hundred people per cooperative would be appropriate, although some may have several hundred and others only a few dozen.

3. It is a good idea to organize cooperatives of the blacksmiths and carpenters who make the rounds of the villages to repair farm implements and serve agricultural production; the peasants will certainly welcome this. That is what handicraftsmen in China have been doing for thousands of years. Organized in cooperatives, the craftsmen can improve their skills and serve the peasants better.

4. You have said that the masses were dissatisfied because production was centralized in the repair and service trades and too many service stations were closed during the high tide of the transformation of handicrafts. That was too bad! What is to be done now? "The general trend under heaven is that there is bound to be unification after prolonged division and division after prolonged unification."

5. The highest labor productivity in mechanized and semimechanized production is over thirty times the lowest in handicraft production. The annual value of output per capita is 20,000 to 30,000 yuan in modernized state industry, 5,000 yuan in mechanized and semimechanized cooperatives, 2,000 yuan in big cooperatives with more than 100 handicraftsmen, 1,500 yuan in small cooperatives and 800 to 900 yuan among independent handicraftsmen. Compare the differences in labor productivity and it becomes clear that the handicrafts must develop in the direction of semimechanization and mechanization and that labor productivity must be raised.

6. All the handicraft trades perform useful services. They provide food, clothing, and other things for daily use. They also

produce arts and crafts, such as cloisonné or the glass grapes blown by "the five spinsters of the Chang family." Besides, the technique of roasting Peking duck is exportable. . . .

Mind you, don't let our fine handicraft products be discarded. Pock-marked Wang's and Chang Hsiao-chuan's kitchen knives and scissors must not be discarded, no, not even ten thousand years from now. Anything good and characteristically Chinese that has been discarded must be restored and even improved.

7. It is a good idea to improve the quality of arts and crafts and to look after the old master craftsmen, and you should start now and speed up the work. You can set up organizations, open schools and call meetings. Yang Shih-hui, the ivory carver, is actually a very fine artist. Once he and I ate at table together, and while observing me he was able to carve my likeness. I could have observed him for several days without being able to draw a picture of him, I'm afraid.

8. The prices of equipment and materials allocated by the state to the cooperatives should be reasonably fixed and must not be set at the normal allocation prices. Cooperatives are not the same as state enterprises and there is a difference between socialist collective ownership and socialist ownership by the whole people. At the outset the economic foundations of the cooperatives are not strong enough and they need assistance. It is a good idea for the state to allocate to the cooperatives at low prices old machines which have been replaced as well as the machinery and factory buildings rendered surplus by the amalgamation of privately owned plants under joint state-private management. "Give in order to take." When the foundations of the cooperatives have become strong enough, the state will collect a larger tax from them and raise the prices of raw materials too. By that time, the cooperatives will be owned by the collective in form but in reality by the whole people.

The state should help the cooperatives to achieve semi-mechanization and mechanization, and they themselves should strive for the same goal. The greater the speed of mechanization, the shorter the life of your handicraft cooperatives. The more your "kingdom" shrinks, the better it is for our common cause. You should exert yourselves to hasten mechanization and make a greater contribution to the state.

9. Since the value of handicraft output forms a quarter of the total value of the country's industrial output, why is it that the supply of raw materials for the handicrafts as well as their production and sales have not been made part of the state plan? The handicrafts assume such large proportions that they should be included in the state plan.

10. In some places the party committees are so occupied with other tasks that they don't put handicrafts on the agenda; this is not good. Why are some cadres rather unwilling to undertake this work? I myself would very much like to do it, as it is very important.

11. You should select outstanding examples from among the sixty-thousand-odd handicraft cooperatives and compile material on their typical experience.

5. THE 1956 WAGE REFORM

The Eighth Party Congress of 1956 consolidated the sweeping wage reform which began with the August 31, 1955, directive completing the shift from the supply system to a wage system and from the new democratic to the socialist era. The 1956 wage reform ended the use of the basically egalitarian free supply system of government and army during the Anti-Japanese War in favor of a wage system designed to increase productivity based on the socialist principle "to each according to one's work." This system introduced three separate wage scales for workers, for technicians, managers and scientists, and for party and state cadres with limited but significant income incentives for skilled and dedicated labor. In the steel industry the reform increased the differential between the highest and lowest paid worker to 3.2 times, with salaries ranging from 34.5 yuan to 110.4 yuan per month. Including chief engineers or directors, the ratio between highest and lowest wages was roughly six times, with maximum salaries pegged at 202 yuan

Liu Tzu-chiu: Wage Reform in China. *People's China*, October 16, 1956.

per month. University professors and research scientists could earn still higher salaries, with a range of 149.5 to 345 yuan per month plus bonuses. The eight grade wage system instituted at that time and maintained subsequently was geared to increasing rationalization of the wage and incentive structure, to unify salary scales within each industry, and to stimulate higher productivity.

After several years of substantial increases in productivity and little rise in wages, the reform provided substantial increases averaging 14.5 percent for workers in the state sector and increased differentials within the factory. It also tended to increase urban-rural and industrial-agricultural income differentials and sharpened differences between specialists and managers on the one hand and workers on the other.

The wage problem is closely linked with the development of the national economy and the improvement of the workers' standard of living. Today, an all-round wage reform is taking place in China. . . .

We raise wages in China on the following principle: that increases are based on rising production and higher productivity of labor, always provided that wages rise more slowly than labor productivity.

In other words, when productivity rises fast, so do wages; if it lags, wages do too. The reason why wages must increase more slowly than labor productivity is, of course, that we have to accumulate funds for socialist construction, to expand production and the state reserves. . . .

We follow this principle because it is an objective law of socialist economy, to flout which would not only harm socialist construction but the working class itself.

Looking back over wage increases in China in the past, we find two entirely different situations.

In the years when the national economy was being restored (1950-1952), labor productivity rose by 33.3 percent and real wages by 36 percent: wages rose faster than productivity. This is explained by the appallingly low wages the workers received before liberation—far below the subsistence level. So that our workers no longer had to exist on starvation wages, so as to raise their living standards to a certain extent, we had to raise wages without waiting for a corresponding increase in labor productivity. That was obviously the right thing to do.

Wages Lag Behind

But when the state started on planned economic construction in 1953, the situation changed. It is envisaged that during the first five-year plan labor productivity in state-owned industry will rise by 64 percent and the average wages of workers and staff throughout the country by 33 percent—an average increase of 5.8 percent per annum.

But while the principle behind this new trend is right, in practice we have somewhat fallen down. Between 1953 and 1955 labor productivity in various branches of industry rose by 41.8 percent, but the real wages of the workers rose by a mere 6.9 percent. Now the government has drawn attention to this serious state of affairs and is taking speedy steps to close the gap.

We have to admit that we failed to understand the principle that proper consideration must be given to the interests of both the state and the individual—a principle which the Chinese Communist Party has said we must observe. We made the bad mistake of carrying out the plan lopsidedly, failing to see that expansion of production and improvement of the workers' standards of living went hand in hand. What usually happened was that plans for wage increases and plans to raise productivity were worked out at the beginning of the year. Then at the end of the year the plan for labor productivity was more than fulfilled, but no proper adjustment was made in the plan for the increase of wages. Some enterprises did not even act on their original plan.

Wage Reform

So in this year's overhaul of wages we are setting out to put these things right. Wages will go up pretty substantially all round. Before the year is out, the average wage of all workers will be 14.5 percent higher than in 1955, that is, they will get a raise nearly two and a half times as great as the 5.8 percent envisaged in the five-year plan. The total wage bill will increase by 1,255 million yuan, which works out at nearly 80 yuan a head.

As a result of the wage reform this year, a worker of average skill in the iron and steel or nonferrous metals industries, or a coal miner of average skill, will get a basic wage of 70 to 80 yuan a month. Actually his earnings will normally be higher, because of bonus payments for overfulfillment of his norms.

A System of Grading

During the wages overhaul, besides raising wages steps are being taken by introducing a well-graded wage system to do away with the bad old system, a holdover from old China of paying a man a flat rate rather than the proper rate for the job he does. In the past you just "hired labor" and as far as wages were concerned it didn't make much difference if the work was skilled or unskilled, heavy or light, or whether it was time work or piece work. Contrariwise, there were cases where, in the same enterprise, you found workers of comparable skill doing exactly the same job and getting widely different wages. Then again, in the same region, among workers of the same trade, some got regional bonuses and others did not. Because of this lack of proper differentials and utter lack of any proper uniformity in our wage system, wages had virtually ceased to be an incentive to greater output.

What we are now doing is working out a proper system of grading which will be a real expression of the formula "to each according to his work"—the kind of system which meets the needs of a country in process of industrialization. In other words, we are fixing wage standards which correspond with the workers' technical skill, intensity of work and the place the particular factory or enterprise occupies in the national economy. In the course of the reform we are properly widening wage differentials as between workers of varying degrees of skill. . . .

How It Will Work Out

Let us see how the planned wage overhaul is going to work out in, for example, Northeast China. Workers at the iron and steel smelting works, whose job is arduous, who need quite a high degree of skill, and who work in an industry which plays an important part in the development of the national economy, will be on a wage scale rising from 34.5 yuan in the lowest grade to 110.4 yuan in the highest. That is, wages in the highest grade are 3.2 times as high as in the lowest. In a cigarette factory in the same region—that is, in an industry that calls for less skill, in which work is less arduous and which is less important to the development of the national economy—the scale rises from 28.5 yuan to 71.3 yuan, the highest grade getting two and a half times as much as the lowest. A similar system of differentials will apply to the workers in responsible positions, engineers and technicians in an enterprise. Taking Northeast China again, the highest wage a director or chief engineer of a first-class iron and steel smelting plant can get is 229 yuan. The upper limit for a director or chief engineer of a first-class cigarette factory is 202 yuan. . . .

We want to encourage such skilled workers to go inland to man the new industrial bases. We shall try to persuade them to do so by patient explanation of the social and political need to move, but we also have to give them a material incentive.

That explains another feature of the wage reform. Wage rates for workers, engineers, and technicians in key construction areas inland are to be higher than elsewhere. For instance, the average wage of engineering workers in Shanghai is going up by 9 percent, but engineering workers in T'ai-yuan are getting an average raise of 20 percent. In remoter areas like Ch'ing Hai, Sinkiang, and parts of Kansu where living conditions are comparatively poor, besides encouraging workers to move there by higher wages, we are giving them incentive bonuses and subsidies of various kinds—regional bonuses, subsidies, and so on. Workers in the Yumen oilfield in Kansu get 11.5 yuan a month more than oil workers in Szechuan, where conditions are better, with a regional subsidy which may amount to another 25 percent of their wages on top of that.

China is admittedly still very backward as far as culture and technology go. To remedy this situation, the Chinese Communist Party has been popularizing the slogan, "Forward to science," because we want China to reach the scientific and technical level of the most advanced countries in the next twelve years. We hope that everyone will respond, so besides political education we are giving material incentives. With this end in view, the present wage reform plan provides for a substantial increase in the wages of all senior scientists and technicians. The salaries of university professors and research fellows in the Chinese Academy of Sciences in Peking have gone up by 36 percent. Their lowest rate is now 149.5 yuan a month and the highest 345 yuan. As for senior scientists and technicians who have made important contributions to the state, they are not only getting higher salaries but also pretty large bonus awards which are a coveted honor. These special awards amount to 30 to 50 percent of their basic salary.

Understanding of Socialism

This far-reaching overhaul of the wage system can hardly fail to convince workers by personal experience that socialism takes into full account the interests of both the state and the individual and that there is no conflict between long-term and immediate interests. It will give them a better understanding of socialism, will give them greater enthusiasm for completing the five-year plan.

6. MAO TSETUNG,
ON THE TEN MAJOR RELATIONSHIPS

The high tide of agricultural cooperation following Mao's July 31, 1955, speech precipitated a dramatic acceleration in the pace of socialist transition of the countryside; in the early months of 1956, a related movement rapidly completed the transfer to ownership by the whole people of China's industry and commerce far ahead of the schedule projected in the first five-year plan. The stage was set for defining a distinctive Chinese socialist development path independent of, yet simul-

Speech to the Political Bureau of the Central Committee, April 25, 1956. In: *Peking Review* (PR), January 1, 1977. Compare the unofficial text which circulated in 1967 in: Stuart Schram, ed., *Chairman Mao Talks to the People* (New York: Pantheon, 1974).

taneously drawing on, both positive and negative features of the Soviet model.

"On the Ten Major Relationships" is the basic synthesis, perhaps Mao's single most important statement in the process of formation of a distinctive dialectical approach to development applied to China's concrete conditions during the socialist transition. Starting from the question "How can China mobilize all positive factors in order to serve socialism?" Mao analyzed ten major contradictions in Chinese society. On this basis he offered both the first serious Chinese criticism of Soviet development strategy and a clear definition of a self-reliant Chinese road to development.

In recent months the Political Bureau of the Central Committee has heard reports on the work of thirty-four industrial, agricultural, transport, commercial, financial, and other departments under the central authorities and from these reports has identified a number of problems concerning socialist construction and socialist transformation. In all, they boil down to ten problems, or ten major relationships.

It is to focus on one basic policy that these ten problems are being raised, the basic policy of mobilizing all positive factors, internal and external, to serve the cause of socialism. In the past we followed this policy of mobilizing all positive factors in order to put an end to the rule of imperialism, feudalism and bureaucrat-capitalism and to win victory for the people's democratic revolution. We are now following the same policy in order to carry on the socialist revolution and build a socialist country. Nevertheless, there are some problems in our work that need discussion. Particularly worthy of attention is the fact that in the Soviet Union certain defects and errors that occurred in the course of their building socialism have lately come to light. Do you want to follow the detours they have made? It was by drawing lessons from their experience that we were able to avoid certain detours in the past, and there is all the more reason for us to do so now. . . .

The Relationship Between Heavy Industry on the One Hand and Light Industry and Agriculture on the Other

The emphasis in our country's construction is on heavy industry. The production of the means of production must be given priority, that's settled. But it definitely does not follow that the production of the means of subsistence, especially grain, can be neglected. Without enough food and other daily necessities, it would be impossible to provide for the workers in the first place, and then what sense would it make to talk about developing heavy industry? . . .

The problem now facing us is that of continuing to adjust properly the ratio between investment in heavy industry on the one hand, and in agriculture and light industry on the other in order to bring about a greater development of the latter. Does this mean that heavy industry is no longer primary? It still is, it still claims the emphasis in our investment. But the proportion for agriculture and light industry must be somewhat increased.

What will be the results of this increase? First, the daily needs of the people will be better satisfied; second, the accumulation of capital will be speeded up so that we can develop heavy industry with greater and better results. Heavy industry can also accumulate capital, but, given our present economic conditions, light industry and agriculture can accumulate more and faster.

Here the question arises: Is your desire to develop heavy industry genuine or feigned, strong or weak? If your desire is feigned or weak, then you will hit agriculture and light industry and invest less in them. If your desire is genuine or strong, then you will attach importance to agriculture and light industry so that there will be more grain and more raw materials for light industry and a greater accumulation of capital. And there will be more funds in the future to invest in heavy industry.

There are now two approaches to our development of heavy industry: one is to develop agriculture and light industry less, and the other is to develop them more. In the long run, the first approach will lead to a smaller and slower development of heavy industry, or at least will put it on a less solid foundation, and when the overall account is added up a few decades hence, it will not prove to have paid. The second approach will lead to a greater and faster development of heavy industry, and, since it ensures the livelihood of the people, it will lay a more solid foundation for the development of heavy industry.

The Relationship Between Industry in the Coastal Regions and Industry in the Interior

In the past our industry was concentrated in the coastal regions. . . . About 70 percent of all our industry, both light and heavy, is to be found in the coastal regions and only 30 percent in the interior. This irrational situation is a product of history. The coastal industrial base must be put to full use, but to even out the distribution of industry in the course of its development we must strive to promote industry in the interior. We have not made any major mistakes on the relationship between the two. However, in recent years we have underestimated coastal industry to some extent and have not given great enough attention to its development. This must change.

In the past, fighting was going on in Korea and the international situation was quite tense; this could not but affect our attitude towards coastal industry. Now, it seems unlikely that there will be a new war of aggression against China or another world war in the near future, and there will probably be a period of peace for a decade or more. It would therefore be wrong if we still fail to make full use of the plant capacity and technical forces of coastal industry. . . .

It does not follow that all new factories are to be built in the coastal regions. Without doubt, the greater part of the new industry should be located in the interior so that industry may gradually become evenly distributed; moreover, this will help our preparations against war. But a number of new factories and mines, even some large ones, may also be built in the coastal regions.

Making good use of and developing the capacities of the old industries in the coastal regions will put us in a stronger position to promote and support industry in the interior. To adopt a negative attitude would be to hinder the latter's speedy growth. . . .

The Relationship Between Economic Construction and Defense Construction

National defense is indispensable. Our defense capabilities have now attained a certain level. As a result of the war to resist U.S. aggression and aid Korea and of several years of training and consolidation, our armed forces have grown more powerful and are now stronger than was the Soviet Red Army before World War II, also, there have been improvements in armaments. Our defense industry is being built up. Ever since Pan Ku separated heaven and earth, we have never been able to make planes and cars, and now we are beginning to make them.

We do not have the atom bomb yet. But neither did we have planes and artillery in the past. We defeated the Japanese imperialists and Chiang Kai-shek with millet plus rifles. We are stronger than before and will be still stronger in the future. We will not only have more planes and artillery but we will also have atom bombs. If we are not to be bullied in the present-day world, we cannot do without the bomb. Then what is to be done about it? One reliable way is to cut military and administrative expenditures down to appropriate proportions and increase expenditures on economic construction. Only with the faster growth of economic construction can there be more progress in defense construction. . . .

In the period of the first five-year plan, military and administrative expenditures accounted for 30 percent of total expenditures in the state budget. This proportion is much too high. In the period of the second five-year plan, we must reduce it to around 20 percent so that more funds can be released for building more factories and turning out more machines. . . .

The Relationship Between the State, the Units of Production, and the Producers

The relationship between the state on the one hand and factories and agricultural cooperatives on the other, and the relationship between factories and agricultural cooperatives on the one hand and the producers on the other should both be handled well. To this end we should consider not just one side, but must consider all three—the state, the collective, and the individual. . . .

Take the workers for example. As their labor productivity rises, there should be a gradual improvement in their working conditions and collective welfare. . . . With the growth of our economy as a whole, wages should be appropriately adjusted. We have recently decided to increase wages to some extent, mainly the wages of those at the lower levels, the wages of the workers, in order to narrow the wage gap between them and the upper levels. . . .

Here I would like to touch on the question of the independence of the factories under unified leadership. It's not right, I'm afraid, to place everything in the hands of the central or the provincial and municipal authorities without leaving the factories any power of their own, any room for independent action, any benefits. . . . In principle, centralization and independence forming a unity of opposites, there must be both centralization and independence. . . . Every unit of production must enjoy independence as the correlative of centralization if it is to develop more vigorously.

Now about the peasants. Our relations with the peasants have always been good, but we made a mistake on the question of grain. In 1954 floods caused a decrease in production in some parts of our country, and yet we purchased 7,000 million more catties of grain. A decrease in production and an increase in purchasing—this made grain the topic on almost everyone's lips in many places last spring, and nearly every household talked about the state marketing of grain. The peasants were disgruntled, and there were a lot of complaints both inside and outside the party. . . . After discovering [a shortage], we purchased 7,000 million less catties in 1955 and introduced a system of fixed quotas for grain production, purchasing and marketing and, what's more, there was a good harvest. . . .

The Soviet Union has taken measures which squeeze the peasants very hard. It takes away too much from the peasants at too low a price through its system of so-called obligatory sales and other measures. This method of capital accumulation has seriously dampened the peasants' enthusiasm for production. You want the hen to lay more eggs and yet you don't feed it, you want the horse to run fast and yet you don't let it graze. What kind of logic is this!

Our policies toward the peasants differ from those of the Soviet Union, and take into account the interests of both the state and the peasants. Our agricultural tax has always been relatively low. In the exchange of industrial and agricultural products we follow a policy of narrowing the price of scissors, a policy of exchanging equal or roughly equal values. The state buys agricultural products at standard prices while the peasants suffer no loss, and, what is more, our purchase prices are gradually being raised. . . .

Except in case of extraordinary natural disasters, we must see to it that, given increased agricultural production, 90 percent of the cooperative members get some increase in their income and the other 10 percent break even each year, and if the latter's income should fall, ways must be found to solve the problem in good time. . . .

The Relationship Between the Central Authorities and the Local Authorities

The relationship between the central authorities and the local authorities constitutes another contradiction. To resolve this contradiction, our attention should now be focused on how to enlarge the powers of the local authorities to some extent, give them greater independence and let them do more, all on the premise that the unified leadership of the central authorities is to be strengthened. . . .

If we are to promote socialist construction, we must bring the initiative of the local authorities into play. If we are to strengthen the central authorities, we must attend to the interests of the localities. . . .

We want both unity and particularity. To build a powerful socialist country it is imperative to have a strong and unified central leadership and unified planning and discipline throughout the country; disruption of this indispensable unity is impermissible. At the same time, it is essential to bring the initiative of the local authorities into full play and let each locality enjoy the particularity suited to its local conditions. . . .

The provinces, municipalities, prefectures, counties, districts, and townships should all enjoy their own proper independence and rights and should fight for them. To fight for such rights in the interest of the whole nation and not of a local department cannot be called localism or an undue assertion of independence. . . .

The Relationship Between China and Other Countries

We have put forward the slogan of learning from other countries. . . . It must be admitted that every nation has its strong points. If not, how can it survive? How can it progress? On the other hand, every nation has its weak points. . . .

Our policy is to learn from the strong points of all nations and all countries, learn all that is genuinely good in the political, economic, scientific, and technological fields and in literature and art. But we must learn with an analytical and critical eye, not blindly, and we mustn't copy everything indiscriminately and transplant mechanically. . . .

We should adopt the same attitude in learning from the experience of the Soviet Union and other socialist countries. Some of our people were not clear about this before and even picked up their weaknesses. . . .

Some people never take the trouble to analyze, they simply follow the "wind." Today, when the north wind is blowing, they join the "north wind" school; tomorrow, when there is a west wind, they switch to the "west wind" school; afterwards when the north wind blows again, they switch back to the "north wind" school. They hold no independent opinion of their own and often go from one extreme to the other.

In the Soviet Union, those who once extolled Stalin to the skies have now in one swoop consigned him to purgatory. Here in China some people are following their example. It is the opinion of the Central Committee that Stalin's mistakes amount to only 30 percent of the whole and his achievements to 70 percent, and that all things considered Stalin was nonetheless a great Marxist. . . .

In the social sciences and in Marxism-Leninism, we must continue to study Stalin diligently wherever he is right. What we must study is all that is universally true and we must make sure that this study is linked with Chinese reality. It would lead to a mess if every single sentence, even of Marx's, were followed. Our theory is an integration of the universal truth of Marxism-

Leninism with the concrete practice of the Chinese
Revolution. . . .

In the natural sciences we are rather backward, and here we
should make a special effort to learn from foreign countries.
And yet we must learn critically, not blindly. In technology I
think at first we have to follow others in most cases, and it is
better for us to do so, since at present we are lacking in
technology and know little about it. . . .

We must firmly reject and criticize all the decadent bourgeois
systems, ideologies, and ways of life of foreign countries. But
this should in no way prevent us from learning the advanced
sciences and technologies of capitalist countries and whatever is
scientific in the management of their enterprises. In the industrially developed countries they run their enterprises with fewer
people and greater efficiency and they know how to do
business. . . .

In my opinion, China has two weaknesses, which are at the
same time two strong points.

First, in the past China was a colonial and semicolonial
country, not an imperialist power, and was always bullied by
others. . . .

Second, our revolution came late. Although the 1911 Revolution which overthrew the Ch'ing emperor preceded the Russian
Revolution, there was no Communist Party at that time and the
revolution failed. The victory of the people's revolution came in
1949, more than thirty years after the October Revolution. On
this account, too, we are not in a position to feel conceited. . . .

Our two weaknesses are also strong points. As I have said
elsewhere, we are first "poor" and second "blank." By "poor" I
mean we do not have much industry and our agriculture is
underdeveloped. By "blank" I mean we are like a blank sheet of
paper and our cultural and scientific level is not high. From the
standpoint of potentiality, this is not bad. The poor want
revolution whereas it is difficult for the rich to want revolution.
Countries with a high scientific and technological level are
overblown with arrogance. We are like a blank sheet of paper,
which is good for writing on. . . .

7. MAO TSETUNG,
ON THE CORRECT HANDLING
OF CONTRADICTIONS AMONG THE PEOPLE

*This is Mao's single most important theoretical contribution
to the understanding of socialist transition.*

*Delivered at a moment when the party's leading body, the
Eighth Congress, had just declared that class contradictions in
Chinese society had been resolved, Mao held that while "large-
scale and turbulent class struggles of the masses have in the
main ended," class contradictions and class struggles, particularly between the proletariat and the bourgeoisie, continued to
exist and would long define the arena of politics. The tasks of
socialist politics and mobilization did not end with the completion of ownership transformation from private to state and
collective hands.*

*Indeed, Mao delivered his remarks in the context of the
effort to launch a new movement which would illustrate contradictions not only in society but between party and people. Mao
distinguished here between* antagonistic *contradictions between
the people and the enemy and* nonantagonistic *contradictions
among the people. While the former could only be resolved by
war and violent struggle as in the case of the Japanese invasion,
the latter under appropriate conditions could be resolved peacefully through criticism, education, and transformation, as in the
party's effort to buy out and then integrate the factory owners
under state leadership.*

*Here Mao's critical concern was the intellectuals, both as
valued contributors to and critics of society, and as a group
derived predominantly from elite family backgrounds for whom
socialist transformation posed difficult problems. The speech
initiated the Hundred Flowers Movement, in which intellectuals
throughout the spring of 1957 sharply criticized the leadership
of party and state. At its most effective these critics exposed
bureaucratic and elitist tendencies in the party at variance with*

Speech to the Eleventh Session (enlarged) of the Supreme State Conference, February 27, 1957. Published with amendations in: JMJP June 19,
1957. SR.

its egalitarian and mass line heritage and stated principles. When the party counterattacked, silencing its intellectual critics as rightists in the summer of 1957, the pendulum had already swung sharply from the conservative mood of 1956 and the Eighth Party Congress and China would move shortly toward the Great Leap Forward. Then and subsequently Mao's speech would provide guidelines for the continued class struggle and the role of social criticism.

Two Different Types of Contradictions

Never before has our country been as united as it is today. The victories of the bourgeois-democratic revolution and the socialist revolution and our achievements in socialist construction have rapidly changed the face of old China. . . . The unification of our country, the unity of our people and the unity of our various nationalities—these are the basic guarantees of the sure triumph of our cause. However, this does not mean that contradictions no longer exist in our society. To imagine that none exist is a naive idea which is at variance with objective reality. We are confronted by two types of social contradictions—those between ourselves and the enemy and those among the people themselves. The two are totally different in their nature. . . .

The contradictions between ourselves and the enemy are antagonistic contradictions. Within the ranks of the people, the contradictions among the working people are nonantagonistic, while those between the exploited and the exploiting classes have a nonantagonistic aspect in addition to an antagonistic aspect. There have always been contradictions among the people, but their content differs in each period of the revolution and in the period of socialist construction. In the conditions prevailing in China today, the contradictions among the people comprise the contradictions within the working class, the contradictions within the peasantry, the contradictions within the intelligentsia, the contradictions between the working class and the peasantry, the contradictions between the workers and peasants on the one hand and the intellectuals on the other, the contradictions between the working class and other sections of the working people on the one hand and the national bourgeoisie on the other, the contradictions within the national bourgeoisie, and so on. Our people's government is one that genuinely represents the people's interests, it is a government that serves the people. Nevertheless, there are still certain contradictions between the government and the people. These include contradictions among the interests of the state, the interests of the collective, and the interests of the individual; between democracy and centralism; between the leadership and the led; and the contradiction arising from the bureaucratic style of work of certain government workers in their relations with the masses. All these are also contradictions among the people. Generally speaking, the people's basic identity of interests underlies the contradictions among the people.

In our country, the contradiction between the working class and the national bourgeoisie belongs to the category of contradictions among the people. By and large, the class struggle between the two is a class struggle within the ranks of the people, because the Chinese national bourgeoisie has a dual character. In the period of the bourgeois-democratic revolution, it had both a revolutionary and a conciliationist side to its character. In the period of the socialist revolution, exploitation of the working class for profit constitutes one side of the character of the national bourgeoisie, while its support of the constitution and its willingness to accept socialist transformation constitute the other. The national bourgeoisie differs from the imperialists, the landlords and the bureaucrat-capitalists. The contradiction between the national bourgeoisie and the working class is one between the exploiter and the exploited, and is by nature antagonistic. But in the concrete conditions of China, this antagonistic class contradiction can, if properly handled, be transformed into a nonantagonistic one and be resolved by peaceful methods. However, it will change into a contradiction between ourselves and the enemy if we do not handle it properly and do not follow the policy of uniting with, criticizing, and educating the national bourgeoisie, or if the national bourgeoisie does not accept this policy of ours.

Since they are different in nature, the contradictions between ourselves and the enemy and the contradictions among the people must be resolved by different methods. To put it briefly, the former are a matter of drawing a clear distinction between ourselves and the enemy, and the latter a matter of drawing a clear distinction between right and wrong. . . .

Marxist philosophy holds that the law of the unity of opposites is the fundamental law of the universe. This law operates universally, whether in the natural world, in human society, or in man's thinking. Between the opposites in a contradiction there is at once unity and struggle, and it is this that impels things to move and change. Contradictions exist everywhere, but they differ in accordance with the different nature of different things. In any given phenomenon or thing, the unity of opposites is conditional, temporary, and transitory, and hence relative, whereas the struggle of opposites is absolute. Many dare not openly admit that contradictions still exist among the people of our country, although it is these very contradictions that are pushing our society forward. Many do not admit that contradictions continue to exist in a socialist society, with the result that they are handicapped and passive when confronted with social contradictions; they do not understand that socialist society will grow more united and consolidated through the ceaseless process of the correct handling and resolving of contradictions. . . .

The basic contradictions in socialist society are still those between the relations of production and the productive forces and between the superstructure and the economic base. However, they are fundamentally different in character and have different features from the contradictions between the relations of production and the productive forces and between the superstructure and the economic base in the old societies. . . .

To sum up, socialist relations of production have been established and are in harmony with the growth of the productive forces, but they are still far from perfect, and this imperfection stands in contradiction to the growth of the productive forces. Apart from harmony as well as contradiction between the relations of production and the developing productive forces, there is harmony as well as contradiction between the superstructure and the economic base. The superstructure consisting of the state system and laws of the people's democratic dictatorship and the socialist ideology guided by Marxism-

Leninism plays a positive role in facilitating the victory of socialist transformation and the establishment of the socialist organization of labor; it is suited to the socialist economic base, that is, to socialist relations of production. But survivals of bourgeois ideology, certain bureaucratic ways of doing things in our state organs, and defects in certain links in our state institutions are in contradiction with the socialist economic base. We must continue to resolve all such contradictions in the light of our specific conditions. . . .

A constant process of readjustment through state planning is needed to deal with the contradiction between production and the needs of society, which will long remain as an objective reality. Every year our country draws up an economic plan in order to establish a proper ratio between accumulation and consumption and achieve a balance between production and needs. Balance is nothing but a temporary, relative unity of opposites. By the end of each year, this balance, taken as a whole, is upset by the struggle of opposites; the unity undergoes a change, balance becomes imbalance, unity becomes disunity, and once again it is necessary to work out a balance and unity for the next year. Herein lies the superiority of our planned economy. . . .

Today, matters stand as follows. The large-scale and turbulent class struggles of the masses characteristic of the previous revolutionary periods have in the main ended, but class struggle is by no means entirely over. . . .

The Question of the Intellectuals

The contradictions within the ranks of the people in our country also find expression among the intellectuals. The several million intellectuals who worked for the old society have come to serve the new society, and the question that now arises is how they can fit in with the needs of the new society and how we can help them to do so. This, too, is a contradiction among the people.

Most of our intellectuals have made marked progress during the last seven years. They have expressed themselves in favor of the socialist system. Many are diligently studying Marxism, and some have become communists. The latter, though small in number, are steadily growing. Of course, there are still some intellectuals who are skeptical about socialism or who do not approve of it, but they are a minority.

China needs the services of as many intellectuals as possible for the colossal task of socialist construction. We should trust the intellectuals who are really willing to serve the cause of socialism, and should radically improve our relations with them and help them solve any problems requiring solution, so that they can give full play to their talents. Many of our comrades are not good at uniting with intellectuals. They are too crude in dealing with them, lack respect for their work, and interfere in certain matters in scientific and cultural work where interference is unwarranted. We must do away with all such shortcomings.

The mass of intellectuals have made some progress, but they should not be complacent. They must continue to remold themselves, gradually shed their bourgeois world outlook and acquire the proletarian, communist world outlook so that they can fully fit in with the needs of the new society and unite with the workers and peasants. This change in world outlook is something fundamental, and up till now most of our intellectuals cannot be said to have accomplished it. . . .

Our educational policy must enable everyone who receives an education to develop morally, intellectually, and physically and become a worker with both socialist consciousness and culture. . . .

On "Let a Hundred Flowers Blossom, Let a Hundred Schools of Thought Contend" and "Long-Term Coexistence and Mutual Supervision"

"Let a hundred flowers blossom, let a hundred schools of thought contend" and "long-term coexistence and mutual supervision"—how did these slogans come to be put forward? They were put forward in the light of China's specific conditions, on the basis of the recognition that various kinds of contradictions still exist in socialist society, and in response to the country's urgent need to speed up its economic and cultural development. Letting a hundred flowers blossom and a hundred schools of thought contend is the policy for promoting the progress of the arts and the sciences and a flourishing socialist culture in our land. Different forms and styles in art should develop freely and different schools in science should contend freely. We think that it is harmful to the growth of art and science if administrative measures are used to impose one particular style of art or school of thought and to ban another. Questions of right and wrong in the arts and sciences should be settled through free discussion in artistic and scientific circles and through practical work in these fields. They should not be settled in summary fashion. . . .

The class struggle is by no means over. The class struggle between the proletariat and the bourgeoisie, the class struggle between the different political forces, and the class struggle in the ideological field between the proletariat and the bourgeoisie will continue to be long and tortuous and at times will even become very acute. The proletariat seeks to transform the world according to its own world outlook, and so does the bourgeoisie. In this respect, the question of which will win out, socialism or capitalism, is still not really settled. Marxists are still a minority among the entire population as well as among the intellectuals. Therefore, Marxism must still develop through struggle. Marxism can develop only through struggle, and not only is this true of the past and the present, it is necessarily true of the future as well. . . . Such struggles will never end. This is the law of development, of truth and, naturally, of Marxism as well.

It will take a fairly long period of time to decide the issue in the ideological struggle between socialism and capitalism in our country. The reason is that the influence of the bourgeoisie and of the intellectuals who come from the old society will remain in our country for a long time to come, and so will their class ideology. . . .

People may ask, since Marxism is accepted as the guiding ideology by the majority of the people in our country, can it be criticized? Certainly it can. Marxism is scientific truth and fears no criticism. If it did, and if it could be overthrown by criticism, it would be worthless. . . .

What should our policy be toward non-Marxist ideas? As far as unmistakable counter-revolutionaries and saboteurs of the socialist cause are concerned, the matter is easy: we simply deprive them of their freedom of speech. But incorrect ideas among the people are quite a different matter. Will it do to ban such ideas and deny them any opportunity for expression? Certainly not. It is not only futile but very harmful to use summary methods in dealing with ideological questions among the people, with questions concerned with man's mental world. You may ban the expression of wrong ideas, but the ideas will still be there. . . .

At first glance, the two slogans—let a hundred flowers blossom and let a hundred schools of thought contend—have no class character; the proletariat can turn them to account, and so can the bourgeoisie or other people. But different classes, strata, and social groups each have their own views on what are fragrant flowers and what are poisonous weeds. What then, from the point of view of the broad masses of the people, should be the criteria today for distinguishing fragrant flowers from poisonous weeds? . . . We consider that, broadly speaking, the criteria should be as follows:

(1) Words and actions should help to unite, and not divide, the people of our various nationalities.

(2) They should be beneficial, and not harmful, to socialist transformation and socialist construction.

(3) They should help to consolidate, and not undermine or weaken, the People's Democratic Dictatorship.

(4) They should help to consolidate, and not undermine or weaken, democratic centralism.

(5) They should help to strengthen, and not discard or weaken, the leadership of the Communist Party.

(6) They should be beneficial, and not harmful, to international socialist unity and the unity of the peace-loving people of the world.

Of these six criteria, the most important are the socialist path and the leadership of the party. These criteria are put forward not to hinder but to foster the free discussion of questions among the people. . . .

B. SOCIALIST TRANSITION
IN THE CHINESE COUNTRYSIDE

1. ON MUTUAL AID
AND COOPERATION IN AGRICULTURE

Basic completion of land revolution in 1952 concluded the first stage of rural transformation, the heart of the new democratic revolution, and opened the way to the next, phase one in the transition to socialism. The initial step beyond land revolution lay in the voluntary organization of mutual aid teams (MATs). Built on the foundation of traditional self-help groups which had enjoyed a long and complex history in China, MATs rationalized production principally through small-scale labor sharing within a private agrarian economy.

A December 1951 draft resolution initiated mutual aid on an experimental basis in advanced areas throughout North China. The success of mutual aid, chiefly in old liberated areas, together with the need to increase agricultural production and to combat re-emerging class stratification, led to the nation-wide movement to form MATs. In 1952 40 percent of all peasant families belonged to MATs; by 1954 this figure had risen to 60 percent and an additional 11 percent had organized more ambitious agricultural producers' cooperatives.

The step-by-step approach outlined in the document underscores the party's efforts to ensure smooth passage through progressively higher stages of cooperation based on voluntary

Central Committee Decision on Mutual Aid and Cooperation in Agriculture. Draft original December 15, 1951; revised draft decision issued by the Central Committee December 15, 1952; officially adopted February 15, 1953. JMJP March 26, 1953. CB 240.

*participation. In charting the advance of cooperation, the direc-
tive emphasizes the importance of raising income for cooperative members and avoiding errors of commandism which
breach guidelines for voluntary participation. While maintaining
that, in the long run, solution of the agrarian problem depended
on large-scale mechanized collective farms, in early 1953 the
party promoted gradual social transition via mutual aid and
rudimentary cooperatives which retained private land ownership.*

(1) The active productive zeal of peasants built up on the
foundations of agrarian reform is being manifested in two
directions: active zeal in the development of individual economy, and active zeal in the development of mutual aid and
cooperation. The productive zeal of the peasants manifested in
these directions constitutes a basic factor contributing to the
rapid restoration and development of the national economy and
the promotion of the industrialization of the country. For this
reason, the party's correct leadership in rural production is of
the greatest significance.

(2) It is inevitable that the peasants after their liberation
have become active in the development of individual economy.
The party has taken full cognizance of the special characteristic
of the peasants to acquire small private holdings, and has
pointed out that this active nature of the individual economy
must not be neglected or crudely suppressed. In this connection
the party has persisted in its policy of consolidating unity with
the middle peasants. Even the economy of the rich peasants is
allowed to continue its development. On the basis of the economic conditions of the country today, the individual peasant
economy must exist to a considerable extent over a long period
of time. . . .

(3) However, the Central Committee of the party has always
considered it necessary to overcome the difficulties of many
peasants arising out of their scattered enterprises, to enable the
broad masses of the poor peasants to promptly increase production and march toward the goal of being well-clothed and
well-fed, to enable the state to get far greater supplies of goods,
grain and industrial raw materials than before, and at the same
time to raise the purchasing power of the peasants to assure a

broad market for the manufactured goods of the state. To achieve these ends, we must promote "organization," and on the principles of voluntary participation and mutual benefit, develop the active nature of mutual aid and cooperation among the peasants.

Such mutual aid and cooperation, at this stage, consists of collective labor built on the foundations of individual economy, that is, the foundations of private property holdings of the peasants. Ahead lies the prospect of the future development of the collectivization or socialization of agriculture. . . .

(4) The development of mutual aid and cooperation in agricultural production among peasants in different areas varies according to the development of the rural economy in different places and the different needs of the peasants. The history has been varied and the forms are complex. Generally speaking, however, there are three main types of mutual aid and cooperation in China.

The first form is that of simple mutual aid. This is the lowest form, organized chiefly on a seasonal or temporary basis. This form has been most numerous in the old liberated areas from the very beginning to the present day. In the new liberated areas it is also suited to the established habits of peasants for mutual aid, and can be easily developed extensively. This sort of organization is generally of small size, and apart from the needs of special individual cases, it is generally only suited to small-scale operation.

The second type is the long-term mutual aid organization, which is a higher form compared with the first. Some of these organizations have started the coordination of mutual aid in agriculture with mutual aid in subsidiary occupations, have mapped out simple production plans, and gradually achieved coordination between labor mutual aid and the improvement of technique, realizing to some extent a division of labor in technique, with the acquisition, in some cases, of common property in the form of draft animals and tools, and even accumulated common wealth. Such organizations are still few in number. . . .

Peasants participating in the mutual aid organizations of the two aforementioned types at present include 60 percent of all peasants in the North China region, and in the Northeast region they include as many as 70 percent.

The third type is the agricultural producers' cooperative,

which is characterized by the contribution of land as investment, and is thus also known as the *land cooperative.* This
organization includes certain important characteristics already
existing in some areas in the organization of the second type,
such as the coordination between mutual aid in agriculture and
mutual aid in subsidiary occupations, production planning to a
certain extent and division of labor in technique, as well as the
ownership of some common property. But these features have
been developed to a greater extent. For with the acquisition of
jointly owned tools of improved or new types, the carrying out
of division of labor, the undertaking of irrigation works and the
reclamation of wasteland, there has naturally arisen the demand
for the unified working of land for production. Such is the
nature of the agricultural producers' cooperative founded on
the basis of the private ownership of land. Investment of land in
the organization is still effected on the principles of freedom of
action and mutual benefit, and investments may be withdrawn
on the same principles.

In the field of production, however, these cooperatives are
able to plan the management of their land in a unified way and
cultivate those crops most suited to the soil and so utilize the
land effectively. On the other hand, they render easier the work
of the regulation of labor power and semi-labor power (women,
children, aged, and handicapped), and release the creative
energies of the peasants through the division of labor. Thus,
certain weaknesses of the small peasant economy can gradually
be overcome. . . . These cooperatives exist today in only a few
hsien and their number is not large. However, in the North
China and Northeast regions, there are more than 300 of these
cooperatives and they are still growing. . . .

Following the general law of the development of the movement and the necessity for developing rural productivity, the
policy of the party on the development of the present mutual
aid and cooperation movement should have the following three
aspects:

First, leadership should be directed to organize the first type
namely, the simple, temporary and seasonal mutual aid organizations on a mass scale throughout the country, particularly in
the new liberated areas and in areas where the foundations of
the movement are weak. It is a mistake to hold in contempt this

lowest form of the organization which is acceptable to the broad masses of peasants today. . . .

Second, leadership should be directed to organize step by step the second type, namely the long-term mutual aid organizations with greater content than simple mutual aid organizations, in areas where the movement had its first foundations. It is also a mistake to be satisfied forever with temporary and seasonal mutual aid organizations, and to fail to take a step further to consolidate these organizations and enable the peasants to reap greater benefits from permanent mutual aid.

Third, leadership should be directed to organizing the third type, the agricultural producer cooperatives with investments of land, at key points, in areas where the peasants have rich experience in mutual aid and there is a strong nucleus of leaders. If there is a disregard of the production needs of the masses, the foundations of the mutual aid movement, the existence of a nucleus of leaders, the active zeal of the masses, and the prerequisites for success, but, instead, an attitude of striving for high objectives and an attempt to rely merely on preparations from the higher levels leading down to the lower levels, and to employ the method of commandism in setting about the formation of the third type of organization, the method thus used is that of formalism and rashness, and is naturally also a mistake.

The Central Committee policy of steady advance is based on both the need for the development of production and the practical possibilities. . . .

(5) With reference to agricultural mutual aid and cooperative organizations, there are, generally speaking, two different deviations.

The first of these deviations is the tendency to adopt a passive attitude toward the movement for mutual aid and cooperation. There is here a failure to realize that the movement is a necessary course by which our party is leading the broad masses of the peasants from their individual economy of small production to proceed gradually toward collective economy with the large-scale employment of mechanical power for cultivation and harvesting. There is a failure to appreciate that the various agricultural producers' cooperatives which have already emerged constitute a transitional form of organization on the progress toward the socialization of agriculture, that they contain socialist factors in them. This constitutes the mistake of the rightist trend.

The second deviation is the tendency to adopt an attitude of precipitate haste, disregarding the necessary conditions such as the willingness of the peasants and the economic preparations required. There is the premature and inappropriate attempt at once to deny or limit the private property holdings of peasants participating in the agricultural producers' cooperatives, or the attempt to apply the theories of absolute egalitarianism among the members of mutual aid organizations and agricultural producers' cooperatives, or the attempt to organize rapidly the higher forms of socialized collective farms, thinking it possible to achieve with a single stroke of the hand the full socialization of the rural areas. All those are mistakes of the leftist trend. . . .

A good job must be made of agricultural production. In the rural areas agricultural production is the task that supersedes all other tasks which are to serve agricultural production. . . .

Under favorable local conditions, there must be developed mutual aid which coordinates agricultural activities with subsidiary occupations such as handicrafts, processing works, transportation enterprises, animal husbandry, afforestation, orchard keeping, fishery, and other activities. In accordance with the needs of agriculture and the subsidiary occupations, and individual capabilities, there shall be effected the rational division of labor and division of trade, and the women and other semi-labor forces shall be organized so that all available human power may be fully utilized. . . .

To meet the needs for the expansion of production, and on the basis of the completely voluntary action of members of a mutual aid organization or cooperative, the method of democratic decision may be employed for the organization of capital to purchase common production tools and draft animals. . . . At the moment the proportionate size of the general reserve or general provisions account in the annual income of a mutual aid organization or cooperative must not be too large, and should in general be only from 1 to 5 percent. . . .

Within the internal ranks of an agricultural mutual aid organization or an agricultural producers' cooperative, there shall not be permitted the exploitation of hired labor (that is, the exploitation by rich peasants). Accordingly, members of a team or a cooperative shall not be permitted to hire permanent laborers into the team or cooperative, and the teams and cooperatives shall also not employ permanent hands for the cultivation of land. . . .

Supply and marketing cooperatives shall conclude contracts with agricultural mutual aid organizations and agricultural producers' cooperatives for marketing, placing of orders, and issuance of loans, in order to assist the organizations and producers' cooperatives to overcome their difficulties in production such as lack of working capital, and in marketing such as distance from markets. . . .

State-owned farms must be extended. In addition to the planned development of certain numbers of mechanized and semimechanized state farms, there shall be in each *hsien* at least one or two experimental state farms. These latter shall demonstrate the superiority of adopting advanced farming techniques and new types of farm tools and so educate the whole body of peasants. At the same time technical help and guidance may be given. In certain places, collective farms of a socialist nature may also be set up on an experimental basis with the whole consent of the peasants and in suitable economic conditions. . . .

After the solution of the numerous problems connected with agricultural mutual aid and cooperation, the Central Committee of the party considers it necessary to draw once more the attention of party committees of all levels and all comrades and activists among those who are not party members engaged in rural work, to attend to the care for, assistance to, and patient education of individual peasants with the greatest enthusiasm and without discrimination. Working their land individually is perfectly legal (being provided for in the Common Program as well as in the agrarian reform law). They must not be ridiculed, not be branded backward, and above all it must not be permitted to hit them with threats and restrictions. Agricultural loans must be issued reasonably to both mutual aid and cooperative organizations as well as individual peasants, and should not be restricted to the first and denied, or issued only in limited amounts, to the latter. . . . We must realize that by showing our concern for and appropriate assistance to these individual peasants, it will be possible for them to be gradually taken into the mutual aid and cooperative organizations, it will be possible for us to realize our final objective in the rural areas—the leadership of the entire body of peasants on the road to socialism and communism.

2. THE FORMATION OF AGRICULTURAL PRODUCERS' COOPERATIVES

Publication in October 1953 of the general line for the transition period—industrialization plus socialist transformation of all sectors of the economy—together with the recognition of lagging agricultural yields and of growing polarization between rural rich and poor sharply focused attention on the slow pace of cooperative formation.

Concern within the party over the inability of an agricultural system rooted in a small peasant economy to provide a stable and increasing marketable agricultural surplus both for industry and for consumption provided the primary impetus to accelerate the movement from MATs to cooperatives.

The December 16, 1953, decision to promote agricultural producers' cooperatives sought simultaneously to spur productivity and to check the growing income gap between rich and poor peasants and ultimately to pave the way to higher levels of cooperation.

It has become more and more evident that small-scale agricultural production cannot satisfy the demand of the broad peasantry to improve their living conditions, nor can it meet the increasing need of the entire national economy. To further raise the productive forces of agriculture, the most fundamental task of the party in its rural work is to educate the peasants through

Central Committee Decision on Development of Agricultural Producers' Cooperatives, December 16, 1953. NCNA January 8, 1954; CB 278.

measures most acceptable and understandable to them and stimulate them to gradually get organized and carry out the socialist reform of agriculture. . . .

According to the nation's experiences, the concrete way for the gradual organization of China's peasants is (1) through temporary mutual aid teams which operate as a simple form of collective labor, and year-round mutual aid teams which have certain divisions of labor among their members on the basis of collective labor, and a small amount of property owned in common; (2) through agricultural cooperatives in which the members pool their land as shares and there is unified management and more property owned in common; and finally (3) to agricultural cooperatives of a higher form (collective farms) with collective peasant ownership entirely socialist in character. This is the path laid down by the party for the gradual, step-by-step socialist transformation of agriculture.

For the past several years, China's mutual aid and cooperation movement for agricultural production has been gaining ever greater momentum. Up to the present, there are approximately 47.9 million peasant households participating in temporary and year-round mutual aid teams and agricultural producers' cooperatives. This constitutes 43 percent of the total peasant households of rural villages. The number of agricultural producers' cooperatives has reached upwards of 14,000, with over 273,000 peasant households as members. Although the movement is yet developed in an unbalanced manner in various places, the effects it has brought about in stimulating agricultural production show that the party policy is gradually gaining the support of the broad peasantry and is turning, step by step, from a possibility to a reality. From this it is clear that the party must take an active attitude, instead of a pessimistic, laissez-faire attitude, towards reforming the individual, small peasant economy and developing mutual aid and cooperation in agriculture. If we should adopt a pessimistic, laissez-faire attitude toward the mutual aid and cooperation movement, if we should remain content with the state of small peasant economy, and if we should make no attempt to point out to the small peasants the correct, bright, and broad path of socialist reform, then we would definitely allow ourselves to go to the extent of giving up socialism on the rural front, and helping rural capitalism to exert its latent influence. This would definitely hamper the growth of productive forces of agriculture and the further improvement of the living conditions of the peasants, jeopardize the balance of industry and agriculture, destroy planned economy and national industrialization, and undermine the worker-peasant alliance. Such policy and action are manifestly erroneous. . . .

The superiority and important function of such cooperatives have already been fully demonstrated in the course of the trial and initial stages of development, in the following ways:

(1) The agricultural producers' cooperatives can solve certain contradictions which cannot be solved in mutual aid teams, especially the contradictions in collective labor and separate management, thus providing a proper future for the mutual aid movement which has already been developed to a certain stage.

(2) The practice of unified use of land will permit land to grow what it is most suitable for, the more rational and planned division of labor to be made on the foundation of collective labor, and the rational and centralized use of the labor force, thus to greatly raise the work efficiency.

(3) Centralized management will provide a greater labor force and economic strength to better utilize the new agrotechnique, to carry out agrotechnical reform and basic construction, and thus to more effectively increase agricultural production.

(4) As more labor and time is saved, side production can be better undertaken and the economic position of the peasants strengthened.

(5) As the system of remuneration according to labor is practiced, the peasants will be greatly encouraged to increase their creativeness and enthusiasm for labor and technical study.

(6) Since the agricultural producers' cooperatives can consolidate the unity between the poor peasants and the middle peasants, they can effectively fight the capitalist tendencies and the state of polarization into poor and rich in the rural villages.

(7) The agricultural producer cooperatives can systematically carry out planned production and, therefore, be easily integrated with the state-operated socialist economy in terms of supply, production and marketing, and thus can gradually embark on the path of the economic plan of the state.

3. MAO TSETUNG,
ON AGRICULTURAL COOPERATION

The year 1955, Mao observed, was a year of decision in which the Chinese people must choose between two roads, socialism or capitalism. It also marked the midpoint in the first five-year plan. Lagging agricultural growth rates heightened awareness that the success of the plan in general, and of China's industrialization in particular, depended upon solving the problem of agricultural production.

The party remained divided, however, over the pace of socialist transition and the role of rapid institutional change in raising agricultural yields and the supply of marketable produce. The dissolution of large numbers of cooperatives in 1954 and early 1955 underlined the seriousness of the rift. In May 1955 Teng Tzu-hui, director of the party's Rural Work Department, proposed further dissolution of a substantial number of cooperatives facing difficulties and Liu Shao-ch'i tacitly approved the plan. The dominant view in the party leadership and underlying the first five-year plan was that institutional change in the countryside must proceed gradually. Three five-year plans would be required before industry could supply sufficient tractors and other modern inputs to agriculture. Then and only then would it be possible to eliminate private ownership of land in favor of large-scale collective farming.

In July, in his most dramatic intervention in the early years of the People's Republic, Mao attacked the slow pace of cooperation and called for the formation of 1.3 million cooperatives by October 1956. Mao's speech transformed in a single stroke the pace of cooperativization. The high tide of rural transformation was underway. Though Mao justified his strategy with reference to the Soviet approach to socialist development, the speech marked the first direct challenge to the logic of Chinese planners and the Soviet model enshrined in the first five-year plan.

At the end of March 1955, 14 percent of peasant households

On the Question of Agricultural Copperation. Report to secretaries of provincial, municipal, and autonomous region committees of the CPC, July 31, 1955. SR.

belonged to semisocialist cooperatives. By October, 32 percent had joined and by December, 70 million households or 63 percent of the total number of peasant households had become cooperative members. In the next six months, the majority of these cooperatives transformed themselves into socialist collectives with land owned and managed by the cooperative.

The high tide posed sharp challenges to party leadership and peasant communities: the intense pace of change brought many communities advanced collective forms without the benefit of experience with lower level cooperatives; mobilization frequently swept aside strictures concerning voluntary participation. In some areas resistance took the form of slaughter and sale of pigs and cattle by more prosperous peasants fearing confiscation. Yet on balance, for a movement so profound in its implications, the transformation took place extraordinarily smoothly and without violence. For the vast majority, particularly poorer strata of the peasantry, higher forms of cooperation opened new prospects for equality and mutual benefit. Again, the poor and lower middle peasants, under party leadership, provided the driving force for revolutionary change, and again, it was the peasantry who advanced ahead of the party and forced it to revise its blueprint for development.

A new upsurge in the socialist mass movement is imminent throughout the countryside. But some of our comrades are tottering along like a woman with bound feet and constantly complaining, "You're going too fast." Excessive criticism, inappropriate complaints, endless anxiety, and the erection of countless taboos—they believe this is the proper way to guide the socialist mass movement in the rural areas.

No, this is not the right way; it is the wrong way.

The high tide of social transformation in the countryside, the high tide of cooperation, has already reached some places and will soon sweep over the whole country. It is a vast socialist revolutionary movement involving a rural population of more than 500 million, and it has extremely great and world-wide significance. We should give this movement active, enthusiastic and systematic leadership, and not drag it back by one means or another. Some errors are unavoidable in the process; this is understandable, and they will not be hard to correct. Shortcomings or mistakes found among the cadres and the peasants can be remedied or overcome provided we give them positive help. The cadres and the peasants are advancing under the leadership of the party and, fundamentally, the movement is healthy. In some places they have made certain mistakes in their work; for example, poor peasants have been barred from the cooperatives and their difficulties have been ignored, while well-to-do middle peasants have been forced into the cooperatives and their interests have been encroached upon. All this has to be corrected by education and not by the crude method of reprimands. Reprimands simply cannot solve any problems. We must guide the movement boldly and must not "always fear the dragons ahead and the tigers behind." Both cadres and peasants will remold themselves in the course of the struggles they themselves experience. Let them go into action and learn while doing, and they will become more capable. In this way, fine people will come forward in large numbers. "Always fearing the dragons ahead and the tigers behind" will not produce any cadres. It is necessary to send large groups of cadres with short-term training out to the countryside to guide and assist the cooperative movement. But also it is by taking part in the movement itself that these cadres sent down from above can learn how to work. . . .

In short, the leadership should never lag behind the mass movement. Yet the present situation is precisely one in which the mass movement is running ahead of the leadership, who cannot keep pace with it. This state of affairs must change. . . .

To achieve cooperation step by step throughout our rural areas, we must conscientiously check up on and strengthen the cooperatives already in existence.

This checking-up should be done not just once, but two or three times a year. It was undertaken in a certain number of cooperatives in the first half of this year (in some places, apparently, very sketchily and without any major effort). I suggest a second check-up of these cooperatives should be undertaken in the autumn or winter of this year, and a third in the spring or summer of next. Of the 650,000 existing cooperatives, 550,000 are new, having been set up last winter or this spring, and they include a number of Class I cooperatives which are more or less consolidated. . . .

We should treasure every spark of socialist enthusiasm shown by the peasants and cadres, and not thwart such enthusiasm. We should identify ourselves heart and soul with the members and cadres of the cooperatives and with the county, district and township cadres, and not thwart their enthusiasm.

Cooperatives should not be dissolved unless all, or nearly all, their members are firmly determined not to go on. If some members are determined not to carry on, let them withdraw while the majority stay in and continue. If the majority are firmly against carrying on but the minority are willing, let the majority withdraw while the minority stay in and continue. Even if it comes to that, it will be all right. In one very small cooperative of only six households in Hopei province, the three old middle peasant households firmly refused to carry on and were allowed to withdraw, but the three poor peasant households said they would continue whatever happened. They stayed in and the cooperative was preserved. In fact, the direction in which these three poor peasant households are moving is the one in which the 500 million peasants throughout the country will move. . . .

With the adoption of a policy of what was called "resolute contraction" in Chekiang (not by decision of the Chekiang Provincial Party Committee), out of 53,000 cooperatives in the province some 15,000 cooperatives (comprising 400,000 peasant households) were dissolved at one fell swoop. This caused great dissatisfaction among the masses and the cadres, and it was altogether the wrong thing to do. . . .

This is how things stand: China has an enormous population with insufficient cultivated land (only three mou of land per head taking the country as a whole, and only one mou or even less on the average in many parts of the southern provinces); natural calamities are frequent (every year large areas of farmland suffer from flood, drought, gales, frost, hail or insect pests in varying degrees); and farming methods are backward. Consequently, although the standard of living of the peasant masses since the land reform has improved or has even improved a good deal, many are still in difficulty or are still not well off, there being relatively few who are well off, and hence most of the peasants show enthusiasm for taking the socialist road. Their enthusiasm is being constantly heightened by China's socialist industrialization and its achievements. For them, socialism is the only way out. These peasants make up 60 to 70 percent of the entire rural population. In other words, the only way for the majority of the peasants to shake off poverty, improve their livelihood and fight natural calamities is to unite and go forward along the high road of socialism. This sentiment is growing rapidly among the masses of the poor peasants and of those who are not so well off. The well-to-do or comparatively well-to-do peasants, who make up only 20 to 30 percent of the rural population, are vacillating, with some trying hard to go the capitalist way. As I have already said, because of their low political consciousness many of the poor peasants and those who are not well off are taking a "wait-and-see" attitude for the time being and are also vacillating; however, it is easier for them to accept socialism than it is for the well-to-do peasants. This is how things really stand. But some of our comrades ignore these facts and think that the several hundred thousand newly established small semisocialist agricultural producers' cooperatives have "gone beyond the real possibilities" or "gone beyond the level of political consciousness of the masses." This means that their eyes are on the comparatively small number of well-to-do peasants to the neglect of the great majority of the poor peasants and those who are not well-to-do. That is one kind of wrong thinking.

These comrades also underrate the strength of the Communist Party's leadership in the countryside and the peasant masses' whole-hearted support for the party. They believe that it is difficult enough as it is for the party to consolidate the several hundred thousand small cooperatives already in existence, and that therefore a great expansion of cooperatives is inconceivable. They paint a pessimistic picture of the party's present work in leading agricultural cooperation, holding that it has "gone beyond the level of the cadres' experience." . . .

We must have faith, first, that the peasant masses are ready to advance step by step along the road of socialism under the leadership of the party, and second, that the party is capable of leading the peasants along this road. These two points are the essence of the matter, the main current. If we lack this conviction, it will be impossible for us basically to complete the building of socialism in the period of roughly three five-year plans.

The great historical experience of the Soviet Union in building socialism inspires our people with full confidence in the building of socialism in China. However, even on this question of international experience, there are different views. Some comrades disapprove of our Central Committee's policy of keeping the development of agricultural cooperation in step with our socialist industrialization, although such a policy proved correct in the Soviet Union. They consider that the speed of industrialization as it is set at present is all right, but that agricultural cooperation should proceed at an extremely slow pace and need not keep in step with it. This is to disregard the experience of the Soviet Union. These comrades fail to understand that socialist industrialization cannot be carried out in isolation from agricultural cooperation. In the first place, as everyone knows, China's current level of production of marketable grain and industrial raw materials is very low, whereas the state's need for them is growing year by year, and this presents a sharp contradiction. If we cannot fundamentally solve the problem of agricultural cooperation in a period of roughly three five-year plans, that is to say, if our agriculture cannot make a leap from small-scale farming with animal-drawn farm implements to large-scale mechanized farming, including extensive state-organized land reclamation by settlers using machinery (the plan being to bring 400-500 million mou of wasteland under cultivation in the course of three five-year plans), then we shall fail to resolve the contradiction between the ever-increasing need for marketable grain and industrial raw materials and the present generally low yield of staple crops, we shall run into formidable difficulties in our socialist industrialization and shall be unable to complete it. . . . In the second place, some of our comrades have not given any thought to the connection between the following two facts, namely, that heavy industry, the most important branch of socialist industrialization, produces tractors and other farm machinery, chemical fertilizers, modern means of transport, oil, electric power, etc., for agricultural use, but that all these things can only be used, or used extensively, on the basis of large-scale cooperative agriculture. We are now carrying out a revolution not only in the social system, the change from private to public ownership, but also in technology, the change from handicraft to large-scale modern machine production, and the two revolutions are interconnected. In agriculture, with conditions as they are in our country, cooperation must precede the use of big machinery (in capitalist countries agriculture develops in a capitalist way). Therefore we must on no account regard industry and agriculture, socialist industrialization and the socialist transformation of agriculture as two separate and isolated things, and on no account must we emphasize the one and play down the other. In this matter too, Soviet experience points the way, yet some of our comrades pay no attention and always see these questions as isolated and unconnected. In the third place, some of our comrades have also failed to give any thought to the connection between two other facts, namely, that large funds are needed to accomplish both national industrialization and the technical transformation of agriculture, but that a considerable part of these funds has to be accumulated through agriculture. Apart from the direct agricultural tax, this is done by developing light industry which produces the great quantities of consumer goods needed by the peasants and exchanging them for the peasants' marketable grain and the raw materials for light industry, so that the material requirements both of the peasants and of the state are satisfied and funds are accumulated for the state. Moreover, the large-scale expansion of light industry requires the development of agriculture as well as of heavy industry. For it cannot be brought about on the basis of small-scale peasant production; it awaits large-scale farming, and in our country this means socialist cooperative agriculture. Only this type of agriculture can give the peasants an inestimably greater purchasing power than they now possess. . . .

Altogether eighteen years will elapse between the founding of the People's Republic and the end of the third five-year plan. In that period, simultaneously with the basic completion of socialist industrialization and of the socialist transformation of handicrafts and capitalist industry and commerce, we intend basically to complete the socialist transformation of agriculture. Is this possible? Soviet experience tells us that it is entirely possible. The civil war in the Soviet Union ended in 1920, and agricultural cooperation was completed in the seventeen years from 1921 to 1937, the main part of this work having been done in the six years from 1929 to 1934. . . . This road traveled by the Soviet Union is our model.

Secondly, the method we are using in the socialist transformation of agriculture is one of step-by-step advance. The first step was to call on the peasants to organize agricultural producers' mutual aid teams, which contain only certain rudiments of socialism and comprise from a few to a dozen or so households each, and to do so in accordance with the principles of voluntary participation and mutual benefit. The second step has been to call on the peasants, likewise in accordance with the principles of voluntary participation and mutual benefit, to organize on the basis of these mutual aid teams small agricultural producers' cooperatives, which are semisocialist in nature and are characterized by the pooling of land as shares and by unified management. Then the third step will be to call on the peasants, in accordance with the same principles of voluntary participation and mutual benefit, to unite further on the basis of these small semisocialist cooperatives and organize large agricultural producers' cooperatives which are fully socialist in nature. These steps make it possible for the peasants gradually to raise their socialist consciousness through their personal experience and gradually to change their mode of life, thus lessening any feeling of an abrupt change. These steps can generally avoid any drop in crop yields during, say, the first year or two; indeed, they must ensure a year-by-year increase, and this can be done. More than 80 percent of the existing 650,000 agricultural producers' cooperatives have increased their output, while over 10 percent have shown neither an increase nor a decrease, and less than 10 percent have shown a decrease. . . .

Some comrades have a wrong approach to the vital question of the worker-peasant alliance, proceeding as they do from the stand of the bourgeoisie, of the rich peasants, or of the well-to-do middle peasants with their spontaneous tendency towards capitalism. They think that the present situation in the cooperative movement is very dangerous, and they advise us to "get off the horse quickly" in our present advance along the road of cooperation. "If you do not," they warn us, "you are in danger of breaking up the worker-peasant alliance." We think exactly the opposite. If we do not get on the horse quickly, there will be the danger of breaking up the worker-peasant alliance. There is a difference of only a single word here—one says "off" while the other says "on"—yet it demonstrates the difference between two opposing lines. As everybody knows, we already have a worker-peasant alliance built on the basis of the bourgeois-democratic revolution against imperialism and feudalism, a revolution which took the land from the landlords and distributed it to the peasants in order to free them from the bondage of the feudal system of ownership. But this revolution is past and feudal ownership has been abolished. What exists in the countryside today is capitalist ownership by the rich peasants and a vast sea of private ownership by the individual peasants. As is clear to everyone, the spontaneous forces of capitalism have been steadily growing in the countryside in recent years, with new rich peasants springing up everywhere and many well-to-do middle peasants striving to become rich peasants. On the other hand, many poor peasants are still living in poverty for lack of sufficient means of production, with some in debt and others selling or renting out their land. If this tendency goes unchecked, the polarization in the countryside will inevitably be aggravated day by day. . . . There is no solution to this problem except on a new basis. And that means to bring about, step by step, the socialist transformation of the whole of agriculture simultaneously with the gradual realization of socialist industrialization and the socialist transformation of handicrafts and capitalist industry and commerce; in other words, it means to carry out cooperation and eliminate the rich peasant economy and the individual economy in the countryside so that all the rural people will become increasingly well off together. We maintain that this is the only way to consolidate the worker-peasant alliance. . . .

We must here and now realize that there will soon be a nation-wide high tide of socialist transformation in the countryside. This is inevitable. By the spring of 1958, at the end of the final year of the first five-year plan and the beginning of the first year of the second five-year plan, cooperatives of a semi-socialist type will embrace some 250 million people, about 55 million peasant households (averaging four and one-half persons each), which will mean half the rural population. By that time many counties and some provinces will have basically completed the semisocialist transformation of the agricultural economy, and in every part of the country a small number of semisocialist cooperatives will have become fully socialist. By 1960, during the first half of the second five-year plan, we shall in the main have achieved the semisocialist transformation of the remainder of the agricultural economy involving the other half of the rural population. By then the number of fully socialist cooperatives formed from the semisocialist cooperatives will have increased. All through the first and second five-year plans, this social transformation will continue to be the main feature of the transformation of the countryside, while technical transformation will take second place; the number of big farm machines will certainly increase, but not to any great extent. During the third five-year plan, the social and the technical transformation of the rural areas will proceed side by side; more big farm machinery will be employed year by year, but in the field of social transformation, from 1960 onwards the semisocialist cooperatives will be gradually developing into fully socialist ones, group by group and stage by stage. . . . The country's economic conditions being what they are, the technical transformation will take longer than the social. It is estimated that the basic completion of the nation-wide technical transformation of agriculture will take roughly four or five five-year plans, that is, twenty to twenty-five years. The whole party must fight for the fulfillment of this great task.

4. SOCIALIST UPSURGE
IN THE COUNTRYSIDE

In the fall of 1955, as a weapon to mobilize support among the party and the peasantry for an upsurge in cooperative formation, Mao edited a collection of several hundred accounts of pacesetting experiments in rural collectivization from villages all over China. The message was, if these model coops can do it, why can't we? The collection, and Mao's vivid commentary

Who Says a Chicken Feather Can't Fly Up to Heaven? *Honan Daily,* November 2, 1955. In: Mao Tsetung, ed., *Socialist Upsurge in the Chinese Countryside* (Peking: Foreign Languages Press, 1956).

(editor's note), reveal in rich detail the process of designing, implementing, and modifying cooperative forms in the search for those appropriate to local conditions, experience, and consciousness. It also exemplifies the mass line method at work and particularly the mobilization relationship involving Mao, the party, and the peasantry. Rather than designing and then imposing the "correct blueprint" on 600 million peasants, Mao presents and sums up diverse advanced experiences which can be studied, adapted, implemented and further modified to suit diverse conditions. The collection provided a powerful stimulus both to fence-sitting party officials and peasants to get on with the task of cooperation, which was then sweeping rural China.

Editor's note

This is an excellent article. It will open the eyes of a great many people. The party organization in this place never wavered on the question of cooperation. It stood four-square behind the destitute peasants in their demand for a coop and in their victorious competition with the well-to-do middle peasants; it firmly supported them as they grew from a small coop to a large one, increasing their output year by year, till by the third year the whole village was in cooperatives. The well-to-do middle peasants had jeered: "They've less money than an egg has hair, yet they think they can run a coop. Can a chicken feather fly up to heaven?" But that is just what this chicken feather did.

Here we had a struggle between two alternatives—socialism and capitalism. . . .

Party organizations should follow the example of the Communists in Nantsui village, Anyang county, and firmly support the cooperatives. Unfortunately, not all the rural party branches did so. And where they didn't, confusion arose.

First of all, there were public debates on whether or not a chicken feather can fly up to heaven. Of course this is a serious question. In thousands of years has anyone ever seen one that could? The impossibility of such a feat has practically become a truism. Where the party does not criticize this old saw it may bewilder many a poor peasant and lower middle peasant. Moreover, with regard to administrative staff and, further, with regard to material resources—such as the ability to raise loans—the coops have a hard time if the party and the government do not give them a hand.

The reason the well-to-do middle peasants dared trot out such moth-eaten proverbs as "chicken feathers can't fly up to heaven" was because the coops had not yet increased their output, the poor coops had not yet become prosperous, and the individual, isolated coop had not yet become one of hundreds of thousands of coops. It was because the party had not yet gone to every corner of the land with banners flying and explained the benefits of cooperation. It was because the party had not yet pointed out why, in the era of socialism, the ancient truism that "a chicken feather can't fly up to heaven" is no longer true.

The poor want to remake their lives. The old system is dying. A new system is being born. Chicken feathers really are flying up to heaven. In the Soviet Union they have already got there. In China they've started their flight. Chicken feathers are going to soar up all over the world.

Many of our local party organizations did not give strong backing to the needy peasants. But we cannot put all the blame on them, because the higher authorities had not yet struck a mortal blow at opportunist thinking, nor made an overall plan for the promotion of cooperation, nor improved the leadership of the campaign on a nation-wide scale.

In 1955, we did these things, and in the space of a few months the situation changed completely. The people who had been standing on the sidelines came over, whole groups at a time, to take their stand with the cooperatives. . . .

In short, in the latter half of 1955, a fundamental change took place in the balance of power between classes in our country. Socialism made a mighty advance. Capitalism took a heavy fall.

From a Poor Man's Team to a Poor Man's Coop

The poor peasants of Nantsui village received land during the land reform, but because they had no money, because their soil was poor and because they were short of animals and implements, they still faced many difficulties. Trying to find a way out, in the autumn of 1950, Chang Huai-teh, Chang Huai-fu, and another poor peasant began swapping labor on some jobs and working together on others. In 1951, when the people's government called on the peasants to organize and increase output, they were the first to respond. They expanded their three-family unit to a seasonal mutual aid team of seven poor families. As a result of the team's efforts, their wheat yield that year rose from 100 catties a mou to 120.

In 1952 the team grew to eleven families (ten poor peasant families, one lower middle peasant family) and worked as a team all the year round. Although the team was now larger, it still did not have enough farm tools; it had only seven donkeys and four wheelbarrows. In the busy seasons, men had to drag the ploughs and harrows themselves; manure had to be carried by wheelbarrow or in baskets hung from shoulder poles, and the crops were brought from the fields in the same manner. Some of the well-to-do peasants in the village jeered and called the team "The Paupers' Brigade," "The Shoulder Pole Company," and "The Skinny Donkeys." Nevertheless, its members were able to do many things as a team which they had not been able to do working alone. There was no longer any question of weeds strangling the young plants, or flooded fields, or not being able to plant on time. Yields increased.

By friendly cooperation they were able to minimize or eliminate the effects of natural disasters and human misfortunes. That year, 1952, right in the middle of the spring planting, poor peasant Chang Kuang-li fell seriously ill. The whole team went to visit him. They helped him pay for a doctor and attended to all the work in his fields. So that he could rest with an easy mind, they hoed his seven mou of cotton three times, although the custom was to hoe only twice. . . .

In the winter of 1952, when the Communist Party was busy with a campaign to strengthen the party and to increase membership, Chang Kuang-li and a number of other enthusiastic poor peasants consulted the village party branch about the team becoming a cooperative. Chang Huai-teh, the team leader and secretary of the party branch, made several trips to two cooperatives in neighboring villages to learn how they worked. After the campaign to strengthen the party was concluded, the village branch put forward a plan that Chang Huai-teh's team should combine with another mutual aid team to form a coop.

They Kept Their Chins Up

When the coop was formed, some of the well-to-do peasants ridiculed it, saying, "They've less money than an egg has hair, yet they think they can run a coop. Can a chicken feather fly up to heaven?" The cooperative was just getting started, and it is true it came up against all sorts of problems. At the height of the spring planting only twelve of the eighteen families had enough to eat. Tsui Feng-lung, Chang Shou-sheng, and two other poor peasant families had to hire themselves out as farm hands. Any day they couldn't find work, that day their families had nothing to put in the cooking pot. Worse difficulties were encountered in production. Seven draft oxen were so weak from lack of fodder that if they fell, they couldn't get up. . . .

All that the members had been able to bring to the coop were a dilapidated old cart, two crude ploughs and four seeders—none of them all of a piece. There were no replacements for parts that were missing, and not even a whip to drive the ox. When they used the cart to haul coal, it was always breaking down, because the animals were weak and thin and the drivers didn't know their trade thoroughly. Middle peasants with carts were fed up having to help them out on the road, and finally refused to travel to the mine in company with the coop teamsters. At that time the coop was an isolated little island in the village.

But thanks to the firm leadership of the party branch (six of the seven Communists in the village had joined the coop), the members were determined to make a go of it. . . .

The coop members rallied together and solved their problems one by one. Some of them received loans or subsidies from the government, but they did not rely entirely on this; they helped one another in a spirit of class solidarity. When the family of the coop chairman had nothing to eat, the other members on their own initiative chipped in with three pecks of grain. When there wasn't enough grass to feed the animals, Communist Chang Kuang-li set an example by removing two broken window frames and two cross-beams from his house, selling them and giving the proceeds to the coop to buy fodder. The other members were so stirred that they too set about making their inanimate belongings serve their living possessions. Using Chang Kuang-li's "method," they raised ten-odd yuan—enough to solve the fodder problem temporarily. Later, the government loaned them 10,000 catties of cottonseed cake, which ended the fodder shortage for good. . . .

In this way the coop members not only got through spring— for them a time of empty bins and larders—but they also planted 120 mou of cotton on time and according to plan. By giving them a loan of 550 yuan, even before their wheat ripened, the government encouraged them to expand productive activities. They used the money to buy two mules and a cart. They became more enthusiastic about their work than ever.

"It's not going to be a poor man's coop much longer," said the people in the village.

The Result of the Contest

Not long after Prosperity Cooperative was formed, some of the relatively well-off middle peasants went into action. Tsui Chin-kao and eight other well-to-do middle peasant families plus two poor peasant families organized a mutual aid team (actually it was a cooperative disguised as a mutual aid team). They jeered openly at Prosperity Cooperative and secretly planned to compete with it. These middle peasants were confident that with the rich soil, good carts, good animals, and ready cash at their disposal, they could crush Prosperity Cooperative and strengthen their own position as leaders of the mutual aid team. But the result was that they lost the contest and Prosperity Coop won. The mutual aid team harvested an average of 95 catties of cotton per mou; their millet averaged 160. The coop's 103 mou of millet land gave a yield of 200 catties to the mou; its 118 mou of cotton fields gave a yield of 120 catties per mou on the alkaline-free land and 93 catties per mou as a combined average of the alkaline-free and the alkaline land together. The coop's millet yield was 40 catties a mou above that of the mutual aid team. . . .

How could a new coop, which was so poor, get such good results? First of all, because, led by the party branch, its members were frugal and worked hard. Some of them had been discouraged when they saw the mutual aid team's carts carrying load after load of fertilizer, bought at the supply and marketing coop. They were afraid Prosperity Cooperative was too poor to compete. But the village party branch encouraged them, urged them to use every available moment collecting natural fertilizer. They built three big privies which all the families in the coop agreed to use. They also got "fertilizer" by tearing down the compound walls and brick oven-beds of every member and making good use of the dirty earth thus obtained. In this way they were able to get enough good fertilizer at a very small cost.

Secondly, they responded to the call of the party and the government to improve methods of cultivation. . . .

What impressed people most was the coop's excellent millet harvest. It was obtained by sowing the improved "Huanung Number Four" seed on all 103 mou of the coop's millet fields and using the "single seed and close planting" method. The harvest was a record-breaker. . . .

Prosperity Cooperative achieved such a remarkable increase in production that more peasants wanted to join. The lives of the members took a turn for the better. Even peasants still outside the coop exclaimed:

"It's a poor man's coop no longer. That chicken feather is flying all over the sky!"

Twenty-six peasant families applied for admission. "If you don't let us join, we'll push our way in," cried some of the poor peasants and lower middle peasants.

And the mutual aid team? Not only did no one want to join it, but several of its original members dropped out. Two of them pleaded to be admitted to the coop.

From Small to Big, from Poor to Prosperous

Now that most of the peasants understood the advantages of cooperation, two more coops were formed in the village. The three coops had a total of sixty-four families—over 60 percent of the village's one hundred four households. Prosperity Cooperative increased its membership from eighteen families to thirty-five.

In 1954, its yields were also considerably greater than in

1953. The wheat output rose from 140 catties a mou to 158, millet from 200 to 212, cotton from 93 to 123.5. . . .

In the autumn of 1954, inspired by the achievements of Prosperity Cooperative and the fine results obtained by the coops in Kuowangtu and other villages where mechanized cultivation had been introduced, the three coops combined so as to be big enough to warrant the use of farming machinery. They also increased their membership by another twenty-four families. Except for fourteen families of former landlords, rich peasants, and two families under surveillance for criminal activities, everyone else in the village—including all the eighty-eight poor and middle peasant families—were now in the coop.

In the year that followed, the three-in-one coop operated on a large scale, using farming machinery, and planting in conformity with the national plan for their region (except for the 30-odd mou set aside for grain and a few vegetable plots, their whole 1,100 mou of arable land were planted entirely with cotton). As a result, their 1955 harvest promised to be even more striking than those of the two previous years. Four hundred and twenty mou of wheat fields have averaged 198 catties to the mou. Twenty-six mou sown and cultivated by machinery have brought in an average of 267 catties. . . .

Many poor members have become prosperous. Of the 35 original members of Prosperity Cooperative, at the time of the 1954 autumn harvest twenty-eight families had enough grain over and above what they needed as food for the coming year to be able to sell 3,000 catties to the government. That year they banked 1,500 yuan in the credit cooperative. According to preliminary estimates for 1955, only seven families—widows, old folks and invalids and the family of one man who works on the administrative staff of the township office—will earn less than they did in 1954, though they will still have enough to live on comfortably. All the other 81 families in the enlarged coop will earn more. Chang Shou-sheng, who used to be the poorest member of the coop, had a surplus of 80 yuan in 1954. In 1955 he and his wife earned 445 yuan.

Why was the coop able to continuously increase its output, to grow from small to large, from poor to prosperous, from weak to strong? Because the party branch in Nantsui village firmly carried out the party's class policy in the rural cooperative movement. Following the lead of Prosperity Cooperative, peasants throughout the township formed fourteen more coops. Prosperity Cooperative's chairman and accountant became leader and chief accountant respectively of the network of coops in the townships of Chentsunying and Taochiaying. Prosperity Cooperative has become a model for peasants in all the surrounding townships and a standard-bearer in the forefront of the cooperative movement.

5. THE NATIONAL PROGRAM
FOR AGRICULTURAL DEVELOPMENT, 1956-1967

The first five-year plan and official policy prior to the socialist upsurge in the countryside were preoccupied with an urban and industrial conception of the new China. It was not until promulgation of the National Program in January 1956 that China's peasantry was presented with an overarching vision and concrete strategy for achieving a full range of economic, social, political, educational, and cultural goals through the self-reliant development of new institutions, educational and technological programs, and, in the most fundamental sense, transformation of the natural environment. The foundation of this program and its experiential base, were the cooperatives whose dramatic expansion from the fall of 1955 opened new prospects for expanding labor utilization and agricultural and sideline production. Here is a vision of the countryside of the future, whose flourishing cooperative economy provides the basis for dramatic expansion of education, health, welfare, and culture. In it we see too the first clear suggestion that China's future did not necessarily lie in the cement and steel of the megalopolis. Yet the program quickly became embroiled in struggles over rural policy within the party and was effectively suppressed until

Political Bureau of the Central Committee, January 23, 1956. *The Draft National Program for Agricultural Development 1956-1967* (Peking: Foreign Languages Press, 1956).

*1958. The document, drafted by Mao in cooperation with rural
activists and cadres, contains in embryo important features of
the Great Leap Forward which would emerge full-blown two
years later.*

The great tide of agricultural cooperation that has swept
China is bringing forth an immense, nation-wide growth of
agricultural production, and this in turn is stimulating the
development of the whole national economy and all branches of
science, culture, education and public health.

To give the leading party and government bodies at all levels
and the people of China, particularly the peasants, a long-term
program of agricultural development, the Political Bureau of the
Central Committee of the Chinese Communist Party, after consulting comrades holding responsible positions on party committees in the provinces, municipalities and autonomous
regions, has drawn up a draft national program outlining the
scale of agricultural development during the period from 1956
to 1967 (the last year of the third five-year plan). . . .

(1) Seeing that in 1955 more than 60 percent of all peasant
households were in agricultural producers' cooperatives, all
provinces, municipalities and autonomous regions should, in the
main, complete agricultural cooperation in its elementary form
and set themselves the goal of getting about 85 percent of all
peasant households into agricultural producers' cooperatives in
1956.

(2) Areas where cooperation is on better foundations and
where a number of cooperatives of advanced form are already
functioning should, in the main, complete the change-over to
cooperation of advanced form by 1957. . . .

In going forward to the advanced form of cooperation certain
conditions must be observed: the change must be of the free
will and choice of the members; the cooperative must have
people capable of giving proper leadership; and it must be
possible for over 90 percent of the members to earn more after
the change.

(3) Every agricultural producers' cooperative must make
suitable arrangements to see that those of its members who lack

manpower, are widows or widowers, who have no close relations to depend on, or who are disabled ex-service men, are given productive work, and a livelihood. . . .

(4) During 1956 attempts should be made to settle the question of admitting to the cooperatives former landlords and rich peasants who have given up exploitation and who have asked to join. . . .

(5) Counter-revolutionaries in the rural areas should be dealt with as follows: (a) Those who have committed sabotage or had committed other serious crimes in the past, and against whom there is great public feeling, should be put under arrest and dealt with in accordance with law. (b) Those who committed crimes which were commonplace in the past, but have not committed sabotage since liberation, and against whom public feeling is not great, should be allowed by the *hsiang* people's council to work in the cooperative under supervision, to be reformed by work. (c) Those who have committed minor crimes and since made amends, those who have served their sentence, been released and behaved well, and those who committed crimes but did deserving work in the campaign to suppress counter-revolutionaries, may be allowed to join the cooperative. . . . In no case, however, whether they are admitted as members or not, must they be allowed to take on important posts in the cooperative for a specified time after joining. . . .

(6) In the twelve years starting with 1956, in areas north of the Yellow River, the Ch'in Ling Mountains, the River Pailung, and the Yellow River in Ch'ing Hai province, the average annual yield of grain should be raised from the 1955 figure of over 150 catties to the mou to 400 catties. South of the Yellow River and north of the Huai the yield should be raised from the 1955 figure of 208 catties to 500 catties. South of the Huai, the Ch'in Ling Mountains and the River Pailung it should rise from the 1955 figure of 400 catties to 800 catties per mou.

In the same twelve years the average annual yield of ginned cotton should be raised from the 1955 figure of 35 catties to the mou (the average for the whole of China) to 60, 80 or 100 catties depending on local conditions. . . .

Agricultural producers' cooperatives should encourage their members to grow vegetables on their own private plots by way of improving their standard of living. . . .

(7) All agricultural producers' cooperatives, besides producing enough food for their own consumption and to meet the requirements of the state, should, within twelve years starting from 1956, store enough grain for emergency use for a year, a year and one-half, or two years, according to local conditions. . . .

(8) Livestock breeding should be encouraged. . . .

(9) There are two main ways of increasing the yield of crops: taking steps to increase production, and imparting better techniques.

(A) The chief steps to increase production are: (a) water conservancy projects and water and soil conservation; (b) use of improved farm tools, and gradual introduction of mechanized farming; (c) efforts to discover every possible source of manure and improved methods of fertilizing; (d) extension of the use of the best and most suitable strains; (e) soil improvement; (f) extension of multiple cropping areas; (g) planting more high-yielding crops; (h) improving farming methods; (i) wiping out insect pests and plant diseases; and (j) opening up virgin and idle land and extending cultivated areas.

(B) The chief steps to impart better techniques include the following: (a) provinces, municipalities, and autonomous regions should collect data on the experience of the best cooperatives in their own areas in increasing yields, compile and publish at least one book a year, so as to spread this knowledge as widely and rapidly as possible; (b) agricultural exhibitions; (c) conferences of model peasants called at regular intervals by provinces (municipalities or autonomous regions), administrative regions (autonomous *chou*), counties (autonomous counties), districts, *hsiang* (nationality *hsiang*), with awards and citations to peasants who distinguish themselves in increasing production; (d) visits and emulation campaigns, the exchange of experience; and (e) imparting technical knowledge and encouraging peasants and cadres to take an active part in learning better techniques. . . .

(20) Expansion of state farms. The area cultivated by state farms should be increased in the twelve years starting 1956 from the 1955 figure of 13,360,000 mou to 140 million mou. . . .

(21) In the twelve years starting 1956 we must clothe every

possible bit of denuded wasteland and mountains with greenery. . . .

(22) Energetic steps should be taken to raise the output of marine products and develop fresh-water fisheries. . . .

(23) If agriculture, forestry, livestock breeding, subsidiary rural production, and fisheries are to develop to the full, if the national wealth and the income of the peasants are to grow, cooperatives must make fuller use of manpower and raise labor productivity. In the seven years beginning with 1956, every able-bodied man in the countryside ought to be able to put in at least 250 working days a year. Serious efforts should be made to draw women into the work of agricultural and subsidiary production. Within seven years, every able-bodied woman in the countryside should, besides the time she spends on household work, be able to give at least 120 working days a year to productive work. . . .

(25) Improve housing conditions. . . .

(26) In seven or twelve years from 1956 determined efforts should be made to virtually wipe out wherever possible all diseases from which the people suffer most seriously, such as schistosomiasis, filariasis, hookworm, kala-azar, encephalitis, bubonic plague, malaria, smallpox, and venereal diseases. . . .

To this end every effort should be made to train medical workers and gradually set up health and medical services in counties and districts, and clinics in villages.

(27) Wipe out the "four evils." In five, seven, or twelve years beginning 1956 we should practically wipe out the "four evils" —rats, sparrows, flies and mosquitoes—wherever possible.

(28) We should improve our research in agricultural science, provide better technical guidance for agriculture and train in a planned way large numbers of people to handle the technical side of agriculture. . . . In the twelve years from 1956 agricultural departments at all levels should, to meet the needs of cooperative economy, between them be responsible for training five to six million experts of primary and intermediate grades for technical work in agriculture, forestry, water conservancy, livestock breeding, veterinary work, farm management, and accounting for agricultural producers' cooperatives.

(29) In five or seven years from 1956, dependent on the situation locally, we must virtually wipe out illiteracy. The

minimum standard of literacy must be 1,500 characters. In every *hsiang* we should have part-time schools to raise the educational standard of our cadres and the peasants. In the next seven or twelve years, again depending on the local situation, we should extend to all rural areas compulsory elementary education. Primary schools in the countryside should mostly be run by agricultural producers' cooperatives. In seven or twelve years, too, we should establish in the rural areas a wide network of film projection teams, clubs, institutes, libraries, amateur dramatic groups and other bodies for education and recreation. In the next seven to twelve years, every *hsiang* should have a sports field and sport should be a common sight in the countryside.

(30) Starting from 1956 we shall, in the next seven to twelve years, depending on local circumstances, extend the radio diffusion network to all rural areas. . . .

(32) In a matter of five, seven, or twelve years, starting from 1956, depending on differing local conditions, the whole countryside must be provided with networks of roads. . . .

(36) In 1957 there must be a rural credit cooperative in practically every *hsiang* to provide credit and encourage saving.

(37) Protection of women and children. The principle of equal pay for equal work must be rigidly adhered to wherever women do productive work. During busy times of the year on the farms agricultural producers' cooperatives should run crèches. When work is given out the health and physique of women members must be taken into consideration.

Organizations concerned with health should train midwives for the rural areas, do all they can to see that modern methods of delivering babies are used, provide postnatal care and take steps to cut down the incidence of maternal diseases and the infant mortality rate. . . .

(38) The young people in the rural areas should become the spearhead, the shock force in productive, scientific, and cultural work in the countryside. . . .

(40) Workers in the cities and peasants in the cooperatives must give each other every support. The workers must turn out more and better industrial goods which the peasants need, and the peasants must grow more and better grain and industrial raw materials which industry and town-dwellers need.

6. CH'EN YUNG-KUEI,
THE FORMATION OF ADVANCED COOPERATIVES
AND THE TWO-LINE STRUGGLE AT TACHAI

"Moving to the stage of advanced cooperation was a much sharper struggle than going from mutual aid to elementary cooperation." Ch'en Yung-kuei, peasant leader of the pacesetting Tachai Brigade in the rugged Taihang Mountains of Shansi, in an interview with American writer William Hinton, provides a lively personal account of the clashes in one village— since 1964 the national model for agricultural development. From land reform through stages of mutual aid and on to higher levels of cooperation, the prosperous—many of whom were rich or upper middle peasants in the old society—resorted to speculation, bribery, and the power of wealth and influence to protect their still privileged positions within villages which had eliminated the sharpest inequalities. At each stage contradictions within the cooperatives led the majority of poor and lower middle peasants, and the party leadership, to grasp the necessity for higher levels of cooperation and help to implement them. The twists and turns described here illustrate concretely aspects of the ongoing class struggle and the role of the party leadership at the grassroots level.

The step to advanced cooperatives wrought changes which were in certain respects more profoundly revolutionary than the land reform itself. Though carried out more swiftly and with little physical violence, the transition which occurred throughout most of rural China in a matter of months in 1956 severed the age-old link between ownership of land and means of production on the one hand and income on the other. For with the formation of advanced cooperatives, income distribution came to rest exclusively on inputs of labor to the cooperative. Vestiges of privilege were swept aside. Inequalities based on differences in individual labor contribution of course remained, but with advanced cooperatives the countryside successfully realized the socialist principle "to each according to one's work."

From a 1971 interview with William Hinton in *New China*, Fall 1977.

We will return to the Tachai experience throughout this text as an example of a widely projected model for transforming the countryside for over a decade.

In 1946, right after the landlords were overthrown, we thought there wouldn't be any more class struggle. For a while they didn't dare attack us openly, but then they started in again. In 1957 a landlord tried to slander me. He said that I wanted the brigade to sell more grain to the state so that I could get something out of it for myself. He said that I wanted to eat white flour [the refined food supplied to delegates at area-wide or higher level meetings], that I wanted to please the state in order to win favor. And that was only the beginning. So we have to realize that just because a landlord has no more land is no reason to think he won't struggle. He is still thinking, "Why have I lost my land? Why am I not rich anymore?" The more he thinks about this the more he attacks.

In the years between 1953 and 1956, landlords, rich peasants, and some ordinary peasants thought they would get rich fast by doing something other than working the land. To do that they had to go into trade and try their hand at speculation. A person could buy cotton in Hopei province and sell it in Shansi province, then buy other things in Shansi and sell them in Hopei. The rich peasants led the way in this, the rich peasants and the landlords. They had done a lot of trading before the land reform. They didn't like working hard in the fields. They were always pushing for a chance to go out and do a little trading instead. Some party members supported them in this. At that time, though I didn't think it was a very good idea, I didn't resist it as I should have.

Who Is Leading Whom?

One of the rich peasants from Tachai set up a trading station in Hsingt'ai county, Hopei. He collected merchandise there, then brought it into Shansi by donkey. When he had collected enough material for a shipment he would call up the village and we would send men and donkeys to haul it back. Once we sent six men and twelve donkeys. The poor peasant Chia Jui-shen

and I were in charge. In the morning early when we arrived in
Hsingt'ai, the sun was already well up. But the rich peasant was
still fast asleep in the local inn. We had traveled all night and
now the sun was high in the sky, but this rich peasant was still
snoring away.

Chia knocked on the door, *ka tsa, ka tsa,* over and over again.
And he called out, *"san ye ye, san ye ye."* [They shared the
same family name so the poor peasant called him "third Grand-
father"—a very respectful term.] He called and knocked for
more than ten minutes before that bastard woke up and opened
the door.

I felt terrible. Here landlords and rich peasants sleep while
poor peasants stand outside calling *"san ye ye."* This is the way
it was before liberation. How come such a thing is happening
now?

The rich peasant finally opened the door and we went in.
What a sight! There he was sleeping under a silk quilt on a heavy
felt mat. And the room was very fancy indeed. When we saw
this we really felt angry. We were disgusted. Here he was, even
more comfortable than before liberation, and we had walked
the rough road all night. I thought to myself, "Who, after all, is
leading whom?"

We loaded the donkeys and hauled the cotton back to Shansi.
We hauled it back to the trading coop in our village. Each
donkey could carry 20 catties so all together we brought back
about 1,500 catties of cotton. No sooner did we pile the cotton
in the coop yard then a group of members began to blow water
on it to make it heavier. Next day some forty people went out
to peddle it from door to door. Lots of people went in for this.
Each family had its own scale. They went down the mountain
to sell cotton. They exchanged the cotton for melon seeds, then
took the melon seeds down to Hopei to sell. The idea was to get
the proper amount of melon seeds first, and put them in your
pocket, then hand over the cotton and leave. The buyer
squeezes the cotton and finds water in it. He yells but it is too
late. You're gone.

I thought "Why should all this be going on now?"

I didn't know any theory that said peasants neglecting farming and going in for trade was the wrong line. But I thought,
"We are farmers, we work on the land. Why go in for all this?

Are we peasants, or workers, or merchants? What are we, after all, that we do all this?"

In those years there were four famous things in these parts: (1) Chingshihpo's drama group; (2) Wuchiap'ing's village quarrels; (3) Liuchuang's big Buddhist temple; and (4) Tachai's trading, otherwise known as "production."

I'm talking about the years from 1952 to 1956.

As for Chingshihpo's drama group, it brought all the old empresses onto the stage. A girl who played *lao dan* [female] roles was famous throughout the region for the way she portrayed the old lady empress. She still lives in the village. Everyone came from miles around to see those old plays.

As for Wuchiap'ing's quarrels, this was a village with three clans—the Kuo clan, the Li clan, and the Wu clan. They never stopped quarreling. At the big temple in Liuchuang, ceremonies were held every day. People went there to light incense. A group of monks was always on hand. It was a thriving temple.

That leaves Tachai. After land reform, the dispossessed landlords and rich peasants all went in for trading. They were getting along fine. They were getting richer all the time and Tachai was becoming famous as the center of their buying and selling. What was going on was a real *fup'i* [restoration]. The wind of restoration was blowing hard from all sides. Ex-landlords and rich peasants in Tachai began to buy land with their profits while poor peasants began to sell. Chia Jui-shen had to sell his land in 1952. . . .

The Weasel and the Chicken

By 1956 we began to be conscious of the fact that all these ambitious side occupations, all this trading and blackmarketeering were wrong. We decided to settle accounts for all this. The ex-landlords and rich peasants were wearing fancy clothes, celebrating festivals, inviting cadres to come and eat and sending them presents. We saw all this going on and we woke up. We sent ten militiamen through Honan and Hopei to collect the ex-landlords and bring them back to the village. We said, "Look what you've been doing, mixing us up all these years." But once we called them back, they started trying to buy off the cadres. They sent presents to everyone. Some of the cadres didn't dare take presents. Some dared take a little, but not a lot. And some reported to the party branch. So in the branch we made a decision. Everyone was instructed to accept all the gifts that were offered. The ex-landlords and rich peasants sent gift after gift, until they finally got tired of it and then they didn't send us any more gifts.

As soon as they stopped sending gifts we started our counter-offensive. We took all the gifts to a mass meeting. At the meeting we exposed what was happening. We said they were like a weasel saying happy new year to a chicken—these people giving away all these things! The masses were very angry. Class struggle started then and there. How could the masses let such things continue? We didn't have to do anything more. The people were aroused. They praised us for what we had done. They said, "Our cadres are not corrupted by sugar-coated bullets fired by class enemies. They don't dance to any outside baton."

After this big repudiation we kept all these people in the village. We let them work and reform themselves through manual labor. We didn't let them run free anymore. From that day unto this we haven't let a single one go out of the village to live. We made them behave themselves. Their buying-off methods didn't work. When they saw that soft methods were no use they started getting out their knives. One said to me, "You say I am a big landlord, but you are the biggest landlord of them all." And he threatened me with his knife.

From 1950 to 1957 we struggled with the *ti, fu, fan, huai* [ex-landlords, rich peasants, counter-revolutionaries, and bad elements]. It was continuous struggle from top to bottom, from the elementary coops to the advanced coops, inside the party and outside it, down among the rank and file, and up top among the leaders. The lessons we learned were very deep. They raised people's consciousness of class struggle and line struggle.

Land Shares versus Labor Shares

The struggle was very sharp when we moved to the advanced coop stage. Going from mutual aid to cooperation was a struggle but this was not so tense as when we moved to the higher coop.

We organized our first cooperative in 1953. At this stage of elementary cooperation people got an income based in part on how much land and other property they had pooled. Say they put in 20 mou of land, how much could it produce? We had to estimate not only the amount but the quality of the land and decide what their land share of the crop should be. And the same went for other property such as tools and animals. We recorded how many days their animals were used. We figured out the depreciation of the tools. After all these costs were deducted and paid out, the balance of the crop was divided on the basis of work done. Sometimes there wasn't much left for work points.

So the poor and lower middle peasants had complaints. They said, "We were exploited before and now we are still exploited." It was mainly those poor families who had put in less land and loaned out few animals or tools who felt exploited. Those who put in a lot of land and still owned means of production were getting rich. Those families who put in less got most of their income from work points, but those who put in more got half or more of their income from property payments. This was indeed a form of exploitation. Those who were exploited complained that they worked all year in the coop only to end up with nothing. "We are like a stalk of kaoliang," they said. "Peel off the hard outer layer and there's nothing but pith inside." They worried all the time. In contrast, those with large land shares and other productive property had an iron rice bowl that could not be broken. They had a guaranteed income.

When we first formed the elementary coop we tried to have every family report on the productivity of their land. Most people exaggerated the figures so that they could receive more as their property share. All these false reports of what the land could produce added up to a lot more than any crop that could be harvested. People reported 400 to 500 catties per mou on land that produced 200. Years later, with the high yields that our advanced coop produced, such land rarely yielded 400 catties.

So what could we do? We held democratic discussion. We asked, "Why is your real production so low? Is it because you exaggerated the figures?" In these meetings each person said what his land would produce. Then everyone discussed the figure. If it seemed out of line, the estimate was lowered. Land shares were supposed to be determined by what the people decided. But some people would not agree to this. They insisted on their own figures.

In order to solve this problem we asked party members and cadres to take the lead in giving honest estimates. Did party members ever exaggerate their estimates? Yes. Some did to a certain extent. But those who thought collectively, and had concern for people, reported things as they really were.

With them we went further and asked that they cut down the figures even more so that we could increase the amount of grain distributed as work points and decrease the amount distributed on the basis of land shares.

We had a struggle inside the party over cutting down the land shares. I fought it over with Chia Ch'en-jung, our accountant. In the course of the argument I slapped the table more than once. In my mutual aid team they all knew how much my land would produce—32 tan. The children and the old men came up with this figure and it was down in the account book. My land was good for 32 tan—this was not one bit false. But in order to lead I wanted to cut it even lower. I wanted to cut it to 18 tan. Chia Ch'en-jung wouldn't agree. He said the original figure was accurate. It was reported by others. So I said, "Give me the writing brush and I'll change it myself." He said no individual can change the accounts by himself. "If you do this you will be making a big mistake."

I told him, "This is not a matter of making a mistake. I'm not adding to the figure, I'm cutting it back. The only reason you don't want me to lower mine is because you are afraid you will be forced to lower yours!" So I took the brush and changed the account book to read 18 tan. Then Chia Ch'en-jung cut his yield figure back too. Many other party members did the same.

But there were some slick ones who wouldn't do it. If the party members can't take the lead, how can the masses be expected to cut back their land shares? One person who really harvested only 20 tan insisted that his land could produce 45. With such an estimate for the land and with his earnings from animals and tools added in, he got so much grain at the end of the year that his jars were full, his *k'ang* [sleeping platform] was covered, and there was grain all over the floor.

On the other hand, Chia Chang-yuan, a poor peasant, worked hard but in the end didn't get enough from his labor to feed his family of five. Chia was dissatisfied. But so was this other man. Why? Because, he said, he had no freedom. As a member of the coop he didn't feel free to do what he pleased. He said his land was good and all that grain came from his land. He thought if he hadn't joined the coop he might have reaped even more of a harvest.

So both families were dissatisfied. Which one was right? Of course the poor peasant was right. He worked all day, every day and never missed a day all year. He was exploited by the middle peasant who had more land and draft animals. When this poor peasant complained that he was getting very little after working so hard all year long, we cadres agreed with him. We felt the same way. Those of us who had cut back our property share worked hard every day like he did but couldn't get much at the end of the year either. It was hard for us to survive.

So we discussed what to do about this problem. We decided to move into an advanced coop where income comes only from the labor contributed. We decided to get rid of income derived from property and go to division based on labor. Having decided this, the land question was easy to solve because we had already pooled all the land. But the animals had to be bought from their owners and so did the implements and tools. And so another struggle arose.

With These Communists, You Never Can Tell

We had quite a battle over the price that our collective should pay for the draft animals. A directive from higher level leaders about how to form a higher stage coop said that draft animals should not be appraised at below market price and the same went for tools. As for tools, only those that were needed should be bought. Full payment was to be made within three to five years. We formed a committee to decide on the prices. The committee called an appraiser from the county market to come and help set standards. Once the prices were fixed, some people began to waver. It wasn't the ex-landlords and rich peasants. They didn't have any animals left after land reform. It was the upper middle peasants who had draft animals. They thought the prices were too low. They went to the collective yard and took their animals home. All our price setting went for nothing.

What were these animal owners really worried about? It was the three- to five-year payment schedule. They wondered if they ever would get paid. Those who worried the most tried to sell their animals on the market but found they couldn't get any better price than the coop offered.

I had a sow. In order to consolidate the coop, I turned the sow over to it. This sow was bred and about to farrow. The appraised price was 120 yuan. I asked only 60 yuan. Three days after the appraisal was made, the sow farrowed. She gave birth to twelve pigs. Two died, leaving ten. They were worth 10 yuan apiece, or another 60 yuan. But I stuck to my original offer. Many people said I was crazy. The appraised price was set through consultation according to the system we all agreed upon. . . .

I felt a responsibility toward the coop. Somebody had to take the lead. If no one took the lead, then nothing could be done. All this bickering made me angry. I thought, "Even if I get nothing at all for the things I contribute to the coop, I'm still much better off than before." This had to do with my history. Before liberation I had nothing to my name except my two hands and my mouth. I had no land, no animals, no tools. The only *ti* [land] that I had was *hsieh ti* [the soles of my shoes]. So I didn't feel that I was losing out. Even if I didn't get a cent I was still much better off than before. I made up my mind to support collective thinking.

As you can see, moving to the stage of advanced cooperation was a much sharper struggle than going from mutual aid to elementary cooperation. Step by step we advanced. Later I saw the fight for the advanced coop as a fight to wage revolution against capitalist thinking. We had to cut the umbilical cord of bourgeois thought. The upper middle peasants said, "Before, we depended on land ownership to eat. Now this rice bowl is smashed and we have to depend on our labor alone. We leaned on our land shares, on the earnings of our draft animals. We fought over the returns from both and glared at each other. Depending on labor as we do now is the only thing that is really secure."

This showed that the upper middle peasants had a dual

character. They tended to take the capitalist road but they could be led forward on the socialist road. And through these struggles we learned what the capitalist road was and what the socialist road was.

7. THE SLAVES' CHARTER

China did not universally abolish slavery until the abortive 1959 rebellion by the Dalai Lama in Tibet led to the intensification of struggle in the minority areas. However, by the mid-1950s, with varying rates of speed and taking different forms, class struggle made itself felt in the minority regions. In Yunnan province in the Southwest, an area of many nationalities, the Norsu people maintained a slave society into the mid-1950s. Increasingly frictions arose as policies designed to stimulate production clashed with a slave system which both fettered the productive forces and deprived a substantial portion of the Norsu people of their humanity.

Finally, in the summer of 1956, momentum gathered for abolition of the slave system through peaceful reform emphasizing the education and mobilization of the slaves. A movement unfolded to isolate the "slave-owners," a maximum of 5 percent of the population, while ensuring that they, like the working people, would also have their livelihood ensured.

What then was a slave-owner? As defined in the supplementary regulations to the Slaves' Charter, slave-owners were those who engaged in little or no productive labor, owned ten slaves or more (as a household), owned ten acres of land (per person) and derived 70 percent or more of their income from exploiting the labor of others. These guidelines made it possible to peacefully liberate all the slaves by isolating and struggling against the most powerful slave-owners and providing incentives for others to support the democratic reform. The regulations given here

Measures Adopted by the People's Congress of the Norsu Autonomous County of Ninglang, Yunnan Province for Democratic Reform by Peaceful Negotiation, 1956. In: Alan Winnington, *The Slaves of the Cool Mountains* (London: Lawrence and Wishart, 1959).

reflect the painstaking attention to the diversity of local condi-
tions and customs required for breaking the back of feudal and
slave institutions in the minority regions, and the effort to
complete the transition and land distribution peacefully. The
Norsu experience illustrates, too, the diversity of social, eco-
nomic, and political systems of fifty-five nationalities which
comprise the Chinese nation.

The purpose is to: develop production, consolidate the unity
of the nationalities, develop political, economic and cultural
establishments, improve living conditions in the Norsu areas,
and gradually achieve the transition to socialism.

Section 1: General Principles

Article 1. The slave system is to be abolished. The slaves,
bondsmen, and great mass of working people are to be liberated.
Personal liberty and political equality are to be guaranteed.

These steps are needed to set free the productive power of
the people, gradually improve the living conditions, develop
mutual aid and cooperation, and create the conditions necessary
for the gradual transition to socialism.

Democratic reform by peaceful negotiation is in the interests
of all classes of the working people. Persistence, patience and
education are therefore needed to ensure the unity of the public
leaders. The method of peaceful negotiation from above must
be adhered to. There must be no resort to beatings, struggle or
killing, no arrests other than of persons who commit crimes at
the present time. United efforts may thus be brought to bear on
the enormous task of carrying through the democratic reform.

Section 2: Liberation of the Slaves and
Settlement of the Various Classes

Article 2. The slave system is to be abolished, the slaves freed
and personal liberty and political equality are to be guaranteed.
The system of land monopoly by the slave-owners is to be
abolished and land ownership by those who till substituted.

Arrears in rents and privilege dues dating from before the

reform are to be cancelled without exception. The system of special privileges pertaining to the slave system, together with slave-owners' usury, is to be abolished.

Article 3. In areas where the reform has not yet taken place it is prohibited to kill, maltreat, abduct, sell, or give slaves in dowry.

Article 4. During the reform, the houses, cattle, farming implements, food stocks, ingot silver, and other money belonging to the slave-owners are to be preserved intact.

In cases where the livelihood of slave-owners is reduced as a result of the reform, the government is to take appropriate measures to make up the deficiency.

Article 5. In the case of those persons who work and also possess slaves—some 30 percent of the total families—it is necessary to give them patient explanations as to their actual losses and gains resulting from the reform.

If any are short of labor as a result of the release of the slaves, the government shall make an appropriate settlement so as to maintain their living conditions and enhance their inclination to support the reform.

Article 6. Liberated slaves have low productive power. Patient education, careful arrangements, and a long period of nurturing in work are therefore necessary after their living conditions have been settled.

(a) The authorities shall give adequate help to freed slaves and bondsmen who have difficulty in making a living.

(b) When house slaves are freed they are to take nothing from their owner's house except articles owned by themselves. Means to enable them to produce and live better than before are to be arranged entirely by the authorities.

(c) In arranging the means for house slaves to produce and live better, attention must be paid to the following:

Those with homes should be helped to return to them;

Those who have parents, husbands, wives, brothers, sisters or other kin should be helped to rejoin them;

Those without home or kin should be encouraged to join with others on a voluntary basis to produce a living.

Article 7. Regardless of class, those who are too old to work will be taken care of by the government for life.

Juveniles are to be looked after until they are able to live independently. . . .

Section 3: Differentiation of Classes

Article 8. When differentiating classes during the reform, the only distinction required is that between slave-owners and working people. No further distinction need be made between slaves, bondsmen, and working people.

Article 9. Slave-owners should not exceed 5 percent of the total households. This accords with the spirit of the decisions of the state council concerning the class differentiation of the peasantry, and takes into account the actual conditions in this county, the number of slaves owned, area of land occupied, whether or not labor is performed, the degree of exploitation, and so on. These actual facts should form the data for analysis to achieve a fundamentally satisfactory demarcation.

Article 10. In differentiating classes, data should be carefully gathered so that negotiations may be thorough. Results of the negotiations should be sent to the Rural District People's Congress for approval. . . .

Section 4: Confiscation and Distribution of Land

Article 11. Land owned by the slave-owner is to be confiscated and distributed to those who work. Slave-owners, including those who oppose the reform, shall receive an equal share.

Article 12. The principles of land distribution:

(a) Taking the rural district as a unit, productive capacity should be appraised and land distributed on the basis of what land is actually under cultivation each year.

(b) Generally no change should be made in the landholdings of working people if the land requirements of those with no land or inadequate land can otherwise be satisfied. If a change is necessary it may be only on the principle of not reducing the income of the original holder and only with county approval.

(c) The land should be distributed on an individual basis. A single person should get two shares and a household with two persons three shares.

(d) Those who have sacrificed their lives in the revolution, members of the militia and persons working in public office should be included in the census for land distribution—each to receive one share.

(e) Mountain forests and pasture land are to be devoted to

public use after confiscation and will not be distributed or used as arable.

(f) All customs and religious beliefs of the nationalities must be respected, cemeteries and cremation grounds preserved, and orchards, etc., protected.

(g) Land that will be needed for communications and construction should be set aside at the time of the distribution on the understanding that it may be used until it is needed.

Article 13. Certain matters concerning slave-owners that arise during the distribution shall be dealt with as follows:

(a) In negotiating the compulsory sale of excess draft cattle from slave-owners, the price must be just and reasonable. There must be no forcing down of prices.

(b) To protect the herds and encourage the development of cattle breeding, existing agreements under which cattle are tended should remain valid. Flocks of sheep are to be protected and no dispersal allowed. Herdsmen who were formerly the property of the slave-owners should remain herdsmen if they are willing, being paid wages and having political equality. If slave-owners find difficulty in paying such wages they shall be paid by the authorities.

(c) Firearms owned by slave-owners should be delivered to the authorities in negotiations conducted by special representatives of the county. Compensation will be paid.

(d) In special cases where slave-owners have a labor-deficient family, they should be permitted to hire wage-labor so long as this is done with the free will of the persons concerned.

Article 14. Certain matters that arise concerning working people during the distribution shall be dealt with as follows:

(a) Existing landholding agreements of the working people remain unaltered. Any anomalies should be settled by negotiations in a spirit of unity and for mutual benefit. During the distribution no land may be disposed of as gifts.

(b) Debts outstanding to working people shall not be cancelled.

(c) Firearms possessed by working people shall be assigned for use by the militia.

(d) Working people deficient in labor power may hire labor or invite people to join their households on an equal footing to work and eat together with them.

III

THE GREAT LEAP FORWARD
1958-1959

A. STRIKE WHILE THE IRON IS HOT: THE GREAT LEAP VISION AND THE TRANSFORMATION OF THE COUNTRYSIDE

1. MAO TSETUNG, THE VISION OF THE GREAT LEAP

In 1958 China broke sharply with certain development principles of the first five-year plan and embarked on a new path, the Great Leap Forward. As in the 1955 socialist upsurge, it was Mao who grasped the significance of new currents emerging in farms and factories throughout the country to fashion an overall vision and revolutionary philosophy of development. During the first plan period China achieved impressive successes, notably smooth transition from private to state and collective ownership in agriculture, industry, and commerce, and the establishment of the foundations of a heavy industrial base. But the plan also exacerbated critical contradictions: between industry and agriculture, city and countryside, bureaucratic and mobilization politics, centralization and decentralization, uncritical application of Soviet methods and the desire for self-reliance. By 1957, it was apparent that unless swift steps were taken to reverse growing sectoral and regional imbalances between industry and agriculture and between city and countryside, the success of the socialist development program would be jeopardized. The central position of agriculture in China's economy meant that lagging agricultural growth, reaching near crisis proportions in 1957, threatened industrial and overall

Speech at the Supreme State Conference, January 18, 1958. In: Stuart Schram, ed., *Chairman Mao Talks to the People* (New York: Pantheon, 1974).

development prospects. *Moreover, disparities in living standards and employment opportunities between city and countryside, and the rising power and prestige of managers and technicians, stood in direct conflict with the egalitarian ideals of the revolution.*

The Great Leap Forward initiated a conscious break with important elements of the Soviet-inspired first plan strategy. Lessons of Yenan, self-reliance, decentralized planning, cooperation and mass participation, would be updated and applied to accelerate the pace of socialist development and technological advance. "In making revolution," Mao insisted, "one must strike while the iron is hot—one revolution must follow another, the revolution must continually advance."

Uninterrupted revolution, relying on a mobilized people would shape not only the political front but technology as well. It is often forgotten that the leap was designed to promote major technical advances. The slogan "Catch up with Great Britain in Fifteen Years" required a technical revolution. The leap promoted the qualities of "red and expert," political as well as technical competence. Suddenly, talk of the transition to communism was in the air, a transition which would require major advances in social relations to overcome inequalities and sustained technical progress to spur economic development.

A. Speech at the Supreme State Conference

Now our enthusiasm has been aroused. Ours is an ardent nation, now swept by a burning tide. There is a good metaphor for this: our nation is like an atom. . . . When this atom's nucleus is smashed the thermal energy released will have really tremendous power. We shall be able to do things which we could not do before. When our nation has this great energy we shall catch up with Britain in fifteen years; we shall produce forty million tons of steel annually—now we produce only just over five million tons; we shall have a generating capacity of 450,000 million kwh of electricity—at present we can generate only 40,000 million kwh, which means increasing our capacity ten times, for which we must increase hydroelectric production and not only thermoelectric. We still have ten years to carry out the

Forty Point Program for Agricultural Development, but it looks as if we shall not need ten years. Some people say five years, others three. It would seem that we can complete it in eight. . . . I stand for the theory of permanent revolution. Do not mistake this for Trotsky's theory of permanent revolution. In making revolution one must strike while the iron is hot—one revolution must follow another, the revolution must continually advance. The Hunanese often say, 'Straw sandals have no pattern—they shape themselves in the making.' Trotsky believed that the socialist revolution should be launched even before the democratic revolution is complete. We are not like that. For example, after the liberation of 1949 came the land reform; as soon as this was completed there followed the mutual aid teams, then the low-level cooperatives, then the high-level co-operatives. After seven years the cooperativization was completed and productive relationships were transformed; then came the rectification. After rectification was finished, before things had cooled down, then came the technical revolution. . . .

It is possible to catch up with Britain in fifteen years. We must summon up our strength and swim vigorously upstream.

B. Talks at Ch'engtu

In the period following the liberation of the whole country (from 1950 to 1957), dogmatism made its appearance both in economic and in cultural and educational work. In economic work dogmatism primarily manifested itself in heavy industry, planning, banking and statistics, especially in heavy industry and planning. Since we didn't understand these things and had absolutely no experience, all we could do in our ignorance was to import foreign methods. Our statistical work was practically a copy of Soviet work; in the educational field copying was also pretty bad, for example, the system of a maximum mark of five

Talks at the Ch'engtu Conference, March 10 and 20, 1958. In: Stuart Schram, ed., *Chairman Mao Talks to the People* (New York: Pantheon, 1974).

in the schools, the uniform five years of primary school, etc. We did not even study our own experience of education in the liberated areas. The same applied to our public health work, with the result that I couldn't have eggs or chicken soup for three years because an article appeared in the Soviet Union which said that one shouldn't eat them. Later they said one could eat them. It didn't matter whether the article was correct or not, the Chinese listened all the same and respectfully obeyed. In short, the Soviet Union was tops. In commerce it was less so, because there was more contact and exchange of documents with the center. There was also less dogmatism in light industry. The socialist revolution and the cooperativization of agriculture were not influenced by dogmatism because the center had a direct grasp of them. During the past few years the center has chiefly grasped the revolution and agriculture, and to a certain extent commerce.

Dogmatism appears under different sets of circumstances, which should be analyzed and compared, and reasons for its appearance discovered.

1. We couldn't manage the planning, construction, and assembly of heavy industrial plants. We had no experience, China had no experts, the minister was himself an outsider, so we had to copy from foreign countries, and having copied we were unable to distinguish good from bad. Also we had to make use of Soviet experience and Soviet experts to break down the bourgeois ideology of China's old experts. The greater part of Soviet planning was correctly applied to China, but part of it was incorrect. It was imported uncritically.

2. We lacked understanding of the whole economic situation, and understood still less the economic differences between the Soviet Union and China. So all we could do was to follow blindly. Now the situation has changed. Generally speaking, we are now capable of undertaking the planning and construction of large enterprises. In another five years we shall be capable of manufacturing the equipment ourselves. We also have some understanding of Soviet and Chinese conditions. . . .

Right now there is a gust of wind, amounting to a force of ten typhoons. We must not impede this publicly, but within our own ranks [*nei-pu*] we must speak clearly, and damp down the atmosphere a little. We must get rid of the empty reports and foolish boasting, we must not compete for reputation, but serve reality. Some of the targets are high, and no measures have been taken to implement them; that is not good. In a word, we must have concrete measures, we must deal in reality. We must deal in abstractions, too—revolutionary romanticism is a good thing —but it is not good if there are no measures [for giving it practical effect]. . . .

3. Under the general line of going all out and aiming high to achieve greater, faster, better and more economical results, a wave-like form of progress is the unity of the opposites, deliberation and haste, the unity of the opposites, toil and dreams. If we have only haste and toil, that is one-sided. To be concerned only with the intensity of labor—that won't do, will it? In all of our work, we must use both deliberation and haste. (For example, the party secretary in Wuchang *hsien* did not take account of the peasants' sentiments, and wanted them to go on working on the reservoirs on the twenty-ninth day of the twelfth [lunar] month, so half of the civilian workers just took off.) This means also the unity of hard fighting with rest and consolidation. . . .

C. On Uninterrupted Revolution

Permanent revolution. Our revolutions follow each other, one after another. . . . We must now have a technical revolution, in order to catch up with and overtake England in fifteen years or a bit longer. Because China is economically backward, and its material foundation is weak, we have hitherto been in a passive position. Mentally, we feel that we are still fettered; in this respect, we have not yet achieved liberation. We must summon up our energies, and in another five years, we may be in a somewhat more active position. After ten years, we will be in a still more active position. After fifteen years, when we have more grain and more iron and steel, we will be in a position to

Sixty Articles on Work Methods. January 28, 1958. Translated by Stuart Schram. *The China Quarterly* 46, April-June 1971.

exercise yet greater initiative. Our revolution is like fighting a war. After winning one battle, we must immediately put forward new tasks. In this way, we can maintain the revolutionary enthusiasm of the cadres and the masses, and diminish their self-satisfaction, since they have no time to be satisfied with themselves even if they wanted to; new tasks keep pressing in, and everyone devotes his mind to the question of how to fulfill the new tasks. In calling for a technical revolution, we aim to make everyone study technology and science. The rightists say we are petty intellectuals, incapable of leading the big intellectuals. There are also those who say that the old cadres should be "bought off," paid a bit of money and asked to retire, because the old cadres do not understand science and technology, and only know how to fight and to carry out land reform. . . . We must learn new skills, we must really understand professional work (*yeh-wu*), we must really understand science and technology. Otherwise, we will be incapable of exercising good leadership. . . . Once attention is shifted to the technical side, there is also the possibility of neglecting politics. We must therefore pay attention to integrating technology with politics.

The relation between redness and expertness, between politics and professional activities (*yeh-wu*), is that of the unity of two opposites. We must definitely criticize and repudiate the tendency to pay no attention to politics. On the one hand, we must oppose empty-headed politicians; on the other hand, we must oppose pragmatists who lose their sense of direction.

Those who pay no attention to ideology and politics, and are busy with their work all day long, will become economists or technicians who have lost their sense of direction, and this is very dangerous. Ideological work and political work are the guarantee that economic and technical work will be carried through, they serve the economic basis. Ideology and politics are the supreme commander; they are the soul. Whenever we are even slightly lax in our ideological and political work, our economic and technical work will certainly take a false direction.

At present, there is on the one hand the grave class struggle between the socialist world and the imperialist world. On the other hand, as regards conditions within our country, classes have not yet been finally wiped out, and there is still class struggle. . . . During the period of transition from capitalism to socialism, there are still hidden among the people some anti-socialist hostile elements, such as the bourgeois rightists. In dealing with such elements, we also adopt basically the method of solving the problems by letting the masses air their views. It is only toward serious counter-revolutionary elements and saboteurs that we adopt the method of repression. After the transition period has come to an end, and classes have been completely abolished, then, as far as conditions within the country are concerned, politics will consist entirely of relationships among the people. At that time, ideological and political struggle among man and man, as well as revolution, will definitely still continue to exist, and moreover cannot fail to exist. The law of the unity of opposites, the law of quantitative and qualitative change, the law of affirmation and negation, exist forever and universally. But the nature of struggle and revolution is different from what it was in the past. It is not a class struggle, but a struggle between the advanced and the backward among the people, a struggle between advanced and backward science and technology. The transition from socialism to communism is a struggle, a revolution. Even when we have reached the era of communism, there will definitely still be many, many stages of development, and the relationship between one stage and another will necessarily be a relation leading from quantitative change to qualitative change. Every mutation or leap is a revolution, and they must all go through struggle. The "theory of no clashes" is metaphysical.

Politicians must understand something of specialized work (*yeh-wu*). It is difficult to understand too much, but it won't do to understand too little either; they must definitely understand something of it. Those who do not understand reality are pseudo-red; they are empty-headed politicians. We must integrate politics and technology.

2. LIU SHAO-CH'I,
A BLUEPRINT FOR THE GREAT LEAP FORWARD

As in the case of the land revolution and constitution, Liu Shao-ch'i provided the official party summation of the wide-ranging vision and strategic principles for implementation of the first phase of the leap. Mobilizing all positive factors, and above all abundant labor power, the priority of heavy industry of the first plan was to yield to the simultaneous development of industry and agriculture (heavy industry nevertheless retained priority). The predominance of large-scale industry was to give way to the simultaneous development of small, medium, and large industry, and the emphasis on large cities to balanced and mutually supportive growth of cities and countryside. Overcentralized planning was succeeded by coordination at the local, regional and provincial levels, and the rigid division of labor in the factories gave way to worker participation in management and cadre participation in labor. The Great Leap discarded the essentially urban-industrial vision of the earlier plan in favor of approaches bridging the gap between the rural hinterlands and cosmopolitan urban centers, between industrial workers and peasant farmers, and between workers and peasants on the one hand and the intellectuals and managers on the other. The goal was not merely an economic revolution but a technological, political, social, and cultural revolution to transform the quality of life in city and countryside.

Internationally, all of us know the now famous conclusion drawn by Comrade Mao Tsetung that the world situation has recently reached a new turning point in its development. In extent of popular support, size of populations and rate of development of production, the socialist camp headed by the Soviet Union has long since surpassed the imperialist camp. . . .

Report on the Work of the Central Committee of the Chinese Communist Party to the Second Session of the Eighth National Congress, May 5, 1958. In: Robert Bowie and John Fairbank, eds., *Communist China 1955–1959 Policy Documents with Analysis* (Cambridge, Mass.: Harvard University Press, 1962).

In October and November last year, the Soviet Union launched two artificial earth satellites. This made the whole world acknowledge that in science and technology too the Soviet Union has surpassed the United States, the most developed of the capitalist countries. . . . All this shows that the east wind has prevailed over the west wind, and will continue to do so in the future. . . .

The experience of the rectification campaign and the anti-rightist struggle once again shows that throughout the transition period, that is, before completion of the building of a socialist society, the main contradiction inside our country is and remains that between the proletariat and the bourgeoisie, between the socialist road and the capitalist road. In certain fields this contradiction manifests itself as a fierce life and death struggle between the enemy and ourselves; that was the case in the attack launched by the bourgeois rightists in 1957. This attack was repelled, but in the future they will try again to make trouble whenever opportunity arises. We must, therefore, be prepared to wage prolonged and repeated struggles against the bourgeois rightists before their contradictions with the people can be fully resolved. . . .

The spring of 1958 witnessed the beginning of a leap forward on every front in our socialist construction. Industry, agriculture and all other fields of activity are registering greater and more rapid growth.

To begin with industry. The total value of industrial output for the first four months of this year was 26 percent higher than in the same period last year; the April increase was 42 percent. According to estimates made on the basis of the present situation, China's steel output this year will be over 7.1 million tons; coal output will reach 180 million tons; 60,000 machine tools will be produced and irrigation machinery with more than 3.5 million horsepower; the output of chemical fertilizers will amount to 1.35 million tons. . . .

An upsurge is shaping up in capital construction in industry this year. Nearly one thousand above-norm projects will be under construction this year; this is more than the total number of such projects under construction in the first five-year plan period. In addition, construction work has already started on thousands of medium and small-sized coal mines, power stations, oil refineries, iron and steel plants, nonferrous mines, chemical fertilizer plants, cement plants, engineering works, and agricultural and animal products processing plants.

The output of local industry this year will show a considerable increase as a result of widespread industrial capital construction undertaken by local authorities. Take iron and steel for example. The amount of iron to be produced by local enterprises this year will reach 1,730,000 tons (as against the 593,000 tons produced last year) and that of steel will reach 1,410,000 tons (as against the 790,000 tons of last year). The rapid growth of the local industries is one of the outstanding features of this year's industrial upswing. . . .

In agriculture, the most striking leap took place in the campaign of the cooperative farmers to build irrigation works. From last October to April this year, the irrigated acreage throughout the country increased by 350 million mou, that is, 80 million mou more than the total added during the eight years since liberation and 110 million mou more than the total acreage brought under irrigation in the thousands of years before liberation. At the same time, more than 200 million mou of low-lying and easily waterlogged farmland was transformed and irrigation facilities were improved on another 140 million mou of land. The loss of water and soil was brought under control over an area of 160,000 square kilometers. This gives proof of the power to conquer nature which the masses of the people have demonstrated in the field of agriculture following the great socialist revolution on the economic, political, and ideological fronts and the release on a tremendous scale of our social productive forces.

In the same period, the peasants all over the country accumulated about 310,000 million tan of fertilizers (including all kinds of fertilizers, mostly clay and mud fertilizers). . . .

In the first four months of this year, over 290 million mou of land was afforested in the country, one and a half times the total acreage afforested in the past eight years. . . .

A mass movement to improve farm tools is now spreading throughout the countryside. Tens of millions of peasants have made all sorts of improved and semimechanized farm implements, water lifts, means of transportation, and equipment for processing farm produce. Thus the centuries-old tradition of primitive manual labor has begun to change and labor productivity has increased enormously. At the same time, the peasants in various places have made energetic efforts to improve systems and methods of cultivation in accordance with local conditions. This is the budding of a great technical revolution in the rural areas.

Rapid developments are also taking place in the fields of culture, education, and public health. Energetic efforts are being made in many villages throughout the country to eliminate illiteracy and establish large numbers of primary and secondary schools financed by the people. Cultural and artistic activities among the masses are advancing quickly. The public health campaign centered on the elimination of the four pests has already spread to every urban and rural district and achieved notable results.

The fact is that the growth of the social productive forces calls for a socialist revolution and the spiritual emancipation of the people; the victory of this revolution and emancipation in turn spurs a forward leap in the social productive forces; and this in turn impels a progressive change in the socialist relations of production and an advance in man's ideology. In their ceaseless struggle to transform nature, the people are continuously transforming society and themselves. . . .

In the light of the practical experience gained in the people's struggle and of the development of Comrade Mao Tsetung's thinking in the past few years, the Central Committee of the party is of the opinion that the following are the basic points of our general line, which is to build socialism by exerting our utmost efforts, and pressing ahead consistently to achieve greater, faster, better, and more economical results:

To mobilize all positive factors and correctly handle contradictions among the people;

To consolidate and develop socialist ownership, that is, ownership by the whole people and collective ownership, and consolidate the proletarian dictatorship and proletarian international solidarity;

To carry out the technical revolution and cultural revolution step by step, while completing the socialist revolution on the economic, political, and ideological fronts;

To develop industry and agriculture simultaneously while giving priority to heavy industry;

With centralized leadership, overall planning, proper division of labor and coordination, to develop national and local industries, and large, small, and medium-sized enterprises simultaneously; and

By means of all this to build our country, in the shortest possible time, into a great socialist country with a modern industry, modern agriculture, and modern science and culture. Based on the requirements of this general line, what are the main tasks facing the party and the people in the technical and cultural revolutions?

The main tasks of the technical revolution are as follows:

To put the national economy, including agriculture and handicrafts, systematically and in a planned way on a new technological basis, that is, the technological basis of modern, large-scale production, so that machinery can be used wherever feasible and electrification is brought to all the cities and villages of the country;

To turn all big and medium-size cities throughout the country into industrial cities; and to build up new industrial bases in those places where the necessary conditions exist, to enable all the county towns and many townships to have their own industries, and to increase the value of industrial output of all the provinces and autonomous regions and even most of the special administrative regions and counties so that it exceeds the value of their agricultural output;

To set up a transport network and post and telecommunications services equipped mainly with modern facilities, reaching every part of the country; and

While introducing as far as possible the world's up-to-date techniques, to launch a widespread mass movement in the cities and villages throughout the country to improve tools and introduce technical innovations so that semimechanized or fully mechanized operations can be properly combined with the necessary hand work.

To meet the requirements of the technical revolution, we must at the same time carry through a cultural revolution, promoting culture, education, and public health in the interest of economic construction. The main tasks in this are as follows:

To wipe out illiteracy, to institute compulsory primary education and step by step to bring secondary schools to the townships in general, and higher educational institutions and scientific research bodies to the special administrative regions in general and to many counties;

To complete the work of devising written languages for the national minorities or improving those already in existence and to make energetic efforts to reform the written languages used by the Han people;

To wipe out the "four pests," improve sanitary conditions, promote sports, eliminate the principal diseases, break down superstitions, reform customs and change habits, and invigorate the national spirit;

To promote cultural and recreational activities among the masses and develop socialist literature and arts;

To train new intellectuals and remold the old intellectuals in order to establish a gigantic force of tens of millions of working-class intellectuals, consisting of technicians, who will account for the greatest number, professors, teachers, scientists, journalists, writers, artists, and Marxist theoreticians. . . .

Why is it that, to increase the speed of construction, industry and agriculture must be developed simultaneously? This is because ours is a large agricultural country, and of our over 600 million people, more than 500 million are peasants who constitute a most powerful force both in the revolutionary struggle and construction. Only by relying on this powerful ally and giving full play to the peasants' initiative and creativeness can the working class of our country achieve victory. The paramount importance of the peasantry as an ally is just the same in the period of construction as it was in the period of revolution.

Some comrades are worried that, though the development of agriculture can accumulate funds for industrialization, it will for the present at least divert some funds which could be used by the state for industrialization. The upsurges in agriculture in 1956 and 1958 have proved such worries unnecessary. So long as we know how to rely on this great force of our 500 million peasants, we can greatly expand the scope of agricultural construction even if there is no increase in state investments in agriculture. The state has invested 1,450 million yuan to harness the Huai River, and completed over 1,600 million cubic meters of masonry and earth work in the past eight years. But by depending mainly on the labor, money and material resources of the peasants themselves, in six months of the winter of 1957 and spring of 1958, more than 12,000 million cubic meters of masonry and earth work were completed in Honan and Anhwei provinces alone. . . .

Why is it necessary to undertake the simultaneous development of national and local industries, and of large, small, and medium-sized enterprises to increase the speed of construction? . . . Big enterprises which have a big output and a high technical level can solve key problems having a decisive bearing on the national economy. They form the backbone of the force that pushes forward the industrial development of the country. But small and medium-sized enterprises have the advantages which big enterprises do not have: they require less investments and can more easily absorb funds from scattered sources; they require less time to build and produce quicker results; they can be designed and equipped locally; they can make do with various simple types of equipment which are readily available in the localities. They can be set up over a wide area so as to facilitate industrialization of the country as a whole, promote the training of technical personnel throughout the country and a balanced development of the economies of the various regions. They can produce a great variety of goods and can be flexibly adapted to produce new types of goods. Close to the sources of raw materials and markets, they can reduce transport costs and make flexible use of available resources, making it easier to bring about a satisfactory relation between supply, production, and sales. It is easier for them to make flexible use of the labor power available in the countryside and of casual labor, depending on the amount of work to be done, and thus help reduce the differences between city and countryside, between workers and peasants.

In the period of the first five-year plan, we paid attention first of all to the development of industries run by the central government, to giant enterprises; this was absolutely necessary. But not enough attention was paid to the development of local industries and small and medium-size industries; this was a shortcoming. In the past two years or more, the Central Committee has repeatedly pointed out that this shortcoming must be rectified. . . . This will inevitably result in: (1) quickening the pace of the nation's industrialization; (2) quickening the pace of mechanization of agriculture; and (3) quickening the speed at which differences between city and countryside are reduced. . . .

The party's general line for socialist construction is the application and development of its mass line in socialist construction. We must fully combine centralized leadership with decentralized management, and coordinate the resources of the central government with those of the local authorities, the resources of the state with those of the masses, the giant undertakings with small and medium-size plants, the striving to raise the quality of work with popularization—all this is applicable not only to industry but also to other economic and cultural undertakings, and to the technical and cultural revolutions as a whole.

3. THE BIRTH
OF THE PEOPLE'S COMMUNES

In the fall of 1957, the revival of the National Program for Agriculture as a comprehensive blueprint for rural development placed a premium on expanded resources and better coordination within and between cooperatives. In addition, the vastly expanded scale of water conservation and fertilizer collection beginning in late 1957 together with sprouts of rural industry repeatedly exceeded the capacities of individual cooperatives.

Local communities began to experiment with enlarged cooperatives capable of directing an increased scale and scope of operations. The amalgamation of cooperatives into a single unit, popularly initiated as early as the spring of 1958, months before official party endorsement of the commune system, provided a framework that could integrate the scattered resources of individual cooperatives.

Tentative Regulations (Draft) of the Weihsing (Sputnik) People's Commune, August 7, 1958. In: Robert Bowie and John Fairbank, eds., *Communist China 1955–1959. Policy Documents with Analysis* (Cambridge, Mass.: Harvard University Press, 1962).

The 43,000 member Weihsing (Sputnik) Commune, established in April 1958 in Honan province was China's first commune. Its success provided important guidelines for the party when the Central Committee formally approved the concept and the name "people's commune" in August 1958. The radical Weihsing regulations which include arrangements for free supply of grain and wide-ranging services offer a detailed account of one model advanced unit which was widely studied throughout the countryside.

In August 1958, after top party leaders toured rural areas, the Central Committee met at Pei-tai-ho and officially endorsed the rural people's commune as the institution responsible for the transition to communism:

> The establishment of people's communes with all-round management of agriculture, forestry, animal husbandry, side occupations and fishery, where industry (the worker), agriculture (the peasant), exchange (the trader), culture and education (the student) and military affairs (the militiaman) merge into one, is the fundamental policy to guide the peasants to accelerate socialist construction, complete the building of socialism ahead of time and carry out the gradual transition to communism.

And within months communes formed everywhere throughout the countryside.

In certain areas the Pei-tai-ho Resolution treads cautiously, particularly in warning against undue haste in eliminating private property and in transfer of property ownership from the cooperative to the commune and from the commune to the state. Yet it squarely places on the agenda the issue of transition to higher forms of ownership, productivity, distribution, and consciousness, reinforcing a feeling of the imminence of communism to inspire the newly formed communes.

The Central Committee's December 1958 Wuhan Resolution is the party's fullest exposition of the role of the commune in reorganizing every facet of rural life and paving the way for the future—and not only the future—transition to communism. The commune provides the basis both for a leap in socialist relations and the industrialization, mechanization, and electrification of the countryside. The changes wrought by the communes pave the way for the material as well as the institutional and spiritual *transition to communism which is to take place fifteen to twenty or more years hence.*

While warning against utopian efforts to achieve communism prematurely, the resolution specifies that the first shoots of communism are already to be found in the free supply system (partial implementation of the communist principle "to each according to one's need") and in rural industrialization (reducing the distinction between city and countryside, industry and agriculture) and other features of communal life.

From early 1958 many cities had begun to experiment with communal forms. The Wuhan Resolution was the first, however, to officially sanction urban communes. While urging discretion and emphasizing important differences between city and countryside, it points to the commune as the basis for both urban and rural life. In short, just two years after the basic completion of socialist ownership of the means of production, China confronted the issues of the radical transformation of rural and urban life auguring the transition to communism.

A. Weihsing: The First People's Commune

Article 1. The people's commune is a basic unit of society in which the working people unite of their own free will under the leadership of the Communist Party and the people's government. Its task is to manage all industrial and agricultural production, trade, cultural and educational work, and political affairs within its own sphere.

Article 2. The intent and purpose of the people's commune is to consolidate the socialist system and energetically create the conditions for the gradual transition to the communist system.

To this end, we must exert our utmost effort, and press ahead consistently to achieve greater, faster, better, and more economical results in developing industry, agriculture, and cultural and educational work, to carry through the technical and cultural revolutions, to gradually reduce the differences between town and country and between mental and manual labor.

As the social product becomes abundant and the people have high political consciousness, so will the transition from the principle of "from each according to his ability, to each according to his work" to the principle of "from each according to his ability, to each according to his needs" be gradually effected. . . .

Article 4. When the agricultural producers' cooperatives merge into the people's commune, they must, regardless of excess or deficiency, turn over all their collectively owned property to the commune in the communist spirit of wide-scale coordination. Their former debts shall be paid off by the commune, excluding those for use in that year's production expenses, which should be settled by the cooperatives themselves. . . .

Article 5. In changing over to the commune, the members of the cooperatives must turn over to the common ownership of the commune all privately owned plots of farmland and house sites and other means of production such as livestock, tree holdings, etc., on the basis that common ownership of the means of production is in the main in effect. However, the cooperative members may keep a small number of domestic animals and fowls as private property. Privately owned livestock and tree holdings when turned over to the common ownership of the commune should be evaluated and counted as the private investment of the cooperative members. . . .

Article 6. To ensure a continuously expanding agricultural output the commune must continue to build irrigation works, apply more manure, improve the soil, use good strains of seed over large areas, breed draft animals, prevent and control insect pests and plant diseases, apply rational close-planting, and practice deep ploughing and careful cultivation. It must make vigorous efforts to improve farm implements and carry into effect the mechanization of agriculture and the electrification of the countryside in the shortest possible time.

The communes must develop industry as rapidly as possible. The first things to be done in this field are to set up mines, iron and steel plants, and factories for manufacturing ball bearings, farm tools, fertilizer, and building materials and for processing farm produce, repairing machinery, building hydroelectric power projects, installations for utilizing methane, and other enterprises. . . .

Article 9. The commune should, step by step, train its members to be cultured working people with professional skill and all-round qualifications.

The commune should institute a system of universal, compulsory education combined closely with labor. Primary schools and part-time continuation schools should be set up on a wide scale so that by degrees all school-age children may attend school and all young people and the middle-aged may reach the educational level of senior primary school. . . .

The commune should encourage and help its members to engage in scientific studies on a wide scale, first of all, studies and experiments in good seed cultivation, soil improvement, tree planting, livestock breeding, elimination of insect pests and plant diseases, and the improvement of farming technique and tools.

Article 10. A system of citizen soldiery shall operate throughout the commune. . . .

Article 11. As the commune has the same confines as a township, that is, one commune to a township, the township should be merged with the commune for the convenience of work. . . .

Article 12. The highest organization of management in the commune is the congress of the commune which will discuss and reach decisions on all important matters of the commune. The congress of the commune shall include representatives of all production brigades and all sections of the people, such as the women, youth, old people, cultural and educational workers, medical workers, scientific and technical workers, the personnel of industrial enterprises, traders, and minority people.

The management committee shall be elected by the congress of the commune to take charge of the commune's affairs. . . .

Article 13. The commune shall institute a system of centralized leadership, with management organs at various levels, in order to operate a responsibility system in production. In accordance with the principle of facilitating production and leadership, the commune shall organize its members into a number of production contingents which will divide up into a number of production brigades. The production contingent is a unit responsible for production and business accounting while its profits and losses are managed by the commune under a unified system. The production brigade is a basic unit for organizing labor. . . .

Article 14. The commune shall operate a wage system when it acquires stability of income and adequate funds and when the members are able voluntarily to consolidate labor discipline. Wages of members will be fixed by the masses through discussion, taking into account the intensity and complexity of the work, physical conditions, technique and attitude towards work. Wages will be paid monthly. Technical allowances may be paid to those who have special skill. One month's wage may differ from another. In months when the commune gets more income and the members need more, the members may get more pay; in other months they may get less. In case of a serious natural calamity the commune may, according to circumstances, pay less to its members. . . .

Until conditions are mature for the institution of the wage system, the system of piece-work wages may be introduced, with a fixed value calculated per workday. The members may be paid monthly, in part or in full, according to the numbers of workdays done. . . .

Article 15. A grain supply system should be operated when grain production reaches a higher level and all the members of the commune agree to it. All members as well as each person of their families will then be supplied with grain gratis in accordance with standards laid down by the state, irrespective of how many of the family can work. . . .

Article 17. The commune shall set up community canteens, nurseries and sewing teams to free women from household labor. . . .

Article 18. The commune will gradually set up and improve the work of medical establishments so that step by step the commune will have a central hospital with in-patient wards for serious cases. . . .

Medical care shall be given in the commune on a cooperative basis. Members will pay a yearly amount in accordance with the number in the family. No other fees will be charged for any benefits they get from the medical establishments. . . .

Article 19. The commune shall make necessary arrangements concerning production and living conditions for the aged, the bereft, the disabled members, and people in bad health who have less or no ability to work and nobody to depend on, so that they can be ensured the means of living. . . .

Article 21. The commune shall encourage cultural, recreational, and sports activities among the masses so as to bring forward communist people healthy in body and in mind. Steps should be taken to ensure that each commune has its own library, theater and film projector teams; that each production contingent has its own club room, amateur theatrical troupe, choir and sports team; and that each production brigade has a small reading room and radio sets.

Article 22. . . . The distribution of income shall be based on the principle of ensuring high speed in expanded reproduction. With the development of production, wages shall be increased every year, but the rate of increase must be slower than the rate of increase in production.

B. The Pei-tai-ho Resolution:
Communes Transform the Countryside

1. The people's communes are the logical result of the march of events. Large, comprehensive people's communes have made their appearance, and in several places they are already widespread. They have developed very rapidly in some areas. It is highly probable that there will soon be an upsurge in setting up people's communes throughout the country and the development is irresistible. The basis for the development of the people's communes is mainly the all-round, continuous leap forward in China's agricultural production and the ever-rising political consciousness of the 500 million peasants. An unprecedented advance has been made in agricultural capital construction since the advocates of the capitalist road were funda-

Central Committee Resolution on the Establishment of People's Communes in the Rural Areas, August 29, 1958. In: Robert Bowie and John Fairbank, eds., *Communist China 1955-1959. Policy Documents with Analysis* (Cambridge, Mass.: Harvard University Press, 1962).

mentally defeated economically, politically, and ideologically. This has created a new basis for practically eliminating flood and drought, and for ensuring the comparatively stable advance of agricultural production. Agriculture has leaped forward since right conservatism has been overcome and the old technical norms in agriculture have been broken down. The output of agricultural products has doubled or increased several-fold, in some cases more than ten times or scores of times. This has further stimulated emancipation of thought among the people. Large-scale agricultural capital construction and the application of more advanced agricultural technique are making their demands on labor power. The growth of rural industry also demands the transfer of some manpower from agriculture. The demand for mechanization and electrification has become increasingly urgent in China's rural areas. Capital construction in agriculture and the struggle for bumper harvests involve a large-scale cooperation which cuts across the boundaries between cooperatives, townships, and counties. The people have taken to organizing themselves along military lines, working with militancy, and leading a collective life, and this has raised the political consciousness of the 500 million peasants still further. Community dining rooms, kindergartens, nurseries, sewing groups, barber shops, public baths, happy homes for the aged, agricultural middle schools, "red and expert" schools, are leading the peasants toward a happier collective life and further fostering ideas of collectivism among the peasant masses. What all these things illustrate is that the agricultural cooperative with scores of families or several hundred families can no longer meet the needs of the changing situation. In the present circumstances, the establishment of people's communes with all-round management of agriculture, forestry, animal husbandry, side occupations, and fishery, where industry (the worker), agriculture (the peasant), exchange (the trader), culture and education (the student), and military affairs (the militiaman) merge into one, is the fundamental policy to guide the peasants to accelerate socialist construction, complete the building of socialism ahead of time, and carry out the gradual transition to communism.

2. Concerning the organization and size of the communes. Generally speaking, it is at present better to establish one

commune to a township with the commune comprising about two thousand peasant households. Where a township embraces a vast area and is sparsely populated, more than one commune may be established, each with less than two thousand households. In some places, several townships may merge and form a single commune comprising about six or seven thousand households, according to topographical conditions and the needs for the development of production. As to the establishment of communes of more than 10,000 or even more than 20,000 households, we need not oppose them, but for the present we should not take the initiative to encourage them. . . .

The township governments and the communes should become one, with the township committee of the party becoming the party committee of the commune and the township people's council becoming the administrative committee of the commune. . . .

3. . . . The merger of smaller cooperatives into bigger ones and their transformation into communes must be carried out in close coordination with current production to ensure that it not only has no adverse effect on current production, but becomes a tremendous force stimulating an even greater leap forward in production. Therefore, in the early period of the merger, the method of "changing the upper structure while keeping the lower structure unchanged" may be adopted. . . .

5. Concerning the name, ownership, and system of distribution of the communes. . . .

After the establishment of people's communes, there is no need immediately to transform collective ownership into ownership by the people as a whole. It is better at present to maintain collective ownership to avoid unnecessary complications arising in the course of the transformation of ownership. In fact, collective ownership in people's communes already contains some elements of ownership by the people as a whole. These elements will grow constantly in the course of the continuous development of people's communes and will gradually replace collective ownership. The transition from collective ownership to ownership by the people as a whole is a process, the completion of which may take less time—three or four years—in some places, and longer—five or six years or even longer—elsewhere. Even with the completion of this transition, people's communes, like state-owned industry, are still socialist in character, where the principle of "from each according to his ability and to each according to his work" prevails. After a number of years, as the social product increases greatly, the communist consciousness and morality of the entire people are raised to a much higher degree, and universal education is instituted and developed, the differences between workers and peasants, town and country, and mental and manual labor—legacies of the old society that have inevitably been carried over into the socialist period—and the remnants of unequal bourgeois rights which are the reflection of these differences, will gradually vanish, and the function of the state will be limited to protecting the country from external aggression but it will play no role internally. At that time Chinese society will enter the era of communism where the principle of "from each according to his ability and to each according to his needs" will be practiced.

After the establishment of people's communes it is not necessary to hurry the change from the original system of distribution, in order to avoid any unfavorable effect on production. The system of distribution should be determined according to specific conditions. Where conditions permit, the shift to a wage system may be made. But where conditions are not yet ripe, the original system of payment according to workdays may be temporarily retained (such as the system of fixed targets for output, workdays, and costs, with a part of the extra output as reward; or the system of calculating workdays on the basis of output). This can be changed when conditions permit.

Although ownership in the people's communes is still collective ownership and the system of distribution, either the wage system or payment according to workdays, is "to each according to his work" and not "to each according to his needs," the people's communes are the best form of organization for the attainment of socialism and gradual transition to communism. They will develop into the basic social units in communist society.

6. At the present stage our task is to build socialism. The primary purpose of establishing people's communes is to accelerate the speed of socialist construction and the purpose of building socialism is to prepare actively for the transition to communism. It seems that the attainment of communism in

China is no longer a remote future event. We should actively use the form of the people's communes to explore the practical road of transition to communism.

C. The Wuhan Resolution:
Communes and the Transition to Communism

In 1958 a new social organization appeared, fresh as the morning sun, above the broad horizon of East Asia. This was the large-scale people's commune in the rural areas of our country which combines industry, agriculture, trade, education, and military affairs and in which government administration and commune management are integrated. . . .

The movement to set up people's communes has grown very rapidly. Within a few months starting in the summer of 1958, all of the more than 740,000 agricultural producers' cooperatives in the country, in response to the enthusiastic demand of the mass of peasants, reorganized themselves into over 26,000 people's communes. Over 120 million households, or more than 99 percent of all China's peasant households of various nationalities, have joined the people's communes. . . .

Under the unified leadership of the commune, industry, agriculture (including farming, forestry, animal husbandry, side occupations and fisheries), trade, education, and military affairs have been closely coordinated and developed rapidly. In particular, thousands and tens of thousands of small factories have mushroomed in the rural areas. To meet the pressing demands of the masses, the communes have set up large numbers of community dining rooms, nurseries, kindergartens, "homes of respect for the aged" and other institutions for collective welfare, which have, in particular, completely emancipated women from thousands of years of kitchen drudgery and brought broad smiles to their faces. As the result of the bumper crops many

Central Committee Resolution on Some Questions Concerning the People's Communes, December 10, 1958. In: Robert Bowie and John Fairbank, eds., *Communist China 1955-1959. Policy Documents with Analysis* (Cambridge, Mass.: Harvard University Press, 1962).

communes have instituted a system of distribution that combines the wage system with the free supply system; the mass of peasants, both men and women, have begun to receive their wages and those families which in the past constantly worried about their daily meals and about their firewood, rice, oil, salt, soya sauce, vinegar, and vegetables are now able to "eat without paying." . . .

The development of the system of rural people's communes has an even more profound and far-reaching significance. It has shown the people of our country the way to the gradual industrialization of the rural areas, the way to the gradual transition from collective ownership to ownership by the whole people in agriculture, the way to the gradual transition from the socialist principle of "to each according to his work" to the communist principle of "to each according to his needs," the way gradually to lessen and finally to eliminate the differences between town and country, between worker and peasant and between mental and manual labor, and the way gradually to lessen and finally to eliminate the internal function of the state. . . .

People's communes have now become the general rule in all rural areas inhabited by our people of various nationalities (except in Tibet and in certain other areas). Some experiments have also begun in the cities. In the future urban people's communes, in a form suited to the specific features of cities, will also become instruments for the transformation of old cities and the construction of new socialist cities. . . . There are, however, certain differences between the city and the countryside.

Firstly, city conditions are more complex than those in the countryside.

Secondly, socialist ownership by the whole people is already the main form of ownership in the cities, and the factories, public institutions, and schools, under the leadership of the working class, have already become highly organized in accordance with socialist principles (with the exception of some of the family members of the workers and staffs). Therefore, the switch-over of cities to people's communes inevitably involves some requirements different from those in the rural areas.

Thirdly, bourgeois ideology is still fairly prevalent among

many of the capitalists and intellectuals in the cities; they still have misgivings about the establishment of communes—so we should wait a bit for them.

Consequently, we should continue to make experiments and generally should not be in a hurry to set up people's communes on a large scale in the cities. . . .

2

The people's commune is the basic unit of the socialist social structure of our country, combining industry, agriculture, trade, education, and military affairs; at the same time it is the basic organization of the socialist state power. Marxist-Leninist theory and the initial experience of the people's communes in our country enable us to foresee now that the people's communes will quicken the tempo of our socialist construction and constitute the best form for realizing, in our country, the following two transitions.

Firstly, the transition from collective ownership to ownership by the whole people in the countryside; and,

Secondly, the transition from socialist to communist society. It can also be foreseen that in the future communist society, the people's commune will remain the basic unit of our social structure.

From now on, the task confronting the people of our country is: through such a form of social organization as the people's commune, and based on the general line for socialist construction laid down by the party, to develop the social productive forces at high speed, to advance the industrialization of the country, the industrialization of the communes, and the mechanization and electrification of agriculture; and to effect the gradual transition from socialist collective ownership to socialist ownership by the whole people, thus fully realizing ownership by the whole people in the socialist economy of our country and gradually building our country into a great socialist land with a highly developed modern industry, agriculture, science, and culture. During this process, the elements of communism are bound to increase gradually and these will lay the foundation of material and spiritual conditions for the transition from socialism to communism. . . .

Though the pace at which we are advancing is fairly rapid, it will still take a fairly long time to realize, on a large scale, the industrialization of our country, the industrialization of the communes, the mechanization and electrification of agriculture, and the building up of a socialist country with a highly developed modern industry, agriculture, science, and culture. This whole process will take fifteen, twenty, or more years to complete, counting from now. . . .

To gradually promote the transition from collective ownership to ownership by the whole people, every county should set up its federation of communes. In coming years, on the basis of the energetic development of production and the raising of the people's political understanding, such federations should take suitable steps gradually to increase the proportion of their means of production that is owned by the whole people and the proportion of their products that is subject to unified distribution by the state, and, when conditions mature, should change collective ownership into ownership by the whole people. . . .

This transition will be realized, by stages and by groups, on a national scale only after a considerable time. Those who, because they fail to understand this, confuse the establishment of people's communes with the realization of ownership by the whole people, making impetuous attempts to abolish collective ownership in the countryside prematurely, and trying hastily to change over to ownership by the whole people, will not be doing the right thing and therefore cannot succeed.

Furthermore, the change from socialist collective ownership to socialist ownership by the whole people is not the same thing as the going-over from socialism to communism. . . .

True, the free supply system adopted by the people's communes contains the first shoots of the communist principle of "to each according to his needs"; the policy carried out by the people's communes of running industry and agriculture simultaneously and combining them has opened up a way to reduce the differences between town and countryside and between worker and peasant, and when the rural people's communes pass over from socialist collective ownership to socialist ownership by the whole people, the communist factors will grow further. All this must be acknowledged. Moreover, with social products becoming increasingly plentiful thanks to the continuous advance of industry and agriculture throughout the country; with the proportion of what is supplied gratis under the distribution system of the people's communes gradually growing larger and the standards of free supply being gradually raised; with the consistent raising of the level of the people's communist understanding; with the constant progress of education for the whole people; with the gradual reduction of the differences between mental and manual labor; and with the gradual diminution of the internal function of the state power, etc., the conditions for the transition to communism will also gradually mature. It is of course not proper to ignore or even impede this course of development and relegate communism to the distant future.

Nevertheless every Marxist must soberly realize that the transition from socialism to communism is a fairly long and complicated process of development and that throughout this entire process society is still socialist in nature. . . . In order to encourage the working enthusiasm of commune members and also to facilitate the satisfaction of their complex daily needs, the communes must strive gradually to increase the wages of their members and, for a number of years to come, must increase them at a rate faster than that portion of their income which comes under the heading of free supply. Even after the transition from collective ownership to ownership by the whole people, the people's communes will, during a necessary period of time, retain the system of "to each according to his work," owing to the fact that there is not as yet an abundant enough supply of social products to realize communism. Any premature attempt to negate the principle of "to each according to his work" and replace it with the principle of "to each according to his needs," that is, any attempt to enter communism by overreaching ourselves when conditions are not mature—is undoubtedly a utopian concept that cannot possibly succeed. . . .

We are advocates of the Marxist-Leninist theory of uninterrupted revolution; we hold that no "Great Wall" exists or can be allowed to exist between the democratic revolution and the socialist revolution and between socialism and communism. We are at the same time advocates of the Marxist-Leninist theory of the development of revolution by stages; we hold that different stages of development reflect qualitative changes and that these stages, different in quality, should not be confused. . . .

3

People in the past often worried about our "overpopulation" and relatively small amount of available arable land. But this idea has been overturned by the facts of our 1958 bumper harvest. Insofar as we succeed in seriously popularizing the rich experience gained in getting high yields through deep ploughing, intensive cultivation, layer-by-layer fertilization and rational close planting, it will be found that the amount of arable land is not too small but very considerable, and that the question is not so much overpopulation as shortage of manpower. . . .

People's communes must go in for industry in a big way. The development of industry by the people's communes will not only accelerate the industrialization of the whole country but also promote the realization of ownership by the whole people in the rural districts, and reduce the differences between town and country. . . . Industrial production in the people's communes must be closely linked with agricultural production; it should first of all serve the development of agriculture and the mechanization and electrification of farming; at the same time it should serve to meet the demands of commune members for staple consumer goods, and serve the country's big industries and the socialist market. . . . With regard to production techniques, the principle should be carried out of linking handicraft with mechanized industry, and indigenous methods with modern methods of production. . . . The mechanized industries must also make full use of indigenous methods and iron, steel, machine tools, other raw materials and equipment produced by indigenous methods; they will gradually advance from indigenous to modern, from small to large and from a low to a high level. . . .

Continued development of commodity production and continued adherence to the principle of "to each according to his work" are two important questions of principle in expanding the socialist economy. The whole party should have a common understanding of them. Some people, attempting to "enter communism" prematurely, have tried to abolish the production and exchange of commodities too early, and to negate at too early a stage the positive roles of commodities, value, money, and prices. This line of thinking is harmful to the development of socialist construction and is therefore incorrect. . . .

4

The more socialism develops and the more abundant social products become, the more abundant will certainly become the means of livelihood allotted to each individual. Some people think that the switch to communes will call for a redistribution of existing property for personal use. This is a misconception. It should be made known among the masses that the means of livelihood owned by members (including houses, clothing, bedding, and furniture) and their deposits in banks and credit cooperatives will remain their own property after they join the commune and will always belong to them. . . .

5

Communes must ensure the successful running of primary and secondary schools and adult education. Universal primary school education should be instituted in the rural areas throughout the country. . . . The principle of combining education with productive labor must be carried out thoroughly in all schools, without exception. . . .

6

Unified leadership as well as management at different levels should be put into effect in the people's commune. The administrative set-up of the commune may in general be divided into three levels, namely: the commune administrative committee, the administrative district (or production brigade) and the production team. The administrative district (or production brigade) is in general the unit which manages industry, agriculture, trade, education, and military affairs in a given area and forms a business accounting unit, with its gains and losses pooled in the commune as a whole. The production team is the basic unit of labor organization. Under the unified leadership of the commune administrative committee, necessary powers should be given to the administrative district (or production brigade) and the production team over such matters as the organization of production work and capital construction, finances and welfare, in order to bring their initiative into full play. . . .

There must be both discipline and democracy in the organizations of labor in the people's commune. What we describe as getting organized along military lines means getting organized on the pattern of a factory. . . .

4. INDIGENOUS STEEL
AND RURAL INDUSTRIALIZATION

During the summer of 1958 small-scale indigenous iron and steel furnaces mushroomed on a vast scale throughout the countryside, providing the most widely publicized demonstration of the industrial capacities of the newly formed people's communes and the effort to narrow the gap between city and countryside. Lushan's pig-iron "sputnik" reveals the basic strategy of utilizing surplus labor and local resources to provide iron to directly serve the countryside while rapidly upgrading technological levels.

Yet as Mao himself admitted less than a year later, despite the millions of tons of iron produced by native methods, the experiment was a costly failure. Within months of the construction of an estimated one million furnaces, all but a handful had closed down as a result of the inferior quality of the product, high costs, and above all the negative impact of drawing substantial labor from agriculture.

The story of decentralized steelmaking and rural industry did not end there, however. In phase two, several thousand "small, modern, mass" iron and steel furnaces were built and considerable gains were registered in raising their efficiency. Nevertheless, in the backlash against the leap in the early 1960s the leadership concluded that these plants too were excessively costly and inefficient. Most were dismantled.

In short, the first attempt to fulfill the promise of the rural people's commune as the locus of industry as well as agriculture in most areas ended in failure. More accurately, as subsequent experience proved, the experiment was cut off before it could be adequately tested. As we will observe, less than a decade

Tan Man-ni. Lushan's Pig-Iron 'Sputnik.' *China Reconstructs,* January 1959.

later rural industrialization would be revived during the Great Proletarian Cultural Revolution on firmer technical foundations and with the benefit of both experience and careful advance planning. Successful rural industrialization would then create the basis of a new countryside and breathe fresh life into the people's communes. But its antecedents lay in the indigenous steel making and other new industries of the Great Leap.

Furnace fields are everywhere in Lushan county, southern Honan province—plots of hundreds of small earthen furnaces were "growing," in late autumn when I was there, alongside fields of sweet potatoes and tobacco. From a distance the leaping flames and columns of smoke look like some new construction site accidentally ablaze. On the scene the atmosphere is like a fairground, with scores of people bustling in and out of the rows of furnaces.

Small red flags fly overhead indicating the sections belonging to the various companies and squads of farmer-steelworkers, who are organized like militia units. The air is filled with the high-pitched melodies of local operas pouring through an amplifier above the site and accompanied by the hum of blowers, the panting of gasoline engines, the honking of heavily-laden lorries, and the bellowing of oxen hauling ore and coal.

At one of the ten-foot-high furnaces, a man climbs a wooden ladder to dump coke and firewood through the top. After a few minutes beside the 1,000-degree heat, he descends and another worker goes up to tamp the fuel down with his rake. A third man follows to pull the hot rake away from the blast of the fire. Beside the furnace another crew is pushing the handle of the huge homemade wooden bellows. With all his might one of them pulls the handle, half as tall as himself, and pushes it back with the weight of his body. Three other men standing by to take their turns jokingly cheer him on.

Washing for Ore

The river a few miles away from the county town is another scene of activity. Undaunted by cold north wind, 25,000 students, women, and local government workers are ankle-deep in the water, washing for the iron-bearing sand that has been carried down from the nearby mountains. On the banks, groups of students off their working shift hold classes, and a crew of older women minds the children for the mothers beside the temporary living quarters made for workers from distant parts of the county. At night, lamps on the washing frames outline the river like two pearl necklaces.

The office of the county Communist Party committee where I stayed in the county town of Lushan is like the headquarters of an army, for the party has undertaken direct leadership of the iron campaign. Any time of the day or night, one can hear someone shouting into the telephone, "Long distance . . . urgent . . . coal . . . tons."

Showed the Country

This is the verve which enabled Lushan, the small mountainous county which six months ago possessed neither a blast furnace nor an engineer, or even an automobile, to startle the entire country by proving it could turn out 1,000 tons of iron a day. That record on last August 28 opened a new page in the nation-wide campaign for iron and steel, for it did away with the belief that smelting by local methods does not add up to much.

Lushan's achievement was called a "sputnik," and within the next month it inspired seventy-three more counties to reach that level. Now the record has been surpassed hundreds of times, but the county's 430,000 people are still seized by the iron and steel fever. Each day 100,000 of them work directly in its production, and many thousands more "at the rear" help transport ore after a day's work in the fields.

The people of Lushan began making small amounts of iron early in the summer, in line with the country's policy of developing small local industry as well as large plants, and to meet their own needs in making labor-saving farm machinery. On exploration they found that they had fine natural conditions for iron. Prospectors have located ore in sixty places in the county, including one deposit with an estimated reserve of 10,000 million tons. Much of it is in surface seams or outcroppings which the people began to mine immediately.

The large river whose floods used to plague the area is now paying its debt. A simple wooden washing frame can isolate from the riverbed up to 5,000 chin (2,500 kg) per day of the dark red, high iron content sand washed down from the mountains. The county can also get an abundant supply of coal from the large Pintingshan mine, located nearby on one of the richest deposits discovered since liberation, whose seams also extend into Lushan.

A Start from Nothing

Initial problems of equipment and training for iron production were solved in much the same way as in other counties. In Lushan, local materials and simple homemade tools were used to cut down initial investment and half of the funds were contributed by the people themselves. A dozen blacksmiths who at the beginning did not know how to smelt ore, led by the party vice-secretary, studied and experimented until they found a suitable process, and then passed the technique on to 600 other farmer-steelworkers.

Between May and August, they built 400 small earthen furnaces in various parts of the county. . . . The county was turning out 8.5 tons of pig iron a day by early August.

"We thought that was pretty spectacular at the time," recalled party secretary Ke, "but we wanted to produce 150,000 to 200,000 tons by the end of the year. . . .

Shooting a Sputnik

"We had heard of the 'sputniks' in high crop yields the farmers in many parts of the country were getting. So the party committee decided that Lushan could try to shoot a 'sputnik' too, and aim at producing 1,000 tons of iron in one day. If we maintained this rate, we could meet the year's target."

The proposal meant that iron had to take precedence over all other jobs. The farming had to be done with as few people as possible so as to free as many workers as possible to build and operate more furnaces, and mine and transport ore and coal. . . .

Some Had Doubts

The people put forth their views through a spirited campaign of big character posters put up on the walls of the villages. Among 1.5 million of them throughout the county, only 4 percent actually opposed making more iron. Some of the writers saw the importance of iron in improving local conditions but feared that it would divert too much effort from regular farm work and endanger the crops. Others believed that although native methods could make iron in small amounts, production of any substantial size could be achieved only by "experts" with large modern facilities. "Ten fingers to pick up ore, two hands to mold clay pots, three mud walls to make a furnace—with such primitive means it is simply nonsense to think of making so much iron," they said. . . .

As the work could not go ahead without full mass support and understanding, the meetings to discuss the proposal became hot debates—a struggle of ideas. It was through this that the farmers came to realize their real power to produce. Party leaders put the need for iron in terms of the county's own needs—it could bring hydroelectric power stations on every one of the 600 reservoirs the people had built in the spring, better farm tools and machines, multi-storied buildings. They also pointed out that more iron for national construction would mean more tractors, rail lines and other improvements for all, and that the way to do this quickly was through small-scale production in communities like Lushan all over the country. . . .

The way, most people agreed, was large-scale organization. Lushan's mountains had ore but few people to do the mining. On the plains, on the other hand, there was manpower to spare. So their coops decided that only by merging could they better deploy the working force. This later formed the basis for the people's commune which now embraces all of Lushan county.

Suggestions for nurseries and canteens to release more women were also adopted. In one large village alone, these measures freed 2,100 women for productive work. . . .

When the time came to sign up for iron work, 95 percent of the county's able-bodied persons applied, and 65,000 were soon actually making iron. Shock teams were organized to man the furnaces, mine the ore, mold crucibles, and repair roads to facilitate transport. They built 500 new furnaces, and methods were developed to make the older ones yield twenty times as much iron per heat.

The Big Day

In the fortnight which preceded the target date of August 28, few people got a full night's sleep. It was just in those weeks that news came of the aggressive military build-up by the United States in the Taiwan Straits area and of provocations against the mainland. Determination became even greater. On August 27, just as the furnaces were being lit, word arrived about the nation-wide call to raise the 1958 national production of steel to 10.7 million tons, twice as much as the year before. On August 28, Lushan's furnaces yielded 1,068 tons of pig iron. The "sputnik" had succeeded and Lushan had set a new standard for local iron production.

Soon the daily average was far surpassing this one-time figure. In the autumn, 40,000 more workers came from neighboring counties. By early November 150,000 tons were being produced in one day—as much as had been planned for the whole year.

Now a new stage has begun. Local iron is being turned into blowers, gasoline engines, and other equipment which will change many of the hand-operated furnaces into semimechanized ones. More than 320 machinery plants, 20 cement works and 4 power stations have been opened. On the site of one furnace field a modern medium-size iron and steel mill, designed and equipped by the provincial authorities, is now being built. It will turn out half a million tons of rolled steel this year.

5. RURAL WOMEN ADVANCE IN THE GREAT LEAP

Spiraling demands for labor created unprecedented opportunities for women to enter the workforce. As local industry

Wang Yin: Women's New Life in Rural People's Communes. China News Service, February 24, 1959. SCPRP 1975.

and major construction projects initiated by the communes relied heavily on men drawn from the agricultural sector, women took responsibility for numerous jobs in agriculture, but many also learned new industrial skills or worked in schools, day care centers and other service occupations. As women joined production units, the communes responded to the need to ease the burden of household chores by expanding child care services and introducing communal dining halls.

The Great Leap was thus second only to the land revolution in providing a setting in which women liberated themselves from the confines of subordinate, household situations. Many of the experiments which favored women's emancipation, particularly the communal dining halls and day care, would be sharply curtailed in subsequent years of economic hardship. But these were now on the agenda of Chinese socialism, goals to strive for in coming years. As women played a larger productive role they hastened the day when these reforms would be achieved on solid foundations; they created, that is, a new basis for subsequent rounds in the struggle for women's emancipation.

During the Great Leap Forward of agricultural production last year, the broad mass of rural women in the country displayed tremendous revolutionary fervor and revolutionary vigor. By participating in all forms of agricultural production, they played an important part in securing the bumper harvest last year. Now that the people's communes are operating collective welfare undertakings, domestic labor has been socialized and the women are no longer compelled to attend at once to the two conflicting jobs of participation in social production and housekeeping. Statistical returns show that to date, there are 2,650,000 dining halls in the rural people's communes in the country, serving meals to 90 percent of the total rural population. There are 4,750,000 nurseries and kindergartens, taking care of 24,000,000 children. In some areas, the number of children thus taken care of accounts for over 85 percent of the total number of children under school age. Practically all rural women in the country have been able to take part in productive labor. Because they are no longer tied down by household matters, they can work and study more attentively than before. . . .

The rural people's communes engage in all forms of production, but women take part mostly in agricultural production. When the male labor force has been transferred to industry, water conservancy construction, and capital construction, it is for the women to take up the greater part of the work in agricultural production. In many people's communes last autumn, it was the women that were mainly responsible for the work of autumn harvesting and winter plowing. So that women may well accomplish their tasks in production, the people's communes have conducted training courses to teach women techniques in agricultural production. In Weihsing people's commune, Kaoan *hsien*, Kiangsi, last autumn, 7,000 to 8,000 men out of the total male labor force of 9,700 men went to smelt iron and build water conservancy projects. The work of autumn harvesting and winter sowing in the 204,000 mou of land was mainly entrusted to the women numbering 9,400 or more. The party committee of this commune opened training classes with production teams as the units, to teach the women the techniques of plowing, raking, seed mixing, and manure application. . . .

The rural people's communes are implementing the directive of attending both to industry and to agriculture. All the people's communes are operating industry on a large scale. They have been operating iron smelting plants, farm tool factories, lathe factories, fertilizer works, and agricultural product processing factories. Many rural women, too, have participated in commune-operated industry and are learning techniques in the factories. In the "March 8" Ball Bearings Works in Yaochin people's commune, T'aiho *hsien*, Anhwei, 60 percent of the workers are women. In Hsiench'iao people's commune, Hangchow, Chekiang, twelve women operated a cement works. Some of them were sent to learn techniques in large cement works. When they came back, they took on apprentices. There are now 103 workers in this cement works, turning out 50 to 60 tons of cement each day. The cement is being used in the construction projects in the commune. . . .

In the social welfare undertakings operated by the people's

communes, especially in the dining halls, nurseries, and maternity homes, most of the personnel are women. The people's communes in all parts of the country have been paying attention to the training of nurses, kindergarten teachers, and midwives. Such training is conducted by the opening of training classes or the serving of apprenticeship under experienced persons. . . .

Many women, since they ceased to be illiterate, have joined part-time schools. In Kweichow and Anhwei, 70 to 80 percent of the women who should attend schools are attending schools. In Sankai people's commune, T'aiho *hsien*, Anhwei, all 135 young and middle-aged illiterate women ceased to be so in March last year. They are now attending part-time schools. . . .

In many people's communes, provisions have been made for granting of forty to fifty days' maternity leave and for the payment of normal wages during this leave of absence. In addition, lying-in women are provided with nourishing food, such as eggs, meat, and sugar. . . .

When the women are asked to describe their new life after the building of people's communes, they say that such description will take more than three days and three nights. They are now leading the life for which they have long yearned. In the morning, the whole family goes to the mess hall for breakfast. The children are then sent to the nursery or the kindergarten as the case may be. The adults are free to attend to their own work. In the afternoon, after the work is finished, the whole family is reunited to enjoy the comfort of home.

The women have participated in social productive labor and have been earning their own wages. In family life, their position has been raised to that of the other adult members of the family. This has removed the last vestige of the feudal family system left behind by history. In production as well as in studies, women's political consciousness and cultural and technical level are rising higher every day. Their ability and wisdom have found better molding and expression. Thus, by actual deed, the difference between women and men politically, culturally, and technologically is being reduced.

6. AWAY WITH ALL PESTS!
THE ELIMINATION OF SCHISTOSOMIASIS
AND THE PRINCIPLES OF HEALTH CARE

*China is the first nation to control and in large areas elimi-
nate, schistosomiasis (snail fever), the scourge of 250 million
people in the tropical and semi-tropical regions of Asia, Africa,
and Latin America. The explanations for this phenomenon take
us to the heart not only of the principles of the Chinese health
system but to the intersection of the interrelated priorities of
health and development and provide a vivid example of mass
line principles at work.*

*China's first National Health Conference in 1950 established
four major guidelines which distinguish the health system from
that of many other nations. Their application can be seen as
instrumental in the elimination of schistosomiasis, opium addiction, and venereal disease, and the effective control of malaria,
Kala-azar, and other dread diseases. These are: (1) health work
should primarily serve the masses of the laboring people; (2)
chief emphasis should be placed on the prevention of disease; (3) close unity should be fostered between traditional and
modern doctors; and (4) health work should, wherever appropriate, be conducted by mass campaigns with the active participation of medical workers.*

*On the basis of these principles and strengthened from 1958
by commune organization, the entire people, under the direction of trained health workers, could be called into play to fight
schistosomiasis and other diseases. Dr. Joshua Horn, a British
physician who worked in China from 1954–1969, has described
the mobilization to eliminate the disease: "Twice a year the
entire population in county after county, supplemented by the
voluntary labor of all available armymen, students, teachers,
and office workers, turned out to drain the rivers and ditches,
dig away and bury their banks and tamp down the buried
earth." . . . To mobilize them, he went on, "does not mean to*

Ling Yang: An End to Plague! Battle Against Schistosomiasis. *Peking
Review* (PR), February 2, 1960.

issue them with shovels and instructions; it means to fire them with enthusiasm, to release their initiative and to tap their wisdom. " *Characteristic methods of the Great Leap in national economic life, the mass line, reliance on mobilized peasants and workers, and the beginnings of cooperative health systems have produced striking gains in health.*

The ghastly plague, schistosomiasis, caused untold suffering to great numbers of Chinese people in the South. In old China, it was prevalent in the twelve provinces and municipalities south of the Huai River and east of the Lan-ts'ang River in Yunnan province. The Kuomintang reactionaries, turning a blind eye to this disastrous situation, did nothing to eradicate the disease or even contain it. And the people themselves, impoverished as they were by the rapacious regime, were helpless against it.

Forty years ago, Shangyangpan village in Yushan county, Kiangsi province, had a population of 500. At the time of liberation, scarcely 144 remained, of whom 115 were schistosomiasis victims. There were widows in almost every household and many families experienced three generations of women widowed in succession. Shangyangpan became known as the "Village of Widows." And such villages were frequently found in the affected areas. The people bitterly lamented their fate in verse:

> *In the daytime few are in the fields.*
> *At night, ghosts sing under the moon.*
> *When shall we see the end of our suffering?*
> *And when shall happiness touch us?*

Many fled their homes to seek safety elsewhere. The population in the plague areas continued to shrink. Large tracts of land lay waste. Even where they were cultivated, the yields were low owing to insufficient labor.

Tortured by this affliction and not understanding what caused it, the people in the worst-stricken areas were extremely superstitious. They pleaded to the gods for mercy but the gods turned a deaf ear to their suffering. In desperation, some victims even sought salvation in death. Shortly before liberation in Fenghwangtai village, Siangyin county, Hunan province, eleven ended the nightmare of their existence by suicide.

Party and People Fight Back

This situation was brought to an end after liberation. Knowing the eagerness of the people to free themselves from schistosomiasis, the Communist Party and Chairman Mao Tsetung specifically set forth the task of wiping out this scourge. To move the whole party and nation to support this movement, the elimination of schistosomiasis was included as an important goal in the National Program for Agricultural Development (1956–67). The Central Committee of the party also formed a special nine-man group to lead the work. . . . A huge campaign was initiated which has advanced with greater speed since the big leap forward in 1958.

To eliminate the snails—the intermediate host to the disease-breeding schistosome—the people worked with a will. In areas crisscrossed by rivers and canals, they drained thousands of streams. Wiping out the snails was combined with digging up silt for fertilizer and building water conservancy projects. Vast tracts of land were reclaimed from the encroaching lakes and swamps thus simultaneously eliminating the snails and enlarging the cultivated area. By the end of September 1959, work to wipe out the snails extended over a region comprising more than 6,350 million square meters. This reduced by one-third the snail-infested sections of residential districts and districts frequented by the people.

An attack on the eggs of the schistosome was made through a night soil control system. This served the fivefold purpose of reducing the dispersal of the eggs, increasing the quantity of manure, improving its quality, contributing to better environmental sanitation, and curtailing the cases of infectious intestinal diseases. The people called this system "a firecracker with five kicks."

As a preventive measure, people in the plague-ridden areas were advised to wear leggings or apply protective medication to their legs when taking part in such activities as the collection of weeds or catching fish. Consequently the infection of large numbers of people living or working in the environs of lakes and swamps has been essentially eliminated. Another preventive measure, the treatment of water used by the people, has also proved very effective.

To cure those suffering from schistosomiasis, the Communist Party and the people's government dispatched scores of thousands of medical workers—both Western-style doctors and practitioners of Chinese medicine. They made the rounds of the stricken areas and provided much needed medical treatment. A large-scale campaign to extend this treatment to the greatest possible number of victims went into high gear. As a result of technical advances, a three-day antimony treatment was developed which proved highly effective. It is also much less costly than the previous one-month treatment. *By the end of September 1959, some 4.9 million patients suffering from schistosomiasis, or 70 percent of all the 7 million cases in the country, had received treatment. About 3.5 million were cured.* Since, on the average, the disease causes a 40 percent loss in the patient's capacity to work, this extensive cure was equivalent to reinforcing the agricultural labor force by more than 1 million people. In addition, more than 140,000 draft oxen suffering from schistosomiasis have also been restored to health.

Schistosomiasis has now been completely brought under control after years of zealous struggle. The affected area is being steadily reduced.

This great victory in combating schistosomiasis stems from the correct principle of combining prevention and cure with production. Both were part of one unified whole. Both made great leaps forward under unified leadership and coordination. While the more serious cases are dealt with all the year round, treatment on a mass scale is timed to coincide with the slack season. The aged, children, the disabled, and the gravely ill are dealt with during the active seasons whereas the young and middle-aged are treated, one group after the other, during the quieter seasons. In this way treatment of the disease does not interfere with production.

In practical terms this means alternating high tempo shock-brigade type actions with routine consolidation. That is, concentrating every effort at the opportune moment, to launch an all-out attack on the disease. This is immediately followed up by routine arrangements such as promulgating the necessary regulations, improving the public health organizations at the grassroots level, solidifying and further developing the gains of the preceding movement and laying the groundwork for the next big push.

The great advances registered in the conquest of schistosomiasis also stem from the principle of combining the mass movement with science and technique. Schistosomiasis infects vast areas. It spreads in a very complicated manner. A large number of human victims and domestic animals must be treated. This is a colossal technical undertaking which can only be successfully accomplished with the conscious initiative, energy, and cooperation of the people firmly united with correct scientific and technical guidance. Only by a fusion of the two can greater, faster, better, and more economical results be achieved. The large number of medical personnel organized to go among the people in the stricken regions, carry out experiments, demonstrate preventive measures, and train others by tens of thousands to form the backbone of the movement for prevention and cure. At the same time they popularize and educate the people in science and technique. The policy of "walking on two legs," of combining Chinese and Western, and modern and indigenous methods was promoted. In this way, mass drives have been set going which draw the entire local population into action and bring into full play all available resources and talents.

Farewell to the God of Plague

As a result of these tremendous efforts a fundamental change has taken place. The scenes described in Chairman Mao Tsetung's poem "Farewell to the God of Plague,"

> *Weeds choked hundreds of villages, men wasted away;*
> *Thousands of households dwindled, phantoms sang with glee.*

have given way to new vistas evoked by the same poet:

> *The spring wind blows amid ten thousand willow*
>   *branches,*
> *Six hundred million in this Sacred Land all equal*
> *Yao and Shun.* *

The population trend in the plague areas has been reversed. Death rates plummeted while birth rates rose rapidly. In the formerly desolate Shangyangpan village, there are now forty-four children under nine years of age—as many as one-fourth of the village's population. Their laughter and singing is music to the people of Shangyangpan after the long years of silence. The villagers have celebrated their new life in a poem of praise:

> *Thousand-year-old iron tree blossoms;*
> *Wives barren for years bear babies.*
> *Everywhere in the village children sing*
> *Bountiful harvests and people spring up together.*

The schistosomiasis victims in this village have all been cured. Those who deserted their homes to flee the plague have returned. Labor is more abundant, causing production to expand and the livelihood of the people to improve.

The campaign to prevent and cure schistosomiasis has helped to alter old customs and habits, enhanced the general health conditions for the country, and transformed the mental perspective of the people. In Yukiang county of Kiangsi province, the first where this plague was eradicated, a fortuneteller who had done a thriving business for twelve years was soon out of customers. Those who had previously turned to him in hopelessness and desperation had found a real cure. People are confident that they will succeed in completely eliminating the plague. One hears such remarks as: "What the gods failed to cure is not insurmountable to the communists at all. With the Communist Party and the people's communes there's nothing on earth that cannot be done."

---

* Two ancient sage kings.

7. TIDYING UP THE PEOPLE'S COMMUNES

Beginning in early 1959 the party reassessed the managerial responsibilities of commune, brigade, and team to determine appropriate levels for ownership and accounting. The first moves were initiated to curb absolute egalitarianism and centralization of all resources at the commune level, both of which had undermined the productive efficiency of the communes.

At their inception, the communes typically coordinated ownership and accounting and assumed authority for overall management. Conflicts soon arose between the commune and lower levels over labor power allocation and resource distribution, particularly between the commune, the primary accounting unit and the team, the primary unit for organizing agricultural work. Commune cadres, tending to focus on new industrial enterprises and construction projects, often slighted the labor requirements of the brigades and teams. Frequently they also lost sight of the primacy of agriculture. These problems were the product of inexperience, overzealousness, pressures from higher levels, and the nationwide mood of imminent transition to communism. Centralization of ownership and management at the commune level led to dissatisfaction, especially among more prosperous brigades and individuals. And with the expansion of partial free supply systems and income distribution calculated on the basis of total communal yields, the direct link between labor input and remuneration became remote and production enthusiasm declined.

From early 1959 decentralization of managerial responsibilities transferred increased responsibility to the brigade and team levels. The commune retained responsibility for overall planning, organizing large-scale construction projects and managing major industries. But limits were placed on communal authority to mobilize labor for major construction projects and in order to guarantee stable work groups at lower levels. Brigades gained

Shantung Provincial Party Committee: Draft Regulations on the System of Production Management in People's Communes, January 11, 1959, *Ta-chung Jih-pao*, January 12, 1959. SCPRP 1962.

*control of land, draft animals, and tools and became the pri-
mary unit of accounting. At this time the free supply system
was being cut back in many areas. These adjustments consolidated the communes by harmonizing more closely the goal of
rural transformation with present levels of political consciousness, scale of production, and management capabilities.*

People's communes are now being energetically tidied up and
consolidated in all districts of the province. How to manage
production successfully in people's communes is an important
question urgently demanding an answer. The provincial committee and provincial people's council have drafted regulations
for distribution to all districts. It is hoped that all districts will
enforce them in light of local conditions and at the same time
start discussion among cadres and the masses and send reports
to the provincial committee on their suggestions concerning
revisions to the draft regulations so that they may be promulgated as an official document after revisions.

The administrative set-up of a commune may generally be
divided into three levels—commune administrative committee,
administrative districts (or production brigades) and production
teams. The administrative districts (or production brigades) are
in general units having under their control workers, peasants,
traders, students, and soldiers and work on a basis of business
accounting for all gains and losses. Production teams are basic
units of labor organization. Under the unified leadership of the
commune administrative committee, the administrative districts
and production teams should be given the necessary powers to
organize production and capital construction and manage their
fiscal affairs and welfare undertakings so that they can bring
their initiative into play. . . .

Production plans. On the basis of unified state plans and on
the principle of suiting local conditions, the commune administrative committee should draw up unified plans and set tasks for
the administrative districts (or production brigades) and production teams. . . .

Industrial production. In general, large factories that involve
large investments and a high technical level and which serve the
whole *hsien* and even other *hsien* areas should be operated and

managed by the *hsien* federation of communes. Small factories that involve small investments and simple equipment and which mainly serve the commune production and members' livelihood should be operated and managed by the commune itself, provided fulfillment of the tasks assigned by the *hsien* federation is insured and provided the commune subordinates itself to the *hsien* plans for transfer of products. Industries that turn out and repair small farm tools and produce granular fertilizer as well as flour mills and tailoring factories that serve the livelihood of commune members—industries that should be properly scattered—may in general be turned over to production brigades for management so that they can display their initiative in production and operation.

On the basis of the agricultural production plans drawn up by the commune administrative committee, the commune should require the administrative districts and production teams to undertake fulfillment of assignments and assume responsibility. For example, in the case of large-scale forestry, the commune may either set up a special team to manage it or transfer its management to the neighboring production team; scattered forestry may be turned over to production teams for management. . . .

Fiscal management. The commune shall pool gains and losses, with the administrative districts and production teams assuming responsibility for business accounting and fiscal obligations. Except for certain amounts of reserve supplies and funds to be kept by the commune for miscellaneous purposes, all outlays in the category of production expenses should be fixed down to the level of teams along with the organization of production plans. Where it is desirable to fix fiscal obligations, expenses should be fixed down to the team level; where it is desirable to fix a norm of consumption, the norm should be fixed down to the team level. . . .

The commune and administrative districts (or production brigades) should show serious respect for the rights of production teams and help them institute responsibility systems for production and livelihood so that they can genuinely become basic units for organizing labor and production under unified leadership. . . .

The people's communes must improve the present state of

labor organization immediately, continue to implement the system of responsibility for production and other tasks, perfect labor inspection and the system of awards, raise labor efficiency and improve the quality of labor. Our present experience indicates that the following measures should be taken to institute the production responsibility system:

(1) The commune should fix "six things" for production teams in its management of agricultural production. That is, the commune administrative committee should hold production teams responsible for fixed farming area, labor power, output, measures, expenses, and livestock tools. A production team shall be given proper award if its production target is exceeded due to good management; a production team shall be properly penalized if its production falls off due to poor management.

(2) The production teams shall fix "four things," that is, output, measures, production cost, and administrative personnel. Further, the teams shall carry out periodic check-ups and comparisons, praising and rewarding those who show a good record of management and criticizing and, if necessary, penalizing those who show a poor record of management. The "army group" type of operation carried out by the communes at present may be adopted in special cases but must not upset the normal production organization and responsibility system.

(3) Labor norms must be maintained in farming jobs. In ordinary cases, labor norms for various farming jobs may be set by fixing the tasks, quality, quantity, time, and personnel. These labor norms should be fulfilled by production teams, production divisions or individuals. . . .

(4) According to different farming seasons and different stages, the administrative districts should help production teams concretely organize farming jobs and labor power and see that long-range plans are worked out and immediate arrangements are made. A state of affairs is widespread in communes at the present moment where production is not planned and jobs are extemporaneously assigned every day. This state of affairs must be changed immediately. . . .

The people's communes must implement the following basic labor systems:

(1) Except for the old, the weak, the disabled, and the sick who are physically unfit for labor, all persons with labor power must perform labor.

(2) The cadres of people's communes must take part in physical labor; the functionaries of production team cadres shall not divorce themselves from production; the heads of production brigades shall devote at least 150 days a year to productive labor and leave their posts for a certain time to act as members. The commune-run schools shall practice the system of education integrated with labor: primary school pupils shall perform labor one hour a day, higher primary school pupils two hours a day and junior middle school students three hours a day. For students of senior middle schools and above, a system of part work and part study shall be instituted in ordinary times and separate provisions shall be made during the busy farming season or in special cases.

(3) Ensure commune members the necessary hours for rest. In ordinary times, they shall perform labor for eight hours and conduct studies for two hours a day. Working hours may be appropriately extended during the busy farming season or during a particular press of other rural work but eight hours for sleep and four hours for meals and rest must be insured.

(4) The day-off system. Commune members shall have two days off each month (or half a day off each week): women members may be allowed proper time to attend to household work. There will be a one-day holiday on New Year's day, May first, and National Day, and a three-day holiday during the Spring Festival. Women members shall not work in water and shall not do heavy work during menstruation nor the latter stage of pregnancy, and shall rest for forty days during the period of confinement; they shall receive the usual pay.

B. THE GREAT LEAP IN INDUSTRY AND THE CITIES

1. DECENTRALIZATION OF PLANNING AND ADMINISTRATION

In the early years of the People's Republic, it was imperative to establish central control over such economic lifelines as planning and finance in order to combat spiraling inflation, unify taxation, and ensure efficient allocation of scarce resources. Launching of the first five-year plan in 1953 further strengthened centralized management of the economy. Learning from "advanced Soviet practice," China created a vast bureaucracy organized along vertical (departmental, ministerial) lines to direct the emerging industrial and national planning structures. It became increasingly apparent, however, that centralized bureaucratic control not only conflicted with revolutionary aims to broaden participation in decision-making but was impractical as well, in a country as large, diverse, and complex as China.

Mao's 1956 speech, "On the Ten Major Relationships" (see this volume, II, 6), initiated a reassessment of issues of centralization and decentralization in economic planning and management. In late 1957 three State Council directives delegated authority to provincial governments over industrial, commercial, and financial management. The first conclusive steps had been taken en route to the Great Leap in industry. The main aim of decentralization, a People's Daily *editorial noted, was to*

State Council Directive Concerning Improvement of Industrial Management System. JMJP, November 18, 1957. SCPRP 1665.

"enhance the initiative and positiveness of local government and enterprises and fulfill the country's unified plan in a way most suitable to local conditions."

Management of a large number of factories, particularly those of light industry, was transferred from central to provincial jurisdiction. Heavy industry and foreign trade remained under the control of the center. However, provincial governments assumed expanded powers over all enterprises within their borders, including those which remained principally under central direction. This allowed provincial governments to draw up regional economic plans to coordinate the operations of all enterprises to better adapt to local needs.

Effective regional planning in turn depended upon establishing a more independent financial base. Previously, the central government collected revenue from the provinces and profits from state enterprises, set a ceiling for provincial expenditures, and then allocated funds to meet the state-determined provincial budget. The new regulations transferred control over some revenues to provincial governments, permitting them to retain a share of the surplus of local enterprises to allocate locally.

Our country is a socialist country and our country's construction is planned construction; the production and construction work of various enterprises in various places throughout the country must invariably abide by and never run counter to the unified plan of the state. Our industrial management system at present basically conforms with this requirement. However, judged from existing conditions, the industrial management system in force has two main shortcomings. One is that some enterprises suitable for local management are now still directly managed by the industrial departments of the central government; at the same time, local administrative organs enjoy too little authority over industrial management with respect to material distribution, financial control, and personnel management. The other shortcoming is that the person in charge of an enterprise has too little authority over that enterprise, while the central industrial administrative department has too much control over the business in that enterprise. These two major shortcomings restrain the initiative and positive work of local administrative organs and leading personnel in enterprises. In the unified plan of the state, it is completely necessary to empower local governments with a certain degree of authority to do what is suitable to local circumstances. This degree of flexible power to be enjoyed by local governments and enterprises within the scope of the unified plan of the state is precisely to fulfill the state's unified plan in the manner most suitable to local circumstances, and is what the state's unified plan needs. . . .

1. To Appropriately Enlarge the Authority of Provinces, Autonomous Regions, and Municipalities Directly Under the Central Government, in the Management of Industry

(1) Adjust the present control of enterprises, and let provinces, autonomous regions, and municipalities directly under the central government take over some of the enterprises now under direct control of the central government.

Most of the enterprises now under the Light Industry Ministry and the Food Industry Ministry, with the exception of certain enterprises which must be controlled by the central authority, are to be taken over by provinces, autonomous regions, and municipalities directly under the central government. In the textile industry, for the present only a small number of enterprises are to be thus decentralized, and further steps will be decided upon according to concrete conditions in the future.

As to enterprises belonging to the various departments of heavy industry, all large-scale mines, large-scale metallurgical enterprises, large-scale chemical industrial enterprises, important coal bases, large power stations and electricity networks, oil refineries, factories manufacturing large and precision machines, factories manufacturing electric motors and instruments, the military industry, and other industries which need complicated skills are still to be controlled by the various industrial departments of the central government. Apart from these, all other factories suitable for local administration are to be decentralized step by step according to actual conditions. . . .

In all enterprises still under the jurisdiction of various departments of the central government, the central-local dual leadership system—with the central authority as the main one—is to be followed, and the leadership and supervision exercised by local authorities over these enterprises are to be strengthened.

(2) Increase the authority of provinces, autonomous regions, and municipalities directly under the central government, in the distribution of materials. . . .

(3) Of the profits of enterprises which were formerly under the control of various central ministries but are now decentralized and put under the management of local governments, 20 percent goes to local authorities and 80 percent goes to the central government.

Local governments are not entitled to profits gained by enterprises belonging to the Second Ministry of Machine Building, the Ministry of Railways, the foreign sale section of the Ministry of Foreign Trade, and the Civil Navigation Bureau; or to those gained by large-scale mines, large-scale metallurgical plants, large-scale chemical industries, large-scale coal mines, large electricity networks, oil refineries, and large factories manufacturing machinery and electric motors; or to those gained by interprovincial marine transport enterprises along the Yangtze River and the seacoast. Except these, local governments may receive 20 percent of the total profits gained by other enterprises, such as textile enterprises, which are still under the management of the central ministries.

The fixed 2 to 8 ratio of profits shall remain unchanged for three years in all enterprises in which local governments are entitled to share profits.

The profits of enterprises which have been under local management from the very beginning still go entirely to local governments.

(4) Increase the power of local authorities in personnel management. The personnel management in decentralized enterprises is to be handled as in local enterprises. . . .

2. To Appropriately Enlarge the Authority of Persons in Charge of Enterprises in the Internal Management of the Enterprises

(1) In controlling a plan, fewer targets should be fixed as orders, and more responsibility should be entrusted to persons in charge of the enterprises.

In respect of production plans, formerly there were twelve compulsory targets which were fixed by the State Council and not to be changed without approval of the State Council. They were: total output value, quantities of important products, new variety of products to be trial manufactured, important technical economic quotas, rate of reduction of costs, amount of reduction of costs, total number of staff and workers, number of workers at the end of the year, total wage bill, average wage, labor productivity, and profit. Now the number of targets fixed by the State Council is to be reduced to four, namely: (i) quantities of important products; (ii) total number of staff and workers; (iii) total wage bill; (iv) profit. . . .

In respect of plans for capital construction, nonflexible targets fixed by the State Council for the year 1957 are four in number, namely: (i) total amount of investment; (ii) above-norm items; (iii) mobilization of productive power; (iv) amount of construction and installation work.

2. THE DEVELOPMENT OF LOCAL INDUSTRY

Concentration during the first five-year plan on large, modern, heavy industrial plants under the jurisdiction of central ministries intensified conflicting demands for limited resources between local communities and the state, and between industry and agriculture. A lagging agricultural growth rate and a widening gap between urban and rural areas precipitated a reassessment of the prevailing strategy.

The 1957 and 1958 directives initiating decentralization of

Develop Local Industry on the Principle of Achieving Greater, Faster, Better and More Economical Results. JMJP editorial, May 12, 1958. In: *600 Million Build Industry* (Peking: Foreign Languages Press, 1958).

financial and administrative controls gave local leaders the authority and financial base from which to vigorously promote local industry as a central part of coordinated regional and local development efforts. During the Great Leap local industry proliferated rapidly, particularly at the county and commune levels to serve the diverse needs of city and countryside.

Generally small in scale and capable of integrating indigenous and modern techniques, local industry was flexible enough to adapt to diverse conditions and changing requirements. Based on local sources of raw materials, local production and local distribution systems, small industry utilized scattered resources, provided employment, overcame transportation bottlenecks, and contributed to technical revolution.

Local industries are being founded throughout China at a striking pace. All the provinces, many special administrative regions, counties, and even townships have made daring plans for a leap forward to make the total output value of their local industries outstrip that of agriculture within five years or so. In most places decisions are carried out immediately, because of the enthusiastic support of the masses. Small industrial plants, mines and power stations have come up like mushrooms. Once such enthusiasm for building local industries is brought into play it acts like the fission of an atomic nucleus, releasing tremendous energy that creates a rate of progress in our industry hitherto unprecedented. . . .

As far back as April 1956, Comrade Mao Tsetung, in "On the Ten Major Relationships," stated the principle of developing industries under the central authorities (mainly giant enterprises), and at the same time developing industries under the local authorities (mainly medium and small enterprises).

Comrade Mao Tsetung set forth this principle as a result of the experiences in industrial construction both at home and abroad, especially China's experiences in industrial construction during the first five-year plan (1953–1957). During that period, we paid special attention to the development of industry administered by the central authorities. This was absolutely necessary and as a result of the rapid development of industry under central management, China has already built the preliminary foundation for industrialization. During the same period, because the socialist transformation was not yet complete and because not enough attention had been paid to it, the development of local industry was comparatively slow. During the first five-year plan great efforts were made to establish giant enterprises, but not enough attention was paid to medium and small enterprises. Previously, it was thought that only giant enterprises were economical, while medium and small enterprises were not worthwhile. . . . But giant enterprises alone are not enough. It is also necessary to establish large numbers of medium and small enterprises for they do not cost much, can be set up locally, take a short time to build and can go into production quickly.

The simultaneous development of large, medium, and small enterprises will remove the fetters that hamper the growth of medium and small enterprises. The development of all three types should be interrelated and act as a stimulus to each other's progress. This is the specific road to the industrialization of China at a high speed.

The third plenary session of the Central Committee of the party held in October 1957 again decided to change the system of management in industry, commerce and finance, passing a large part of the administrative power formerly under the central authorities to the local authorities. All these, plus the fight against conservatism and waste in the course of the rectification campaign, have greatly stirred the initiative of the local authorities to found industries. . . .

In 1958 the rate of growth of local industries in the country will probably reach 37 percent or even more. In Kansu, which has always been a rather poor province, the people, with the aim of building up industry, collected funds amounting to more than the total investment made by the state in the local industries in the last three years. They did this in a few weeks. Where the region is comparatively backward industrially, the initiative in building industry is also higher. . . .

In counties with adequate resources (mainly coal and iron), it is estimated that it is possible, within a few years, to build at least one small coal mine, one small chemical fertilizer plant, one small coal tar plant, one small iron smelting plant, one small cement works, one small power station, and one integrated machinery repair plant. The construction of these factories will need a total investment of around 12 million yuan. On a county level it is not very difficult to raise that amount of money in about five years. Once these factories are built up, then industrialization of that county is a reality. There are over 2,000 counties in our country. According to present statistics, there are over 1,500 counties with coal resources and over 200 counties with iron resources. . . .

The basic task of local industries is to serve agriculture. They must also serve the big state industries, the people's daily needs, both in town and countryside, and foreign trade (mainly by processing farm produce and making native and special products for export). . . . All the provinces and autonomous regions, while making every effort to fulfill the plan for a leap forward in agriculture, must strive to make the total output value of the local industries outstrip that of agriculture in five to seven years. . . .

With the exception of the relatively large and important projects which will be financed mainly by the central authorities, all other construction projects will be financed mainly by the localities themselves. Local funds will, in large part, come from the treasuries of local organizations and from the funds accumulated by the local industrial enterprises, the handicraft cooperatives and the agricultural producers' cooperatives. This year, in view of the fact that the agricultural coops and the peasants have already invested heavily in water conservancy construction, it is generally not advisable to burden them too much with investments in industrial construction. . . .

Handicraft industry must also be reconstructed and developed. Attention must be paid first to developing it into handicraft production that serves agriculture and the needs of the people in the locality. Next, it is necessary to develop actively the manufacture of special handicrafts to meet the needs of both the home and export markets.

In view of the fact that this year most of the money, materials and manpower of the various regions will be devoted to the Great Leap Forward in agriculture, we should mainly build small enterprises, especially those making improved farm tools, repairing agricultural machinery and exploiting nonferrous metals and coal pits, which require small investments, take less time to build and bring quick results.

3. WORKER PARTICIPATION
AND THE TRANSFORMATION
OF THE CHINESE FACTORIES

In 1956 widespread dissatisfaction with Soviet managerial practices introduced in China, particularly the method of "one-man management," led the party to modify the system by placing individual managers under the overall leadership of factory party committees. Party committees enjoyed greater authority over major policy decisions such as investment and work assignments, but managers retained responsibility for the day to day operation of the factory. Reliance on a core of administrative and technical experts, most of bourgeois origin, threatened to perpetuate and reinforce sharp divisions in power and income between managers and workers. The party committee managerial system opened the possibility of expanded worker decision-making through the party, yet the fundamental question of worker control of industry could only be resolved through movements which embodied direct participation of workers in factory decisions.

But did the mobilization techniques perfected in the countryside apply to modern industry? After a full decade in the cities, little experience had been gathered in this area.

Li Hsueh-feng, head of the Central Committee Department of Industry and Communication, noted in 1958 the pervasiveness of the view that

> *management of highly unified and centralized modern enterprises can only depend on engineers, technicians, proficient functionaries, and the so-called immutable 'scientific' rules and institutions. The mass movement, it is said, is a method of rural work. It will disturb production order and upset the balance of plans. The mass movement is therefore undesirable in the case of industrial management.*

The prerogatives of managerial authority and technical imperatives clashed with the mass line. In the Great Leap workers for the first time took the initiative and began to challenge mana-

An Important Beginning for Reform of Industrial Management. JMJP editorial, May 7, 1958. SCPRP 1774.

gerial prerogatives in fundamental ways and bid for direct control of management, technology, and planning.

The Chinghua Machine Tools Plant and Chienhua Machinery Factory in Heilungkiang province were among the first to experiment with new forms of industrial management which expanded worker participation in management and technical innovation, and transformed the role of managers. An April 1958 national industrial conference endorsed the Chinghua and Chienhua guidelines, touching off a burst of efforts in the factories to overcome the gap between mental and manual labor and between workers, cadres, and technicians, and to devise effective means of ensuring worker initiative and participation in management in ways which increased productivity. In the Great Leap Forward factories joined the countryside as major arenas of class struggle, illustrating the proposition that socialist industry requires not merely state ownership of the means of production but the direct role of workers in the management of industry.

A. Reform of Industrial Relations

The bold reform of industrial management initiated by the worker masses of the Chinghua Machine Tools Plant in Heilungkiang on the basis of the rectification campaign is a beginning of great significance. The experiences acquired by the plant consist of three aspects:

(1) Administrative cadres of departments and workshops take part in half-day physical labor every day and the leading cadres of the plant take part in one-day physical labor every week.

(2) Under the leadership of the shop administration the workers take a direct part in some of the everyday administrative work of the production teams.

(3) We must improve industrial management and operation, i.e., reform irrational rules and systems. Coordination of the work in these three spheres will fundamentally improve the relations between the leading cadres and the worker masses and enhance workers' sense of responsibility and activity, thereby setting in motion a leap forward in production.

With cadres performing half-day physical labor and workers taking a direct part in the everyday administrative work of production teams, a profound change will take place in the relations between the administrative cadres and the worker masses. As we know, in socialist enterprises the means of production belong to all the people and both the administrative personnel and the workers strive for one great common objective—building socialism. Politically they are absolutely equal and their relations in work are comradely relations which are fundamentally different from the relations of exploitation and oppression between the administrative personnel and workers of the old society. But this does not mean that no problem exists between them at all. Certain survivals of old relations of production are still constantly found between them. For instance, some administrative personnel, standing head and shoulders above others and not treating the workers as equals, regard themselves as persons exclusively charged with the task of directing and controlling others; they merely issue orders from above, seldom going to the production sites and taking no part in physical labor. In their opinion, an enterprise can be managed well if only they set up a huge machinery with multifarious rules and systems and issue administrative orders. For this reason, they disregard the position and role of the worker masses as masters and run the enterprise without relying on the creativeness and consciousness of the masses. They disregard the fine party tradition of following the mass line. And the result is that they divorce themselves from the masses and reality. This is what we call official airs. . . . This gives expression to some survivals of the old relations of production, survivals which hamper the political activity and production activity of the worker masses to a certain extent and hinder the rapid development of the productive forces. The main aim of the party center in directing cadres to take part in physical labor and in launching a rectification campaign in enterprises is to radically change the thinking and working style of cadres and heighten the consciousness of the worker masses so as to overcome such survivals of old relations of production, achieve socialist equality, mutual help and cooperation in the relations between the leader and the led, thereby to develop further the productive forces.

In this respect, the leading cadres and worker masses of the Chinghua Machine Tools Plant manifested revolutionary creativeness. This plant has not only introduced a system whereby the leading cadres performed physical labor for one to one and a half days each week but also introduced a system whereby the administrative cadres of departments and workshops took part in half-day physical labor every day; simultaneous with this, the workers under the leadership of the shop administration took a direct part in some of the everyday administrative work of production teams. The practical action taken by cadres in performing physical labor, and particularly the practical action taken by the workers in doing the administrative work of production teams, are strong proof that in a socialist enterprise there is only a difference in division of labor and duties and no difference in social status between the leader and the led, between administrative personnel and workers. Thus, the administrative cadres should not only do administrative work but should also take part in certain physical labor; the workers should not only engage in production but should also do certain administrative work. This will bring about a change in thinking, heighten workers' sense of responsibility, form a habit of loving the factory and taking good care of state property, develop criticism and self-criticism and manifest collectivism. . . .

We have introduced two basic systems—the superintendent responsibility system and the workers' council under party leadership. . . . By integrating the superintendent responsibility system with the system of workers' councils and by constantly acquiring new experiences in their application, a set of socialist industrial systems relatively integrated and capable of ensuring the mass line can gradually be established.

The Chinghua and Chienhua factories also successfully carried out reform designed to change irrational rules and systems. In these two factories as in other factories there existed some outdated rules and systems and multifarious procedures that restricted mass activity and hindered the development of production and the improvement of management. The obstruction of these outdated rules and systems to production was brought into more striking relief after cadres took part in physical labor and workers took part in administration. . . . Relying on the wisdom and creativeness of the masses, the Chinghua Machine

Tools Plant did away with and simplified 263 kinds of forms and revised 158 systems in a few days. . . . Many of the rules and systems worked out by the administrative organs over the past years are still applicable but a considerable part of those rules and systems have become obstacles to mass enthusiasm and productive force and must be revised or done away with.

B. Experiments in Factory Management Reform

Our factory is a large modern enterprise devoted to the manufacture of measuring instruments and cutting tools. In the course of the continued leap forward over the past years, we have become deeply aware of the fact that trust in the party and reliance on the masses are the basic guarantees of success in the socialist cause. . . .

Insist on Cadres Participating in Labor

Participation for a certain period of time by cadres in manual labor, particularly by cadres in leadership posts, is of great significance for cementing the relations between cadres and masses, for improving the method of leadership, for overcoming bureaucratism, for consolidating enterprise management, and for realizing a continued leap forward in production.

In the past two years, cadres of our factory have participated in labor generally in the following ways.

(a) The method of leadership relating to the operation of "experimental farms" has been promoted among the cadres from the highest level in the factory to the level of the workshop. The method provides for the timely summing up and promotion of advanced experiences gained in different fields and the extension of aid to backward units to enable them to catch up with the advanced.

The New Socialist System of Enterprise Management. CCP Committee for the Measuring Instruments and Cutting Tools Factory, Ch'engtu. JMJP, June 24, 1960. SCPRP 2295.

(b) Within the factory, a system has been established under which the cadres work regular shifts and bind themselves as apprentices to the workers. The idea is to enable them to realize and solve ideological, production and work problems through actual practice in labor.

(c) The cadres have taken the lead in organizing technical personnel for shock efforts to solve key problems of production by the use of the method of "triple combination." They go wherever there are difficulties and make shock efforts whenever the weakest link in the chain of production is found. The scope of this kind of labor is wide, the number of participants is large, the time is long and the effect on production is great. . . .

The participation by workers in management has lessened the burden of routine work on the shoulders of cadres and has created the necessary condition for the latter to participate in labor, thereby enabling them to learn from actual practice better methods of leadership over production. While participating in labor, the cadres help production teams set up the necessary production control systems and adopt the necessary measures. This enables close coordination to be effected between professional management and management by the masses and an improvement to be made in the management of production teams. . . .

Without cadres participating in labor, there can be no workers taking part in management. The participation by cadres in labor has prompted the workers to take part in management and the participation by workers in management has created the necessary condition for the cadres to take part in labor. . . .

Fully Mobilize the Workers for Participation in the Management of Enterprises

From our experience in launching the mass movement in our factory, we find that there are many forms whereby workers can participate in management and that participation in the management of the small production team is the most fundamental form at the present moment. . . .

The process of strengthening the management of the production team and delegating administrative power to lower levels in our factory is a process of implementing the policy of "two participations, one reform and triple combination'' and the system of control at different levels. We started with the workers taking part in the routine management of production and gradually extended the process to the handling of the economic accounting of the production team and to participation in economic and technical controls until the workers are firmly in the seat of overall administration. This has enriched the content of the management of the production team and has accorded professional management a comprehensive mass base. It has enabled close coordination to be effected between professional management and management by the masses, has led to the full implementation of the party's policy of coordination between the centralization of leadership and the launching of the mass movement in a big way, has constantly adjusted the relationship between the productive forces and the relations of production, and has kept up the leap forward in production. . . .

The economic accounting system for the production team must be coordinated with the voluntary labor emulation of the workers and the distribution of appropriate material rewards to them. On the basis of the overall regulations for the granting of rewards and in the light of the concrete conditions in our factory, we worked out a set of regulations offering rewards to production teams which had accomplished remarkable successes. The production teams were to accomplish the three targets of production value, quantity, and expenses set for them on a monthly basis and were to overfulfill their production goals provided this achievement was not accompanied by any serious accidents, and they should be relatively successful in political work, rate of attendance and maintenance of equipment. They would then be given rewards calculated on the basis of the amount of work which they had accomplished in excess of the quotas allotted to them. . . . The concrete measure for the distribution of rewards was: No individual was to receive any reward until his team received it. Rewards for individuals were divided into three grades on the basis of the work they accomplished in the production teams, and those individuals who performed no satisfactory service even though rewards were granted to the teams to which they were attached would not be given any reward. The distribution of rewards was closely coordinated with labor emulation. Comparisons were periodically held and banners and certificates of merit were distributed together with cash as rewards. This method, which was very well received by the masses, gave full expression to the spirit of coordination between the assumption of politics in command and the apportionment of appropriate material rewards, and prevented the occurrence of the economist tendency which was unfavorable to the full display of enthusiasm and ingenuity and which was prevalent in the past when wages were paid according to the amount of work accomplished. The economic accounting system, the labor emulation, and the distribution of appropriate material rewards made up a regular system of control for the production teams. . . .

In this situation, some of the original systems for technical control could no longer meet the needs arising from the development of production. Some of them even cramped the work enthusiasm of the masses. The workers felt the increasing need to participate in technical management. We decided to delegate the power of industrial planning and product designing to the production team.

Technology is the summation of the practical experiences of the toiling masses. The more the masses create, the richer is the content of technology. Previously some of our technical personnel deliberately wrapped technology in a shroud of mystery and regarded its laws as sacrosanct. The workers' criticism of this viewpoint ran like this: "While there are lines in the sketches and charts, there is, however, no mass line." The antirightist struggle raised the ideological consciousness of the technical personnel who, now possessed of a stronger mass viewpoint, became more attached to the workers and volunteered to work in the production teams and suggested the delegation of power on industrial arts to these teams. . . .

The simplification of industrial arts and participation by the workers in designing set the technical personnel free from the narrow confines of routine matters and gave them more time for the discussion and inspection of the new industrial arts designed by the workers in the production teams and for studying technical problems, summing up and promoting the advanced experiences already well tried out in the teams. In this way, there was not only the delegation of power but also the control of this power. Thus, the argument that the sending down of power would throw everything in confusion was without foundation. . . .

Having participated in the overall management of the production teams and particularly technical management, the workers became increasingly interested in learning scientific, technical, cultural, and theoretical knowledge. Many of the production teams worked out plans coordinating immediate with long-range studies, and launched activities for fostering technical personnel and for learning science with appropriate arrangements made for the completion of the work within a set period of time and for the administration of mutual help. Within the factory, an educational system was set up comprising a spare-time college, a secondary technical school, a junior grade middle school a primary school and an anti-illiteracy class. Now over 99.6 percent of the workers in our factory are taking part in the movement for learning culture and techniques. . . . We have recently decided to promote 200 of our workers to the positions of engineers or technical personnel. This indicates the steady narrowing of the gap between the workers and the technical personnel and paves the way for the eventual elimination of that gap.

Steady Improvement in the Management of Enterprises

The continued development of the system of "two participations, one transformation and triple combination" has created the necessary conditions for the ultimate elimination of the difference between mental labor and manual labor and for the transition to communism. Of course, it will be some time before we can realize that objective and we shall have to raise the cultural and moral levels of our workers and grapple with different sorts of bourgeois thought.

4. PIECE WORK AND SOCIALIST CONSCIOUSNESS: REFORM OF THE WAGE SYSTEM

Simultaneous with the attack on one-man management, workers vigorously protested against the piece-work system which had been widely adopted since the mid-1950s. The challenge lay in devising a wage system which maximized production and innovation incentives while reinforcing cooperative values.

Noting the important role that piece work had played in some plants in the early years after liberation, the present article analyzes a series of contradictions intensified by the Great Leap which rendered the system anachronistic. Piece work intensified conflicts and blocked cooperation among workers both by tending to reward the disproportionately young and unskilled more than highly skilled master workers, and by fostering individual acquisitiveness as opposed to collective advance. For example, piece-work systems retarded the spread of technical innovation by placing a premium on the individual's *ability to exceed quotas; sharing knowledge could raise everyone's quota, thus reducing the income advantage of the innovator. Piece work also tended both to increase inequalities and to focus worker goals on individual material incentives, thus conflicting with political goals of socialist consciousness geared toward equity and national development. In the context of the Great Leap mobilization, piece work stood out as an anachronism impeding the overall advance.*

The solution advocated here and widely practiced in Chinese factories until 1966 was the system of hourly wages plus bonuses (especially collective bonuses) for achievement, with emphasis placed on the honor of achievement and modest cash rewards provided only secondarily. In this manner Chinese factories adhered to the socialist wage principle "to each ac-

Liu Ch'eng-jui, Hung Sui-chih, Yang Chen, K'ang Tso-wu, and Ko Liang-p'ing: Contradictions in the Piece-Rate System Enforced in Industrial Enterprises. *Chiao-hsueh yu Yen-chiu* (Teaching and Research), September 4, 1958. SCPRM 153.

cording to one's work," while downgrading individual acquisitiveness, emphasizing full cooperation of workers in technical innovation, and raising factory output.

The piece-rate system, for a time after its nation-wide introduction, stimulated labor productivity, promoted elevation of workers' technical level and proficiency and gave impetus to the improvement in labor organization and production organization. In a word, it played a certain part in developing production and improving industrial management. . . . But in the last few years its active role has gradually declined and its negative role has gradually become apparent. Wages were greatly in excess of standard scale, and the piece-rate system did not show good results economically, politically, or ideologically. The piece-rate system has more and more manifested itself as a restriction on productive forces and mass enthusiasm. . . .

How is it that the piece-rate system has increasingly lost its positive part and shown its negative part?

1. The piece-rate system enlarges the contradictions among workers, affects their solidarity, and seriously restricts the activity and creativeness of the worker masses. To begin with, it enlarges the contradiction between piece-rate workers and hour-wage workers. Piece-rate workers generally get more than hour-wage workers. . . . The preponderant difference in wages between piece-rate workers and hour-wage workers causes variance and destroys the unity of workers. Some piece-rate workers are proud of their high wages and look down on hour-wage workers, saying: "Hour-wage workers dawdle over their work." . . . Some hour-wage workers say the piece-rate workers "charge with bayonets" for money. Some of them grumble and demand piece rates. Further, the system enlarges contradictions between old workers (generally high-grade workers) and new workers (generally low-grade workers and young workers). Old workers are mostly the backbone elements in production and political matters but, under the piece rate system, their wages do not exceed the standard wages as much as the wages earned by new workers. This is because young workers are strong and fast in their work. . . .

Figures from the processing shop of the Peking No. 2 Lathe

Plant show that between July and December 1957 the lower the grade of workers the higher the piece wages in excess of standard wages. On average, workers of low grade got piece wages which were higher than the standard wages for the next two or three higher grades. . . . New workers get more wages but their labor efficiency is not necessarily higher than that of old workers. . . .

2. The piece-rate system obstructs technical innovations. It hinders all-round elevation of production technique. In particular, it comes into conflict with the present Great Leap Forward in production. To begin with, techniques are now constantly innovated, norms are constantly broken, and labor efficiency is rapidly raised; yet, norms cannot be constantly revised with the result that there is no way to pay wages that are in excess of standard wages. Meanwhile, it is incompatible with the present demand for trial production of new products. High-grade workers have to take part in trial production of new products but, being paid on the basis of hour wages, they generally get less than piece-rate workers. . . . This circumstance is likely to dampen workers' enthusiasm in trial production of new products. Further, it hinders all-round elevation of techniques. Under the piece-rate system, a worker, as long as he can proficiently handle a certain working process, can earn more wages even without getting a promotion and raising his technical level. Thus the piece-rate system cannot give incentive to workers to raise their technical level in an all-round way. This is contrary to the demand for "all-round hands." . . . In addition to this, the piece-rate system obstructs exchange of advanced experiences and revision of norms. Advanced experiences are taken as "secret methods" which are not made known to others lest others should raise their efficiency and revise norms which would affect their own wages. . . .

3. The piece-rate system lends itself to the growth of bourgeois ideas among workers and enlarges contradictions between the state and workers, between the leadership and the masses. The piece-rate system inclines workers to set big store by their own material benefits, and chase after higher wages. It lends itself to individualism and economism among workers and to the tendency toward neglect of politics. . . . The result is that workers' minds are corrupted. It also adds difficulties to the

distribution of labor power, distribution of production tasks, computation of wages, and checking of jobs. . . .

In a word, judging by the practical results of introducing the piece-rate system in some enterprises, the present system of piece rates has more disadvantages and less advantages. It is disadvantageous to the development of production, to the unity of workers, and to their ideological awakening. . . .

At the early stage of economic rehabilitation and construction in our country, the piece-rate system, despite the above contradictions, played a certain part in stimulating production. This was because of the following reasons. First, the wage system in old China showed extremely irrational features; in the early days of liberation, we abolished the old wage system marked by exploitation of workers, and instituted a new socialist wage system. The new wage system was essentially adapted to the development of social productive forces.

The introduction of the piece-rate system at the time did not reveal its inherent contradictions; on the contrary, it conspicuously demonstrated its role in stimulating the development of productive forces. Second, persons just freed from the fetters of the old society bore the imprint of the old society ideologically or morally. They were still interested in material benefits to themselves, were accustomed to the standard of bourgeois right and were unlikely to detect the defects of the "distribution according to labor" principle and the contradictions inherent in the piece-rate system.

Third, as the piece-rate system was not introduced in an all-round manner, the sphere in which its contradiction manifested itself was comparatively narrow. But when conditions gradually changed, i.e., when the socialist economic system was brought to perfection, the productive forces rapidly developed, the consciousness of the masses was generally raised and the piece-rate system was introduced in an overall manner, the contradiction in the piece-rate system gradually became acute, particularly at the time the Great Leap Forward was taken in production. . . . Today we should not negate the "distribution according to labor" principle, otherwise it will lead to serious mistakes. But at the same time we cannot but foresee that the tendency toward the development of socialism is "to each according to his need" which will gradually replace the "distribution according to labor" principle. . . . When we realize that, with the intensification of contradictions, the piece-rate system is no longer in keeping with the Great Leap Forward in production and is contrary to the communist spirit, we should look for a wage form which will promote the Great Leap and the growth of communist rudiments and conform with the "distribution according to labor" principle. . . .

We are of the opinion that the abolition of the piece-rate system will not negate the "distribution according to labor" principle and material stimulation. The hour-wage system still accords with the "distribution according to labor" principle. The irrational distribution of wages caused by the piece-rate system between piece-rate workers and hour-wage workers and between old and new workers is precisely an indication that the piece-rate system does not fully embody the "distribution according to labor" principle. In combating egalitarianism we should also combat preponderant differences in wages. As to material stimulation, we think it is essential to give it due importance but should not overstress it. A wage form advantageous to political and ideological work and combined with material stimulation is more likely to bring into correct play the material stimulation in pressing forward production. . . .

The system of hour wages plus bonuses, which we recommend, is as follows: in addition to basic wages paid according to technical grades of workers, bonuses are to be paid to advanced workers and advanced units. Bonuses should be granted with honorary awards as the main thing and with material awards included; they should be granted mainly to collective bodies while awards to individuals are also to be included. The masses are to mobilize periodically to review the bonuses in democratic ways. This form can implement the "distribution according to labor" principle, eliminate the contradictions enlarged by the piece-rate system among workers, strengthen the unity of workers and facilitate the development of workers' productive activity. At the same time, it can combine material stimulation with political leadership and change the tendency towards material stimulation and personal benefits to the neglect of spiritual stimulation and collective benefits, thereby strengthening workers' urge towards advancement and the collective concept. It will help political and ideological education for workers, raise workers' communist consciousness, and promote technical advancement. In a word, it is advantageous to the development of production, to the unity of the workers, and to the elevation of workers' consciousness. It can cope with the situation of the Great Leap Forward and facilitate the transition from the socialist to the communist principle of distribution.

5. THE URBAN PEOPLE'S COMMUNES

Entering the cities in the late 1940s after an absence of more than twenty years, the party faced the complex task of managing the densely populated, economically diversified urban areas. It rapidly sought to streamline municipal organization and transform urban administration and social services. While important, these changes, relying extensively on the services of former government personnel, were far less thoroughgoing than those in rural leadership in the wake of the land revolution. Moreover, streamlining was accompanied by increased centralization of decision-making in urban affairs. The establishment in 1956 of residents' committees provided informal links between the urban administration and neighborhoods. Citizens gained greater control over basic level administrative tasks such as safety and security. Yet the residents' committees lacked the resources and authority to solve more fundamental concerns of unemployment, social services, and housing. The capital-intensive first plan had failed to solve the problem of large-scale urban unemployment, especially in the case of disguised unemployment and women. New jobs failed to keep pace with the influx of people from the countryside, despite repeated efforts to curb it. The urban communes sought to redefine the essential nature of the cities. Focusing on rapid economic expansion, they initiated a vast increase of social services and redefined the role of citizens, community, and state.

Lu Hsiao-p'ing: Birth of the People's Commune of the Chengchow Textile Machine Plant. HC (Red Flag) 10, October 16, 1958. SCPRM 150.

Residents' committees organized the first urban communes around neighborhoods. By pooling community resources, neighborhoods quickly set up labor-intensive workshops and street industries. Often small satellite factories were established to meet the specific needs of large industries, for example, through the manufacture of spare parts and recycling of industrial waste. Women played the key role in the development of urban communes. They initiated, directed, and staffed the expansion of residents' committees into productive activities through the establishment of street industries. Enlarged employment opportunities were of particular importance to urban women who had limited access to scarce urban jobs. When household demands curtailed their working hours, women took the lead in establishing collective social services such as dining halls and nurseries.

Based on these street communes and collective social services, a more mature form of urban commune emerged, centered around large industries, public agencies, and schools, in some instances embracing whole districts. In the model commune organized around the Spinning and Weaving Machine Plant in Chengchow City, commune members included the workers, their dependents, and those employed in the commercial and service establishments in the area. In addition, suburban agriculture was incorporated, laying a foundation for greater self-reliance and coordinating needs between town and country. The commune served as the chief administrative unit, assuming control of industrial and commercial enterprises within its boundaries, and as the basic level of state power.

The commune embodied a radical new vision of urban planning designed to eradicate the differences between city and countryside. Chengchow planners, for example, looked forward to a time when "the cities will have been built like an orchard with green fields and forests separating one industrial area from another and with numerous small cities lying hidden in the green sea like small islands."

From the outset, however, urban communes posed extremely difficult problems. Cities embraced an immense variety of economic enterprises whose market and service areas often extended beyond the immediate vicinity of a large factory, school, or office. Moreover, both state and collective ownership co-

existed within a single commune, resulting in a dual wage system. Unlike the rural communes, rooted in a unity of work and community, urban employment and residential patterns tended to be scattered. Husband and wife might belong to different urban communes on the basis of jobs in different factories or offices while living in a residential area located within a third commune. In the face of these and other difficulties, the urban communes represented an ambitious attempt to restructure political, economic, and social institutions, to stimulate economic growth and to meet the needs of city residents in ways which fostered community and led ultimately to the transition to communism. Plans envisaged radical innovation in urban planning and redevelopment, with the commune as the core, to overcome problems of overlapping and conflicting economic units and to integrate city and countryside, industry and agriculture. In the end the great majority of the urban communes proved to be short-lived. Though some continue to function today, after 1960 mention of the communes in the press virtually ceased. They marked China's boldest effort to date to recreate urban community preparatory to the transition to communism. Many of the experiments in industry, agriculture, and community organization would be developed further and on a firmer foundation during the Great Proletarian Cultural Revolution, but without the comprehensive reorganization of the commune.

A. Birth of the Urban Commune

Among the factories and mines in Honan province, the Chengchow Spinning and Weaving Machine Plant was the first to hoist the red flag of the people's commune. Established at the end of June of this year, this people's commune now has been developed into a basic-level social unit combining industry, agriculture, commerce, and culture with military affairs, and integrating economic activity with political activity, education with production and "labor with military exercise."

This people's commune is centered around the Chengchow Spinning and Weaving Machine Plant. Of the total of 10,559 persons who live around the plant, including dependents of its office employees and workers, handicraftsmen working for the plant, residents, and peasants, all of those who are qualified for membership have joined this people's commune.

This people's commune consists of manifold "satellite" factories. All commercial departments and service units established by the Chengchow Municipal Government to serve the plant in question have been handed over to this commune for management. Also, the two brigades for agricultural production and a sheep dairy farm have been transferred to the control of the commune. In this commune there is a dining hall, a kindergarten, a nursery, nursing rooms, and various organizations for service. The Red and Expert University established by this commune includes the nine colleges of Technical Research, Marxism-Leninism, Industry, Agriculture, Finance and Economics, Medical Science, Military Affairs and Physical Education, Culture and Education, and Foreign Language. There is also a school combining study with work, a part-time middle school, a part-time primary school, a part-time polytechnic school, a day middle school, and a day primary school.

The whole commune is run along military lines and organized into an army corps. The plant, according to workshops, the commercial departments, according to units, and the agricultural organization, according to brigades, are organized into regiments, battalions and companies. . . .

At present the commune has established over ten small "satellite" factories around the Chengchow Spinning and Weaving Machine Plant. For instance, the major plant leaves much remnant material and waste material. So the commune has established a small hardware factory to process them. The carpenters' workshop of the major plant has always turned out a large amount of sawdust and many short planks which in the past were thrown away as useless materials, but now are processed in three new factories. One is an alcohol brewery using sawdust as a raw material. The second is a chemical factory processing sawdust into chemical boards. And the third is a carpenters' factory utilizing waste materials to make furniture and other household utensils. . . .

As the major plant has constantly burned up a great deal of waste paper, the commune has established a large paper mill to process it. The commune has also established an iron and steel mill, a coke refining factory, a toy plant, a shoemaking factory, a washing and dyeing factory, a knitting and weaving factory, and a sewing factory.

These factories are established for two purposes. One purpose is to serve the major plant. For instance, with the establishment of the small hardware factory, the major plant need not send its odd parts to other cities for processing. The coke refined by native methods may be used to smelt steel, thereby lowering the cost of steel. Chemical boards may replace the iron plate fixed on the machines to stiffen cloth with starch. This item alone may save the plant over twenty tons of rolled steel a year. The other purpose of these factories is to serve the staff members and workers. The small factories weave and knit woolen clothes or make shoes for the department store. . . .

In previous days the office employees and workers of the Chengchow Spinning and Weaving Machine Plant would go to the aid of nearby agricultural producer cooperatives only upon the instruction of superior governments and at the invitation of the agricultural producers' cooperatives concerned. It was a very passive act. Since the two brigades for agricultural production in the suburbs were incorporated into the people's commune, it is no longer so. Over 700 mou of land farmed by the two brigades are near the living quarters for the office employees and workers of the plant. On rainy days the dirty water of the living quarters would flow into the field and inundate the crops. Recently the people's commune mobilized over 4,000 of its members to excavate a long and deep ditch to settle the long-standing problem. It took only one morning. . . .

This people's commune has established a mess hall, a kindergarten, a nursery, and various service organizations, enabling the dependents of the workers to take part in production. . . .

As the whole family of each office employee and worker eats at the mess hall, the women are free from housework and may join production to create wealth for the society, increase their income, and raise their living standard. Besides, the mess hall turns out more economical food than their own home cooking. Compared with the decentralized cooking, about 500 tons of coal a year may be saved. . . .

With the children placed in the kindergarten or nursery, women can take part in production work. . . .

The means of production of the people's commune are basically owned by the whole people. This is because the Chengchow Spinning and Weaving Machine Plant is a state enterprise; and the small "satellite" factories are under the assistance of the plant. For instance, their machines were produced by the plant. Raw materials used by the processing factories are also the plant's waste and remnant materials. . . .

The "satellite" factories and the new service trades have "worked to success barehanded." In order to accumulate funds, the dependents of the office employees and workers who join these enterprises advanced the slogan "hard combat for two months." During the first month of their work, they did not draw wages. All proceeds from sales were used for the expansion of production. . . . This may illustrate the fact that, aside from agriculture, this commune still retains the system of collective ownership over part of its property.

In response to the above conditions, the commune as a whole adopts two wage systems. *First*, the office employees and workers of state-operated enterprises such as the Chengchow Spinning and Weaving Machine Plant, the commercial departments, and state-operated service trades, are paid with the same wage as before. *Second*, the brigades for agricultural production, "satellite" factories, and the new service organizations, respectively, adopt a low wage system in accordance with the development of their production. The wage system adopted by the agricultural production brigades is different from that of the "satellite" factories as well as that of the service trades. Each system varies its wages according to the attitude toward work, ability to work, and skill.

As to welfare service, the commune members are invariably equal in principle. But under the present conditions there is a difference in free medical treatment. The personnel of the state-operated enterprises still enjoy medical treatment at public expense and the dependents of the office employees and workers enjoy semi-free medical treatment now as before. The personnel of the agricultural brigades and other units who previously got medical treatment at their own expense enjoy semi-free treatment now.

B. Urban Communes
and the Transition to Communism

People's communes are set up in cities mainly for the purpose of accelerating the pace of socialist construction now and creating suitable conditions for gradually passing over to communism in the future. Therefore, the central link in the chain of consolidation and elevation of urban people's communes should consist in developing production and building a powerful material base.

From our experience in setting up people's communes in Chengchow, we have come to realize that there are many favorable conditions for developing production in cities. The economic strength of state-owned factories, enterprises, and schools is powerful enough to aid the development of commune production. Meanwhile, commune production consists mainly in socialist commodity production; production is fast, profits are greater, development is rapid, and technical conditions are better. The production policy of urban people's communes should be: to serve state industry, agricultural production, and people's livelihood in cities; to suit local conditions, obtain materials locally and rely on the masses; to run communes industriously and thriftily, and gradually build the material base for communes with the aid and support of the state economy.

In Chengchow, commune production takes on the following forms:

(1) Commune-run factories. These factories organize production of desired articles; taking into account the needs of state industry, obtaining materials locally, utilizing waste products and materials, and maintaining direct contact with state factories and work sites. The products are sold either through commercial departments or by the communes themselves.

(2) Production to serve large factories and enterprises. The commune-run factories are organized to meet the needs of large factories and enterprises or to do processing jobs for state-owned factories, enterprises, and commercial departments under processing contracts.

Wang Li-chih: More on the Question of Setting up Urban People's Communes. Honan Jih-pao, January 19, 1959. SCPRP 1965.

(3) Service production. For instance, tailoring, shoemaking, dry cleaning, dyeing, etc., are organized to meet the people's daily needs.

(4) Agricultural and subsidiary production and processing of foods to ensure supply of nonstaple foods to cities.

To develop commune production, a mass movement must be launched for finding production outlets in every possible way and expanding multiple production. Existing facilities and waste material must be fully utilized. A technical revolution must take place to ensure progress by transferring from crude methods to modern methods and from handicraft to mechanization in order to raise production efficiency.

In order to further develop commune production, it is essential to incorporate commune production into state plans so as to avoid a situation in which certain units sometimes cannot carry on normal production because of the lack of raw materials. At the same time, existing small plants of the same character should be systematically merged, where possible, into larger plants on the principle of facilitating production, leadership, and the gradual transition from collective ownership to ownership by the whole people. But some production units that serve the masses should be scattered. Street communes, as they exist today, should gradually grow into large production enterprises. . . .

The communes should see to it that, provided socialist accumulation is strenuously expanded, the portion allotted to commune members for consumption is above the living standard they maintained before joining the communes, and that the wage level is gradually raised along with the development of production in order to constantly improve the material and cultural life of commune members. . . . Since the production in urban people's communes mainly consists of commodity production, and since production is developed fast, it is entirely possible for the overwhelming majority of communes to bring their accumulations up to 60 to 70 percent and distribution up to 30 to 40 percent of their income and bring the average monthly wage to 20 yuan per capita. . . .

At the moment, multiple methods of distribution are being adopted. They may be divided into three categories:

(1) Fixed wages plus awards. The monthly wages vary from 12 to 20 yuan and go as high as 30 to 40 yuan.

(2) Wage system combined with free supplies. A technical allowance is given monthly to persons having special technical skill.

(3) Piece rate and other forms of labor are still retained by some communes at the moment.

In the present circumstances, it is advisable for urban people's communes to adopt diversified methods of distribution and to allow certain differences at wage levels between communes and between various production units within a commune.

Under present conditions, it is inadvisable to overexpand the living amenities in urban communes. The communes should mainly operate such welfare organizations as public mess halls, nurseries and kindergartens to serve production. Where suitable conditions exist, communes should provide some free medical treatment. Subsidy should be granted to those commune members whose life is hard and whose income is reduced for want of adequate labor power. . . .

In accordance with the directives of the Central Committee and in the light of local conditions, the communes set up in Chengchow assume the following forms:

(1) Communes formed with a large factory, enterprise, or school as its backbone and with the dependents of workers, neighboring inhabitants, stores and individual villages drawn in.

(2) Communes jointly formed by several factories, schools, and streets.

(3) Communes formed by inhabitants of several streets.

(4) Big communes.

Establishment of a big commune, taking the twenty-seventh *ch'u* as a unit, has been tried out. This big commune is actually a federation in character. Other *ch'u* are prepared to set up similar communes. . . .

The basic characteristics of cities and the special features of people's communes, which are both large and public, make it possible to set up people's communes in the future with municipalities as units. For the present, big communes are set up and individual units are allowed to set up their communes separately. It is advisable for *ch'u* communes to assume the character of a federation for the time being. . . .

With the *ch'u* communes set up, we have decided to transfer some municipally owned factories, enterprises, schools, hospitals, and retail shops that can be so managed to *ch'u* communes for management. This does not amount to the reduction of ownership by the whole people to collective ownership; on the contrary, the transfer greatly increases the element of ownership by the whole people in the communes, provides more favorable conditions for expanding the material foundation of the communes, and facilitates the transition to ownership by the whole people.

The *ch'u* commune exercises all-round leadership over the work of street communes and manages the fiscal affairs and personnel work of the municipality-owned enterprises and services transferred to the commune while ensuring fulfillment of state plans, delivery of profits to the treasury and implementation of policies. . . .

The process of establishing and elevating urban people's communes is one of transforming old cities and building new socialist cities. Despite a series of transformations of old cities since liberation, old cities remain backward in many aspects: small areas, concentrated population, narrow streets, dilapidated houses, unsatisfactory sanitation conditions, great density of commercial networks, few large-sized production units, a certain disparity between production and life, separation of service trades from the productive population, strained communications and transport, waste of manpower and resources. All this is disadvantageous to production and the people's living conditions. For this reason, we contemplate systematic transformation of the old city area on the principle of gradually eliminating the differences between town and country, between workers and peasants, and between mental labor and physical labor and on the principle of combining industry and agriculture, labor and education, and production and life.

The transformation is to be effected mainly in the following ways. First, gradually move the dependents of workers, who now reside in scattered parts of the old city area, to the housing areas of the factories and enterprises concerned. Second, readjust the commercial network by transferring superabundant commercial service units in the old city area to the industrial area. Third, gradually move away the dwellers in the old residential areas which impede city planning. Fourth, on the basis of readjustment of houses and on the principle of making arrangements for housing before removal, gradually tear down some of the old houses that impede transformation of the old area, and turn the vacated plots into orchards. Fifth, on the basis of municipal planning, expand some of the factories on existing streets and completely rebuild the streets in the old city area. The transformation of the old city area is a complex task and must be effected gradually at separate stages along with the development of production. We plan to fulfill this task in three to five years or a little longer.

The newly built units are to be spread over the suburban area or the *hsien* areas so as to gradually form several satellite cities and independent industrial areas inhabited by a population of 30,000 to 50,000 or in the case of larger areas, 80,000 to 100,000 persons. At the same time, the existing factories are to be appropriately renovated and several people's communes centered on big production units or jointly organized by several production units and villages are to be formed gradually so as to transform the rural areas into cities. The farmland lying between different industrial areas and the vacant plots vacated in the old city area are to be fully utilized for developing agriculture and subsidiary industry. Certain areas will use such land for planting trees.

It is conceivable that in the not distant future our cities will become areas in which several big factories form the backbone, where workers, peasants, traders, students, and soldiers are closely combined, and complete facilities are available for cultural, educational, and welfare work. By that time, the cities will have been built like an orchard with green fields and forests separating one industrial area from another, with numerous small cities lying hidden in the green sea like small islands. One city area alone will have clear creeks, calm lakes, rows of buildings separated by fruit trees and flowers, broad streets and winding paths. Busy markets are in the depth of orchards, and orchards are near busy markets. This is a picture of the new socialist and communist cities we are now building.

IV

THE TWO-LINE STRUGGLE
IN CITY AND COUNTRYSIDE
1959-1965

A. THE GREAT LEAP UNDER ATTACK

1. MAO TSETUNG, THE GREAT LEAP FORWARD AND THE "COMMUNIST WIND"

By the early months of 1959 continued reports of promethean achievements of the Great Leap were increasingly tempered by signs of dislocation and crisis in the countryside. In February and March the emphasis shifted from dynamic expansion and grassroots initiative to consolidation and coordination, in a word, caution. "Take the Whole Country as a Single Chessboard" was the theme of a major People's Daily *editorial and a report by Chou En-lai.*

At this time Mao vigorously defended the overall strategy and accomplishments of the Great Leap Forward. But he also subjected its shortcomings to a withering critique and called for "tidying up" measures to consolidate the gains and avert the crisis looming in the countryside.

The central error of the leap, in Mao's words "the communist wind" or adventurism, stemmed from excessive desire to advance immediately to communism before material conditions were ripe. In practice this took such forms as excessive concentration of resources in the collective at the expense of the individual (e.g., eliminating private plots of land and privately tended pigs, orchards, etc.) and setting ownership and administrative levels too high. By making the commune the level of

Speech at Chengchow, February 27, 1959. Translated by Pierre Perrolle. In: *Chinese Law and Government*, 1977.

ownership, management and distribution, rather than the smaller brigade or team, formidable problems of coordination arose and, most important, the productive efforts of more successful units were discouraged as their income levels dropped and they felt that they were subsidizing the less diligent. Like earlier cooperative forms, unless the communes could fulfill the promise of increased income for the vast majority of peasants, they were doomed to failure. A socialism which condemned working people to a meager livelihood, which undercut their efforts to improve living standards, was unacceptable. Mao likened this danger to Stalin's primary error with regard to the peasantry of attempting to drain the pond to catch the fish.

China's peasants, Mao insisted, are still peasants. Step by step they could take the path of full collectivization through ownership by the commune and eventually ownership by the whole people, but instant solutions, omitting stages of development and ignoring immediate welfare needs and existing inequalities, could only produce demoralization and disaster.

While the leap continued to advance on many fronts during the next year or more, the optimistic phase of radical change now yielded to consolidation and retrenchment.

In 1958 we achieved great successes on every front. On the ideological and political front, the industrial front, the agricultural front, the communications and transport front, the commercial front, the cultural and educational front, the national defense front, as well as in other areas, no matter where, it was the same in all. Especially remarkable was the fact that there was a magnificent leap forward in the area of industrial and agricultural production. In 1958 people's communes were established everywhere throughout the rural areas of the entire nation.

The establishment of the people's communes has enlarged the original system of collective ownership of the means of production and raised it to a higher level and, moreover, it begins to embody certain elements of the system of ownership by the whole people. The scale of the people's communes is much larger than that of the agricultural producers' cooperatives and, morever, has put into operation the unity of workers, peasants, merchants, students, and soldiers, and of agriculture, forestry, animal husbandry, subsidiary productive activities, and fish culture. This has given a powerful push to the development of agricultural production and the entire rural economy. . . .

In a new and historically unprecedented social movement that involves several hundred million people and for which previous experience is lacking, like the setting up of the people's communes, both the people and their leaders can only acquire experience step by step, from their practice, and step by step deepen their knowledge of the essence of things, expose the contradictions within things, solve these contradictions, and affirm the achievements and overcome the shortcomings of their work. Anyone who says that a broad social movement can be completely without shortcomings is nothing but a dreamer, or a tide-watcher, or an account-settler, or simply a hostile element. As for the relationship between our achievements and defects, it is, just as we have often said, like the relationship between nine of the ten fingers, and the one remaining finger. There are some people who doubt or deny the achievements of the Great Leap Forward of 1958, and doubt or deny the superiority of the people's commune. This kind of viewpoint is completely mistaken. . . .

Now I'm going to talk a little bit about the problems of the people's communes. I think that there is a contradiction in the people's communes, a contradiction that should be said to be quite serious, which has not yet been recognized by many comrades. Its nature has not been revealed, and thus it has not been solved. And I think that this contradiction must be resolved quickly, and that only then will the situation be favorable to mobilizing the still greater enthusiasm of the broad masses of people, only then will it be favorable to improving our relationship with basic-level cadres, which is essentially the relationship between the *hsien* party committee or the people's commune party committee and the basic-level cadres. In the final analysis what kind of contradiction is this? As everybody can see, there exists at present in our relationship with the peasants a rather tense state of affairs in some matters. The outstanding phenomenon in this regard is the fact that the state's task of purchasing agricultural products, such as food grains, cotton, edible oils, and so on after the bumper harvest of

1958, is to date still partly uncompleted. Furthermore, throughout the entire country (except in a small number of disaster areas) there has appeared almost everywhere the practice of the peasants' "concealing production and dividing it among themselves" and great unrest about food grains, edible oils, pork, and vegetables being "insufficient." The large scale of the unrest clearly surpasses that of both the 1953 and the 1955 periods of unrest over food. . . . I think that we should look for the answer to the problem mainly in the area of what we know about the ownership system in the rural people's commune and the policies we have adopted.

Should the system of ownership in the rural people's commune go through a process of development? Or should the commune, as soon as it is set up, immediately have a complete system of ownership by the commune, and can it immediately eliminate ownership by the production brigade . . . (which generally corresponds to the former higher-level agricultural producers' cooperative)? Even now there are a good many people who still don't recognize that the system of ownership by the commune must go through a process of development. Within the commune there needs to be a process of transition from ownership by a small collective, the production brigade, to ownership by a large collective, the commune, and this process requires a period of several years before it can be completed. They mistakenly believe that as soon as the people's commune is set up, the means of production, the manpower, and the products of each production brigade can all be directly controlled by the leadership organs of the commune. They mistake socialism for communism, they mistake distribution according to labor for distribution according to need, and they mistake collective ownership for ownership by the whole people. In many places they deny the law of value, and deny the necessity for exchange at equal value. Thus, within the confines of the commune they carry out the leveling of the poor and the rich, and equal distribution. They have transferred the ownership of some of the property of the production team upward without compensation; in the area of banking, they have recalled all loans in a good many rural areas, too. What is known as "equalization, transferring, and recalling loans" has given rise to great fear and anxiety among the broad masses of peasants. So this is a most fundamental problem in our present relationship with the peasants. . . .

Before the system of ownership by the whole people in the countryside has been put into effect, peasants are still always peasants, and on the path of socialism they still always have a definite dual character. We can only lead the peasants step by step to divorce themselves from the system of ownership by a relatively small collective, and move, by way of the system of ownership by a relatively large collective, toward ownership by the whole people. We cannot demand that they complete this process all at once, just as in the past we could only lead the peasants step by step to divorce themselves from the system of ownership by individuals and move toward the system of ownership by the collective. To move from an incomplete system of ownership by the commune to a complete, unitary system of ownership by the commune is a process of raising the comparatively poor production brigades to the level of production of the comparatively rich production teams. It is also a process of expanding the commune's capital accumulation, developing the commune's industry, accomplishing agricultural mechanization and electrification, and accomplishing the industrialization of the commune and the industrialization of the nation. The things owned directly by the commune at the present time are still not many, such as commune-run enterprises, commune-run undertakings, the common fund and the welfare fund controlled by the commune, etc. Although this is the case, our great, glorious, and brilliant hope also lies right here. Because the commune can draw its capital accumulation from the production brigades year by year and it can increase its capital accumulation from the profits of the commune-run enterprises, and add to this the state's investment, its development will not be very slow, but rather will be very rapid.

With regard to the question of state investment, I propose that within seven years the state invest in the communes between several billion and more than ten billion yuan to help the communes develop industry, and help the poor production brigades develop their production. I believe that it won't be very long before the poor communes and poor brigades will be able to catch up with the rich communes and rich brigades, and develop tremendously. Once the communes have acquired great economic power, we will be able to put into effect a complete system of ownership by the commune, and can also proceed to put into effect the system of ownership by the whole people besides. As for time, about two five-year plans are needed. Hurrying won't do. . . . This is also precisely what the Pei-tai-ho Resolution said, that it will take three or four years, or five or six years, or even a bit longer. After that, we will go through several more developmental stages, and in fifteen or twenty years or a bit longer, the socialist commune will develop into the communist commune. . . .

We must first investigate and correct two tendencies of our own, namely the tendency toward egalitarianism and the tendency toward excessive concentration. By the tendency toward egalitarianism I mean the tendency to deny that there should be differences in income among the various production brigades and various individuals. And to deny such differences is to deny the socialist principles of "to each according to his labor," and "the more work, the more reward." By the tendency to excessive concentration I mean the tendency to deny the system of ownership by the production brigade, and to deny the rightful authority of the production brigade, and to arbitrarily transfer the property of the production brigade upward to the commune. At the same time, a good many communes and *hsien* have extracted too much capital accumulation from the production brigades and, moreover, the administrative expenditures of the communes include a great deal of waste. (For example, there are some large communes that have as many as a thousand or more working personnel who eat without doing any labor, and there are even cultural work teams which are divorced from production altogether.) The two above-mentioned tendencies both incorporate the kind of thinking that denies the law of value and denies exchange at equal value. . . .

At the time of the unified decision on distribution, the commune should recognize that there are reasonable differences in income between one production brigade and another and between one commune member and another, and that there should be differences in food and wages between poor production brigades and rich production brigades. When it comes to wages, we should act on the principle of "fixed grades and flexible assessment." The commune should implement a downward transfer of authority, a three-level system of accounting, and, moreover, use the accounting of the production brigade as the basis. Between the commune and the production brigade and between production brigades we should carry out exchange at equal value. . . .

After the communes were set up in the autumn of 1958, for a while there blew up a "communist wind." It consisted mainly of three elements: the first was the leveling of the poor and the rich brigades, the second was that capital accumulation by the commune was too great, and the commune's demand for labor without compensation was too great, and the third was the "communization" of all kinds of "property." This so-called "communization" of all kinds of "property" included all kinds of different situations. Some of it was things that should have belonged to the commune, like the greater part of the private plots, some of it should simply have been borrowed by the commune, like some of the buildings, tables, chairs, benches, and stools needed for the commune's public undertakings, and the knives, cooking pots, bowls, and chopsticks needed for the dining hall. Some were things that belonged to the commune when they should not have, like chickens, ducks, and some of the pigs, which belonged to communes without being paid for. . . . The phenomenon of uncompensated takeover of the fruits of other people's labor is something we do not permit. Just take a look at our history. The only things we took without compensation were the means of production of Japanese, German, and Italian imperialism, of feudalism and bureaucratic-capitalism, and some of the landlords' houses, food, and other means of livelihood. . . .

In addition to the tendencies to egalitarianism and excessive concentration, at present there are also very irrational aspects to the allocation of the rural labor force. These are, specifically, that the labor force used in agriculture (including agriculture, forestry, animal husbandry, subsidiary production, and fish culture) is generally too small, while too many personnel are used in industry, the service industries, and administration. The latter three types of personnel must be reduced. . . .

We must simultaneously take into consideration, and do unified planning for, our work in making arrangements for these three areas: the livelihood of the people, the commune's accumulation of capital, and satisfying the needs of the state. Only in this way can it be said that we have truly succeeded in doing things as if the affairs of the entire nation were a single game of chess. Otherwise, the so-called chess game is actually only half a chess game, or it is an incomplete chess game. Generally speaking, the accumulation of the communes in 1958 was a little in excess. Therefore each area should fix an appropriate limit, on the basis of concrete conditions, for the commune's accumulation in 1959, and should announce this to the people in order to set people's minds at ease and increase the broad masses' enthusiasm for production.

2. THE GREAT LEAP ASSAILED AND DEFENDED: THE CLASH AT LUSHAN

General P'eng Teh-huai spearheaded the inner-party criticism of the Great Leap Forward in an attack at the July 1959 Lushan meeting of the Central Committee. Speaking informally, P'eng derided the leap:

> *One has to take off one's trousers by oneself. Don't let others pull them down. Kiangsi is still talking now about its 67 percent increase of production last year. It's taking off only the outer trousers but keeping the inner ones on. One should be stripped once and for all to save others the trouble.*

Taking aim at its excesses and hyperbole, P'eng went on:

> *Is this slogan of "Make steel by the whole people" truly correct? In the program of running industries by the whole people, over 13,000 sub-norm projects were undertaken. . . . In our party, it has always been difficult to correct "leftist" mistakes and comparatively easy to correct rightist ones.*

P'eng lashed out at the core institution of the period, the people's communes; they "appeared somewhat too early. . . . Moreover, no experiments were made in communalization." He placed the blame for economic reverses at the feet of the chairman himself. "Everybody had a share of the responsibility, including Comrade Mao Tsetung."

P'eng's denunciation of the Great Leap is perhaps most vividly captured in a 1958 poem, following an inspection tour of Hunan province: "Grain scattered on the ground, potato leaves withered, strong young people have left for steel-making, only children and old women reaped the crops, how can they pass the coming year? Allow me to appeal for the people."*

With the battle lines drawn P'eng formally summarized his criticisms in a "Letter of Opinion" to Chairman Mao. In this document P'eng's criticisms are far more muted and lip service is paid to some aspects of the Great Leap. Nevertheless the document, which locates the heart of the problem in petty bourgeois fanaticism, remains the most comprehensive critique of the full constellation of Great Leap policies and the sharpest challenge to Mao Tsetung's leadership to emerge from within the ranks of the party.

At Lushan, Mao defended the overriding achievements of the Great Leap and the communes. But he did so from a defensive position, delivering probably the most severe self-criticism he had made since assuming leadership of the party more than two decades earlier. Mao acknowledged the heavy cost of "blowing a communist wind" which impeded production and alienated people. While insisting that the most serious problems had already been solved, he accepted personal responsibility for some errors, notably indigenous steelmaking and errors associated with the early phases of the people's communes. At the same time he warned that he was prepared to return to the countryside to lead the peasants once again should the government fail to respond to their needs. At Lushan Mao turned back the attack on the leap and P'eng was deprived of his army and party posts (while retaining his Politburo membership). Nevertheless P'eng's views were widely shared among party leaders and conflicting assessments of the leap remained at the heart of the intra-party debate over the future of China's socialist development. At Lushan the party officially inaugurated a retrench-

---

* Mao returned from his own tour of Hunan in June 1959, including his return to his native village after 32 years, sounding a more optimistic note in a poem which ended with these lines:

Bitter sacrifice strengthens bold resolve
Which dares to make sun and moon shine in new skies.
Happy I see wave upon wave of paddy and beans,
And all around heroes homebound in the evening mist.

ment which eventually led to dismantling many of the experiments of the leap. At the same time it continued to set extremely ambitious production targets for 1959.

The "Resolution on Developing the Campaign for Increasing Production and Practicing Economy" reaffirmed the centrality of the communes to China's rural development, while mandating a downward transfer of authority and ownership from the commune to the brigade, the first of a series of steps to set the communes on a firmer footing, by bringing ownership levels closer to familiar levels of face to face relations and functioning productive units. This initiated a process, however, of curbing the powers of the communes to command labor and initiate and sustain many of the projects begun during the leap.

A. P'eng Teh-huai,
The "Petty-Bourgeois Fanaticism" of the Great Leap

July 14, 1959

Chairman:

I am a simple man like Chang Fei,* though I have only his roughness without his cautiousness. For this reason, whether this letter is of reference value or not is for you to decide. If what I say is wrong, please correct me.

A. The achievements made in the Great Leap Forward of 1958 are affirmed and undoubted.

According to the several figures after verification by the State Planning Commission, gross output value of industry and agriculture in 1958 rose by 48.4 percent as compared with 1957. Industry grew by 66.1 percent and agriculture and subsidiary production by 25 percent (the increase in grain and cotton output being definitely 30 percent). State financial receipts increased by 43.5 percent. Such a rate of growth has never been achieved in other parts of the world.

It now seems that some projects for capital construction in

Letter of Opinion, July 14, 1959. SCPRP 4032.

* A warrior in the *Romance of the Three Kingdoms*.

1958 were too hasty or excessive, with the result that a portion of capital was tied up and some essential projects were delayed. This is a drawback, and the basic cause for this is lack of experience. We had not understood this sufficiently, and when we understood it, it was too late. As a result, in 1959, instead of slowing down a bit and appropriately controlling the speed, the Great Leap Forward was pushed ahead.

Now there are still some articles in short supply and weak links, with the result that the production system cannot be complete. Highly necessary stocks of some commodities are lacking, so that when signs of dislocation and new imbalances appear, they cannot be readjusted in time. This is our present difficulty. In view of this, while drawing up plans for next year (1960), we should all the more seriously consider them on the basis of seeking truth from facts and on a reliable foundation.

The formation of rural communes in 1958 was of great significance. This will not only enable our peasants to free themselves completely from poverty, but it provides the correct way to speed up the building of socialism and transition to communism. Nevertheless, there has been a period of confusion regarding the question of the system of ownership and some shortcomings and errors appeared in our concrete work; this of course is a serious phenomenon. However, after a series of conferences held in Wuch'ang, Chengchow, and Shanghai, this phenomenon has been in the main corrected. The chaotic condition is basically over and we are embarking step by step on the normal path of distribution according to labor.

In the course of the Great Leap Forward of 1958, the problem of unemployment was solved. Its rapid solution in a country with a large population and economic backwardness such as ours is not a small but a great thing.

In the course of refining steel by the whole people, some small and indigenous blast furnaces which were not necessary were built, with the consequence that some resources (material and financial) and manpower were wasted. This is of course a relatively big loss. But a preliminary geological survey on a huge scale was carried out throughout the country, and many technical personnel were trained. The broad masses of cadres have tempered and improved themselves in this movement. Although a tuition fee was spent (in the amount of 2 billion yuan), even in this respect there have been losses and gains. . . .

B. How to sum up the experiences and lessons in work. . . .

In my view, some of the shortcomings and errors that appeared in the course of the Great Leap Forward of 1958 were unavoidable. As in the case of the many movements led by our party over the last thirty years and more, there are always shortcomings among great achievements. These are two sides of a matter. The outstanding contradiction with which we are faced in our work now is the tension and strain in various quarters caused by disproportions. Essentially speaking, the development of such a situation has affected the relationships between the workers and peasants, between the various strata in the cities and between the various strata among the peasants. Therefore, the problem is also political in character. It is the key to whether we can mobilize the broad masses to continue the Great Leap Forward in the future.

In the past, some shortcomings and mistakes appeared in our work. The cause is many-sided, and the subjective factor is that we are not familiar with the work of socialist construction and lack integral experiences. . . .

On the other hand, the objective situation is that our country is poor and blank (there are still a number of people who do not have enough to eat. Last year, there was an average of only eighteen feet of cotton cloth for every person, enough for a shirt and two pairs of pants). The people urgently demand a change of the present conditions. . . .

In the past, a lot of problems were also exposed in our way of thinking and our style of work. These problems are worthy of our attention. The principal ones are as follows:

1. The habit of exaggeration bred and spread rather universally. Last year, at the time of the Pei-tai-ho meeting, a higher estimate of grain output was made than was warranted. This created a false phenomenon. Everybody felt that the problem of food had been solved, and that our hands could be freed to engage in industry. There was serious superficiality in our understanding of the development of the iron and steel industry. . . .

The habit of exaggeration spread to various areas and departments, and some unbelievable miracles were also reported in the press. This has surely done tremendous harm to the prestige of the party.

At that time, from reports sent in from various quarters, it would seem that communism was around the corner. This caused not a few comrades to become dizzy. In the wake of the wave of high grain and cotton output and the doubling of iron and steel production, extravagance and waste developed. The job of autumn harvesting was handled crudely and without consideration of cost, and we considered ourselves rich while actually we were still poor. More serious, in a rather long period of time, it was not easy to get a true picture of the situation. . . . Although the chairman had last year called on the whole party to combine sky-rocketing zeal with scientific analysis and set forth the policy of walking on two legs, it appears that both the call and the policy had not been appreciated by the majority of leading comrades. I am of course no exception.

2. Petty bourgeois fanaticism renders us liable to commit "left" mistakes. In the course of the Great Leap Forward of 1958, like many comrades, I was bewitched by the achievements of the Great Leap Forward and the passion of the mass movement. Some "left" tendencies developed to quite an extent; we always wanted to enter into communism at one step. Our minds swayed by the idea of taking the lead, we forgot the mass line and the style of seeking truth from facts which the party had formed over a long time. . . .

For instance, the slogans raised by the chairman, such as "grow less, produce more, and reap more" and "catch up with Britain in fifteen years," were strategic and long-range policies. But we did not study them well; we failed to give attention to and study the current concrete conditions, and we failed to arrange work on a positive, steady and reliable basis. . . . As a result, divorced from reality, we failed to gain the support of the masses. For instance, the law of exchange of equal values was negated prematurely; and free supply of meals was effected too early. . . .

In the view of some comrades, putting politics in command could be a substitute for everything. They forgot that putting politics in command was aimed at raising the consciousness of labor, ensuring improvement of products in both quantity and quality, and giving full play to the enthusiasm and creativeness of the masses in order to speed our economic construction. Putting politics in command is no substitute for the economic principles, still less for the concrete measures in economic work. . . .

Just as the chairman has pointed out at this meeting: "The achievements are tremendous, the problems are numerous, the experience is rich, and the future is bright." We must take the initiative to unite the whole party and work hard. Conditions for continued leap forward are present. The plans for this year and next and for the next four years can surely be victoriously fulfilled. The target of catching up with Britain in fifteen years can be basically accomplished in the next four years. For certain important products, we will undoubtedly surpass Britain. These are our great achievements; this is our bright future.

B. Mao Tsetung, The Great Leap Assessed

Now that you have said so much, let me say something will you? I have taken sleeping pills three times, but I can't get to sleep. . . .

We are under combined attack from within and outside the party. The rightists say: Why was Ch'in Shih Huang overthrown? Because he built the Great Wall. Now that we have built the T'ien An Men we shall collapse. . . .

Gentlemen, all of you have ears, so listen. They all say we are in a mess. Even if it is hard to listen to it, we must listen to it and welcome it. As soon as you think in this way, it ceases to be unpleasant to the ears. Why should we let the others talk? The reason is that China will not sink down, the sky will not fall. We have done some good things and our backbones are strong. The majority of comrades need to strengthen their backbones. Why

Speech at the Lushan Conference, July 23, 1959. In: Stuart Schram, ed., *Chairman Mao Talks to the People* (New York: Pantheon, 1974).

are they not all strong? Just because for a time there were too few vegetables, too few hair-grips, no soap, a lack of balance in the economy and tension in the market, everyone became tense. . . .

People say that we have become isolated from the masses, yet the masses still support us. I think this was temporary, just for two or three months before and after the Spring Festival. I think that we and the masses are now combining well. There is a bit of petty bourgeois fanaticism, but not all that much. . . . "The people in Honan and Hopei have created the truth from experience, they have smashed Roosevelt's 'freedom' from want." How should we look upon such enthusiasm for communism? Shall we call it petty bourgeois fanaticism? I don't think we can put it that way. It's a matter of wanting to do a bit more, it's nothing else but wanting to do a bit more, a bit faster. Is this analysis appropriate? In these three months, there were three times 300,000 people going to the mountains to burn incense. We must not pour cold water on this kind of broad mass movement. We can only use persuasion and say to them: Comrades, your hearts are in the right place. When tasks are difficult, don't be impatient. . . .

Could the people's communes collapse? Up to now not one has collapsed. We were prepared for the collapse of half of them, and if 70 percent collapsed there would still be 30 percent left. If they must collapse, let them. If they are not well run they are sure to collapse. . . .

But comrades, in 1958 and 1959 the main responsibility was mine, and you should take me to task. In the past the responsibility was other people's—En-lai, XX—but now you should blame me because there are heaps of things I didn't attend to. Shall the person who invented burial puppets be deprived of descendants? Shall I be deprived of descendants too (one son was killed, one went mad)? Who was responsible for the idea of the mass smelting of steel? K'o Ch'ing-shih or me? I say it was me. . . . Small native-type blast furnaces were built . . . I read a lot of discussion reports; everyone said it could be done. Provided that we came to grips with the problem and worked really hard, we could raise the quality, reduce cost, lower the sulphur content, and produce really good iron. . . .

When I said that the inventor of burial puppets should have no descendants, I was referring first to the target of smelting 10,700,000 tons of steel, which resulted in ninety million people going into battle and the expenditure of —— dollars of people's currency. "The gain did not compensate for the loss." This was my suggestion and my resolution. Next I was referring to the people's communes. I do not claim to have invented the people's communes, only to have proposed them. The Pei-tai-ho Resolution was drafted according to my suggestion. At that time, it was as though I had found a treasure in the regulations of the Cha-ya-shan [commune]. When I was in Shantung a reporter asked me: "Are the people's communes good?" I said: "They are good," and he published it in a newspaper. There was a spot of petty bourgeois fanaticism there, too. In future reporters should keep away.

I have committed two crimes, one of which is calling for 10,700,000 tons of steel and the mass smelting of steel. If you agreed with this, you should share some of the blame. But since I was the inventor of burial puppets, I cannot pass on the blame: the main responsibility is mine. As for the people's communes; the whole world opposed them; the Soviet Union opposed them. . . .

Will our present work also fail, like what happened in 1927? Or will it be like the 25,000 li Long March, when most of our bases were lost and the soviet areas were reduced to one tenth of their former size? No, it will not be like these. Have we failed this time? All the comrades present say there have been gains; it is not a complete failure. Is it mainly a failure? No, it's only a partial failure. We have paid a high price. A lot of "communist wind" has blown past, but the people of the whole country have learned a lesson.

C. Revising Commune Management

The eighth plenary session of the Eighth Central Committee of the Chinese Communist Party holds that the central task confronting the whole party and the people of all nationalities throughout the country now is to develop intensively a vigorous mass campaign for increasing production and practicing economy and strive for the fulfillment and overfulfillment of the production and construction plan of 1959. . . .

The total output value of industry in the first half of this year was 65 percent more than that in the corresponding period of last year. Pig iron reached 9.5 million tons; coal, 174 million tons; and metal-cutting machine tools, 45,000 units. In each case output was more than double that in the corresponding period of last year. Steel (excluding steel made by indigenous methods) amounted to 5.3 million tons, an increase of 66 percent over the corresponding period of last year. Cotton yarn amounted to 4,147,000 bales, and sugar, 780,000 tons; both represented an increase of 40 percent and more over the corresponding period of last year. . . .

In agriculture, although the acreage planted to summer crops this year was somewhat reduced, and there were floods and drought, yet the average per mou yields of wheat, early rice and rapeseed greatly surpassed those of last year and their total outputs also exceeded those of last year.

A check-up has been carried out in the rural people's communes throughout the country. . . . During the check-up the principles of management and business accounting at different levels, of "to each according to his work" and more income for those who do more work have been implemented. It has been decided that at the present stage a three-level type of ownership of the means of production should be instituted in the people's communes. Ownership at the production brigade level consti-

Resolution on Developing the Campaign for Increasing Production and Practicing Economy, August 16, 1959. In: *Eighth Plenary Session of the Eighth Central Committee of the Communist Party of China* (Peking: Foreign Languages Press, 1959).

tutes the basic one. Ownership at the commune level constitutes another part (in addition to ownership of the public economic undertakings run by the commune, the commune can draw each year a reasonable amount for its capital accumulation fund from the income of the production brigades). A small part of the ownership should also be vested in the production team. In this way, the people's communes, which are large in size, which integrate industry, agriculture, trade, education, and military affairs and which combine government and commune administration into one, have overcome the tendencies which, owing to lack of experience, occurred during the initial period of their founding, such as the tendencies to overcentralization, to egalitarianism and extravagance, and have rapidly taken the road of sound and consolidated development. . . .

To sum up, the various branches of the national economy in the first half of this year were on the whole in good shape and the situation is favorable for the realization of this year's continued leap forward.

In the light of the verified figures on last year's agricultural output, the actual implementation of the national economic plan in the first half of this year and recent occurrence of natural calamities, the eighth plenary session of the Eighth Central Committee recommends that the State Council submit to the Standing Committee of the National People's Congress a proposal for appropriate readjustment of the 1959 plan, fixing the following targets: steel (excluding that made by indigenous methods), 12 million tons (an increase of 50 percent over last year's output of 8 million tons of steel produced with modern equipment; in view of the shortage of labor power in the rural areas, it is suggested that this year the production of steel by indigenous methods should be decided upon by the local authorities themselves in accordance with local conditions and will not be included in the state plan); coal, 335 million tons (an increase of 24 percent over last year's coal output of 270 million tons); grain, about 10 percent above last year's verified output of 500,000 million catties (250 million tons); cotton, about 10 percent above last year's verified output of 42 million tan (2.1 million tons). It is quite clear that the readjusted national economic plan remains a plan for a continued leap forward; it is also one which can be overfulfilled and hence can all the more encourage the initiative of the working people. . . .

The experience of 1958 very clearly proved that the wisdom and strength of the masses is unlimited. Enlightened and led by our party and Comrade Mao Tsetung, and inspired by and organized under our party's general line, this wisdom and strength has become as irresistible as a mighty force under whose impact high mountains bow their heads and broad rivers make way. . . .

3. PO I-PO, THE SEVENTY ARTICLES ON INDUSTRY

Vice Premier Po I-po's seventy articles on industry were presented to the secretariat in 1961 as a synthesis of the party's industrial policy for the post-leap period of retrenchment.

The seventy articles underline the sharp cutbacks ordered in industrial construction while highlighting policies of centralization of resources and the use of profit as the principal yardstick for both individual enterprises and workers. Thus all units which were unable to show a profit at the height of the setbacks of the three hard years were enjoined to cease operations. At the same time, piece work and individual bonuses were elevated to become the center of the industrial wage policy in contrast to the emphasis during the Great Leap Forward on collective and nonmaterial incentives. The seventy articles also reversed the process which had been accelerated by the Great Leap of transferring cooperative factories to ownership by the state, calling for their transfer back again to producers' cooperatives.

If each of these measures marked steps backward from the socialist transformation of Chinese industry, the seventy articles also stipulated certain basic rights for workers such as a forty-five day leave with pay for women workers following the birth of a child, and designated principles for rationalizing the labor process through cost, resource and quality controls. The articles would become the object of attack during the Great Proletarian Cultural Revolution.

Main Content of the 70 Articles
of Industrial Policy

1. This year's industrial policy is aimed at adjustment, consolidation, filling up, and elevation.

2. The object of service in industry this year is "market as the primary."

3. In view of the present industrial policy, all capital construction projects except those specially provided for should stop.

4. Unless specially approved all the expansion or new construction projects formerly planned should stop without exception.

5. Capital construction units as well as factories, mines, and enterprises should check in detail all their new and old equipment (distinguishing between the indigenous and the modern and stating the years of make, the designed capacity, and the existing capacity) and draw up statements to be forwarded to the higher bodies. . . .

9. Except with special instructions, all industrial units which show themselves to be losing concerns in "business accounting" should stop operation from now on.

10. *Hsien* factories (local state-owned) should arrange their production plans on the basis of local resources.

11. *Hsien* factories (local state-owned) should produce daily necessaries for the people of the *hsien* concerned to meet people's needs of livelihood.

12. In order to overcome overexpansion of enterprise operations, all the local state-owned factories, which were formed through the merging of producers' cooperatives in 1958, should, with the exception of those with special qualifications, be gradually changed into producers' cooperatives at separate stages and in separate groups.

13. After the change the producers' cooperatives will come

From Documents of the Chinese Communist Party Central Committee, 1956–1969, URS, Vol. 1.

under collective ownership and assume responsibility for their own profit and loss.

14. All trades should strengthen their leadership over the producers' cooperatives.

15. The state-owned factories should investigate in detail the commodities transferred to them on the "communist wind" during the "Great Leap Forward" period. They should be returned, item by item, by the secretaries of the party committees for the units under their responsibility. . . .

18. From now on, factory workers' working hours shall not exceed eight.

19. It is stipulated that the workers shall take four days off each month. . . .

21. Lest it should take up workers' rest time, the eight-hour-a-week study time should be cut down as far as possible.

22. From now on all industrial units shall not call upon the workers to fight a "hard battle."

23. Lying-in woman workers shall have forty-five day leave with pay. . . .

25. Factories shall put piece-work systems into practice if they are in a position to do so.

26. Where it is not possible to put the piece-work system into practice, collective piece-work systems may be put into practice.

27. If the work cannot be paid for at a rate based on the amount done, it shall be paid for at a rate based on the time employed. From now on wages shall be paid at the rate of basic wages plus bonus, but the amount of bonus may not exceed 30 percent of the basic wages.

28. Evaluation of bonus shall be carried out once every month for the workers and once every quarter for the administrative personnel. . . .

30. From now on all factories and mines should bring into full play the advanced method of three-in-one combination of "leaders, technicians, and workers."

31. From now on the industrial units may not arbitrarily transfer workers. If they find it necessary to transfer skilled workers, they should do so with the consent of the shop directors.

32. In the next three years the industrial units may not recruit labor force in the countryside.

33. In the next three years local governments may not arbitrarily transfer workers. Any transfer of workers should be made through the *hsien* or provincial committee. . . .

55. Institute a system of workers' congress.

56. Workers' delegates shall be elected by the workers.

57. The factory superintendent and the party committee shall periodically make reports to the workers' delegates on the factory affairs.

58. Workers' delegates have the right to remove the factory superintendent or the personnel under the superintendent from their duties.

63. The party committee should arouse the office and factory workers to develop creations and inventions energetically and should give material and spiritual awards to those who have made innovations and inventions.

64. The party committee should arouse the administrative cadres to take part regularly in shop production.

65. It is permitted to have half a chairman separated from production in the case of a trade union with 50 members or more, one chairman separated from production in the case of a trade union with 200 members and more, and two chairmen separated from production in the case of a trade union with more than 500 members.

4. MAO TSETUNG, CRITIQUE OF SOVIET ECONOMICS

Mao's commentary on the authoritative Soviet political economy text which was prepared under Stalin's direction in the early 1950s, constitutes his most comprehensive, incisive, and mature statement of political economy and the process of

Reading Notes on the Soviet Text *Political Economy*. Translation by Moss Roberts in: *A Critique of Soviet Economics* (New York: Monthly Review Press, 1977).

socialist transition. Here Mao reveals the depth of his grasp of Marxist dialectics, categories of development, and the concrete practice of Soviet and Chinese experiences. Building on insights first explored in "On the Ten Major Relationships," Mao defines a development path attuned to China's unique conditions and appropriate for continuing the advance toward higher levels of socialism and communism. But the interest of this text transcends the particularities of the Chinese experience to provide larger insights into the problem of socialist transition, stages of development, and capitalist restoration.

In the analysis of balance and imbalance, self-reliance, the relationships among heavy industry, light industry, and agriculture, between city and countryside and between worker and peasant, the development opportunities for the backward and the advanced, and the preconditions for the transition to communism, Mao provides perhaps the clearest statement of his concept of the goals and methods of the Chinese road to socialism and a devastating, yet balanced and thoughtful, critique of Stalin and of the political economy of the Soviet Union.

If there is a single feature which distinguishes Mao's political economy from that of Stalin—and certainly no less of Stalin's successors—it is Mao's grasp of the production relations and the continuing class struggle, that is, the revolutionary human role in the development process. Mao clearly outlines the ways in which institutions and human relations formed during the early phases of socialist transition may prefigure the realization of a classless and prosperous communist society—or contribute to the restoration of capitalism.

Steel mills, power plants, and tractors are, to be sure, essential components of Mao's vision of the future of the Chinese economy. But for Mao, like Marx, at the heart of the development process, and central to the continued march toward socialism and prosperity, is the human factor. The speed and direction of advance as well as the quality of life are shaped by relations of participation, authority, and remuneration among the immediate producers, and between laboring people on the one hand, and cadres and managers on the other. While inequalities cannot be entirely eliminated under socialism so long as scarcity exists, the nature of the transition requires their systematic restriction precisely to stimulate the creative contributions of more and more working people, to create a situation, in short, in which work is transformed from a necessity to life's highest satisfaction. The advance toward higher stages of socialism, far from impeding economic development, has the potential to increase productivity. Moreover, excessive preoccupation with technology, and the failure to progressively curb inequalities, invites the resurgence of new elites and leads ultimately to the erosion of socialism. Exclusive preoccupation with the productive forces may set the stage for a capitalist restoration. Though Mao in 1960 was not yet prepared to conclude that precisely this stage had been reached in the Soviet Union, the seeds of this analysis are clearly present in his critique.

Because of the nature of this text as a commentary, I have taken the liberty in this case alone of rearranging Mao's comments topically to highlight his most distinctive and original theses.

I. Principles of Political Economy

A. Relations of Production and Productive Forces

In economics the main object of study is the production relations. All the same, political economy and the materialist historical outlook are close cousins. It is difficult to deal clearly with problems of the economic base and the production relations if the question of the superstructure is neglected. (15)*

We need to use balance and imbalance among the productive forces, the production relations and the superstructure as a guideline for researching the economic problems of socialism. (41)

---

*Numbers in parentheses refer to chapters in the text.

B. Revolution, Stages of Development, and Productive Forces

From the standpoint of world history, the bourgeois revolutions and the establishment of the bourgeois nations came before, not after, the Industrial Revolution. The bourgeoisie first changed the superstructure and took possession of the machinery of state before carrying on propaganda to gather real strength. Only then did they push forward great changes in the production relations. When the production relations had been taken care of and they were on the right track they then opened the way for the development of the productive forces. . . . In England the Industrial Revolution (late eighteenth–early nineteenth centuries) was carried through only after the bourgeois revolution, that is, after the seventeenth century. All in their respective ways, Germany, France, America, and Japan underwent change in superstructure and production relations before the vast development of capitalist industry.

It is a general rule that you cannot solve the problem of ownership and go on to expand development of the productive forces until you have first prepared public opinion for the seizure of political power. (28) . . .

In the various nations of the West there is a great obstacle to carrying through any revolution and construction movement; that is, the poisons of the bourgeoisie are so powerful that they have penetrated each and every corner. . . .

Lenin says, "The transition from capitalism to socialism will be more difficult for a country the more backward it is." This would seem incorrect today. Actually, the transition is less difficult the more backward an economy is, for the poorer they are, the more the people want revolution. In the capitalist countries of the West the number of people employed is comparatively high, and so is the wage level. Workers there have been deeply influenced by the bourgeoisie, and it would not appear to be all that easy to carry through a socialist transformation. . . . Countries of the East, such as China and Russia, had been backward and poor, but now not only have their social systems moved well ahead of those of the West, but even the rate of development of their productive forces far outstrips that of the West. Again, as in the history of the development of the capitalist countries, the backward overtake the advanced as America overtook England, and as Germany later overtook England early in the twentieth century. (14) . . .

It is possible to divide the transition from capitalism to communism into two stages: one from capitalism to socialism, which could be called underdeveloped socialism; and one from socialism to communism, that is, from comparatively underdeveloped socialism to comparatively developed socialism, namely, communism. This latter stage may take even longer than the first. But once it has been passed through, material production and spiritual prosperity will be most ample. People's communist consciousness will be greatly raised, and they will be ready to enter the highest stage of communism.

In the period of communism there will still be uninterrupted development. It is quite possible that communism will have to pass through a number of different stages. How can we say that once communism has been reached nothing will change, that everything will continue "fully consolidated," that there will be quantitative change only, and no partial qualitative change going on all the time. (21)

C. Contradictions and Development During the Transition

[The text] recognizes only the unanimity of solidarity but not the contradictions within a socialist society, nor that contradiction is the motive force of social development. Once it is put this way, the law of the universality of contradiction is denied, the laws of dialectics are suspended. Without contradictions there is no movement, and society always develops through movement. In the era of socialism, contradictions remain the motive force of social development. (23)

D. Balance and Imbalance

The national economy of a socialist society can have planned proportional development which enables imbalances to be regulated. However, imbalance does not go away. "Unevenness is in the nature of things." Because private ownership was eliminated it was possible to have planned organization of the economy. Therefore, it was possible to control and utilize consciously the objective laws of imbalance to create many relative temporary balances.

If the productive forces run ahead, the production relations will not accord with the productive forces; the superstructure will not accord with the production relations. At that point the superstructure and the production relations will have to be changed to accord with the productive forces. Between superstructure and production relations, between production relations and productive forces—some say balance is only relatively attainable, for the productive forces are always advancing, therefore there is always imbalance. Balance and imbalance are two sides of a contradiction within which imbalance is absolute and balance relative. If this were not so, neither the superstructure nor the production relations, nor the productive forces, could further develop; they would become petrified. Balance is relative, imbalance absolute. This is a universal law which I am convinced applies to socialist society. Contradiction and struggle are absolutes; unity, unanimity, and solidarity are transitional, hence relative. The various balances attained in planning are temporary, transitional, and conditional, hence relative. Who can imagine a state of equilibrium that is unconditional, eternal? (41)

E. Planning and the Law of Value

The law of value serves as an instrument of planning. Good. But the law of value should not be made the main basis of planning. We did not carry through the Great Leap on the basis of the demands of the law of value but on the basis of the fundamental economic laws of socialism and the need to expand production. If things are narrowly regarded from the point of view of the law of value the Great Leap would have to be judged not worth the losses and last year's all-out effort to produce steel and iron as wasted labor. The local steel produced was low in quantity and quality, and the state had to make good many losses. The economic results were not significant, etc. The partial short-term view is that the campaign was a loss, but the overall long-term view is that there was great value to the campaign because it opened wide a whole economic construction phase. Throughout the country many new starts in steel and iron were made, and many industrial centers were built. This enabled us to step up our pace greatly.

In sum, we put plans ahead of prices. Of course we cannot ignore prices. A few years ago we raised the purchase price for live pigs, and this had a positive effect on pigbreeding. But for the kind of large-scale, nation-wide breeding we have today, planning remains the main thing we rely on. (45)

II. Socialist Transition

A. Transforming Production Relations

It is not enough to assert that the development of large industry is the foundation for the socialist transformation of the economy. All revolutionary history shows that the full development of new productive forces is not the prerequisite for the transformation of backward production relations. Our revolution began with Marxist-Leninist propaganda, which served to create new public opinion in favor of the revolution. Moreover, it was possible to destroy the old production relations only after we had overthrown a backward superstructure in the course of revolution. After the old production relations had been destroyed new ones were created, and these cleared the way for the development of new social productive forces. With that behind us we were able to set in motion the technological revolution to develop social productive forces on a large scale. At the same time, we still had to continue transforming the production relations and ideology. (15)

Prolonged coexistence of ownership by the whole people with ownership by the collectives is bound to become less and less adaptable to the development of the productive forces and will fail to satisfy the ever increasing needs of peasant consumption and agricultural production or of industry for raw materials. To satisfy such needs we must resolve the contradiction between these two forms of ownership, transform ownership by

the collectives into ownership by the whole people, and make a unified plan for production and distribution in industry and agriculture on the basis of ownership by the whole people for an indivisible nation. (19) . . .
The text says that it is necessary to make a transition from collective ownership to indivisible ownership by the whole people. But from our point of view it is first necessary to turn collective ownership into socialist ownership by the whole people, that is, to make the agricultural means of production entirely state owned, and to turn the peasants entirely into workers under uniform contract to the state for wages. At present nation-wide, each Chinese peasant has an average annual income of 85 yuan. In the future, when this amount will reach 150 yuan and the majority of workers are paid by the commune, it will be possible to make a commune ownership system basically work. In this way taking the next step to state ownership should be easy. (58)

B. Self-reliance
and the International Division of Labor

The text goes on to express the view that the reason why countries dominated by precapitalist economic forms could carry through a socialist revolution was because of assistance from advanced socialist countries. This is an incomplete way of putting the matter. After the democratic revolution succeeded in China we were able to take the path of socialism mainly because we overthrew the rule of imperialism, feudalism, and bureaucratic capitalism. The internal factors were the main ones. While the assistance we received from successful socialist countries was an important condition, it was not one which could settle the question of whether or not we could take the road of socialism, but only one which could influence our rate of advance after we had taken the road. With aid we could advance more quickly, without it less so. (3)

We advocate all-round development and do not think that each province need not produce goods which other provinces could supply. We want the various provinces to develop a variety of production to the fullest extent, provided there is no adverse effect on the whole. One of the advantages Europe enjoys is the independence of the various countries. Each is devoted to a set of activities, causing the European economy to develop comparatively quickly.

I wonder why the text fails to advocate each country's doing the utmost for itself rather than not producing goods which other countries could supply? The correct method is each doing the utmost for itself as a means toward self-reliance for new growth, working independently to the greatest possible extent, making a principle out of not relying on others, and not doing something only when it really and truly cannot be done. Above all, agriculture must be done well as far as possible. Reliance on other countries or provinces for food is most dangerous. (60)

C. Incentives: Community and Individual

Even if the importance of material incentive is recognized, it is never the sole principle. There is always another principle, namely spiritual inspiration from political ideology. And while we are on the subject, material incentive cannot simply be discussed as individual interest. There is also the collective interest to which individual interest should be subordinated, long-term interests to which temporary interests should be subordinated, and the interests of the whole to which partial interests should be subordinated. (42)

We have always spoken of joint consideration of public and private and long ago made the point that there is no such thing as all the one or the other, but that the public takes precedence over the private. The individual is a part of the collective. If the collective interest advances, the individual's lot will improve in consequence. (51)

As to the distribution of commodities, the text has to be rewritten, changing its present approach altogether. Hard, bitter struggle, expanding reproduction, the future prospects of communism—these are what have to be emphasized, not individual material interest. The goal to lead people toward is not "one spouse, one country house, one automobile, one piano, one television." This is the road of serving the self, not the society. A "ten-thousand-league journey begins where you are standing." But if one looks only at the feet without giving thought to the future, then the question is: What is left of revolutionary excitement and ardor? (66)

D. *Transforming Ideology*

Landlords, bureaucrats, counter-revolutionaries, and undesirable elements have to be remolded; the same holds true for the capitalist class, the upper stratum of the petty bourgeoisie, and the middle peasants. Our experience shows that remolding is difficult. Those who do not undergo persistent repeated struggle cannot be properly remolded. To eliminate thoroughly any remaining strength of the bourgeoisie and any influence they may have will take one or two decades at the least and may even require half a century. In the rural areas, where basic commune ownership has been put into effect, private ownership has been transformed into state ownership. The entire country abounds with new cities and new major industry. Transportation and communications for the entire country have been modernized. Truly the economic situation has been completely changed, and for the first time the peasants' world view is bound to be turned around completely step by step. (6)

E. *The Transition to Communism*

The transition to communism certainly is not a matter of one class overthrowing another. But that does not mean there will be no social revolution, because the superseding of one kind of production relations by another is a qualitative leap, that is, a revolution. The two transformations—of individual economy to collective, and collective economy to public—in China are both revolutions in the production relations. So to go from socialism's "distribution according to labor" to communism's "distribution according to need" has to be called a revolution in the production relations. Of course, "distribution according to need" has to be brought about gradually. Perhaps when the principal material goods can be adequately supplied we can begin to carry out such distribution with those goods, extending the practice to other goods on the basis of further development of the productive forces. (25)

III. Rural Development

A. Land Revolution

[The text] says that the land taken from the rich peasants and given to the poor and middle peasants was land the government had expropriated and then parceled out. This looks at the matter as a grant by royal favor, forgetting that class struggles and mass mobilizations had been set in motion, a right deviationist point of view. Our approach was to rely on the poor peasants, to unite with the majority of middle peasants (lower middle peasants) and seize the land from the landlord class. While the party did play a leading role, it was against doing everything itself and thus substituting for the masses. (9)

B. Cooperation, Mechanization, and Rural Industrialization

Our worker-peasant alliance has already passed through two stages. The first was based on the land revolution, the second on the cooperative movement. If cooperativization had not been set in motion the peasantry inevitably would have been polarized, and the worker-peasant alliance could not have been consolidated. In consequence, the policy of "unified government purchase and sale of private output" could not have been persevered in. The reason is that that policy could be maintained and made to work thoroughly only on the basis of cooperativization. At the present time our worker-peasant alliance has to take the next step and establish itself on the basis of mechanization. . . . When state ownership and mechanization are integrated we will be able to begin truly to consolidate the worker-peasant alliance, and the differences between workers and peasants will surely be eliminated step by step. (10)

The book sees socialist industrialization as the precondition for agricultural collectivization. This view in no way corresponds to the situation in the Soviet Union itself, where collectivization was basically realized between 1930 and 1932. Though they had then more tractors than we do now, still and all the amount of arable land under mechanized cultivation was under 20.3 percent. Collectivization is not altogether determined by mechanization, and so industrialization is not the precondition for it. (12)

The text states, "The machine and tractor stations are important tools for carrying through the socialist transformation in agriculture." Again and again the text emphasizes how important machinery is for the transformation. But if the consciousness of the peasantry is not raised, if ideology is not transformed, and you are depending on nothing but machinery—what good will it be? The question of the struggle between the two roads, socialism and capitalism, the transformation and re-education of people—these are the major questions for China. (20)

In a future time, because of inadequate machinery, we will be calling for partial mechanization and improvement of our tools. For now we are holding off on general automation. Mechanization has to be discussed, but with a sense of proportion. If mechanization and automation are made too much of they are bound to make people despise partial mechanization and production by native methods. In the past we had such diversions, when everybody was demanding new technology, new machinery, the large-scale, high standards; the native, the medium or small in scale were held in contempt. We did not overcome this tendency until we promoted concurrently native *and* foreign, large *and* medium *and* small. (48)

C. Two Forms of Ownership: State and Collective Ownership

Consider the development of our people's communes. When we changed from basic ownership by the team to basic ownership by the commune, was a section of the people likely to raise objections or not? This is a question well worth our study. A determinative condition for realizing this changeover was that the commune-owned economy's income was more than half of the whole commune's total income. To realize the basic commune-ownership system is generally of benefit to the members of the commune. Thus we estimate that there should be no objection on the part of the vast majority. But at the time of changeover the original team cadres . . . would *they* object to the changeover?

Although classes may be eliminated in a socialist society, in the course of its development there are bound to be certain problems with "vested interest groups" which have grown content with existing institutions and are unwilling to change them. (25)

IV. Industrialization

A. Industry and Agriculture

In Stalin's time, due to special emphasis on priority development of heavy industry, agriculture was neglected in the plans. Eastern Europe has had similar problems in the past few years. Our approach has been to make priority development of heavy industry the condition for putting into effect concurrent promotion of industry and agriculture, as well as some other concurrent programs, each of which again has within it a leading aspect. If agriculture does not make gains few problems can be resolved. How highly we regard agriculture is expressed by the quantity of steel materials we are allocating to agriculture. In 1959 we allocated only 590,000 tons but this year (including water conservancy construction) we allocated 1.3 million tons. This is truly concurrent promotion of industry and agriculture. . . .

The experience of the Soviet Union, no less than our own, proves that if agriculture does not develop, if light industry does not develop, it hurts the development of heavy industry. (38)

"Industry developing faster than agriculture" has to be posed in an appropriate way. One cannot emphasize industry to an inappropriate degree or trouble is sure to occur. Take our Liaoning: with its many industries, this province has an urban population that is one-third the total. In the past they had always put industry in first place, without attending at the same time to the vigorous development of agriculture. The result was that the province's agriculture could not guarantee supplies of grain, meats, and vegetables for the urban markets, and they always had to ship these items in from other provinces. . . . What we had failed to understand was that it was precisely in such places as the Northeast, particularly Liaoning, where we should have taken firm hold of agriculture. So one cannot emphasize only taking firm hold of industry.

Our position is that industry and agriculture should be developed together with priority given to developing heavy industry.

The phrase "concurrent promotion" in no way denies priority in growth or faster development of industry than agriculture. At the same time, "concurrent promotion" is not equal utilization of our strength. For example, this year we estimate we can produce about 14 million tons of steel materials, of which 10 percent is to be applied to agricultural technological transformation and water conservancy construction. The remaining 90 percent is to be used mainly in heavy industry and communication and transportation construction. Under this year's conditions this is concurrent promotion of industry and agriculture. (54)

After the Soviet Union's first five-year plan had been completed, when the value of all large industrial production was 70 percent of the value of all industrial and agricultural production, they promptly declared that industrialization had been made a reality. We too could quickly reach such a standard, but even if we did, we still would not claim that industrialization had become a reality, because we have over 500 million peasants devoting themselves to agriculture. . . .

In the long term, we expect to be known as an industrial-agricultural nation. Even if we make over 100 million tons of steel it will still be so. If our per capita output were to surpass Great Britain's we would need to be producing 350 million tons of steel at least! (Supplement 1)

B. City and Countryside

Since they want to eliminate the difference (the book says "basic difference") between urban and rural, why does the text make a point of saying that it is not "to reduce the functions of the big cities?" The cities of the future need not be so large, Residents of large cities should be dispersed into the rural areas. Building many smaller cities is a relative advantage in case of nuclear war. (59)

In eliminating the problem of excess population, rural population is the major problem, the solution of which calls for vast development of production. In China over 500 million people are devoting themselves to agriculture. But they do not eat their fill, although they toil year in year out. This is most unreasonable. In America the agricultural population is only 13 percent and on the average each person has 2,000 catties of grain. We do not have so much. What shall we do to reduce the rural population? If we do not want them crowding into the cities we will have to have a great deal of industry in the countryside so that the peasants can become workers right where they are. This brings us to a major policy issue: Do we want to keep rural living conditions from falling below that in the cities, keep the two roughly the same, or keep the rural slightly higher than the urban? Every commune has to have its own economic center, its own upper-level schools to train its own intellectuals. There is no other way to solve the problem of excess rural population really and truly. (Supplement 8)

C. Large, Medium, and Small Industry

The text touches on our broad development of small- and medium-scale enterprise but fails to reflect accurately our philosophy of concurrent promotion of native and foreign, small, medium, and large enterprise. . . . Under the guidance of the larger enterprises we are developing the small and the medium; under the guidance of the foreign we are adopting native methods wherever we can—mainly for the sake of achieving the high rate of industrialization. (18)

From small plants have come many creations and discoveries. Larger factories may have superior facilities, newer technology, and for that very reason the staff all too often assume airs of self-importance, are satisfied with things as they are and do not seek to advance and reach out ambitiously. All too often their creativity does not compare at all with that of the staff of the smaller factory. (Supplement 2)

D. Management

Throughout, the text speaks of "managing production according to the principle of the single-leader system." All enterprises in capitalist countries put this principle into effect. There should be a basic distinction between the principles governing management of socialist and capitalist enterprises. We in China have been able to distinguish our methods strictly from capitalist management by putting into effect factory leader responsibility under the guidance of the party. (34)

After the question of the ownership system is solved, the most important question is administration—how enterprises owned either by the whole people or the collective are administered. . . . With respect to administration of enterprises owned by a whole people, we have adopted a set of approaches: a combination of concentrated leadership and mass movement; combinations of party leaders, working masses, and technical personnel; cadres participating in production; workers participating in administration; steadily changing unreasonable regulations and institutional practices. (66)

5. ON KHRUSHCHEV'S PHONY COMMUNISM

The party's Tenth Plenum in 1962 endorsed Mao's formulation for the basic line during the period of socialist transition:

Socialist society covers a considerably long historical period. In the historical period of socialism, there are still classes, class contradictions and class struggle, there is the struggle between the socialist road and the capitalist road, and there is the danger of capitalist restoration. We must recognize the protracted and complex nature of this struggle. We must heighten our vigilance. We must conduct socialist education. We must correctly understand and handle class contradictions between ourselves and the enemy from those among the people and handle them correctly. Otherwise a socialist society like ours will turn into its opposite and degenerate, and a capitalist restoration will take place. From now on we must remind ourselves of this every year, every month and every day so that we can maintain a rather sober understanding of this problem and have a Marxist-Leninist line.

The struggle which reached fever pitch within the Chinese leadership and at the grassroots in the years following the Great

Editorial departments of JMJP and HC: On Khrushchev's Phony Communism, and Its Historical Lessons for the World. PR July 17, 1964.

Leap was enacted simultaneously in the international arena. "On Khrushchev's Phony Communism," written with the collaborative authorship of Mao, sums up the central role of the dictatorship of the proletariat and class struggle in sustaining China along the road of socialist development.

In perhaps the most brilliant polemic to emerge from the fierce Sino-Soviet debate, the article establishes the basis of China's strategy of uninterrupted revolution in direct opposition to central propositions advanced by Khrushchev: that the Soviet Union had eliminated classes and class struggle; that the dictatorship of the proletariat was therefore obsolete; that the Soviet state represented no single class or bloc of classes, but the whole people. Showing that these propositions constituted the theoretical bases for undermining socialism in the Soviet Union, the article spelled out in detail the measures required if China—or any other society—was to avoid the pitfalls of capitalist restoration and was to continue to advance toward communism through the elimination of the three great differences (between city and countryside, workers and peasants, and mental and manual labor) and of all forms of privilege. In so doing it anticipated many themes of the Great Proletarian Cultural Revolution which would erupt less than two years later.

The theories of the proletarian revolution and the dictatorship of the proletariat are the quintessence of Marxism-Leninism. The questions of whether revolution should be upheld or opposed and whether the dictatorship of the proletariat should be upheld or opposed have always been the focus of struggle between Marxism-Leninism and all brands of revisionism, and they are now the focus of struggle between Marxist-Leninists the world over and the revisionist Khrushchev clique.

At the Twenty-second Congress of the CPSU, the revisionist Khrushchev clique developed their revisionism into a complete system not only by rounding off their antirevolutionary theories of "peaceful coexistence," "peaceful competition," and "peaceful transition" but also by declaring that the dictatorship of the proletariat is no longer necessary in the Soviet

Union, and advancing the absurd theories of the "state of the whole people" and the "party of the entire people." . . .

In socialist society, the dictatorship of the proletariat replaces bourgeois dictatorship and the public ownership of the means of production replaces private ownership. The proletariat, from being an oppressed and exploited class, turns into the ruling class and a fundamental change takes place in the social position of the working people. . . .

However, one cannot but see that socialist society is a society born out of capitalist society and is only the first phase of communist society. It is not yet a fully mature communist society in the economic and other fields. It is inevitably stamped with the birth marks of capitalist society. . . .

Throughout this stage, the class struggle between the bourgeoisie and the proletariat goes on and the question of "who will win" between the roads of capitalism and socialism remains, as does the danger of the restoration of capitalism.

Throughout the stage of socialism the class struggle between the proletariat and the bourgeoisie in the political, economic, ideological, and cultural and educational fields cannot be stopped. It is a protracted, repeated, tortuous, and complex struggle. . . . Whether a socialist society will advance to communism or revert to capitalism depends upon the outcome of this protracted struggle.

The class struggle in socialist society is inevitably reflected in the Communist Party. . . . The old and new bourgeois elements, the old and new rich peasants and the degenerate elements of all sorts constitute the social basis of revisionism, and they use every possible means to find agents within the Communist Party. The existence of bourgeois influence is the internal source of revisionism, and surrender to imperialist pressure is the external source. . . .

The development of socialist society is a process of uninterrupted revolution. In explaining revolutionary socialism Marx said:

> This socialism is the *declaration of the permanence of the revolution*, the *class dictatorship* of the proletariat as the necessary transit point to the *abolition of class distinctions generally*, to the abolition of all the relations of production on which they rest, to the abolition of all

the social relations that correspond to these relations of production, to the revolutionizing of all the ideas that result from these social relations.

In his struggle against the opportunism of the Second International, Lenin creatively expounded and developed Marx's theory of the dictatorship of the proletariat. He pointed out:

> The dictatorship of the proletariat is not the end of class struggle but its continuation in new forms. The dictatorship of the proletariat is class struggle waged by a proletariat which has been victorious and has taken political power in its hands against a bourgeoisie that has been defeated but not destroyed, a bourgeoisie that has not vanished, not ceased to offer resistance, but that has intensified its resistance.

Judging from the actual situation today, the tasks of the dictatorship of the proletariat are still far from accomplished in any of the socialist countries. In all socialist countries without exception, there are classes and class struggle, the struggle between the socialist and the capitalist roads, the question of carrying the socialist revolution through to the end and the question of preventing the restoration of capitalism. All the socialist countries still have a very long way to go before the differences between ownership by the whole people and collective ownership, between workers and peasants, between town and country, and between mental and manual laborers are eliminated; before all classes and class differences are abolished and a communist society with its principle, "from each according to his ability, to each according to his needs" is realized. Therefore, it is necessary for all the socialist countries to uphold the dictatorship of the proletariat. . . .

Since Khrushchev usurped the leadership of the Soviet party and state, there has been a fundamental change in the state of the class struggle in the Soviet Union.

Khrushchev has carried out a series of revisionist policies serving the interests of the bourgeoisie and rapidly swelling the forces of capitalism in the Soviet Union. . . .

Khrushchev has substituted "material incentive" for the socialist principle, "from each according to his ability, to each according to his work." He has widened, and not narrowed, the gap between the incomes of a small minority and those of the workers, peasants, and ordinary intellectuals. He has supported the degenerates in leading positions, encouraging them to become even more unscrupulous in abusing their powers and to appropriate the fruits of labor of the Soviet people. Thus he has accelerated the polarization of classes in Soviet society.

Khrushchev sabotages the socialist planned economy, applies the capitalist principle of profit, develops capitalist free competition and undermines socialist ownership by the whole people.

Khrushchev attacks the system of socialist agricultural planning, describing it as "bureaucratic" and "unnecessary." Eager to learn from the big proprietors of American farms, he is encouraging capitalist management, fostering a kulak economy and undermining the socialist collective economy. . . .

Going forward to communism means moving towards the abolition of all classes and class differences. A communist society which preserves any classes at all, let alone exploiting classes, is inconceivable. Yet Khrushchev is fostering a new bourgeoisie, restoring and extending the system of exploitation and accelerating class polarization in the Soviet Union. A privileged bourgeois stratum opposed to the Soviet people now occupies the ruling position in the party and government and in the economic, cultural and other departments. Can one find an iota of communism in all this?

Going forward to communism means moving towards a unitary system of the ownership of the means of production by the whole people. A communist society in which several kinds of ownership of the means of production coexist is inconceivable. Yet Khrushchev is creating a situation in which enterprises owned by the whole people are gradually degenerating into capitalist enterprises and farms under the system of collective ownership are gradually degenerating into units of a kulak economy. Again, can one find an iota of communism in all this?

Going forward to communism means moving towards a great abundance of social products and the realization of the principle of "from each according to his ability, to each according to his needs." A communist society built on the enrichment of a handful of persons and the impoverishment of the masses is inconceivable. . . .

Going forward to communism means moving towards enhancing the communist consciousness of the masses. A communist society with bourgeois ideas running rampant is inconceivable. Yet Khrushchev is zealously reviving bourgeois ideology in the Soviet Union and serving as a missionary for the decadent American culture. By propagating material incentive, he is turning all human relations into money relations and encouraging individualism and selfishness. Because of him, manual labor is again considered sordid and love of pleasure at the expense of other people's labor is again considered honorable. . . .

Khrushchev's "communism" takes the United States for its model. Imitation of the methods of management of U.S. capitalism and the bourgeois way of life has been raised by Khrushchev to the level of state policy. . . .

Thus it can be seen that Khrushchev's "communism" is indeed "goulash communism," the "communism of the American way of life" and "communism seeking credits from the devil." No wonder he often tells representatives of Western monopoly capital that once such "communism" is realized in the Soviet Union, "you will go forward to communism without any call from me."

There is nothing new about such "communism." It is simply another name for capitalism. It is only a bourgeois label, sign, or advertisement. . . .

How can the restoration of capitalism be prevented? . . .

First, in socialist society there are two kinds of social contradictions, namely, the contradictions among the people and those between ourselves and the enemy. These two kinds of social contradictions are entirely different in essence, and the methods for handling them should be different, too. Their correct handling will result in the increasing consolidation of the dictatorship of the proletariat and the further strengthening and development of socialist society. . . .

Second, socialist society covers a very long historical period. Classes and class struggle continue to exist in this society, and the struggle still goes on between the road of socialism and the road of capitalism. The socialist revolution on the economic front (in the ownership of the means of production) is insufficient by itself and cannot be consolidated. There must also be a thorough socialist revolution on the political and ideological fronts. . . .

Third, the dictatorship of the proletariat is led by the working class, with the worker-peasant alliance as its basis. This means the exercise of dictatorship by the working class and by the people under its leadership over the reactionary classes and individuals and those elements who oppose socialist transformation and socialist construction. Within the ranks of the people democratic centralism is practiced. . . .

Fourth, in both socialist revolution and socialist construction it is necessary to adhere to the mass line, boldly to arouse the masses and to unfold mass movements on a large scale. . . .

Fifth, whether in socialist revolution or in socialist construction, it is necessary to solve the question of whom to rely on, whom to win over and whom to oppose. The proletariat and its vanguard must make a class analysis of socialist society, rely on the truly dependable forces that firmly take the socialist road win over all allies that can be won over and unite with the masses of the people, who constitute more than 95 percent of the population, in a common struggle against the enemies of socialism. . . .

Sixth, it is necessary to conduct extensive socialist education movements repeatedly in the cities and the countryside. . . .

Seventh, one of the basic tasks of the dictatorship of the proletariat is actively to expand the socialist economy. . . .

Eighth, ownership by the whole people and collective ownership are the two forms of socialist economy. The transition from collective ownership to ownership by the whole people, from two kinds of ownership to a unitary ownership by the whole people, is a rather long process. . . .

Ninth, "Let a hundred flowers blossom and a hundred schools of thought contend" is a policy for stimulating the growth of the arts and the progress of science and for promoting a flourishing socialist culture. . . . It is necessary to build up a large detachment of working-class intellectuals who serve socialism and who are both "red and expert," that is, who are both politically conscious and professionally competent, by means of the cultural revolution, and revolutionary practice in class struggle, the struggle for production and scientific experiment.

Tenth, it is necessary to maintain the system of cadre participation in collective productive labor. The cadres of our party and state are ordinary workers and not overlords sitting on the backs of the people. . . .

Eleventh, the system of high salaries for a small number of

people should never be applied. The gap between the incomes of the working personnel of the party, the government, the enterprises, and the people's communes, on the one hand, and the incomes of the mass of the people, on the other, should be rationally and gradually narrowed and not widened. . . .

In the light of the historical lessons of the dictatorship of the proletariat Comrade Mao Tsetung has stated:

> Class struggle, the struggle for production, and scientific experiment are the three great revolutionary movements for building a mighty socialist country. These movements are a sure guarantee that communists will be free from bureaucracy and immune against revisionism and dogmatism, and will forever remain invincible. They are a reliable guarantee that the proletariat will be able to unite with the broad working masses and realize a democratic dictatorship. . . .

Comrade Mao Tsetung has pointed out that, in order to guarantee that our party and country do not change their color, we must not only have a correct line and correct policies but must train and bring up millions of successors who will carry on the cause of proletarian revolution.

B. THE STRUGGLE SHARPENS
IN THE COUNTRYSIDE

1. MAO TSETUNG,
LETTER TO TEAM LEADERS

On November 29, 1959, Mao wrote directly to the hundreds of thousands of team leaders throughout the countryside in a personal effort to stem the "communist wind." He attributed excesses such as inflated reporting to pressure from "higher levels" and instructed basic level cadres where necessary to ignore instructions from above and concentrate on realistic possibilities for raising output. In contrast to those who saw the solution to the production setbacks which began in some areas in 1959 in retreat to individual farming and the free market, Mao called for hard realism (and an end to "trumpet blowing") rooted in the continued expansion of communal activities within a framework of decentralized planning. Mao sought in short to combat utopian tendencies which had produced hyper-inflated rhetoric, extreme imbalances, and chaos in planning. At the same time he reaffirmed the basic soundness of the course initiated during the Great Leap in the countryside. Here we see Mao attempting to slice through the layers of bureaucracy and party officialdom to implement a mass line relationship based on direct communication with activists at the grassroots level.

Comrades of the Provincial, Administrative District, *Hsien,* Commune, Brigade, and Team Levels:

I want to discuss with you comrades a few questions, all of which concern agriculture.

A Letter to Production Team Leaders, November 29, 1959. CB 89.

The first one is the question of fixing output quotas. Transplanting is being carried out in the South and spring farming is also underway in the North. The fixing of output quotas must be carried out to the letter. Basically, you should pay attention not to the instructions from a higher level but to the realistic possibilities. For example, the per-mou yield amounted to only 300 catties last year, and it will be good if the yield could be increased by one or two hundred catties this year. It is no more than trumpet blowing to say that the yield will amount to 800 catties, 1,000 catties, 1,200 catties and even more. This is actually unattainable, and what is the use of blowing the trumpet in this way? Those places that managed to bring in 500 catties per mou will be doing a great job if they can increase the yield by 200 or 300 catties this year. Generally speaking a greater increase is not possible.

The second one is the question of close planting. Crops should not be planted too wide apart nor too close. Due to their lack of experience, many young cadres and some organs at a higher level are bent on advocating close planting. Some people actually say the closer the better. This is undesirable and the old peasants and middle-aged people are also skeptical of the idea. It will be nice for these two kinds of people to hold a meeting to work out the proper density. Since production quotas have to be fixed, the question of close planting should be discussed and determined by the production brigades and teams. Any rigid order concerning close planting from a higher level is not only useless but also harmful. Therefore such rigid orders basically should not be issued. The provincial committees may suggest the range of close planting, not for issue as an order to the lower level, but for the reference of the lower level. Apart from this, the higher level should seriously study what is the ideal degree of close planting and lay down a more scientific set of rules concerning the degree of close planting according to the climate, the locality, the soil, water supply and seed, the conditions of various crops, and the high or low level of field management. It will be nice if a practicable criterion is reached within a given number of years.

The third one is the question of economy of grain. It is necessary to exercise a tighter grip and fix the quantity on a per capita basis. More grain should be consumed in the busy season and less grain should be consumed in the slack season. In the busy season, people should feed on solid rice and in the slack season they should feed alternately on solid rice and rice porridge mixed with sweet potatoes, vegetables, carrots, gourds, beans, taroes, etc. A tight grip should be exercised on this matter. Every year, the matter of harvesting, storage and consumption must be firmly grasped. Furthermore, the matter must be grasped in the nick of time and no opportunity should be missed since time and tide wait for no man. There must be reserve grain and it is necessary to store away some grain every year. The quantity of grain stored should increase year by year. After eight or ten years of struggle, the grain problem can be solved. Within the next ten years we should never indulge ourselves in big and high-flown talk because this is very dangerous. It should be known that ours is a big country with a population of 650 million people and feeding them is an important matter.

The fourth one is the question of planting a greater acreage to crops. The plan of reaping a bigger harvest by planting a smaller number of high yield crops is a long-term one which can be carried out, but it is not possible to carry out the whole or the greater part of it in the next ten years. Most of the plan cannot be carried out in the next three years. In the next three years, it is necessary to strive to plant more crops and simultaneously carry out the policies of the past few years—to plant a greater acreage to low-yield crops and to reap a bigger harvest through planting a smaller number of crops in bumper-harvest fields.

The fifth one is the question of mechanization. The fundamental way out for agriculture lies in mechanization. This requires ten years of time. It is necessary to solve the question on a small scale in four years, on an intermediate scale in seven years and on a large scale in ten years. Over the period of four years—that is, this year and the three following years—we should mainly rely on improved farm implements and semi-mechanized farm implements. There must be a farm implements research center in every province, every administrative district, and every *hsien*, and a number of scientific and technical personnel and experienced blacksmiths and carpenters in the countryside should be concentrated to gather together the more progressive types of farm implements of the whole province, the whole administrative district, the whole *hsien* for comparison, testing, and improvement. After that, it is possible to start mass production of farm implements for popularization. Whenever mechanization is mentioned, it is necessary to take into consideration the mechanized production of chemical fertilizer. It is most important that the supply of chemical fertilizer should be increased year by year.

The sixth one is the question of telling the truth. When output quotas are fixed, we should make known the actual output quotas we can guarantee. We must not tell lies by fixing the output quotas at a level which are actually beyond our means to fulfill. We must not tell lies about various measures for increasing production and the enforcement of the Eight Point Charter. Those who are honest and dare to tell the truth are in the final analysis beneficial to the cause of the people, and they themselves also have nothing to lose. Those who are fond of telling lies will do harm to the people as well as themselves and they always are at a disadvantage. It should be said that many lies are told due to the pressure of a higher level. When the higher level resorts to trumpet blowing, applying pressure and making promises, it makes things difficult for the lower level. Therefore, while one must have drive, one must never tell lies.

You comrades are requested to study the six questions mentioned above. You may put forward different views with the object of getting at the truth. Our experience is still rather inadequate in agricultural work. By accumulating experience year after year, in another ten years the objective necessity can be gradually known to us, and there will be some degree of freedom for us. What is called freedom? Freedom is the knowledge of necessity.

Compared with the high-flown talk that is in vogue at present, what I have said here is low-keyed. My purpose is to arouse enthusiasm in the true sense and to attain the end of increasing production. If things are not as low as I talk about and a higher objective is achieved, thus turning me into a conservative, then I'll thank heaven and earth and feel greatly honored.

2. FIRMLY OPPOSE THE "COMMUNIST WIND": THE CONSOLIDATION OF THE COMMUNES

Issued at the nadir of economic difficulty in November 1960, the Central Committee's urgent directive provides guidelines to preserve peasant income and security by scaling down several of the most radical features of the communes. The directive unequivocally criticized the "communist wind" and provided assurances that with the transfer of ownership from the commune to the production brigade and with the resurrection of private plots, the system would be stabilized for at least seven years. The directive provides the clearest indication of the end of the Great Leap.

Two editorials in the People's Daily, *November 20 and November 25, 1960, define the consolidation and downward transfer of authority within the communes and the balance of collective and individual incentives. While the brigade had replaced the commune as the major unit of accounting since 1959, the team had already emerged as the basic level for organizing agricultural production. A basic contradiction in the communes at this time, not resolved until 1961 when the unit of accounting was transferred to the team, flowed from the division between brigade-level accounting and production management by the team.*

The November 25th editorial raises another critical issue: incentives. The system of "three guarantees and one reward" here applied to team units opened the way in 1960–1962 to the breakdown of cooperative farming in some areas with individuals simply contracting to fill quotas, a policy subsequently attacked and attributed to Liu Shao-ch'i.

A. Central Committee
Urgent Directive on the Rural People's Communes

Central Committee letter to the Party Committee of Each Province and District:

1. At the present stage make certain that ownership by the production brigade is basic in the three-level system of ownership.

2. Firmly oppose the "communist wind" of one equalization and two transfers [absolute egalitarianism and excessive transfer of personnel] and thoroughly rectify it.

3. Strengthen the system of basic ownership by the production brigade.

4. Stabilize the system of partial ownership by the production team. Carry out the "four fixed allocations" policy [fixed assignment of manpower, land, farm tools, and draft animals] and the "three responsibilities and one reward system" [fixed targets for output, workdays, and costs, with bonuses for over-fulfillment] and ensure peasant rights to subsidiary agricultural products.

5. Permit commune members to cultivate private plots and engage in family sideline activities.

6. Lessen deductions, enlarge distribution and ensure income increases for 90 percent of the commune members.

7. Enforce the principle "from each according to one's ability, to each according to one's work," and divide income in the ratio of three parts free supply and seven parts wages.

8. Economize labor and strengthen the first line of agricultural production.

9. Handle the distribution of grain well and manage the communal dining halls well.

10. Restore rural free markets under proper leadership and stimulate the village economy.

11. Genuinely integrate labor and rest and put into effect the holiday system.

12. Boldly mobilize the masses and carry out readjustment of the communes.

Urgent Directive Concerning Present Policy Problems in the Rural People's Communes, Central Committee, November 1960. In: Ajiya Keizai Kenkyūjo, ed., *Jimmin Kōsha Soron* (Tokyo: 1965). Translated by Mark Selden.

We will not change the above measures for at least seven years. The entire nation must study, but cadres especially must study every year during the winter season. Continue this for at least three years.

B. Take the Brigade as the Accounting Unit in the People's Communes

The authority for production management and administration should be transferred chiefly to the production brigade. However, the communes and the administrative divisions which are organs of the commune (known in some places as production brigades) naturally cannot abandon their role of supervising the production brigades and ensuring the carrying out of production plans; but they cannot direct production blindly or interfere in production without reason. The communes should formulate their production plans on the basis of the production plans of production brigades and production teams. However, while we put special stress on strengthening the production brigade's basic system of ownership, under no circumstances should we neglect the economic development of the communes. The economy of communes represents the great hope and bright future and must be developed positively.

But the important thing is that the commune economy must be gradually developed by the communes themselves based on their own economic strength. . . .

Speaking of the relations between the production brigade and production teams, production brigades are the basic unit of accounting and auditing in a commune and also the unit for unified distribution of agricultural and subsidiary products. . . .

C. Develop the Role of the Team

Production teams are the fundamental basic-level organizational units of people's communes and are the fundamental basic-level combat units on the agricultural front. They are

---

JMJP editorial: Sum Up the Experiences of Communes and Strengthen the Development of Communes, November 20, 1960. SCPRP 2388.

JMJP editorial: Fully Develop the Fighting Role of Production Teams, November 25, 1960. SCPRP 2394.

charged with the task of making the most direct and specific arrangements for the production and livelihood of the commune members. All the principles and policies of the party must be introduced to and carried out by the masses through the production teams. . . .

(1) The allocation of manpower, land, draft animals, and farm tools should be made according to fixed assignments. . . .

Combat units must be used in fighting battles. Production teams are combat units right on the agricultural front; they must have, first of all, sufficient manpower. The CCP Central Committee has repeatedly pointed out that "the principal manpower resources should be concentrated to strengthen the first line of agricultural production." . . .

Only after receiving sufficient manpower of required standards can production teams greatly raise their productivity and fulfill their production tasks with better and faster results. . . .

CCP organs and rural people's communes in the various localities should adopt realistic measures to ensure the allocation of the greatest amount of manpower to production teams. . . .

It is more convenient and better to let production teams feed, care for, and use draft animals than to place them under the care of production brigades and communes; this is because, by so doing, the draft animals will be cared for and used more properly and will propagate more rapidly. . . .

The experience of many localities shows that the allocation of manpower, land, draft animals, and farm tools to production teams by fixed assignment is a prerequisite in fully developing the combative role of the production teams and in rapidly developing agricultural production. . . .

(2) The production brigade should adopt the system of establishing contracts with production teams to guarantee production, manpower, and costs, and to award bonuses for over-fulfillment of contracts. The production teams should properly implement the labor quota and wage-point systems with regard to the commune members.

If it can be said that the implementation of the "four fixed allocations" policy is the prerequisite for fully developing the combative role of production teams, then the "three guarantees and one bonus" system and the labor quota and wage-point systems are the material guarantees for production teams in developing their combat potential. We hold that the policy of "politics in command" should be coordinated with these material guarantees. The "three guarantees and one bonus," the labor quota, and the wage-point systems are the concrete guarantees in carrying out the principle of "to each according to his work" on the basis of placing politics in command. The "three guarantees" will provide the people with actual targets in order to develop fully their struggle enthusiasm. Bonuses for overfulfillment of contracts should be awarded in the form of both material rewards and political citations. . . .

In carrying out the policy of "three-level ownership with ownership by the production brigade as the foundation," the "partial ownership" of production teams should be faithfully guaranteed.

Under the premise of guaranteeing the fulfillment of production tasks the production teams have the authority to decide what crop to cultivate according to land conditions, and adopt necessary technical measures, and to set different farm tasks. . . .

Some differences may result in the grain ratio standards, wage levels, and the calculation of wage points for each workday of labor between different production teams in the same production brigade. This difference is reasonable. It will play a part in encouraging emulation for the backward to catch up with the advanced and will benefit the development of production. . . .

Production teams are the basic-level organizations of the people's communes. They are the key in perfecting the people's commune system and consolidating the people's communes and constitute an important link in the chain of tasks to promote the rapid development of agricultural production. . . .

3. THE PEOPLE'S COMMUNES
AND THE FUTURE OF AGRARIAN DEVELOPMENT

At the Tenth Plenum of 1962, summing up four years of the people's communes and the lessons of the three hard years, the party leadership assigned agriculture the first priority in national development for the first time. The priority ranking subsequently was agriculture, light industry, and finally heavy industry, recognizing not only the needs of the vast majority of the Chinese people but also the critical role which agriculture played in the development of other sectors. The plenum designated the commune the heart of a strategy of socialist development in the countryside, while reaffirming the 1961 decision to take the team as the basic unit of accounting and stipulating that it should remain so for thirty years.

The Sixty Articles on the communes, drawn up under Mao's personal direction and ratified by the Tenth Plenum, provided the most comprehensive program of rural development since the National Program of 1956. Drawing on the lessons of the leap, they outline the role of the commune, stressing the centrality of the team level and the importance of principles of mutual benefit, equal exchange and the right to cultivate private plots.

While the overriding emphasis of the document is on the role of the team as a cooperative unit, article 31 opened the possibility of contract labor both by teams and individuals. This practice, which had become increasingly widespread as the economic pinch increased in the late 1950s and early 1960s, could in the end threaten the continued advance to higher levels of communal economic life. More bluntly, as critics would later charge, the practice could open the way to the restoration of capitalism in the Chinese countryside.

A. Tenth Plenum Resolution on the People's Communes

The Central Committee believes that the unified plan for the national economy must take the expansion of agriculture as its starting point. The order of priority of the economic plan is, first, agriculture, then light industry, and finally heavy industry. That is to say, we must begin our socialist construction with the expansion of agriculture. It is an error to disregard the extremely important position of agriculture in socialist construction. The state must draft long-term plans for the support

Resolutions on the Further Strengthening of the Collective Economy of the People's Communes and Expanding Agricultural Production. Tenth Plenum, Eighth Central Committee, September 27, 1962. In: C. S. Chen, ed., *Rural People's Communes in Lien-chiang* (Stanford, Ca.: The Hoover Institute, 1969).

of agriculture by all sectors of the national economy. The plans set up and the measures adopted by the state planning sectors—economic, industrial (both heavy and light), and handicraft, communications and transportation, commercial, fiscal and financial, and the scientific and cultural—must acknowledge agriculture as their foundation, direct their attention to the villages and put the support of agriculture and the collective economy in first place. . . .

We must redetermine the ratio of investment for each sector of the national economy in conformity with the planning and economic sectors' policy of designating agriculture as the foundation for industry. The Central Committee believes that investment in agriculture, including investments in industry, transportation, and scientific research which directly serve agriculture, should be systematically raised in proportion to the gross investment for economic construction. . . .

With the exception of a minority of regions in which the brigade continues to be the basic accounting unit, the production teams should undertake independent accounting, bear the responsibility for profit and loss, directly organize production, and organize the distribution of their output. According to the draft regulations, once the basic accounting system has been determined, there should be no change for at least thirty years. . . .

B. The Sixty Articles on the Communes

The Nature, Organization and Scale of Rural Communes at the Present Stage

1. Rural people's communes are organizations combining government and cooperative into one, are primary units of our socialist society in the countryside, and are primary units of our socialist state power in the countryside. . . .

The state should support the collective economy of the people's communes and develop agricultural production as far as possible, gradually effect agrotechnical reform and, within the period of several five-year plans, realize mechanization and

Regulations on the Work of the Rural People's Communes Central Committee (Revised Draft) approved at the Tenth Plenum, Eighth Central Committee, September 1962. CC Documents.

electrification of agriculture on the basis of agricultural collectivization.

2. The basic accounting units of people's communes are production teams. . . .

Communes

10. The main tasks of the commune administrative committee are: direct its attention to the production teams, fully summon the enthusiasm of member masses, and develop productive undertakings of agriculture, stock-breeding, forestry, side occupations, and fisheries. . . .

11. Bearing in mind the production requirement and available manpower and material and financial resources and after discussion by the congresses of the production brigades and production teams concerned or the general meeting of commune members, the commune administrative committee may, with approval of the higher body, build capital construction projects like water conservation, afforestation, water and soil conservancy, and soil improvement for the whole commune or for several production brigades and production teams, and build water conservation projects or other capital construction projects for several communes provided such projects do not hinder the growth of production for the current year and do not hinder the growth of commune members' income for the current year. . . .

12. In order to ensure protection, cultivation, and rational utilization of the forest resources, the forests owned by the commune should in general be transferred to production team ownership; the forests not suitable for transfer to production teams shall remain under the commune or brigade ownership. . . .

13. The commune administrative committees shall generally not run new enterprises for years to come. All the enterprises already undertaken, which are not qualified for normal production and are not welcomed by the masses, should be stopped without exception. After discussion and decision by commune members' congress, these enterprises should be transferred to the handicraft cooperatives and production teams for manage-

ment or changed into individual handicrafts and family side occupations. . . .

All the enterprises run by the commune should directly serve agricultural production and peasants' livelihood. . . . Enterprises must strictly carry out business accounting and democratic management and periodically make their accounts public. . . .

14. The commune administrative committee should actively promote development of handicraft production.

The rural handicraft producers' cooperatives and cooperative teams are independent units under the dual leadership of the *hsien* federation of handicraft cooperatives and the commune. . . .

16. The commune and production brigades will in general not draw reserve fund and public welfare fund from the production teams for several years to come. . . .

Production Brigades

19. Under the leadership of the commune administrative committee the brigade administrative committee shall manage the productive work and administrative work of the production teams within the brigade.

(1) Help the production teams draw up production plans;

(2) Correctly direct, check up and supervise the productive work, fiscal management and distribution work of the production teams, and help the production teams improve their management; . . .

(3) Guide, undertake and manage the water conservation and other farm capital construction projects within the brigade or common to several production teams; . . .

(4) Properly keep and use the large and medium-sized agricultural machinery and means of transportation belonging to the brigade;

(5) Properly run all the forests and enterprises belonging to the brigade; . . .

(6) Urge the production teams within the brigade to fulfill the state targets for requisition and procurement of grain and other agricultural products and by-products; help the production teams organize members' livelihood properly;

(7) Manage the civil affairs, militia, public security, culture, education, and public health in the whole brigade;

(8) Carry out ideological and political work and implement the center's policies and decrees. . . .

Production Teams

20. Production teams are the basic accounting units in a people's commune. They carry on independent accounting, assume responsibility for their profits and losses, directly organize production of grains. Once established this system shall remain unchanged for at least thirty years.

21. All the land within the production teams belongs to the production teams. [The commune] is not allowed to rent, buy, or sell the land owned by the production teams, including the private plots, private hills and residential land of commune members. . . .

The labor forces within the production teams are at the production teams' disposal. The commune or production brigades must consult the members of the production teams concerned if they want to transfer labor forces from them and, in the absence of their consent, they are not allowed to transfer labor from them. . . .

All collective forests, water surface, and grassland should be owned by production teams if it is advantageous for the production teams to own them. . . .

22. The production teams have the right to freely manage production and distribute gains. . . .

24. The production teams in general should lay emphasis on the development of grain production while at the same time actively developing production of cotton, oil-bearing crops and other industrial crops according to local conditions; further, the production teams should fully utilize the natural resources and the by-products of farm crops to develop stockbreeding, forestry, fishery, and other side occupations. . . .

25. The production teams should actively expand multiple undertakings.

The production teams may, in the light of local needs and facilities, actively develop the shops for processing agricultural by-products formerly found in the rural districts (mills, vermicelli shops, oil shops, bean-curd shops, etc.), handicrafts (farm implements, kilns; native paper, plaiting and knitting, etc.), breeding (female and pedigree animals, ducks, geese, bees, etc.), transport, picking, fishing, hunting, etc. . . . All the production pursuits run by the commune or production brigades should be transferred to production team ownership and run by them if they are suitable for production team management and if they can be run by the production teams without hindering their agricultural production; . . .

When the basic number of workdays is fixed for women members, their physical conditions and household chores should be taken into consideration. . . .

31. In order to facilitate the organizing of production, the production team may set up fixed or temporary work teams, according to localities, and contract work may be subscribed by period, by season or by the whole year so that a rigid responsibility system may be established. The system may apply to stock-breeding, forestry, fisheries, and other sideline production and also to the administration of draft animals, farm tools, irrigation, and other public properties. The production team or an individual may be subjected to such a system. . . .

32. The production team should give rational remuneration to its members according to the quality and quantity of labor performed, and egalitarianism should be avoided when labor is accounted for among these members.

The production team should gradually introduce the system of fixed labor quota and exercise control over such quota. . . .

Equal pay for equal work should be effected, regardless of sex, age, cadres, or commune members. . . .

Each and every commune member with labor power should perform a definite amount of productive capital construction work each year as fixed by a general meeting of commune members, as a labor contribution to the collective economy. Such capital construction work in general should be restricted within approximately 3 percent of the basic workdays performed by each commune member during the whole year, and any number of workdays spent on such work over and above the fixed standard should be paid for out of the public accumulation funds. . . .

36. A certain amount of public welfare fund may be de-

ducted from the total income of the production team each year to cover social insurance and collective welfare. . . . but in no case should it exceed 2 to 3 percent of the total amount of income to be distributed. . . .

38. The production team must practice democratic management and bring to the full the activism of making commune members the masters.

All important things such as the team's production and income distribution must be decided through discussion at a general meeting of commune members, and not by the cadres. . . .

Commune Members' Family Sideline Production

39. The family sideline production of the commune members is a necessary ancillary part of the socialist economy. It comes under the collective ownership and all people's ownership economy and is their assistant. . . .

40. . . . The private land generally accounts for 5 to 7 percent of the production team's total cultivated land. This is allotted to a commune member for his own use on a permanent basis. . . .

41. The products and income from family sideline production of the commune members shall be owned by them and distributed as they like. . . . The state will not collect any agricultural tax on them and will not consider them as agricultural products subject to unified purchase.

4. STATE FARMS

China's state farms form a little known but important segment of the rural economy. Frequently established on reclaimed land, and providing models for intensive mechanization, advanced cultivation techniques and diversified agriculture and

Wang Chen: China's State Farms—Production Bases of Farm and Animal Products. HC April 1, 1961. PR April 28, 1961.

animal husbandry, state farms rapidly expanded at the time of the Great Leap Forward. With nearly three million workers in the early 1960s (and five million in 1978), state farms accounted for less than 10 percent of China's farm output. They represented, however, important rural experiments in ownership by the whole people, widely regarded as a model for the future to eradicate distinctions between city and countryside and between prosperous and poor communities. The People's Daily *has emphasized that state farms "should demonstrate the greater superiority of mechanized production under the system of all-people ownership; should continue to exert their effect as demonstrators in respect of mechanized production, labor productivity, per unit area farm yields, cost of production and collective welfare; should help the people's communes in development; and should guide them to make the transition gradually to the system of all-people ownership and then to communism." Wang Chen, minister in charge of state farms, commanded the famed 359th Brigade based at Nanniwan during the Anti-Japanese War, the model of self-reliance in attaining basic self-sufficiency in grain and supplies and of serving the people under arduous conditions.*

The state farms, which constitute an important force on the agricultural front, are a component of the socialist economy based on ownership by the whole people. They possess advanced technical equipment and have largely replaced manual production by modern large-scale mechanized production. Their output level is relatively high and they are in a position to provide the country with large quantities of farm and animal products. . . .

In the eleven years since the founding of the People's Republic, China's state farms have started from scratch and developed smoothly and steadily. By 1952, the last year of the period of national economic rehabilitation, 52 relatively large mechanized farms with over 3.3 million mou of land had been set up and each county had at least one or two local ordinary experimental farms. By 1957, the last year of the first five-year plan, there were 710 larger farms (not including those run by the special administrative regions and counties) with a cultivated area of more than 15 million mou, half a million workers and staff members, about 10,000 tractors (in terms of 15 h.p. units) and a total grain yield of 1,190 million chin. The state farms, guided by the party's general line, have advanced with giant strides since the Great Leap Forward in 1958. By the end of 1960, there were over 2,490 state farms under the Ministry of State Farms and Land Reclamation, with 2.8 million workers and staff members, or 5.6 times the 1957 figure; a cultivated area of more than 78 million mou, 5 times the 1957 acreage; 28,000 tractors (in terms of 15 h.p. units), more than 2.7 times the 1957 number; and a total grain yield of over 5,000 million chin, more than 4.7 times the 1957 output....

In the course of their development, the state farms have increasingly demonstrated their superiority....

In the National Program for Agricultural Development 1956–1967, it is once more pointed out that "all state farms should unite with and help their neighboring agricultural cooperatives and set good examples in farming technique as they are expected to." Even in the early days of their existence, the state farms fulfilled this role. In 1952, for instance, the average wheat yield of mechanized state farms exceeded the national average by 21.7 percent; their average cotton yield was 48.7 percent higher than the national average; and their average soya bean yield topped the national average by 11 percent. Again, in 1956, average grain and cotton yields of all state farms exceeded those of all agricultural coops by 4 percent and 66 percent respectively....

The state farms play a particularly important role in reclaiming large tracts of wasteland and in the construction of the border areas. Land reclamation is one of the basic measures for developing agricultural production and stock-breeding....
Large-scale reclamation in sparsely populated areas calls for large-scale resettlement organized by the state and the employment of modern machines. The state farms have contributed much to land reclamation and building the border areas in the past eleven years. In Sinkiang, to cite a case in point, more than 180 mechanized farms were set up both north and south of the Tienshan Mountains. By 1959, their cultivated acreage encompassed 8.03 million mou. In 1960, an additional 3.57 million mou was opened up and the sown area nearly doubled com-

pared with the preceding year. State farms in Heilungkiang, Inner Mongolia, Hainan Island, and Yunnan have also reclaimed large expanses of wasteland. These farms have become the country's important commodity bases producing large amounts of farm and animal products. The development of the state farms promoted the growth of industry, communications and transport, building construction as well as culture, education, and public health in these border areas, rapidly transforming their backwardness.

The Chinese People's Liberation Army has played a significant part in the establishment and development of the state farms. . . .

In production and management the state farms should adhere to the following policy: take agriculture as the foundation and develop a diversified economy in an all-round manner, making grain production the key link while simultaneously developing farming and stock-breeding.

The task of the state farms is to provide the state with marketable grain, cotton, meat, and many other types of farm and animal products. In order to supply the country with the necessary products for national construction and export, the state farms, in their production and management, must handle correctly the relations between farming and stock-breeding on the one hand and the other lines of production in a diversified economy on the other. . . .

Since the Great Leap Forward the state farms have advanced considerably in the development of diversified economies and have essentially overcome the shortcoming of some farms which in the past evolved only single economies. The proportion of stock-breeding and industry and sidelines in the economy of all state farms in the country rose from 10 and 12 percent respectively in 1957 to 25 and 32 percent respectively in 1959. . . .

The correct way to develop a diversified economy is to take agriculture as the foundation, simultaneously develop farming and stock-breeding while making grain production the key link, and develop those industries, sidelines, and other lines of production that serve farming and stock-breeding on the condition that the normal development of farming and stock-breeding is ensured. . . .

5. THE TWO-LINE STRUGGLE
IN LIEN-CHIANG COUNTY

More vividly than any other available document of the period, this inner-party report from a Fukien county provides a glimpse into the fierce struggle at the grassroots level between two classes and two roads and of the sharply depressed economic conditions of the early 1960s.

Powerful forces were at work in the county to restore individual enterprise and to harness individualistic and superstitious values. At one level the problem manifested itself in the reappearance of Bodhisattvas, divination, such feudal practices as marriage by sale and cadre corruption. A more immediate threat, however, lay in the revival of individual enterprise, sapping the vitality and challenging the legitimacy of communal institutions. In addition to the private plots officially sanctioned for every family, the document describes the significant emergence of contract labor whereby households merely fulfilled individual production contracts with the brigade or team. The result in some teams was a sharp overall drop in the range of collective activities. Contributions of fertilizer fell, workers increasingly withdrew from collective production to engage in sideline (often illicit) enterprises, or drifted to the cities, and class polarization increased. Faced with nothing less than the threat of disintegration of the communal order in the countryside, the Tenth Plenum moved to strengthen the communes and restore confidence in their efficacy as the basis for eliminating poverty and exploitation. The task would prove an arduous one in the face of the resurgence of feudal and capitalist tendencies throughout the countryside.

Wang Hung-chih: Implementation of the Resolutions of the Tenth Plenum of the Eighth Central Committee on Strengthening the Collective Economy and Expanding Agricultural Production. From Lien-chiang County, Fukien. In: C. S. Chen, ed., *Rural People's Communes in Lien-chiang*, 1962. This is a captured document released by the Kuomintang on Taiwan. Its authenticity cannot be verified, but the weight of internal evidence of the document and the collection of which it is a part is strongly suggestive of conditions of rural crisis at the time.

Since October our country has begun the initial implementation of the essence of the Tenth Plenum. Within the county we held meetings of cadres above the team level and through them have launched propaganda education for the masses in which, for the most part, we have used the methods of recollection, contrast, airing complaints, and reckoning of accounts as [means of] criticism of the error of the spirit of individual enterprise. . . . The spread and growth of the spirit of individual enterprise was effectively halted. All household contract production land in the county, with the exception of that used for sweet potatoes not yet harvested, has reverted to the collective. The majority of those who drifted to the cities have returned to the villages, and the peddlers and speculators have sharply decreased in numbers. All these events have had a great effect in promoting the autumn harvest and the winter planting. But this is only a beginning. . . . Superficially, it appears that individual contracting has been stopped, but we have not yet solved the fundamental ideological problem. The general attitude is one of waiting to see what happens. . . .

1. The Problem of Conditions

First, there has been a recovery and an expansion in all phases of production, in agriculture, fishing, forestry, animal husbandry, and subsidiary enterprises. As preliminary estimates show, this year's total food production may reach 130 million catties, which is 86.7 percent of the yearly average of 150 million catties. Of this, the collective accounts for 111 million catties. The area occupied by the collectives has decreased by more than 20,000 mou since last year, principally because of an increase in private plots and vegetable farming; however, production in the collectives has increased over last year's 109 million catties. . . .

Second, there has been an increase in the standard of living of the masses. The level of their food rations was better this year than last. According to statistics, the average basic ration last year (except that for the nonagricultural population) was 23 catties per person per month. Although the amount of state levies and purchases has increased over last year, the net ration from the collective, together with that from private plots, may reach 29 catties, an increase of 26 percent. If supplements from the private plots are added, there will be quite a number of production teams that will have enough food. The masses say: "Life is better from year to year. The year before last we ate the 'three heads' (of betel nuts, bananas, and the sago palm); last year was the melon and vegetable era; and this year we eat as we please." In addition, income in money has increased. On the basis of statistics from seventy-one brigades, this year's collective total income is 8.78 million yuan, an increase of 3.7 percent over last year. . . .

Third, there has been brisk activity in the market. Commodities in the community increased, and industrial goods and supplementary foodstuff supplied by the state increased 26.7 percent over last year (amounting in value this year from January through October to 1,032 million yuan and last year for the same period to 839 million yuan). . . .

Fourth, the social order has become more stable. Petty thieves are noticeably absent. This is reflected in the popular saying: "Last year we had to compete with thieves in gathering the sweet potatoes. This year we can leave them in the open, and no one will steal them." Furthermore, there has been a sharp decrease over last year in fighting and disorder among the masses. . . .

What caused these favorable conditions? We believe that there are three major factors. First, party leadership has been correct, as have the three red banners. . . .

Second, the thorough implementation of a series of party policies has stimulated the enthusiasm of the masses. The implementation of the twelve articles, the rectification of the communist wind at the end of 1960, and the implementation last year of the sixty draft regulations gave the commune members private plots and gave individuals permission to reclaim barren land on a limited basis. This year, provisions for lowering the administrative level of the basic accounting units and for allowing brigade-contract production were put into effect. . . .

Third, the strong support given to agriculture by the state, the support of agriculture by industry, and the support of the villages by the cities were further causes of improvement. The party policy of taking agriculture as the foundation, together with the two times that the number of workers and crowded urban populations have been reduced, strengthened the first line of agriculture. This year, loans for agriculture and fishing for the entire county are 1.70 million yuan (of this amount, the portion for agriculture is 730,000 yuan), and the investment in basic construction and water conservancy was 600,000 yuan, making a total of 2.3 million yuan. The supply of chemical fertilizer was 33,000 tan, an increase of 30 percent over last year, allowing 16.5 catties of chemical fertilizer to be spread on each mou of cultivated land. . . .

Two different points of view exist concerning the reason for these improved conditions. The majority of the people believe that the improvement is due to party leadership, the strength of policies, and state support. Some, however, are confused in their ideology and say that these favorable conditions have resulted from the "small freedoms"; others say that these conditions result from the use of private plots, reclaimed land, and free markets. . . .

Our major difficulty at present is that food production has not yet completely regained the highest post-liberation level. Our best food year was 1959, when the total volume of production of the county was 160 million catties. We have not reached this level this year. . . . Because of the influence of the spirit of individual enterprise, market management is also in disorder, and varying degrees of ideological confusion exist among some of the masses and cadres. However, these are all temporary phenomena. . . .

2. Class

In the last three years, because of continual natural disasters and errors and deficiencies in our work, all sectors have encountered certain temporary difficulties. Beginning last autumn, class enemies have greatly increased, and up to the spring of this year some landlords and rich peasants would not participate in collective labor and openly took away collective farm tools and plough oxen. They raised a commotion over household contract production. . . .

The class struggle is therefore prolonged, complex, repetitive, alternately resurgent and recessive, and sometimes acute. The reasons are as follows.

First, there is the power of old customs. The peasants have gone through several thousand years of feudal control and more than a hundred years of semifeudal-semicolonial control. Feudal, semifeudal, and semicolonial thought is deep-rooted and cannot be corrected overnight. Although they have received ten years of education in socialist ideology since the liberation, the peasants fall back on the old customs when the opportunity occurs, thereby producing class struggle on the battle fronts of politics and ideology. For example, since the liberation, by consistently opposing superstition and marriage by sale, we were able to correct these old patterns of thought to some extent. Last year, however, when we encountered difficulties, marriage by sale began to reappear, and the masses once again began to engage in activities inspired by superstition, such as worshipping Bodhisattvas, divination, and fortunetelling. . . .

Second, the overthrown classes do not willingly die out, and they come to life when opportunity permits. . . .

Third, in addition to classes, there are class strata. Lenin said, "Small producers are daily, hourly giving rise to capitalism and the bourgeoisie." Our China is a large country, a nation with a vast number of small producers. For this reason, it is difficult to avoid the continual production of a bourgeoisie. What are small producers? Individual producers and handicraft industries are examples. Although we have collectivized, domestic industries and private plots still exist. These are all instances of small-scale production. They are supplements to the collective economy, required by the collectives, which we cannot do away with. However, they are also capable, at each instant, of giving rise to capitalism and bringing about the struggle between the two roads. . . .

According to the statistics through October, 768 teams had taken up private contracting (26.5 percent of the total number of teams in the county). Altogether there are 7,178 mou of land under private contract. This amounts to 2.05 percent of the total area of the county and includes 395 mou of land for paddy rice (0.28 percent of the total rice paddy area), 3,783 mou of land for sweet potatoes (8.2 percent of the total sweet potato area), and 326 mou of land for economic crops (3.0 percent of the total economic crop area). . . .

Another manifestation of the spirit of individual enterprise is emphasis on the individual and neglect of the collective, as when commune members do not hand over fertilizer to the collective and when they fail to participate in collective labor; and when a large amount of uncultivated land is reclaimed for private planting. According to an investigation of the twelve model teams at Shan-pien, there was a 50.2 percent decrease in the quantity of fertilizer handed over this year from January to September, compared with last year for the same period. On the average, only 13.8 days of labor power per month were devoted to work for the collective, and for the third team in Shan-pien only 8.0 days. Where does the labor force go if it does not work on the collective? It engages in subsidiary production, miscellaneous work, and peddling. In the Lien-teng Brigade of the Ao-chiang commune, after the summer harvest 96 workers out of 190 drifted outside (50 percent). . . . Small freedoms land (including private plots) makes up, on the average, more than 30 percent of the county collective area. In a minority of teams, it has reached more than 50 percent.

In addition, individuals have encroached upon the collective farms by usurping collective land for basic construction. They have "reclaimed" collective land. . . .

Before liberation, all farmers were individual entrepreneurs and the masses of peasants were oppressed and exploited. They did not have enough to eat and wear. Can that be called freedom? Actually, when these people demand freedom, what they demand is freedom to engage in peddling, freedom to hire labor, and freedom to lend money at high interest—in short, a freedom allowing them to exploit others—and it is this kind of freedom that we will not allow and that we must firmly oppose. As far as being a cadre is concerned, this is a worthy thing. Engaging in socialism is troublesome, but what is there to fear?

6. THE FIRST TEN POINTS
ON PROBLEMS IN RURAL WORK

The first ten points drafted under Mao's direction provided philosophical and practical guidance for the socialist education movement initiated by the Tenth Plenum and the forerunner of the Cultural Revolution in the countryside. The directive emphasized mobilization politics and class struggle at a time when these themes were notably absent in the subdued pronouncements of party leaders seeking to restore production.

It was precisely the persistence of feudal and capitalist ideas, and the continued existence of the classes which embodied them—deprived of their monopoly on property but ever hopeful of a comeback—whose surfacing in the aftermath of the Great Leap produced sharp struggle with emerging socialist currents in the countryside. Mao emphasized the "three great revolutionary movements"—the struggle for production, class struggle, and scientific experiment—as the means to avoid the pitfalls of capitalist restoration and continue the advance to socialist development and prosperity.

The socialist education movement was thus launched in the countryside to overcome incipient tendencies toward rural capitalism, to spur production through mass education and mobilization, and deepen the socialist content of ideas and institutions.

From the outset, however, the movement was plagued by conflicts over rural policy and class struggle within the party leadership; thus the first ten points would be followed by the later ten points and finally the revised later ten points while the mass movement remained at low ebb.

Where do correct ideas come from? Do they drop from the skies? No. Are they innate in the mind? No. They come from social practice, and from it alone; they come from three kinds

Draft Resolution of the Central Committee of the Chinese Communist Party on Some Problems in Current Rural Work (The First Ten Points), May 20, 1963. In: Richard Baum and Frederick Teiwes, *Ssu-Ch'ing: The Socialist Education Movement* (Berkeley: Center for Chinese Studies, 1968).

of social practice—the struggle for production, the class struggle, and scientific experiment. It is man's social being that determines his thinking. Once the correct ideas characteristic of the advanced class are grasped by the masses, these ideas turn into a material force which changes society and changes the world. . . . The one and only purpose of the proletariat in knowing the world is to change it. Often, a correct idea can be arrived at only after many repetitions of the process leading from matter to consciousness and then back to matter, that is, leading from practice to knowledge and then back to practice. Such is the Marxist theory of knowledge, the dialectical materialist theory of knowledge. . . . It was groundless for some comrades to entertain pessimistic views in the past towards the rural situation and the conditions of agricultural production. All this also proves the total correctness and greatness of the party in raising high the three red banners of the general line, the people's communes, and the Great Leap Forward.

2. *The Problem of Whether Class, Class Contradiction, and Class Struggle Still Exist in a Socialist Society*

At the Central Committee's working conference at Pei-tai-ho in August 1962, and at the Tenth Plenum of the Eighth Central Committee in September of the same year, Comrade Mao Tsetung repeatedly pointed out that the socialist society is a relatively long historical stage; that in this stage there still exist class, class contradiction, and class struggle; and that also existent is the struggle between socialism and capitalism and the danger of a comeback of capitalism. . . .

3. *The Present Emergence of Severe and Sharp Class Struggle in Chinese Society*

Many facts brought to light concerning today's society prove the correctness of this assertion on class struggle.

(1) The exploiting class, landlords, and rich peasants who have been overthrown are always trying to stage a comeback. They are waiting for an opportunity to counterattack in order to carry out class revenge, and to deal a blow against the poor peasants and lower middle peasants.

(2) Landlords and rich peasants who have been overthrown

are employing all kinds of schemes in an attempt to corrupt our cadres in order to usurp the leadership and power. In some communes and brigades the leadership and power actually have fallen into their hands. In some sectors of other organizations they also have their agents.

(3) In some places landlords and rich peasants are carrying out activities for the restoration of feudalistic patriarchal rule, putting out counter-revolutionary propaganda, and developing counter-revolutionary organizations.

(4) Landlords, rich peasants, and counter-revolutionaries are making use of religion and the reactionary *hui-tao-men* [secret, religious, and welfare societies] to deceive the masses and carry out criminal activities.

(5) Various sabotage activities of the reactionaries, such as sabotage of public properties, collection of intelligence, or even murder and arson, have been discovered in many places.

(6) In commerce, the activities of speculation and profiteering have reached serious proportions. In some places, such activities are rampant.

(7) The phenomena of exploiting hired hands, high-interest loans, buying and selling of land have also occurred.

(8) In addition to the old bourgeoisie who continue to engage in speculation and profiteering activities, there also emerge in today's society new bourgeois elements who have become rich by speculation.

(9) In organizations and the collective economy, there have emerged a group of corrupt elements, thieves, speculators, and degenerates who have ganged up with landlords and rich peasants to commit evil deeds. These elements are a part of the new bourgeoisie, or their ally.

These facts have combined to give us a most serious lesson: Never at any moment should we forget the class struggle, forget the proletarian dictatorship, forget to rely on the poor and the lower middle peasants, forget the party policies, forget the party work.

4. *The Question of Whether Our Comrades Have Clearly Seen the Seriousness of This Hostile Situation*

It should be stated that not all our comrades have paid attention to the various kinds of class struggle phenomena mentioned above. . . .

5. The Question of Whom to Rely Upon

In rural areas, the proletarian dictatorship can be realized only by relying upon the poor peasants and the lower middle peasants. They are the only ones to rely upon for the formation of a strong alliance of workers and peasants, for the expert management of the nation, for achieving a good collective economy, for the effective suppression and remolding of all the hostile elements, and for smashing the encirclement formed by the spontaneous capitalistic forces. . . .

6. The Problem Regarding the Correct Method and Policy for Carrying out the Socialist Education Movement in Rural Areas at Present

Basing itself on Comrade Mao Tsetung's directives issued at the Pei-tai-ho conference in August 1962 in relation to class, situation, and contradiction, the Central Committee considers a socialist education movement must be universally carried out in rural areas in order to demarcate the contradictions between ourselves and the enemy, and the internal contradictions of the people. It is also to distinguish right from wrong, thereby rallying together more than 95 percent of the peasant masses and the rural cadres to jointly deal with the enemy of socialism, to continue with the thorough execution of the revised draft of the sixty articles on sending down the basic accounting units to the countryside, all for the development of agricultural production. The method of education lies in teaching the cadres and masses the directives of Comrade Mao Tsetung, the Central Committee resolutions on the strengthening of collective economy and on agricultural production, the revised draft of the sixty articles, and this current resolution of the Central Committee. Such lectures should also cover the specific situation, concrete cases, and work of that locality, so as to bring out the initiative of local cadres and people. . . .

7. The Problem of How to Organize a Revolutionary Class Army

The Central Committee is of the conviction that in order to strengthen the proletarian dictatorship and the collective economy, and to develop agricultural production, the work of setting up organizations of the poor and lower middle peasants in the rural collective economic system is wholly essential. . . .

Members of organizations of the poor peasants and lower middle peasants should be the poor and lower middle peasants of the time of agrarian reform and agricultural collectivization. When the organizations are first established, it is necessary to see to it that the foundation of the new organizations is firmly laid. No corrupt elements, thieves, speculators, and degenerates should be admitted. . . .

8. The "Four Cleans" Problem

When cadres of the Paoting special district committee in Hopei went to conduct rural village investigations, they found that the peasants had an urgent demand that communes and brigades do a serious job of cleaning up account books, cleaning up granaries, cleaning up properties, and cleaning up workpoints (called four cleans in short). Today the contradiction of four uncleans is prevalent in the communes and brigades. This is principally a contradiction between the cadres and the masses. It should be resolved, and it is not difficult to solve. . . .

Now, the first thing to be done is to set the masses in motion to conduct an all-out, thorough check of accounts, warehouses, properties, and work points starting from last year to the present. This investigation should include the assets procured with state investments, bank loans, and proceeds accrued from credit sales of the business departments. This will be a large-scale movement of the masses coordinated with socialist education, its principal purpose being the resolution of internal contradictions of the people. And as far as the corrupt elements, thieves, speculators, and degenerates are concerned, it will be a very serious class struggle. . . .

This is the policy of our party: education by persuasion; washing hands and bodies; going to the front with a light load; unity against the enemy. . . .

9. The Problem of Cadres Joining the Collective Production Labor Force

Ours is a party of the proletariat, an advanced political party of the laboring masses. We must place the root organizations of our party in the hands of the active, advanced elements of the laboring masses. The secretaries of the party branches in rural areas must be not only the most advanced elements in politics, but also the most advanced among the laboring masses. They should strive to be good hands in production work, to be models of labor. . . .

10. The Problem of Marxism's Scientific Methods of Carrying Out Investigation and Research

In addition to the most convenient method for understanding conditions, that is, participating in collective productive labor, responsible comrades of party organizations at various levels must also in a planned and selective manner squat at points, humbly listen to the opinions of the masses, discover problems in good time, and summarize experiences. . . .

The party's Central Committee hereby calls upon comrades of the party to learn and to comprehend this directive of extraordinary importance issued recently by Comrade Mao Tsetung:

Class struggle, production struggle, and scientific experiment are the three great revolutionary movements that build up a powerful socialist nation. They are a guarantee for the communists to do away with bureaucratism, to avoid revisionism and dogmatism, to stand eternally invincible. They are an assurance for the proletariat to be able to unite with the massive labor populace in order to realize democratic dictatorship of the proletariat. Otherwise, the landlords, the rich peasants, the counter-revolutionaries, the bad elements and the evils would all come out. . . . It would then become a certainty that the party of Marxism and Leninism would turn into a party of revisionism, of fascism. The whole of China would then change color. . . .

With cadres and masses joining hand in hand in the productive labor and scientific experiments, our party will take another stride forward in becoming a more glorious, greater, and more correct party; our cadres will be versed in politics as well as in business operations, become red as well as expert. They will then no longer be toplofty, no longer bureaucrats and overlords, no longer divorced from the masses. They will then merge themselves with the masses, becoming truly good cadres supported by the masses.

V

THE GREAT PROLETARIAN CULTURAL REVOLUTION 1966-1976

A. POLICY GUIDELINES

1. A CALL TO ACTION

Why, given the socialist transformation of the economy and state since 1949, did Mao and others both at the grassroots and the central leadership levels believe that a sweeping revolutionary movement was necessary? Although the landlords and the bourgeoisie had been overthrown and socialist institutions implanted, the class struggle to shape China's future continued. In the early 1960s, for example, conflict centered on attempts to restore the individual economy in the countryside. By the mid-1960s the focus of contention was the realm of culture, customs, and ideas, that is, the superstructure. Old values and ideas die slowly. If China was to continue to advance, not only would new socialist ideas have to replace deeply ingrained Confucian, hierarchical, and bureaucratic values but they would also have to overcome new impulses derived from the bourgeoisie or new party or managerial elites seeking to maximize their personal power or to turn back the clock on the advance of socialism.

The series of People's Daily *editorials of June 1966 made the clash in the realm of customs, culture, and ideas the focus of nation-wide mobilization. As Mao put it at the time, "there is no construction without destruction, no flowing without damming and no moving forward without a holding back." "Destruction here means criticism, means revolution," the* People's Daily *explained. "Destruction necessarily calls for reasoning,*

JMJP editorial: Sweep Away All Monsters, June 1, 1966. In: David Milton, Nancy Milton, and Franz Schurmann, eds., *People's China* (New York: Random House, 1966).

*and reasoning is construction; destruction comes first, and in
the course of it there is construction."*

*But destruction of what, criticism of whom? During the
Anti-Japanese Resistance and civil war, in the land revolution
and cooperative movements, the national and class targets of
attack could be clearly defined and, on this basis, unity
achieved. The Great Proletarian Cultural Revolution provided a
greater challenge: to distinguish clearly contradictions with class
enemies from those among the people, and to isolate, struggle
with, and transform the remnants of bourgeois and feudal ideas
in every individual and institution.*

*The editorials discussed and dissected in study groups
throughout China provided a call to action for millions of
people, particularly at this stage youth, students, and intellectuals, to participate in a cultural revolution.*

An upsurge is occurring in the Great Proletarian Cultural
Revolution in socialist China whose population accounts for
one-quarter of the world's total.

For the last few months, in response to the militant call of
the Central Committee of the Chinese Communist Party and
Chairman Mao, hundreds of millions of workers, peasants, and
soldiers and vast numbers of revolutionary cadres and intellectuals, all armed with Mao Tsetung's thought, have been
sweeping away a horde of monsters that have entrenched themselves in ideological and cultural positions. With the tremendous
and impetuous force of a raging storm, they have smashed the
shackles imposed on their minds by the exploiting classes for so
long in the past, routing the bourgeois "specialists," "scholars,"
"authorities," and "venerable masters," and sweeping every bit
of their prestige into the dust.

Chairman Mao has taught us that class struggle does not cease
in China after the socialist transformation of the system of
ownership has in the main been completed. He said:

> The class struggle between the proletariat and the bour-
> geoisie, the class struggle between different political forces,
> and the class struggle in the ideological field between the
> proletariat and the bourgeoisie will continue to be long
> and tortuous and at times will even become very acute.

The proletariat seeks to transform the world according to its own world outlook, and so does the bourgeoisie. In this respect, the question of which will win out, socialism or capitalism, is still not really settled.

The class struggle in the ideological field between the proletariat and the bourgeoisie has been very acute right through the sixteen years since China's liberation. The current Great Proletarian Cultural Revolution is precisely a continuation and development of this struggle. The struggle is inevitable. The ideology of the proletariat and the ideology of all the exploiting classes are diametrically opposed to each other and cannot coexist in peace. The proletarian revolution is a revolution to abolish all exploiting classes and all systems of exploitation; it is a most thoroughgoing revolution to bring about the gradual elimination of the differences between workers and peasants, between town and country, and between mental and manual laborers. This cannot but meet with the most stubborn resistance from the exploiting classes.

In every revolution the basic question is that of state power. In all branches of the superstructure—ideology, religion, art, law, state power—the central issue is state power. State power means everything. Without it, all will be lost. Therefore, no matter how many problems have to be tackled after the conquest of state power, the proletariat must never forget state power, never forget its orientation, and never lose sight of the central issue. . . . The exploiting classes have been disarmed and deprived of their authority by the people, but their reactionary ideas remain rooted in their minds. . . .

In order to seize state power, the bourgeoisie during the period of the bourgeois revolution likewise started with ideological preparations by launching the bourgeois cultural revolution. Even the bourgeois revolution, which replaced one exploiting class by another, had to undergo repeated reversals and witness many struggles—revolution, then restoration, and then the overthrow of restoration. It took many European countries hundreds of years to complete their bourgeois revolutions from the start of the ideological preparations to the final conquest of state power. Since the proletarian revolution is a revolution aimed at completely ending all systems of exploitation, it is still less permissible to imagine that the exploiting classes will meekly allow the proletariat to deprive them of all their privileges without seeking to restore their rule. The surviving members of these classes who are unreconciled will inevitably, as Lenin put it, throw themselves with a tenfold furious passion into the battle for the recovery of their lost paradise. The fact that the Khrushchev revisionist clique has usurped the leadership of the party, army, and state in the Soviet Union is an extremely serious lesson for the proletariat throughout the world. At present the representatives of the bourgeoisie, the bourgeois "scholars" and "authorities" in China are dreaming precisely of restoring capitalism. Though their political rule has been toppled, they are still desperately trying to maintain their academic "authority," mold public opinion for a comeback and win over the masses, the youth and the generations yet unborn from us. . . .

The Proletarian Cultural Revolution is aimed not only at demolishing all the old ideology and culture and all the old customs and habits, which, fostered by the exploiting classes, have poisoned the minds of the people for thousands of years, but also at creating and fostering among the masses an entirely new ideology and culture and entirely new customs and habits— those of the proletariat. This great task of transforming customs and habits is without any precedent in human history. As for all the heritage, customs, and habits of the feudal and bourgeois classes, the proletarian world outlook must be used to subject them to thoroughgoing criticism. It takes time to clear away the evil habits of the old society from among the people. Nevertheless, our experience since liberation proves that the transformation of customs and habits can be accelerated if the masses are fully mobilized, the mass line is implemented and the transformation is made into a genuine mass movement. . . .

The scale and momentum of the Great Proletarian Cultural Revolution now being carried on in China have no parallel in history, and the tremendous drive and momentum and boundless wisdom of the working people manifested in the movement far exceed the imagination of the lords of the bourgeoisie. Facts have eloquently proved that Mao Tsetung's thought becomes a moral atom bomb of colossal power once it takes hold of the masses. The current Great Cultural Revolution is immensely advancing the socialist cause of the Chinese people and undoubtedly exerting an incalculable, far-reaching influence upon the present and future of the world.

2. THE SIXTEEN POINTS: GUIDELINES FOR THE GREAT PROLETARIAN CULTURAL REVOLUTION

Throughout June and July 1966 proponents and opponents of the Cultural Revolution clashed at the highest levels of the party, in the universities and in cultural circles. At the Eleventh Plenum in August 1966, as the delegates filed into the meeting they confronted Mao's own big character poster "Bombard the Headquarters" charging that "some leading comrades from the central down to the local levels . . . have enforced a bourgeois dictatorship and struck down the surging movement of the Great Cultural Revolution of the proletariat." The struggle at the highest levels of the party had been bared. The plenum, though deeply divided, endorsed a sixteen point decision which provided basic guidelines for the Cultural Revolution.

The movement, which unfolded from the summer of 1966, sought to transform the entire realm of culture, customs, and ideas in line with China's evolving socialist institutions. But that was not all. In the sixteen points, the basic programmatic document of the Cultural Revolution, the Central Committee designated the main target as "those within the party who are in authority and are taking the capitalist road." They would be attacked, isolated, removed from power and, when possible, transformed by means of education. Since opposition to the Cultural Revolution centered in the upper ranks of the party itself, Mao and others turned first to revolutionary youth who, organized as red guards and supported by the army, spread the movement and Mao's thought throughout the country.

Decision of the Central Committee of the Chinese Communist Party Concerning the Great Proletarian Cultural Revolution, August 8, 1966. PR August 12, 1966.

1. A New Stage in the Socialist Revolution

The Great Proletarian Cultural Revolution now unfolding is a great revolution that touches people to their very souls and constitutes a new stage in the development of the socialist revolution in our country, a deeper and more extensive stage. . . .

Although the bourgeoisie has been overthrown, it is still trying to use the old ideas, culture, customs, and habits of the exploiting classes to corrupt the masses, capture their minds and endeavor to stage a comeback. The proletariat must do just the opposite: it must meet head-on every challenge of the bourgeoisie in the ideological field and use the new ideas, culture, customs, and habits of the proletariat to change the mental outlook of the whole of society. At present, our objective is to struggle against and crush those persons in authority who are taking the capitalist road, to criticize and repudiate the reactionary bourgeois academic "authorities" and the ideology of the bourgeoisie and all other exploiting classes and to transform education, literature, and art and all other parts of the superstructure that do not correspond to the socialist economic base, so as to facilitate the consolidation and development of the socialist system.

2. The Main Current and the Zigzags

The masses of the workers, peasants, soldiers, revolutionary intellectuals, and revolutionary cadres form the main force in this Great Cultural Revolution. Large numbers of revolutionary young people, previously unknown, have become courageous and daring pathbreakers. They are vigorous in action and intelligent. Through the media of big character posters and great debates, they argue things out, expose and criticize thoroughly, and launch resolute attacks on the open and hidden representatives of the bourgeoisie. . . .

Since the Cultural Revolution is a revolution, it inevitably meets with resistance. This resistance comes chiefly from those in authority who have wormed their way into the party and are taking the capitalist road. It also comes from the old force of habit in society. At present, this resistance is still fairly strong and stubborn. However, the Great Proletarian Cultural Revolution is, after all, an irresistible general trend. There is abundant evidence that such resistance will crumble fast once the masses become fully aroused. . . .

3. Put Daring Above Everything Else and Boldly Arouse the Masses

The outcome of this Great Cultural Revolution will be determined by whether the party leadership does or does not dare boldly to arouse the masses. . . .

What the Central Committee of the party demands of the party committees at all levels is that they persevere in giving correct leadership, put daring above everything else, boldly arouse the masses, change the state of weakness and incompetence where it exists, encourage those comrades who have made mistakes but are willing to correct them to cast off their mental burdens and join in the struggle, and dismiss from their leading posts all those in authority who are taking the capitalist road, and so make possible the recapture of the leadership for the proletarian revolutionaries.

4. Let the Masses Educate Themselves in the Movement

In the Great Proletarian Cultural Revolution, the only method is for the masses to liberate themselves, and any method of doing things on their behalf must not be used.

Trust the masses, rely on them and respect their initiative. Cast out fear. Don't be afraid of disorder. Chairman Mao has often told us that revolution cannot be so very refined, so gentle, so temperate, kind, courteous, restrained, and magnanimous. . . .

5. Firmly Apply the Class Line of the Party

Who are our enemies? Who are our friends? This is a question of the first importance for the revolution and it is likewise a question of the first importance for the Great Cultural Revolution.

Party leadership should be good at discovering the left and developing and strengthening the ranks of the left, and should firmly rely on the revolutionary left. During the movement this is the only way to isolate thoroughly the most reactionary rightists, win over the middle, and unite with the great majority so that by the end of the movement we shall achieve the unity of more than 95 percent of the cadres and more than 95 percent of the masses. . . .

The main target of the present movement is those within the party who are in authority and are taking the capitalist road. . . .

6. *Correct Handling of Contradictions Among the People*

A strict distinction must be made between the two different types of contradictions: those among the people and those between ourselves and the enemy. Contradictions among the people must not be made into contradictions between ourselves and the enemy; nor must contradictions between ourselves and the enemy be regarded as those among the people.

It is normal for the masses to hold different views. Contention between different views is unavoidable, necessary, and beneficial. In the course of normal and full debate, the masses will affirm what is right, correct what is wrong, and gradually reach unanimity.

The method to be used in debates is to present the facts, reason things out, and persuade through reasoning. Any method of forcing a minority holding different views to submit is impermissible. The minority should be protected, because sometimes the truth is with the minority. Even if the minority is wrong, they should still be allowed to argue their case and reserve their views.

When there is a debate, it should be conducted by reasoning, not by coercion or force. . . .

7. *Be on Guard Against Those Who Brand the Revolutionary Masses as "Counter-Revolutionaries"*

In certain schools, units, and work teams of the Cultural

Revolution, some of the persons in charge have organized counterattacks against the masses who put up big character posters against them. These people have even advanced such slogans as: opposition to the leaders of a unit or a work team means opposition to the party's Central Committee, means opposition to the party and socialism, means counter-revolution. In this way it is inevitable that their blows will fall on some really revolutionary activists. This is an error on matters of orientation, an error of line, and is absolutely impermissible. . . .

8. The Question of Cadres

The cadres fall roughly into the following four categories: (1) good; (2) comparatively good; (3) those who have made serious mistakes but have not become anti-party, antisocialist rightists; (4) the small number of anti-party, antisocialist rightists.

In ordinary situations, the first two categories (good and comparatively good) are the great majority.

The anti-party, antisocialist rightists must be fully exposed, hit hard, pulled down, and completely discredited and their influence eliminated. At the same time, they should be given a way out so that they can turn over a new leaf.

9. Cultural Revolutionary Groups, Committees and Congresses

Many new things have begun to emerge in the Great Proletarian Cultural Revolution. The cultural revolutionary groups, committees and other organizational forms created by the masses in many schools and units are something new and of great historic importance.

These cultural revolutionary groups, committees and congresses are excellent new forms of organization whereby under the leadership of the Communist Party the masses are educating themselves. They are an excellent bridge to keep our party in close contact with the masses. They are organs of power of the Proletarian Cultural Revolution.

The cultural revolutionary groups, committees, and congresses should not be temporary organizations but permanent, standing mass organizations. They are suitable not only for colleges, schools, and government and other organizations, but generally also for factories, mines, other enterprises, urban districts, and villages.

It is necessary to institute a system of general elections, like that of the Paris Commune, for electing members to the cultural revolutionary groups and committees and delegates to the cultural revolutionary congresses. . . .

10. Educational Reform

In the Great Proletarian Cultural Revolution a most important task is to transform the old educational system and the old principles and methods of teaching.

In this Great Cultural Revolution, the phenomenon of our schools being dominated by bourgeois intellectuals must be completely changed.

In every kind of school we must apply thoroughly the policy advanced by Comrade Mao Tsetung, of education serving proletarian politics and education being combined with productive labor, so as to enable those receiving an education to develop morally, intellectually, and physically and to become laborers with socialist consciousness and culture.

The period of schooling should be shortened. Courses should be fewer and better. The teaching material should be thoroughly transformed, in some cases beginning with simplifying complicated material. While their main task is to study, students should also learn other things. That is to say, in addition to their studies they should also learn industrial work, farming, and military affairs, and take part in the struggles of the Cultural Revolution as they occur to criticize the bourgeoisie.

11. The Question of Criticizing
by Name in the Press

Criticism of anyone by name in the press should be decided after discussion by the party committee at the same level, and in some cases submitted to the party committee at a higher level for approval.

*12. Policy Toward Scientists, Technicians,
and Ordinary Members of Working Staffs*

As regards scientists, technicians and ordinary members of working staffs, as long as they are patriotic, work energetically, are not against the party and socialism, and maintain no illicit relations with any foreign country, we should in the present movement continue to apply the policy of "unity, criticism, unity." Special care should be taken of those scientists and scientific and technical personnel who have made contributions. Efforts should be made to help them gradually transform their world outlook and their style of work.

*13. The Question of Arrangements for Integration
with the Socialist Education Movement in
City and Countryside*

The cultural and educational units and leading organs of the party and government in the large and medium cities are the points of concentration of the present Proletarian Cultural Revolution.

The Great Cultural Revolution has enriched the socialist education movement in both city and countryside and raised it to a higher level. Efforts should be made to conduct these two movements in close combination. . . .

*14. Take Firm Hold of the Revolution
and Stimulate Production*

The aim of the Great Proletarian Cultural Revolution is to revolutionize people's ideology and as a consequence to achieve greater, faster, better, and more economical results in all fields of work. If the masses are fully aroused and proper arrangements are made, it is possible to carry on both the Cultural Revolution and production without one hampering the other, while guaranteeing high quality in all our work.

The Great Proletarian Cultural Revolution is a powerful motive force for the development of the social productive forces in our country. Any idea of counterposing the great Cultural Revolution against the development of production is incorrect.

15. The Armed Forces

In the armed forces, the Cultural Revolution and the socialist education movement should be carried out in accordance with the instructions of the Military Commission of the Central Committee and the General Political Department of the People's Liberation Army.

16. Mao Tsetung's Thought Is the Guide for Action in the Great Proletarian Cultural Revolution

In the Great Proletarian Cultural Revolution, it is imperative to hold aloft the great red banner of Mao Tsetung's thought and put proletarian politics in command. The movement for the creative study and application of Chairman Mao Tsetung's works should be carried forward among the masses of the workers, peasants and soldiers, the cadres and the intellectuals, and Mao Tsetung's thought should be taken as the guide for action in the Cultural Revolution. . . .

Party committees at all levels must abide by the directions given by Chairman Mao over the years, namely that they should thoroughly apply the mass line of "from the masses and to the masses" and that they should be pupils before they become teachers. They should try to avoid being one-sided or narrow. They should foster materialist dialectics and oppose metaphysics and scholasticism.

3. MAO TSETUNG, ASSESSING THE CULTURAL REVOLUTION

In a talk with an Albanian military delegation in August 1967 Mao offered his personal assessment of the first two years of the Cultural Revolution, analyzing the struggle between the bourgeoisie and the proletariat in the realm of ideas and culture on the one hand and state power and policy on the other.

A Talk by Chairman Mao With a Foreign Military Delegation, August 31, 1967. SCPRP 4200.

Mao's extremely pessimistic view of intellectuals expressed here underlined his central point: the necessity to continue to contest world views, to re-educate a nation through participation in revolutionary struggle.

Mao pinpointed another critical issue: that those who pioneered in the national liberation and democratic revolutions would not necessarily lead the way in subsequent phases in which the principal enemy was neither foreign invaders nor the landlord class but the bourgeoisie. (Both of Mao's assessments would become subjects of sharp debate in the 1970s.)

Yet even as he pointed to the dangers of capitalist restoration, Mao reaffirmed a theme which runs through his entire revolutionary career: basic optimism that both the vast majority of cadres and people (his figure here is 95 percent) continue to support revolutionary advance and if properly mobilized will provide the basis for continuing the revolution.

I said at a rally of 7,000 people in 1962 that the struggle between Marxism-Leninism and revisionism had not yet come to a conclusion, that it was quite probable that revisionism would win while we would lose. We reminded everyone of the possibility of defeat in order to help everyone's vigilance against revisionism and to strengthen the effort to oppose and prevent revisionism. As a matter of fact, the struggle between the two classes and two lines has always existed in the party. . . .

Our Great Proletarian Cultural Revolution should begin with Yao Wen-yuan's criticism of *Hai Jui's Dismissal from Office* in the winter of 1965. At that time some departments and areas of our country were dominated to such an extent by revisionists that they were watertight and could not even be penetrated with a needle. At that time I suggested that Comrade XX should organize the writing of criticism against *Hai Jui's Dismissal from Office*. But nothing could be done even in this red city, and so it had to be done in Shanghai. When the essay was completed, I read it three times and thought it would do basically. So I let Comrade XX have it published. . . .

Comrade Yao Wen-yuan's essay was only a signal for the Great Proletarian Cultural Revolution. So we especially supervised the formulation of a May 16 circular at the center. . . .

The circular clearly raised the question of struggle of line. At that time most people disagreed with me. Sometimes I was all alone. They said that my ideas were out of date. So I had to bring my views to the Eleventh Plenary Session of the CCP Eighth Central Committee for discussion. Through the discussion I was able to secure the consent of slightly more than half of those present. . . .

After the Eleventh Plenary Session of the party's Eighth Central Committee, the focal point was on the criticism against the bourgeois reactionary line in the three months of October, November, and December 1966. That openly provoked contradictions within the party. . . .

With regard to policy and strategy, the Great Proletarian Cultural Revolution may roughly be divided into four stages:

The period from the publication of Comrade Yao Wen-yuan's essay up to the Eleventh Plenary Session of the CCP Eighth Central Committee may be regarded as the first stage. It was primarily a mobilization stage.

The period from the Eleventh Plenary Session of the CCP Eighth Central Committee to the January Storm may be regarded as the second stage. It was primarily a stage for correcting the orientation.

The power seizure in the January Storm and the revolutionary great alliance and three-in-one combination may be regarded as the third stage.

The fourth stage began with the publication of Ch'i Pen-yu's "Is It Patriotism or National Betrayal?" and "The Essence of Self-cultivation Is Betrayal of the Proletarian Dictatorship."

The third and fourth stages are both concerned with the question of power seizure. The fourth stage, however, involves ideological seizure of power from revisionism and the bourgeoisie. Therefore it is a crucial stage of decision for the struggle between the two classes, two roads, and two lines. . . .

It was desired to bring up some successors among the intellectuals, but now it seems a hopeless task. As I see it, the intellectuals, including young intellectuals still receiving education in school, still have a basically bourgeois world outlook, whether they are in the party or outside it. This is because for seventeen years after the liberation the cultural and educational circles have been dominated by revisionism. As a result, bourgeois ideas are infused in the blood of the intellectuals. So revolutionary intellectuals must successfully reform their world outlook at the crucial stage of the struggle between the two classes, two roads, and two lines, or they may head in a direction opposite that of the revolution.

Here I'll ask you a question: Tell me, what is the object of the Great Proletarian Cultural Revolution? (Someone answered that it was to struggle against the capitalist roaders in the party.) The struggle against the capitalist roaders in the party is the principal task, but not the object. The object is to solve the problem of world outlook and eradicate revisionism.

The center has repeatedly stressed the importance of self-education, because a world outlook cannot be imposed on anyone, and ideological remolding represents external factors acting on internal factors, with the latter playing the primary role. If world outlook is not reformed, then although 2,000 capitalist roaders are removed in the current Great Cultural Revolution, 4,000 others may appear the next time. We are paying a very high price in the current Great Cultural Revolution. The struggle between the two classes and two lines cannot be settled in one, two, three, or four cultural revolutions, but the results of the current Great Cultural Revolution must be consolidated for at least fifteen years. Two or three cultural revolutions should be carried out every hundred years. So we must keep in mind the uprooting of revisionism and strengthen our capability to resist revisionism at any time.

Here I wish to ask you another question: What are the capitalist roaders? (No reply) Capitalist roaders are power-holders who follow the capitalist road. During the democratic revolution they took an active part in the fight against the three big mountains. But in the fight against the bourgeoisie after the nation-wide liberation, they were not so enthusiastic. They actively took part in the war against local tyrants and in the redistribution of land, but they were not so enthusiastic when it came to collectivization of farming after the nation-wide liberation. They do not take the socialist road, but they now hold power. Isn't it right to call them power-holders who take the capitalist road?

When a veteran comes face to face with a new problem, he will resolutely take the socialist road if he has the proletarian world outlook, but if he has the bourgeois world outlook, he will take the capitalist road. That is why we say the bourgeoisie will want to reform the world according to the bourgeois world outlook. Some people who have made mistakes of orientation and line in the Great Proletarian Revolution also try to excuse themselves by saying that veteran revolutionaries have met new problems. But since they have made mistakes, it shows that these veteran cadres have not yet thoroughly reformed their bourgeois world outlook. From now on, veteran cadres will yet have to meet with many more new problems. To ensure that they will resolutely follow the socialist road, they must bring about a proletarian revolution of their mind. . . .

In dealing with cadres, we must first of all believe that more than 95 percent of them are good or comparatively good. Our confidence cannot be separated from this class viewpoint. Revolutionary cadres and those who want to make revolution must be protected. They must be protected without fear and liberated from their mistakes. Even those who have followed the capitalist road should be allowed to make revolution when after prolonged education they have corrected their mistakes.

Those who are really bad are not many. They form at most 5 percent of the masses and 1 or 2 percent in the party and CYL. The inveterate capitalist roaders are only a small handful. But we must hit at this small handful as the main target, because their influence and poison is deep and great. So their overthrow is the principal task of our current Great Cultural Revolution.

Bad men among the masses cannot be more than 5 percent, but they are scattered and therefore ineffectual. . . .

All the same, we must sharpen our vigilance, particularly at crucial stages of the struggle, when it will be necessary to prevent bad men from infiltrating our ranks. Therefore the revolutionary great alliance should be conditioned by two prerequisites—one is destruction of self and establishment of devotion to public interest, and the other, struggle. An alliance without struggle will not be effective.

The fourth stage of the current Great Cultural Revolution is a crucial stage of the struggle between the two classes, two roads, and two lines.

4. REVOLUTIONARY COMMITTEES AND THE ATTACK ON BUREAUCRACY

Beginning in early 1967 the emphasis in the Cultural Revolution shifted from destruction to construction, from attack to seizing power and reconstituting the political order. The most important institutional innovation emerging from the movement to combat bureaucracy and extend democracy was the revolutionary committee. Revolutionary committees became the highest organs of authority at virtually every level and in all institutions from factories and communes to schools, hospitals, offices, and municipal and provincial governments. Composed initially of "three-in-one combinations" of revolutionary cadres who had weathered the storm of criticism, younger activists who emerged during the Cultural Revolution, and PLA representatives who helped to ease frictions among conflicting groups, the revolutionary committees faced the formidable task of restoring effective administration while deepening the critique of bureaucracy and authoritarianism. It remained to be seen whether the revolutionary committees which challenged bureaucratic authority and seized power on the basis of the mass line could lead the nation forward without succumbing to routinization.

The spring breeze of Mao Tsetung's thought has reached every corner of our motherland. The revolutionary committees which have come into being one after another stand like red flags flying in the wind. To date, revolutionary committees have been established in seventeen provinces and municipalities and in one autonomous region. More are in the preparatory stage in other areas. Vast numbers of units at the grassroots levels have set up their own revolutionary committees. . . .

When the newborn revolutionary committees appeared on the eastern horizon a year ago, our revered and beloved leader Chairman Mao, with his Great Proletarian Revolutionary genius, pointed out with foresight: "In every place or unit

Revolutionary Committees are Fine. JMJP, March 30, 1968. PR, April 5, 1968.

where power must be seized, it is necessary to carry out the policy of the revolutionary 'three-in-one' combination in establishing a provisional organ of power which is revolutionary and representative and enjoys proletarian authority. This organ of power should preferably be called the revolutionary committee."

Our great leader Chairman Mao again recently pointed out: "The basic experience of revolutionary committees is this—they are threefold: they have representatives of revolutionary cadres, representatives of the armed forces, and representatives of the revolutionary masses. This forms a revolutionary 'three-in-one' combination. The revolutionary committee should exercise unified leadership, do away with redundant or overlapping administrative structures, have 'better troops and simpler administration' and organize a revolutionized leading group which is linked with the masses." Chairman Mao's brilliant directive sums up the experience of revolutionary committees at all levels and gives the basic orientation for building revolutionary committees. . . .

The "three-in-one" revolutionary committee is a great creation of the hundreds of millions of the revolutionary masses that appeared in the course of their struggle to seize power from the handful of party people in authority taking the capitalist road. It has shown enormous vitality in leading the proletariat and the revolutionary masses in the fight against the class enemy over the past year and more.

This "three-in-one" organ of power enables our proletarian political power to strike deep roots among the masses. Chairman Mao points out: "The most fundamental principle in the reform of state organs is that they must keep in contact with the masses." The representatives of the revolutionary masses, particularly the representatives of the working people—the workers and peasants—who have come forward en masse in the course of the Great Proletarian Cultural Revolution are revolutionary fighters with practical experience. Representing the interests of the revolutionary masses, they participate in the leading groups at various levels. This provides the revolutionary committees at these levels with a broad mass foundation. Direct participation by the revolutionary masses in the running of the country and the enforcement of revolutionary supervision from below over the organs of political power at various levels play a very important role in ensuring that our leading groups at all levels always adhere to the mass line, maintain the closest relations with the masses, represent their interests at all times and serve the people heart and soul.

The great Chinese People's Liberation Army is the main pillar of the dictatorship of the proletariat and a Great Wall of steel defending the socialist motherland. The revolutionary "three-in-one" combination carries our army-civilian unity to a completely new stage. In its work of helping the left, helping industry and agriculture, exercising military control and giving military and political training, the People's Liberation Army has made big contributions over the past year and more and has been well steeled in the process. . . .

Revolutionary leading cadres are the backbone of the "three-in-one" organs of power. They have rich experience in class struggle and are a valuable asset to the party and people. By going through the severe test of the Great Proletarian Cultural Revolution and receiving education and help from the masses, they were touched to the soul and remolded their world outlook further. The combination of the revolutionary leading cadres and representatives of the PLA and of the revolutionary masses in the revolutionary committees makes them better able to carry out Chairman Mao's proletarian revolutionary line, grasp and implement the party's policies, and correctly organize and lead the masses forward. At the same time, veteran cadres and young new cadres work together in the revolutionary committees, learn from each other and help each other so that, as Chairman Mao teaches, the veterans are not divorced from the masses and the young people are tempered. Organizationally, this guarantees the work of training successors to the proletarian revolutionary cause.

This "three-in-one" organ of power has absolutely nothing in common with the overstaffed bureaucratic apparatus of the exploiting classes in the old days. It has an entirely new and revolutionary style of work of its own and it functions in a way which is beneficial to the people. . . . "Remain one of the common people while serving as an official." Maintain "better troops and simpler administration," and drastically reform old methods of office and administrative work. Have a small leading body and a small staff, as certain revolutionary committees have begun doing, so that there is no overlapping or redundancy in the organization and no overstaffing, so that bureaucracy can be prevented. . . .

In order to become genuinely revolutionary headquarters with proletarian revolutionary authority, the revolutionary committees should hold fast to the general orientation for the struggle, consistently direct the spearhead of attack against China's Khrushchev* and the handful of other top party persons in authority taking the capitalist road and their agents, distinguish the contradictions between ourselves and the enemy from contradictions among the people, carry on revolutionary mass criticism and repudiation, continue to consolidate and develop the revolutionary great alliance and the revolutionary "three-in-one" combination and constantly sum up experience and draw lessons. . . .

Of all the good things characterizing the revolutionary committees, the most fundamental is the creative study and application of the thought of Mao Tsetung and the doing of this well. . . .

The revolutionary "three-in-one" provisional organs of power which have sprung up all over the country will lead the proletariat and the revolutionary masses in establishing proletarian authority and in playing a vital revolutionary role in the momentous struggle to win all-round victory in the Great Proletarian Cultural Revolution.

5. CHOU EN-LAI,
ON CLASSES, CUSTOMS,
AND CULTURAL REVOLUTION

In a wide-ranging series of discussions with American author William Hinton in 1971, Premier Chou En-lai spelled out the rationale for the Great Proletarian Cultural Revolution in terms of the continued existence of classes, class struggle, and the

Premier Chou Talks to William Hinton About Classes and Customs in Chinese Society (May 1971). *New China*, Spring 1975.
    * Liu Shao-ch'i

persistence of feudal and capitalist ideas in China. Analyzing China's class structure, Chou pointed out that the old exploiting classes—the landlords and rich peasants, the capitalists, and the petty bourgeoisie—deprived of their base of power but in many cases clinging to old ideas, may numerically exceed the proletariat, despite the rapid growth of the latter since the revolution. Moreover, a new party and managerial elite may seek to consolidate power and bring the revolution to a halt. In this context the importance of the worker-peasant alliance as the bulwark of a political process carrying forward the socialist revolution, and the necessity for continued struggle in the realm of culture and ideas, take on added significance.

Hinton: We have been impressed by the progress and enthusiasm for socialism we've seen everywhere. Why does political conflict continue?

Have you ever heard about the old-fashioned method of childbirth that is still practiced in some parts of Shansi? Did you investigate that? In Shansi some people still follow a very bad custom. After a woman has given birth to a child, she must sit up on the *k'ang*. She is not allowed to eat anything and has to sit upright. Many women have ruined their backs in this way. In the course of childbirth a woman has already lost a lot of strength but in Shansi she can't eat anything nourishing—not even bean milk, to say nothing of an egg or two. She is given only a little rice or millet gruel. . . .

Of all the provinces, Shansi's population has increased the least. To this day it has not topped 20 million. Before liberation there were quite a few provinces with a population below 20 million—Fukien, Kwangsi, Yunnan, Kweichow, Shensi, and Shansi. Now all but the last exceed 20 million, even neighboring Shensi. And the reason for this is not because Shansi has done well in birth control but only because, though a lot of babies are born, many don't live. In Shansi infant mortality is still high. We have done a lot of work on this but we still haven't found a lasting solution.

It is very hard to change old customs. West Shansi is the worst. In one county there is a brigade made up of immigrants from Honan. They pay much attention to hygiene. Their children survive and grow up in good health. But the Shansi villagers all around won't learn from the immigrants. Instead they look down on Honan people.

In the last few years we have sent them a number of medical teams. Some of them have been People's Liberation Army teams, others have been regular government teams. When they demonstrate modern methods, the people appear to pay attention, but when the teams leave they go right back to their old habits. Some even go back to consulting witch doctors (there still are some in Shansi today) when they get sick. In the old days the Eighth Route Army stayed in those mountains. They never lost control of them during the Japanese War (1937–1945) or the Liberation War (1946–1949) either. They were in revolutionary hands right up until liberation. Yet these backward things still exist. . . .

There are thousands and thousands of backward phenomena. But no matter how you look at it, Chinese society is advancing. . . . But to get rid of these backward things during the course of making progress is not easy. The thinking of feudal society over several thousand years is stamped in people's minds. And so are the old class habits. In the countryside, even though the former poor and lower middle peasants are in the majority and the former landlords and rich peasants make up only a minority of around 7 percent, still these old exploiters continue to exist. Their thinking influences others. They make up a reactionary force that must be struggled against.

In the countryside, under socialism, classes still exist. There are, of course, some special places where old exploiters are few in number or even absent. In Tachai, in Shansi province, not many landlords or rich peasants remain. . . . In most cases land reform took place only twenty years ago (1949–1952), so there are ex-landlords and rich peasants in large numbers almost everywhere.

As for the offspring of these people, if they were young at the time of liberation they never took part in exploitation. Some have become students, others have become laborers. Nevertheless, the influence of their parents on them may be quite deep.

If you take the total as 7 percent and realize that there are over 600 million rural people, then the ex-landlords and rich peasants number over 40 million. If half of them have been transformed, the total of unreconstructed persons is still over 20 million, and this is putting the best light on the matter because it is not easy to transform them. . . .

So classes still exist even though the old rulers no longer hold any power but on the contrary are supervised by our people's power.

As for the cities, before the Cultural Revolution the class situation was even more clear. There was a bourgeois group that owned and operated profit-making enterprises. At first we adopted a policy for the transition period (1949–1955) of use, restrict, and transform. Then at the end of 1955 and in the spring of 1956, with drums beating and cymbals clashing, this bourgeois group marched into socialist society all together. Some gave up their enterprises and turned them over to the public, some entered joint state-private management schemes, others set up cooperatives, as in the handicraft field. All this occurred as collectivization, the move toward higher-stage cooperatives, went forward in the countryside.

After this shift to socialist ownership, we paid interest to the capitalists based on the estimated value of their property. Naturally our estimates were somewhat low. The proletariat is not likely to over-value the property of the bourgeoisie. At that time we estimated the total capital in private hands at 2 billion, 200 million yuan, or 900 million U.S. dollars. At 5 percent we paid out 110 million yuan or 45 million U.S. dollars annually to the former owners. From 1956 through 1966, for ten years, right up until the first year of the Cultural Revolution, we paid out this money. Then the payments stopped. It was a coincidence—our payments went on for just ten years, not more, not less. . . .

As interest payments, they got back just about half of what they had invested—450 million U.S. dollars. Of course, this isn't applicable in every case. Some people never took the interest due them. Others became "democratic personages" and drew a salary for the job they held. They were reluctant to accept any interest. Some people refused the money because their share was so small. Once you accept any of it you are called a capitalist. For some it was hardly worth it. So not all of the money due was actually paid out to capitalists.

When the Cultural Revolution broke out, the masses wouldn't allow the banks to pay out any more interest on private capital. At this point the bourgeoisie didn't dare demand it, so the payments ended. But after all, these people still constitute a bourgeois class. They still exist. Furthermore, their number is quite large. Their percentage in the cities might well be higher than that of the landlords in the countryside. We figure 10 million people altogether, counting all family members.

Then there is another bourgeois category—the petty bourgeoisie. For example, the upper middle peasants in the countryside. They retained their land in the land reform, they worked, they became commune members, but they still have some rich peasant or upper middle peasant thought. If you divide the peasants into three categories—upper, middle, and lower—among the middle peasants there is also some individualist thinking and this is petty bourgeois thinking. Even ordinary poor peasants and lower middle peasants have a lot of petty bourgeois thinking. Before they had no economic status at all, so that they could be called semi-proletarian. But after land reform they held and worked their own private land for a period. After they joined cooperatives and communes they pooled their land and held it collectively, but each family still saved out a private plot. Places like Tachai, where no one has private plots today, are in the minority. . . .

The brigades that don't have private plots are a minority and they are socially advanced. The majority still have them. But of course we are not like the Soviet Union where agricultural production is concentrated on private plots. There people expend little energy on their collective land; most of their time is spent on their plots. . . .

We do not follow the Soviet example in the way private plots are used, but we still need to have them. In order to stimulate the initiative and enthusiasm of the peasants we still advocate private plots, so that in addition to their collective income they can earn something on the side and also ensure some variety in their diet. . . .

What I want to stress is that in the countryside petty bourgeois thinking still exists on a wide scale. From a Marxist point of view the petty bourgeoisie belongs to the bourgeois class and not to the working class or proletariat. In the cities the little merchants and storekeepers have merged their enterprises into cooperatives but there are still people who go around with carrying poles, who buy from state enterprises at wholesale prices, and who sell to the public at retail prices, and there are still household inns, restaurants, and shops—what we call husband-and-wife inns or shops.

This shows that the petty bourgeoisie are quite numerous. While at the same time the working class, the true proletariat, is quite small. How many workers do we have? We have no more than 30 million industrial workers. If we count workers, doctors, teachers—that is, all salaried and wage-earning personnel—there are still only 50 million. If we count only real workers who satisfy Marx's definition as commodity producers, there are no more than 30 million. Looked at in this way America certainly has more workers than we do, and even Japan, where industry is growing very rapidly, may surpass us in this category. This 30 million figure refers to individual employed workers. If you count family members, dependents, and children, then of course there will be a lot more people in the working class.

In China, as a general rule, everyone works. Sometimes the woman in the family stays at home, but in many cases both husband and wife work. Thus 50 million workers does not mean 50 million families. The figures tend to double up.

We estimate the urban population at 100 million, and the rural population at 600 million.

Obviously the 50 million wage and salaried workers are not all in the cities. . . .

My basic point is this—in China's socialist society there are still classes. Classes still exist. On this question there are people who disagree, but once you point out the objective facts, how can they refute you?

Given the figures mentioned above, it is obvious that, in terms of ideology, proletarian class rule is minority rule. The minority dictates to the majority. But if we look at the question in terms of class alliances, then it is the other way around: we have a majority of workers and peasants dictating to the

minority of former exploiters. But within the great alliance of the workers and peasants, proletarian thinking is not universal. There is still a lot of petty bourgeois thinking.
One can talk about this in two ways:
(1) China is a socialist society. We have established a socialist system with two kinds of ownership—public and collective. From this point of view we can say that this society is a worker-peasant society, a socialist society. It represents the majority dictating to the minority of former exploiters.
(2) The working class must lead in everything. That is to say, the proletarian world outlook must predominate. This then is minority leadership.

So, once again, in China's socialist society there are classes, there are class contradictions, and there is class struggle.

Internal factors are influenced by external ones. Internally we are encircled by capitalists and revisionists, and the revisionist ideas are especially corrosive. So to say that in China there is only ideological struggle, only a struggle between the advanced and backward, is wrong. Advanced and backward thinking itself reflects class struggle. Even among working people there is backward thinking which reflects the thinking of the exploiting classes. . . .

Hinton: What about newly generated bourgeois forces, those capitalist roaders who arise due to privilege? If one looks only at former landlords isn't one apt to be disarmed before the newly emerging bourgeoisie?

Yes. I was just about to discuss that. I started with a static analysis and said that certain classes exist, secondly that these reactionary classes are influencing the petty bourgeoisie and the working class. Thirdly, bourgeois elements will be newly generated. In the development of socialism right up until today, if the directors of industry—the accountants, engineers, managers, etc.—expand and consolidate special privilege, a new privileged class will be generated and its members will be the capitalist roaders whom you have just mentioned. . . .

Thus we have: (1) old exploiters still around; (2) newly generated bourgeois class forces; (3) ideological influence and corrosion.

This last, the old habits, customs, and ways of thinking left over from the past, are widespread. Lenin had especial hatred for such things, the bad things left over from the exploiters. The old way of childbirth in Shansi which I discussed at the start is one of the bad things left over. In highly industrialized societies this kind of thing is less common, or even absent. But in a backward country like ours there are lots of things of this sort. . . .

Liu Shao-ch'i thought that after the three great transformations [of agriculture, of industry, and of commerce] class struggle would die out. . . . In over 20 years of socialist revolution, the struggle against such ideas has been very sharp. But if we didn't admit class struggle, how could we direct our work? What would be our guiding principles?

6. THE 1975 CONSTITUTION

The Fourth National People's Congress adopted a new constitution defining the principles for carrying forward socialist revolution and economic construction. This document, which replaced the 1954 Constitution, emphasized the danger of capitalist restoration throughout the period of socialism and the importance of the dictatorship of the proletariat. In essence, it represents a synthesis of principles for the transition to socialism as they emerged from the Cultural Revolution.

Preamble

The founding of the People's Republic of China marked the great victory of the new democratic revolution and the beginning of the new historical period of socialist revolution and the dictatorship of the proletariat, a victory gained only after the Chinese people had waged a heroic struggle for over a century and, finally, under the leadership of the Communist Party of China, overthrown the reactionary rule of imperialism, feudalism, and bureaucrat-capitalism by a people's revolutionary war.

For the last twenty years and more, the people of all nation-

The Constitution of the People's Republic of China, adopted January 17, 1975, by the Fourth National People's Congress. PR January 24, 1975.

alities in our country, continuing their triumphant advance under the leadership of the Communist Party of China, have achieved great victories both in socialist revolution and socialist construction and in the Great Proletarian Cultural Revolution, and have consolidated and strengthened the dictatorship of the proletariat.

Socialist society covers a considerably long historical period. Throughout this historical period, there are classes, class contradictions, and class struggle, there is the struggle between the socialist road and the capitalist road, there is the danger of capitalist restoration, and there is the threat of subversion and aggression by imperialism and social-imperialism. These contradictions can be resolved only by depending on the theory of continued revolution under the dictatorship of the proletariat and on practice under its guidance.

We must adhere to the basic line and policies of the Communist Party of China for the entire historical period of socialism and persist in continued revolution under the dictatorship of the proletariat, so that our great motherland will always advance along the road indicated by Marxism–Leninism–Mao Tsetung thought.

We should consolidate the great unity of the people of all nationalities led by the working class and based on the alliance of workers and peasants, and develop the revolutionary united front. We should correctly distinguish contradictions among the people from those between ourselves and the enemy and correctly handle them. We should carry on the three great revolutionary movements of class struggle, the struggle for production, and scientific experiment; we should build socialism independently and with the initiative in our own hands, through self-reliance, hard struggle, diligence, and thrift and by going all out, aiming high and achieving greater, faster, better, and more economical results; and we should be prepared against war and natural disasters and do everything for the people. . . .

Chapter 1
General Principles

Article 1. The People's Republic of China is a socialist state of the dictatorship of the proletariat led by the working class and based on the alliance of workers and peasants.

Article 2. The Communist Party of China is the core of leadership of the whole Chinese people. The working class exercises leadership over the state through its vanguard, the Communist Party of China.

Marxism-Leninism-Mao Tsetung thought is the theoretical basis guiding the thinking of our nation.

Article 3. All power in the People's Republic of China belongs to the people. The organs through which the people exercise power are the people's congresses at all levels, with deputies of workers, peasants, and soldiers as their main body.

The people's congresses at all levels and all other organs of state practice democratic centralism.

Deputies to the people's congresses at all levels are elected through democratic consultation. The electoral units and electors have the power to supervise the deputies they elect and to replace them at any time according to provisions of law.

Article 4. The People's Republic of China is a unitary multinational state. The areas where regional national autonomy is exercised are all inalienable parts of the People's Republic of China.

All the nationalities are equal. Big nationality chauvinism and local nationality chauvinism must be opposed.

All the nationalities have the freedom to use their own spoken and written languages.

Article 5. In the People's Republic of China, there are mainly two kinds of ownership of the means of production at the present stage: socialist ownership by the whole people and socialist collective ownership by working people.

The state may allow nonagricultural individual laborers to engage in individual labor involving no exploitation of others, within the limits permitted by law and under unified arrangement by neighborhood organizations in cities and towns or by production teams in rural people's communes. At the same time, these individual laborers should be guided onto the road of socialist collectivization step by step.

Article 6. The state sector of the economy is the leading force in the national economy.

All mineral resources and waters as well as the forests, undeveloped land, and other resources owned by the state are the property of the whole people.

The state may requisition by purchase, take over for use, or nationalize urban and rural land as well as other means of production under conditions prescribed by law.

Article 7. The rural people's commune is an organization which integrates government administration and economic management.

The economic system of collective ownership in the rural people's communes at the present stage generally takes the form of three-level ownership with the production team at the basic level, that is, ownership by the commune, the production brigade and the production team, with the last as the basic accounting unit.

Provided that the development and absolute predominance of the collective economy of the people's commune are ensured, people's commune members may farm small plots for their personal needs, engage in limited household sideline production, and in pastoral areas keep a small number of livestock for their personal needs.

Article 8. Socialist public property shall be inviolable. The state shall ensure the consolidation and development of the socialist economy and prohibit any person from undermining the socialist economy and the public interest in any way whatsoever.

Article 9. The state applies the socialist principle: "He who does not work, neither shall he eat" and "from each according to his ability, to each according to his work."

The state protects the citizens' right of ownership to their income from work, their savings, their houses, and other means of livelihood.

Article 10. The state applies the principle of grasping revolution, promoting production, and other work and preparedness against war; promotes the planned and proportionate development of the socialist economy, taking agriculture as the foundation and industry as the leading factor and bringing the initiative of both the central and the local authorities into full play; and improves the people's material and cultural life step by step on the basis of the constant growth of social production and consolidates the independence and security of the country.

Article 11. State organizations and state personnel must earnestly study Marxism–Leninism–Mao Tsetung thought, firmly put proletarian politics in command, combat bureaucracy, maintain close ties with the masses and wholeheartedly serve the people. Cadres at all levels must participate in collective productive labor.

Every organ of state must apply the principle of efficient and simple administration. Its leading body must be a three-in-one combination of the old, the middle-aged and the young.

Article 12. The proletariat must exercise all-round dictatorship over the bourgeoisie in the superstructure, including all spheres of culture. Culture and education, literature and art, physical education, health work, and scientific research work must all serve proletarian politics, serve the workers, peasants, and soldiers, and be combined with productive labor.

Article 13. Speaking out freely, airing views fully, holding great debates and writing big character posters are new forms of carrying on socialist revolution created by the masses of the people. The state shall ensure to the masses the right to use these forms to create a political situation in which there are both centralism and democracy, both discipline and freedom, both unity of will and personal ease of mind and liveliness, and so help consolidate the leadership of the Communist Party of China over the state and consolidate the dictatorship of the proletariat.

Article 14. The state safeguards the socialist system, suppresses all treasonable and counter-revolutionary activities, and punishes all traitors and counter-revolutionaries.

The state deprives the landlords, rich peasants, reactionary capitalists, and other bad elements of political rights for specified periods of time according to law, and at the same time provides them with the opportunity to earn a living so that they may be reformed through labor and become law-abiding citizens supporting themselves by their own labor.

Article 15. The Chinese People's Liberation Army and the people's militia are the workers' and peasants' own armed forces led by the Communist Party of China; they are the armed forces of the people of all nationalities.

B. THE GREAT PROLETARIAN CULTURAL REVOLUTION IN INDUSTRY AND THE CITIES

1. THE CULTURAL REVOLUTION IN THE CITIES

The Cultural Revolution launched by intellectuals and students and initially centered on culture and ideas quickly spread to the factories. In late September and October 1966, long-simmering conflicts involving workers, technicians, managers, and the party exploded. From this time the proletariat became central actors in the national political context and in the striving of working people to become masters not only of the workplace but of urban politics and society as a whole.

The "Twelve-Point Directive" of 1966 framed guidelines to expand worker political activity and sustain industrial production through transforming the relations of production while attempting (futilely as it turned out) to restrict the scope of activity to individual workplaces and nonworking hours.

As the movement spread, workers initiated power seizures, overturned the leadership of managerial and party cadres, and inaugurated administrative and technological reforms. Struggle within the factories sharpened as party, managerial, and union leadership sought to ease criticism and curry favor with the workers through bonuses and cash payments. The focal point of workers' struggles centered on seizure of power and transformation of production relations in the factories and municipal governments.

In response to the widespread anarchy and sharp divisions among worker groups, in January 1967 the People's Liberation Army was called in to back up rebel organizations and to help restore order by consolidating the revolution in many areas. Functioning primarily in an educational and administrative

*capacity rather than as a fighting force, the army was directed
to support the left, counter revisionist currents, and restore
production. The Central Committee's "Letter to Revolutionary
Workers" defines this new stage as leading to the establishment
of great alliances of workers, cadres, and PLA members to
sustain the revolution, promote production and forge unity.*

*In the months that followed, these alliances became the basis
for forming revolutionary committees which eventually established combinations of workers, technicians, and managerial
personnel to run the factories.*

A. The Twelve-Point Directive:
The Cultural Revolution in the Factories

1. The Great Proletarian Cultural Revolution is to propagate
forcefully Mao Tsetung thought, to reform the society with the
proletarian world view, to eradicate the ideologies of the bourgeoisie and other exploiting classes, to destroy the four olds of
the bourgeoisie and to establish the four news of the proletariat,
for the sake of consolidating the proletarian dictatorship, uprooting the revisionist roots, preventing the capitalist restoration, guaranteeing the permanence of our socialist regime, and
greatly promoting the development of socialist productivity.

The working class is the leading strength and the most active
element of the Cultural Revolution; workers are shouldering a
specially great responsibility for this Great Proletarian Cultural
Revolution; and the rising up of worker masses in factories,
mines, and enterprises to carry on the Great Cultural Revolution which is required by the general situation, is just excellent,
and is unpreventable.

2. Party committees at all levels and leaders of all factories
and mines must seriously carry out the directive of "grasping
revolution and promoting production" laid down by Chairman

Twelve-Point Directive of the Central Cultural Revolution Group Concerning the Great Proletarian Cultural Revolution in Factories and Mines
(Draft), November 17, 1966. CC Documents.

Mao and the party Central Committee; they must not be afraid of the rising up of the masses, must not shirk their responsibilities, and must not oppose the masses. They must stand firmly with the masses, against the small handful of degenerate, ungrateful, selfish persons in authority taking the capitalist road who suppress the masses. They must also dare to mobilize the masses to criticize their own mistakes, and must not instigate workers to struggle against workers, or masses to struggle against masses.

3. The current problem is that the leaders of certain units erroneously put the Cultural Revolution Movement in opposition to production. Some use the pretext of grasping the movement to suppress the revolutionaries and protect themselves, neglecting production; others use the pretext of grasping production to boycott the Cultural Revolution movement. These two mistakes are both a disregard of the whole situation, a violation of the policies of the party, and a serious violation of the directive to "grasp revolution and promote production." . . .

5. The party Central Committee calls on the leaders at all levels to go actively to the workers, according to the decision of the party Central Committee concerning the Great Proletarian Cultural Revolution, that is, the sixteen articles, to explain clearly to the masses the great meaning of "grasping revolution and promoting production," to let the masses carry on full discussions, so that they may consciously grasp revolution while promoting production, and may make proper arrangements according to the conditions in their own units. There must not be mistakes such as doing all things for the masses, suppressing the masses, adhering obstinately to set patterns, and being afraid of the masses. Revolutionary masses who were branded counter-revolutionary workers must be rehabilitated. . . .

6. Many workers in factories, mines, and enterprises have suggested that there should be proper regulations for the time spent for cultural revolution and for production. For instance, the eight-hour work system must be maintained; the Cultural Revolution must be carried on after working hours, ranging from three to four hours without taking up production time; meantime the worker comrades must be allowed to have necessary rest.

7. In order that the revolutionary movement to grasp revolu-

tion and promote production might develop smoothly, there should be organized two mutually cooperating leaderships, which should be laid down solidly at each level. . . . The leading organs of the Cultural Revolution are the Cultural Revolution committees, leading groups, and congresses. These organs must not be manipulated from behind the scenes, but must be elected according to the system of the Paris Commune, after full consultation and repeated discussion of the masses, in the practice of a general election, and with the members capable of being changed and re-elected at any time. The production command system of the factories must not be interrupted. Where the original administrative organs and party committees have not been paralyzed, the leadership should be reorganized, with experienced and politically reliable old workers as the bulwark and with the participation of technicians, in order to direct production. . . .

8. According to provisions in the constitution of the People's Republic of China, worker comrades have the right to establish all kinds of Cultural Revolution organizations; all revolutionary comrades must act according to the principles and policies of the party. . . . We must guard against factionalism, refrain from armed struggle, protect production from being affected by troubles, and prevent work stoppage.

9. Collective organizations of the workers should adopt the forms of associations, representative conferences, congresses, etc., which are suitable for the worker masses. All good organizations should retain the characteristics of the working class of diligence and plainness, without being detached from the masses, and without organs and material equipments detached from the masses. Personnel in workers' organizations should as a rule not be detached from production.

10. Working masses must stand firmly at their own posts, must be mindful of the general situation, and must not abandon productive labor and go out in groups for exchange of revolutionary experience so as to affect the production of their own units and other units. . . .

11. Workers' organizations of factories and mines may go to other factories and mines in their own locality after working hours for visits, and to exchange experiences in the Great Proletarian Cultural Revolution.

12. Revolutionary student organizations may send representatives to factories, mines, and enterprises for the exchange of revolutionary experience. Student representatives should first make contact with workers' organizations in factories and mines.

B. Forming Revolutionary Great Alliances

Comrade workers and staff members!

Comrade revolutionary cadres of factories and mining enterprises!

The working class is the leading force in our country's socialist revolution and socialist construction.

Chairman Mao and the party Central Committee call upon you to carry the Great Proletarian Cultural Revolution through to the end and hope that you will, during this Great Proletarian Cultural Revolution and under this new condition, exert still greater efforts to strive for prosperity and prove yourselves the most distinguished models for the whole country's laboring masses in grasping revolution and promoting production at the present stage.

It is hoped that you will become models in firmly executing the proletarian revolutionary line represented by Chairman Mao and criticizing and repudiating the bourgeois reactionary line.

It is hoped that you will become models in firmly carrying out the party Central Committee's decision on the Great Proletarian Cultural Revolution.

It is hoped that you will become models in struggling against the handful of party persons in authority taking the capitalist road.

It is hoped that you will become models in achieving the revolutionary great alliance, models in opposing the small group mentality, anarchism, mentality of seeking the limelight, economism, and selfishness.

Central Committee Letter to Revolutionary Workers and Staff Members and Revolutionary Cadres of Factories and Mines All over the Country, March 18, 1967. SCPRM (Supplement), January 15, 1968.

You should consolidate labor discipline, firmly uphold democratic centralism and establish a good order in the socialist production and in the Great Cultural Revolution. You should stick firmly to the eight-hour work system specified by the party Central Committee and persevere in the Cultural Revolution during the rest of the time apart from these eight hours of work. Under no circumstances should you leave your posts of production and work without permission during the time of production. . . .

You should follow the regulations laid down by the party Central Committee and, during the Cultural Revolution, promote the revolutionizing of your thinking, carry out production with greater, faster, better, and more economical results, ensure the quality of products, and strive to improve the quality of products to a high level. You must struggle against some undesirable phenomena of disregarding quality and wasting the state's materials and supplies.

In the course of the Great Proletarian Cultural Revolution, all workers and staff members of factories and mining enterprises must study the experience of "having fewer and better troops and simpler administration." They must retrench the nonproductive staff and heighten efficiency of work to a large extent. They must pay close attention to practicing economy while making revolution. The working personnel of workers' organizations must generally not be taken away from production.

During the Great Proletarian Cultural Revolution, all workers and staff members of factories and mining enterprises must heighten their great sense of responsibility as masters of the country and protect state property well. Those who sabotage state property must be seriously punished according to the state's law.

The party Central Committee calls upon all revolutionary cadres working in factories and mining enterprises to take the lead in doing all branches of work well and to exert their utmost efforts to fulfill and overfulfill the state's production plan and construction plan. . . .

The party Central Committee has decided that the People's Liberation Army must vigorously assist the local administration and support industrial production. You should cooperate very well with comrades of the People's Liberation Army. . . .

Let us unite together under the guidance of the great thought of Mao Tsetung!

We hope you will fight bravely to secure a double bumper harvest in the Great Proletarian Cultural Revolution and in industrial production.

(This letter must be read in public and put up in all factories, mining enterprises, and units of capital construction.)

2. THE TACH'ING OIL FIELD, NATIONAL MODEL FOR INDUSTRY

In 1964 Mao designated the Tach'ing oil field the national model in industry. The development of Tach'ing, China's first major oil strike and still the largest, demonstrated fundamental principles of the road to socialist construction which have been summed up as "combining revolutionary zeal with a strict scientific approach, launching mass movements, and working hard and self-reliantly to build socialist enterprises, with greater, faster, better, and more economical results." Geologic surveys had been conducted throughout the fifties with Soviet technicians and aid, but it was not until 1960, in the very year that the Soviets withdrew all assistance, that China discovered a large oil field on the Sung-liao basin in Heilungkiang. For an oil-poor nation (prior to 1960, each year China imported between 55 and 73 percent of her oil) the discovery bolstered hopes for self-reliant development.

China has not only been spared energy dependence and debt accelerated by spiraling oil prices, but has already become a modest oil exporter. Some current projections suggest that by the early 1980s China is likely to become a major oil supplier, perhaps exporting 50 million tons a year or 25 percent of her projected oil production which some predict will be on a scale with that of Saudi Arabia in the 1980s. What is certain is that

Hsu Chin-ch'iang: Hold High the Great Red Banner of the Thought of Mao Tsetung, Further Deepen the Revolutionization of Enterprises: Basic Experience in Revolutionization of the Tach'ing Oil Field. *Ching-chi Yen-chiu* (Economic Research) April 20, 1966. SCPRM 538.

*oil exports have become the pivot of ambitious modernization
plans emphasizing purchase of foreign plant and equipment.
Tach'ing embodies the theme of self-reliance in other striking
ways, above all in combining industry and agriculture, city and
countryside, and exercising ingenuity in reducing costs. The oil
fields, rapidly constructed in the midst of economic hardship in
the early 1960s, relied heavily on worker initiative to overcome
equipment and transport shortages, inexperience, and financial
strictures.*

*Tach'ing rejected the convention of building a single petrol-
eum city on the outskirts of the field which would require a
large state investment, separate workers from their families,
produce a large population of consumers and be vulnerable to
foreign attack. Instead it decentralized operations, organized in
effect an agricultural-petroleum commune and promoted land
reclamation for farming in order to achieve food self-
sufficiency. Tach'ing thus became the model for China's urban-
rural planning. Combining industrial and agricultural pursuits,
Tach'ing has not only achieved food self-sufficiency but since
the Cultural Revolution it has initiated more than one hundred
small industries, many of which use waste products of the oil
refinery, to produce chemical fertilizer, pharmaceuticals, roof-
ing, screws, and other products.*

Under party leadership and thanks to the concern and support of various related quarters, workers of the Tach'ing oil
field in the 1960–1963 period overcame innumerable difficulties and succeeded in completing this huge oil field at a very
high speed. Since 1964, holding even higher the great red
banners of the thought of Mao Tsetung and of the general line
for socialist construction, taking class struggle and the struggle
between the road of socialism and the road of capitalism as the
key link, and using the "one dividing into two" theory as a
weapon, the oil field has been learning from the Liberation
Army and other advanced units, and has continued to revolutionize its operations. . . .

*It is essential to follow the mass line and
conduct a large-scale mass movement*

Unreservedly promote democracy in politics, production, and economy.

Promoting political democracy is aimed principally at ensuring that the whole body of workers, led by the party, will continue to enhance their proletarian political consciousness and fully exercise "five major rights":

(1) the right to struggle against all acts which run counter to the policies and guidelines of the party and the state and against foul wind and evil atmosphere;

(2) the right to examine the revolutionization of leading organs and the observance of rules and regulations by the leading cadres;

(3) the right to criticize the cadres at any conference;

(4) the right to hear and discuss reports by leading cadres on work; and

(5) the right to elect basic-level cadres through the democratic process.

Giving free rein to production democracy is aimed at ensuring that the workers will participate in production and technical management, combining specialized management with management by the masses. . . .

In order to safeguard the right of the workers to run their own house, Tach'ing has provided for workers at production posts "five big functional rights":

(1) the right to refuse to take orders having nothing to do with their production posts;

(2) the right to refuse to operate a machine which is due for overhaul;

(3) the right to refuse to let unqualified personnel operate a machine;

(4) the right to report immediately to the higher level on hidden dangers in production and, should the higher level fail to give any instruction or take any action, to suspend production when suspension is the only way to avoid accidents; and

(5) the right to refuse to commence production where there are no working regulations, quality standards, and safety measures.

As for capital construction workers, they are also empowered not to carry out construction under five conditions; namely,

(1) they may not start operation if their task is not clearly defined and the construction blueprints are not clear;

(2) they may not start operation if the quality, specifications, and technical measures are not clear;

(3) they may not start operation when the materials necessary for construction are not well prepared;

(4) they may not start operation if the construction equipment is not in good condition; and

(5) they may not start the next operation sequence if the quality of the previous operation sequence is not up to standard.

Promotion of economic democracy is designed to ensure that the masses will take part in the economic and food management of the enterprise and exercise four rights:

(1) the right to fight against all phenomena of extravagance and waste;

(2) the right to participate in the economic accounting of the enterprise;

(3) the right to participate in the dining hall management and to examine the accounts of the dining hall; and

(4) the right to participate in the distribution of farm and subsidiary production. . . .

It is necessary to develop the party revolutionary traditions of hard work and plain living. . . .

How to promote the party's revolutionary traditions of hard work and plain living? Our way is:

To promote the spirit of "storming a fortress." That is, with regard to production and construction we must seek new techniques and high quality, while our living facilities should be simple and indigenous. Whether it is plant construction or living facilities, we must give attention to practicality and must not chase after formalism and grandeur. We should not build tall buildings including office buildings, auditoriums, hostels and reception houses. Size should be determined by local conditions and local materials must be used. We must save construction funds for the state and establish the idea of taking pride in plain living among the workers. . . .

Promote the "one penny" spirit. That is, we must not waste one drop of oil, one unit of electricity, one tael of coal, one inch of steel or timber. Everybody must practice austerity. Austerity must be practiced everywhere, in everything, and at all times.

Promote the spirit of never letting a flaw in quality pass unnoticed. We must give top priority to quality.

*It is necessary to launch the technical innovation
and technical revolution movement on a large scale
and catch up with and surpass the advanced world levels. . . .*

"Triple combination" is the most effective way for technical innovations and technical revolution.

In effecting this "triple combination," it is essential to bring into full play the roles of the leading cadres, workers, and technicians. "Triple combination" must be effected from investigation and study, formulation of plans, drafting of designs, organization of supply of equipment and materials, manufacture of equipment, experiments on the spot and application of results of experiments in production all the way to the summarization and popularization of results of experiments. The workers call this "a dragon's triple combination."

*It is necessary to revolutionize the leadership
and organs. . . .*

In revolutionizing the leadership and the organs during these years, our way has been to:

1. Go to the front in person and go to stay at the basic level.

Leading cadres must persist in staying at selected spots and regard this as a system. Through staying at selected spots, they must continuously seek to understand the work the masses are doing, what they think and what they want. . . .

2. Adopt the work methods of "first and second lines," "three-three system" and face to face leadership.

Tach'ing has upheld the principle laid down by Chairman

Mao to the effect that "big power must be centralized while small power must be decentralized. Decisions reached at the party committee must be implemented by various quarters, and they must be implemented resolutely and on the basis of principles. The party committee should be responsible for inspection of work." It has persistently executed the system of division of work and responsibility under the collective leadership of the party committee. We have introduced the work methods of "first and second lines," "three-three system" and face to face leadership in a way consistent with the fact that Tach'ing is a large modern enterprise.

The "second line" of the "first and second lines" is composed of the principal leading cadres of the party committee of the oil field. They do not command production directly and do not concern themselves with complicated routine affairs. Instead, they attach special importance to bringing politics to the fore. In the main they are faced with four tasks: (1) they must acquaint themselves with the thought of Mao Tsetung, the policies and guidelines of the party center and the directives of the higher authorities concerned; (2) they must go to the basic level to stay at selected spots and carry out investigations and research; (3) they must size up the general situation, see the main stream, point out the direction, and grasp the central issues; (4) they must examine and assist in the work of the "first line," seek out shortcomings and mistakes, and sum up experiences.

The "first line" is composed of three units—the political headquarters, the production office, and the livelihood office. Leading comrades of the "first line" are to concretely organize the execution of decisions made by the party committee in various fields—political, production, and livelihood. They exercise unified command over daily production.

Introduction of the division of work of the "first and second lines" gives everyone a clear goal to work for and urges him to work hard. In this way, work may be done well with uniform steps. This avoids division of work according to departments and types of operation, for such division would lead to competition for selfish reasons.

The "three-three system" is that one-third of the working personnel of an organ stay in the office to handle routine work, another one-third do field work, and still another one-third stay and work at selected basic-level spots. In this way, the higher and lower levels, and the points and the whole area, are connected. . . .

3. Insist that leading cadres abide by "three agreements."

These "three agreements" are as follows:

(1) To persevere in the fine traditions of hard work and plain living without claiming any special privileges.

They will not build office buildings, auditoriums, hostels, and reception houses; they will live in "makeshift dwellings" or single-story houses. They will hold no parties and present no gifts; they will neither dance nor put a sofa in their office. They will eat in collective dining rooms. And they will teach their children not to seek privileges for themselves.

(2) They must persist in participating in physical labor and must never be bureaucrats sitting high above the people.

Cadres should participate in labor at fixed hours. They must submit to the leadership of team and group leaders. They must create material wealth. Moreover, they must effect "five combinations": combination of participation in labor with leadership work, with work on experimental plots, with the carrying out of investigations and studies and the solution of problems, with the learning of operating techniques, and with their own administrative work.

(3) Persist in being "honest" and "strict"; never feel conceited or tell lies. . . .

Combine industry with agriculture and town with
countryside, and progressively reduce
the three differences. . . .

If we build an industrial or mining enterprise of a foreign pattern, we shall have to build or expand a city; we shall have to build a welfare district with tall buildings and use walls to keep the peasants away. This is bound to lead to separation from the masses to a serious extent and to expansion of the differences between industry and agriculture and between town and countryside; it will jeopardize the worker-peasant alliance and be harmful to socialist construction and the transition to a communist society. . . .

The construction of the mining district must be based on the principle of integrating industry with agriculture and town with countryside for the benefit of production and the people's livelihood. Workers' living quarters should be scattered and not concentrated in one area. A large city should not be built. The dependents of the workers must be properly organized to take part in labor and develop production. . . .

At present, Tach'ing has preliminarily built a new socialist mining district where town and countryside, industry and agriculture, and government and enterprise are integrated.

Tach'ing does not build a concentrated urban area; instead it has built residential points in scattered places. At the moment, it has completed three workers' towns and several dozen central residential points (each consisting of 300-400 households) and residential points (each with 100-200 households). Every central residential point with four or five residential points surrounding it becomes a livelihood base. Within this base are set up a mechanized farming station, an agricultural technical research station, a primary school, a part-work (farming) and part-study middle school, a bookstore, a health clinic, a nursery, a mess hall, a shoe repair shop, a sewing and mending unit, a post and telecommunication agency, and a savings office. These are establishments for production, livelihood, culture, education, and health. Their presence contributes to production and to the improvement of living standards. Within residential points all houses built are single-story houses of earth. . . .

At present, the dependents whom the oil field has organized to take part in various kinds of collective productive labor represent 95 percent of the total number of dependents with labor capacity. They are engaged in farm and subsidiary production in the entire mining district. In addition, they are also charged with the task of maintaining several hundred kilometers of highways; they work in industry as auxiliary laborers and are engaged in service trades. Today, the residential points and production teams are managed by the dependents themselves— and are managed well. The dependents constitute an important force for the construction of the mining district. Their spiritual outlook has undergone a marked change. . . .

In organizing the dependents to engage in productive labor, Tach'ing has put into force the principle of "taking the team as the foundation, practicing unified accounting, assessing work performance and recording work points, and paying according to work." All products are without exception delivered to the proper authorities. Whether they are engaged in industry or agriculture or engage in service work or work as teachers, the dependents do not receive salaries; their work is assessed and work points are recorded for them, and those who work more are paid more. . . .

Tach'ing oil field is actively enforcing two systems of labor and two systems of education. Today, it has introduced universal primary education and junior middle education and established an education network ranging from primary school to university, including primary schools, part-farming and part-study junior middle schools, part-work and part-study schools and a part-work and part-study petroleum college. . . .

In order to strengthen centralized and unified leadership in the mining district, Tach'ing has established an administration in the mining district so as to effect integration of government with enterprise. The party committee of the oil field is the party committee of the mining district. The work of the government and that of the enterprise are carried out under the unified leadership of the party committee.

Through the construction of the Tach'ing mining district, we have gained the following points of understanding with respect to reduction in the differences between town and countryside, between industry and agriculture, and between mental and physical labor:

1. We must develop the Yenan spirit. Using simple and indigenous equipment and local materials, Tach'ing has built residential points in scattered places. It builds no walls and no welfare zone with tall buildings. Thus it has inherited and developed the Yenan spirit. By so doing, the living standards of the workers and dependents are similar to those of the local peasants. . . .

2. We must develop the Nanniwan spirit and the working style of the old Eighth Route Army. Utilizing the favorable conditions created by the large size of the oil field and by plenty of wasteland, Tach'ing has reclaimed the wasteland and put it under the plough, thereby achieving an abundance of food and clothing. While putting the wasteland under cultiva-

tion, it has educated the dependents of workers and organized them to participate in collective productive labor, thereby promoting their revolutionization. . . .

3. We must develop the spirit of the Anti-Japanese Resistance University. We must operate schools arduously by relying on our own efforts. We must enforce two systems of education and set up part-work and part-study, part-farming and part-study schools on a large scale. We must train new-type laborers who can write and labor so as to create conditions for the gradual reduction of the differences between mental and physical labor. . . .

Only if we run the enterprise and construct the mining district in such revolutionary spirit, shall we be able to turn the enterprise into an ideological position for the proletariat, a scientific and technical position for industry and agriculture, and a position for socialist culture and education. We shall integrate town with countryside and industry with agriculture and progressively reduce the three great differences.

<h3 style="text-align:center">3. MAO TSETUNG, ON
THE ANSHAN CONSTITUTION</h3>

The Anshan Iron and Steel Works, constructed in the period of Japanese rule in Manchuria, was China's first large modern enterprise and the center of its heavy industry. The focus of industrialization during the first five-year plan, today it is an advanced complex with more than 100,000 workers supplying 25 percent of the nation's steel, the foundation of the industrial economy. The constitution of the Anshan Steel Company was proposed by the workers of Anshan and approved by Mao in March 1960. The constitution encapsulates the major lessons derived from the Great Leap in industry, particularly the rejection of Soviet one-man management in favor of collective responsibility and mass participation. Its five principles include:

Mao Tsetung: Note on "Charter of the Anshan Iron and Steel Company." JMJP March 22, 1960. PR April 1, 1977.

(1) stick to putting politics in command; (2) strengthen party leadership; (3) go in for mass movements in a big way; (4) institute the two-one-three system of management; and (5) vigorously carry out technical revolution. Although written in 1960 it was not widely disseminated until 1968 during the Cultural Revolution.

In the post-leap retrenchment principles of worker participation were never explicitly abandoned, though attempts to rationalize the experiments in "two participations, one reform, and the triple combination" tended to curb the role of workers in management and favor stronger central and managerial control. Debate over industrial efficiency and the respective roles of profits and politics in industry led to a limited resurgence of hierarchical structures, material incentives and the primacy of the profit motive as illustrated by the seventy articles in industry prepared by Po I-po in 1961. Struggles nevertheless continued within the factories.

The Cultural Revolution reaffirmed the need to revolutionize factory management touching off another wave in the working class movement. In 1968 the Anshan Constitution gained nation-wide acclaim as the most succinct and thoroughgoing Chinese attempt to define managerial principles embodying socialist relations in the factory. The Anshan Constitution seeks to transform the workplace by reducing hierarchical distinctions within the factory and actively involving workers in decision-making, planning, technical innovation, indeed in all aspects of factory and industrial life.

This report of the Anshan party committee is very good. The more one reads it the more delighted one gets. It doesn't strike one as too long, in fact, one would be willing to read it even if it were longer; this is because the problems raised in the report are factual, well reasoned, and very absorbing. With more than 100,000 workers and staff members, the Anshan Iron and Steel Company is the country's biggest enterprise. Formerly, people there thought that their enterprise was a modernized one and there was no need for technical revolution. They were opposed to launching vigorous mass movements, to the principle of cadre participation in productive labor and worker participation in

management, of reform of irrational and outdated rules and
regulations and of close cooperation among cadres, workers,
and technicians, and opposed to putting politics in command;
they relied on just a few people working in seclusion. Many
favored the system of placing responsibility solely on the factory director and were against the system of the factory director designated to undertake responsibility under the leadership
of the party committee. They held that the "Charter of the
Magnitogorsk Iron and Steel Combine" (a set of authoritative
rules practiced in a big steel plant in the Soviet Union) was
sacred. That was the situation up to the Great Leap Forward in
1958, which marked the first stage. The year 1959 marked the
second stage, when people began to think things over, began to
have faith in the mass movement, and began to question the
system of placing responsibility solely on the factory director
and the Charter of the Magnitogorsk Iron and Steel Combine.
During the Lushan Meeting of July 1959, the Central Committee received a good report from them, which spoke in favor of
the Great Leap Forward, of opposing the right deviation and
making utmost exertions; it also put forward a high but practicable target. The Central Committee was extremely pleased
with the report and had it circulated to the comrades concerned
with its comment. They immediately relayed it by telephone to
their respective provinces, municipalities and autonomous regions, thus helping the struggle going on at the time to criticize
right opportunism. The present report (March 1960) takes another step forward; it does not smack of the Charter of the
Magnitogorsk Iron and Steel Combine, but has given birth to a
Charter of the Anshan Iron and Steel Company. Here emerges
the Charter of the Anshan Iron and Steel Company in China, in
the Far East. This marks the third stage. Now this report is
being passed on to you and you are asked to transmit it to the
large and medium-sized enterprises under your administration
and to the party committees of all large and medium-sized cities
and, of course, you may also transmit it to prefectural party
committees and other cities. It should be used as a document
for study by cadres in order to stimulate their minds and make
them think about the affairs in their own units, so that under
due leadership a great Marxist-Leninist movement of economic
and technical revolution will be carried out link by link and

wave upon wave in the cities and the countryside during the whole year of 1960.

4. WAGES AND THE RESTRICTION OF BOURGEOIS RIGHT

Inequality persists and must persist under socialism under conditions of scarcity. China has nevertheless sought (and with striking success) to reduce the major inequalities while refining socialist distribution systems which allocate income on the basis of work. Under the eight-grade wage system workers within a particular industry receive wages according to skill, diligence, political consciousness, and length of service. But the differential between the highest and lowest wage is unusually small, usually on the order of 3:1. Differences nevertheless persist within individual factories, between state and cooperative industries, between state employees and contract workers, and between city and countryside.

The present discussion of wages by workers in Shanghai underlines the key tensions within the wage system. Drawing on the model of the Paris Commune, it suggests that equitable patterns characteristic of communism can gradually emerge with economic growth and class struggle during the socialist era.

Throughout the decade of the Cultural Revolution focus on curbing inequality meant, among other things, that the income of the industrial workforce remained essentially frozen to reduce the urban-rural gap. Documents like this one defended such policies against the drive by many workers to raise salaries, a drive which eventually bore fruit in the 1977 wage hike. Even then, however, the impact of egalitarian thinking is clear as the principal beneficiaries are workers in the lowest grades, while salaries for higher paid workers and technicians reportedly remain frozen.

Comrades from the Shanghai Hutung Shipyards and the Sixth Economic Group of the Shanghai Municipal May Seventh Cadre Schools: *Two Kinds of Society, Two Kinds of Wages* (Shanghai, 1974). Translated by Donald Long and Robert Salasin.

In the old society, we workers worked for the capitalists and received wages; in the new society we labor for socialism and still receive wages. But how are the wages and distribution of these two societies fundamentally different? Today, in our socialist society, how exactly should we treat questions of distribution and wages? In these questions where will the struggle between the two classes and the two class lines manifest itself? . . .

Socialism has eliminated the system of hired labor, and has also liberated the worker's wage level from the limits of capitalism, has expanded it to whatever is permissible according to society's current productive power, even to the extent of caring for everyone based on the limits of what is permitted within both long- and short-term interests. . . .

Socialist accumulation and the basic interests of the working people are completely consistent, but this is not to imply that there are no contradictions between accumulation and consumption. Each year the way in which the national income is distributed especially since our country is not yet really well-off, necessarily creates contradictions between accumulation and consumption. . . . Chairman Mao's directive: "In questions of distribution, we must pay attention to national interest, collective interest, and individual interest" is our fundamental principle to correctly handle the contradiction between accumulation and consumption. On the basis of the continual development of socialist production, we must gradually raise the level of working people's living standards. However, our nation is a developing country and the economy is still relatively backward; in order to lead our nation to progress another step toward prosperity and power, we must maintain a relatively high level of accumulation, and pass through a period of several decades of hard and bitter struggle. . . .

The socialist wage is the socialist nation's basic principle, based on "from each according to his ability, to each according to his work"; it is the basic form through which the workers carry out the distribution of consumer goods to the individual. "From each according to his ability, to each according to his work" is to say that each individual laborer must give his greatest effort for socialist labor, while society distributes differing amounts of consumer goods based on the conditions of the individual's labor, the size of his contribution to society. "From each according to his ability" is a premise of this division according to labor. . . .

Why must a socialist society put "from each according to his ability, to each according to his work" into effect rather than "to each according to his need"? . . . The supply of goods has still not reached the stage of abundance necessary for the latter stage. . . . It is absolutely impossible to jump over the current objective socioeconomic conditions in order to arbitrarily determine the social distribution system. It is only in forwarding the principle of "from each according to his ability, to each according to his work" that it is possible to match the level of the development of socialist society's productive power and the stage of human consciousness, only then is it possible to match understanding with what the vast laboring peoples receive.

The establishment of the previously mentioned type of socialist distributive system, "from each according to his ability, to each according to his work," is the negation of the capitalist system of distribution in which "the worker does not get, and the getter does not work"; it is a deeply etched revolution against the exploiting class's distributive system. Labor truly becomes the measure of society's distribution of consumer goods. . . .

But we must still see that the principle "from each according to his ability, to each according to his work" is a manifestation of equal right still limited by the framework of the bourgeoisie. This framework is that of bourgeois right, because under the principle of "from each according to his ability, to each according to his work," exchange is most commonly still governed by the rules of commodity exchange: one form of labor may be exchanged for another type of equal labor. Under this mode of distribution, each and every person's labor is rewarded on the basis of an equal standard—labor is the measure and from that perspective [the reward] appears equal. But great differences exist in the conditions of individual laborers: some are stronger, some weaker; some have a high cultural level, some a lower one; some have more mouths to feed, some fewer, and so forth. Therefore, to use a unified measure of labor as the measure of distribution and to apply this to very unequal individuals must result in real inequality and differences of living standards. The peculiarities of bourgeois right manifest themselves; equal right will in fact be the premise of inequality. . . . But this type of corrupt practice is unavoidable in a socialist society, for as Marx pointed out, "Right can never be higher than the economic structure of society and its cultural development conditioned thereby." (*Critique of the Gotha Program*). . . .

How ought we to treat this kind of bourgeois right? In order to thoroughly and correctly implement "from each according to his ability, to each according to his work" we must oppose these two tendencies: (1) to deny that inequality exists or to play at egalitarianism and (2) to allow the differences to grow. . . .

In a socialist society, if differences are not acknowledged, if the principle of distribution according to labor is rejected, if one pays no attention to whether the laborer's work is good or bad, and if one uniformly averages distribution of consumer goods to individuals, this can only damage the activism of the socialist labor of the masses and become detrimental to productive power. . . .

The principle of distribution in a socialist society is "from each according to his ability, to each according to his work." But this is not the proletariat's final ideal. The final goal of the proletariat is the institution of communism. On the banner of communism is inscribed: "From each according to his ability, to each according to his need." In a socialist society it is necessary to acknowledge differences in the rewards for labor, but the differences ought not to be too great, and certainly should not be allowed to grow larger. We must actively create the conditions for communist society's stage, "from each according to his ability, to each according to his need," and should constantly strive to lessen the three great differences and unceasingly extirpate the influence of bourgeois right. While a socialist society is actualizing the fundamental principle "from each according to his ability, to each according to his work," it must pay attention to gradually lessening differences and gradually increasing the factor of distribution according to need. Various types of welfare measures and so forth are in reality the sprouts of communist distribution according to need. . . .

We ought to rationally and gradually shrink, not expand, the distance between the individual incomes of the masses of people and those of functionaries in the party, the national government, in industry, and in the people's communes. We must prevent all functionaries from using professional status to obtain any special privilege. To resolutely uphold the principle of the Paris Commune and to oppose a system of high salaries (for the few) has the advantage of promoting intimate relations between party and masses, provides a style of frugality and struggle, and contributes to the revolutionization of the thinking of many cadres.

5. THE PROLETARIAT IN THE EDUCATIONAL REVOLUTION

Educational revolution was an integral part of the Cultural Revolution's program to transform culture and ideas consistent with the emergence of the proletariat to predominance in the workplace and society. In the late 1960s as all state universities and high schools closed to permit students and faculty to participate in the movement as well as to restructure the basic character and method of higher education, new schools proliferated designed to integrate mental and manual labor and to combat elitism. These included May Seventh cadre schools which combined physical labor, theoretical and practical study and self-criticism and a variety of educational experiments in factories and communes across the country.

Shanghai was at the forefront of the educational revolution and Mao designated the Shanghai Machine Tools Plant a national model in providing advanced education for factory workers. The goal: to train a corps of technicians from the ranks of factory workers combining practical experience, theory, and political awareness through advanced technical education integrated with the productive process. At this time many factories initiated worker universities which provided courses linking theory and practice and ranging from a few weeks to several years. Along with the insistence that technical cadres participate in productive labor and that three-in-one combinations of work-

*ers, technicians, and cadres assume responsibility for techno-
logical innovation, the new educational opportunities for
workers provided the backbone of the system of reducing and
overcoming the differences between workers and technicians,
between workers and managers, and between those who work
with their hands and those who work with their minds. Since
the Cultural Revolution these principles have been applied and
developed in commune-run universities, in hospital-run medical
schools, and in a variety of other educational institutions which
responded to the needs of working people for higher education.
Many of these new schools followed the work-study formula
which had flourished during the Great Leap and whose roots
can be traced back to the Anti-Japanese Resistance. The model
for such schools was the Kiangsi Communist Labor University
which Mao singled out for special praise in 1961 at a time when
its nearly 100 campuses had enrolled 50,000 students—and
when such experiments were being curtailed by the Liu Shao-
ch'i leadership in many regions: "A school run on the basis of
part-work and part-study," Mao commented, "self-supporting
through hard work, without having to ask the state for a single
cent, a school embracing primary school, middle school, and
college courses and functioning mostly in the hilly regions of
the province though also on the plains—such a school is a very
fine one indeed."*

A. The Factory as University

Editor's Note:
    In these penetrating words Chairman Mao recently pointed
out:

> It is still necessary to have universities; here I refer
> mainly to colleges of science and engineering. However, it
> is essential to shorten the length of schooling, revolu-
> tionize education, put proletarian politics in command and
> take the road of the Shanghai Machine Tools Plant in

The Road for Training Engineering and Technical Personnel Indicated
by the Shanghai Machine Tools Plant. JMJP, July 22, 1968. Foreign
Languages Press Pamphlet.

training technicians from among the workers. Students should be selected from among workers and peasants with practical experience, and they should return to production after a few years' study.

This great call of Chairman Mao's is our militant program for carrying the proletarian revolution in education through to the end. . . .

The Shanghai Machine Tools Plant is a large factory famous for its production of precision grinding machines. It has a technical force of more than 600 engineers and technicians which is made up of people from three sources: 45 percent of them are from the ranks of the workers, 50 percent are post-liberation college graduates and the remainder are old technicians trained before liberation. The tempest of the Great Proletarian Cultural Revolution has brought about a profound change in the ranks of the technicians of this plant.

This great revolutionary change manifests itself mainly in the following ways:

First, . . . many technicians of worker origin, revolutionary young technicians, and revolutionary cadres are now the masters in scientific research and technical designing. . . .

Second, the counter-revolutionary, revisionist line pushed by China's Khrushchev in the technical sphere and the reactionary bourgeois world outlook have been sharply criticized. . . . The mental outlook of many of the young technicians has now undergone a marked change. They understand that the desire for fame and gain is the root cause of revisionism and that one should not seek bourgeois laurels. . . . All the technicians have volunteered to work in the shops alongside the workers. Together they study and improve designs. . . .

Third, relations between the workers and technicians have changed. The few capitalist roaders and reactionary "authorities" in the plant advocated a "one-to-one" combination, that is, one worker serving one technician. This so-called combination meant "the engineer gives the word and the worker does the job," or "the engineer has the idea and the worker carries it out." . . . They put out a set of rules and regulations to control, check and suppress the workers. Every worker was expected to memorize and act on the more than 170 rules in the "Handbook for a Worker in Production." All this further widened the gap between workers and technicians. During the Great Cultural Revolution, a "three-in-one" combination of workers, revolutionary technicians, and revolutionary cadres was introduced in the plant. The rank-and-file workers now take part in designing and the technicians go to operate machines in the first line of production, closely linking theory with practice. As a result, there is a big improvement in the relations between workers and technicians.

Road for Training Engineering and Technical Personnel

... At present, the overwhelming majority of the technical personnel of worker origin have become the technological backbone of the plant and about one-tenth of them are capable of independently designing high-grade, precision, and advanced new products. . . .

Selecting technical personnel from among the workers is the road for training proletarian engineers and technicians. . . .

The Orientation for Educational Revolution Indicated by the Plant

In accordance with Chairman Mao's thinking on education and in view of the actual conditions in the plant, the workers and technical personnel put forward the following opinions and ideas in respect to the revolution in education:

First, schools must train "workers with both socialist consciousness and culture," as pointed out by Chairman Mao and not "intellectual aristocrats" who are divorced from proletarian politics, from the worker and peasant masses and from production, as the revisionist educational line produced. . . .

Second, school education must be combined with productive labor. . . . Workers and technical personnel at this plant suggest that schools should have experienced workers as teachers and let workers appear on the classroom platform. Some courses can be given by workers in the workshops.

Third, as to the source of engineering and technical personnel, they maintain that, apart from continuing to promote technical personnel from among the workers, junior and senior middle school graduates who are good politically and ideologically and have two to three or four to five years of practical experience in production should be picked from grassroots units and sent to colleges to study. All conditions now exist for this to be done. . . .

Fourth, on the question of reforming the present technical force in factories and raising its level, they point out that large numbers of school-trained technical personnel have for a long time been poisoned by the revisionist educational line and the revisionist line in running enterprises. . . .

B. Higher Education Walks on Two Legs

Shanghai has sixteen institutions of higher learning. They include universities, engineering, medical, and teachers' colleges, and fine arts institutes. Their enrollment is over 26,000 worker-peasant-soldier students.

But this is not the whole picture. Many factories run workers' universities; communes and state farms run part-time universities; and some hospitals have set up medical schools. Universities and technical institutes maintain correspondence schools for middle school graduates who have gone to work in the countryside, and run short training courses in various specialties for factories, communes, and other units. The number of people in this new kind of study is several times the number in the sixteen regular institutes of higher learning.

This policy of both running ordinary universities and developing various other forms of higher education is called "walking on two legs." It was adopted to train more people better able to meet the needs of the rapid development of socialist revolution and construction.

The Cultural Revolution thoroughly criticized the revisionist

Higher Education in Shanghai "Walks on Two Legs." *China Reconstructs*, April 1975.

line that divorced schools from proletarian politics, real life, and work. The resulting revolution in education broke the ideological fetters of the old concept of universities, changed institutions of higher learning, and led to the creation of other forms of university-level education. . . .

Short Training Courses

There are two types of students at many of Shanghai's universities. One is the regular student in the three-year courses, most of whom are around twenty years old. The other is the student in the short training courses run especially for factories, communes, and other units. Their ages vary, for many are workers with long years of practical experience. These have been sent to study to meet the requirements of their jobs and continue to receive their regular pay. Some of them study half a day and work the other half.

Not long ago the chemistry department of Futan University ran a short course in the analysis of trace quantities of mercury with a new instrument used in monitoring industrial waste. The students were all doing antipollution work. They studied the principles, structure and use of the new instrument, exchanged experience on mercury analysis, and tested samples of food or water from their own units. Learning through actual practice, they mastered the necessary theoretical and practical knowledge and returned to their units with the new instruments made for them by the university.

As such short courses expanded, teachers from many schools went out to run courses in factories, communes, and army units. Teaching on the spot makes it possible to link teaching more closely with reality and to reach more students.

The subjects are decided after thorough study of the needs of the units concerned. This makes what the students learn of immediate practical use. For instance, Chiaot'ung University ran fifteen courses on cold extrusion, training a core of 2,000 technicians for some 200 factories. . . .

Correspondence Courses

Since the Cultural Revolution began in 1966, a million Shanghai middle school graduates have gone to help build a new socialist countryside. They realize that to do a better job in production—to become more skilled in serving the people—they need more education.

Shanghai's answer is correspondence courses. Since last year thirteen universities have set up part-time correspondence courses in twenty-three subjects for 30,000 young people in five provinces. . . .

The courses are closely related to the needs of rural life. Grouped mainly under politics, language, agricultural techniques, and medicine and health, they run for six months to a year. Students form study groups by subject, study the material sent from the school by themselves, then meet to discuss it. They can write to the school to ask questions. The school answers but it also regularly sends teachers to make the rounds of the study groups, where they run supplementary short training courses for the correspondence students. . . .

Factory-Run Universities

In a directive July 21, 1968, Chairman Mao said that educational work should "take the road of the Shanghai Machine Tools Plant in training technicians from among the workers. Students should be selected from among workers and peasants with practical experience, and they should return to production after a few years' study."

Two months later this 6,000-worker plant set up the "July 21" Workers' University.

The students all had experience in machine building. Some of the teachers came from polytechnic institutes, others were experienced workers and technicians in the plant. The first course was on the design and construction of grinders. The students took part in political movements, studied Marxism–Leninism–Mao Tsetung thought, did some work and spent two-thirds of their study time on seven professional courses: mechanical drawing, mathematics, engineering mechanics, hydraulics, electrical devices, design and construction of grinders, and foreign language.

A special feature was that the three-year course was divided into four stages closely linked with the actual design and building of products in the plant: a brief study of basic knowledge, practice and study, raising theoretical level, and more practice. This helped students understand theory on the basis of practice. After the course, they were able to do calculations for and design machine tools or major sub-assemblies on their own. The school has graduated over 150 worker-students in the past six years. . . .

Similar workers' universities have been set up by many other plants. Some are run by one plant, some by several plants, others in cooperation with universities or research institutes. By December 1974 there were 130 "July 21" workers' universities in Shanghai with an enrollment of 10,000. Today 3,600 graduates have gone back to become the technical core of their plants. . . .

Farm Universities

Ch'ungming Island near Shanghai has a number of state farms. In 1974, to meet the needs of expanding production, these farms set up ten part-time universities offering ten courses including politics, Chinese language, agriculture, fundamentals of industry, water conservancy, animal husbandry, medicine, and revolutionary art and literature. Three thousand young people of middle school level enrolled.

These schools teach on the farms, setting the length of the course by the amount and nature of the study material. The students continue to do farm work and their study time is shortened during the busy season. The teachers are experienced workers, peasants and farm technicians, and also include university professors and scientists doing research work in the countryside. The schools have compiled teaching materials suited to local farming conditions. . . .

Hospital-Run Medical Schools

Medical schools alone cannot train enough doctors to meet the growing demands of medical and health work in town and country. Shanghai's Huashan Hospital and the First and Sixth People's Hospitals have made a bold attempt to deal with this problem by setting up their own medical schools. Huashan Hospital started a three-year experimental course in 1970.

Forty-two students enrolled, all with two years or more of work in industry or agriculture. Eighteen of them had been "barefoot doctors" or army health workers. This class graduated in 1974 and their training proved sound. They diagnose and treat common illnesses, and handle emergency cases of heart failure, insecticide poisoning, shock and hemorrhage. Surgeons among them can do appendix and hernia operations, and with guidance from experienced doctors they can also do more difficult upper-abdominal surgery such as removal of the spleen, gall bladder, and most of the stomach. Ninety-eight students enrolled in 1973 and 120 in 1974.

C. THE UNINTERRUPTED REVOLUTION
IN THE COUNTRYSIDE

1. CH'EN YUNG-KUEI,
MANAGEMENT, REMUNERATION, AND CONSCIOUSNESS
IN THE TACHAI BRIGADE

What has made Tachai the quintessential model for the road to socialism in the countryside? Ch'en Yung-kuei, the brigade's party secretary, subsequently a vice premier and Politburo member, in this lecture provides a detailed account of the brigade's step-by-step advance through struggle and experimentation toward higher forms of socialist practice consonant with the development of the productive forces and popular consciousness and closely attuned to the concrete problems of village life.

Above all Tachai symbolizes the community-based self-reliant struggle to simultaneously transform human relations and the harshest of natural environments through the conscious implementation of mass line principles. In its approach to management and remuneration we see embodied the tension between the socialist principle "to each according to one's work" and embryonic "sprouts of communism" in the planned effort to reduce income inequality, and to break through the distinction between laborer and cadre, between those who work with their hands and those who work with their minds. Tachai's development of a system designed to maximize the collective conscious-

A Vivid Lesson in Bringing Politics to the Fore: On Tachai Brigade's Experience in Firmly Following the Socialist Direction of Labor Management. JMJP March 22, 1966. SCPRP 3675.

ness and contribution of each of its members crystallized out of the crisis conditions precipitated by the 1963 floods which threatened to wipe out the community's hard-won gains. Ch'en summed up the essence of the system which made Tachai a model not only of socialist practice but of high and increasing productivity in these words: "The object was to enable commune members to raise generally their ideological awareness, so that they might know that in order to increase their personal income, they must increase output, and to increase output, they must labor carefully and ensure the good quality of farm jobs done." In Tachai and throughout the countryside the challenge to rural leadership lies in devising systems which work to the mutual advantage of the individual and collective so as to progressively strengthen the collective, develop scientific farming and mechanizations, and bring prosperity to the countryside, which in turn provides the basis for higher socialist consciousness.

In Carrying Out Operations and Management, It Is Necessary to Persevere in the Struggle Between the Two Roads

Chairman Mao tells us that in the period of transition there will still be class struggle in our country. This class struggle between the two roads is reflected in our rural areas largely in operations and management. . . .

To wage struggle, two things are essential. The basic thing is to carry out political work well with the thought of Mao Tsetung as a weapon. In other words, it is necessary to educate cadres and commune members so that they may increase their socialist and communist ideological consciousness, raise the level of their understanding of policy, realize that class struggle is long term, not short term, and set up the splendid will to rely on themselves, work hard for the future, work boldly and practically, and build socialism with a heaven-and-earth-changing effort.

The other thing is a system of management capable of consolidating and developing the collective economy, so as to enable every commune member to work according to the regulations and systems of the collective economy.

When these two things are well done, politics will have been put in command. Then there will be no need to worry that production may not go up and work may not be done well. . . .

First, the socialist direction should be firmly followed and capitalist influence prevented, so that collective economy may be consolidated and developed. This is the kingpin in all work, especially in the work of business operations and management. . . .

We want to implement, taking local conditions into consideration, the guideline of all-round development of agriculture, forestry, livestock breeding, sideline production and fisheries, while some people advocate simultaneous development of agriculture and commerce, and abandon cultivation of food crops in favor of sideline production, saying: "For food we depend on the collective; for spending money we must depend on ourselves."

—We want to develop the advantages of collective economy and improve the system of management of the collective economy, but some people extol the advantages of individual farming and advocate the underwriting of production by groups, the underwriting of labor by households, decentralization of livestock, and individual undertaking of sideline production.

—We want to rely on poor and lower middle peasants, but some people say that poor peasants should be relied on only for agrarian reform, while the middle peasants should be relied on for production and merchants should be relied on for sideline production. They also say that since landlords no longer own land and rich peasants are no longer rich, and since both live on the work points they earn, everyone is on the same footing.

—We want to put politics in command in all things and recognize differences in wages, but some people stress the primacy of work points and material incentives and demand high work points.

—We want to combine immediate interests with long-term interests, but some people want to share everything and consume everything, preferring to lead a hand-to-mouth existence.

—We want everyone to be honest, speak the truth, and act according to the policies of the state, but some people want to report a smaller output, exaggerate natural calamities, conceal food grain, and engage in free trade.

Is that not open class struggle? . . .

Since we are building socialism, our regulations must have as their object the maintenance of the collective interests of socialism. . . . We have to take care of our own unit, but more important still, the whole country and the whole world. If our regulations and systems do not let us do that, they will be of no use. On the contrary, they will let capitalism gain the ascendancy.

Second, the socialist principle of distribution should be put into effect, so as to further boost the enthusiasm of the great masses of commune members. . . .

Some people say that to boost the enthusiasm of commune members for work, it is necessary to have recourse to material incentives. I say that we must resolutely uphold the socialist principle of distribution, that we cannot adopt absolute egalitarianism. Absolute egalitarianism cannot be adopted now or at any time in the future. But we cannot on the other hand resort to material incentives, nor can we confuse the principle of more pay for more labor with material incentives. In other words, we have to recognize some difference, but the differences must not be too great.

Only in this way can we better realize the socialist principle of distribution, whip up the eagerness for collective production of the great masses of commune members and not just some of them, and help to make a success of the collective economy.

Third, we must insist on simplicity, feasibility, and helpfulness to the masses in a system so that it will not be too complicated and vexatious. If systems are made too complicated and vexatious, they may as well be nonexistent in practice. What everyone does every day is productive labor, not enforcing systems. Coming home with one's feet covered with mud after a hard day's work, who would trouble one's self about systems? . . .

Fourth, the principle of taking measures to suit local needs must be firmly upheld, and concrete measures must be worked out in conformity with local conditions. In other words, there must be no mechanical imitation, separation from reality or subjective imaginings. . . .

Fifth, the system of having cadres participate in labor must be firmly upheld. Some people think that a great contradiction exists between official work and labor, that they cannot labor if they are to do their work well, and that they cannot do their work well if they take part in labor. I say that we cannot view it that way. Labor itself is part of our work. If we do not take part in labor, we shall not be doing our work well. That is a simple truth. . . .

How can a cadre "labor dynamically"?

(1) He must do three jobs, namely, heavy jobs, dirty jobs, and key jobs, and set a good example for commune members. . . .

(2) He must carry out scientific experiment while taking part in labor and thoroughly grasp the "temperament" of nature, otherwise all may suffer greatly at the hands of nature. . . .

(3) He must do politico-ideological work while taking part in labor and must not separate labor from political work. Apart from eating their meals and going to bed at night, commune members spend all their time doing labor every day and that is the important time for politico-ideological work. It is also easy to detect problems in the course of labor and once problems are detected, it is possible to solve them in time. . . .

Sixth, the principle of having politics dominate management must be firmly upheld, and the system of management must be built on the basis of the consciousness of the masses. . . .

A System Must Be Built on the Basis of Ideological Awakening of Commune Members

Pacesetter work points, personal reporting, and public assessment—such a system of labor management is a product of accumulation of experience in production and management, particularly of a heightening in the ideological awakening of commune members. In this system the socialist line of operation is firmly upheld and the principle of distribution according to labor is observed, so that the enthusiasm of commune members for collective production is boosted. It is also simple and easy to enforce, and meets the requirements of the present large-scale production.

A New System that Combines Politics with Management

Pacesetter work points, personal reporting and public assessment. In labor management in Tachai at present, what sort of system is in force with regard to computation of wages? To give it a name, we may call it a system of "pacesetter work points, personal reporting and public assessment." It works concretely as follows:

In everyday labor, the work recorder puts down what kind of job a commune member does, how much time he puts in, that is, whether he works in the early morning, forenoon, or afternoon, and what specific job each commune member does.

An evaluation, comparison, and summing up will be made at the end of each month. This is done by first finding out which of the commune members of a group have the best attitude toward labor, put in the most time, and do jobs of the highest quality. These are called pacesetters.

Then the work points a pacesetter should get for each working day are fixed.

With pacesetters and pacesetter work points we have a standard. The rest of the commune members then report their own work and say how many work points they should receive a day in accordance with their physical strength, level of skill, and attitude toward labor. When each commune member has reported his own work and made claims to work points, his claims are evaluated and examined. . . .

Why is it necessary to elect pacesetters? Because with pacesetters, we have not only a standard by which to measure our work when fixing work points, but also a model whom everyone may emulate in everyday labor. To the pacesetters themselves, the distinction is a sort of encouragement. Moreover, commune members may learn from one another and compete among themselves. It is in fact a system that combines politics with management. . . .

The Advantages of Pacesetter Work Points and Personal Reporting and Public Assessment. . . .

First, the complicated and vexatious system of fixed quotas is done away with so that more time is available.

As it is no longer necessary to assess work and record work points every evening, commune members may now have more time for studying Chairman Mao's works and learning culture and techniques. . . .

Second, there is no great difference in remuneration, and the socialist principle of distribution according to labor is better realized.

In the past, work points were entered according to the job undertaken, so that some people earned only a few points while others might earn several score. The gap was very wide between the two extremes. Now persons with different labor power and skills get different wages, but the difference is not great.

Take, for example, the situation last year. With regard to difference in labor power, a skilled laborer with strong labor power got an average of 11 points a day, one with average labor power got 9.5 points, one with half labor power got 7 points, and an auxiliary laborer got 5 points. The difference between the highest and the lowest was 2.2 times. . . .

Third, selfishness is gradually changed and communist ideas are gradually established.

In the first place, the practice of vying for work points is overcome and attention is paid to the quality of farm jobs done. Before the present system came into effect, members always wrangled and clamored for more work points. After the system came into effect, fixed quotas were abolished and commune members now need not fear being punished for failure to fulfill quotas or being cheated by some who may get more work points by taking unfair advantage of the quota system. What they all think and talk about is how they may learn and improve their farming techniques and guarantee a certain standard for their farm jobs. . . .

Moreover, at the assessment and comparison, what is assessed is not only how much work a certain man has done, whether the work is done well or poorly, and how much skill is required for the job. The basic thing is assessment of thought and attitude toward labor. If his thought is not fit, then he must be given assistance. The root must be traced, the dangers recognized, and the reason examined. . . .

Fourth, cadres no longer monopolize the work and democracy is promoted still further.

In the past, it was the commune members who labored while the cadres checked and okayed the farm jobs and recorded work points for commune members. If the commune members made a mistake, the cadres would criticize them. As a result, the cadres could not make the masses appreciate their work and it was impossible to develop the enthusiasm and initiative of the masses. An undesirable impression was created in which it appeared that cadres were there to rule the people and commune members were to be ruled.

After the present system came into force, the masses themselves discuss and deal with such matters as the allocation of work points, checking and approving of farm jobs, ascertaining the quality of the jobs done, etc. . . .

Fifth, checking farm jobs and approving them is made simpler.

With the change in wage computation and intensification of politico-ideological work by the party branch on the masses of commune members, the mass line is now truly implemented in checking on and approving farm jobs. Everyone has a part in it and it is carried out all the time. . . .

As time went on, most comrades formed the habit of using their eyes, ears, brains, hands, feet, and mouths diligently. Checking on and approving farm jobs is now done principally with the guidance of the cadres during work hours and under the mutual supervision of commune members. . . .

The New System Was Evolved Gradually from the Old One

The new system was evolved from the old following the gradual development of production in our brigade and the constant rise of the socialist ideological awareness of the masses of commune members, and on the basis of the principle of consolidation of the collective economy and development of agricultural production. In the past more than ten years we have passed through roughly four stages:

First stage: Fixed work points and flexible assessment.

In the period of agricultural cooperatives, wage computation in Tachai was done according to a simple system of "fixed work points and flexible assessment."

Every day after work was done, an assessment of work was carried out in the fields according to the basic work points allotted to each and the amount of work done that day. Because the ideological level of all was low and the method poor, assessment was begun every day while the sun was still high in the sky. Those whose work was assessed highly were silent, but those whose work was underassessed protested vociferously. Very often nothing came out of such assessment sessions. They ended with the team leader deciding the work points to be allotted and the work point recorder putting them down in his book. . . .

Second stage: Quota control and crediting of work by piece was put into effect.

When the higher agricultural producers' cooperative was inaugurated in 1956, Tachai learned the experience of Yao-shangkou Brigade of Wuhsiang *hsien* in "setting quotas on farm jobs." All farm jobs were divided into classes and graded according to their demands on physical exertion and skill, the degree of responsibility required, and their degree of difficulty. "Quotas were then set according to the grades, and wages were reckoned by the piece."

This system helped at the time to whip up the enthusiasm of members for collective production. Work points were entered according to the job done. There was no longer any arguing or wrangling over work assessment and allotment of work points for most farm jobs. After this system was put into effect, the labor enthusiasm of members rose higher, it was easier to assign some farm jobs to members, and collective production was promoted. However, new problems arose.

First of all, farm work reckoning was quite complex and farm jobs were divided into many classes. Land in Tachai was divided into tiny plots, each of a different character. It was extremely difficult to set quotas for such land. . . .

Another problem was the impossibility of ensuring the good quality of farm jobs. . . .

We realized that this system would encourage the tendency to fight for trifles. . . . In the fields people would do only as much as they had undertaken to do and no more. It was everyone for himself. Those whose job was to hoe land would not get rid of weeds at the sides, while those who were to trim the sides would not pick up stones in the earth. If you asked one of them why he did not remove the rock which he could see, he would tell you that there was no work point for removing rocks. . . .

Third stage: Wage computation according to different items. The above-described system remained in force for three or four years, altogether 130 or 140 quotas were set for farm jobs in the field alone. Scarcely had old problems been solved when new ones arose. More and more members were dissatisfied with the system.

In 1960, to solve the above-mentioned contradictions, the party branch and the management committee of the brigade consulted with the masses and amended the system, a new one—"wage computation according to different items of farm work"—being put into effect.

By this system, different methods of computing wages were adopted for different farm jobs. Wages continued to be computed by the piece according to the labor quota for "open" jobs—that is, jobs such as carrying manure, removing weeds, and transporting harvested crops, which could easily be reckoned quantitatively and qualitatively and easily checked. For capital construction on farmland and farm jobs in general the method of rating of pacesetters and personal reporting and public assessment was adopted. This in practice is the method which is currently in use. . . .

Fourth stage: Pacesetter work points, personal reporting and public assessment.

In the summer of 1963 there was a flood. Houses collapsed, soil was washed away, crops in the fields were also washed away or lodged. Men and labor were needed everywhere.

In view of the situation, members urgently wanted to fight the calamity and would not wait for any quotas or fixing of work points. Men, women, teenagers, and the young all turned out. They worked day and night, doing whatever work they could or whatever work that it was their turn to do. Sometimes one man would do the work of two or three. Sometimes one man would do four or five farm jobs.

After some time, the question of recording work points had the cadres stumped. What was to be done? Finally it was decided to let members discuss the matter and hear what they had to say and find the suitable solution.

In the discussion the majority of the members said, "Whether it is assessment of work and allotment of work points or allotment of work points by the piece, the object is to boost the enthusiasm of members for production and make production a success. Anyone knows how to earn more work points, but if the quality of farm jobs is completely disregarded, how can production be made a success? How can the quality of farm jobs be maintained at a high level?"

It appeared that it would not do to rely solely on checking on farm jobs. The important thing was the consciousness of members. In their own words, "To set quotas, it is necessary to set the mind first." . . .

We began to work out a system which conformed to the principle of distribution according to labor and which was simple. It was decided to place the politico-ideological work of the party in the primary position and strengthen ideological education of commune members.

Accordingly, the party branch explained repeatedly to commune members the relationship between the quality of farm jobs and output and the relationship between output and the value of work points and members' personal income. The object was to enable commune members to raise generally their ideological awareness, so that they might know that in order to increase their personal income, they must increase output, and to increase output, they must labor carefully and ensure the good quality of farm jobs done.

2. THE CULTURAL REVOLUTION IN THE COUNTRYSIDE

Initially, as the Cultural Revolution spread inexorably from intellectuals and students to the factories, efforts were made to shield the countryside from its impact. Thus, as late as its directive of September 14, 1966, the party center emphasized the absolute priority of producing a bumper harvest and enjoined red guards from going down to the grassroots levels except under carefully controlled circumstances. Not until December 15, 1966, with the peak agricultural season past, did the Central Committee issue its "Draft Directive on the Great Proletarian Cultural Revolution in Rural Districts" calling on the peasantry, above all the poor and lower middle peasants, to "grasp revolution and promote production." This basic directive for the countryside emphasized the self-liberation of the masses —led by the poor and lower middle peasants—through over throwing the "small handful of capitalist roaders in authority within the party." It called for broad unity and stressed the use of reason not violence as it called for destroying the four olds and ensuring the supremacy of the new thought, culture, customs, and habits of the proletariat. Nevertheless, though the movement had profound consequences for the rural areas, it never reached the intensity or spawned the factionalism and violence witnessed in the cities.

Directives of February and March 1967 reflected the sense of rhythm which must pervade all effective rural work. As peasants prepared for spring planting, the party center once again stressed the tasks of production and stated explicitly that: "During the busy season for spring farm work, struggle for seizing power should not be carried out in production brigades and production teams." Yet with the breakdown of party authority as a result of the conflicts of the preceding year, the center could not enforce these guidelines.

The final document included here is the Central Committee directive of December 4, 1967, the first to explicitly condemn the policies associated with Liu Shao-ch'i and the capitalist road in the countryside. Again the theme of linking revolution and production is emphasized in the context of projecting Tachai as a model, and the three-in-one combination which was restruc- turing urban and industrial leadership patterns was put forward as an appropriate model for the countryside as the party sought to restore unity and continue the revolution on the basis of the "revolutionary great alliance."

Yet where were the class enemies? The difficulty in answer- ing this question frequently produced a tendency to either attack the helpless remnants of the former landlord class or (spurred on by urban students) arbitrarily overthrow local leadership.

A. Directive on the Cultural Revolution in the Countryside

(For discussion and trial application)

1. Firmly implement the "grasp revolution, promote production" directive proposed by Chairman Mao and the party center, lay firm hold on the Great Proletarian Cultural Revolution, promote revolutionization of one's mind, and move the agricultural production forward.

2. Carry out the Great Proletarian Cultural Revolution in rural districts according to the principles laid down in the decision, that is, the sixteen points of the CCP Central Committee concerning the Great Proletarian Cultural Revolution and in the first ten points and the twenty-three articles concerning the socialist education movement. It is imperative that the masses take responsibility, educate and liberate themselves and rise to make revolution. As a rule, no work team will be sent. A few skilled observers may be sent.

3. The center of gravity in the Great Proletarian Cultural Revolution in the rural districts consists in purging the small handful of capitalist roaders in authority within the party and the landlords, rich peasants, counter-revolutionaries, bad elements, and rightists not well reformed.

Bring the four cleans campaign into the orbit of the Great Cultural Revolution. Solve the four cleans problems and the problems of four-clean-up re-examination in the Great Cultural Revolution.

Destroy the old thought, old culture, old customs, and old habits of the exploiting class and establish the new thought, new culture, new customs, and new habits of the proletariat.

Styles of bureaucracy and commandism among cadres must be rectified and the system of cadres' participation in labor implemented in the Great Cultural Revolution.

4. It is imperative to rely firmly on the poor peasants and lower middle peasants, unite with the middle peasants and gradually unite with more than 95 percent of the masses and

Directive of the Central Committee on the Great Proletarian Cultural Revolution in Rural Districts (Draft), December 15, 1966. CB 852.

more than 95 percent of cadres during the Great Cultural
Revolution in the rural districts.

5. The power organs leading the Great Cultural Revolution
in the rural districts are the Cultural Revolution committees of
poor and lower middle peasants, which are to be elected democratically by the congresses of poor and lower middle peasants.
If they are unequal to their duties they may be re-elected and
changed any time.

Streamline or re-elect the production leadership groups
through mass discussions. These production leadership groups
are responsible for production, distribution, procurement, and
supply work.

6. Build and develop red guards with young poor and lower
middle peasants as the backbone during the Great Cultural
Revolution. Red guards may join the militia.

As a rule, the children of leading cadres of various levels in
the rural districts may not take up the leadership duties of red
guards.

The children of landlords and rich peasants who work and
study in other localities may not return to their home towns for
building revolutionary ties. A policy of standing off as practiced
during the agrarian reform must be adopted.

7. Four bigs—big contending, big blooming, big character
poster, and big debate—and extensive democracy must also be
introduced to the Great Proletarian Cultural Revolution in the
rural districts. Revolutionary ties may be built between brigades
and between communes during the leisure hours of production.
A group of revolutionary students may also be organized to go
to the rural districts to build revolutionary ties, to eat, live, and
work together with the poor and lower middle peasants and to
take part in the Great Cultural Revolution in the rural districts,
but they must not monopolize things and take the place of
others.

Struggle must be waged by placing facts on the table and
reasoning things out. Persist in struggle by reasoning and refrain
from struggle by violence.

Guard against the factional strife stirred up by bad characters.

8. It is not permitted to attack and retaliate against the
revolutionary masses who express dissident views to leading

)odies and put up big character posters, nor is it permitted to educe their wage points. The revolutionary masses who have)een denounced as "counter-revolutionaries" and "saboteurs" because they have expressed dissident views should be vindicated.

Landlords, rich peasants, counter-revolutionaries, bad elements and rightists are the targets of dictatorship. They are absolutely not permitted to rebel against the proletariat. They are absolutely not permitted to rebel against the poor and lower middle peasants.

9. Intermediate schools will take a vacation and make revolution until the summer vacation next year. In the work-study universities and middle schools the Cultural Revolution should be properly arranged on the guiding principle of grasping revolution and stimulating production and in the light of concrete circumstances.

The Cultural Revolution in the rural primary schools should be carried out by the schools together with the communes and brigades in their localities and under the single leadership of the Cultural Revolution committees of communes and brigades in their localities.

10. During the Great Cultural Revolution, Chairman Mao's works must be studied and applied in flexible ways, the class struggle taken as the leading theme, and emphasis placed on "application." Through the Great Cultural Revolution change the rural districts into big schools for studying the thought of Mao Tsetung.

B. Revolution and the Rhythm of Rural Life

Party Committees at All Levels:

Since the CCP Central Committee promulgated its directive on the Great Cultural Revolution in the countryside, the broad masses of poor and lower middle peasants have held high the

Central Committee Notice on Stopping Seizure of Power in Production Brigades and Production Teams During the Spring Farming Period, March 7, 1967. SCPRM Supplement 17 great red banner of Mao Tsetung's thought and vigorously rebelled against the handful of party persons in authority taking the capitalist road and against the landlords, rich peasants counter-revolutionaries, bad elements, and rightists who cling to their reactionary standpoint. The situation of the Cultural Revolution in the countryside is excellent. The present is the very busy season for spring farming. Under this excellent situation, rural areas all over the country should earnestly implement Chairman Mao's directive, "grasp revolution and promote production," and immediately whip up an earth-shaking upsurge of spring farm work. This is a matter of first importance bearing on "preparedness for war and famine and everything for the people" as well as the annual harvest and the consolidation of the dictatorship of the proletariat.

The CCP Central Committee has therefore made this decision:

1. During the very busy season for spring farm work, struggle for seizing power should not be carried out in production brigades and production teams.

2. The leading groups, which have been approved by the revolutionary masses and the higher authorities, of production brigades and production teams where power has been seized should concretely shoulder the two heavy loads of revolution and production and apply Mao Tsetung's thought in directing the battle of spring farming. In production brigades and production teams where leadership is paralyzed, the activists among poor and lower middle peasants and the revolutionary cadres should organize a provisional leading group to grasp spring farm work.

3. The majority of rural cadres (including full-time cadres) are good or comparatively good. We should adhere to Chairman Mao's directive of "learning from past mistakes to avoid future ones and curing the sickness to save the patient," criticize and educate those cadres who have made mistakes, and help them rectify their mistakes. We must allow them to turn over a new leaf and encourage them to make amends, providing they are not anti-party and antisocialist elements, do not persist in their mistakes and do not refuse to correct their mistakes after repeated education.

4. In localities where the four-cleans movement has been

completed, under no circumstances are those cadres who take the capitalist road and have been dismissed from office and the landlords, rich peasants, counter-revolutionaries, bad elements, and rightists allowed to vindicate themselves. The fruit of the four-cleans movement must be protected without fail.

CCP Central Committee
March 7, 1967
(This notice may be read in public and posters of it put up in rural villages.)

C. Spring Planting and Cultural Revolution

The spearhead of the struggle should always be directed against the biggest of the small handful of persons in authority in the party taking the capitalist road and their agents in all places. We must resolutely rely upon the poor peasants and the lower middle peasants. We must mobilize the masses without reservation, let the masses educate themselves, and not send work teams to do a lot of gesticulation. Workers, town residents, cadres in organs, and students should all refrain from going out for exchange of revolutionary experience. Peasants are not to go to cities for exchange of revolutionary experience. When necessary, the People's Liberation Army may organize small but well-selected Mao Tsetung thought propaganda teams to propagandize Mao Tsetung thought and the principles and policies of the party.

All units of municipalities, counties, people's communes, production brigades, and production teams should participate in Mao Tsetung thought study classes. The vast commune members, cadres, and militia should all take part in the study. We should hold aloft the great red flag of Mao Tsetung thought, take "combat self-interest and repudiate revisionism" as the theme, and carry on education by positive example. We should

Directive of the Central Committee Concerning the Great Proletarian Cultural Revolution in the Countryside This Winter and Next Spring, December 4, 1967. CC Documents.

profoundly study the "three constantly read articles" and study Chairman Mao's important directives concerning the Great Proletarian Cultural Revolution. We should develop revolutionary great repudiation, to expose deeply and repudiate thoroughly the reactionary absurdities advocated by the biggest person taking the capitalist road in China. . . .

The current system in the rural people's communes by which ownership is held at three levels with the team as the basis, and the system of private plots should not be changed as a rule, and there should not be movements for donations.

On the basis of organizing Mao Tsetung thought study classes, problems of the revolutionary great alliance and the revolutionary three-in-one combination at the county level and the commune level should be solved, and revolutionary leadership at the county and the commune level should be established, so as to better lead the Great Proletarian Cultural Revolution in the production brigades and production teams. As a rule, there should not be power seizure in the production teams. In production brigades where power seizure is needed, the question should be solved by firmly relying upon the poor and lower middle peasants, realizing the revolutionary great alliance and the revolutionary "three-in-one combination," and re-electing the leadership. It should be affirmed that the majority of the rural cadres are good or relatively good.

Revolutionary masses should sharpen their class-alertness and strengthen the proletarian dictatorship. . . . In areas controlled by persons taking the capitalist road and by landlords, rich peasants, counter-revolutionaries, bad elements, and rightist elements, leadership must be seized and put into the hands of proletarian revlutionaries composed mainly of poor and lower middle peasants. We should realize the revolutionary great alliance, oppose factionalism, persist in unarmed struggle, and prevent the small handful of persons in authority from instigating armed struggle and instigating the masses to fight among themselves.

3. MECHANIZATION, COOPERATION, AND DECENTRALIZATION

Among rural developmental issues posed by the Cultural Revolution, the question of tractors, their number, their allocation, and their control, was central. In the Great Leap Mao had insisted that "the way out for agriculture lies in mechanization," but mechanization rooted in effectively functioning communal organization. Immediately following the leap the state took control over tractors which had been assigned to the communes. The communes, particularly those remote from major centers, found themselves deprived of access to the means of mechanization. The Cultural Revolution reversed many of the trends of the early 1960s in the field of mechanization through implementation of three policies:

(1) Mechanization must be implemented on the basis of cooperation by making the means of mechanization available to the brigades and communes. This would strengthen the communes and accelerate technological transfer throughout the countryside.

(2) Combine mechanization, semi-mechanization, and farm tool improvement with primary emphasis on self-reliance but with increasing support by urban industry.

(3) Disperse the means of mechanization throughout the countryside rather than concentrate them in opening virgin land (and in state farms).

The seventeen-year history of agricultural mechanization is the history of the struggle between the proletariat and the bourgeoisie, between socialism and capitalism, and between the

Take-over Committee of the Heilungkiang Provincial Department of Agricultural Machinery: Let the Brilliance of Mao Tsetung Thought Forever Shine on the Road to Agricultural Mechanization. Thoroughly Eradicate Poisons on the Front of Our Province's Agricultural Mechanization Spread by the Revisionist Line Promoted by China's Khrushchev. *Agricultural Machinery Technique,* July 8, 1967. URS, vol. 48.

revolutionary line and the reactionary line. The focus of the struggle from beginning to end has been over the question of what road should China take in agricultural mechanization.

As early as 1955, in his report on the question of agricultural cooperativization, Chairman Mao comprehensively explained our party's basic line in agriculture. That was: After the accomplishment of the antifeudal agrarian reform, the first step is to achieve agricultural collectivization, and the second step is, on the basis of collectivization, to achieve mechanization and electrification. This is our party's basic line for persisting in socialism and defeating capitalism in the struggle between the two roads in rural areas. Chairman Mao said: "The social and economic physiognomy of China will not undergo a complete change until the socialist transformation of the social and economic system is accomplished and until, in the technical field, machinery is used, whenever possible, in every branch of production and in every place."

But the top party person in authority taking the capitalist road and his lackeys have done things quite the reverse. They frenziedly opposed Chairman Mao's basic line in agriculture. They said: "China has a huge rural population and enormous manpower with a complex agricultural system. Therefore agricultural mechanization cannot be achieved." . . . The handful of party persons in authority taking the capitalist road in our province have faithfully carried out their master's black instruction. Over the past years, they have all along promoted a counter-revolutionary revisionist line of bourgeois economism and pragmatism, by means of which they altered the political orientation of socialist agricultural mechanization. They did not take agricultural mechanization as the basic line, basic orientation, and basic way out for agriculture, but took it as only an expedient. They vigorously advocated putting profit in command and energetically trumpeted the economic advantages of agricultural mechanization.

In the allotment of tractors, they paid more attention to counties with extensive land, scanty animal power, wilderness for reclamation and a high commodity rate of food grains. They took agricultural mechanization as "patching up," "filling in holes," "cleaning out corners" and "making immediate profit" and as a temporary measure to make up for the disadvantages of barren, hard, and thin land. . . .

China's Khrushchev came to our province in October 1965 to peddle his revisionist black goods and energetically advocated that mechanization must be "run by government." He said blatantly: "Agricultural mechanization requires state investment; the state should appoint personnel to take charge of operation, distribution and management. . . . In ten years the state should invest a big sum to be recalled after ten years. With this money, the state can then equip another area. In several decades, to achieve total mechanization, the state will have to invest 10 to 20 billion. Afterwards, the state may rely on the money to make more money." With these words, he frenziedly opposed Chairman Mao's great instructions. In 1962, in a document approved by the handful of top party persons in authority taking the capitalist road, it was said: "The people's commune now takes the production team as the basic accounting unit. It is even more difficult for a commune or a production brigade to run the tractor station." This denied the possibility of running mechanization by collective economy and self-reliance. It fanned an evil wind to strangle mechanization by the masses themselves. The handful of party persons in authority taking the capitalist road in our province . . . put up three objections that the communes and brigades "cannot afford to buy machines, maintain them and operate them," to echo their master and oppose Mao Tsetung thought. They also viciously denied the success achieved by the use of tractors during the period when these tractors were sent to the countryside in 1958; they attacked only shortcomings and made no mention of merits. . . . They insisted that the masses could not run mechanization properly, much less handle large farming machines. Arbitrarily and against the strong wishes and protests of the communes and production brigades, they adopted radical measures to take over all the tractors owned and managed by the communes and production brigades and put them under state ownership. Consequently, the prosperous self-run mechanization of our province was seriously damaged. . . .

In 1958 the Ch'engtu Conference passed the "Opinions on the Problem of Agricultural Mechanization." It stated:

The conference unanimously approves Chairman Mao's instructions concerning the farm tool renovation movement. The mass farm tool renovation movement which has the participation of the broad peasantry is the germination of technological revolution and a great revolutionary movement. The whole nation should actively popularize it and, through it, gradually pass over to semi-mechanization and mechanization.

The renovation of farm tools, whether mechanization (including hand-driven machines and machine-drawn tools), semi-mechanization (the so-called new-type animal-power farm tools) or the preliminary renovation of old-fashioned farm tools (the so-called improved farm tools), is beneficial to the enhancement of the productivity of agricultural labor. We should not merely wait for agricultural machines and ignore the popularization of the new-type animal-power farm tools and the improved farm tools.

Agricultural machines should be mainly of small size, and an appropriate number of those of large and medium-size may be used in coordination.

However, a handful of top party persons in authority taking the capitalist road and their black henchmen have made the utmost efforts to suppress this important document and refused to transmit and implement it. . . . Nobody cared about the renovation of farm tools and nobody looked after the new-type horse-drawn implements, causing serious damage and loss. (In eight counties alone, more than 13,000 machines worth more than 3 million yuan were either lost or damaged.) They thus suppressed the nation-wide mass farm tool renovation movement which was initiated by Chairman Mao personally and developed all over the broad countryside of our province in the period of the Great Leap Forward in 1958. . . .

They openly disobeyed Chairman Mao's instruction that "every province, district and county must set up a farm tool research institute, call together scientists, technicians, experienced blacksmiths, and carpenters and collect all kinds of comparatively advanced farm tools from the whole province, district and county for comparison, experiment, and improvement to trial make new types of farm tools." By merging and abolition, they reduced the fifty-two farm tool research institutes estab-

lished in the various counties and municipalities to only a few
agricultural mechanization professional research institutes in
some special districts and municipalities. . . .
As early as 1956, Chairman Mao taught us: "What we should
attend to at present is promoting local activism and let every
place do more things on its own under the unified planning of
the Central Committee." In the "Opinions on the Problem of
Agricultural Mechanization," decided upon in 1958, Chairman
Mao also pointed out: "Agricultural machines (including
machine-drawn tools, new-type animal-power tools and improved tools), except large ones and those of high technique,
should be manufactured mainly by the localities." But the
handful of top party persons in authority taking the capitalist
road madly put forth the absurd proposal that "[The Ministry
of Agricultural Machinery] should serve agriculture better and
also consider the formation of a trust to supervise manufacture
and management." Its evil aim was to prevent local party
committees from having a hand in the work of agricultural
mechanization, isolate agricultural mechanization from party
leadership and establish an independent kingdom of capitalist
operation.

4. DELAYED MARRIAGE AND PLANNED BIRTH: A SOCIALIST POPULATION POLICY

*China's population will pass the one billion mark in the early
1980s according to U.S. Commerce Department estimates.
While holding to a philosophy that "people are the most pre-
cious," China is vigorously promoting planned birth. As India,
Puerto Rico, and other nations experiment with forced sterilization, how has China accomplished the reduction of the birth
rate from 45 per thousand in 1953 to below 25 in the late
1970s? The answer lies in linking modes of social development*

Planned Birth Leadership Group, Kwangtung Provincial Revolutionary
Committee: Delayed Marriage and Planned Birth (1972). Translated by
Loren Fessler, *Field Staff Reports, East Asia,* Series XXX, 1, 1973.

which ensure food, jobs, and security for everyone with a comprehensive program to transform marriage and fertility patterns while fully integrating women into the mainstream of economic and social life. In this way the need for large families to ensure security of parents in their old age and the wherewithal for planned birth in terms of information and supplies have made possible impressive successes in family planning. The most difficult challenge has been and remains the countryside.

Planned birth is currently a major priority with a national program to reduce the present natural increase estimated at 1.5 percent to 1 percent between 1978 and 1980.

"Delayed Marriage and Planned Birth," a popularly written birth manual distributed in Kwangtung province in 1972 highlights four basic principles of the Chinese approach. First, active encouragement of delayed marriage, which has shifted the typical marriage age from ages 18-21 to 23-26 in the countryside and 25-28 in the cities, thereby sharply reducing the childbearing years. Second, the provision of free contraception and birth information to parents at the grassroots level with encouragement (and pressure) to limit births to two per family and to space children by several years. Third, active encouragement and opportunity for women's full participation in the workforce and in society. Fourth, and most important, the provision of collective guarantees of popular welfare which removes the overriding pressure for large families and male children, the key factors which have frustrated population control programs in most Third World nations to date.

While emphasizing the contributions to the revolution of planned birth, the manual shows how it serves the interests of the mother, the children, and the entire family.

Delayed marriage and planned birth are two aspects of a single question; the main goal is through advocating delayed marriage and practice of planned birth to change the situation regarding births from the former phenomenon of "early, frequent, and many" to "late, spaced, and few," so that in this way we can change the situation in population growth from one which is unplanned to one which is planned, and thereby better adapt to the needs of the planned and proportional development of the national economy, and improve the people's health. . . .

1. Why Advocate Delayed Marriage?

Delayed marriage means that unmarried young men and women in a well-considered manner delay their age of marriage according to the needs of the revolution and to the circumstances of their own physical and intellectual development and marry at a more appropriate age.

Early marriage is an old custom left over from the old society, and it is beneficial neither to the task of socialist revolution and construction nor to the physical and ideological growth of young people. . . .

It is stipulated in our country's marriage law that men at the age of 20 may marry and women at the age of 18. This is the minimum marriage age, and marriages earlier than this are impermissible and illegal; but this is definitely not to be taken to mean that these ages are the most suitable for marriage. Generally speaking, it is more suitable for men to marry at ages 25 and 26 or so and women at 23 and 24 or thereabouts. . . . If young people marry too early, their study, work, and physical growth will all be affected because of family and other burdens. . . .

2. What are the Advantages of Planned Birth?

Planned birth is the practice of birth planning for the sake of revolution. . . . Specifically, it advocates that couples of child-producing age, on the basis of revolutionary requirements and the concrete situation of the individual, through using scientific methods, will properly arrange the timing and number of births, and when not desiring children, will practice contraception; and if no longer wanting to continue having children, then they will be able to undergo sterilization.

Practicing planned birth does *not* mean opposing the bearing of children, but seeks birth with planning. Generally speaking, it is advocated that it is best for every couple to have two children, and moreover that it is best to have four or five years between the two births. . . .

The significance of practicing planned birth is as follows.

First, it is advantageous in enabling the broad masses of the people to have more time and energy to read and study, to participate in political activity, to elevate their thoughts and political consciousness in revolutionary practice, and constantly reform their world view. Especially for the broad masses of women the practice of planned birth lightens the burden of household tasks, of having too many children at too frequent intervals, and enables them to study Marxism, Leninism, and the writings of Chairman Mao. Thus they have the drive, second they have the time, and third they will get results which further the revolution of women's thought. . . .

Second, it is beneficial to "grasping revolution, promoting production, promoting work, and being prepared for war," accelerating the building of socialism and supporting world revolution. . . . The implementation of planned birth keeps the population growth rate at a reasonable level, and in this way, on one hand, consumption can be decreased, savings increased, and construction expanded; on the other hand, the labor power of women can be better liberated, production further developed, and more social wealth created. . . .

Third, planned birth is beneficial to elevating the standard of people's health. Too many and too frequent births will affect the health of both mothers and children. . . .

Fourth, planned birth is beneficial to the education of future generations and to better cultivating successors to the tasks of the proletarian revolution. In the past, many school-age children in rural areas lost the opportunity to go to school because their brothers and sisters were too numerous, and because elder children had to take care of younger ones. . . .

Fifth, planned birth is beneficial to the rational arrangement of individual and family life. Following our nation's continuous development in socialist construction, and following the consolidation and strengthening of our rural collective economy, the living standard of the broad masses of workers and peasants has been continuously elevated. But in some villages at present there are still some among the masses who, because of having too many children and excessively heavy household burdens, have had their work attendance affected and their incomes decreased; likewise, because of too many children, expenditures are also increased, and in this way, economic problems are created and family life affected. Therefore, the implementation of planned birth is not only beneficial to promoting production and consolidating the collective economy, but is also greatly advantageous to elevating the people's living standard.

5. EQUAL PAY FOR EQUAL WORK FOR WOMEN

Issues of women's equality were broached more fully and directly during the 1974 campaign to criticize Lin Piao and Confucius than perhaps at any time since liberation. One pivotal issue concerned the socialist principle of distribution "to each according to one's work" and its relationship to the question of housework. Despite public commitment to equal pay for equal work, throughout rural China and regardless of their productivity or skill, women were often limited to a maximum of eight points while men could receive up to ten—and in some areas women were automatically lowered in the pay scale after marriage. The result of this system, rooted in traditional notions of male supremacy, was to retain in effect a two-tier system reinforcing the notion of women's inferiority and to hold back the desire of women to contribute to the collective economy. The experience of the Hsiaochinchuang Brigade outside Tientsin, until late 1976 a model in the area of women's equality (it was singled out as a model and promoted by Chiang Ch'ing), reveals some of the complexity and tenacity of the issues. Should the primary standard applied to income distribution be physical strength, technical skill, or political consciousness? Should women be penalized for failure to develop technical skills when they are barred from working with machinery? Is the principle "to each according to one's work" inherently discriminatory against women under present conditions in which physical strength plays an important role? What should

Chou Ke-chou: How Our Village Got Equal Pay for Equal Work. *China Reconstructs*, March 1975.

be the primary criteria for evaluating the work of each individual?

So long as women rank significantly lower than men in workpoint ratings the logic of maximizing family earning power is to delegate household tasks among women, since to take the major earner from paid labor would sacrifice earning power. While the issue of socialization of household labor has been actively discussed, notably in those periods of mobilization when large numbers of women advanced into social labor, rarely has the issue of men's responsibility for sharing it been raised. An article in the September 1971 issue of Red Flag is a notable exception. It noted that "some household chores must be done by both women comrades as well as by men comrades"; however, no significant national movement has ever developed around this issue. In the countryside at least, housework remains women's work despite women's gains in the collective economy and politics.

In our village east of Peking in Hopei province there used to be an old saying:

> Donkey in the shafts and
>   horse pulling on the side,
> Woman ruling the house—
>   neither will go right.

The usual way of pulling a cart around here is to have the horse in the shafts and the donkey in the traces. The saying means that when a woman assumes a leading role it's like the donkey taking the place of the horse, which can only lead to trouble.

Before the Cultural Revolution, some of the men in the commune not infrequently used such sayings in our faces. We women were offended, but we had nothing to answer back with. In the years after liberation of the country, we married women had come out to work in the collective fields, but only at the height of the harvest. At other times we stayed home doing the cooking and caring for the children. In our spare time we made straw mats which brought in a little money, but we were not the main family income earners. . . .

In the summer of 1972, twenty-seven hectares of corn were withering in a long dry spell. Most of the able-bodied men were called off to work on a commune project to dig a waterway, a measure against drought. "Watering the corn will just have to wait till we get back," the brigade leader said to me as he left. As soon as they were gone we women held a heated discussion. "How can we wait?" some asked. "If the crop dies we won't have any harvest at all from those fields."

We all knew about the Tachai Brigade, where women really did "hold up half the sky," so about thirty of us, mostly middle-aged women, formed a shock team for watering. For forty days without stop we carried water with shoulder poles. We watered the young plants three times and replaced those that didn't revive. When the men came back and saw what we had done they said, not without admiration, "Without these women our crop would have been lost."

Once we saw our own strength, we determined to do even more for farm production in the future. Since then, because the men are often needed on special projects for permanent improvement like transforming saline soil or digging irrigation canals, we women have become the main force in tending the crops. But just because we'd shown our strength didn't mean the male supremacist ideas of thousands of years were going to leave people's heads. We had a real struggle when we started implementing the national policy of equal pay for equal work in our brigade.

Inequality Destroys Unity

After liberation Chinese men and women working for the state and many in rural communes began receiving equal pay for equal work. But here because of the remnant influence of male supremacist ideas, the highest base rate for men was 10 work points a day, while the highest a woman could get was 7½, even though she did the same amount of work. This was only natural, thought many men cadres and brigade members, "because men and women have been different since ancient times." Seeing that they were not as strong and—at least at first—not as skilled as the men at some jobs, the women didn't dare say anything. But among themselves some women would refer to their baby girls as "my little 7½-pointer."

Our base rate is determined at meetings held once a year. Each brigade member says what he thinks his work is worth and the others discuss it. At a meeting not long ago, while two-thirds of the men confidently stated 10 points, only one strong woman had the courage to bid even 9½. None of the other strong women dared bid over 8. That was when the brigade Communist Party branch asked that the evaluation be stopped and organized a series of meetings to criticize male supremacy.

Our study brought out the fact that such thinking stemmed from the 2,000-year-old doctrines of Confucius and Mencius. To maintain the rule of the slave-owners, which centered around the patriarchs, Confucius spread the idea of male supremacy, saying "Women and slaves are hard to manage" and putting the two in the most subservient position. Later the feudal ruling class, too, used male supremacy to hamper women's thinking and action. . . .

To counter this we studied Chairman Mao's words, "When women all over the country rise up, that will be the day of victory for the Chinese Revolution." Brigade members began to realize that the question of equal pay for equal work was much more than just a matter of a few work points for an individual. . . .

What Criterion?

When we began the evaluation, some men had said, "All a man has to do is stick out his fist and he does as much as a woman does in six months. If women want the same base rate, they have to do just as we do in ploughing, planting, digging ditches, and carrying sacks of grain." We pointed out that women had never had the chance to learn some of these jobs. If you make only strength and skill the basis of your comparison you'll be pitting men's strong points, physiologically and historically, against women's weak points. First and foremost, the comparison should be on attitude toward work, on patriotic and collectivist thinking, and contribution to the collective.

We took comparison of two brigade members as an example. One is the strongest man in the village. He can lift the diesel engine off a two-wheeled tractor and is a master at almost any farm job. The other, a woman production team leader, can't compete with him in this, though on most jobs she can keep up with the men. And when it comes to taking the lead in revolutionary criticism and theoretical study, or making arrangements for collective labor and mobilizing people, his contribution to the collective can't compare with hers. Everyone finally agreed that both had their strong points and both deserved a 10-point rating.

This kind of evaluation made a dent in the thinking of many of the men. Some of the men team leaders pointed out that in many ways the women showed greater concern for the collective than the men. For instance, when they were all out weeding, the woman each brought back a bundle of weeds for the brigade's compost heap, while the men came home empty-handed. . . .

After comparison on these various aspects, two-thirds of the men still got 10 points. Out of 136 women, 16 got 10 points and 40 others got 9 or over. A total of 116 women got a higher rating than before.

Managing Things Together

Since equal pay for equal work was instituted the women have shown more enthusiasm for their tasks and even more concern for the collective. . . . With help from the men, many young women have learned to drive tractors and carts and to plough, all things they were not allowed to learn before. The men haven't fallen behind either. They voluntarily take on the heaviest jobs and even have started doing household chores that were once all left for women. . . .

Wang Hsien, a twenty-year-old middle school graduate, gives well-organized classes in the brigade night school. Men and women militia members do their military training together. Last year a woman was chosen to become team leader and another as bookkeeper and I was elected to the brigade party branch committee. It's fine for women to be running things together with the men!

6. UP TO THE MOUNTAINS
AND DOWN TO THE COUNTRYSIDE:
EDUCATED YOUTH IN THE COMMUNES

The dispatch of close to 15 million educated youth from the cities to the countryside in the decade after 1966 is among the most distinctive Chinese attempts to speed rural development and eliminate the gap between town and country.

Su hsien in Hopei province was a model of successful work in integrating youth from the large cosmopolitan city of Tientsin into the pattern of rural life. While stressing its achievements the report is particularly illuminating in suggesting the broad range of problems and tensions which confront the experiment everywhere throughout the Chinese countryside: how to fully accommodate the presence of dynamic new elements into rural society in ways that maximize their contribution to the local economy and society; how to provide fulfillment both to those used to the amenities of urban life and to the villagers they are joining; how to ease the cultural barriers between people of vastly different experience; and how to reassure not only the youth but their urban parents of the promise of life in the countryside. What about marriage—will urban youth marry among themselves or locally? Most difficult of all, will they settle permanently in the countryside or, after a few years, return to the cities? The answers to these questions and the success of the program hinge in large part on the success of present mechanization and modernization programs to transform the countryside.

In some areas educated youth assume leadership and technological roles after overcoming the first barriers of unfamiliarity and inexperience. Yet dealing effectively with potential strains and conflicts of millions who seek to make their permanent home in the countryside is at best a difficult, long-term task. It

The Placement is Good, the Education is Good, the Utilization is Good: An Investigation of Su Hsien's Good Job in Working with Educated Youths Going Up to the Mountains and Down to the Countryside. In: *Have a Warm Regard for the Growth of Educated Youths in the Country- side* (Peking, 1973). *Chinese Education*, 2, 3, 1975.

is, of course, one which is central to the effort to bridge the gap between city and countryside. Like many others, this program has been reassessed since 1976, with an emphasis on greater flexibility for youth going to the countryside and with early indications that fewer will settle permanently and more will have the opportunity to continue their education.

Since 1964, 2,030 educated youths from Tientsin, Peking, and other cities have come to Su *hsien* in Hopei province to join the brigades and settle down. Party organizations on every level and the poor and lower middle peasants of Su *hsien* have worked hard to achieve good placement, education, and utilization of educated youths who have gone up to the mountains and down to the countryside so that they may put down roots, grow, and continually develop more active usefulness in the vast universe of the villages. . . .

In 1969, five educated youths from Tientsin arrived at Chien-niu-kung Brigade to join the brigade and settle down. The poor and lower middle peasants greeted them as though welcoming back their own children; they had made careful preparations for them: they raised houses, bricked in pig pens, and even thought of crocks for salty vegetables and sacks for food, so that the educated youths upon arrival could enter the houses and begin cooking and go out to the fields and begin laboring. Secretary Chang Shou-ts'ai of the brigade party branch, who had suffered much class bitterness in the old society, was especially concerned about the educated youths, and he frequently went to the homes of educated youths to inquire about their living conditions. On December 29, 1970, he returned from a meeting at the *hsien* with other cadres from the brigade. Even before entering his own home, he went to look in on the educated youths. When he saw that the educated youths had not finished preparing their things for the New Year's festivities, he felt badly about it. He felt that he had not done his work well, so he immediately called the cadres to a meeting to propagate Chairman Mao's directive on doing a good job of working with educated youths who go up to the mountains and down to the countryside, and he asked everyone to treat educated youths with "even greater regard than for our own children and be whole-heartedly concerned." Under the leadership of the old party secretary, everyone immediately helped the educated youths prepare things for the New Year, so that the educated youths and the poor and lower middle peasants together happily celebrated the Spring Festival in a revolutionary way. Immediately after the Spring Festival he deputed the branch deputy secretary to escort the educated youths back to Tientsin to visit their parents. This branch deputy secretary, house by house, home by home, reported to the parents the many different ways in which their children were growing in the villages. . . . With the addition of two youths who joined this brigade in 1970, all seven young people have joined the league, and among them two young persons have gloriously joined the Chinese Communist Party.

Su *hsien's hsien* committee has learned from the experience of Chien-niu-kung Brigade that to do a good job of managing and educating educated youths who have gone up to the mountains and down to the countryside it is necessary to place them well. It is necessary to be concerned about their living, to actively create conditions for them to settle in the villages to carry out the revolution. . . .

When placing the educated youths, the *hsien* committees of Su *hsien* and every level of the party organization conscientiously attended to every concrete problem. Chief among these were:

(1) The problem of housing. In the beginning, some cadres and masses thought that the educated youths would not stay long in the villages, that they would be there no more than three years or so for re-education, and that temporary living quarters would be all right. For this reason, some communes and brigades did not grasp firmly the problem of finding housing for educated youths settling in the countryside. . . . The party organization on every level in Su *hsien* decided to motivate the masses of poor and lower middle peasants, and with a spirit of self-reliance, take appropriate measures to help the educated youths prepare materials to build houses and then help them build them. While building, they looked to the future and built housing sufficient for today, and sufficient also for the future when the educated youths would have families. At

present, the entire *hsien* has built for the educated youths who collectively joined the brigade 1,189 rooms, averaging 0.8 rooms per person. Thus when the educated youths marry, each family can have a living area of 1.5 rooms, generally equivalent to the average living space of the local commune members. . . .

(2) The problem of self-sufficiency. The *hsien* committee of Su *hsien* opportunely summed up and propagated the experience of Tung-shih-ku commune in order to solve the problem of livelihood for the educated youths who have gone up to the mountains and down to the countryside. Most of the educated youths going to Tung-shih-ku commune in 1970 were not able to support themselves. They were dissatisfied, their parents were worried, and the poor and lower middle peasants were unsympathetic. The party committee of the commune was very concerned, and it organized a special investigatory group which discovered three main reasons why educated youths in the countryside were unable to realize self-sufficiency: Their work attendance was low; the educated youths, on the average, reported for work on two hundred days or so, about one-third less frequently than the local commune members. The compensation was not just; on the average the male educated youths were about two points lower than local commune members, and the female educated youths more than one point lower. They had only a single economic source and no auxiliary income.

In response to these problems revealed by the investigation, the commune party committee adopted measures to solve them. First, they strengthened education in enthusiasm for work, so that the educated youths would strengthen their attitude toward labor. Thereafter their work attendance increased yearly. Now the average educated youth is already close to the labor level of local commune members. They also helped educated youths set up collective auxiliary projects like raising pigs, ducks, and rabbits, planting vegetables, and setting up collective dining rooms. At the same time, they educated them in economizing their ways of living and changing their wasteful attitude of "a kitchenful of firewood, a potful of rice." After these measures were taken, most of the educated youths in the commune had surplus grain, and had raised their standards of living, which made them feel secure. They became more indus-

trious in their work and developed into very useful persons. . . .
(3) The *hsien* committee of Su *hsien* and the party organization at every level are also very concerned about the question of marriage for the educated youth in the countryside.

Enthusiastically Educate and Ceaselessly Raise Ideological Consciousness

The Yu-ku-chuang Brigade of Yu-ku-chuang commune in this *hsien* accepted eight educated youths to the countryside in 1969. . . .

After this study, the educated youths made encouraging progress. In 1972 each person worked an average of 269 days, 64 days more than in 1971. At the same time, some of them undertook jobs as teachers, bookkeepers, agricultural technicians, and so on. . . .

In order to work well with educated youths who go to the countryside, it is even more important to strengthen their ideological and political education than to settle them well, so that they will make great strides in following the revolutionary line of Chairman Mao. . . .

(1) They organized the educated youths to study earnestly books by Marx and Lenin and books by Chairman Mao, to criticize deeply revisionism, and to reconstruct painstakingly their world view. . . .

(2) Class education is a main subject. They adopted the method of inviting old, poor peasants to describe the bitterness of the past and the sweetness of the present to the educated youths; organized educated youths to view exhibits on class education, to visit the monuments to dead revolutionary heroes and other types of education in order to advance class education and education in revolutionary heritage. . . .

(3) They extensively advanced education on ideals and the future. In response to the restlessness of some educated youths in the villages, and their inability to think correctly about the needs of the revolution, they organized discussions on "the ideals and future of youth" and on "putting down roots in the villages for a lifetime or for a brief while." . . .

(4) They initiated activities for learning from progressive models. . . .

(5) The city and the countryside cooperated in the work of administering education to educated youths in the countryside. Every year the *hsien* committee of Su *hsien* organizes cadres from the *hsien*, the communes, and the brigades to visit the parents of the educated youths and the schools and streets where they used to live and report to them on the growth of the educated youths, ask for their opinions, and obtain the cooperation of parents and society. . . .

Promote the Utility of Educated Youths in the Countryside by Boldly Using Them

The *hsien* committee of Su *hsien* also educated the party organization on every level to actively cultivate and boldly use the educated youths in accordance with the special qualities of each, and to develop fully their special abilities, so that the educated youths feel that the villages really need them, that in the villages they may do great deeds. . . . At present, among the educated youths who have joined the brigades and made a home in the *hsien*, some have been elected into the leading groups of the *hsien*, communes, brigades and production teams; some have separately taken on the duties of teacher, barefoot doctor, bookkeeper, agricultural mechanic, agricultural technician, and so on. . . .

The educated youths are a most active and most energetic force in the construction of the new socialist villages. . . .

7. THE SEVEN-YEAR PLAN FOR DEVELOPMENT OF THE HSINCHING BRIGADE

Planning. The word gleams of steel and concrete structures spiraling skyward, of the mentality of the center, the ministry, and the technocrat shaping the lives and the futures of working people. Here is a plan drafted by a production brigade in a

The Program for Agricultural Development 1974–1980 of Hsinching Production Brigade, Ant'ing Commune, Chiating Hsien (revised draft), June 1974. *Study and Criticism* No. 7 and HC No. 8, August 1, 1974. SCPRM 74-14.

suburban commune which concretely surveys the prospects for change in a single rural community. It reflects the concerns of peasants in a relatively prosperous and advanced setting on the outskirts of Shanghai.

The future they project rests on the growing viability of the collective and continued progress in mechanization, industrialization, and diversification. While adhering to the three-level accounting system with the team as primary, this blueprint projects the rising share of income contributed by the brigade and commune with the expansion of industry and sideline production; likewise it suggests the steady growth of free and subsidized services such as health and education at the brigade and commune levels.

With a view to further consolidating the collective economy of the people's commune, expediting agricultural production, gradually raising the living standard of commune members, consolidating the rural socialist position, and fulfilling the task of consolidating the dictatorship of the proletariat at the grass-roots level, we cadres and commune members of Hsinching Production Brigade have drawn this seven-year program. . . .

1. Under the guidance of Chairman Mao's revolutionary line, bring the superiority of the collective economy of the people's commune into full play, correctly enforce the basic system of the people's commune at the present stage marked by "three-level ownership with the production team as the foundation," actively bring the role of the production brigade level into play, lead and assist all production teams in taking the socialist road toward common affluence, and continue criticizing capitalist tendencies. . . .

2. Strive to raise the output of grain, cotton, and edible oil to the level of "two, two, three." This means that by 1980 the average per mou output of grain will reach 2,000 catties, an increase by 46 percent over 1973's 1,370 catties, and the state will be supplied with 1,740,000 catties of commodity grain (over 1,000 catties per capita); the average per mou output of ginned cotton will reach 200 catties, an increase of 96 percent over 1973's 102 catties; the average per mou output of rapeseed

will reach 300 catties, an increase of over 200 percent over 1973's 98 catties.

3. Develop a diversified economy with priority given to hog raising. By 1980, the number of live hogs bred by the brigade, teams and commune members will reach 4,500 head, an average of 1.5 head per mou, representing an increase of 55 percent over 1973; 2,300 head will be sold to the state for slaughter, representing an increase of 50 percent over 1973. Seven reservoirs of the brigade will be turned into fish ponds to contain 8,000 fish. Vacant spaces on livestock farms will be used for planting 2,000 fruit trees and 1,500 grape trees. Forty catties of pearls will be cultured. Mushrooms will be grown in 20,000 square feet of land. Poultry will be raised energetically. Income from side occupations in 1980 will account for 20 percent of the gross revenue from farm and sideline production. Hsinching will be turned into a land of fish and rice in name and in fact, supplying more farm and subsidiary products to the state.

4. Make the "four sides" green. Beginning from 1974, 3,000 trees and a number of willow trees are to be planted each year by the side of houses, villages, roads, and streams. . . .

5. Build high- and stable-yield fields. In this way, "a dry spell of a hundred days will not be feared and a downpour of six inches of rain will cause no flooding." . . .

6. Land will be leveled to make garden farming possible. The more than 1,800 plots of land of varying sizes in the whole brigade will be realigned in a manner suited to actual conditions into some 1,300 rectangular plots of fields with three specifications, measuring 2 mou, 2.4 mou, and 2.5 mou respectively. (Up to this spring more than 400 such plots have been formed). . . .

7. Accumulate more natural manure. In line with the policy of self-reliance, hog manure will be accumulated, green manure crops will be grown, and manure will be fermented all year. . . .

8. The brigade will set up a seed base and production teams will set up seed fields so as to cultivate fine strains. . . .

9. Prevent and eliminate diseases and pests. Strenuous efforts will be made to basically wipe out and control such diseases and pests as rice borer and streak rust, army worms and scabs ravaging the wheat, and red spiders, red boll worms, and damp-off ravaging cotton. . . .

10. The brigade should set up a "scientific farming center" and production teams should each set up "a group" (scientific farming group) and appoint four full-time persons (to take care of seeds, protect plants, breed seedlings, and control inlet of water to the fields). . . .

11. Further effort will be made to raise the level of mechanization with emphasis on improving the "four back-breaking jobs" of pulling out seedlings, transplanting seedlings, harvesting, and ploughing. By 1980, the eleven production teams will each have ten kinds of machines: small tractors, small hoisting machines, seedling pullers, seedling transplanters, harvesters, ploughing machines, bulldozers, soil loosening machines, spraying machines and hulling machines. . . .

12. Build passages for farm machines, adjust pedestrian paths, and complete a rural road network which is practical and low cost. . . .

13. Develop the collective economy of the brigade. Within the next seven years, further efforts will be made to run well brigade-run factories, increase accumulation of funds, and promote capital construction on the farms. Apart from the existing lens-processing factory, farm machine repair workshop, and farm and subsidiary products processing plants, a small factory is to be built to produce components serving the big industries. In the wake of development of mechanization, the redundant manpower will be used for side occupations of the brigade. By 1980, net income from the brigade-level economy will increase to 150,000 yuan from 20,000 yuan in 1973.

14. On the basis of increased production, commune members' income will be gradually increased. By 1980, income of commune members from collective distribution will increase to 230 yuan from 176 yuan per capita in 1973.

15. Grain reserves are to be increased year after year. By 1980, the brigade will assuredly have 1,200,000 catties of grain in reserve, sufficient for one and a half years' consumption for all commune members. . . .

16. The brigade's commerce should be better run. . . .

17. Old houses will be gradually rebuilt and new housing estates built.

18. Universal secondary education will be introduced and

illiteracy among young and middle-aged people will be eliminated. In the past, due to domination by the revisionist line in education, a part of poor and lower middle peasants received no schooling. At the moment our brigade still has 195 adult illiterates. With the political evening school as the base, the method of one teaching one and one helping one should be adopted. While efforts should not be relaxed in ordinary times, intensive studies should be organized in the winter. By 1976, illiteracy should disappear among all young and middle-aged commune members. In the future new peasants will generally reach the middle school cultural standard.

19. Eliminate pests and diseases and raise the level of health of commune members. Patriotic health campaigns of a popular nature will be actively unfolded, and everyone will be urged to attend to hygiene and form good sanitary habits. . . .

20. Further efforts will be made to improve the cooperative medical service and to consolidate and develop the ranks of "barefoot doctors." . . . Charges for medical service should be gradually reduced and subsidies should be increased. By 1980, the annual contribution each person will have to make toward the cooperative medical service fund will be reduced from two to one yuan and his medical subsidy will be increased to sixty from thirty yuan at present. . . .

21. Every production team should run its nursery well during busy farming seasons. Kindergartens in various areas should be operated efficiently. . . .

22. The part-time cultural and sports life among commune members will be activated. . . .

23. Late marriage and planned childbirth should be encouraged. . . .

24. Train a contingent of Marxist theorists among poor and lower middle peasants. . . . By 1980, each production team will have a contingent of five to ten theorists who will not be detached from production. These theorists will be required to serve as "teaching assistants in the political evening school, correspondents for newspapers and broadcasting stations, and propagandists of policies to be enforced." . . .

25. Step up the building of the brigade's militia company. In accordance with the principle of "combining labor with military

training," we should continue to consolidate and develop the militia organization and to put it on a sound footing organizationally, politically, and militarily. . . .

26. The number of days for brigade cadres to take part in collective labor should not be less than 120 days in a year.

VI

CLASS STRUGGLE, MODERNIZATION, AND THE FUTURE OF THE CHINESE REVOLUTION
1975–

1. REVOLUTION AND MODERNIZATION:
THE GREAT DEBATE

In 1975, with both Mao and Chou En-lai rapidly approaching death, struggle erupted at the highest levels of the party. The documents which follow present both sides in the most important of the polemics to define the future of the revolution. The debate is most pointed in the writings of Chang Ch'un-ch'iao and Teng Hsiao-p'ing. Stripped to essentials, Chang stresses class struggle to extend the Cultural Revolution through the restriction of bourgeois right. The documents drafted under Teng's direction constitute a program to implement the "four modernizations" to accelerate China's industrialization and economic growth. Yet both essays proclaim the importance of properly combining revolution and production; both praise the accomplishments of the Cultural Revolution; and both quote extensively from Mao.

The documents presented here provide a rare glimpse of the political process at work at the highest levels of the party. They clarify not only the struggle which rocked the party in 1975–1976 but the highly charged issues at the center of the continuing revaluation of the Cultural Revolution and the effort to define China's course in the post-Mao era. The central issues remain as they have for three decades: defining the appropriate relationship between class struggle and the struggle for production, and between centralism and democracy. But they hinge as well on conflicting evaluations of the Cultural Revolution and its aftermath.

Chang Ch'un-ch'iao's essay "On Exercising All-Round Dictatorship over the Bourgeoisie" spearheaded the 1975 attack on bourgeois remnants, calling for restriction of bourgeois right, that is, curbing remaining elements of privilege and inequality of income and opportunity. Chang, who rose to leadership during the Cultural Revolution, hailed "new socialist things" in the realm of factory and commune, management, education, etc. as vital elements in the movement to restrict bourgeois right and eliminate the three great differences.

In 1977 following the fall of the "gang of four," and continuing in 1978, the article was subject to a series of attacks in the Chinese press. Chang has been criticized for confusing contradictions between the people and the enemy with contradictions among the people and hence distorting the concept of the dictatorship of the proletariat; for ignoring the importance (in Mao's words) of protecting "the people so that they may carry on peaceful labor and build our country into a socialist state with modern industry, modern agriculture, and modern science and culture." He has also been criticized for attacking the basic socialist principle "to each according to one's work" thus ignoring Marx's stricture that "right can never be higher than the economic structure of society and its cultural development conditioned thereby"; for ignoring the decisive differences between bourgeois right which rests on exploitation under capitalism and its remaining manifestations under socialism which serve the interest of adjusting relations among state, collective, and individuals and between workers and peasants; and, finally, for pitting revolution against production by carrying political struggle to dictatorial extremes of violence against the people and negating science and technology.

In the summer and fall of 1975 Teng Hsiao-p'ing directed the State Council to draft three documents: "On the General Program for All Work of the Whole Party and the Whole Country," "Some Questions on Accelerating the Development of Industry" (The Twenty Articles), and "The Outline of the Summary Report on the Work of the Chinese Academy of Sciences." Together they constitute the core of Teng's program for implementing the goals outlined by Chou En-lai in February 1975: "Modernization of agriculture, industry, national defense, and *science and technology, so that our country will join the front ranks of the world" by the year 2000.*

In the spring and summer of 1976 following Teng's purge, the media labeled the documents the "three poisonous weeds" and the "program for capitalist restoration." The central charge was that the documents negated class struggle and opposed continuing the revolution under the dictatorship of the proletariat. In failing to note the problems of capitalist roaders in the party and reviling only those who "attack revisionism while holding the anti-revisionist banner," critics charged that the program ignored the main danger of revisionism and the necessity to restrict bourgeois right. By downplaying class struggle and socialist revolution in the economic sphere, it "draws the development of the national economy into the orbit of the revisionist theory of the productive forces." Moreover, in calling for reliance *on foreign technology, in advocating greatly accelerated resource exports and deficit financing, it negates the principle to "rely mainly on our own effort making external assistance subsidiary."*

The three draft documents in question have never been officially issued by the Chinese government; but they have been quoted extensively (and, since 1977, approvingly) in the Chinese press.

The issues debated in these documents posed critical issues not only of theory but of policy priorities which profoundly affect China's future: the nature and financing of foreign technology; the allocation of resources between city and countryside, industry and agriculture; the utilization of natural resources for domestic or export use and in what proportions; wage and income levels in city and countryside; the role of intellectuals and technical personnel in the development process.

A. Chang Ch'un-ch'iao,
On Exercising All-Round Dictatorship
over the Bourgeoisie

The question of the dictatorship of the proletariat has long been the focus of the struggle between Marxism and revisionism. Lenin said: "Only he is a Marxist who *extends* the recognition of the class struggle to the recognition of the *dictatorship of the proletariat.*" And it is for the very purpose of enabling us to go in for Marxism and not revisionism in both theory and practice that Chairman Mao calls on our whole nation to get a clear idea of the question of the dictatorship of the proletariat. . . .

[In the Soviet Union] the new bourgeois have been engendered in one batch after another, and their representative is none other than the Khrushchev-Brezhnev renegade clique. These people generally have a good class background; almost all of them have been brought up under the red flag; they have joined the Communist Party organizationally, received college training and become so-called red experts. But they are new poisonous weeds engendered by the old soil of capitalism. . . . At no time should we forget this historical experience in which "the satellites went up to the sky while the red flag fell to the ground," especially at a time when we are determined to build a powerful country.

We must be soberly aware that there is still the danger for China to turn revisionist. This is not only because imperialism and social imperialism always set their minds on aggression and subversion against us, and the old landlords and capitalists, unreconciled to their defeat, are still there, but also because new bourgeois elements are, as Lenin put it, being engendered daily and hourly. . . .

Chairman Mao pointed out recently: "In a word, China is a socialist country. Before liberation she was much the same as a capitalist country. Even now she practices an eight-grade wage system, distribution according to work and exchange through

On Exercising All-Round Dictatorship Over the Bourgeoisie. HC April 1975. PR April 4, 1975.

money, and in all this differs very little from the old society. What is different is that the system of ownership has been changed." In order to gain a deeper understanding of Chairman Mao's instruction, let us take a look at the changes in the system of ownership in China and the proportions of the various economic sectors in China's industry, agriculture, and commerce in 1973.

First, industry. Industry under ownership by the whole people accounted for 97 percent of the fixed assets of industry as a whole, 63 percent of the industrial population, and 86 percent of the value of total industrial output. Industry under collective ownership accounted for 3 percent of the fixed assets, 36.2 percent of the industrial population, and 14 percent of the total output value. Besides these, individual handicraftsmen made up 0.8 percent of the industrial population.

Next, agriculture. Among the agricultural means of production, about 90 percent of the farmland and of the irrigation-drainage machinery and about 80 percent of the tractors and draft animals were under collective ownership. Those under ownership by the whole people made up a very small proportion. Hence, over 90 percent of the nation's grain and various industrial crops came from the collective economy. The state farms accounted for only a small proportion. Apart from these, there still remained the small plots farmed by commune members for their personal needs and limited household sideline production.

Then, commerce. State commerce accounted for 92.5 percent of the total volume of retail sales, commercial enterprises under collective ownership for 7.3 percent, and individual peddlers for 0.2 percent. Apart from these, there still remained a sizable amount of trade conducted at rural fairs.

The above figures show that socialist ownership by the whole people and socialist collective ownership by working people have indeed won great victory in China. The dominant position of ownership by the whole people has been very much enhanced and there have also been some changes in the economy of the people's commune as regards the proportions of ownership at the three levels—the commune, the production brigade, and the production team. On Shanghai's outskirts, for example, income at the commune level in proportion to total income rose from

28.1 percent in 1973 to 30.5 percent in 1974, that of the brigades rose from 15.2 percent to 17.2 percent, while that of the teams dropped from 56.7 percent to 52.3 percent. The people's commune has demonstrated ever more clearly its superiority of being larger in size and having a higher degree of public ownership. Insofar as we have, step by step in the past 25 years, eliminated ownership by imperialism, bureaucrat-capitalism, and feudalism, transformed ownership by national capitalism and by the individual laborer, and replaced these five kinds of private ownership with the two kinds of socialist public ownership, we can proudly declare that the system of ownership in China has changed, that the proletariat and other working people in China have in the main freed themselves from the shackles of private ownership, and that China's socialist economic base has been gradually consolidated and developed. . . .

However, we must see that the issue has not been entirely settled with respect to the system of ownership. We often say that the issue of the system of ownership "has in the main been settled"; this means that it has not been settled entirely, neither has bourgeois right been totally abolished in the realm of the system of ownership. Statistics cited above show that private ownership still exists in part of industry, agriculture, as well as commerce, that socialist public ownership does not consist purely of ownership by the whole people but includes two kinds of ownership, and that ownership by the whole people is as yet rather weak in agriculture, the foundation of the national economy. The nonexistence of bourgeois right in the realm of the system of ownership in a socialist society, as conceived by Marx and Lenin, implies the conversion of all the means of production into the common property of the whole society. . . .

Speaking at the First Plenary Session of the Ninth Central Committee of the party on April 28, 1969, Chairman Mao said: "It seems that it won't do not to carry out the Great Proletarian Cultural Revolution, for our foundation is not solid. Judging from my observations, I am afraid that in a fairly large majority of factories—I don't mean all or the overwhelming majority of them—leadership was not in the hands of genuine Marxists and the masses of workers. Not that there were no good people among those in charge of the factories. There were. There were good people among the secretaries, deputy secretaries, and members of party committees and among party branch secretaries. But they were following that line of Liu Shao-ch'i—simply resorting to material incentives, putting profit in command and, instead of promoting proletarian politics, handing out bonuses, and so forth. . . .

"But there were indeed bad people in the factories. . . . This showed that the revolution remained unfinished." Chairman Mao's remarks not only explain the necessity of the Great Proletarian Cultural Revolution but enable us to see more clearly that on the problem of the system of ownership, as on all other problems, we should pay attention not only to its form but also to its actual content. It is perfectly correct for people to attach importance to the decisive role of the system of ownership in the relations of production. But it is incorrect to attach no importance to whether the issue of the system of ownership has been resolved in form or in reality, to the reaction exerted on the system of ownership by the two other aspects of the relations of production—the relations between men and the form of distribution—and to the reaction exerted on the economic base by the superstructure; these two aspects and the superstructure may play a decisive role under given conditions. Politics is the concentrated expression of economics. The correctness or incorrectness of the ideological and political line, and the control of leadership in the hands of one class or another, decide which class owns a factory in reality. . . .

Also, we must see that what we practice today is a commodity system. Chairman Mao says: "Our country at present practices a commodity system, the wage system is unequal, too, as in the eight-grade wage scale, and so forth. These can only be restricted under the dictatorship of the proletariat. So if people like Lin Piao come to power, it will be quite easy for them to rig up the capitalist system." This state of affairs which Chairman Mao pinpointed cannot be changed in a short period. Take, for instance, the rural people's communes on the outskirts of Shanghai where the economy at the commune and production brigade levels has developed at a rather fast pace. The commune accounts for 34.2 percent of the fixed assets owned at all three levels, the brigade accounts for only 15.1 percent, while the production team still accounts for 50.7 percent. Therefore, considering the economic conditions in the commune alone, it will take a fairly long time to effect the transition from the team to the brigade and then to the commune functioning as the basic accounting unit. Even when the commune is made the basic accounting unit, it will still remain under collective ownership. Thus, within a short period no basic change will take place in the situation in which there are both ownership by the whole people and collective ownership. So long as these two kinds of ownership still exist, commodity production, exchange through money, and distribution according to work are inevitable. Since "these can only be restricted under the dictatorship of the proletariat," the growth of capitalist factors in town and country and the emergence of new bourgeois elements are likewise inevitable. If these are not restricted, capitalism and the bourgeoisie will grow faster. Therefore, on no account should we relax our vigilance just because we have won great victory in the transformation of the system of ownership and carried out a Great Proletarian Cultural Revolution. We must realize that our economic base is not yet solid and that bourgeois right, which has not yet been abolished entirely in the system of ownership, is still prevalent to a serious extent in the relations between men and holds a dominant position in distribution. In the various spheres of the superstructure, some aspects are in fact still controlled by the bourgeoisie which is predominant there; some are being transformed but the results are not yet consolidated, and old ideas and the old force of habit are trying obstinately to hold back the growth of socialist new things. New bourgeois elements are engendered, group after group, in the wake of the development of capitalist factors in town and country. The class struggle between the proletariat and the bourgeoisie, the class struggle between the different political forces, and the class struggle in the ideological field between the proletariat and the bourgeoisie will continue to be long and tortuous and at times will even become very acute. . . .

"Are you out to stir up a wind of 'communization'?" To fabricate rumors by posing such a question is a tactic which some persons have recently resorted to. To this we can answer explicitly: the wind of "communization" as stirred up by Liu Shao-ch'i and Ch'en Po-ta shall never be allowed to rise again. We have always held that instead of having too big a supply of commodities, our country does not yet have a great abundance of them. So long as the communes cannot yet offer much to be "communized" with production brigades and teams, and enterprises under ownership by the whole people cannot offer a great abundance of products for distribution according to need among our 800 million people, we will have to continue with commodity production, exchange through money, and distribution according to work. . . .

We would rather call comrades' attention to the fact that it is another kind of wind which is blowing—the "bourgeois" wind. This is the bourgeois style of life Chairman Mao has pointed out, an evil wind stirred up by those "parts" of the people who have degenerated into bourgeois elements. The "bourgeois" wind blowing from among those communists, particularly leading cadres, who belong to these "parts," does the greatest harm to us. Poisoned by this evil wind, some people are permeated with bourgeois ideas; they scramble for fame and gain and feel proud instead of ashamed of this. . . . Those who are communists in name but new bourgeois elements in reality manifest the features of the decadent and moribund bourgeoisie as a whole. . . .

Under the leadership of the party Central Committee headed by Chairman Mao, the mighty proletarian revolutionary contingents formed by the masses in their hundreds of millions in China are striding forward. With twenty-five years of practical experience in the dictatorship of the proletariat and the international experience since the Paris Commune, and as long as the few hundred members of our party Central Committee and the several thousand senior cadres take the lead and join the vast numbers of cadres and masses of people in reading and studying assiduously, conducting investigation and study, and summing up experience, we can certainly translate Chairman Mao's call into reality, get a clear idea of the question of the dictatorship of the proletariat, and ensure the triumphant advance of our country along the course charted by Marxism-Leninism-Mao Tsetung thought.

B. How Chiang Ch'un-ch'iao Tampered with
the Theory of the Dictatorship of the Proletariat

In 1957, Chairman Mao made the report "On the Correct Handling of Contradictions Among the People," in which he explicitly explained the meaning of the dictatorship of the proletariat (or the people's democratic dictatorship) as follows:

> Our state is a people's democratic dictatorship led by the working class and based on the worker-peasant alliance. What is this dictatorship for? Its first function is internal, namely, to suppress the reactionary classes and elements and those exploiters who resist the socialist revolution, to suppress those who try to wreck our socialist construction, or in other words, to resolve the contradictions between ourselves and the internal enemy. . . . The second function of this dictatorship is to protect our country from subversion and possible aggression by external enemies. . . . The aim of this dictatorship is to protect all our people so that they can devote themselves to peaceful labor and make China a socialist country with modern industry, modern agriculture, and modern science and culture. Who is to exercise this dictatorship? Naturally, the working class and the entire people under its leadership. Dictatorship does not apply within the ranks of the people. The people cannot exercise dictatorship over themselves, nor must one section of the people oppress another." . . . Our socialist democracy is the broadest kind of democracy, such as is not to be found in any bourgeois state. Our dictatorship is the people's democratic dictatorship led by the working class and based on the worker-peasant alliance. That is to say, democracy operates within the ranks of the people, while the working class, uniting with all others enjoying civil rights, and in the first place with the peasantry, enforces dictatorship over the reactionary classes and elements and all those who resist socialist transformation and oppose socialist construction.

Here Chairman Mao dealt not only with the two functions of

Wang Kuei-hsiu and Chang Hsien-yang: How Chang Ch'un-ch'iao Tampered with the Theory of the Dictatorship of the Proletariat. JMJP June 11, 1977. PR January 20, 1978.

the dictatorship of the proletariat but with the aim and essence of this dictatorship as well. Applying the law of the unity of opposites, he classified the contradictions in socialist society into two types of contradictions, those between ourselves and the enemy and those among the people, which are different in nature, and pointed out that different methods must be employed to handle and resolve them. . . .

From Chairman Mao's explanation it can be seen that "dictatorship of the proletariat" and "dictatorship over the bourgeoisie" are not one and the same concept but two concepts which are associated with and at the same time differ from each other. For the proletariat to exercise dictatorship over the bourgeoisie is an extremely important content, but not the entire content, of the dictatorship of the proletariat.

The dictatorship of the proletariat refers to the proletarian state system which embraces not only the relationship of the proletariat to the bourgeoisie with the former exercising dictatorship over the latter but also the relationship of the proletariat to the peasants and other laboring people as well as the relevant systems and methods for handling these two relationships.

Chang Ch'un-ch'iao, however, deliberately confounded the above-mentioned two concepts. When he quoted Marx's and Lenin's famous theses concerning the dictatorship of the proletariat in that article of his, he changed nearly all their references to the "dictatorship of the proletariat" into the "dictatorship over the bourgeoisie." His aim in doing this was to drain the former of its rich content.

What then did he lop off from the content of the dictatorship of the proletariat? It can be summarized as follows:

First, the dictatorship of the proletariat constitutes a unity of two aspects—exercising dictatorship over the reactionaries and practicing democracy within the ranks of the people. But in his article Chang Ch'un-ch'iao did not make any mention of the latter.

Second, the words "led by the working class and based on the worker-peasant alliance" were completely out of sight in his article which claimed to deal with the dictatorship of the proletariat. Hence the question: How can a dictatorship not led by the working class through the Communist Party and not based on the worker-peasant alliance be regarded as the dictatorship of the proletariat?

Third, the aim of this dictatorship is to build China into a powerful, modern socialist country, ultimately abolish all classes and class distinctions and realize communism, for the accomplishment of which a vigorous development of the productive forces is indispensable. But the necessity for the dictatorship of the proletariat to develop the socialist economy was swept under the rug by Chang Ch'un-ch'iao.

"Dictatorship means everything and there is nothing else"—this was Chang Ch'un-ch'iao's formula. . . .

The kind of "dictatorship" of Chang Ch'un-ch'iao's brand was devoid of democracy for the proletariat and the people, of party leadership and of the worker-peasant alliance; it did not undertake to organize the socialist economy, nor did it pay attention to the people's well-being. Although he vociferously called it "exercising dictatorship over the bourgeoisie," it actually amounted to nothing but a fascist dictatorship of the bourgeoisie over the proletariat.

C. Teng Hsiao-p'ing,
A General Program for the Nation

The Second Plenary Session of the Tenth Party Central Committee and the Fourth National People's Congress, acting on Chairman Mao's proposals, put forward a grand task for the development of the national economy in our country over the next twenty-five years. As the first step, we should build, before 1980, an independent and comparatively complete industrial system and national economic system; as the second step, before the end of this century, realize modernization of agriculture, industry, national defense, and science and technology, so that our national economy will join the front ranks of the world.

On the General Program for All Work of the Whole Party and the Whole Country (Draft, October 7, 1975). SCPRM 921, April 25, 1977.

Meanwhile, Chairman Mao issued a directive on studying the theory of proletarian dictatorship, a directive on promoting stability and unity, and a directive on pushing the national economy forward. These three important directives issued by Chairman Mao are not only the general program for work in all fields of the whole party, the whole army, and the country at present, but will also be the general program in the whole course of struggle for achieving the grand objectives of the next 25 years. Carrying out these three important directives is tantamount to carrying out the party's basic line, the party's line of unity for victory, and the party's general line for building socialism. . . .

For many years Chairman Mao has set for us a complete line and a set of principles, policies, and methods, and it can be said with certainty that after the Great Proletarian Cultural Revolution, these have been mastered by the vast number of cadres. The leadership power of many industrial and mining enterprises and grassroots units is already in the hands of Marxists and the worker and peasant masses. The socialist consciousness of the masses of people is soaring with every passing day, their enthusiasm for socialist contruction is rising considerably, and the socialist cause is flourishing. . . .

1.

In his directive on studying theory, Chairman Mao pointed out: "Why did Lenin speak of exercising dictatorship over the bourgeoisie? This question must be made clear. Lack of clarity on this question will lead to revisionism. This must be made known to the whole nation."

Studying the theory of proletarian dictatorship and combating and preventing revisionism are a matter of top priority in the three important directives. . . . The only yardstick that measures our results in studying the theory of proletarian dictatorship—whether these results are good or bad, large or small—is whether we can apply this theory, and in such a manner as to benefit the carrying out of the task of the dictatorship of the proletariat at the grassroots level, the creation of a political situation favorable to stability and unity, and the development of the national economy at an accelerated pace. . . .

Anti-Marxist class enemies, who inherited Lin Piao's mantle, always take over our revolutionary slogans, twist them, cut them up and fill them with their private stuff so as to confuse black and white and confound right and wrong. They create confusion in the thinking of some of our comrades and of some sections of the masses, and in some localities and units disrupt the party organization and split the party, the working class, and the rank and file. They practice revisionism while holding the antirevisionist banner and promote restoration while holding the antirestoration banner. . . . The contradiction between these anti-Marxist class enemies and the masses of people is a contradiction between the enemy and ourselves, and their struggle with the working class, the poor and lower middle peasants, revolutionary cadres, and revolutionary intellectuals is a life-and-death struggle. This struggle is a concentrated manifestation of the current struggle between the two classes, two roads, and two lines. . . .

2.

Chairman Mao has said: "The Great Proletarian Cultural Revolution has gone through eight years. Now let us have stability. The whole party and the whole army must unite." In studying theory and grasping the line, we aim at promoting stability and unity. "Unite for one purpose, that is, the consolidation of the dictatorship of the proletariat in every factory, village, government office, and school." . . .

But there are contradictions of all kinds among the people, and these contradictions can only be resolved through the formula of unity–criticism–unity, as referred to by Chairman Mao. This means that a new unity is to be achieved on a new basis, starting from the desire for unity, through criticism and struggle, by distinguishing what is correct from what is incorrect. . . .

3.

The aim of the dictatorship of the proletariat, as Chairman Mao has pointed out, "is to protect the whole people so that they may carry out peaceful labor and build our country into a socialist state with modern industry, modern agriculture, and modern science and culture." Studying the theory of proletarian dictatorship, carrying out the tasks of the proletarian dictatorship at the grassroots level, correctly distinguishing between and handling the two different types of contradictions, and promoting stability and unity the country over—these are the tasks for adjusting the socialist superstructure. To push the national economy forward is a task for strengthening the socialist economic base. Between these tasks there are mutual relations, that is, the relations between revolution and production, relations between politics and economics, and relations between the superstructure and the economic base. . . .

In accordance with Chairman Mao's teachings, we must dialectically understand the relations between politics and economics as a unity of opposites. We must not only recognize the role of politics as the commander but also recognize that political work guarantees the fulfillment of economic work and serves the economic base. Even now, however, some comrades of ours still use metaphysics to deal with the relations between politics and economics and between revolution and production. They always cut politics off from economics, and revolution off from production. They talk only about politics, but not economics; they talk only about revolution, but not production. The moment they hear of the need to boost production and make a success of economic construction, they would put on you the cap "theory of productive forces," and charge you with practicing revisionism. Such views are utterly untenable. . . .

Lenin said: "The results of political education can only be measured by the improvement of the economic condition." Chairman Mao also said: "The good or bad, large or small effects exerted among the Chinese people by the policies and practices of all political parties in China depend, in the last analysis, on whether they are helpful, and in what degree, to the productivity of the Chinese people, on whether they restrict or release the productive forces."

D. Teng Hsiao-p'ing,
On Accelerating the Development of Industry

Rectification of Enterprise Management

Since the beginning of the Great Proletarian Cultural Revolution, many enterprises have adhered to the charter of the Anshan Iron and Steel Company, aroused the masses boldly, improved enterprise management, and enlivened all kinds of work. But there are still quite a number of enterprises whose ideological and political work is weak, management chaotic, and labor productivity low. The quality of their products is bad, their consumption of raw materials is great, their production cost is high, and they are involved in many accidents, thereby inflicting heavy losses on the state and the people. These enterprises, while rectifying and strengthening their leading groups, must rectify their enterprise management and make their rules and regulations more strict.

We must not relax our effort to continue to criticize in depth the revisionist line on running enterprises. The aim of doing this is to strengthen, not weaken, socialist enterprise management. Production control and rules and regulations are needed at all times, even ten thousand years from now. The question is what line to follow and on whom we rely in enforcing them. Wholesale opposition to enterprise management and rules and regulations is bound to lead to anarchy. "Anarchy is incompatible with the interests and wishes of the people."

All enterprises must persevere in putting proletarian politics in command and ideological and political work first. . . . All political movements of the enterprises must proceed under the condition of maintaining production; under no circumstances should production be suspended to make revolution.

In all of its work, an enterprise must keep to the mass line, unfold a mass movement on a large scale, and mobilize the masses boldly do the work, instead of letting a small number of people work quietly in seclusion. It must launch a socialist

Some Questions on Accelerating the Development of Industry (Draft, September 2, 1975). SCPRM 926, May 23, 1977.

labor emulation drive. Cadres at all levels in the enterprise must keep to the system of regular participation in collective productive labor and intermingle with the masses, instead of claiming special privileges for themselves. Workers must take part in the enterprise management. It is imperative to put into practice extensively the three-in-one combination of leading cadres, workers, and technicians.

All enterprises must, under the unified leadership of their party committees, set up an effective and independent production management command system, which will be responsible for managing and directing the daily production activities of the enterprises and for handling in time problems arising from production so as to ensure the normal operations in production. . . .

All enterprises must grasp the following principal economic and technical targets: (1) output target; (2) variety target; (3) quality target; (4) consumption target for raw materials, other materials, fuels, and power; (5) labor productivity target; (6) cost target; (7) profit target; (8) target of ratio of working capital, and so on and so forth. Failing to achieve these targets and to fulfill the supply contracts according to the quality and quantity prescribed and according to the schedule laid down means failing to fulfill the state plans in an all-round manner, and where the state plans have not been fulfilled for a long time, the responsibility of leadership must be investigated. . . .

All enterprises must rely on the masses and, proceeding from actual needs, establish and strengthen the following principal production management systems: (1) the system of responsibility at each post (or personal responsibility); (2) the system of checking attendance; (3) technical operating procedures; (4) the system of quality inspection; (5) the system of equipment control and maintenance; (6) the system of production safety; (7) the system of economic accounting, and so on and so forth. The specific content of these systems should be constantly changed and gradually perfected along with the change of objective conditions. But these systems are essential and must be strictly enforced. . . .

The system of responsibility is the core of an enterprise's rules and regulations. Without a strict system of responsibility, production can only proceed in a chaotic manner. We must establish the system of responsibility and regard it as an important step of rectifying enterprise management. Someone must be put in charge of every piece of work and every station, and every cadre, every worker, and every technician must have clearly defined duties. We must coordinate the system with the mass movement properly, strengthen ideological and political work, and translate observance of rules and regulations into a conscious action of the masses. . . .

Adoption of Advanced Technology

It is by the adoption of the most advanced technologies that the industrially backward countries catch up with the industrially advanced countries in the world. We must also do the same. Every department and every industry must know the world's advanced level and map out plans and measures for catching up with and surpassing it.

We must make a big effort to develop a mass movement for technical innovation and scientific experimental activities. We must respect the pioneering spirit of the masses and pay attention to summing up, elevating, and popularizing the achievements of innovation and creation of the masses. We must develop the backbone roles of specialized research agencies and forces and enable them to cooperate closely with the masses in studying and solving major scientific and technological problems of a crucial nature. . . .

In regard to the importation of advanced technologies from foreign countries, we must train the necessary technical forces to master them as speedily as possible. In accordance with the principle of "first, use; second, criticize; third, convert; and fourth, create," we must, in the course of applying them, know them, transform them, and develop them. We must oppose copying wholesale and applying mechanically, and we must also oppose the practice of transforming them without first mastering them. . . .

Increasing Export of Industrial and Mineral Products

If we are to import more advanced technologies from abroad, we must increase exports and raise the proportion of industrial and mineral products among export commodities.

Every industrial department must study the requirements of the international market and energetically increase the output of products which can be exported and have a high exchange value. We must develop production as fast as possible and increase our exports as much as possible. We must not consider only our import requirements without considering the need to increase export resources. Our country gives the main emphasis to the domestic market, which is supplemented by the external market. But the external market is very important and must not be neglected.

In order to accelerate the exploitation of our coal and petroleum, it is possible that on the condition of equality and mutual benefit and in accordance with accepted practices of international trade such as deferred payment and installment payment, we may sign long-term contracts with foreign countries and fix several production points, whereby they will supply complete sets of modern equipment required by us and then we will pay for them with the coal and oil we produce.

From Each According to His Best, To Each According to His Work

On the question of wages, our party's consistent policy has been to oppose not only wide differentials between high and low wages but also egalitarianism in respect to wages.

We must restrict bourgeois right, oppose the extension of differences, and oppose material incentives. Failure to do this will aid the growth of capitalist factors as well as endanger the consolidation of the dictatorship of the proletariat.

We cannot restrict bourgeois right by ignoring the material and spiritual conditions at the present stage, by negating the principle of to each according to his work, by disavowing the necessary differences, and by practicing egalitarianism. Egalitarianism does not work now and will not work in the future.

From each according to his best, to each according to his work, and he who does not work shall not eat—these are socialist principles. At the present stage, these principles basically meet the needs of the development of the productive forces and must be resolutely enforced. . . .

We must gradually raise the wages of workers receiving low wages and reduce the gap between high and low wages.

We must enforce the system of regular promotions. Every year or every two years we should raise the wages of a number of workers in accordance with the labor attitude of the workers, their technical and vocational capabilities, and their contribution in labor and work, in accordance with the number of promotions granted in the state plan, and after evaluation by the masses and approval by the leadership. . . .

We must not separate "to each according to his work" from "from each according to his best." We must explain to the broad masses that we are still a developing country, that our living standard can only be improved on the basis of developing production and raising labor productivity, and that we must continue to display the fine tradition of hard work and plain living.

E. A Critique of
Teng Hsiao-p'ing and the Twenty Articles

Fraud always has to be practiced by the capitalist roaders in power within the party when they push the counter-revolutionary revisionist line, and the so-called "everything for modernization" is just a fraud used by Teng Hsiao-p'ing. . . .

Is Teng Hsiao-p'ing really more anxious than anyone else to achieve four modernizations? Certainly not! "Certain Questions of Accelerating the Development of Industry" ("Twenty Articles"), cooked up on his personal instruction, has entirely exposed the ferocious features of this commander in whipping up the right deviationist wind to reverse verdicts. . . .

Kung Hsiao-wen, "Teng Hsiao-p'ing and the 'Twenty Articles,' " *Hsueh-hsi yu p'i-p'an* (Study and Criticism), June 14, 1976. SCPRM 879, July 12, 1976.

His "taking the three directives as the key link" was written into the "General Work Program." He attacked the excellent situation since the start of the Great Cultural Revolution, and the document also exaggerated this onesidedly and listed a large number of so-called "dark aspects" such as "lax discipline," "confusion in management," "poor quality and many accidents." . . .

The article "from each according to his best, to each according to his work" was added. Why give prominence to this article? . . .

On Teng Hsiao-p'ing's order, the draft was revised and it stated emphatically: "In the socialist period, it (distribution according to work) basically conforms to the requirements of the developing productive forces and must be resolutely enforced." The special feature of this article is that it embraces "all sides"; "this side," "that side," "not only opposing material incentives," "but also opposing egalitarianism," etc. But once the crucial issue is involved, it does not embrace "all sides." Here it is permissible only to talk about "basic conformity," "this side." As regards the Marxist thesis that distribution according to work is a birthmark of the old society and the idea that bourgeois right manifested in distribution according to work must be restricted under the dictatorship of the proletariat—sorry, they do not deserve to be written into the article. Don't you want to restrict and criticize bourgeois right? The document would accuse you of "departing from the material and spiritual conditions at the present stage," and put on your head the big hat of "practicing egalitarianism." What a champion of bourgeois right!

Bourgeois right is the lifeblood of the capitalist roaders. Teng Hsiao-p'ing is of course particularly resentful of the criticism and restriction of bourgeois right. . . .

The article "increasing the export of industrial and mineral products" was added. This proposal was also made by Teng Hsiao-p'ing at the August 18 discussion meeting. He said: "We must use more things to exchange for the best and the latest equipment of foreign countries," adding this policy "is most reliable" and "a major policy" at that.

Here what is raised is not the question of how much should

be "relied" on in bringing about four modernizations. According to Teng Hsiao-p'ing's logic, only "importing foreign advanced technology" is "most reliable," only "exchanging for
the best and the latest equipment of foreign countries" is "most
reliable." Does this mean that maintaining independence and
achieving rejuvenation through self-reliance and calling into play
the creative power of the masses of people are all "unreliable"?
"Relying" on such a "major policy" not only will make it
impossible to bring about four modernizations but also will
cause China to be reduced into an appendage of imperialism and
social imperialism. . . .

In the new text, Teng Hsiao-p'ing's revisionist program of
"taking the three directives as the key link" suddenly dis-
appears. . . . "Taking the three directives as the key link" van-
ished from the front door, but re-entered through the back
door. After "General Work Program" was deleted and a lot of
nonsense about "penetratingly conduct education in the party's
basic line" was said, in the last article "The Whole Party Should
Get Mobilized to Fight for Accelerating the Speed of Industrial
Development," it was nevertheless stated that "the three directives" were "so closely interrelated that they were inseparable
from one another and must be enforced in an all-round manner," a repetition of an old tune. . . .

In carrying out education in the party's basic line, it is
necessary to criticize revisionism and the bourgeoisie. Where is
the bourgeoisie? The document said: "Leadership in a small
number of enterprises is usurped by bad people. They practice
restoration under the 'anti-restoration' banner and exercise a
bourgeois dictatorship over the vast numbers of cadres and
masses."

Aren't these words entirely the same as those in the first two
drafts? Here, the Marxist principle that the main danger is
revisionism and the proposition that the main target of the
struggle is party persons in power taking the capitalist road are
subtly evaded. They use more insidious language, such as "practice restoration under the 'anti-restoration' banner" in an attempt to finish off at one stroke the revolutionary cadres and
masses who rise up to expose and criticize Teng Hsiao-p'ing's
scheme of restoring capitalism. The only difference is that here

they add the fraud "carrying out education in the party's basic line." . . .

What is worth mentioning with emphasis is that "Twenty Articles" is not something new. If we contrast it with that "Seventy Articles for Industry" formulated under Teng Hsiao-p'ing's direction before the Great Proletarian Cultural Revolution, one finds a great deal of similarity. In 1968, under the blow of the tempest of the Great Cultural Revolution, Teng Hsiao-p'ing could not but admit: "This document did not stress putting politics, namely, Mao Tsetung thought, in command. It contained many serious errors. I must take the main responsibility. . . ." Once he went back to work, he denied what he had said. In August and September last year, he referred to the "Seventy Articles" on several occasions. Once he said: "In industry there has been a set of regulations [meaning the 'Seventy Articles']. They may be revised, but not abolished." . . .

"Twenty Articles" is nothing less than a reprint under the new situation of the "Seventy Articles" of fifteen years ago. Teng Hsiao-p'ing himself admitted voluntarily: This document "basically replaces the former Seventy Articles for industry." . . . "Seventy Articles" reversed the verdicts on the general line, the Great Leap Forward and the people's communes, and "Twenty Articles" reverses the verdicts on the Great Proletarian Cultural Revolution. The spearhead of both documents is directed at the great leader Chairman Mao and his revolutionary line. If only we seriously analyze "Seventy Articles" and "Twenty Articles" formulated under Teng Hsiao-p'ing's direction, we shall fully recognize that this unrepentant capitalist roader is not, as he has boasted of himself, an expert interested in four modernizations, but an old hand in right deviationist reversal of verdicts and practice of revisionism.

2. HUA KUO-FENG,
BUILD TACHAI-TYPE COUNTIES
THROUGHOUT THE COUNTRY

Hua Kuo-feng's speech to the First National Conference on Learning from Tachai in Agriculture provides the most comprehensive statement on the political economy of rural development since the sixty points of 1962. Hua's command of rural affairs, his commitment to development of rural cooperation, and his abundant experience as a local and provincial official concerned with the Hunan countryside, paved the way to his rise to the chairmanship of the Chinese Communist Party.

The report, which launched the nation-wide movement to build Tachai-type counties, is built around the interrelated goals of revolutionary change (deepening class struggle and formation of socialist institutions and consciousness) and coordinated development of the productive forces, emphasizing mechanization, rural industrialization, and capital construction. Hua defines a central role in rural development for the county party while continuing to stress the role of the commune in agricultural mechanization and capital construction.

1. Militant Task of the Whole Party

China's socialist revolution and socialist construction at present are in an important historical period of development, and the nation-wide mass movement—In agriculture, learn from Tachai—has also reached a new important stage. A great militant task before us is to get the whole party mobilized for a vast effort to develop agriculture and build Tachai-type counties throughout the country. This is an urgent task in implementing Chairman Mao's important directive on studying theory and combating and preventing revisionism and in consolidating the dictatorship of the proletariat; it is also an urgent task in

Let the Whole Party Mobilize for a Vast Effort to Develop Agriculture and Build Tachai-Type Counties Throughout the Country. Report to the National Conference on Learning from Tachai, October 15, 1975 (Peking: Foreign Languages Press, 1975).

pushing the national economy forward so that China will be advancing in the front ranks of the world before the end of this century, as well as an urgent task in racing against the enemy for time and speed and doing a good job of getting prepared against war. . . .

To build Tachai-type counties throughout the country means building every county in China into a fighting bastion which adheres to Chairman Mao's proletarian revolutionary line and the socialist road. In this way, the leading bodies at all levels in the country will be further revolutionized. . . .

To build Tachai-type counties all over the country means enabling every county in China to achieve stability and unity on the basis of Chairman Mao's revolutionary line and go all out to build socialism with millions united as one. It means that every county will implement the general principle of *taking agriculture as the foundation and industry as the leading factor* in developing the national economy, undertake large-scale farmland capital construction, basically realize the mechanization of agriculture, *take grain as the key link and ensure an all-round development* so that production of grain, cotton, oil-bearing crops, pigs, all industrial crops and forestry, animal husbandry, side occupations, and fishery will surpass the targets set in the National Program for Agricultural Development and outstrip the state plans. . . .

When agricultural mechanization is basically attained throughout the country, and the major processes in farming, forestry, animal husbandry, side occupations, and fishery are 70 percent mechanized, the use of machinery in ploughing, in irrigation and drainage, and in transportation alone will more than double today's total rural labor power. This will bring about tremendous development in the economy of the people's communes and the national economy as a whole. . . .

Since 1970, the Hsiyang experience in building itself into a Tachai-type county in three years has been popularized and the movement to learn from Tachai in agriculture has gathered ever greater momentum. Tachai-type communes and production brigades have emerged in great numbers, more than 300 counties in various parts of the country have excelled as advanced units in learning from Tachai, and a revolutionary torrent involving vast numbers of people in learning from Tachai has taken shape in many areas and a number of provinces. In the movement to learn from Tachai, the cadres and people have mounted powerful attacks on the class enemies and capitalist forces and this has led to a tremendous rise in the socialist forces and a drastic fall in the capitalist forces. Farmland capital construction has been carried out on a large scale, and during the past four years some 100 million people have taken part in each winter-spring period, bringing an average of 1.6 million more hectares of land each year under irrigation. The rate of mechanization of agriculture has been gradually stepped up. The amount of irrigation and drainage equipment, chemical fertilizer, and tractors supplied in the past four years exceeded the total supplied in the previous fifteen years, and a number of production brigades, communes, and counties have attained a relatively high degree of mechanization. Mass scientific experiment in farming has spread far and wide. Three provinces and 2 municipalities, 44 prefectures and 725 counties have topped their targets for per-hectare yield of grain set in the National Program for Agricultural Development. Another 11 provinces and 1 municipality are nearing their respective targets. Thirty counties in the north have reached the target set for areas south of the Yangtze River, 6 of them topping the 7.5-ton-per-hectare mark, and 4 counties in the south have doubled the yield set by the program.* These facts indicate that in our country the conditions by and large are ripe for building Tachai-type counties everywhere.

At the same time, however, we must take note of the fact that the development of this movement is very uneven. . . . In a few rural areas class struggle remains very acute and capitalist activities are fairly serious. . . .

---

* The grain yield targets set by the National Program for Agricultural Development for different areas of the country are: 200 kilograms per mou (one-fifteenth of a hectare) for areas north of the Yellow River (the section inside Ch'inghai province), the Ch'ing Ling Mountains, and the Pailung River; 250 kilograms per mou for areas south of the Yellow River and north of the Huai River; 400 kilograms per mou for areas south of the Huai River, the Ch'ing Ling Mountains, and the Pailung River.

2. Key to Success Lies in County Party Committees

Tachai's fundamental experience lies in its adherence to the principle of putting proletarian politics in command and placing Mao Tsetung thought in the lead, to the spirit of self-reliance and hard struggle, and to the communist style of loving the country and the collective. . . .

The criteria for a Tachai-type county at present should be: (1) The county party committee should be a leading core which firmly adheres to the party's line and policies and is united in struggle. (2) It should establish the dominance of the poor and lower middle peasants as a class so as to be able to wage resolute struggles against capitalist activities and exercise effective supervision over the class enemies and remold them. (3) Cadres at the county, commune, and brigade levels should, like those in Hsiyang, regularly participate in collective productive labor. (4) Rapid progress and substantial results should be achieved in farmland capital construction, mechanization of agriculture, and scientific farming. (5) The collective economy should be steadily expanded, and production and income of the poor communes and brigades should reach or surpass the present level of the average communes and brigades in the locality. (6) All-round development should be made in farming, forestry, animal husbandry, side occupations, and fishery with considerable increases in output, big contributions to the state, and steady improvement in the living standards of the commune members. . . .

After this conference all county party committees must conscientiously study the theory of proletarian dictatorship and the conference documents and link their study with the specific situation in their respective counties. . . .

To ensure success in the county party committees' rectification, the stress should be on ideological rectification, with organizational adjustment where really necessary. . . .

3. Deepening Education in Party's Basic Line

In the historical period of socialism, the principal contradiction always remains the struggle between the proletariat and the bourgeoisie and between the socialist road and the capitalist road. Deepening education in the party's basic line in the countryside is the fundamental guarantee for building Tachai-type counties. . . .

The traditional influence of small production still remains among the peasants, and there are still fairly serious spontaneous tendencies toward capitalism among the well-to-do middle peasants. . . .

Many cases of the tendency toward capitalism in the countryside are problems among the people. They must be solved by means of persuasion and education, and criticism and self-criticism. It is also necessary to solve those problems concerning the consolidation and development of the collective economy appropriately in line with the party's policies. For instance, people who have gone to other localities to work individually should be called back; scattered craftsmen working on their own should be organized; private plots or wasteland reclaimed by commune members in excess of the amount allowed by party policy should go to the collective; the wrong tendency in distribution of dividing and eating up everything, leaving no public accumulation, must be corrected. In short, constant effort must be made to consolidate and further the positions of socialism. . . .

The class struggle in society inevitably finds expression within the party. Where there are wanton attacks by the bourgeoisie, its agents are likely to be found in the party. . . . In some communes and brigades political power is in the hands of bad elements, political degenerates, those who yearn to take the capitalist road, "jolly good fellows," or people whose thinking still remains at the stage of the democratic revolution. This question must be solved discriminatingly and seriously. . . .

4. Speeding Up the Building of Large-Scale Socialist Agriculture

The experience of the Tachai-type counties in different parts of the country shows that where great achievements have been made in farmland capital construction, the superiority of the people's commune as an institution large in size and with a high degree of public ownership has been fully demonstrated, the old features of small production have undergone tremendous changes, and better conditions have been created for the development of mechanized farming than elsewhere. . . .

In order to build themselves into Tachai-type counties, all counties must map out overall plans for their farmland capital construction. These should center on improving the soil and building water conservancy projects, while the mountains, rivers, farmland, forests, and roads should be tackled in a comprehensive way. . . . Conditions must be created for the gradual spread of the county, commune, and brigade farmland capital construction contingents, a new emerging thing specialized in transforming nature and vigorously building socialism.

The equipping of agriculture with machinery is the decisive condition for a big and integrated expansion of farming, forestry, and animal husbandry. In the course of building Tachai-type counties throughout the country, the provinces, municipalities, and autonomous regions must energetically develop their own farm machinery industry in the light of local conditions so as to supply the communes and production brigades with equipment and other products needed for the mechanization of agriculture. The prefectures and counties, for their part, must according to their own resources and other conditions set up small industrial enterprises producing iron and steel, coal, chemical fertilizer, cement, and machinery in order to provide the rural areas with more farm machinery, chemical fertilizer, and insecticide suited to local needs. We must publicize among the masses Chairman Mao's teaching that *the fundamental way out for agriculture lies in mechanization,* bring the enthusiasm and initiative of the hundreds of millions of people into full play, work energetically for the technical transformation of agriculture, and gradually raise the level of mechanized farming in a planned way. We must train a mighty contingent of people for mechanized farming, people who are both workers and peasants and well acquainted with modern techniques. The development of farm mechanization will greatly raise labor productivity in agriculture and give the peasants plenty of time to develop a diversified economy and build a new, prosperous, and rich socialist countryside. It will also have a great significance in bringing into play the role of the people's commune as an organization that combines industry, agriculture, commerce, education, and military affairs, in enabling the commune to display its superiority—big in size and with a high degree of public ownership—and in narrowing the differences between town and country, between worker and peasant, and between manual and mental labor. Therefore, the various departments concerned under the State Council and the leading organs of the provinces, prefectures, and counties must make very great efforts to speed up the progress of this work, make various practical arrangements, take effective measures, check on its progress every year and sum up experience, so as to ensure that the great task of mechanizing agriculture will be accomplished in the main by 1980.

In order to build Tachai-type counties and achieve high and stable yields, it is necessary to implement the Eight Point Charter for agriculture in an all-round way and go in for scientific farming. . . . Each county must set up and strengthen agricultural scientific experiment organizations at the county, commune, production brigade, and production team levels and weld them into a complete network, encourage the masses to carry out widespread scientific experiments, and bring into full play the function of professional scientific and technical personnel. . . .

The expansion of commune- and brigade-run enterprises strengthens the economy at the commune and brigade levels; it has given effective help to the poorer brigades and teams, accelerated farm production, supported national construction and speeded up the pace of mechanization of agriculture. . . .

For most parts of China, the rural people's communes' present system of "three-level ownership, with the production team as the basic accounting unit" is in the main still in harmony with the growth of the productive forces in the countryside. However, we must also note that, with the spread and deepening of the movement to build Tachai-type counties, with the expansion of large-scale socialist agriculture, and especially with the growth of the economy at the commune and brigade levels, this system of ownership will make a step-by-step transition to the system of ownership that takes the production brigade or even the commune as the basic accounting unit when conditions are ripe. In the still more distant future, the people's commune will undergo the transition from the system of collective ownership to the system of ownership by the whole people and then from the socialist system of ownership by the whole people to the communist system of ownership by the whole people. . . .

5. All-Round Planning and the Strengthening of Leadership

After five years of hard struggle, that is, by 1980, more than one-third of the counties in the country are expected to have become Tachai-type counties, and more Tachai-type brigades and communes should have been built up in the other counties. . . .

3. YU CH'IU-LI, THE TACH'ING MODEL AND THE FUTURE OF SOCIALIST INDUSTRIALIZATION

Vice Premier Yu Ch'iu-li's May 1977 speech at the First National Conference on Learning from Tach'ing provides the first authoritative statement of the Hua administration's industrialization strategy. The conference inaugurated a movement to emulate Tach'ing as the focus of a drive to intensify the pace of socialist industrialization. It also endorsed Hua Kuo-feng's call to construct ten more oil fields on the scale of Tach'ing within the century. Oil thus joins steel as the center of industrial development in providing both fuel and capital for domestic development and as the major source of foreign exchange.

Yu's speech underlined and concretized the continuing commitment to mass line features of industrial policy including:

(1) A reduction in managerial personnel to ensure that a maximum of 18 percent of the payroll of each enterprise is allocated for management.

(2) A provision for ensuring that managers and specialists engage in specified quantities of productive labor, for example,

Mobilize the Whole Party and the Nation's Working Class and Strive to Build Tach'ing-Type Enterprises Throughout the Country. Speech to the First National Conference on Learning from Tach'ing, May 4, 1977. PR May 27, 1977.

150 days per year in the case of brigade-level cadres, and that workers participate in management.

(3) Assurances of stepped-up industrial contributions to agriculture in the form of machinery, fertilizer, pesticides, and consumer goods to support agricultural modernization.

(4) Comprehensive plans for combining industry and agriculture. While emphasizing industrial activity, where conditions permit, workers also engage in agriculture and other sideline activities, thus linking industry and agriculture, city and countryside.

(5) Principles of red and expert for workers, managers, and technicians implemented through theoretical study, technical education, and practice.

At the same time, no mention is made of the revolutionary committees which would shortly be officially abolished in the factories.

The conference, with more than 7,000 participants, was the industrial counterpart to the National Tachai Conference in agriculture. Its targets include the creation of 400 or more Tach'ing-type enterprises per year so that one-third of China's industrial enterprises could be so designated as such by 1980.

A critical question in Chinese industry concerns the relationship between the independent self-reliant route associated with Tach'ing and the purchase of large-scale expensive foreign technology associated with the program to achieve the "four modernizations." Will the latter prove compatible with breaking down distinctions between workers, technicians, and cadres, and between city and countryside, or will it contribute to widening divisions and block worker attempts to become masters of the factory and industry? Will it, in conjunction with the first significant pay raise for a large portion of industrial workers in more than a decade, raise labor enthusiasm in the factories?

The opening and construction of the Tach'ing oil field is an example of a thorough rupture with outdated conventions and foreign stereotypes, conscientious application of Chairman Mao's teachings and comprehensive implementation of the "Charter of the Anshan Iron and Steel Company." . . .

Building Tach'ing-type enterprises throughout the country means getting every enterprise to emulate Tach'ing and assiduously study Marxism–Leninism–Mao Tsetung thought, constantly criticize revisionism, capitalism, and all kinds of erroneous ideas, apply the whole set of experience of the Liberation Army in doing political work to the industrial front and, in the course of the three great revolutionary movements of class struggle, the struggle for production, and scientific experiment, build a leading body that firmly follows Chairman Mao's revolutionary line, perseveres in taking part in collective productive labor, maintains close ties with the masses, and unites in struggle, and train a contingent of industrial workers who are ideologically sound, full of drive and technically proficient and who have a good style of work, and strictly observe discipline. . . .

Building Tach'ing-type enterprises throughout the country means getting every enterprise to emulate Tach'ing and work hard and self-reliantly, surmount all difficulties with heaven-storming and death-defying revolutionary enthusiasm, display the revolutionary spirit of "going ahead with the task when the conditions are available, and, when they are not available, going ahead by creating the necessary conditions," dare to think, speak, and act and dare to scale the world peaks of science and technology and, at the same time, combine high revolutionary spirit with a strict scientific approach, and establish and perfect rules and regulations that reflect the new socialist relations of production and objective laws of production. . . .

Building Tach'ing-type enterprises throughout the country means getting every enterprise to emulate Tach'ing and adhere to the "May Seventh" road; while engaging mainly in industrial activity, the workers should be urged to do other things and where conditions permit, organize them and their families to take up farming, forestry, animal husbandry, side occupations, and fisheries. In doing so, we will be able to arrange for everyone to live in collective communities, do a good job of revolutionizing our thinking, and improve the workers' livelihood. This helps restrict bourgeois right and narrow step by step the differences between town and country, between worker and peasant, and between manual and mental labor.

What is most valuable in Tach'ing's experience is that the Tach'ing people really hold high the great banner of Chairman Mao on the industrial front and persevere in continuing the revolution under the dictatorship of the proletariat. . . .

Speed Up China's Industrial Growth, Strive to Catch Up and Surpass Advanced World Levels

At the first session of the preparatory meeting for the Eighth Party Congress in 1956, Chairman Mao compared the conditions of our country with those of the United States, and suggested that we overtake it economically in fifty or sixty years. He said: "This is an obligation. You have such a big population, such a vast territory and such rich resources, and what is more, it has been said that you are building socialism, which is supposed to be superior; if after much ado for fifty and sixty years you are still unable to overtake the United States, what a sorry figure you will cut! You should be read off the face of the earth. Therefore, to overtake the United States is not only possible, but absolutely necessary and obligatory. . . ."

In view of the advances in China's socialist revolution and construction, Chairman Mao in 1963 mapped out a grand plan for building a powerful, modern socialist country. In line with Chairman Mao's instructions, Premier Chou in his reports on the work of the government to the Third and Fourth National People's Congresses proclaimed the envisaged two-stage development of our national economy. First, to build an independent and relatively comprehensive industrial and economic system before 1980; second, to accomplish the comprehensive modernization of agriculture, industry, national defense, and science and technology before the end of the century, so that our national economy will be advancing in the front ranks in the world. The decade 1976–1985 is crucial for accomplishing the grand plan of the two-stage development. In this period, we are first of all to build a nation-wide, independent, and relatively comprehensive industrial and economic system and basically complete the technical transformation of the national economy; then, on this basis, the six major regions of Northeast, North, East, Central-south, Southwest, and Northwest China are to build up step by step their respective economic systems, which vary as regards standards and characteristics and which function self-reliantly while working in close coordination, and have a fairly harmonious development of agriculture and light and heavy industry. . . .

Soon after smashing the "gang of four," the party Central

Committee headed by Chairman Hua called the Second National Conference on Learning from Tachai in Agriculture and now it is holding this large-scale National Conference on Learning from Tach'ing in Industry. The day before the conference opened, Chairman Hua gave the instruction that we should not only build the Tach'ing oil field more successfully and continue concentrating on production in breadth and depth, but should build some ten more oil fields as big as Tach'ing within this century. Chairman Hua's instruction not only sets a grand plan for China's oil industry to catch up with and surpass the most developed capitalist countries in the world, but gives great encouragement and impetus to our comrades in all fields of endeavor. . . .

Agriculture is the foundation and industry is the leading factor of the national economy. While vigorously developing large-scale socialist agriculture, we must greatly speed up industrial development. It is possible to strengthen leadership by the working class and further consolidate the worker-peasant alliance on a new basis only when industry develops faster and supplies agriculture with more and better farm machinery, chemical fertilizer, pesticides, and other such goods, turns out large quantities of light industrial products to exchange for farm products, and ensures the mechanization of agriculture by and large by 1980, and then proceeds to achieve the modernization of agriculture. Only when industry develops faster will it be possible to push the entire national economy forward rapidly and strengthen the material basis for consolidating the dictatorship of the proletariat. . . .

Some Questions Concerning Straightening Out Enterprises

All enterprises should take Tach'ing as the example, conscientiously learn from the experience of the Liberation Army, establish and improve their organizations and rules and regulations for political work, and take effective steps to strengthen political and ideological work. Political work should be linked with economic work and carried out carefully on the workshop floor, in the workers' living quarters, and among the workers' families. . . .

The administrative structure of enterprises should be simplified and superfluous office functionaries sent to grassroots units, and cadres must take part in collective productive labor. The number of nonproductive personnel in general should not exceed 18 percent of the total payroll in an enterprise. Overstaffing exceeding this percentage should be reduced step by step. Theoretical contingents, theatrical and propaganda groups, sports teams, and militia organizations should be run well but only on the principle that the members are not divorced from productive labor. Each leading member and office cadre in Tach'ing participates in productive labor at least 60 days a year, each cadre at the factory and divisional levels at least 100 days, each brigade cadre at least 150 days, and every cadre in grassroots units works regular shifts. What is being done in Tach'ing, other enterprises should strive to do the same.

Enterprises should create the conditions for workers and staff members to become both red and expert, raise their political and technical level, and train their own proletarian technicians and engineers. . . .

Enterprises should strengthen centralized party leadership and institute the system of division of labor and responsibility under the leadership of the party committee. Responsibility for the daily work in production, construction, and management in an enterprise rests with the chairman of the revolutionary committee. . . .

The Key to Building Tach'ing-Type Enterprises Lies in Provincial and Municipal Party Committees

The party committee of each enterprise is the key to its success in becoming a Tach'ing-type enterprise. In the case of a city, the city party committee is the key to the successful building of its enterprises into Tach'ing-type enterprises. As for a province or autonomous region, the key to such success lies in the party committee of the province or autonomous region. . . .

In line with discussions at this conference on the criteria for a Tach'ing-type enterprise at the present stage, we propose the following six points as the standard for evaluation and comparison: (1) It should conscientiously study Marxism-Leninism-Mao Tsetung thought and adhere to the party's basic line and the socialist orientation in running the enterprise; (2) it should have a core of party leadership which combines the old, middle-aged and young and firmly carries out the party's line, principles, and policies, maintains close ties with the masses and is united in struggle; (3) it should have a contingent of workers and staff members capable of fighting hard battles in the three great revolutionary movements of class struggle, the struggle for production, and scientific experiment and imbued with the revolutionary style of being honest in thought, word, and deed and setting itself strict standards for work, organization, attitude, and observance of discipline; (4) it should adhere to the principle of cadre participation in productive labor and worker participation in management, reform of irrational and outdated rules and regulations and close cooperation among cadres, workers, and technicians, and institute scientific rules and regulations for management which rely on the masses and meet the needs for expanding production; (5) it should constantly make new achievements in technical innovations and technical revolution, fulfill state targets in all-round way, and reach the advanced national levels in major technical and economic indices; (6) it should keep to the "May Seventh" road, that, is, while mainly engaging in industrial activity, the workers also do other things and, where conditions permit, do a good job of farming, forestry, animal husbandry, side occupations, and fisheries, and make good arrangements for the workers' daily life while improving production.

We should build one-third of the enterprises in the country into Tach'ing-type units within the current fifth five-year plan. . . . Of the large and medium-sized enterprises throughout the country, an average of 400 or more should be turned into Tach'ing-type enterprises every year from 1977 through 1980. . . .

4. FOR A POWERFUL AND MODERN SOCIALIST CHINA: TASKS FOR THE NEW ERA

The Eleventh Party Congress in August 1977 officially proclaimed the conclusion of the Great Proletarian Cultural Revolution and the beginning of a period of great unity.

The Fifth National People's Congress in March 1978 completed the institutional transition to the new era and provided the fullest expression of the leadership's vision for China's modern future.

The constitution, replacing the 1975 constitution, in many respects resembles its predecessor, reflecting the deep influence of the Cultural Revolution and the concept of continuing the revolution under the dictatorship of the proletariat.

In one significant area it breaks new ground, however, that is, in the explicit focus on modernization including economic development, new technology, education, and culture. It is here that we find the distinctive stamp of the Hua Kuo-feng administration. The new constitution thus explicitly recognizes the important role of scientists and educators in the ambitious modernization programs endorsed by the congress and to encourage their participation revives the themes of 1957: "Let a hundred flowers bloom and a hundred schools of thought contend."

The congress, following shortly after conclusion of the $20 billion seven-year Sino-Japanese trade agreement, established the basic development priorities for the next decade. To achieve its central goals for 1985—400 billion kilograms of grain and 60 million tons of steel a year, 85 percent mechanization of farmwork, and completion of 120 major construction projects—will require a substantial acceleration of the pace of development. The congress set goals, for example, of 4 to 5 percent annual production increases in agriculture and over 10 percent in industry.

As in the first five-year plan, great attention is being paid to modern and heavy industry. But the present leadership clearly recognizes the importance of and obstacles to rural development, mechanization, and industrialization. Thus agriculture is designated the foundation of the economy and industry the leading sector. China's leaders in emphasizing the Tachai model stress the predominant role of self-reliant rural communities. Yet the state is also committed to stepped-up industrial assistance to agriculture in the form of steel, tractors, fertilizer, electricity, and consumer goods. The outcome of the rural modernization drive will be shaped in part by the ability of the state to make good its promises, in part by the success of efforts to reduce population growth to less than 1 percent within three years, but ultimately it rests on the success of communal institutions in mobilizing local resources.

China's largest science conference, convened the week following the National People's Congress, emphasized the priority commitment to modern science and technology. In the new policy toward scientists we have the clearest articulation of a departure from the tone and priorities of the Cultural Revolution and an attempt to rectify its excesses. Teng Hsiao-p'ing's guidelines for scientists are clearly designed to protect them from political pressures to devote full attention to advancing the four modernizations with all possible speed. Thus in contrast with Mao's insistence on the integration of science and technology with politics, Teng defined as "red and expert" anyone who works hard in the service of China's science. Nevertheless, while Teng assured scientists of the freedom to work essentially independent of political pressures, he reaffirmed the party's leadership in all scientific institutes.

The central promise of the Hua-Teng leadership to the Chinese people is the fulfillment of the four modernizations (in industry, agriculture, defense, and science and technology) leading to a prosperous, strong socialist economy and flourishing culture. Since 1977 the overriding emphasis has been placed on modernization, on advancing the forces of production, yet the framework of analysis remains socialist. The central issue of the coming decades is whether China can achieve rapid development within the framework of the four modernizations while continuing the revolution.

A. The 1978 Constitution

Preamble

After more than a century of heroic struggle the Chinese people, led by the Communist Party of China headed by our great leader and teacher Chairman Mao Tsetung, finally overthrew the reactionary rule of imperialism, feudalism, and bureaucrat-capitalism by means of People's Revolutionary War, winning complete victory in the new democratic revolution, and in 1949 founded the People's Republic of China.

The Constitution of the People's Republic of China, adopted March 5, 1978. PR March 17, 1978.

The founding of the People's Republic of China marked the beginning of the historical period of socialism in our country. Since then, under the leadership of Chairman Mao and the Chinese Communist Party, the people of all our nationalities have carried out Chairman Mao's proletarian revolutionary line in the political, economic, cultural, and military fields and in foreign affairs and have won great victories in socialist revolution and socialist construction through repeated struggles against enemies both at home and abroad and through the Great Proletarian Cultural Revolution. The dictatorship of the proletariat in our country has been consolidated and strengthened, and China has become a socialist country with the beginnings of prosperity.

Chairman Mao Tsetung was the founder of the People's Republic of China. All our victories in revolution and construction have been won under the guidance of Marxism–Leninism–Mao Tsetung thought. . . .

The triumphant conclusion of the first Great Proletarian Cultural Revolution has ushered in a new period of development in China's socialist revolution and socialist construction. In accordance with the basic line of the Chinese Communist Party for the entire historical period of socialism, the general task for the people of the whole country in this new period is: to persevere in continuing the revolution under the dictatorship of the proletariat, carry forward the three great revolutionary movements of class struggle, the struggle for production, and scientific experiment, and make China a great and powerful socialist country with modern agriculture, industry, national defense, and science and technology by the end of the century.

We must persevere in the struggle of the proletariat against the bourgeoisie and in the struggle for the socialist road against the capitalist road. We must oppose revisionism and prevent the restoration of capitalism. We must be prepared to deal with subversion and aggression against our country by social imperialism and imperialism.

We should consolidate and expand the revolutionary united front which is led by the working class and based on the worker-peasant alliance, and which unites the large numbers of intellectuals and other working people; patriotic democratic parties, patriotic personages, our compatriots in Taiwan, Hongkong, and Macao, and our countrymen residing abroad. We should enhance the great unity of all the nationalities in our country. We should correctly distinguish and handle the contradictions among the people and those between ourselves and the enemy. We should endeavor to create among the people of the whole country a political situation in which there are both centralism and democracy, both discipline and freedom, both unity of will and personal ease of mind and liveliness, so as to help bring all positive factors into play, overcome all difficulties, better consolidate the proletarian dictatorship, and build up our country more rapidly. . . .

Chapter 1
General Principles

Article 1. The People's Republic of China is a socialist state of the dictatorship of the proletariat led by the working class and based on the alliance of workers and peasants.

Article 2. The Communist Party of China is the core of leadership of the whole Chinese people. The working class exercises leadership over the state through its vanguard, the Communist Party of China.

The guiding ideology of the People's Republic of China is Marxism-Leninism-Mao Tsetung thought.

Article 3. All power in the People's Republic of China belongs to the people. The organs through which the people exercise state power are the National People's Congress and the local people's congresses at various levels.

The National People's Congress, the local people's congresses at various levels, and all other organs of state practice democratic centralism.

Article 4. The People's Republic of China is a unitary multinational state.

All the nationalities are equal. There should be unity and fraternal love among the nationalities and they should help and learn from each other. Discrimination against, or oppression of, any nationality, and acts which undermine the unity of the nationalities are prohibited. Big nationality chauvinism and local nationality chauvinism must be opposed.

All the nationalities have the freedom to use and develop their own spoken and written languages, and to preserve or reform their own customs and ways.

Regional autonomy applies in an area where a minority nationality lives in a compact community. All the national autonomous areas are inalienable parts of the People's Republic of China.

Article 5. There are mainly two kinds of ownership of the means of production in the People's Republic of China at the present stage: socialist ownership by the whole people and socialist collective ownership by the working people.

The state allows nonagricultural individual laborers to engage in individual labor involving no exploitation of others, within the limits permitted by law and under unified arrangement and management by organizations at the basic level in cities and towns or in rural areas. At the same time, it guides these individual laborers step by step on to the road of socialist collectivization.

Article 6. The state sector of the economy, that is, the socialist sector owned by the whole people, is the leading force in the national economy.

Mineral resources, waters, and those forests, undeveloped lands, and other marine and land resources owned by the state are the property of the whole people.

The state may requisition by purchase, take over for use, or nationalize land under conditions prescribed by law.

Article 7. The rural people's commune sector of the economy is a socialist sector collectively owned by the masses of working people. At present, it generally takes the form of three-level ownership, that is, ownership by the commune, the production brigade, and the production team, with the production team as the basic accounting unit. A production brigade may become the basic accounting unit when its conditions are ripe.

Provided that the absolute predominance of the collective economy of the people's commune is ensured, commune members may farm small plots of land for personal needs, engage in limited household sideline production, and in pastoral areas they may also keep a limited number of livestock for personal needs.

Article 8. Socialist public property shall be inviolable. The state ensures the consolidation and development of the socialist sector of the economy owned by the whole people and of the socialist sector collectively owned by the masses of working people.

The state prohibits any person from using any means whatsoever to disrupt the economic order of the society, undermine the economic plans of the state, encroach upon or squander state and collective property, or injure the public interest.

Article 9. The state protects the right of citizens to own lawfully earned income, savings, houses, and other means of livelihood.

Article 10. The state applies the socialist principles: "He who does not work, neither shall he eat" and "from each according to his ability, to each according to his work."

Work is an honorable duty for every citizen able to work. The state promotes socialist labor emulation, and, putting proletarian politics in command, it applies the policy of combining moral encouragement with material reward, with the stress on the former, in order to heighten the citizens' socialist enthusiasm and creativeness in work.

Article 11. The state adheres to the general line of going all out, aiming high and achieving greater, faster, better, and more economical results in building socialism; it undertakes the planned, proportionate, and high-speed development of the national economy, and it continuously develops the productive forces, so as to consolidate the country's independence and security and improve the people's material and cultural life step by step.

In developing the national economy, the state adheres to the principle of building our country independently, with the initiative in our own hands and through self-reliance, hard struggle, diligence, and thrift, it adheres to the principle of taking agriculture as the foundation and industry as the leading factor, and it adheres to the principle of bringing the initiative of both the central and local authorities into full play under the unified leadership of the central authorities.

The state protects the environment and natural resources and prevents and eliminates pollution and other hazards to the public.

Article 12. The state devotes major efforts to developing science, expands scientific research, promotes technical innovation and technical revolution and adopts advanced techniques wherever possible in all departments of the national economy. In scientific and technological work we must follow the practice of combining professional contingents with the masses, and combining learning from others with our own creative efforts.

Article 13. The state devotes major efforts to developing education in order to raise the cultural and scientific level of the whole nation. Education must serve proletarian politics and be combined with productive labor and must enable everyone who receives an education to develop morally, intellectually, and physically and become a worker with both socialist consciousness and culture.

Article 14. The state upholds the leading position of Marxism–Leninism–Mao Tsetung thought in all spheres of ideology and culture. All cultural undertakings must serve the workers, peasants, and soldiers and serve socialism.

The state applies the policy of "letting a hundred flowers blossom and a hundred schools of thought contend" so as to promote the development of the arts and sciences and bring about a flourishing socialist culture.

Article 15. All organs of state must constantly maintain close contact with the masses of the people, rely on them, heed their opinions, be concerned for their weal and woe, streamline administration, practice economy, raise efficiency, and combat bureaucracy.

The leading personnel of state organs at all levels must conform to the requirements for successors in the proletarian revolutionary cause and their composition must conform to the principle of three-in-one combination of the old, the middle-aged, and the young.

Article 16. The personnel of organs of state must earnestly study Marxism–Leninism–Mao Tsetung thought, wholeheartedly serve the people, endeavor to perfect their professional competence, take an active part in collective productive labor, accept supervision by the masses, be models in observing the constitution and the law, correctly implement the policies of the state, seek the truth from facts, and must not have recourse to deception or exploit their position and power to seek personal gain.

Article 17. The state adheres to the principle of socialist democracy, and ensures to the people the right to participate in the management of state affairs and of all economic and cultural undertakings, and the right to supervise the organs of state and their personnel.

Article 18. The state safeguards the socialist system, suppresses all treasonable and counter-revolutionary activities, punishes all traitors and counter-revolutionaries, and punishes new-born bourgeois elements and other bad elements.

The state deprives of political rights, as prescribed by law, those landlords, rich peasants, and reactionary capitalists who have not yet been reformed, and at the same time it provides them with the opportunity to earn a living so that they may be reformed through labor and may become law-abiding citizens supporting themselves by their own labor.

Article 19. The chairman of the Central Committee of the Communist Party of China commands the armed forces of the People's Republic of China.

The Chinese People's Liberation Army is the workers' and peasants' own armed force led by the Communist Party of China; it is the pillar of the dictatorship of the proletariat.

B. Hua Kuo-feng,
To Build a Modern, Powerful Socialist Country

Speed Up Socialist Economic Construction

In order to make China a modern, powerful socialist country by the end of the century, we must work and fight hard in the political, economic, cultural, military, and diplomatic spheres, but in the final analysis what is of decisive importance is the rapid development of our socialist economy. . . .

By the end of this century, the output per unit of major agricultural products is expected to reach or surpass advanced world levels and the output of major industrial products to approach, equal, or outstrip that of the most developed capitalist countries. In agricultural production, the highest possible degree of mechanization, electrification, and irrigation will be achieved. There will be automation in the main industrial processes, a major increase in rapid transport and communications services, and a considerable rise in labor productivity. We must apply the results of modern science and technology on a broad

Unite and Strive to Build a Modern Powerful Socialist Country. Report to the Fifth National People's Congress, February 26, 1978. PR March 10, 1978.

scale, make extensive use of new materials and sources of energy, and modernize our major products and the processes of production. Our economic and technical norms must approach, equal, or surpass advanced world levels. As our social productive forces become highly developed, our socialist relations of production will be further improved and perfected, the dictatorship of the proletariat in our country consolidated, our national defense strengthened, and our people's material well-being and cultural life substantially enriched. By then, China will have a new look and stand unshakably in the East as a modern, powerful socialist country. . . .

In the space of ten years we are to lay a solid foundation for agriculture, achieve at least 85 percent mechanization in all major processes of farmwork, see to it that for each member of the rural population there is one mou of farmland with guaranteed stable high yields irrespective of drought or waterlogging, and attain a relatively high level in agriculture, forestry, animal husbandry, sideline production, and fisheries. The plan calls for the growth of light industry, which should turn out an abundance of first-rate, attractive, and reasonably priced goods with a considerable increase in per capita consumption. Construction of an advanced heavy industry is envisaged, with the metallurgical, fuel, power, and machine-building industries to be further developed through the adoption of new techniques, with iron and steel, coal, crude oil, and electricity in the world's front ranks in terms of output, and with much more developed petrochemical, electronics, and other new industries. . . . We shall in the main have built up a regional economic system in each of the six major regions, that is, in Southwest, Northwest, Central-south, East, North, and Northeast China, and turned our interior into a powerful, strategic rear base.

According to the ten-year plan, by 1985 we are to produce 400 billion kilograms of grain and 60 million tons of steel. In each of the eight years from 1978 to 1985, the value of agricultural output is to increase by 4 to 5 percent and of industrial output by over 10 percent. The increase in our country's output of major industrial products in the eight years will far exceed that in the past twenty-eight years. In these eight years, state revenues and investments budgeted for capital construction will both be equivalent to the total for the past twenty-eight years. . . .

In the eleven years from 1966 to 1976, despite serious interference and sabotage by Liu Shao-ch'i, Lin Piao, and particularly the "gang of four," grain output still registered an annual increase of over 4.3 percent in a third of the provinces, municipalities and autonomous regions, with a maximum of 5.5 percent, and the value of industrial output went up annually by more than 12 percent likewise in a third of the provinces, municipalities and autonomous regions, with a maximum of 18.5 percent. . . .

Mobilize the whole nation and go in for agriculture in a big way

Agriculture is the foundation of the national economy. If agriculture does not develop faster, there will be no upswing in our industry and economy as a whole, and even if there is a temporary upswing, a decline will follow, and there will be really serious trouble in the event of major natural calamities. . . .

The state is planning to take the following measures to develop agricultural production:

(1) While attaining a country-wide increase in grain production, focus on the two following tasks. One, run the twelve large commodity grain bases and all our state farms efficiently and enable them to achieve a twofold or threefold increase in marketable grain in a space of eight years. Two, help low-yield, grain-deficient areas to become self-sufficient and achieve a surplus within two or three years.

(2) While ensuring a rise in yields per unit, organize planned reclamation of wasteland by the state farms and people's communes. . . .

(3) In accordance with the principles of specialized planting and rational distribution, build a number of bases for the production of cotton, edible oil, sugar, and other cash crops where conditions are suitable, and turn them into the state's main sources of supply for these products.

(4) Strive to develop forestry, animal husbandry, sideline production, and fisheries, and do a good job of developing the forest regions, plant trees around every house and every village, by roadsides and watersides, build livestock breeding areas, set up freshwater and marine fishing grounds, and actively promote

rural sideline occupations and commune- and brigade-run enterprises. . . .

(5) Mobilize the masses to forge ahead with farmland capital construction and stress soil improvement and water control. . . .

(6) From the top organs to the grassroots units, set up and perfect a system of agro-scientific research and agro-technical popularization; implement the Eight Point Charter for Agriculture in an all-round way, with stress on cultivating and popularizing fine strains of seed, improving farming methods, extensively exploring various sources of fertilizer, making a big effort to develop organic fertilizer, and making proper use of chemical fertilizer.

(7) In order to hasten the mechanization of agriculture, strive to manufacture more, better, and cheaper farm machinery, chemical fertilizer, and insecticide that meet specific needs, do a good job of supplying complete sets of farm machinery and of their maintenance, repair, and management, and step up the training of farm technicians.

(8) Make an extra effort to build up mountain areas and in particular give attention and assistance to construction in the old revolutionary base areas so as to accelerate their economic progress.

(9) Strengthen the leadership of the poorer production teams and help them to transform themselves economically and catch up with the richer teams as soon as possible.

In order to ensure the implementation of the above measures, the state has planned to make appropriate increases in the proportion of its financial expenditures allocated to investments in agricultural capital construction and to operating expenses and to make corresponding arrangements for materials and equipment.

*Speed up the development of the basic industries
and give full scope to the leading role of industry*

As the economy becomes modernized, the leading role of industry, and especially that of the basic industries, becomes more and more prominent. We must *take steel as the key link*, strengthen the basic industries and exert a special effort to step up the development of the power, fuel, and raw and semifinished materials industries and transport and communications. . . .

The state plans to build or complete 120 large-scale projects, including ten iron and steel complexes, nine nonferrous metal complexes, eight coal mines, ten oil and gas fields, thirty power stations, six new trunk railways, and five key harbors. The completion of these projects added to the existing industrial foundation will provide China with fourteen fairly strong and fairly rationally located industrial bases. This will be decisive in changing the backward state of our basic industries.

Uphold the principle of
"from each according to his ability,
to each according to his work"
and steadily improve the livelihood of the people

Throughout the historical period of socialism, we must uphold the principles of "he who does not work, neither shall he eat" and "from each according to his ability, to each according to his work." In applying them we must firmly put proletarian politics in command, strengthen ideological and political work, and teach and encourage everybody to cultivate the communist attitude toward labor and to serve the people wholeheartedly. With regard to distribution, while we should avoid a wide wage spread, we must also oppose egalitarianism and apply the principle of more pay for more work and less pay for less work. The enthusiasm of the masses cannot be aroused if no distinction is made between those who do more work and those who do less, between those who do a good job and those who do a poor one, and between those who work and those who don't. All people's communes and production brigades must seriously apply the system of fixed production quotas and calculation of work points on the basis of work done and must enforce the principle of equal pay for equal work irrespective of sex. The staff and workers of state enterprises should be paid primarily on a time-rate basis with piece work playing a secondary role, and with additional bonuses. . . .

Develop Socialist Science, Education, and Culture

Modern science and technology, which are characterized mainly by the use of atomic energy and the development of electronic computers and space science, are experiencing a great revolution leading to the emergence of new industries and spurring the advance of technology by leaps and bounds. To catch up quickly with the dramatic changes in modern science and technology and rapidly transform our backwardness in these fields are important and indispensable steps for the speedy development of our economy and the strengthening of our national defense. . . .

By 1985, in the main, eight-year schooling should be made universal in the rural areas and ten-year schooling in the cities. We should fully tap the potential of existing institutions of higher learning, actively expand the student enrollment, rapidly set up new colleges and institutes, and endeavor to run the vocational and technical schools and colleges well. . . .

The repertoires of the performing arts should be enlarged to enrich the people's cultural life. Literature and art must keep to the orientation of serving the workers, peasants, and soldiers. . . . There should be variety in the subject matter of our literature and art. Modern revolutionary themes should be dominant, particularly those reflecting the three great revolutionary movements of the socialist period, but attention should also be given to historical and other themes. Revolutionary realism combined with revolutionary romanticism should be encouraged in artistic creation. . . .

In health work, we should continue the policy of putting the stress on the rural areas and run county and commune hospitals well. The rural cooperative medical service should be strengthened and expanded and the professional proficiency of barefoot doctors raised. At the same time, medical and health work in the cities and in factories and mines should also be done well. . . .

Planned control of population growth is conducive to the planned development of the national economy and to the health of mother and child. It also benefits the people where production, work, and study are concerned. We must continue to give it serious attention and strive to lower the annual rate of growth of China's population to less than 1 percent within three years. . . .

Giving full scope to the abilities of intellectuals is important for speeding up the development of our science, education, and other cultural undertakings and building a modern, powerful socialist country. The overwhelming majority of the intellectuals are devoted to the party and socialism and support Chairman Mao's revolutionary line. . . . The "gang of four" maligned the intellectuals as "the stinking ninth category." . . . We must make a clean sweep of the gang's pernicious influence and correctly and comprehensively carry out the party's policy of uniting with, educating, and remolding the intellectuals. We must give due weight to their work, improve their working conditions, turn their specializations to account, and commend their achievements. At the same time, we must warmly help and encourage them to make a real effort to remold their world outlook in the three great revolutionary movements, persevere in identifying themselves with the workers and peasants and advance along the "red and expert" road. . . .

"Let a hundred flowers blossom, let a hundred schools of thought contend" is the basic policy for making China's socialist science and culture flourish. Its essence is to adopt a policy of "opening wide" within the ranks of the people while adhering to the six political criteria so as to constantly expand the positions of Marxism in matters of ideology and to promote science and culture. . . .

To accelerate the development of socialist science and culture we must stick to the policy of "making the past serve the present" and "making foreign things serve China." We must conscientiously study the advanced science and technology of all countries and turn them to our account. We must be critical in assimilating things from our ancient culture and from the culture of foreign countries, taking the essence and discarding the dross and weeding through the old to bring forth the new, in order to promote a socialist culture which is national in its traits and rich in the characteristics of the age.

C. Teng Hsiao-p'ing,
On Science and Modernization

Comrades!

The successful convocation of the national science conference is a matter of great joy for us and for the people throughout the country. ... Never before has work in science and
technology received such attention and concern from the whole
party and the whole people. ...

Among those attending the present conference are outstanding scientists and technicians from various fronts, first-rate
technical innovators, model laborers who excel in scientific
farming, and cadres devoted to the party's scientific undertakings. ...

Our people face the great historic mission of comprehensively
modernizing agriculture, industry, national defense, and science
and technology within this century, making our country a
modern, powerful socialist state. We have waged a sharp and
bitter struggle against the "gang of four" on whether to accomplish the four modernizations. The "gang of four" made the
absurd claim that "if the four modernizations are carried
through, capitalist restoration will happen on the same day."
Their wild sabotage brought our national economy for a time to
the brink of collapse and was increasingly widening our distance
from advanced world scientific and technological standards. ...
What they did serves as a negative example, making us appreciate more deeply that under conditions of proletarian dictatorship, if we do not modernize our country, raise our scientific
and technological level, develop the social productive forces,
strengthen our country, and improve the material and cultural
life of the people, our socialist political and economic system
cannot be fully consolidated and there will be no sure guarantee
for our country's security. By adhering to the party's basic line
formulated by Chairman Mao, the more up-to-date our agriculture, industry, national defense, and science and technology, the
greater our strength in the struggle against capitalism and all
forces of restoration, and the more our people will support the
socialist system. ...

Speech at Opening Ceremony of National Science Conference, March
18, 1978. PR March 24, 1978.

The crux of the four modernizations is the mastery of modern science and technology. Without modern science and technology, it is impossible to build modern agriculture, modern industry, or modern national defense. Without a high-speed development of science and technology, it is impossible to develop the national economy at high speed. . . . Today, I am going to give some opinions on pertinent questions.

The first question—the question of understanding that science is part of the productive forces. On this point, the "gang of four" raised a hue and cry confounding right and wrong and causing much confusion. Marxism has consistently held that science and technology are part of the productive forces. . . . Modern science has opened the way for the progress of production techniques and determined the direction of their development. Many new instruments of production and technological processes have come into being first in the laboratory. . . .

Since science is becoming an increasingly important part of the productive forces, are people engaged in scientific and technological work to be considered workers or not? . . .

In a socialist society, brain workers trained by the proletariat itself differ from intellectuals in any exploiting society in history. . . . Generally speaking, the overwhelming majority of them are part of the proletariat. The difference between them and the manual workers lies only in a different role in the social division of labor. Those who labor, whether by hand or by brain, are all working people in a socialist society. With the advancement of modern science and technology and progress toward the four modernizations, a great deal of heavy manual work will gradually be replaced by machines. Manual labor will steadily decrease for workers directly engaged in production and mental work will continuously increase. Moreover, there will be an increasing demand for more people in scientific research and for a larger force of scientists and technicians. The "gang of four" distorted the division of labor between mental and manual work in our socialist society today, calling it class antagonism. Their aim was to attack and persecute the intellectuals, undermine the alliance of the workers, peasants, and intellectuals, disrupt the social productive forces and sabotage our socialist revolution and construction.

Correctly understanding that science and technology belong to the productive forces and that brain workers who serve socialism are a part of the working people has a close bearing on the rapid development of our scientific undertakings. . . .

Our science and technology have progressed enormously since the founding of new China and played an important role in economic construction and national defense construction. . . . But we must see, with a clear head, that there is still a very big gap between our science and technology and advanced world levels and that our scientific and technical forces are still very weak, far from meeting the needs of modernization. . . .

How do things stand with the technical level of our production? Several hundred million people are busy producing food. We still have not really solved the grain problem. Average annual output of grain per farm worker is about 1,000 kilograms in China, whereas in the United States the figure is over 50,000 kilograms, a disparity of several dozen times. Labor productivity in our iron and steel industry, too, is only a small percentage of advanced levels abroad. The gap in the newly emerged industries is still wider. . . .

Backwardness must be perceived before it can be changed. A person must learn from the advanced before he can catch up and surpass them. Of course, to raise China's scientific and technological level we must rely on our own efforts, develop our own inventions, and adhere to the policy of independence and self-reliance. But independence does not mean shutting the door on the world, nor does self-reliance mean blind opposition to anything foreign. Science and technology are a kind of wealth created in common by all mankind. Any nation or country must learn from the strong points of other nations and countries, from their advanced science and technology. . . .

The second question is, the building of a mammoth force of scientific and technical personnel who are both red and expert.

For the modernization of science and technology, we must have a mighty scientific and technical force of the working class which is both red and expert, and a large number of scientists and experts in engineering and technology who are first rate by world standards. . . .

An important question here is that we must have a correct understanding of being both red and expert, and set reasonable standards for it. . . .

Chairman Mao advocated intellectuals becoming both red and

expert, encouraging everyone to remold the bourgeois world outlook and to acquire the proletarian world outlook. The basic question about the world outlook is whom to serve. If a person loves our socialist motherland and is serving socialism and the workers, peasants, and soldiers of his own free will and accord, it should be said that he has initially acquired a proletarian world outlook and, in terms of political standards, cannot be considered white but should be called red. Our scientific undertakings are an important part of our socialist cause. To devote oneself to our socialist science and contribute to it is an important manifestation of being red, the integration of being red with being expert.

Imbued with Mao Tsetung thought, our scientists and technicians have made truly rapid progress in the last twenty-eight years. . . . Many showed a high level of political awareness in the eleventh struggle between the two lines. The smashing of the gang unleashed in them great revolutionary enthusiasm. They wholeheartedly support the party Central Committee headed by Chairman Hua and work still harder for the four modernizations. How invaluable are these scientists and technicians! They are worthy of the title "red and expert," fit to be called our working class's own scientific and technical force. . . .

This appraisal naturally does not mean that these scientists and technicians all have a very high level of political and ideological consciousness or that there are not shortcomings and mistakes of one kind or another in their ideology, their work style or their specific work; it means that judged by the basic criterion of political stand, the overwhelming majority of them take the stand of the working class, and these revolutionary intellectuals constitute a force our party can rely on. They should not be complacent or come to a halt, but should continue the effort, constantly seeking new progress both politically and in their specific fields. Their shortcomings and mistakes are a matter for education and assistance, something to be overcome through criticism and self-criticism. No one is free from shortcomings and mistakes. Take people like us, our cadres doing political work and our veteran cadres who have been in the party for decades; do we not also have shortcomings or errors of this kind or that? Why be especially exacting toward vocational cadres and technical experts! . . .

There is a section of scientists and technicians whose bourgeois world outlook has not fundamentally changed, or who are rather deeply influenced by bourgeois ideology. They often waver in the midst of sharp, fierce, and complicated class struggle. As long as they are not against the party and against socialism, we should, in line with the party's policy of uniting with, educating, and remolding the intellectuals, bring out their specialized abilities, respect their labor, and take an interest in their progress, giving them a warm helping hand. . . . Scientists and technicians should concentrate their energy on scientific and technical work. When we say that at least five-sixths of their work time should be left free for their scientific and technical work, this is meant to be the minimum demand. It is still better if even more time is available for this purpose. If some persons work seven days and seven evenings on end to meet the needs of science or production, that shows their lofty spirit of selfless devotion to the cause of socialism. . . . Scientists and technicians who have flaws of one kind or another in their ideology or their style of work should not be called "white," if they are not against the party and socialism. How can our scientists and technicians be accused of being divorced from politics when they work diligently for socialist science? The cause of socialism calls for a division of labor. On condition that they keep to the socialist political stand, comrades of different trades and professions are not divorced from politics when they do their best at their posts; on the contrary, this is a concrete manifestation of their service to proletarian politics and of their socialist consciousness. . . .

On the question of talented people, we must particularly stress the need to break with convention in the discovery, selection, and training of those with outstanding talent. This was one of the big issues muddled by the "gang of four." They vilified scientists, professors, and engineers distinguished for their contributions as bourgeois academic authorities, and all outstanding young and middle-aged scientists and technicians trained by our party and state as revisionist sprouts. . . .

Rapid development of science and technology hinges on good party leadership in these fields. . . .

During the unprecedented Great Proletarian Cultural Revolution, our party concentrated maximum efforts on the political revolution. Today, after victory in the struggle to expose and criticize the "gang of four," while continuing to eliminate their pernicious influence and deepen the socialist revolution on the ideological and political fronts, the whole party must take firm hold of the work of modernization and carry out the great political and economic revolution and the great scientific and technical revolution, tasks which history has conferred on us.

The party committees at various levels should learn from Tach'ing and Tachai and make an earnest effort to grasp simultaneously the three great revolutionary movements of class struggle, the struggle for production, and scientific experiment. Following the examples of Tach'ing and Tachai, they should unfold mass movements for scientific experiment, with new technical progress and new production records every year. . . . At the same time, we must work energetically for the success of specialized scientific research institutes. Professional scientists and technicians form the mainstay of the revolutionary movement for scientific experiment. . . .

The Central Committee has stipulated that a system of individual responsibility for technical work be established in scientific research institutes and that the system of division of responsibilities among institute directors under the leadership of party committees be set up. These are important organizational measures which help strengthen the leading role of the party committees while bringing into full play the role of the specialists. . . .

As to divergent views on academic questions, we must follow the principle of letting a hundred schools of thought contend and encourage free discussion. . . . As we are engaged in socialist modernization and are advancing toward the mastery of modern science and technology, the important task for our political work today is to make every scientist and technician understand how his work relates to the grand goal of the four modernizations, encourage and mobilize them to work together with one heart, and coordinate their efforts in the spirit of revolution, so as to storm the citadels of science.

SUPPLEMENT
MAO TSETUNG, ECONOMIC PROBLEMS
AND FINANCIAL PROBLEMS

Economic Problems and Financial Problems is Mao Tsetung's formative statement on political economy. The book-length manuscript, hastily prepared in late 1942 for an important inner-party meeting and never completed, sums up for the first time core principles of the political economy of people's war. Moreover it elucidates important features which subsequently characterized the Chinese road to socialist development.

In 1952, when excerpts were prepared for inclusion in the Selected Works, *at a time when the Chinese leadership stressed its fidelity to the Soviet development path, the following passage was added to the text:*

This self-supporting economy, which has been developed by the troops and the various organizations and schools, is a special product of the special conditions of today. It would be unreasonable and incomprehensible in other historical conditions, but it is perfectly reasonable and necessary at present.

It is clear, however, that in preparing the original and in his subsequent economic thought, Mao saw the significance of the wartime economic experiments in self-sufficiency and mobilization in more sweeping if not universal terms. "We have established a new model for the national economy," Mao stated in a passage not included in the Selected Works. *"What is new about*

Ching-chi wen-t'i yu ts'ai-cheng wen-ti (Economic Problems and Financial Problems) (Hong Kong: Hsin-min-chu, 1947). Translated by Mark Selden. Excerpts in *Selected Works of Mao Tse-tung III.* [Full translation and analysis of the document forthcoming by Andrew Watson, Cambridge University Press.]

this model is that it is neither the old Bismarckian model of national economy nor the new Soviet model of national economy. It is the national economy of the new democracy or the three people's principles." It was in short a Chinese model rooted in national conditions and the national revolutionary heritage.

Summing up the wartime economic experience of the Shen-Kan-Ning base area, Mao pinpointed and elaborated a series of economic measures which, particularly after 1958, would be resurrected and further developed in the service of socialist development. The most important of these were principles of self-reliance and self-support, rural cooperation, centralized leadership and dispersed administration of the economy, turning labor into capital through the mobilization of women and others, the stress on government and military contributions to economic life, the narrowing of differences between mental and manual labor through economic contributions of officials and soldiers, the commitment to raising the income of the peasants, the use of labor models, and the stress on consciousness and activism in transforming the economy.

Mao's report makes clear the process of experimentation inspired by wartime crisis conditions which gave rise to the political economy of people's war in the base areas. It also reveals Mao in one of his central roles, that of an advocate for agriculture and the peasantry. Here he stresses the primacy of agriculture (industry and commerce would be secondary), a conclusion to which the party would return in the early 1960s. And he states, perhaps more forcefully than at any time, the necessity for party and army to serve the peasantry, concretely and above all by ensuring improvement in their livelihood and wealth.

The general policy guiding our economic and financial work is to develop the economy and ensure supplies. But many of our comrades stress public finance and do not understand the importance of the economy; engrossed purely in matters of revenue and expenditure, hard as they try they cannot solve the problem. The reason is that an outmoded and conservative standpoint is doing mischief in their minds. They do not know that while a good or a bad financial policy affects the economy, it is the economy that determines finance. Without a firmly based economy it is impossible to solve financial difficulties, and without a growing economy it is impossible to attain financial sufficiency. . . . We shall simply be resigning ourselves to extinction unless we develop both the private and public sectors of the economy. Financial difficulties can be overcome only by down-to-earth and effective economic development. . . .

In the last five years we have passed through several stages. Our worst difficulties occurred in 1940 and 1941, when the two anticommunist drives created friction. For a time we were virtually without clothing, cooking oil, paper, and vegetables, footwear for the soldiers or winter bedding for the civilian personnel. The Kuomintang tried to strangle us by cutting off the funds due to us and imposing an economic blockade; we were indeed in dire straits. But we pulled through. Not only did the people of the border region give us grain but, in particular, we resolutely built up the public sector of our economy with our own hands. The government established many self-supporting industries. The troops engaged in a large-scale production movement and expanded agriculture, industry, and commerce to supply their own needs. The tens of thousands of personnel in various organizations and schools also developed similar economic activities to support themselves. By such means we have been overcoming our difficulties. Do not these indisputable historical facts prove that supplies can be ensured only through economic development? . . .

We must refute all one-sided views and advance the correct slogan of our party: "Develop the economy and ensure supplies." With regard to the relation between public and private interests, our slogans are: "Pay attention to both public and private interests" and "pay attention to both troops and civilians." We consider only such slogans to be correct. The only guarantee of our financial needs is to expand both the public and private sectors of the economy in a realistic and practical way. Even in difficult times we must take care to limit taxation so that the burdens, though heavy, will not hurt the people. And as soon as we can, we should lighten the burdens so that the people can build up strength. . . .

On the Development of Agriculture

I shall discuss several important lessons to be drawn from our work.

First, act according to local conditions and the season. Agricultural regions and seasons differ, and methods of development also differ. . . . In directing agriculture we must adopt various different methods in different regions. In one region we should emphasize deep ploughing, and in another expanding the cultivated area. We must also make distinctions with respect to timing. When there is fallow land that can be cultivated, we should emphasize encouraging the opening up of new land. . . . In the past general propagation of slogans for deep ploughing, opening new lands, water conservancy, and increasing production by 400,000 tan or 200,000 tan actually contained much subjectivism. Many peasants were neither interested in nor influenced by them. From this we may conclude that in future we must carry out deep, factual investigative research, and solve problems on the basis of concrete times, places, and conditions.

Second, as yet the peasants in a great many areas still pay heavy rents and heavy interest rates. The policy of reducing rent and interest has not been thoroughly carried out. On the one hand peasants must bear the burden of paying rent and interest to the landlords, and on the other they must pay grain and money taxes to the government. They get too little for themselves so that they cannot increase their enthusiasm to produce and cannot increase production. From this we may conclude that we must conscientiously implement the decrees to reduce rent and interest rates.

Third, the effect of the increase in grain tax, and the newly levied fodder tax, sheep tax, and salt transport requirement is a decline in the peasants' enthusiasm for production. . . . From this we may conclude that we must restrict the grain and fodder tax, and at the same time we must raise tax collection standards so as to promote agricultural production.

Fourth, policies should be thoroughly implemented. For example, we stipulated that for three years we would not take grain tax from new immigrants or from those planting cotton, but in fact we have both "welcomed" grain tax from immigrants and levied one half the grain tax on land planted in cotton. . . .

Fifth, more equitable adjustment in the use of labor power and numerous other methods to help the peasants, such as mutual aid teams, contract labor teams and so forth have strongly promoted agricultural growth. But with the exception of some localities like Yenan and other counties, we have still not done enough organization and promotion. . . .

Adjusting Labor Power

All of the following methods assist in adjusting the use of labor power: providing mutual aid labor, mobilization of women, mobilization of loafers, emphasizing support for families of resistance soldiers, granting leave of absence to take part in production, obtaining help from the troops, and so forth. . . .

Mutual aid labor. Within one village or among several villages not only does each peasant household plough and plant its land independently, but in busy seasons it also carries out mutual aid. For example, five, six, seven, or eight households can voluntarily form one group. Those who have labor power provide labor power, those who have animal power provide animal power, those who have more provide more, those who have less provide less. In rotation and collectively they can plough, plant, hoe, and harvest for each household in the group, and after the autumn harvest they can settle accounts. Work can be repaid by equal amounts of work. Those who supply more can receive supplementary wages from those who supply less, according to the wage rate of the village. This method is called mutual aid labor. . . .

Mobilizing women to participate in production. Although many of the women of the border region have bound feet, still they are second only to men as a large labor force. They can participate in all kinds of supplementary agricultural work such as planting vegetables, sowing seeds, hoeing weeds, feeding livestock, delivering food to the fields, drawing water, and gathering the harvest, etc. There are also some who can do basic labor. They have already participated rather extensively in the past. From now on we should propagate, encourage, and stimulate their enthusiasm for labor so as to raise agricultural production. Comrades in the leading women's organizations of the border region party and mass organizations have as yet not found the orientation for their work, feeling that there is nothing that they can do. In fact, their first task should be to investigate and help the women masses of the border region to play a wider role in productive labor, to enable all those women who can take part in labor to go to the production front and, together with the men, solve the great problem of increasing production. There are still a large number of women in the border region who have not untied their bound feet. This greatly impedes labor productivity. We should use the two methods of propaganda and compulsion so that within a few years we make them unbind their feet. From now on no one, no matter who, may again bind the feet of young girls. . . .

On the Development of Self-Sufficient Industry

In 1939 . . . we were facing a serious situation in finance and supplies. This compelled us to devise a movement for complete mobilization to become economically self-sufficient. At that time we already raised the following questions at the congress for cadre mobilization. Do you want to starve to death? Shall we disband? Or shall we set to ourselves? No one advocated starving to death and no one advocated disbanding. Let's set to ourselves—this was our answer. . . . This time we no longer wanted merely to improve out livelihood, but also wanted to meet part of our general needs. The scope of mobilization was not limited to the army and we called on all forces, official organizations and schools to carry out production. . . . This call not only mobilized the several tens of thousands of people in the party, government, army, and schools, but also mobilized the common folk of the border region who opened up over one million mou of new land that year. . . .

In the new stage when our economic base is already rather firm and our experience fairly wide, we should put agriculture in first place, industry, handicrafts, transport, and animal husbandry in second place. . . .

Why should unified self-sufficient industry be run in such a dispersed way? The main reason is that labor is dispersed among the various branches of the party, government, and army. If it were centralized, this would destroy their activism. For example, we encouraged the 359th Brigade to establish the Takuang

Textile Mill and did not order it to combine with a government mill because most of the mill's several hundred employees were selected from among the officers and men of the 359th Brigade. They work to produce the bedding and clothing requirements of the brigade and their enthusiasm is high. If we centralized, that would destroy this enthusiasm. Another important reason for dispersed operation is that raw materials are dispersed and transport is inconvenient.

This process of dispersal first and centralization later is perhaps unavoidable. Dispersal makes it possible to use the activism of all departments to better obtain supplies. But it is especially important that dispersed management not forget centralized leadership. This enables us to take quite a few steps toward unified planning, balanced supplies, rational management and proper distribution. Up to now we have had great shortcomings in this respect and they must be corrected in future. To sum up, our policy is "centralized leadership, dispersed operations." This is so not only for industry but for agriculture and commerce too. . . .

In the five years since 1938, the public sector of the economy has had some very great success. This success is worth treasuring for ourselves and for our nation. That is, we have established a new model for the national economy. What is new about this model is that it is neither the old Bismarckian model of national economy nor the new Soviet model of national economy. It is the national economy of the new democracy or the three people's principles. . . .

On Grain Work

All empty words are useless, we must give the people visible material wealth. The minds of many of our comrades have still not completely turned into the minds of communists. They only do one kind of work, that is, asking the people for this and that, for grain, fodder, taxes, and for this and that kind of mobilization work and do not know how to do the other kind of work, namely, striving to the utmost to help the people develop production and raise their cultural level. . . . The primary aspect of our work is not to ask things of the people but to give things to the people. What can we give the people?

Under present conditions in the Shen-Kan-Ning border region, we can organize, lead, and help the people develop production, increase their material wealth, and, on this basis, step by step raise their political consciousness and cultural level. For this we must scorn all discomforts and night and day, diligently and thoroughly study and concretely help to resolve problems of people's livelihood and production. . . . We must concretely help the people to solve these problems and not use empty words. This work is the primary aspect of work for every Communist Party member working in the countryside. Only after we have done this aspect of work and achieved real results can we get the people's support when we do the second aspect of our work, which is to ask things of the people. Only then will they say that our requests are necessary and just. Only then will they understand that if they do not provide grain, fodder, and other things to the government, their livelihood will not be good and will not improve. Only in this way will our work avoid coercion, will things go smoothly, and only in this way will we be truly united with the people. This is the basic line of our party.

Suggested Reading and Reference Works

The basic official source of information on contemporary China is Peking Review. *Western periodicals providing extensive China coverage range from the popular magazine* New China *to journalistic coverage in the weekly* Far Eastern Economic Review *(the view of Hong Kong China watchers) to scholarly periodicals, including the* Bulletin of Concerned Asian Scholars, The China Quarterly, *and* Modern China.

Andors, Stephen. *China's Industrial Revolution*. New York: Pantheon, 1977.

Belden, Jack. *China Shakes the World*. New York: Monthly Review Press, 1970.

Bettelheim, Charles. *Cultural Revolution and Industrial Organization in China*. New York: Monthly Review Press, 1974.

Bianco, Lucien. *Origins of the Chinese Revolution, 1915-1949*. Stanford, Calif.: Stanford University Press, 1971.

Boorman, Howard, ed. *Biographical Dictionary of Republic China*. 4 vols. New York: Columbia University Press, 1967.

Bowie, Robert, and John Fairbank, eds. *Communist China, 1955-1959. Policy Documents with Analysis*. Cambridge, Mass.: Harvard University Press, 1962.

Brugger, William. *Contemporary China*. London: Crook, Helms, 1977.

————. *Democracy and Organisation in the Chinese Industrial Enterprise (1948-1953)*. Cambridge: Cambridge University Press, 1976.

Chen, Jack. *Inside the Cultural Revolution*. New York: Macmillan, 1976.

Ch'en, Jerome. *Mao and the Chinese Revolution*. London: Oxford University Press, 1965.

Clark, Anne, and Donald Klein. *Biographical Dictionary of Chinese Communism 1921-1965*. Cambridge, Mass.: Harvard University Press, 1971.

Collection of Important Documents of the Great Proletarian Cultural Revolution. Peking: Foreign Languages Press, 1970.

Committee of Concerned Asian Scholars. *China! Inside the People's Republic*. New York: Bantam, 1972.

Crook, David, and Isabel Crook. *Revolution in a Chinese Village: Ten Mile Inn*. London: Routledge and Kegan Paul, 1959.

Davin, Delia. *Woman-Work: Women and the Party in Revolutionary China.* London: Oxford University Press, 1976.

Daubier, Jean. *A History of the Chinese Cultural Revolution.* New York: Vintage, 1974.

Fei Hsiao-t'ung. *China's Gentry.* Chicago: University of Chicago Press, 1953.

Gittings, John. *The Role of the Chinese Army.* New York: Oxford University Press, 1967.

Gurley, John. *China's Economy and the Maoist Strategy.* New York: Monthly Review Press, 1976.

Harrison, James. *The Long March to Power: A History of the Chinese Communist Party, 1921-1972.* New York: Praeger, 1972.

Hinton, William. *Fanshen: A Documentary of Revolution in a Chinese Village.* New York: Monthly Review Press, 1966.

Horn, Joshua. *Away With All Pests.* New York: Monthly Review Press, 1969.

Joint Economic Committee of the United States Congress. *China: A Reassessment of the Economy.* Washington: Government Printing Office, 1975.

Lippit, Victor. *Land Reform and Economic Development in China: A Study of Institutional Change and Development Finance.* White Plains, N.Y.: International Arts and Sciences Press, 1974.

MacFarquhar, Roderick. *The Origins of the Cultural Revolution.* Vol. 1: *Contradictions Among the People.* New York: Columbia University Press, 1974.

Mao Tsetung. *Selected Works.* 5 vols. Peking: Foreign Languages Press, 1961.

——. *Selected Readings.* Peking: Foreign Languages Press, 1967.

——. *A Critique of Soviet Economics.* Translated by Moss Roberts. New York: Monthly Review Press, 1977.

——. *Socialist Upsurge in the Chinese Countryside.* Peking: Foreign Languages Press, 1977.

——. *Mao Tse-tung Unrehearsed: Talks and Letters, 1956-1971.* Edited by Stuart Schram. New York: Pantheon, 1974.

——. *Poems of Mao Tse-tung.* Edited by Wong Man. Hong Kong: Eastern Horizon Press, 1974.

Meisner, Maurice. *Mao's China: A History of the People's Republic.* New York: The Free Press, 1978.

Milton, David, and Nancy Milton. *The Wind Will Not Subside: Years in Revolutionary China, 1964–1969.* New York: Pantheon, 1976.

————, Nancy Milton, and Franz Schurmann. *People's China.* New York: Vintage, 1974.

Myrdal, Jan. *Report from a Chinese Village.* New York: Pantheon, 1965.

Nee, Victor, and James Peck. *China's Uninterrupted Revolution. From 1840 to the Present.* New York: Pantheon, 1975.

Robinson, Joan. *Economic Management in China.* London: Anglo-Chinese Educational Institute, 1975.

Schram, Stuart. *Mao Tse-tung.* New York: Simon and Schuster, 1967.

————, ed. *Authority, Participation and Cultural Revolution in China.* Cambridge: Cambridge University Press, 1973.

Schran, Peter. *The Development of Chinese Agriculture, 1950–1959.* Urbana: University of Illinois Press, 1969.

Schurmann, Franz. *Ideology and Organization in Communist China.* Berkeley: University of California Press, 1966.

Smedley, Agnes. *The Great Road: The Life and Times of Chu Teh.* New York: Monthly Review Press, 1956.

Snow, Edgar. *Red Star Over China.* New York: Grove Press, 1968.

Stavis, Benedict. *Making Green Revolution. The Politics of Agricultural Development in China.* Ithaca, N.Y.: Rural Development Committee, Cornell University, 1974.

State Statistical Bureau. *Ten Great Years.* Peking: Foreign Languages Press, 1960.

Union Research Institute, ed. *Documents of the Chinese Communist Party Central Committee.* 2 vols. Hong Kong: Union Research Institute, 1971.

Wheelwright, E. L., and Bruce McFarlane. *The Chinese Road to Socialism: Economics of the Cultural Revolution.* New York: Monthly Review Press, 1970.

Wilson, Dick, ed. *Mao Tse-tung in the Scales of History.* Cambridge: Cambridge University Press, 1977.

Wong, John. *Land Reform in the People's Republic of China: Institutional Transformation of Agriculture.* New York: Praeger, 1973.

Young, Marilyn, ed. *Women in China.* Ann Arbor: University of Michigan Center for Chinese Studies, 1973.